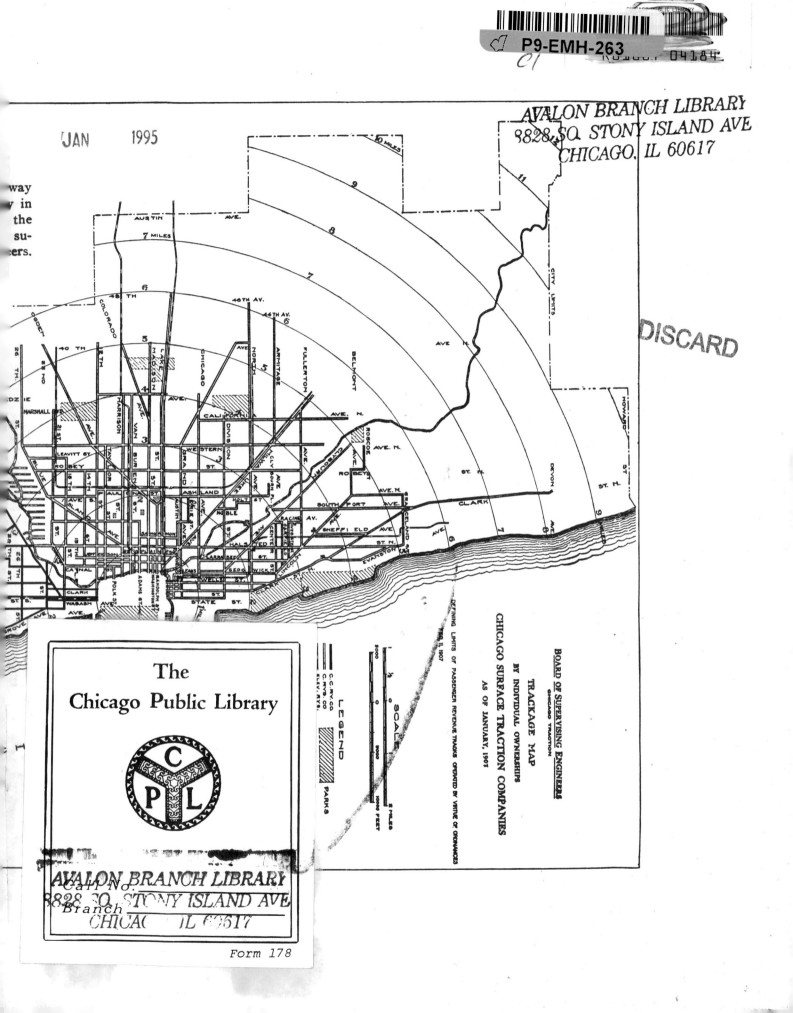

JAN 1995

BOARD OF SUPERVISING ENGINEERS
CHICAGO TRACTION

TRACKAGE MAP
BY INDIVIDUAL OWNERSHIPS

CHICAGO SURFACE TRACTION COMPANIES

AS OF JANUARY, 1907

LEGEND

C.C. RY. CO.
C. RYS. CO.
ELEV. RYS.

PARKS

Chicago Surface Lines

An Illustrated History

By Alan R. Lind

International Standard Book Number: 0-934732-00-0
Library of Congress Catalog Card Number: 74-75870

Copyright © 1974, © 1979, and © 1986 by Alan R. Lind.
All rights reserved.
Third Edition August, 1979.
Second Printing March, 1986.
Published by Transport History Press,
Box 201, Park Forest, Il 60466.

• Opposite page. Inbound 1936 PCC car 4049 passes outbound mate 7022 on the Madison Street route at Madison and Hamlin Boulevard. Photo from St. Louis Car Co. • Above. Old Pullman 373 waits for departure time at the Grand and Armitage terminal of the Armitage-Downtown line. Barney Neuberger photo from Railway Negative Exchange.

2

Introduction

Do you remember when scarlet and cream trolley cars swayed down the streets of Chicago? The trolley wheel sang as it turned against the overhead wire, the car motors whined, and the motorman banged the bell as you stood waiting for the car. It stopped with a hiss of the air brake, and you scrambled aboard the big rear platform. The conductor took your 7¢ fare, rang it up on a large round register, and yanked the bell cord twice.

Responding to that "go" signal, the motorman notched up his controller. Motors began to hum, tickled to life by 600 volts of direct current. You were on your way, bound for work, the beach, the ball game, to shop, to sightsee, or just to cool off on a hot day.

From your yellow cane seat you saw a panorama of people and places. The cars served the whole city, from the Gold Coast to the Ghetto, from the fashionable shops on State Street to the stinking stockyards. The cars ran past Comiskey Park, through Chinatown, along Lincoln Park, and out to the city limits.

To haggle with the merchants of Maxwell Street you took the Halsted car, to watch the Black Hawks play you rode the "Blue Goose" PCC cars on Madison Street. A dozen crosstown lines served the lakefront beaches, and the Broadway car took you to Lincoln Park Zoo.

Just watching the cars go by was fun. Old Pullman cars trundled along North Side lines, noisy but dependable. Nearside cars rolled along Cottage Grove Ave. They were known as "Muzzleloaders," since for years they were the only two-man cars in the city to load passengers at the front. On other busy South Side lines big Brill cars in the 5000 series handled the traffic. The first modern PCC cars arrived in 1936.

At the very end of the Surface Lines era, in 1947, the post-war streamlined PCC cars arrived, replacing the "Sedans" on the Clark-Wentworth route. They also saw service on the heavy Broadway-State line.

In winter a special sort of trolley — a work car with a snow plow — came out on the streets to buck deep drifts. Behind the plows came the snow sweepers, rattan brooms twirling, to keep the lines clear. When summer came, ponderous sprinkler cars spurted water on the streets to keep the dust down. Mild days also brought out the trolley cranes, concrete mixers, and other work cars used in track maintenance.

Long ago a special streetcar shuttled the insane between the county's psychiatric hospital and outlying asylums. Other cars distributed mail, collected garbage, and took the dead and the mourners to the cemetery.

Memories of this era are fading fast. Thirty years ago thousands of streetcars trundled down a hundred streets. Fifteen years ago they were all gone. Today there is scarcely a trace of them anywhere in the city.

Those who call Chicago home are not surprised that few traces remain of what was once the world's largest street railway system just 15 years after its last cars ran. Natives are used to seeing the cityscape shift rapidly, for Chicago has always restlessly rebuilt itself. Chicago's spectacular rise from swamp to metropolis is too well known to require retelling here. But a bit of that story helps in understanding how and why the streetcar system grew.

The city took its shape from a plat drawn by James Thompson in 1830 for the State Canal Commissioners. A year earlier the Commissioners had been appointed to plan a canal linking Lake Michigan with the Mississippi River. Chicago, at the northeast end of the canal, and Ottawa, at the southwest end, were platted at this time.

On this original survey Chicago was laid out on a grid street pattern, and this pattern persisted as the city grew through annexation. The original map included the area bounded by State St. on the east, Desplaines St. on the west, Madison St. on the south, and Kinzie St. on the north. Major streets beyond the area covered by the map were located at one mile intervals under the Ordinance of 1785. This law provided for the dividing of the United States into squares one mile on each side. CSL cars operated on virtually every one of these major streets, and on many of the half-section streets between them.

Chicago grew first to the north and to the west of the original settlement along the Chicago River. Horse car, cable car, and electric car service was most intensive in these sections of the city, for mass transit thrives in areas of dense population. Even today as one moves north or west of downtown Chicago, population density remains fairly high right to the borders of the adjacent suburbs. On the other hand, large tracts of the far South Side are thinly populated even today.

The South Side was settled later than the North and West Sides, experiencing its most rapid growth after the Chicago Fire of 1871. Many of these early settlements clustered around what were then rural railroad stations. When streetcars came to the South Side they linked these pioneer communities, and provided the means to settle the gaps between them.

Lake Michigan, Chicago's eastern boundary, had a strong influence on the city's development. North of the Loop the lake cuts westward, slicing off many north-south streets. For example, at Madison St. in the heart of the Loop the lake shore is more than a half-mile east of State St. At Howard St., the city limits some nine and one-half miles north of Madison St., the lake shore is one and one-half miles west of State St. North Side streets such as Clark and Broadway run on the diagonal, parallel to the lake shore.

In addition to the diagonal streets along the lake shore, the North Side has a number of important roads which

● Opposite page. Seven streetcars spaced along State Street are visible in this 1913 view looking northeast from Jackson Boulevard, including CCRy standard wood semiconvertibles 5023, right, and 5580, center. Kaufmann & Fabry photo from Dave Kleiman.

run on the bias. Among them are Lincoln, Milwaukee, Clybourn, Grand, and Elston Aves. Some of the North Side's crosstown streetcar lines got started as extensions of the routes that ran on these diagonal streets. Although the South Side has fewer diagonal streets, they were equally important to the growth of crosstown car lines in that part of the city. Among the most important diagonal streets on the South Side are Ogden, Archer, South Chicago, Vincennes, and Cottage Grove Aves.

In understanding the CSL it helps to know what sort of competition for riders and street space the company faced. For most of the period covered by this book, three major public transportation companies fought for passengers: the Chicago Surface Lines, the Chicago Rapid Transit Co., and the Chicago Motor Coach Co. CSL ran the streetcars, and the bus lines that fed them traffic, the CRT ran the ''L'' and subway trains, and the CMC ran its double-deck buses mostly on the boulevards, which cut through the city parks.

The densely populated North and West Sides received the bulk of ''L'' and subway service. But on the South Side ''L'' service didn't reach even 69th St. until 1907. Aside from this light-density branch line to Normal Park, there was no ''L'' service south of 63rd St. until the CTA opened its Dan Ryan Expressway median strip line in 1969, 11 years after streetcar service ended in Chicago.

All in all, CSL's North and West Side lines were more closely spaced, had more circuitous routings, had more cars assigned to them, and had more frequent headways than the South Side routes. On the other hand, the South Side lines were often the only means of transportation for thousands of people who lived south of 63rd Street and west of State St.

By far the heaviest routes on the South Side were those on the major north-south streets, such as Halsted. These were the lines that had Through Route cars to the North and West Sides, as well as local service. They were the only lines south of Madison Street to have trailer operation and multiple-unit trains, and the only South Side lines to get PCC cars, except for 63rd Street.

Although this is a book on the Chicago Surface Lines, it would not be complete without mentioning the horse cars and cable cars that preceded CSL or the conversion to gas, diesel and trolley bus that marked the end of the CSL era. So the first chapter begins with the start of horse car service, and throughout the book you will find references to operations after CTA took over from CSL.

The first chapter is a history of the Cottage Grove line from the start of horse car service in Chicago in 1859 until the unification of 1914, which created the Surface Lines. It is included to give you some understanding of the development of transit service in Chicago prior to the creation of the CSL.

In writing about the Surface Lines, one quickly becomes aware that the subject is big enough to fill a half-dozen books. A volume could be written on the streetcars alone, another on the routes, and a third on the CSL's buses and trolley buses. Other subjects which deserve book-length treatment are the relationship between CSL and the political powers of city and state, and the life and times of a streetcar man, which could include the growth of the Amalgamated Association of Street & Electric Railway Employees of America.

This book covers all aspects of the Surface Lines, and so some detail about each aspect must be left out. To present all this information as concisely as possible, many tables, rosters, and maps are used.

Old Pullman 620 was one of a series of 600 identical cars built by Pullman in 1908-09 for Chicago Railways. They were the first Pay-As-You-Enter cars built for CRys. Car is stopped on Western near 79th. Barney Neuberger collection.

Acknowledgments

Although the Surface Lines went out of business almost three decades ago, interest in the company remains surprisingly high. It seems that everyone who lived in Chicago rode the cars at least occasionally, and that many visitors used them to sightsee. Many Chicagoans had friends or relatives who worked for CSL. Even the one-time visitor to Chicago who drove through could hardly fail to notice the swarms of scarlet and cream cars which hummed through the city.

This book was made possible through the generosity of those who preserved mementos of the time when the streetcar was king of local transportation. These pages contain many photos and much information not available from libraries or other public sources.

A special word of thanks is due Roy Benedict. He supplied many photos from his own collection, and much roster material. On all aspects of the CSL, Roy made many valuable suggestions based on his years of research into CSL operations. He also reviewed the photos used, suggesting much caption material.

Zenon Hansen furnished car and bus plans, roster material, and many car and bus photos. John White, Jr., of the Smithsonian Institution granted permission to use several photos of early street railway equipment made from glass plate negatives in the Smithsonian collection. George Krambles allowed the author to use many of the negatives in his extensive collection, and Arthur Peterson processed them for use in the book.

Pullman-Standard public relations men Tom O'Rourke and John McHugh allowed the author access to Pullman records, and also supplied construction photos of experimental car 4001. Mel Lamb and Thomas Taylor of the St. Louis Car Company supplied several photographs and much technical material, including

Far from the Northwest Highway route indicated by the side route sign, Chicago Railways 510 poses on the Midway Plaisance near the University of Chicago campus. This 1935 White Model 684 had seats for 32. Photo from Zenon Hansen.

blueprints of the 1936 and 1948 PCC cars. Bob Heinlein of the Chicago Transit Authority, successor to the Chicago Surface Lines, supplied all of the photos credited to the CTA.

Much of the material on the personal side of CSL came from Walter Blix. This material included a history of Division 241, copies of CSL's *Surface Service* magazine, operating timetables, and a CSL rule book. Augie Pritzlaff contributed much information about CSL's street railway post office cars and routes. He also supplied information on the tangled web of properties held by CSL's predecessor companies. Michael Jarosak of the Mobile Post Office Society also sent material on streetcar post offices. Nick Kalman, who has a virtually complete collection of CSL transfers, assisted the author in making up the unofficial guide to CSL transfer variations. He also provided several CSL route maps, street guides, and official reports from his large private collection.

Allan Williams kindly permitted the author to use prints and negatives from his collection, including many negatives from the last years of streetcar operation. Steve Maguire, Transit Topics editor of *Railroad* magazine, allowed the author to select photos from the hundreds of CSL negatives in his collection. Warren Miller of the Railway Negative Exchange in Moraga, Calif., searched out many rare CSL photos. Mr. Miller has purchased the photo collection of the late Barney Neuberger, perhaps the largest collection of CSL photos assembled by one man.

W. David Randall helped secure much material, including rosters and photos. Jeff Wien supplied several PCC car pictures, and gave information about preserved equipment. Photos from the collection of Alan Simms and a valuable track map were secured by Eugene W. Anderson.

From his own collection and that of his father, Bernard Rossbach contributed several photos and much memorabilia. Douglas Wornom of the Owen Davies bookstore located several rare official reports, as well as some trolley RPO material. Joe Diaz, editor and publisher of the *Street Railway Review,* gave his encouragement and advice, as well as permission to use several of his excellent CSL photos.

Arthur Dubin gave enthusiastic support and encouragement to this project while it was still in the planning stage, and helped to secure much material for the book.

Special thanks are due two photographers who opened their extensive negative and print files to the author. David R. Phillips kindly allowed the author to search his thousands of glass plate negatives and prints, which cover every aspect of life in Chicago. From this source have come some of the finest full-page illustrations in the book, including the photo used on the back of the dust jacket. Bill Richmond was kind enough to open his large collection of street railway negatives and prints for use in this volume. Many of these fine photos were once part of the Neuberger collection.

James Prokes, president of the National Association of Timetable Collectors, supplied several rare Surface Lines timetables and brochures, as well as some photos.

Among those who contributed photos are Tom Mangan, Richard J. Cook, Theodore P. Taetsch, Al Shade, Jack Hedrich of Hedrich-Blessing photographers, and Dave Kleiman of the Kaufmann & Fabry Company.

In the captions the photographs are credited to the photographer whenever possible. When the photographer is unknown, the picture is credited to the man who supplied the photo.

While many persons contributed material and suggestions for the book, all facts and opinions expressed in these pages are the responsibility of the author.

Just a little more than a mile from the end of its run, Chicago City Railway 1946 PCC 7161 was photographed at 73rd and Vincennes October 28, 1955, by A. C. Williams.

Chicago Surface Lines

Abbreviations used in this book

BOSE	Board of Supervising Engineers
C&IT	Chicago & Interurban Traction
C&SC	Calumet & South Chicago
C&WT	Chicago & West Towns
C&W	Chicago & Western Railway
CCRy	Chicago City Railway
CER	Chicago Elevated Railways
CMC	Chicago Motor Coach
CRT	Chicago Rapid Transit
CRys	Chicago Railways
CSL	Chicago Surface Lines
HW&EC	Hammond, Whiting & East Chicago
PAYE	Pay-As-You-Enter
PCC	Presidents Conference Committee
SSR	Southern Street Railway

The Cottage Grove line: 1859 to 1914

The story of rail transit on Cottage Grove Avenue begins in 1858, when the Chicago Common Council (City Council) passed legislation permitting horse car lines on State St., Madison St., and Cottage Grove Ave. A year later Franklin Parmelee, one of Chicago's early omnibus operators, and two other businessmen formed the Chicago City Railway Company. The first route built by CCRy, a single track from Madison to 12th on State St., opened April 25th, 1859. By June, two horse cars were running on a twelve minute headway between Madison and a new terminal at 22nd and State.

During the summer of 1859 the route was extended via 22nd and Cottage Grove to 31st and Cottage Grove, with cars running shuttle service at six minute intervals between 31st and the 22nd junction. The first rails laid on

Cottage Grove were spiked directly to the plank road because the CCRy wanted the line ready for the opening of the Illinois State Fair, held at the suburb of Cottage Grove in 1859.

One of the most interesting and amusing incidents in the history of the line occurred during the Civil War. The Greenback money issued by the Federal Government steadily fell in value until the CCRy refused to accept it in payment of fares, demanding currency instead. When their supply of silver coins ran out, passengers began to turn in packets of uncancelled postage stamps. To help its employees unstick themselves from the mass of stamps, the CCRy ran off $150,000 worth of "Emergency Tickets" in 1861.

Although officially the 50¢ tickets were only good for

8

horse car rides, Chicagoans soon accepted them as change in any business transaction, and some turned up in church offerings. Because of extensive counterfeiting, the first issue was called in and exchanged for new tickets in 10¢, 15¢, and 25¢ denominations. Until 1863, when the government provided a more stable medium, the horse car tickets were as good as gold.

In the two decades following the Chicago Fire the Cottage Grove line was rebuilt, converted to cable operation, and doubled in length. In 1871, the year of the fire, cars ran from Randolph and State to 22nd and State once a minute, and to Cottage Grove Avenue and Douglas Place (34th Place) at four minute intervals.

In 1882 horse car operations ended, and cable cars took over, running from the downtown loop to 39th over the former horse car route. Along with the State line completed earlier the same year, Cottage Grove formed the nucleus of what became the world's largest cable car system. In 1887 the Wabash-Cottage Grove line reached 67th, and a one-mile branch opened on 55th between Cottage Grove and Lake Park.

The last extension of cable car operation on Cottage Grove, a half-mile between 67th and 71st, opened in 1890.

By 1892 the single reversing loop in the downtown district could not handle the traffic on the many lines which used State Street or Wabash Avenue. Construction of a new loop for the Wabash Avenue lines, including Wabash-Cottage Grove, began in May of 1892. Running from Wabash to Michigan on Madison and Randolph, the new loop had to be completed before the Democratic National Convention on June 21, 1892. Around-the-clock construction work completed the loop on June 11, 1892, in time for the Democrats to renominate Grover Cleveland, and in time for the heavy 4th of July crowds.

The World's Fair of 1893 drew hundreds of thousands of visitors to the fair grounds in Jackson Park between 55th and 63rd Streets. Connecting Washington and Jackson Parks between 59th and 60th Streets, Midway Plaisance was the exposition's "Midway." The Chicago City Railway prepared for the Fair by electrifying the

• Opposite page. The Jackson Park roof destination sign and the "55" over the headlight indicate that this three-car cable train led by CCRy grip car 662 was running on the 55th Street branch of the Cottage Grove line. CTA photo. • Above. CCRy Nearside 5779 rests at Brookline Loop south of 71st and east of Cottage Grove. Really unsuited for operation on heavy lines, these cars were nonetheless mainstays of the Cottage routes for many years. Photo from Tom Mangan. See page 250 for a picture of a Cottage Grove 1936 PCC car photographed at this same loop.

61st-63rd horse car line on June 6, 1893. The route went from 61st and State to Cottage Grove Avenue, south on the Cottage Grove cable car tracks to 63rd Street, and then east to the World's Fair entrance.

Meanwhile two separate companies, the South Side Elevated Railroad and Illinois Central Railroad with its suburban service, were also making plans to serve the Fair. The Elevated Railroad completed its line from downtown Chicago to the 63rd Street entrance to the Fair on May 1st, the opening day of the Fair.

The ingenious management of the Illinois Central Railroad ran non-stop express trains from downtown Chicago to the Illinois Central World's Fair terminal at 63rd Street-Woodlawn. New station platforms on a level with the car floors were built, and loading and unloading were extremely rapid.

Despite the tough competition the Cottage Grove cable cars did a good job. Both the Cottage Grove main line and the 55th branch served the fair grounds, so riders had the choice of riding the through cars to the dazzling Midway at 59th or taking the branch car to the northern edge of the fair grounds. On October 9, 1893, Chicago Day at the World's Fair, the CCRy carried 500,000 and the Illinois Central carried 541,000 passengers.

Seventy-first Street on the southern end of the Cottage line was also bustling in 1893. Here the cable car connected with the electrics of the Calumet Electric Street Railway Co. Calumet Railway cars ran south down Cottage Grove from a loop at 72nd to 95th, then west on 95th to Michigan, and south on Michigan to a terminal at

119th, a distance of 13.5 miles from the Downtown loop of the Cottage Grove cable cars. In later years the track on 95th became part of the 93rd-95th Street route (Chicago Surface Lines), and the track on Michigan Avenue was used by Broadway-State route cars (CSL).

Calumet Electric ran essentially "fair weather" service, using only 8 to 10 motor cars in a typical February, then bringing out 18 motor cars and 18 trailers for summer operations. Joint fare from the Cottage line to any point on the connecting line was 10 cents.

By transferring several times a passenger could also reach South Chicago from 71st and Cottage. However, the route was not direct down South Chicago Avenue. The hardy traveler who chose this way to reach the Southeast fringe of Chicago first transferred from a Cottage Grove cable car to a CCRy electric shuttle car on South Chicago. At 75th the shuttles connected with a Calumet Electric Railway car. Transferring to this car the intrepid rider went east to Stony Island where he made a final transfer to the Calumet Electric Railway's Roby line car for South Chicago. Direct service on the Cottage Grove line from downtown Chicago to South Chicago via South Chicago Avenue began with the inauguration of Through Route 5 on February 23, 1913.

In 1896 battery-powered streetcars began to run from 63rd and Vernon to 87th and Summit on a route that connected with the Cottage cable cars at 71st. Extended to 91st and Loomis by June, 1897, and electrified with conventional cars on July 1, 1901, the line was discontinued on March 1, 1912.

Until the 1936 PCC cars were transferred to Cottage Grove in 1953, Peter Witts such as 6284 provided service. This 1952 photo, taken at 96th and Cottage by A. C. Williams, shows the car entering side-of-the-road ballasted track. Jog in the track is a remnant of the days when the Cottage line crossed the Illinois Central tracks at grade.

Operating statistics for the years immediately following the World's Fair measure the stimulus which the Fair gave to the growth of Chicago's Southeast Side. For all South Side lines in 1894 there was an increase of 32 million in the number of passengers carried, earnings rose nearly $2 million, and car miles jumped by 5.5 million over 1893. Other figures showed that although cable cars could handle large loads at a profit, the electric car could handle the same loads at a greater profit. For example, in 1898 electric cars cost 12.96¢ per car/mile to operate and earned 22.7¢, cable cars and trailers and electric car trailers cost 10.8¢ per car/mile and earned 16.5¢, and horse cars cost 27.2¢ and earned 16.6¢ per car/mile.

On October 21, 1906 Cottage Grove became a trolley line. The change from cable to electric operation was made under the terms of the Ordinance of June 18, 1906, which authorized temporary electrification of certain CCRy lines. As it turned out, this "temporary" electrification lasted 50 years. Because of the extremely heavy traffic, trolley wire was strung directly over the cable car tracks, and only absolutely necessary repairs were made in the tracks themselves. Later a shoo-fly was built around a short section of track, the track was removed, and new track with steel crossties and rail bonds was laid. The tracks were set in concrete mixed on the site in Drake concrete mixers.

On November 22, 1907, part of CCRy's first order of PAYE cars entered service on the Cottage Grove line, replacing 131 older cars. With a loading capacity of 75 people per minute, these PAYE cars were the first used in the United States, although Montreal had previously used similar cars. The 1907-08 PAYE cars numbered 5301-5600 became models for the conversion of cars 5001-5200 (Brill, 1905-06) and 5201-5300 (Brill, 1906) which were converted to PAYE in 1908-1909. All three series of cars operated on Cottage Grove lines. The introduction of electric cars speeded up Cottage Grove operations by 25 per cent between January, 1906, and January, 1908. In 1906 the cable cars made an average speed of 7.68 mph, in 1907 mixed single and double truck electric cars averaged 8.13 mph, and in 1908 the double truck PAYE cars averaged 8.49 mph.

Fast as they were, the PAYE cars seated only 40 people, so on September 7, 1912, 124 new Brill Nearside cars with maximum traction trucks replaced the PAYE cars. Seating 54 passengers, the new 5703-5827 series cars had Brill 39E1 trucks, two WH 306CA motors, and WH K36g or K36j controls. Both entrance and exit were at the front of the car, with the single "nearside" rear door used as a regular exit at beaches, ball parks, and other places where large numbers of passengers wanted to get off, and as an emergency exit at all other times.

The 1907 PAYE cars and the 1912 Nearsides are good examples of the improvements in streetcars since the first horse cars ran on State Street. The first streetcar was 12 feet long and seven feet wide, with the driver's platform enclosed by a waist-high, semi-circular dash. On these bob-tailed cars the only entrance was at the rear — a broad step, handrail, and side shields surrounding a

Some of the Nearsides were converted to optional one-man/two-man operation. This Barney Neuberger photo shows such a converted car outbound on the Cottage Grove-South Chicago route. Photo from the Bill Richmond collection.

narrow door. A single bench ran along each side of the car, and total seating capacity was 20. There were no heaters, but coal oil lamps lighted the interior of the car. In later horse cars the seating arrangement remained the same, but the cars were double-ended, with two platforms, seated 30 passengers, had side steps, two horses, and a conductor equipped with a fare register. Cottage Grove grip cars were 19', 1" long, 7', 9" wide, and 10', 4" high. The blue, double-ended cars seated 20 people and were numbered 600-699 and 1300-1360. These company-built cars cost $1,000 each. Cable trailers were remodeled horse cars seating 30 people, and identical company-built trailers were later used, along with open trailer cars built for the World's Fair.

Keeping pace with the improvements in the Cottage Grove streetcars, the CCRy built a new barn at 38th and Cottage Grove in 1907. The barn had a capacity of 226 cars, with space for an additional 26 cars on the unsheltered lead-in tracks. Seven bays with four tracks each gave a total of over 12,000 feet of storage and repair track. The end of the barn facing Cottage Grove was two stories high, and contained club rooms, a stage, and trainmen's assembly rooms. Cost of the barn, including later remodeling, was $709,974.

Under the terms of a 1908 Ordinance the South Chicago City Railway, owners of the South Chicago Ave. line, and the Calumet Electric Street Railway, owners of the Cottage line south of 71st, were merged into the Calumet and South Chicago Railway. In 1908 the new company made an operating agreement with the Chicago City Railway Company which made the establishment of long Through Routes possible. Under the Ordinance of February 11, 1910, Cottage Grove from the downtown loop to 71st, the 55th branch, and the South Chicago line to 75th belonged to the CCRy. Cottage Grove south of 71st and South Chicago Avenue south-east of 75th belonged to the Calumet and South Chicago Railway.

Through Routes, lines running from one end of the city to the other over tracks of several separate companies, were proposed in order to eliminate switching downtown and to get the cars through in the quickest time. By 1908 the saturation point had been reached on many downtown streets including Wabash Ave., used by Cottage Grove cars. Many changes were made in the Through Routes between 1908, when they were proposed; July 1, 1910, when the first eight opened; and 1913-1914, when they reached the form in which many of them operate today as CTA bus routes, even retaining the old Through Route numbers on the destination signs.

The following paragraphs, taken from the 1915 report of the Board that supervised the CSL, summarize the changes in service made by the Through Routing.

Although Peter Witt cars provided most Cottage Grove service in the years just prior to the use of PCC cars, other types of equipment made tripper runs to supplement rush hour service. A. C. Williams snapped this "Odd 17" car April 17, 1952 at 111th and Cottage.

"Operation of all surface street railways in Chicago under one management began February 1, 1914 or at the beginning of this fiscal year. The Cottage Grove Avenue service, formerly furnished by the City Railway Company, and the West Pullman service, formerly furnished by the Calumet Company, were consolidated, giving direct through service from 119th Street to Randolph Street in the downtown district. This resulted in increasing the number of cars operating on Through Route No. 4 over threefold.

"The Cottage Grove-Jackson Park service, formerly furnished by the City Railway Company, was consolidated with the Stony Island service, formerly furnished by the Calumet Company, resulting in through service from 93rd Street to Randolph Street by way of Stony Island and Cottage Grove Avenues.

"By means of the foregoing additional through service and through transfer privileges between other lines, the five-cent fare zone was extended into the Calumet district, which heretofore had been in the ten cent zone. The extension of the fare zone resulted in a loss of revenue to the companies in the Calumet territory of from $1,000 to $1,200 per day and a saving of a like amount to the street railway patrons."

Actually the CCRy Cottage Grove line and the Calumet Electric's West Pullman service were through-routed February 23, 1913. Known as Through Route 4, the line ran from the 119th, Morgan, 120th loop via 119th, Michigan, 95th, Cottage Grove, Indiana, 18th, and Wabash to the Washington, Garland Court, Randolph loop. The line was discontinued on August 12, 1918. That same day the designation Through Route 4 was given to a new Cottage Grove-Pullman route. For details of this service look under that route in the route history chapter.

Even a sharp eyed local railfan will find few traces of the Cottage Grove streetcar line today. The Chicago Transit Authority converted the route (4) to bus operation in June, 1955, and civic improvement projects have obliterated most of the features of the line. After streetcar service ended, construction crews sealed off a three block section of Cottage Grove and began preliminary work on a large apartment house development. A few months later the side of the road open track south of 95th was paved over in a street widening project. The old steel line poles gave place to modern lampposts in 1957, and by March, 1958, the 38th Street barn, used exclusively by Cottage cars in the last years of operation, was torn down. CTA has scrapped the PCC cars used at the end of service, and the last of the Peter Witt fleet, standard equipment in pre-PCC days, served as toolrooms at the 77th Street yard.

Parked close together, these prewar PCC cars seem to be coupled together, although of course they ran only as single units. They are waiting for their time just north of 115th Street along Cottage Grove. A. C. Williams took this photo in CTA days.

An introduction to CSL passenger cars

In writing about the Surface Lines fleet of nearly 5,000 passenger cars it is possible to use many methods of presentation. One can arrange the cars in numerical order by series, or under the names of the four companies underlying the CSL which actually owned the cars, or by date of construction. In this section they are arranged in numerical order, starting with 101-700 and ending with 9000-9046. Ownership, some construction details, dates of service, and in some cases route assignments are given for all cars in this section. Detailed scale drawings of some of the cars, as well as a list of car ownership by underlying company, can be found in the Equipment Appendix.

Perhaps the most unusual passenger car to operate over CSL was Cook County Hospital Car 1. Built in CSL's own West Shops in 1918, it carried patients from Cook County Psychopathic Hospital at Polk and Wood Streets to state asylums at Dunning and Manteno. CSL lines were used to reach Dunning, which was served by an extension from the west end of the Irving Park streetcar line. To reach Manteno the car used CSL and Chicago & Interurban Traction Company lines. A single track spur was built from CSL's Harrison Street line down Wood Street and into the County Hospital grounds. A similar spur served Dunning.

The car was divided into two compartments. The men's section had nine double seats for 18 men, two reclining seats for invalids, and two upper and lower berths. The women's section had five conventional double seats for 10 women, two reclining seats for invalids, and one double berth. Each section had its own enclosed flush toilet.

In outward appearance the car resembled an electric interurban car, and in fact it was equipped as such. The MCB trucks had wheels with a three inch tread and a three-quarter inch flange to AREA interurban standards. Four GE-210 motors with a gear ratio of 24:63, identical to Chicago & Interurban Traction electrical equipment, powered Cook County 1. The vestibules at each end of the car had railroad-type trapdoors covering the steps, arranged so that patients could be removed on stretchers.

For operation on the private right-of-way of the C&IT, the car carried an interurban arc headlight, dimmed while running in Chicago. Painted CSL's standard medium green, it was trimmed in red. Its lettering identified it as Cook County Hospital Car 1, and it was evidently owned by the Hospital.

Service between the Hospital and the Dunning asylum lasted from 1918 until 1939, with the car making one trip a

● Opposite page. A cautious motorman on the near track slows his southbound Racine Ave. car to a crawl to avoid trapping pedestrians between streetcars in this scene at State and Washington. David R. Phillips collection. ● Above. Cook County 1 at West Shops. Neuberger collection, from A. C. Williams.

week with a CSL crew. (The service to Manteno had been discontinued earlier, probably with the abandonment of C&IT service in 1927.) The Hospital provided its own attendants for the patients enroute. The Chicago Motor Coach Company is said to have provided the same service after CSL discontinued its Hospital car operation, but details are lacking.

To simplify the CSL passenger car roster, the following table has been prepared. It gives the official designation and/or unofficial nickname for many series of CSL cars. Except for a small fleet of Birney safety cars, the Surface Lines did not buy or build any single truck cars, and those acquired before the 1914 unification by the underlying companies are not included in the table or in the detailed listing of cars by series.

As the table shows there were several series which were alike but carried different series numbers. This is because the cars, though alike, were owned by the four underlying companies. After the unification of 1914, cars were ordered on a 60/40 basis, with sixty per cent going to Chicago Railways and 40 per cent going to Chicago City Railway. Aside from the rebuilding of the funeral cars into passenger cars in 1919, the only Calumet & South Chicago Railway car built after 1914 was 2859, built as a replacement for 2850 in 1924. No new equipment was ever built for the Southern Street Railway Company during the CSL era.

Some general notes on car design and construction are in order here. All CSL cars listed in this chapter were double ended, except for the following: 3322-3381 and 6280-6319 (Peter Witts), 4001-4411 and 7001-7274 (Experimental pre-PCCs and the 1936 and 1947 PCCs) and cars 5703-5827 (the Nearsides). All cars listed had two trucks, except the following series: 2000-2005 and 2900-2903 (Birney cars) 2006, and 4000, the three-truck articulated car. Most of the cars had four motors, although the Surface Lines did use many two-motor cars with maximum traction trucks.

The first decade of the Twentieth Century and the 10 years after World War II marked the periods of greatest change for street railway transportation in Chicago. In the first period of ten years electric cars replaced the last horse cars and cable cars, and double truck electric cars began to replace single truck electrics. The decade following the end of WW II saw the dismantling of the world's largest street railway system and its replacement by various types of buses. During both periods of rapid change the vehicles originally used as feeders to the dominant means of transportation became themselves the dominant means. The early electric cars were feeders to the cable car lines until they replaced all cable car lines. Likewise the early gas bus lines were mostly feeders to the streetcar lines, and ultimately replaced them.

The various city ordinances, state laws, and Illinois Commerce Commission decisions under which CSL operated had an effect on car design. Many car designs were worked out jointly by the CSL and the Board of Supervising Engineers, a board of engineers and accountants set up in 1907 to keep track of expenses and make sure that the companies obeyed the Settlement Ordinance of 1907 and all other street railway legislation. The Board had four members: a chairman and chief engineer, a representative from the City of Chicago, and a representative from Chicago Railways and from Chicago City Railway. After the underlying companies entered receivership, the receivers continued to support the work of the Board, and it functioned until the Chicago Transit Authority took over in 1947.

The Settlement Ordinance of 1907 required the Chicago City Railway to operate at least 800 double truck cars. Chicago Railways was allowed to run 486 closed cars and 564 open cars, but had to increase its

Common Names for CSL Cars

Official Designation or Nickname	Series
Old Pullmans, Big Pullmans	101-700
Pressed Steels	701-750
New Pullmans, Small Pullmans	751-1100
St. Louis Rebuilds, Matchboxes	1101-1423
CUT Rebuilds, Bowling Alleys	1429-1505
CRys Cars, Turtlebacks	1506-1720
169 cars, Broadway-States	1721-1785
Flexible Flyers	1800-1999
Birneys	2000-2006
St. Louis Rebuilds	2501-2625
St. Louis Rebuilds	2701-2780
Interstates	2846-2856
Birneys	2900-2903
CSL Safety Cars, Sewing Machines	2904-2922
CSL Safety Cars, Sewing Machines	3092-3118
169 cars, Broadway-States	3119-3178
Sun Parlors	3179-3201
Multiple Unit Cars	3202-3321
FECE, Peter Witts, Sedans	3322-3381
Pullman Special	4001
PCCs, Blue Geese	4002-4051
PCC, Green Hornets	4052-4411
Little Brills	5001-5200
Big Brills	5201-5600
Crete Suburban Cars (on C&IT)	5651-5665
Nearsides, Muzzleloaders	5703-5827
169 cars, Broadway-States	6155-6198
Multiple Unit Cars	(a) 6199-6279
FECE, Peter Witts, Sedans	6280-6319
Brill Special	7001
PCCs, Blue Geese	7002-7034
Green Hornets	7035-7274

a. Except 6239, built to replace 2726.

Opposite page. For a decade Chicagoans could ride their last miles in style in one of two funeral cars, built in 1910 for the C&SC. When built they carried the numbers 1 and 2, changed to work car numbers Y-301 and Y-302 in 1916. When CSL funeral service ended in 1919, the cars were re-numbered 2857 and 2858 and ran in regular passenger service. Photo courtesy of Chicago Transit Authority.

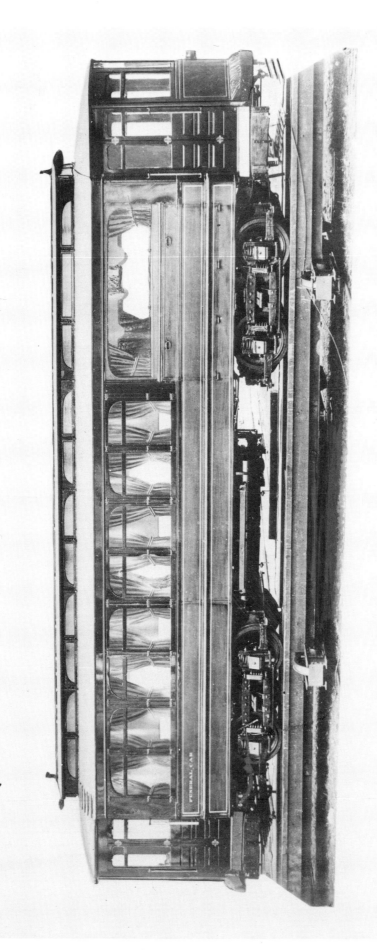

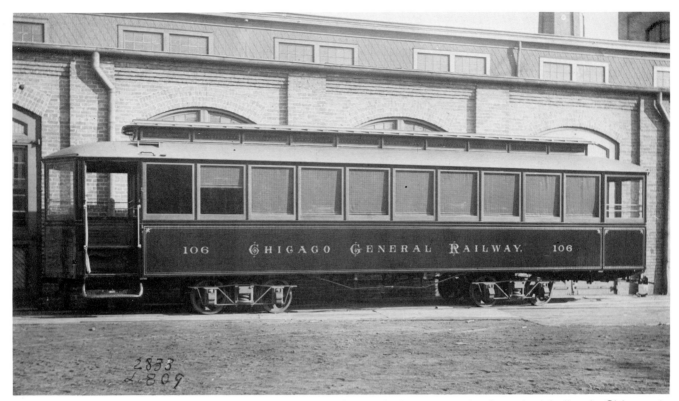

Above. Chicago General Railway, later the Southern Street Railway, was the first electric line in Chicago to use double truck electric streetcars. Car 106 was one of these first cars, built by Pullman in 1895. It was scrapped ca. 1909-1910.

Opposite page and below. Pullman also built a number of single truck cars for Chicago General Railway in 1895. Like the double truck cars, they were painted a dark blue and loaded from the rear. While some early electric cars retained kerosene or gas lights, car 54 also used electricity for lighting. All three photos were taken at the Pullman plant at Pullman, Ill. From the Smithsonian collection, used by permission.

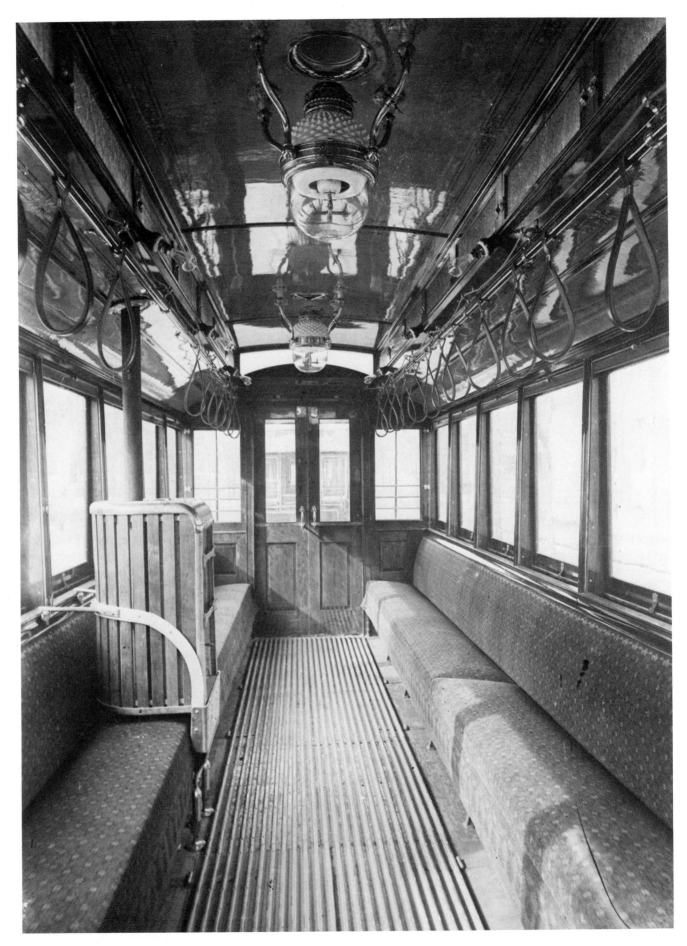

Today the cable cars and the early electric cars may seem toy-like, but in their time they were excellent people movers. Here a State Street grip car and trailer carries an overflow crowd to Chicago Day at the 1893 World's Fair. Photo from CTA.

Opposite page and below. Handsome CCRy car 2176 was built in 1896 by Pullman, and renumbered to 2338 in 1908. The car was painted olive green with white trim on the outside, and had a mahogany finish on the inside. Both photos were taken at the Pullman plant at Pullman, Ill. Prints from the Smithsonian Institution, Washington, D.C., used with their permission.

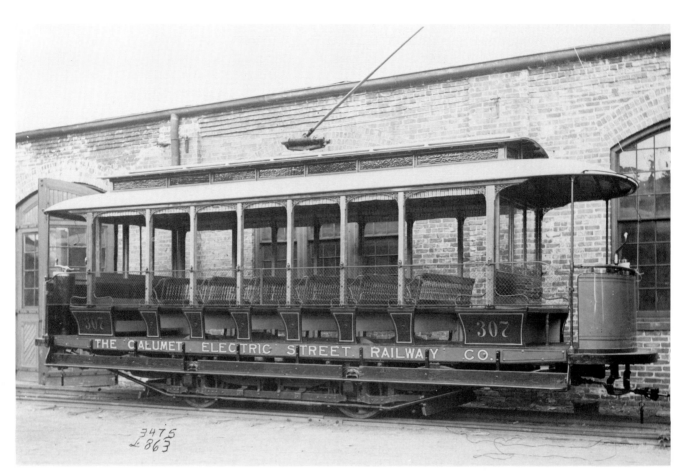

• Above. From the first mild days of spring until the start of winter, the Calumet Electric Street Railway ran single truck open streetcars such a number 307. This Pullman-built car, painted chrome yellow, ran on lines in the far southeast corner of the city. Photo from Smithsonian. • Below. State Street cable trailer poses for an official photo at the Brill plant before shipment to Chicago. Barney Neuberger collection, from Jack Doyle. Though delightful on a warm, clear summer day, open cars were expensive when used in Chicago, since closed cars had to be purchased for use in winter. Some of CSL's predecessor companies reduced this expense by using the same set of trucks under an open car body in summer and a closed body in winter.

• Above. One of the larger cars built at the turn of the century was Chicago Union Traction 4499, a product of the company's own shops. This photo of its crew was taken on the Lake Street line under the Lake "L" on July 18, 1909. Photo from the Bernard Rossbach collection. • Below. Wabash Ave. (Cottage Grove) grip car will drop the last car in its train, an Indiana Ave. horsecar, at 22nd and Wabash for pickup by a team of horses for the trip further south via 22nd and Indiana. Author's collection. For several years after the electrification of the cable car lines, the electric cars continued to haul cable car trailers. Trailers came back into use on heavy lines in 1921-1930. Trailer operation had been forbidden under the Settlement Ordinances of 1907.

Above. Pullman-built CCRy open car was outshopped in 1896 painted yellow. In 1908 the car was modernized with a glass front, and the paint scheme changed to dark green with orange trim. Smithsonian photo.

Opposite page and below. Tiny single truck car 4 was run by the Calumet Electric Street Railway, the first company in the Chicago area to use electric streetcars. Though it was electrically lighted, car 4 depended on muscle power for braking and a stove for winter heat. In later years when electricity was used to pump up air for the brake system and to heat streetcars through resistance grids, the power drain for these auxiliaries — particularly the heating — was quite substantial. Both photos from the Smithsonian collection.

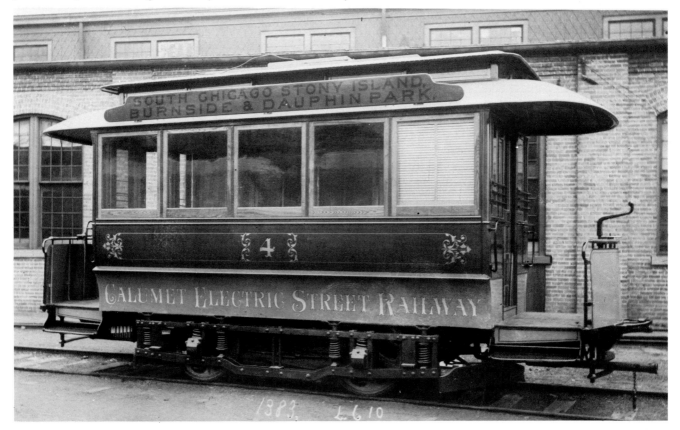

• Above. CSL 5465 southbound on the Halsted-Archer (Halsted-Downtown) line on Clark at Polk. Dearborn Station is in the background. Author's collection. • Below. Same type of car as shown in photo above about 25 years later in the CTA era, still in good condition. Note slightly different paint schemes. CTA photo.

total ownership to 1,200 cars of all kinds at the end of the reconstruction period specified in the Ordinance. The specifications for the cars were general, and were the same for both Chicago Railways and Chicago City Railway.

Among the general specifications was one that called for heating the cars to 50 degrees in winter. From this requirement came the standard thermometer carried on all cars on one of the window posts so that riders could check the temperature. Ads were allowed, but only on the inside of the car, and then only in the space between the top of the windows and the transom. CSL lost much revenue because it could not carry ads on the outside of the cars, but the cars looked better without them. The ordinance did permit the operation of funeral cars and mail cars.

Two men, a motorman and conductor, were required on each car. Train operation was forbidden, and the companies had to dispose of their trailer cars. For some time before the passage of the ordinance the companies had hauled cable car trailers behind electric cars on such busy lines as Madison Street.

Perhaps the most revolutionary change of the 1900-1910 era was the introduction of the Pay As You Enter car, abbreviated PAYE. Chicago City Railway's 5301-5600 series cars were the first PAYE type to enter service in Chicago in 1907. Similar cars in the 5000-5300 series, built in 1905-06, were converted to PAYE in 1908-09. Chicago Railways' first PAYE cars were the 101-700 series Old Pullmans, built in 1908-09. Prior to the development of the PAYE car, fare payment had been something of a hit or miss affair. Passengers could board or get off at either the front or the rear of the car, and the conductor had to always be on the move through the car to collect fares and issue transfers.

With the conductor necessarily always on the move, safety also suffered. A report prepared in 1906 by a traction expert employed by the city showed that 52 accidents involving streetcars took place in a period of 50 days. Twenty-one persons were killed and 86 injured. Mayor Dunne compared this record with that of Liverpool, England, which had only three streetcar-related deaths in an 18-month period.

The PAYE car was such a radical change from the old equipment that Chicago City Railway felt it was necessary to distribute a four-page brochure to its passengers, explaining in detail the passenger flow through the cars. One illustration showed a conductor blocking the platform, urging prospective riders to board the next car. Conductors were instructed to limit passenger loads to a total of 80 seated and standing passengers. Passengers could board the PAYE car at the rear end only, paying their fare to the conductor, who was stationed on the rear platform. He stood behind a railing which channeled riders around him and through a door in the bulkhead and into the carbody. Exit was either front or rear. The single-stream rear exit was forward of the double-stream rear entrance, and access to the rear exit was through a separate door from the carbody to the platform, to assure separation of entering and exiting passengers.

The Chicago City Railway cars were of the 1905 Montreal standard type, with minor modifications to the cross seats, heaters, and vents, and the addition of some safety features. Seating capacity was 44, and a maximum of 36 standing passengers was the seldom-enforced rule. Large platforms at each end of the car were arranged for operation in either direction. The folding rear doors were kept open at all times, although CCRy did consider using Minneapolis folding gates to protect the rear while the car was in motion.

Built just before the PAYE car became the standard in Chicago, this 1905 American Car product was rebuilt into a PAYE car in 1908, and scrapped in 1948. R. H. Kennedy took this photo, which came from the A. C. Williams collection. Photo taken at the 69th and Ashland carbarn.

R-8671
CHICAGO ARCHITECTURAL
PHOTOGRAPHING COMPANY

• Above. Car 2811 has clear running on this part of the Riverdale (Michigan-Indiana) line. Barney Neuberger collection. • Opposite page. Cars trapped by congestion in downtown Chicago. David R. Phillips collection. • Below. At speed on private right-of-way, car 7004 nears the west end of the 63rd Street line. Photo by A. C. Williams. Two cars in background indicate close headways on this busy crosstown line.

After the Cottage Grove line was fully equipped with PAYE cars, surplus cars were assigned to the Indiana Avenue line. This route ran parallel to Cottage Grove, and like the former was a heavily used trunk line. Each streetcar crew received a printed timetable with a number of different running times for their route printed on it. Starters at the end of the line, working under the dispatcher with whom they were in telephone contact, would display a number to a crew and ring a bell. The number corresponded to one of the running times on the timecards the crew had, and the bell was the starting signal. Trainmen also received keys to lineside telephone boxes, where they could call the dispatcher for further orders or summon a wreck wagon. In the Loop District, where even minor delays could seriously disrupt schedules, trainmen could summon wreck wagons directly without going through the dispatcher.

The PAYE car lived up to the expectations Chicago traction men held for it. Accident statistics gathered soon after their introduction showed a 32 per cent reduction in accidents to passengers while boarding the car, leaving the car, or riding the car around curves. Financial men felt pleased with the results for the first 14 months of operation. Total receipts increased 4.4 per cent, car hours fell 8.9 per cent, and receipts per car hour increased 15.2 per cent. Operating men could point to a small but worthwhile improvement in schedule speeds on the lines using PAYE cars.

In these introductory remarks Chicago's first PAYE cars have received detailed attention. They happened to be Chicago City Railway cars. For a full treatment of Chicago Railways' first PAYE cars, see series 101-700 in the next chapter.

Throughout the CSL era there was great emphasis on proper operation of cars to save wear on equipment and cut the cost of electricity. Through tests made on the Van Buren Street line in 1911, it was found that considerable money could be saved if motormen coasted more often. The principal savings came through lower power costs and less brake shoe wear. Pressed Steel cars in the 701-750 series made the test runs, equipped with Railway Improvement Company coasting time recorders. Van Buren Street was chosen for the test because it was narrow and choked with horse-drawn wagons, making it one of the most difficult streets to coast upon. Even so, tests determined that motormen could coast for fully half the time their cars were moving. In late 1922 CSL ordered more than 3,000 watt-hour meters, enough to equip every car on the system. They measured current consumption and provided a check on the motorman's power use.

The PAYE cars were perhaps as much of a standard car as CSL ever had. The Brill Nearsides, which were built for the Chicago City Railway in 1912, had a design made popular in Philadelphia but really unsuited to Chicago. The 1913 Chicago City Railway cars marked somewhat of a return to the old Brill standard cars, but they had arch rather than deck roofs, and platform seats which brought their seating capacity to 54, ten more than the Brills.

Each vestibule of the 1913 cars had a single manually-operated door with an interlocked step mechanism that raised the step when the door closed and lowered it when the door opened. The other side of the platform had a pair of doors, also manually operated, with a step interlock. The single door was used as a front exit under the

At the east end of the 63rd Street line, CTA 391 swings off Stony Island into 64th Street in this A. C. Williams photo taken in April, 1952. Trees in Jackson Park give this scene a tranquil feeling; actually it is in the Woodlawn ghetto. Note the extreme overhang of the car body on this tight curve.

motorman's control. The conductor controlled the pair of rear doors, one an entrance the other an exit.

To reduce accidents caused by moving the car while the rear door was open, a signal light interlocked with the rear doors was installed in each vestibule. This signal gave the motorman a positive indication of door position. In effect the 1913 cars had the safety advantages of the Nearsides' enclosed entrance without their disadvantage of front-end congestion.

As a result of tests conducted in 1910-1911, both Chicago Railways and the Chicago City Railway adopted the maximum traction truck as standard equipment, and the 1913 cars were among the first CCRy cars to have them. They were Brill 39-E-1 trucks with wheels of 34" and 22" diameter. Other equipment included two GE 242-A motors with field taps and K-51-A controllers.

The 1913 Chicago Railways cars in the 1800-1999 series also had maximum traction trucks, field control motors, and greater seating capacity than their PAYE predecessors in the 101-700 series. Built to CRys own design, these Flexible Flyers had two Westinghouse 534-Y1 motors, arch roofs, seats for 53, and heating controlled by a thermostat. Two motors were used for several reasons. One was the truck design: maximum traction trucks could accomodate only one motor per truck. Compared to the four motors previously used on Chicago cars two motors were cheaper to buy and maintain than four motors of equivalent horsepower. Their big disadvantage was motor failure, since the car could barely creep along on its remaining good motor. Motor failure also posed a hazard in tunnel operation, and Chicago had three streetcar tunnels under the Chicago River. Tests showed that a disabled car could climb out of the river tunnels on an 11.5 per cent grade with just one motor in service, but a running start had to be made to make the grade.

The 1907 Settlement Ordinances prohibited one-man car operation in Chicago, but during 1920 the Illinois Public Utility Commission held hearings to determine the feasibility of such operation. The Commission was newly established and struggling to assert its authority over street railways in every part of the state. Expert witnesses, among them Chicago Transportation Supervisor R. R. Kelker, Jr., agreed that one-man cars would never be suitable for operation through the Loop. However Kelker agreed that there were many outlying lines where use of one-man cars could improve service and lower costs. His figures showed that three one-man cars could be run for less than two two-man cars. It seemed a perfect solution to the problem of public demand for more service and CSL's need to economize.

CSL got permission to start one-man service on outlying light lines, and in early 1921 placed Birney cars in operation on the Division Extension. A total of 10 cars were delivered in the usual 60/40 ratio. Cars 2000-2005 went to Chicago Railways, cars 2900-2903 to Chicago City Railway. Only 28', 1" long, these cars had a single Brill 79-E-1 truck with an 8' wheelbase and 26" diameter wheels. There were two GE 264-A motors with K-63 controls. There were seats for 32, the smallest seating capacity of any CSL car.

The Brill Birney was a standardized design built by the hundreds and used in many cities. It did cut CSL's platform costs, but there were drawbacks to Birney operation in Chicago. Their single front door, used as both an entrance and an exit, was always a source of conges-

Motorman and newsboy pose in front of this Birney car loading at Division and Grand for an eastbound run to Division and Austin. Note cream door post, indicating a front entrance car. Photo taken in August, 1921. B. A. Rossbach collection.

Three types of CSL one-man car. • Above. Double truck safety car 3092, built by CSL in 1921, was their answer to the problems they had with the Birney. It became the prototype for two series of cars, 2904-2922 and 3093-3118. • Opposite page. Car 1415 was one of several in the 1101-1423 series (1389-1423) converted to one-man operation in 1924. It is shown in operation on the Webster-Racine line. • Bottom. Looking much the worse for wear, Birney car 2004 rests at the North Avenue carhouse. Though popular in many other cities, the Birney was too small and too light to be successful on even the lightest lines in Chicago. All were scrapped in 1937. Photos from the Neuberger collection. Two factors leading to CSL's use of one-man cars in the early 1920s were the ever-increasing wages paid to trainmen and the need for small cars on streetcar extensions which tapped lightly-settled parts of Chicago.

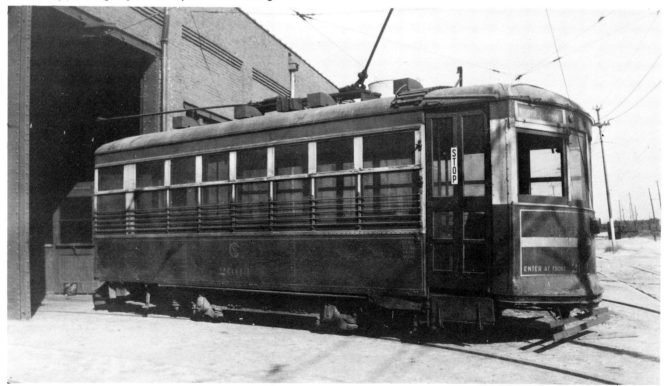

tion. Another bad feature was the conflicting passenger flow through the car, as those who moved to the rear to find a seat struggled past riders moving forward to get off. A third disadvantage was the relatively light construction of the car. It saved power, but the car crumpled easily when hit.

To remedy these faults, CSL built two one-man cars to its own designs in 1921. One was a single-truck car, the other a double-truck. The CSL's own single-trucker was lighter than the Brill cars, yet had heavier front end framing to reduce collision damage, a wider aisle, and separate entrance and exit doors to relieve congestion.

A treadle-operated gate at the exit door permitted passengers to alight, but prevented boarding from the street. The gate on the single-truck car was put in service in September, 1921, and on the double-truck car in December. The success of the gate led to the construction of a full-size model of a treadle-operated door, and such a door was later installed on one of the test cars.

The experimental car with double trucks, 3092, became a prototype for CSL's own two series of one-man safety cars: CCRy 2904-2922 and CRys 3093-3118. However, the production model cars were one window longer than 3092 and seated 50, five more than the prototype. By 1924 at least 14 lines had one-man cars, though of course not all were Birneys or CSL double-truck safety cars. CSL converted some older cars, such as 1398-1423, to one-man operation in 1924.

CSL certainly accomplished what it set out to do when it built its double-truck safety cars. They were much bigger than the Birneys, had seats for 50, wide aisles, and air-operated, treadle-actuated exit doors, yet weighed just 31,800 lbs. CSL saved weight everywhere it could: the two K-68 controllers had aluminum frames and tops, saving 120 lbs. per car.

Throughout this chapter there are references to cars destroyed by fire, the great enemy of the wooden streetcar. The most disastrous blaze was the Devon carhouse fire of January 26, 1922, which claimed 90 cars. Among those destroyed were nine of the trailers built in 1921, 14 of the Old Pullmans which had been rebuilt to haul trailers, 57 other passenger cars, four sprinklers, three snow sweepers, and two snow plows. Half the carhouse was a total loss, and the cars which survived did so only because employees had time to close the firedoors which separated the two halves of the carhouse. The office section of the carhouse also escaped damage. The total loss was set at one million dollars.

Despite the loss of 90 cars, CSL was able to provide full service the next day on those North Side routes served by Devon carhouse. Extra cars were drawn from the reserve cars kept at CSL's 15 other operating stations. At that time CSL had more than 3,000 cars on the roster, and the loss of even 90 cars was not a crippling blow to the system. For details on other cars lost through fire, see the individual series histories in the next chapter. More information on carhouse construction will be found in the chapter on carhouses and shops.

To replace the cars lost in the Devon fire, CSL ordered and built a mixed batch of cars known by their total number as the "169 cars." They included the 1721-1785 series of 1923 steel cars built at West Shops, and the 3119-3178 and 6155-6198 series built by the Surface Lines, Brill, and Cummings. Of this total of 169 cars, CSL built 69, J. G. Brill built 70, and McGuire-Cummings built 30. Orders to build the cars were given in such a way that the complete series would be ready to go into service at about the same time. These cars were the first to carry CSL's new color scheme, red below the belt rail and cream above. Some equipped for hauling

trailers, the 169 cars weighed about 7,700 lbs. less than the Old Pullmans modified for trailer-pulling service.

The 169 cars marked a return to four motor streetcars by the Surface Lines (4 GE-275-B motors with K-35 control and line switches interlocked with the doors). Trucks were Brill 51-E-2 with 28″ wheels. Many of the platform details set these cars apart: aluminum grab rails, use of a fare box, route and destination signs carried over the right hand vestibule window rather than over the center window, and folding rear doors air-operated by the conductor. The motorman controlled the single sliding front door. With their four 60 HP motors these cars were well equipped for running on the tunnel routes or for hauling trailers all day long.

Although the last two cars of series 3179-3201 were equipped with experimental multiple-unit control, it was later removed from these 1923 CSL-built cars. The first regular multiple unit cars were a lot of 100 built in 1924 by the Lightweight Noiseless Streetcar Company of Minneapolis and by the CSL's own West Shops. As usual the 60/40 ratio was used, with Chicago Railways getting 60 cars (3202-3261), and Chicago City Railway receiving 40 cars (6199-6238). Surface Lines reverted to maximum

traction trucks for this series (Brill 39-E-2X) with 28″ and 22″ wheels. Two 60 HP GE 275-B motors were regulated by GE Type M multiple unit control. MU control differed from the traditional "K" type, in which the 600-volt propulsion current passed through the controller. In MU control the controller regulated the speed of a pilot motor, which in turn made and broke the connections between the motors and the resistances. It is the same sort of control used on subway trains and electrified suburban railroads, where a dozen or more cars can be run by one man. On CSL, though, two car MU trains were the rule.

For easy train makeup these cars carried Tomlinson couplers, which automatically made the air connection between cars. However, electrical connections had to be made by hand through jumper cables. When operated as a single car, this series carried a two-man crew; when operated as a two-car train the lead car carried a motorman and conductor and the rear car a conductor. Passengers entered the lead car of a two car train at the rear, and left by either the front or the rear. Passengers entered the rear car at the front door and left via the front or rear. In train operation the lead car had seats for 51, and

• Opposite page. Doing what it was built to do, car 1756 pulls trailer 8049. CTA photo. • Below. Repainted in September, 1942 as an armed forces recruiting car, 1775 carries a load of Navy volunteers along State St. George Krambles collection.

the rear car seats for 54. Door controls were arranged so that all the doors on one side of a car could be opened from either end. This speeded loading at terminals, and was also designed to expedite loading in the proposed streetcar subways. Although 50 of the 100 cars in this series were built by the Lightweight Noiseless Streetcar Company of Minneapolis, they were all built to CSL specifications and did not have the "noiseless" improvements such as band brakes, roller bearing trucks, and light weight.

While experimenting with new ideas such as MU train operation, CSL continued to upgrade and improve its older equipment. In 1923, for example, the Surface Lines added a five and three-eighths inch red semaphore tail light to all its cars without rear platforms (the trailers and the Nearsides).

CSL continued its car experiments in the 1920s by building an articulated streetcar from the bodies of two 1903 St. Louis cars and a drum vestibule. It was designed to handle industrial peak loads on lines which could otherwise be served by much smaller cars. Completed August 3, 1925, the car went into service on the Cicero line to handle shift changes at the Western Electric plant. It also reportedly ran on the Ewing-Brandon line to serve Republic Steel. Although it could seat 91 persons, car 4000 was never very successful and CSL dropped the idea of converting other old cars into articulateds. Car 4000 was withdrawn from service in 1930 and scrapped March 30, 1937.

The Surface Lines asked both Brill and Pullman to come up with what would now be called "state of the art cars" embodying every up-to-date feature. The result was Pullman car 4001, built for Chicago Railways, and Brill car 7001, built for Chicago City Railway. Both cars were completed in 1934, saw service on Through Route 22, made special trips to serve the World's Fair, went on display at the World's Fair, and were soon withdrawn from service. Although they had a brief life, both cars had a deep influence on Surface Lines management. They convinced CSL that builders could come up with a light weight, high speed, smooth running, fast accelerating, comfortable, modern streetcar. Less than two years after the two experimental cars began to run, CSL received its first order of Presidents Conference Committee Cars, known as PCCs. The experimental cars had helped convince CSL that there was a future for the streetcar. Ultimately Chicago ordered 683 PCC cars, the largest fleet of new cars to run in any U.S. city. For further details on the experimental cars and the 1936 PCCs, look under their series numbers in the next chapter. (4001 and 7001, 4002-4051 and 7002-7034).

On March 3, 1945 the Federal Court overseeing the bankruptcy of the underlying companies gave the CSL authority to buy 200 new streetcars. One hundred ten PCC cars were ordered from Pullman and 90 PCC cars from St. Louis, at a cost of a little over $22,000 a car. CSL planned to use 185 of the cars to re-equip Clark-Wentworth, and the remaining 15 to supplement Madison Street service, at that time largely given by 1936 PCC cars. The new cars were nine feet wide, three inches wider than the Madison Street PCCs, with the extra room used to increase aisle width. A windshield slanted back into the car and a shadow apron above the windshield made the motorman's job easier by eliminating night-time reflections from interior lighting.

Dynamic brakes brought the cars almost to a stop,

Pullman thought that a modern mid-Thirties streetcar should look like this. Car 4001 was built by Pullman for Chicago Railways in 1934, and featured an all-aluminum body and acceleration at 4.75 mph/sec. Photo courtesy of Pullman-Standard.

with spring-applied drum brakes completing the stop. No air brakes were used on these cars: in the jargon of the trade they were known as "all-electric" PCCs. Four track brakes, one on each side of each truck, could be used either with or without the other brakes. Battery powered, they could be used even if the trolley pole left the wire. For standing passengers there was the added amenity of small windows above the regular windows, placed to give standees a chance to look out of the car.

Like all other Chicago PCCs, these cars were delivered as two-man cars with hand controls for the motorman. When they were converted for one-man operation on the Cottage Grove and Western lines, pedals replaced the hand controls.

CSL ordered 400 additional PCC cars in December, 1945. In addition to re-equipping Clark-Wentworth and supplementing service on Madison, these cars were intended to replace old streetcars on Broadway-State, Western, and 63rd Street. CSL and later CTA did eventually place PCCs on all these lines, as well as on Halsted and Cottage Grove. However, 63rd got the 1936 PCC cars from Madison Street when 96 post-war PCCs replaced the Madison PCCs in 1948. The pre-war cars and a few converted post-war cars later ran on Cottage Grove. Western Ave. used both pre-war and post-war PCC cars. Broadway-State and Clark-Wentworth used post-war PCCs exclusively.

Of the 83 pre-war PCCs only car 4021 survives. CTA kept it as part of its historical collection, and it is now in storage. Post-war car 4391 was sold to the Electric Railway Historical Society in 1959. It has been restored to operating condition and is on display at the Illinois Railway Museum at Union, Ill. It too is the sole survivor of its class of car.

However, salvaged parts from the post-war cars were used to build 570 new "L" - Subway cars for use on Chicago's rapid transit lines. Like the Surface Lines, the Chicago Rapid Transit Company was taken over by the CTA on October 1, 1947, and needed new equipment even more badly than the Surface Lines. So as the streetcar lines went to bus, CTA shipped PCC car 4394 to Pullman and car 4381 to St. Louis for conversion to experimental rapid transit cars. CTA sent the cars in October, 1952. Both cars were scrapped after conversion experiments in early 1953.

A total of 150 cars (4172-4321) were sold to the St. Louis Car Co. during 1953. They were scrapped at St. Louis. Salvage parts such as trucks, seats, windows, and other components went into rapid transit cars 6201-6350. In early 1954 cars 4122-4171 and 4322-4371 were sold to St. Louis Car., scrapped in St. Louis, and parts used in rapid transit cars 6351-6450. The same use was made of the following cars: 4102-4121, shipped in December, 1954, parts used in cars 6451-6470; cars 4062-4101 and 7045-7085 shipped in December, 1955, used in cars 6471-6550; cars 7086-7135, shipped in March and April, 1956, used in cars 6551-6600; cars 4052-4061, 7035-7044, 7225-7274 shipped from January to April, 1957, used in cars 6601-6670.

Cars 4372-4377, 4379, 4382-4386, 7136-7216, and 7219-7224 were shipped from May to August, 1958 and used in rapid transit cars 6671-6720 and 1 to 50. Only the body fittings were used to build cars 1-4, as these had special high-speed trucks and controls.

Other cars of interest are noted under their respective series numbers in this chapter. More complete technical

Brill experimental car 7001, like its counterpart car 4001, actually served the Chicago World's Fair grounds during 1934. Famed stylist and designer Otto Kuhler gave this car its sleek shape. Paint scheme was aluminum and two-tone green. Photo from the Neuberger collection.

• Above. View from the rear of a 1936 PCC car shows center exit and front entrance. There was also a single rear exit door. Photo from St. Louis Car. • Below. Two postwar PCCs pass at 59th and Wentworth on the Clark-Wentworth line. Photo by Roy Benedict.

• Above. Prewar PCC rests at the 69th and Ashland carhouse after a run on 63rd Street in this April 28, 1951 photo by A. C. Williams. Note tiger stripes on dash. • Below. Just five days before the CTA replaced the streetcars with buses, A. C. Williams snapped 7020 southbound at 95th and Cottage Grove on June 14, 1955.

• Above. Most postwar Chicago PCC cars lasted a decade or less, while the prewar cars lasted some 20 years. Some of the postwar cars, like the one in this photo, were simply scrapped by commercial scrap merchants without any attempt to salvage components. Photo taken in August, 1959 by Jeff Wien in a scrap yard at 67th and Cicero. • Below. CTA sold 570 of its 600 postwar PCCs to St. Louis Car Co., which scrapped them and used the parts to build CTA rapid transit cars 6201-6720 and 1-50. This Neuberger collection photo shows some of the car bodies in a St. Louis scrap yard. Note both light and dark green color schemes on the cars.

• Above. The postwar PCCs contributed some components to CTA's high speed rapid transit cars in the 1-4 series. However, the trucks for these experimental cars were built especially for them and had high horsepower motors. This 1958 St. Louis Car Company photo shows car 2 on the transfer table at the St. Louis plant. • Below. CTA locomotive L-202 has just brought PCC 7060 to the railroad interchange at 84th and Wentworth. From there it will go to St. Louis for scrapping and salvage of parts. A. C. Williams photo on November 16, 1955. L-202 wound up on the rapid transit division too, as locomotive S-343.

• Above. A CSL Peter Witt car painted in the conventional carmine red and cream paint scheme, the CSL's standard colors for conventional equipment from 1921 until the end of the Surface Lines in 1947. Assigned to the Madison route, the car was photographed at the Kedzie and Van Buren carhouse. CTA photo. • Opposite page. Postwar PCC cars painted Mercury Green and Croydon Cream with a Swamp Holly Orange belt rail (note bus in same scheme) contrast sharply with conventional cars in the red and cream scheme. Photo at State and Randolph from the David R. Phillips collection. • Below. Although most CSL cars were red and cream, the Surface Lines did experiment with new colors: Birney 2902 (illustrated elsewhere in this book), experimental cars 4001 and 7001, the 1936 PCC cars, and the postwar PCCs are some examples. A lesser-known color combination was tried on car 3236. It emerged from the paint shop in orange and cream livery. This photo from the A. C. Williams collection shows the car in service on the Armitage Avenue line. In addition to the color of the paint, there are other variations in the experimental scheme. Note that the upper window sash is painted cream, the lower sash orange. Also note that the CSL logo is near one truck, while the car number is near the other truck. Usually they would be centered, with the CSL logo over the car number.

data will be found in the Equipment Appendix, while operating details can be found in the chapter on route histories.

No discussion of CSL cars would be complete without mentioning their paint schemes. Chicago cars were rather somber looking until 1921. They had medium green bodies with red windows and yellow letters, numbers, and striping. In 1921 CSL changed the colors to carmine red below the belt rail on both sides and ends, cream from belt rail to roof, brown door and window sashes, weathered brown roof, black underbody and bumpers, and silver striping, numbers, and CSL emblem. A few years later the letterboards were also painted red rather than cream. By March, 1921, 100 of the newly-painted cars were on the streets of Chicago. Most conventional cars carried this paint scheme until their last runs in 1954. Work equipment retained the somber pre-1921 passenger car green paint until the end of streetcar service in Chicago.

CSL chose the bright new colors for a better psychological effect on riders, to make the cars more visible, and as a symbol of a forward-looking management. The "169 cars" series of 1923 were the first new CSL cars to carry the carmine red and cream scheme.

Since most Chicago streetcars had a rear entrance, front-entrance cars had distinctive paint schemes to alert the public that they should be entered at the front. The Birneys had a cream platform corner post adjacent to the front door. Later front-entrance cars had a single band of silver, later sometimes cream, across the dash. The Peter Witts and the Blue Goose cars had vertical hourglass figures on the dash, painted cream. Those on the Witts appeared like two triangles point to point, while those on the Blue Geese had a more streamlined shape.

On the cars with a post-WW II dark green and cream paint scheme, front entrance cars were indicated by cream wings around the headlight. The wings were used on both PCC cars and on the few conventional "red" streetcars which got green and cream paint jobs. On those PCC cars which could be used in either one or two-man service, a small sign reading "Enter At Front" could be displayed on the dash when the cars were operated by one man. (The cream wings on the one-man PCC cars should not be confused with the small chrome PCC car wings, which all post-war two-man PCC cars had around their headlights. The painted wings on the one-man PCCs were broad and deep, stretching across the entire dash. The wings on the repainted "169 cars" were thick and short.)

There were three basic paint schemes used on the PCC cars. The 1936 cars (4002-4051 and 7002-7034) were dark blue below the belt rail, had a red belt rail, and were cream above the belt rail, including the roof. There was a blue stripe on the lower part of the letterboard. Several of these cars in series 4002-4051 received experimental paint jobs in 1945. You'll find details in the next chapter under that car series.

As delivered, all the post-war PCC cars (4052-4411 and 7035-7274) had a light Mercury Green body below the belt rail, a Swamp Holly Orange belt rail, and a Croydon Cream body above the belt rail, including the roof.

In 1952, prior to going into service on the Cottage Grove line as one-man cars, the pre-war PCCs were repainted. They received an Everglade Green body below the belt rail and a Croydon Cream body above the belt rail, including the roof. Most of the post-war PCCs also got this darker green paint scheme during their short careers.

List of all Preserved Surface Lines Equipment

Car Number	Type of Car	Preserved By
4	Former Chicago Union Traction 4022.	Chicago Transit Authority
6	Chicago Railways United States Mail car.	Chicago Transit Authority
8	North Chicago Street Railroad horse car.	Chicago Transit Authority
10	Chicago City Railway horse car.	Museum of Science & Industry
144	CRys Old Pullman (101-700 series).	Illinois Railway Museum
209	Chicago City Railway cable trailer.	Chicago Transit Authority
225	CRys Old Pullman (101-700 series).	Seashore Trolley Museum
460	CRys Old Pullman (101-700 series).	Chicago Transit Authority
532	Chicago City Railway cable grip car.	Museum of Science & Industry
1374	"Matchbox," salt car AA-63	Illinois Railway Museum
1467	"Bowling Alley," salt car AA-72	Illinois Railway Museum
2843	SCCRy 323, C&SC 828, salt car AA-95	Illinois Railway Museum
2846	SCCRy 332, C&SC 831, salt car AA-98	Illinois Railway Museum
3142	"Broadway-State," "169 Cars"	Illinois Railway Museum
4001	Pullman Experimental, pre-PCC	Illinois Railway Museum
4021	Madison Street car, Blue Goose, PCC	Chicago Transit Authority
4391	Green Hornet, PCC	Illinois Railway Museum
9020	Chicago City Railway 1922 trailer.	Illinois Railway Museum
E-223	Chicago City Railway snow sweeper.	Illinois Railway Museum
X-4	Chicago Railways derrick car.	Illinois Railway Museum

CSL added silver striping to the body panels of the cars with carmine red and cream paint schemes. The striping was dropped during WW II, and the CTA did not use stripes on the cars it repainted.

On CSL's only articulated car, number 4000, there was a solid band of red below the belt rail across both the bodies and doors. Between the belt rail and the roof the body was cream. The continuous bands of color were used to give the car a smooth, streamlined appearance, and to mask the fact that it was built from two old cars.

Pullman experimental car 4001 had a color scheme similar to that later used on the 1936 PCCs, although those cars more nearly resembled Brill experimental car 7001 in design. Car 4001 had a light Royal Blue body below the belt rail, and silver above the belt rail including the roof, with black striping. The Brill experimental car, 7001, was aluminum and two-tone green with orange trim. CSL did experiment with other color schemes through the years.

In 1943 CSL painted 11 cars of the "169 cars" series with patriotic color schemes and appeals to support the war effort. They included three cars advertising War Bonds, six promoting military enlistments, one urging Community Fund contributions, and a CSL house ad summoning men to become "Trolley Pilots." A bus was also painted with a CSL house ad for bus drivers.

Of the thousands of horse cars, cable cars, and electric streetcars operated by the Surface Lines and its predecessors, a score have been preserved by various museums and by the Chicago Transit Authority. The list on page 44 shows where they are located. All the cars except those in the CTA's historical collection are on public display. CTA keeps its own cars under wraps at the Lincoln and Wrightwood barn. The list is strictly numerical by the number the car now carries. The car's original number and details of ownership are given next to the current number.

Some of the cars are in good condition. Old Pullman 144, for example, is regularly run for visitors to the Illinois Railway Museum at Union, Ill. The horse car and cable grip car on display in Chicago's Museum of Science & Industry have also been restored to excellent condition. Mail car 6 in the CTA collection was exhibited as recently as 1967 at the Ford City Shopping Center in Chicago. However, most of the CTA collection is never seen by the public. Green Hornet car 4391 is in operating condition, and the Illinois Railway Museum plans to run it during 1974. Old Pullman 225 at the Seashore Trolley Museum in Kennebunkport, Me., is also operable. Sweeper E-223 and derrick car X-4 have been operated at Union.

Of the remaining cars, those in the best condition are 4, 8, 10, and 209 in the CTA collection. The others may never be restored to operating condition, although some could well go on static display with a new coat of paint and minor repairs. Illinois Railway Museum's all-aluminum Pullman experimental car could be thus restored.

CCRy horse car 10 is preserved at Chicago's Museum of Science and Industry. Visible in this shot by Ray DeGroote, Jr., is State Street grip car 532 (see next page).

• Above. CCRy grip car 532 at the Chicago Railroad Fair in 1949. The car is now back on display in the Museum of Science and Industry, Chicago. Photo from Stephen D. Maguire. • Below. CCRy cable trailer 209 is part of the Chicago Transit Authority's collection of historic cars. Photo from the Neuberger collection.

• Above. North Chicago Street Railroad horse car 8 had a part in the "Wheels a' Rollin" pageant at the Chicago Railroad Fair in 1948-1949. CTA photo. • Below. West Chicago Street Railway single truck electric car 4 was originally Chicago Union Traction 4022, built by Pullman in 1895. The 33-foot car seats 30. CTA photo.

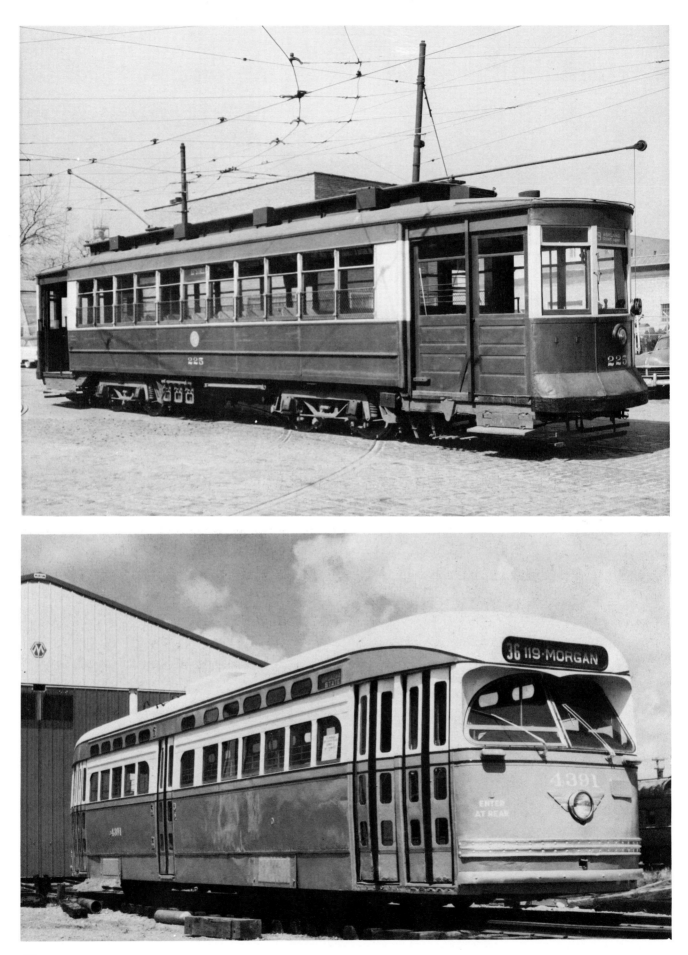

• Opposite page. Old Pullman 225 is now at the Seashore Trolley Museum at Kennebunkport, Me. Other cars in this series are 144, at the Illinois Railway Museum, and 460, saved by the Chicago Transit Authority. • Above. A number of Chicago area trolleys and buses were preserved by the Electric Railway Historical Society in a barn near suburban Downers Grove, Ill. Visible in this shot of the barn under construction are Chicago trolley bus 193 and PCC car 4391, both now at the Illinois Railway Museum at Union, Ill. The 4391 is the only preserved postwar PCC. Photo from the author's collection. Other ERHS cars in the collection now at Union include Chicago & West Towns passenger car 141, an ex-MU car from the LaGrange line. The car next to the trolley bus is CSL double truck snow plow F-305, which was being given a coat of primer paint when this photo was taken in 1959.

• Opposite page and above, left. Two views of PCC 4391 at the Illinois Railway Museum. Freshly painted and refurbished after years of storage, it may run again in 1974. Photos by Jeff Wien. • Above, right. West Chicago 4 in a 1936 parade to mark the opening of the Ashland Ave. bridge. A. C. Williams collection.

Passenger cars of the Surface Lines

The last car in the Old Pullman series, number 700, poses with incomplete platforms for the photographer at the Pullman plant. Note CRys logo. Smithsonian photo.

101-700

Known as the "Old Pullmans" or "Big Pullmans," the 600 cars of this series ran all over the CSL system, although their home was the city's North side. Their sheer bulk, long years of service, and great dependability made them the symbol of the largest street railway system in the United States. They made their last runs on Ashland, Halsted, Halsted-Downtown, and Kedzie-California. They were the last two-man conventional streetcars used in Chicago.

The first cars in this series arrived in the fall of 1908, and went into service on the busy Madison route. They replaced St. Louis-built cars in the 1306-1423 series, which were pulling cable car trailers. The St. Louis cars had replaced the Madison cable cars in August, 1906.

● Opposite page. Closeup of 700's platform shows entrance and exit passages with railing around conductor's station. Smithsonian photo. ● Above. J. Buck took this shot of CSL 118 in post-1920 colors, about to leave on an Armitage-Downtown run. Allan C. Williams collection.

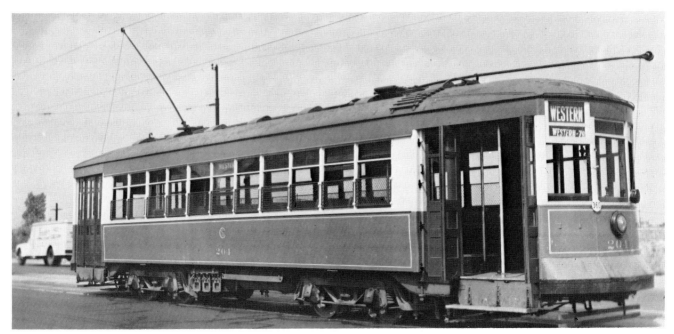

• Above. Rebuilt car 204 had an arch roof, no bulkheads, and indirect lighting. Barney Neuberger collection from Jack Doyle. • Opposite page. Car 229 at the 18th St. terminal of the Cermak line, built for the World's Fair of 1934. Even in CTA days the weed-grown loop handled big crowds. Alan W. Simms photo.

• Above. A. C. Williams caught these two Old Pullmans resting in the Narragansett (west) terminal of the 63rd Street line on April 17, 1952. Loop was needed for PCC operation.

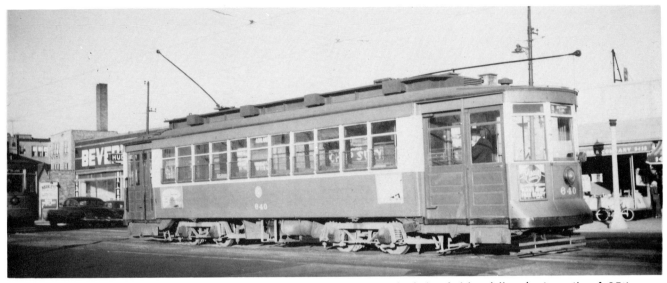

Car 640 was nearly 50 years old when it was snapped at the end of the Ashland line just north of 95th.

Cars 101-700 were the first series to result from the joint efforts of the Chicago Railways and the Board of Supervising Engineers. The Pay As You Enter (PAYE) cars already in operation on busy Chicago City Railway lines strongly influenced the decision to make PAYE cars of the 101-700 series. Among the advantages of the PAYE car were a reduction in passenger accidents caused by falls while boarding or leaving the car, physical separation of entering and alighting passengers, more positive fare collection, and faster schedules through faster loading.

One design problem was how to prevent sagging of the long platforms required for PAYE service. The solution was to use two main platform knees of steel Z section attached to the side sills, and three additional center platform knees of pine. In a test, 46 men were jammed on the platforms and directed to jump up and down together. The platforms held up.

Rectangular sash in the deck roof, linked together to open and close in groups of four, provided ventilation, together with 11 windows on each side. Window guards protected passengers when the windows were open, and storm sash helped hold in heat in winter. A single four-inch Globe ventilator in the roof over each vestibule lifted smoke out of the platforms (in the early days smoking was permitted on the front platforms). Heating was electric, with a switch permitting adjustment to three levels.

Car 560 was one of the cars in the series 501-610 rebuilt in 1921 for hauling trailers. Neuberger photo.

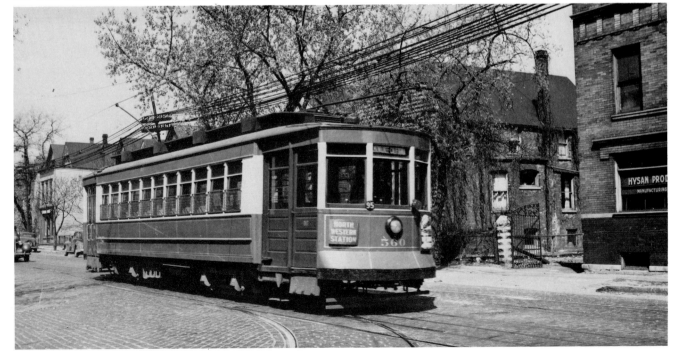

Because of the ever-present danger of fire, great pains were taken to protect the wooden bodies of these cars from the electrical wiring and electric components. All car wiring was enclosed in galvanized iron conduits, and quarter-inch asbestos board protected the body at the resistances, lightning arrestors, choke coils, fuse boxes, and circuit breakers.

It took 21 days to paint the cars in their Chicago Railways colors of medium dark green body, red window sash, and gold lettering and striping. There was a primer coat, three coats of surfacer, three coats of color, and four coats of varnish.

Low bridges, narrow viaducts, and tight curves kept these cars off many lines until track changes could be made. Some carbarn tracks were also off limits for these cars, as well as for the 701-750 series cars built by Pressed Steel Car Co. in 1909. Most of the Old Pullmans were 49', 2" long (53 were six inches longer), and all were 8', 9" wide and 11', 8" high. The "Pressed Steels" of the 701-750 series were all 49', 2" long and 8', 9" wide.

Length and width were the limiting dimensions, and Chicago Railway's next order from Pullman — the 350 cars of the 751-1100 series — were kept to a length of 46' and a width of 8', 6". These dimensions were 3', 2" shorter and 3" narrower than the 101-700 series.

Being Chicago Railways cars, the Old Pullmans saw most of their early service on North and West Side lines. After the establishment of Through Routes with the South Side lines, some were assigned to these routes. After rebuilding in 1921, cars 501-610 went into service on the busy routes whose ever-growing traffic required two car trains.

Trailer operation ended in 1930, and the 501-610 series cars went into service on Milwaukee Ave. Couplers used in train operation were removed in 1936. When Milwaukee Ave. became a motor bus line in 1952, these cars moved to Ashland Ave. Other cars in this series ran out their last miles on the Halsted, Halsted-Downtown, and Kedzie-California lines (See chart on page 44 for cars saved for museums.)

Car 505 was the first to be rebuilt to pull trailers. It was chosen because it was already in CSL's West Shops awaiting heavy repairs. Modifications included a change to K-35-KK control, linebreakers, Van Dorn couplers, and air-operated doors on the rear platform. Of six-panel folding design, the doors were interlocked with the steps — the steps folded up as the doors shut, folded down when the doors opened. The front door and front folding step remained under the control of the motorman.

On car 505 only, the bulkheads which separated the passenger section from the end platforms were removed. This was done to aid passenger flow through the car, and to provide seats for an additional 14 passengers.

Car 505 made test runs on Through Route 22 — Clark-Wentworth — pulling prototype trailer car 8000. The tests revealed just one major problem: car 505's four GE-216 motors built up excessive heat after sustained operation with a trailer. To guard against motor burnouts, CSL specified a three and one-half hour layover for the motor cars between rush hour round trips. This limitation meant that the cars could make just one round trip in each rush hour. Since most lines which used trailers were fairly long, and since the rush hour peaks were fairly short, this layover limitation was not a serious restriction. Car 505 was one of the first of the rebuilt Old Pullmans to be scrapped, going to the torch on January 14, 1946.

As a result of the successful test runs with cars 505 and 8000, CSL ordered an additional 99 trailers and rebuilt 109 other Old Pullmans for trailer-pulling operation.

Car 627 waits for departure from Cermak and Kenton in February, 1946. S. D. Maguire photo.

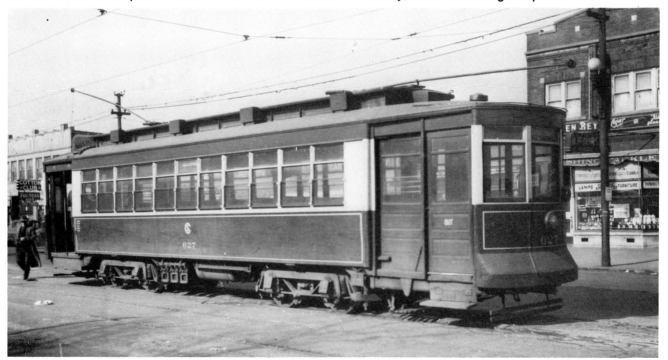

● Above. Southbound on the Ashland line, car 522 swings off Paulina onto Roosevelt Road, where it will run eastbound to Ashland. Barney Neuberger/Railway Negative Exchange. ● Below. On February 23, 1956 CTA scrapped six of the last nine Old Pullmans at South Shops. The remaining cars were preserved for display at museums. Chicago Transit Authority photo.

• Above. On State Street near Congress car 367, southbound on the Racine route, passes Minsky's burlesque show. A. C. Williams captured the scene on July 26, 1951, just a day before buses replaced the streetcars on this line. • Below. Westbound North Avenue car 644 grinds to a stop at Dayton Street in this photo. Barney Neuberger collection from Railway Negative Exchange.

The Old Pullmans ran everywhere on the system. Car 199's destination sign indicates that it was filling in between Nearside cars on Through Route 5, Cottage Grove-South Chicago. Old Pullmans also supplemented Peter Witt service on Through Route 4, Cottage Grove-Pullman. Note trolley shoe in place of trolley wheel on this car. A. C. Williams photo.

Taken September 27, 1935 when Broadway was a separate route, this R. H. Kennedy photo shows car 165 northbound to the Clark and Dewey terminal. A. C. Williams collection.

Fire was the prime enemy of wooden streetcars such as the Old Pullmans, particularly fires in carbarns, which spread quickly among cars parked end to end. The Devon Carbarn fire of January 26, 1922 destroyed the following Old Pullmans: 116, 139, 159, 162, 164, 166, 168, 169, 179, 189, 198, 212, 226, 266, 316, 332, 371, 376, 387, 404, 405, 406, 408, 420, 438, 454, 456, 457, 464, 466, 468, 471, 476, 502, 516, 519, 524, 539, 564, 576, 583, 590, 598, 599, 608, 656. The 46 cars destroyed included 13 rebuilds. After the fire CSL had 457 Old Pullmans and 98 rebuilds on the roster.

Another fire, this one in car 204 at Roosevelt Road and Kostner on October 17, 1934, gave CSL a chance to spruce up an Old Pullman. It emerged from the CSL shops with an arch roof, air doors on all sides, K-35-KK controllers, and line breakers. The bulkheads were removed, as they had been on car 505, and seats for an additional ten passengers were added for a total of 50. The motors were field shunted to increase speed, and self-lapping air brakes were installed. Car 204 was scrapped on November 2, 1948.

Field shunts and self-lapping brakes were also applied to cars 611-620. Cars 621-625 received self-lapping brakes and two-turn motors.

Among other unusual cars was 102, which had a roof like the 751-1100 series with inverted ventilators. Car

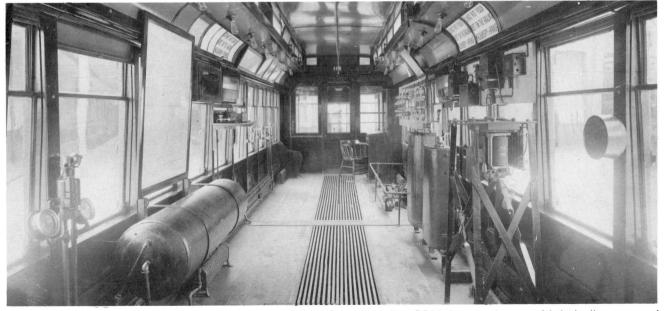

Equipped with several controllers and air brake stands, 114 served as CSL's instruction car. Light bulbs on panel at far right represented traction motors. Photo from Jim Prokes.

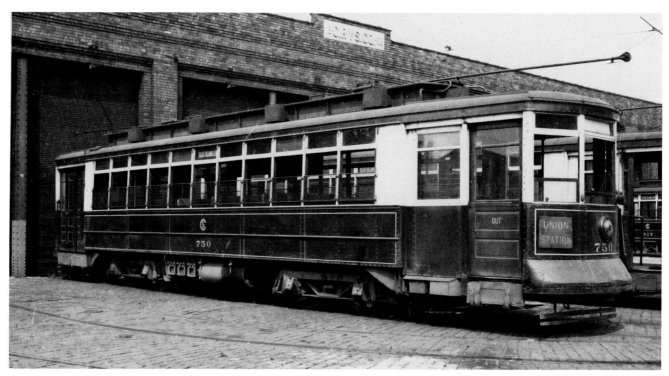

The last built of the Pressed Steels, car 750 rests at the carhouse after a run on the Blue Island-26th line. Neuberger collection from Railway Negative Exchange.

114, scrapped November 10, 1952, was an instruction car in the early years of its life. Car 268 was destroyed by a fire in the Lawndale carbarn on February 14, 1938. Car 357 made the last run on the Kedzie-California line on May 28, 1954, and was scrapped May 26, 1955.

Except for those cars described above, all the cars in the 101-700 series were scrapped between 1946 and 1956. Last to go were 288, 362, 453, 507, and 542 on February 23, 1956. (See the section on preserved cars for details on those cars sold to museums or kept in CTA's historical collection.)

701-750

These cars, known as the "Pressed Steels," continued the basic pattern established by the 101-700 series. Like their predecessors they were PAYE types, and were 49', 2" long, 8', 9" wide, and 11', 8" high.

They were somewhat lighter than the Old Pullmans (52,350 lbs. vs. 53,400 lbs.) and considerably lighter than the rebuilt Pullmans, which weighed 55,500 lbs. The motors were identical to the 101-700 series: four GE-216-A of 50 HP each. The gear ratio remained at

Though built for operation in streetcar subways, the 701-750 cars spent most of their time on the Blue Island-26th route. Car 738 is at 26th and Kenton, west terminal of that line. Neuberger collection.

This photo of 730 at the Lawndale carhouse shows well the close resemblance between the Pressed Steels and the Old Pullmans of the 101-700 series. CTA photo.

71:15, the Pressed Steels rode on identical Baldwin-Pullman 150 trucks with 34″ wheels, and seating capacity was 40, the same as the Old Pullmans. Control was also identical, K-35-C.

The cars were built of steel for five main reasons: for use in the streetcar subways then under active consideration, to make the cars more sanitary, to obtain longer life, to eliminate the risk of fire, and to lower maintenance costs. The streetcar subways were never built, and the Old Pullmans, built of wood just before the Pressed Steels, outlived them.

Like their predecessors in the 101-700 series, these cars ran on the busy North and West Side lines at first, then some went into pool service to help operate the Through Routes. In later years the cars were used mainly on the Blue Island-26th route. No major modifications were made to the cars during their life of nearly a half-century.

First to be scrapped were 705 and 741, which went to the torch in 1945. Cars 724 and 749 followed in 1946, 726 in 1947, 707 and 710 in 1948, and 708, 711, 721, and 733 in 1950. The remaining 39 cars were scrapped in 1951.

751-1100

For this series of 350 cars Chicago Railways returned to Pullman Car Co. Compared to the Old Pullmans of the 101-700 series, these "New Pullmans," also known as "Small Pullmans," were 3′, 2″ shorter (46′, 0″), 3″ narrower (8′, 6″), but 1½″ higher (11′, 9½″). They were 2,900 lbs. lighter than the Old Pullmans, had four WH-319-B motors of 40 HP instead of four GE-216-A of 50 HP, and they rolled on modified Baldwin-Pullman 150-A trucks.

Control was K-35-G rather than K-35-C. Seating capacity remained 40. The cars were built in 1910.

The Division carbarn fire of May 6, 1913 damaged cars 942, 946, 959, 968, 970, and 974. These six cars were rebuilt with arch roofs and seats for 53. In 1926 car 804 was rebuilt with an arch roof, no bulkheads, air operated doors, and 50 seats.

The series held up well through the years: the first four cars were not scrapped until 1945. Twenty-five were scrapped in 1946, 5 in 1947, 32 in 1948, 30 in 1949, and 27 in 1950. In 1951 196 cars were eliminated, and in 1952 the remaining 31 were scrapped.

1101-1423

Known as the "Matchboxes," these 323 cars came from the St. Louis Car Company in two batches. Cars 1101-1305 were built in 1903 and cars 1306-1423 followed in 1906. Chicago Railways rebuilt all of the cars into PAYE types in 1909-1910.

Matchbox was an apt name for these cars, since their seating capacity of 36 was rather low by CSL standards. Their other statistics compared favorably with cars built later: length 41′, width 8′, 6″, and height 11′, 4″. Cars in the 1101-1305 series weighed 44,000 lbs.; those in the 1306-1423 series weighed 46,000 lbs.

The 1903 cars had four GE-70 40 HP motors, while the 1906 cars had four GE-80 40 HP motors. All cars had GE-K-28 control. Trucks were St. Louis 47, rebuilt, with 34″ wheels. Since all cars were delivered prior to the formation of Chicago Railways, they carried Chicago Union Traction Co. numbers in the 4630-4952 series until renumbered in 1909.

• Above. Side shot of 755, signed for a trip on Indiana-Lincoln. Was the man on the back platform the conductor, dressed in an experimental white uniform for summer wear? A. C. Williams supplied the photo, which was taken by R. H. Kennedy on September 27, 1935. • Opposite page. Conflict in front and side signs, the lack of passengers, and the absence of a conductor all indicate that car 952 was brought out on the street just to pose for the company photographer. Credit this classic shot to the files of the Chicago Transit Authority. • Below. Car 810 at the west end of the Fullerton line is all set for a chilly winter with its storm sash applied. Compare this car with the one above, which shows a car equipped for summer service with mesh window guards installed. Barney Neuberger collection from Jack Doyle. Despite the labor costs involved in installing and removing storm sash once a year, the Surface Lines thought it was worthwhile. The storm sash provided extra passenger comfort and also lowered CSL's winter power bills. As those with electrically heated homes know, electric heat takes quite a bit of energy.

• Above. Every time a double ended car like 1044 changed direction, the crew would have to change ends, raising the rear trolley pole and lowering the front pole. CSL cars always operated with the rear trolley pole raised, except for certain work cars which used the front pole. To facilitate changing the pole from the car's vestibule, the platforms had sash which dropped into pockets in the dash, allowing motormen and conductors to lean out backwards far enough to change the pole. This crewman is violating a CSL rule by changing the pole from the street, a dangerous practice which cost more than one CSL man his life in a traffic accident. Barney Neuberger collection from Jack Doyle. • Below. Before the CSL's color scheme was changed to carmine red and cream in 1921, the standard colors were medium green with red trim. Car 922 carries the older colors in this Chicago Transit Authority photograph. The public relations value of a fresh coat of paint in new colors led the Chicago Transit Authority to choose green and cream for its new equipment delivered after 1947. CTA even repainted a few of the older, conventional streetcars in the new colors, and some riders thought that they were new cars too.

● Above. It seems that every large series of CSL cars had to have at least one oddball car. In the 101-700 series it was car 204, illustrated on page 52. In the 751-1100 series the oddball car was 804, shown above running southbound on Through Route 1, Cottage Grove-Broadway, passing the Limits carhouse. Car 804 was rebuilt in 1926 with an arch roof, seats for 50 passengers, air-operated doors, and no bulkheads. The same modifications were made to car 204, but in addition it got self-lapping air brakes and field-shunted motors. The arch roof and the normally closed air doors made an astonishing difference in the appearance of the two cars, making them appear much younger than they were. ● Below. Car 804 operating on the South Cicero shuttle route, an unusual assignment for a car with such a large seating capacity. Both the photos are from the Barney Neuberger collection through the Railway Negative Exchange. Six other cars in the 751-1100 series also received arch roofs, and their seating capacity was increased from 40 to 53. Cars 942, 946, 959, 968, 970, and 974 were rebuilt after suffering damage in the Division barn fire of 1913.

A fire at the Archer carhouse damaged car 1405 (former CUT 4934) in 1916. Rebuilt, it was made one-man in 1924 and later converted to work car X-2. The 1922 Devon carbarn fire claimed cars 1115, 1125, 1127, 1129, 1167, 1195, 1206, 1216, 1247, 1272, and 1298.

Cars 1398-1423 were equipped for one-man operation in 1924. One of them, 1421, received air doors.

In 1925 cars 1101 and 1102 were withdrawn from service and put through the CSL shops. When they emerged on August 3, 1925 they had become single unit experimental articulated car 4000.

This one-of-a-kind car was 83', 7″ long, and rode on three trucks. Withdrawn from service in 1930, it was scrapped in 1937. More details on this unusual car are given under car 4000's listing, and in the Cicero route description.

A fire in the Chicago & West Towns Railways barn on Lake Street destroyed 25 of their cars on December 2,

This view of car 1348 plainly shows the curved side below the rub rail, a carry-over from the days of the horse drawn omnibus. Omnibus bodies had to be narrow at this point in order to clear the wheels. Chicago Transit Authority photograph.

● Above. "Matchbox" 1407 in one-man service on the 87th Street line, at 87th and Vincennes. Built by St. Louis Car Co. in 1906 for the Chicago Union Traction Company (4630-4952), the Matchboxes were rebuilt by Chicago Railways into PAYE cars in 1909-1910. Cars 1398-1423 were converted to one-man operation in 1924. Seating only 36, the Matchboxes were equal in size to the new one-man cars, and by the 1920s were too small for use on the heavy two-man routes. J. Buck took the picture on April 1, 1941. From the A. C. Williams collection. ● Below. Though carrying a CSL logo on its side, car 1317 appears to be painted in the old medium green paint scheme, dating this photo sometime between 1914 and the early 1920s. Chicago Transit Authority photo. Car appears to be at the Pitney Court-Archer terminal of the 31st Street line.

1936. CSL loaned the West Towns ten of the 1306-1423 series cars to see them through their emergency. The cars ran on the West Towns until 1937. They ran at first as two-man cars, but were later made one-man.

Cars in this series had a reputation for being rough riding and noisy. In fact there was considerable opposition to running them on the West Towns in Oak Park, despite the fact that C&WT lost 25 of its cars in the Lake barn fire and had pressed all of its other cars into service. CSL used this car on light lines and secondary routes such as Fulton-21st, Webster-Racine, Taylor-Sedgwick-Sheffield, 26th, 31st, 71st, and 87th.

When the first PCC cars arrived on Madison Street in 1936, equipment shifts forced the retirement of 85 cars of the 1101-1423 series. Other early retirements were given to car 1128, scrapped in 1938 after being caught in a fire at the Lawndale carbarn. Other cars retired during 1938 included 1283, 1327, 1342, 1377, and 1385. After a wreck at 111th Street and Sacramento on the Halsted line, car 1211 was retired January 30, 1939.

Thirty-eight cars from this series ended their days as AA series salt cars. Car 1110 was sold to Detroit in 1946, and car 1178 became a supply car and was scrapped in 1946.

1424-1428

This series of five cars, similar in size and equipment to the 1101-1423 series, was built by J. G. Brill Co. in 1903 for the Chicago Union Traction Co. These cars carried the numbers 4625-4629 on the CUT.

This series was rebuilt by Chicago Railways into PAYE cars in 1910 and 1911. The cars remained two-man until scrapped in April and May of 1937.

1429-1505

Products of Chicago Union Traction Company's own shops, 53 of these cars underwent extensive rebuilding by Chicago Railways. The chart below shows the major modifications.

	As Built 1899-1900	As Rebuilt 1911-1912
Numbers	4475-4554 (a)	1429-1505
Seats	40	36
Length	39', 6"	43", 3¼"
Width	7', 9"	7", 7 ¾"
Height	11', 0"	11", 6 ¾"
Weight	38,000 lbs	42,300 lbs.
Operation	Two-man	Two-man
Motors	4 GE-52	4 GE-226-A
Horsepower	25	35
Control	K-12	K-35-G
Trucks	Curtis, McGuire	Brill 27-GE-1
Wheels	34"	34"
(a) CUT 4475, 4477-4497, 4499-4525, 4526-4554.		

Because of their longitudinal seating, these cars came to be known as "Bowling Alleys." As built they were two-man with a roving conductor. They had no front door, only a rear entrance and exit. They were rebuilt as two-man Pay As You Enter cars with a rear entrance and a front exit. Although figures are not available on the cost of conversion, it probably came to around $1,300 a car. The cost of converting the 1903 St. Louis cars (series 1101-1305) to PAYE was $1,335.50 a car, less $91.53

• Opposite page. Built by Chicago Railways in 1912, car 1590 was scrapped by the CTA on September 12, 1950. This photo from the George Krambles collection shows the car in the Elston carhouse yard. • Below. Part of the 1429-1505 series, car 1433 was built at the turn of the century by Chicago Union Traction and rebuilt by Chicago Railways in 1911-1912. (For a look at this series before rebuilding, see car 4399 on page 23.) R. H. Kennedy photo from A. C. Williams collection.

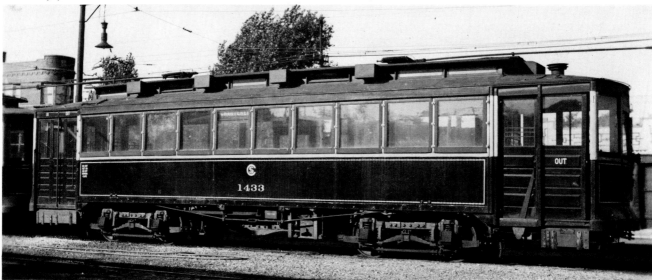

credit for salvaged material. Hourly wages at that time were 28¢ to 39¢ for wood machinists, 26¢ to 30¢ for carpenters, 56¢ for blacksmiths and their helpers, 28¢ for electricians, and 23¢ for truckmen.

The Bowling Alleys numbered 80 on the CUT, but their number was reduced to 77 before rebuilding. As built they all had a large rear platform and a small front platform. Twenty-four of the rebuilt cars kept the original platforms: 1429, 32, 34, 36, 38, 39, 42, 49, 50, 52, 56, 60, 61, 64, 69, 70, 73, 76, 79, 85, 86, 90, 91, and 1505. The others were rebuilt with platforms of equal size. All of the 24 cars with the original platforms were sold to other street railways before 1918, except for 1505, which was retired in 1912.

Quite a few cars in this series were sold to other electric railways. A rebuilt car, 1486, was sold in 1914. The buyer is unknown. Cars 1429, 1456, and 1479 were sold to Gary Railways, Gary, Ind., in 1916. On that property they became cars 601-603. In 1917 car 1485 was also sold to Gary, where it became car 604. These four cars were retired in 1926 and 1927, long before most of the cars that stayed in Chicago.

Eighteen other cars were sold in 1917. They were: 1432, 1434, 1436, 1438, 1439, 1442, 1449, 1450, 1452, 1460, 1461, 1464, 1469, 1470, 1473, 1476, 1490, and 1491.

Some of these 18 cars went to the Tri-City Railway in Davenport, Ia., where they were renumbered in the high 200 series. Disposition of the other cars is not known.

Fifty-two cars from this series became salt cars in 1931. However, they did not receive the work car designation "AA" until several years later. Twenty-five cars carried their original passenger car numbers until 1941, when they became AA-1 to AA-25. The remaining 27 cars did not become AA-64 to AA-90 until 1948.

In 1912 car 1505 was the first to leave the active roster through scrapping. Car 1466 was for many years a training car for new employees to instruct them in streetcar operation. After the Van Buren Street tunnel under the Chicago River was taken out of regular service, car 1466 used the tunnel and its approaches for training purposes. The training car was scrapped March 9, 1951.

Car 1467 had a long and interesting career. After more than three decades of passenger service it became a salt car on November 12, 1931. It was renumbered into the salt car equipment class on April 15, 1948, receiving the number AA-72. On February 27, 1958, when almost all of its contemporaries had gone to the torch, AA-72 was sold to the Electric Railway Historical Society. Car 1467 (AA-72) is preserved at the Illinois Railway Museum site at Union, Ill.

1506-1720

Arch roofs made their first appearance with this series of Chicago Railways cars, built in the company's own shops. Cars 1506-1576 were outshopped in 1911, followed by 1577-1720 in 1912. These cars marked a return to wooden construction, and were some 7,000 lbs. lighter that the Pressed Steel cars of the 701-750 series. The arch roof gave these cars their nickname of "Turtlebacks."

These cars were designed jointly by the Chicago Railways and the Board of Supervising Engineers. The prime objective was to save weight, which not only lowered construction costs but saved electric power and was easier on the track. This meant a return to steel underframes with wood side panels. Even the motors were specified with weight in mind. These cars used 35 HP motors, which were 440 lbs. lighter than the standard 40 HP motor.

The motors were designed to give a maximum speed of 24 mph on level track at 500 volts DC. With an average of seven stops of six seconds each per mile, the cars could maintain a schedule speed of 9 mph. In general appearance these cars were almost identical to the 1910 "New Pullman" cars, except of course for the arch roof and differences in the ventilating system.

The Turtlebacks usually ran on North and West Side lines, including Elston, Grand, Lake, Division-Van Buren, Taylor-Sedgwick-Sheffield, 14th-16th, and Ogden.

The series ran intact for more than three decades — until 1945 — before the first four cars were scrapped. Twenty-five cars reached the end of the line in 1946, three in 1947, 31 in 1948, 22 in 1949, and 127 in 1950.

Through conversion to work cars, 1545, 1609, and 1636 outlasted the others. Car 1545 was made a salt car on July 29, 1947, and received its work car designation as AA-91 on April 15, 1948. It was scrapped August 8, 1955. Car 1609 was converted to car W-18 on December 27, 1946, and was scrapped December 11, 1954. Car 1636 became work car W-56 on June 12, 1946, and was scrapped December 11, 1954.

1721-1785

With the delivery of this series, the Surface Lines had a car specifically designed for pulling trailers. Cars 501-610 of the 101-700 series had been rebuilt to pull trailers in 1921. These modifications had been successful, but cars 1721-1785 were 7,700 lbs. lighter than the rebuilt Old Pullmans, and had four 60 HP motors vs. four 50 HP motors in the rebuilt Old Pullmans. Control was K-35-KK in both series. CSL built 1721-1785 in 1923.

Cars 1721-1785 were identical to two other groups of cars built at the same time: 3119-3178 and 6155-6198. Series 1721-1785 were Chicago Railways cars.

All cars in the 1721-1785 series had Van Dorn couplers for pulling trailers. Trailer operation ended on all lines in

• Opposite page. Passing under the Lawndale Station of the Douglas Park "L," CTA 1739 grinds to a stop to pick up a passenger at 21st and Lawndale while outbound on the Ogden Avenue line. Photo from the A. W. Simms collection. • Below. Car 1513, part of the 1506-1720 series, pauses on its Taylor-Sedgwick-Sheffield run while a trainman tries to fix a balky step. Barney Neuberger collection from Jack Doyle.

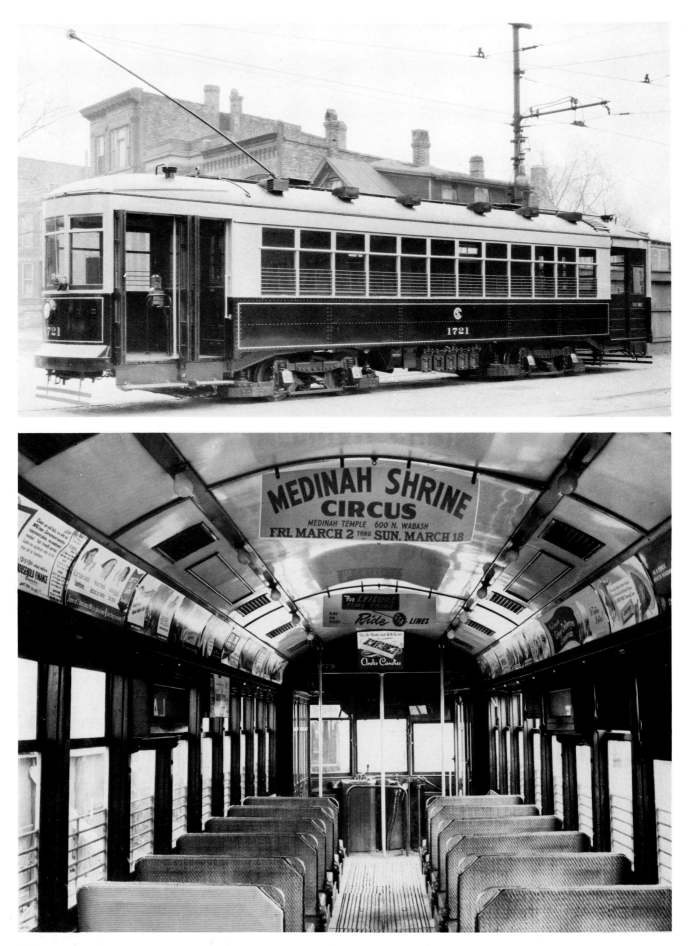

1930, and the couplers were later removed. For details on trailer operations, see the chapter on Surface Lines routes.

Originally two-man cars, those remaining on the roster were converted to one-man operation in 1949 and 1950. Cars scrapped prior to conversion were 1727 (1948), 1738 (1946), 1754 (1946), and 1770 (1946). Although it survived until 1949, car 1763 was not converted. As part of the conversion to one-man operation, the front sliding doors were replaced by folding doors. Six of the one-man cars received CTA green and cream paint jobs: 1723, 1733, 1742, 1764, 1777, and 1779. The last cars in this series were scrapped between 1951 and 1954.

Cars in this series were among the last conventional one-man cars to run in Chicago. They ran out of Kedzie depot to serve the Fifth Avenue shuttle, abandoned February 22, 1954, and the Cermak and Lake routes, both abandoned on May 29, 1954.

1800-1999

This order for Chicago Railways was split among three builders. Chicago Railways built 1800-1899, American Car Co. built 1900-1949, and Southern Car Company built 1950-1999. Actually Chicago Railways assembled cars 1900-1999 after buying the bodies, trucks, and electrical equipment from the manufactur-

ers. All cars were built during 1913 and 1914.

Several features made these cars different from any previously used by Chicago Railways. They had two motors, rather than the customary four, they rode on maximum traction trucks (with wheels of different diameters on the same truck), and they were the first Chicago cars to have seats on the platforms. This novel feature increased seating capacity of this series of cars to 53.

The lack of bulkheads on these cars gave them a peculiar rolling gait as they twisted over uneven track in their last years. Because of this unsettling habit they were nicknamed "Flexible Flyers." They were usually assigned to crosstown lines near the Loop, including Division, Chicago, Grand, and Harrison, although they also ran on Kedzie.

Six cars in this series — 1994 to 1999 — were rebuilt for optional one-man/two-man operation in 1936. One rebuilt car was scrapped in 1948, the other five in 1949.

Among other cars of interest in this series was 1813, first to be retired (1939) and first to be scrapped (1941). Car 1814 had a run-in with a freight train, and emerged from rebuilding with different roof vents. Car 1853 was sent to the material yard at 38th and Halsted Street as a tool shed in 1948, and was scrapped there in 1956. It was the last of its class to be scrapped, all the others having been cut up before 1950.

• Opposite page, top. The first car in the 1721-1785 series in its original paint scheme featuring more cream than later schemes. CTA photo. • Opposite page, bottom. Interior of car 1779 in March, 1951. CTA photo. • Below. Car 1730 resting at the south terminal after a run on the long Broadway-State through route. Made one-man by CTA in 1949, the car was scrapped in 1954. Barney Neuberger collection.

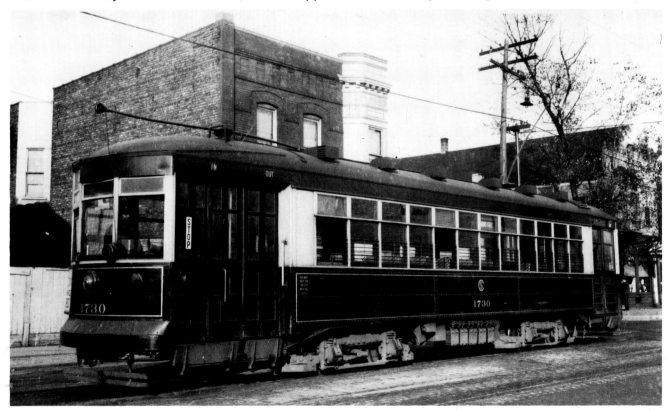

2000-2005

Short-lived but nonetheless fascinating, these single-truck double-end Birney cars ran on short shuttles and light lines. They were Chicago Railways cars. These six cars were identical to CCRy 2900-2903 series cars. All six of the 2000-2005 cars were scrapped in March, 1937.

Although the Birney cars enjoyed a measure of success in other cities, they were really unsuited for even the lightest Chicago lines. It seems as though their popularity in other cities led to their use in Chicago. They did have safety features which permitted one-man operation, but their single front entrance and exit door and limited seating capacity made them highly unsuitable for Chicago, where even the lightest lines had rush hour peaks. Although usually assigned to the 71st and 87th lines, these cars did operate on other routes. They were the first one-man cars run by the Surface Lines.

2006 (one car)

Except for greater length, greater seating capacity, and lighter weight, this car was identical to the five cars of the 2000-2005 series. Built by CSL in 1921, the car was assigned to Chicago Railways. Like the 2000-2005 and 2900-2903 series, this car was scrapped in March, 1937. It was built as a test car to determine if a large single-truck car could handle CSL's needs. It couldn't, and CSL later built the successful double-truck safety car 3092, prototype for the 2904-2922, 3093-3118 cars.

2501-2625

These 125 cars were the lowest numbered CCRy cars to survive long into the CSL era. They were identical to the 2801-2815 class: in fact C&SC bought those 15 cars from CCRy in 1908 and renumbered them in the 700 series. They were renumbered again in 1913 to 2801-2815. Look under that series for details on renumbering.

Five cars from this series — 2543, 2544, 2545, 2547, and 2548 — were sold to the Hammond, Whiting & East Chicago Railway in 1910. On the HW&EC they became 506, 507, 512, 513, and 514 in 1913. In a later renumbering they became 56, 57, 62, 63, and 64. All five cars were scrapped ca. 1935.

A fire in the Archer carbarn in 1916 claimed four cars in this series: 2520, 2526, 2597, and 2621. Other cars retired early were 2515, 2546, 2565, and 2585. All four were off the active roster by 1917, disposition unknown.

Built by St. Louis Car in 1901, these cars were the oldest passenger equipment on the Surface Lines roster after 1915. They were assigned to lines on the far South Side of Chicago, including 106th, 111th, Riverdale, and Ewing-Brandon.

In the shuffle of equipment that took place after the first PCC cars arrived, 55 cars in this series were scrapped in 1937. All of the remaining cars dropped off the roster one by one until all but one was gone by the end of 1947. The sole survivor was car 2605, sent to the Devon carbarn in 1948 and scrapped there in 1954.

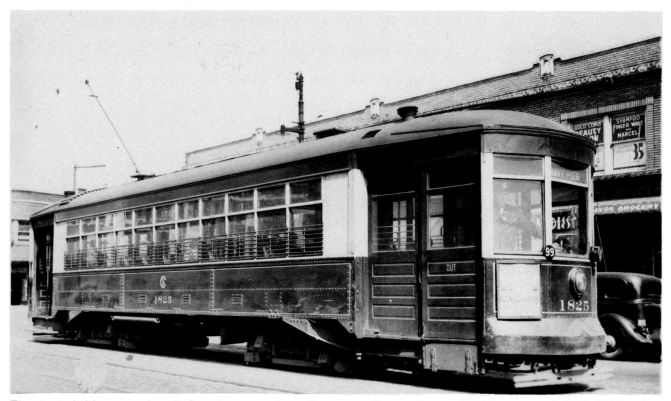

The riveted sides, massive platform knees, and maximum traction trucks combined to give the 1800-1999 series a low-slung, massive appearance. Car 1825 is at the west end of the Grand Avenue line at Grand and Harlem, ready for a run to Navy Pier. These "Flexible Flyers" also ran on Harrison, Chicago, and Kedzie. Photograph from the Barney Neuberger collection, courtesy of Jack Doyle.

2701-2780

Quite similar to the 2501-2625 series, these St. Louis Car Co. products of 1903 were longer and heavier than their predecessors. They also originally ran on McGuire 10-A trucks, changed in 1918 to Brill 51-E-1.

Car 2777 was the first to leave the roster. It was destroyed by fire in 1917 and replaced by car 6154. A 1924 wreck did in car 2726, and it was replaced by car 6239. Car 2765 was used as a supply car before it was scrapped in 1948.

This series survived largely intact until the mid-1940s. Four cars were scrapped in 1945, 11 in 1946, 61 in 1947, and the last two in 1948.

An additional 20 cars, 2781-2800, were ordered but never delivered. They went to the St. Louis & Suburban Railway after a carbarn fire had destroyed much of its equipment. The cars ran as that line's 600-619 series.

Cars 2847 and 2851 in a Neuberger collection photo.

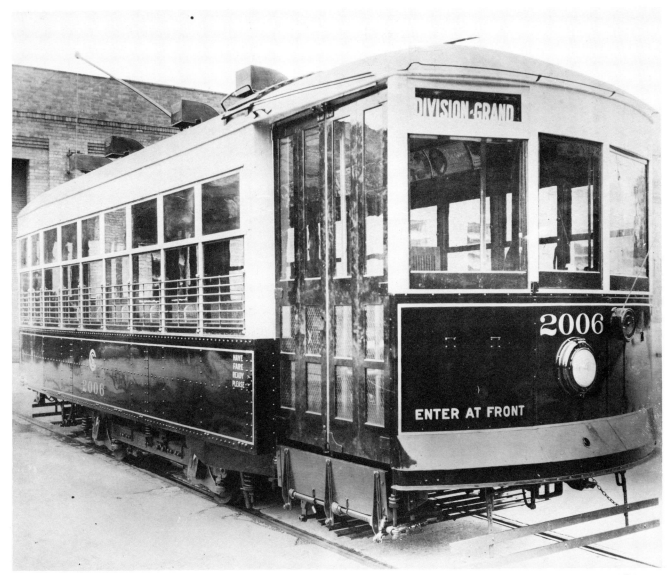

Single truck safety car 2006 was built by CSL to see if a single truck car slightly larger than the standard Birney could handle traffic on light lines. Assigned to Chicago Railways, the car was outshopped with the new paint scheme that featured cream from the belt rail to the roof. CSL built double truck safety car 3002 at the same time, and it proved much better suited to Chicago conditions. CTA photo.

• Opposite page. Cars 2518 and 2599 pass on the Ewing-Brandon (Hegewisch) line. The line was single track here with passing sidings. Photo by Joe L. Diaz. • Above, top. Cars 2620 and 2599 pass on the 111th Street line near Halsted. • Above, middle. Car 2619 at the end of double track on the Hegewisch line at 127th and Brandon. • Above, bottom. Car 2615 at 106th and Torrence Ave. on the 106th Street line. Bottom two photos on this page from the Neuberger collection, top photo from A. Simms.

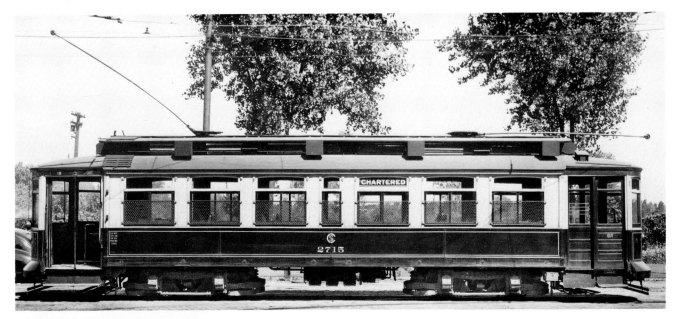

2801-2815

Although assigned to the Calumet and South Chicago Railway Company, this series was made up of CCRy cars sold to the C&SCRy in 1908. On the CCRy they were 2501-2625 series cars. The table below shows ownership changes and renumberings.

CCRyCo number in use until 1908	C&SCRyCo number from 1908-1913	C&SCRyCo number from 1913 on
2572	701	2801
2554	702	2802
2600	703	2803
2590	704	2804
2591	705	2805
2522	706	2806
2536	707	2807
2593	708	2808
2541	709	2809
2528	710	2810
2586	711	2811
2549	712	2812
2582	713	2813
2542	714	2814
2578	715	2815

First to be scrapped was 2801, cut up in 1942. The rest of the cars lasted a few more years, with two surviving the extensive scrappings of 1946 and 1947. Car 2806 was scrapped in 1948, leaving only 2807, which was renumbered as the first AA-99 and used in salt service at the 69th Street carhouse. It was scrapped in 1956.

2816-2823

This series began life as Calumet Electric Street Railway single-end cars with smoking compartments. Built by J. G. Brill as semi-convertibles, they were extensively rebuilt in 1910, emerging as double-end cars without the smoking section. While still on the Calumet Electric Street Railway roster, car 111 was destroyed in an accident. The table below shows ownership changes and renumberings.

CESRyCo in 1903	C&SCRyCo in 1908	C&SCRyCo in 1913
110	801	2816
111 Car 111 destroyed in an accident.		
112	802	2817
113	803	2818
114	804	2819
115	805	2820
116	806	2821
117	807	2822
118	808	2823

A fire in the Lawndale carbarn on February 14, 1938 destroyed car 2823. Car 2817 was scrapped in 1942, and the remaining six cars were scrapped in 1946.

Calumet Electric first used these cars on the Roby line. The front, or smoker end of the car, retained the single bulkhead door even after the car was converted to double-platforms.

2824-2840

The 17 cars in this series are a mixture of two groups and a single car, all built by G. C. Kuhlman Car Co. between 1904 and 1908. Like the 2816-2823 series, they were built as single-end cars with a smoking compartment, and rebuilt as double-end cars without the smoker in 1910.

Like the preceding series, they were built for the Calumet Electric Street Railway (119-135), became Calumet and South Chicago cars in 1908 (809-825), and were again renumbered in 1913 (2824-2840). The chart below presents these changes in graphic form.

The single car in this order, 2829, was like the 2824-2837 with medium-size platforms, except that it

CESRyCo as built	CESRyCo 1908	C&SCRyCo 1913
119	809	2824
120	810	2825
121	811	2826
122	812	2827
123	813	2828
124	814	2829
125	815	2830
126	816	2831
127	817	2832
128	818	2833
129	819	2834
130	820	2835
131	821	2836
132	822	2837
133	823	2838
134	824	2839
135	825	2840

• Opposite page. Top. Side view of car 2715 clearly shows off-center route sign placement required because of tiny center window. Large windows made car seem small, but it had a seating capacity of 44. CTA photo. • Middle. Just a few blocks from the lakefront terminal where it began its run, car 2720 moves west along 75th St. past Coles Ave. on the 74th-75th Street line. Photo from the Barney Neuberger collection. • Bottom. The open windows and the motorman in his shirtsleeves indicate it's a hot, muggy Chicago summer day as car 2776 moves south on the Stony Island-Wabash route at Wacker and Wabash. Barney Neuberger collection.

Waiting for its departure time at the Pitney Court-Archer terminal of the 31st Street line, car 2829 shows traces of its origin as a single end car with a smoking compartment. The smoking section was the short end of the car (the three windows beyond the wide post). Neuberger collection.

The man under the dash sign is a railfan, and he's watching another electric railway enthusiast snap his photo as car 2802 stops for a photo session at 63rd Place just east of Halsted. South Suburban Safeway Lines bus at left ran on former Chicago & Interurban Traction lines. Neuberger collection.

was PAYE on one end only. That is, the rear platform only had a pair of doors through the interior bulkhead with the conductor standing between them, rather than just one wide door in the middle of the bulkhead. The front, or smoker end of the car, retained the single bulkhead door even after the car was converted to double-end operation. It is likely that 2838 was selected as a test car for the PAYE design, since the 2839 and 2840 were also single-end PAYE cars. They had large rear platforms and front platforms only slightly smaller.

A fire at the Lawndale carbarn destroyed car 2825 in 1938. No other cars were scrapped until 1946, when 15 cars were cut up. Two years later the sole survivor of the class, car 2826, was converted to a salt car and a renumbered second AA-92. It was scrapped in 1955.

2841-2845

Like the three previous series, these cars passed through several owners and renumberings. They began as South Chicago City Railway Co. 321-325 (1903), became Calumet and South Chicago Railway Co. 826-830 (1908), and finally became Calumet and South Chicago Railway Co. 2841-2845 (1913). The chart below shows these changes.

SCCRyCo 1903	C&SCRyCo 1908	C&SCRyCo 1913
321	826	2841
322	827	2842
323	828	2843
324	829	2844
325	830	2845

This series — which came through all its renumberings and ownership changes in perfect numerical order — kept that order when all cars in the class were made AA series salt cars in 1948. The work car numbers were AA-93 through AA-97. (Some cars had been converted to salt service as early as 1943, but did not get their official designation as work equipment until 1948). Car 2843 (AA-95) is now preserved at the Illinois Railway Museum.

The operating history of these cars ties into their ownership. From 1902 the Hammond, Whiting & East Chicago Railway and the South Chicago City Railway were under common ownership, and cars were freely exchanged between the two systems. This exchange persisted into the CSL era, and details of joint Surface Lines-HW&EC operations are found under the Hammond and Whiting-East Chicago route descriptions. Cars 321-325 went into interstate service in 1903, and continued to make Hammond and Whiting-East Chicago trips until 1921. CSL then assigned the cars, now renumbered 2841-2845, to light lines on the far South Side such as 111th, 115th, 119th, and Torrence. They were cars noted for their small platforms and high-mounted bodies.

2846-2856

This series of 11 cars emerged from the South Chicago City Railway's own shops in 1907. Originally 332-342, they were changed to C&SCRy 831-841 in 1908, and to 2846-2856 in 1913. As originally built these cars had Minneapolis-type mesh gates protecting an open rear platform, and they also had a smoking section. These 11 cars were built especially for service to Hammond via the HW&EC. They ran on this line and the Whiting-East Chicago route until 1932, when the line was changed from two-man to one-man operation. At that time CSL placed its 6199-6220 cars on the interstate routes. Because of their long service on the Indiana lines, these cars were known as the "Interstates."

SCCRyCo 1907	C&SCRyCo 1908	C&SCRyCo 1913
332	831	2846
333	832	2847
334	833	2848
335	834	2849
336	835	2850
337	836	2851
338	837	2852
339	838	2853
340	839	2854
341	840	2855
342	841	2856

Misfortune struck car 2850 not once but twice during its career, and it was the first to leave the roster. In 1909 it was hit by a train near 94th Street and Cottage Grove Ave., and emerged from the shops with a deck roof in place of its original railroad roof. On January 20, 1924 it was destroyed by fire on Indianapolis Blvd. while making a run on the Whiting line.

All the remaining cars were used in salt service. They received the AA designation in 1948, except for 2847, which became a salt car in 1943 and was scrapped in 1948. Renumberings were: 2846 to AA-98, 2848 to AA-100, 2849 to AA-101, 2851 to AA-102, 2852 to AA-103, 2853 to AA-104, 2854 to AA-105, 2855 to AA-106, and 2856 to AA-107.

Three cars were scrapped in 1951, one in 1952, two in 1954, and two in 1956. The remaining car, AA-98 formerly 2846, is now at the Illinois Railway Museum at Union, Ill.

2857-2858

The specifications of these two cars are fairly typical for their era. But they were unusual: they were built as funeral cars 1 and 2 in 1910. A renumbering changed them to Y-301 and Y-302 in 1916. In 1919 they were converted to passenger cars, and remained in passenger

To replace car 2850, burned at 120th and Indianapolis on the Whiting line January 20, 1924, CSL built car 2859 in its own shops and assigned it to the Calumet & South Chicago Railway. CTA photo.

service until they were scrapped in 1946.

In 1910 the Calumet and South Chicago Railway, the Chicago City Railway, and the Hammond, Whiting & East Chicago offered funeral car service from any point on their lines to four cemeteries. Charges varied from $30 to $40 for a round trip, depending on the distance. On the return trip the funeral car conductor issued transfers good on regular cars of connecting lines. To promote the service the three companies issued a 12-page brochure,

illustrated with pictures of the cars and a large map of South Side streetcar lines. Although built for the Calumet and South Chicago, the funeral cars were operated by the Chicago City Railway over all three lines.

The cars had two compartments, one for the coffin and one for the mourners, separated by a bulkhead. The casket compartment had an outside hinged door which swung down to facilitate loading and unloading the coffin. Opposite the casket compartment was a longitudinal

CSL's paint shop was turned loose on CCRy Birney 2902, and came up with what appears to be either a cream or light yellow paint scheme. Photo from the CTA.

This was CSL's own answer to the Birney car: a one-man, light weight, steel safety car with a seating capacity of 50. Note Brill 39-E-1 maximum traction trucks. CTA photo.

bench for the pallbearers. The mourners' section of the car had 12 cross seats and four stationary longitudinal seats.

Substantially built, the cars had extra reinforcement of the side sill on the casket side. Four sets of half-elliptic window pairs illuminated each side of the mourners' compartment, and a single plate glass window extended the entire length of the pallbearers' compartment.

Interior finish and appointments reflected the car's purpose. Woodwork was cherry, with the doors stained mahogany. The casket compartment was finished in white and gold. All passenger windows had black drapes, adding an air of solemnity to the cars.

Coincident with their conversion to regular passenger cars in 1919, the cars were renumbered 2857 and 2858. They ran on Ashland before they were scrapped in 1946, and few who rode them in later years realized that they had a brief career as streetcar hearses.

Stripped of its destination and route signs, car 2853 is in green paint and obviously a work car. It eventually received the work car number AA-104 in 1948. Neuberger collection.

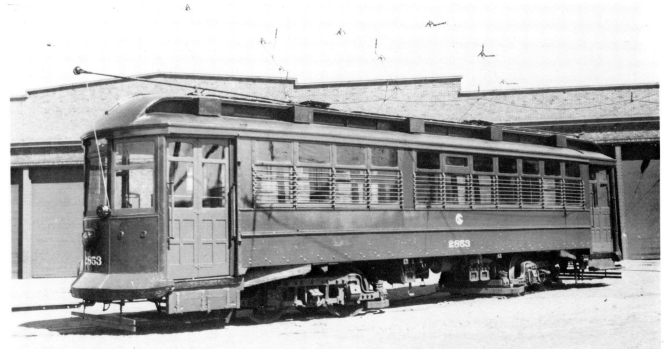

Allan C. Williams captured this close-up of car 3179 at the Navy Pier terminal of the Stony Island line. Note air doors: car 3179 was the only one in the 3179-3201 series to receive them. It also reportedly was equipped with leather seats taken from the two funeral cars. Cars in this series, known as "Sun Parlors," were mainstays of the Stony Island line.

2859 (one car)

Chicago Surface Lines built this car in 1924 as a replacement for car 2850. It was identical to car 6239, built in 1924 to replace car 2726, which was wrecked in 1924. Car 2859 was assigned to the Calumet and South Chicago Railway Co. It was scrapped in 1948. This was C&SC's only modern car, since under CSL they normally received no new streetcars.

2900-2903

These four Chicago City Railway Company cars were identical to Chicago Railways 2000-2005. They were single-truck, double-end, arch-roof steel Birney cars. Like the Chicago Railways cars, all were scrapped in March, 1937.

2904-2922

This series of 19 cars, built by the Surface Lines, was assigned to the Chicago City Railway Company. The cars were identical to the Chicago Railways 3093-3118 series. They were double-truck, arch-roof, double-end steel safety cars. A curious feature was the use of maximum traction trucks with wheel diameters of 28″ and 21″. They were outshopped in 1922.

Like the 3093-3118 series, all the cars in this group were scrapped in 1948. The only exception was 2919, which was scrapped in 1947.

Known as "Sewing Machines," these cars were much better suited to light traffic lines than the Birney cars which CSL tried and found wanting. They were assigned to such lines as 18th, Morgan-Racine-Sangamon, and 87th.

3000-3091

Ninety cars in this series (3000-3089) came from J. G. Brill in 1914-1915, followed by one car (3090) from the American Car Co. in 1918, and one car (3091) from the CSL's own shops in 1919. Cars 3090 and 3091 were built to replace cars 1360 and 1405. The replacement cars had four GE-80 motors and St. Louis 47 trucks, probably taken from 1360 and 1405. Car 3091 was equipped with air doors. Both replacement cars were scrapped in 1948.

Except for the two replacement cars, this series was mounted on Brill maximum traction trucks. Because of the truck design, these were two-motor rather than four motor cars. The 3000-3091 series, assigned to Chicago Railways, was identical to the Chicago City Railway Company's 6000-6137 series built by Brill in 1914-1915.

The Clark-Devon carbarn fire of 1922 claimed eight cars in this series: 3000, 3003, 3004, 3006, 3008, 3012, 3013, and 3014. The remaining cars lasted until 1946, when scrapping began. By mid-1951 all the cars were gone. The cars ran on such lines as Elston, Kedzie, and Halsted.

3092 (one car)

This double-truck, arch-roof, double-end, steel safety car was built by the CSL in 1921. It was designed for one-man operation, and assigned to Chicago Railways. It was scrapped in 1946. It was the prototype car for CSL's double-truck safety car fleet, and is shorter with one less window than the production model cars, such as 3093-3118.

3093-3118

These cars, built by Chicago Surface Lines in 1922, were identical to cars 2904-2922, also built by CSL in 1922. Cars 2904-2922 were assigned to Chicago City Railway Company. Cars 3093-3118 were assigned to Chicago Railways. These cars were double-truck, arch roof, double-end steel safety cars. They were all scrapped in 1948. They ran on such lines as North Ashland, Morgan-Racine-Sangamon, and 16th-18th.

3119-3178

Officially designated as the "169 cars," these 1923 cars came from two builders. J. G. Brill built 3119-3160, and the Cummings Car Company built 3161-3178. They were identical to cars 1721-1785, built by CSL, and cars 6155-6198, built by CSL, Brill, and McGuire-Cummings. The first of these other two series were Chicago Railways cars, the last was assigned to the Chicago City Railway Company. They got their name from the fact that there were a total of 169 cars in the three series.

The first seven cars in this series — 3119-3125 — were equipped with Van Dorn couplers for pulling trailers. Trailer operation ended in 1930.

Built as two-man cars, the entire series was converted to one-man operation in late 1949 and early 1950. As part of the changeover, the sliding front doors were replaced with folding doors.

CTA gave a new look to three cars of this series when it painted 3127, 3162, and 3167 green and cream.

The first car to be scrapped was 3176 in 1945. Cars 3133 and 3170 were scrapped in 1946, followed by 3130, 3150, 3152, 3155, and 3159 in 1948. All but one of the remaining cars was scrapped between 1951 and 1954. Longest-lived of this series was 3142. Converted to one-man operation in 1949, it became a storage shed at South Shops in 1953.

3179-3201

These 23 cars were known as "Sun Parlors." Built by CSL in 1923, they were assigned to Chicago Railways.

Cars 3200 and 3201 received experimental multiple-unit equipment. They also had treadle-operated folding doors like the MU cars in series 3202-3261 and 6199-6238. In 1936 the two experimental cars were converted to optional one-man/two-man operation.

Car 3179 had leather seats and air doors. The seats

came from the two rebuilt funeral cars.

Cars 3195 and 3199 were scrapped in 1946. Between the end of 1950 and the end of 1954 all the other cars were scrapped.

3202-3261

These were the first production-model (as opposed to experimental) multiple-unit cars built for the CSL. They were built in 1924 and 1925 following the test of MU operation with cars 3200-3201, the last two cars of the preceeding series.

This series, assigned to Chicago Railways, was identical to series 6199-6238, assigned to Chicago City Railway Company. The bodies were identical to both later series of MU cars, CRys 3262-3321, and CCRy 6240-6279. The 3202-3261 series could run in multiple-unit with 3262-3321, 6199-6238, and 6240-6279.

As built the cars could run one-man, two-man, or three-man (in a two-car train). After train operation ended in 1930, the Tomlinson couplers were removed.

The cars were converted permanently to one-man operation during 1932.

Like their predecessor series, the "Flexible Flyers," these cars had no bulkheads. Each platform had both folding doors and a single treadle-operated door.

In an effort to give the cars a modern look, CTA painted 3204, 3207, 3228, and 3250 green and cream.

Cars 3202 and 3233 were the first cars scrapped, in 1946. Four cars — 3203, 3221, 3240, and 3256 — followed in 1948. By the end of 1953 all the cars had been scrapped.

3262-3321

These 60 multiple-unit cars, built by three manufacturers, were identical to series 6240-6279, built by the same three manufacturers. Cars 3262-3321 were assigned to Chicago Railways, cars 6240-6279 to Chicago City Railway Co. All 60 cars were built in 1926.

The bodies of these cars were the same as series

• Opposite page, top. It's early in the CTA era, but already car 3085's days are numbered.   Shown here at Kedzie and Bryn Mawr, north terminal of Through Route 17, the car was scrapped August 8, 1949.   Neuberger collection. •   Bottom. Interior of car 3034, taken in March, 1951, three months before it was scrapped. CTA photo. •   Below. Its destination sign indicating it has pulled in after a run on Halsted Street, car 3049 rests at the Limits carhouse.   George Krambles collection.

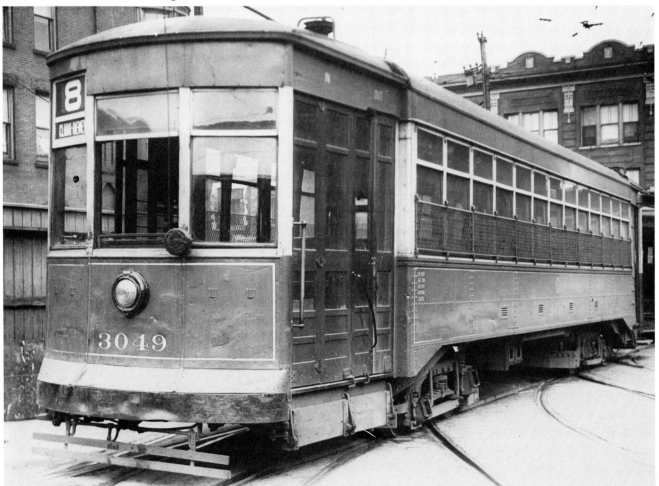

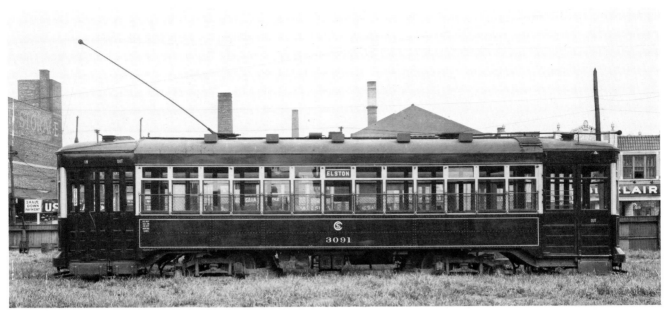

Car 3091 was built to replace car 1360. It was built by the Surface Lines in their own shops in 1919. Note air doors at one end, sliding manual doors at the other end. Photo courtesy of the Chicago Transit Authority.

• Opposite page. Top. In service on Through Route 22 — Clark-Wentworth — car 3154 waits to make a southbound trip from the off-street terminal on Clark Street near Howard. Author's collection. • Middle. Equipped with four 60 HP motors, cars in the 3119-3178 series were well suited to hard service on heavy trunk lines. Here car 3172, a Cummings Car Co. product of 1923, waits its turn to pull into the stub end terminal at 95th and Ashland. Barney Neuberger photo from the A. C. Williams collection. • Bottom. Car 3189 rests behind the Cottage Grove carbarn between runs. Chicago Transit Authority photo.

J. Buck took this photo of Chicago Railways double truck safety car 3094 on March 30, 1941, when it was running on the Morgan-Racine-Sangamon line (Through Route 23). The car was scrapped just a little more than seven years later. Photo from the Allan C. Williams collection.

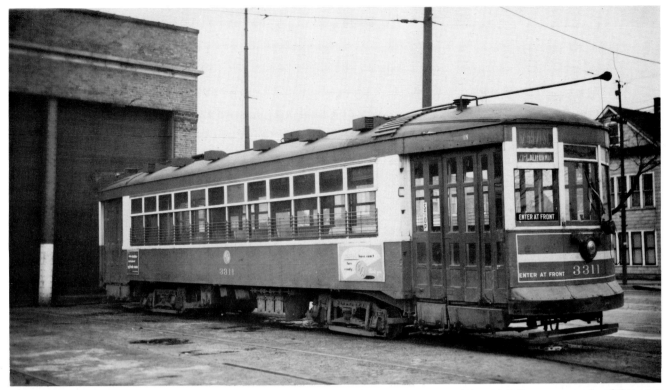

• Opposite page, above. The decline in the fortunes of the CSL can be traced through the uses made of the cars in the 3262-3321 series. Built as multiple-unit cars for use in two-car trains on heavy lines, they ended their days in one-man service on the lighter lines. Here 3266 is ready to depart from its sparsely-settled western terminal at 71st and California Ave. on the 67th-69th-71st Streets line. Neuberger collection from A. C. Williams. • Below. Interior of 3287. St. Louis Car Co. photo. • This page, above. CTA 3311 at the 69th and Ashland carhouse. Neuberger collection. • Below. Car 3303 in one-man service on Armitage Ave. Neuberger collection.

A 1925 product of the Lightweight Noiseless Streetcar Company, car 3249 was built as a multiple-unit car capable of two-car train operation. On August 23, 1932 the Surface Lines converted this car to one-man operation. After nearly 20 years' service as a one-man car, it was scrapped on May 19, 1952 by the Chicago Transit Authority. A. C. Williams photo taken near the end of its career.

Sedans, also known as Peter Witt cars after their designer, were the mainstays of the Clark-Wentworth line (Through Route 22) for many years. Car 3358 was built by Brill in 1929 as part of the 3342-3361 series, owned by Chicago Railways. These cars got their official designation of FECE from the fact that they loaded at the front, and had the exit doors at the center of the car. A. C. Williams collection.

A long line of Sedans shares a bay in the Kedzie carhouse with prewar PCC cars in this photo by Joe L. Diaz. Both types of car were assigned to the heavy Madison Street line: the PCCs making mostly main line runs and the Sedans making trips on the Fifth Avenue branch. The arrival of the postwar PCCs displaced both the Sedans and the Blue Geese on the Madison runs.

Side view of ill-fated experimental articulated car 4000. Photo from the W. R. Keevil collection.

3202-3261 and 6199-6238. The cars could run in multiple-unit with 3202-3261, 6199-6238, and 6240-6279. When multiple-unit operation ended in 1930, the couplers were removed. Most of the cars were converted for one-man operation in 1931-1932.

Of special interest were four experimental cars in this series. In 1929 car 3287 received St. Louis E1B-66 trucks, 50 HP GE 298-A-51 motors, a gear ratio of 8:1, and 26″ wheels. Car 3288 received Timken 52 trucks, 50 HP GE 298-D-51 motors, a 7.75:1 gear ratio, and 28″ wheels. Car 3289 received Brill 277E trucks, 50 HP double-reduction motors, an 8.75:1 gear ratio, and 26″ wheels. Car 3312 received Brill 39E-2 trucks, 60 HP motors, 3.8:1 gear ratio, and 28″ wheels. The first three cars were made one-man in 1931, the fourth in 1932.

Cars in the 3262-3321 series were built without bulkheads, had folding doors with treadle operation, and 22 cars (3282-3303) had foot operated brakes. Scrapping of this series began in 1948, and was completed in early 1954.

3322-3381

This order of Peter Witt cars came from CSL (3322-3341), J. G. Brill (3342-3361), and Cummings Car Co. (3362-3381). All were built in 1929. Known informally as "Sedans," these cars had the official designation "FECE," standing for front entrance, center exit. These were the first CSL cars to have such an arrangement. They were also single-end cars, the only ones of that type besides the Nearsides on the Surface Lines until the arrival of the PCCs in 1936. The 3322-3381 series was assigned to Chicago Railways. An identical series of 40 cars — 6280 to 6319 — was built in 1929 by the same three builders and assigned to Chicago City Railway Company.

These cars were the first on the Surface Lines to have automatic acceleration. This feature gave smooth operation, since acceleration was not subject to the varying skill of the motormen.

Several cars underwent early modification. Car 3322 was rebuilt with a rear exit treadle door in 1932. Car 3341 received re-spaced exit doors and Timken trucks in an early rebuilding.

In 1952 the CTA embarked upon a rebuilding program involving a total of 21 cars. Seventeen cars from this series were involved: 3325, 3347, 3348, 3349, 3351, 3352, 3354, 3355, 3357, 3360, 3361, 3362, 3363, 3368, 3372,

3378, and 3379. The cars were rebuilt for one-man operation, but never ran as one-man cars and were all scrapped within a year of conversion. Six of the cars in this series, including some of the rebuilt cars, received green and cream paint schemes. These cars were: 3326, 3328, 3350, 3354, 3378, and 3381.

Car 3322 was the first to be scrapped, in 1945. All the cars had been scrapped by the end of April, 1953.

The first 10 Peter Witt cars went into service October 3, 1929 on Clark-Wentworth (Through Route 22), and CSL assigned top brass to ride them. In addition to the regular crew of motorman and conductor, each car carried a division superintendent and a traveling motorman. Two assistant superintendents of transportation, the men division superintendents reported to, were also assigned to the inaugural runs. The cars operated out of two barns, Devon and 77th.

The total of 100 cars (3322-3381 and 6280-6319) cost $1.7 million, and the Surface Lines spent an additional $100,000 to modify loop tracks along the line to handle the single-end cars. With a length of 49 feet and seats for 60 passengers, they were the largest standard cars on the Surface Lines. They were luxurious, too, for both passengers and crew, with bucket seats upholstered in leather. Motormen appreciated the windshield wiper and defroster. Other memorable features were the dash-illumination headlight, also used on some trolley buses, and the hourglass and wide horizontal band painted on the dash to indicate a front-entrance car.

In the early 1930s CSL experimented with regenerative braking on one of the Peter Witts. Regenerative braking turned the car's motors into generators which could return from 15 to 25 per cent of the power used to move the car to the overhead trolley wire.

The motorman used a master controller with acceleration points on one side of a central off position, and braking points on the other side. The controller did not make and break the 600 volt power connections to the resistances and the motors as older-style controllers did. Instead it regulated a motor-driven accelerator which had 46 steps of resistance in series with the motors, and 31 steps to weaken the motor field current. During acceleration the accelerator cut out the 46 resistance steps first, then weakened the field in 31 steps to get still higher speeds. In braking the sequence was reversed, with the field weakening steps cut in first to accomplish regenerative braking, followed by the 46 steps of dynamic braking through the resistances. (The CSL's multiple-unit cars and the other Peter Witts also had MU type controls, in which the full 600 volt propulsion current did not go through the controller as it did in the older "K" type control.)

Four WH 50 HP motors designed to work at 300 volts were permanently connected in series to run on the 600 volt circuit. Compound motor windings helped the car accelerate and brake smoothly without external resistance while the car was running on the field weakening notches. Lightweight Standard Steel Car Co. trucks were used on the experimental car, with a double-reduction drive similar to type WN.

Though tests on Clark Street were disappointing, CSL engineers felt that if an entire line were equipped with the cars, schedule speed could rise to 16 mph, with acceleration and braking rates of 4.75 mph/sec. (The Clark Street tests showed a schedule speed of 12 mph and acceleration and braking rates of 1.75 mph/sec.) Under better operating conditions, a fleet of such cars could return fully 25 per cent of the power they consumed, engineers said. Although the regenerative braking scheme was never revived, the 1936 and postwar PCC cars did use dynamic braking.

4000 (one car)

This Chicago Railways Company vehicle began life as two cars, 1101 and 1102. They were in the "Matchbox" series, 1101-1423. When built by the St. Louis Car Company in 1903 they were Chicago Union Traction 4633 and 4634. Car 4633 became 1104 in 1909 and 1101 in 1925. Car 4634 became 1105 in 1909 and 1102 in 1925.

Each car when rebuilt retained one St. Louis 47 rebuilt truck at each end. The other ends of the cars were joined together with a Cincinnati Car Co. steel vestibule drum, and rode on a single Brill 67-F truck with 22″ wheels. Seating capacity of 1101 and 1102 was 36 each as separate cars. When combined into car 4000 they had a combined capacity of 91, accomplished through use of longitudinal seats along one side of each car and the use of platform seats.

This experimental articulated was completed August 3, 1925, and went into service on Cicero to serve the Western Electric plant during rush hours. It was scrapped March 30, 1937. For further details of its operation, see the Cicero Avenue route description.

Each section of articulated car 4000 had longitudinal seats along one side and cross seats on the other side, giving a seating capacity for the whole car of 91, plus plenty of standing room. W. R. Keevil collection.

The front entrance and center exit of Pullman experimental car 4001 are visible in this official Pullman photo. Also quite evident are the tilted windows, which were sealed because the car depended on forced-air ventilation. High curved ceiling gave car spaciousness. Pullman-Standard photo.

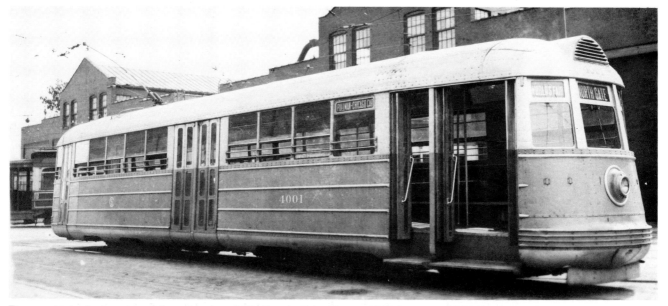

The sealed windows and forced-air ventilation originally provided on car 4001 were soon removed in favor of windows that could be opened. Tubular window guards were then added to prevent passengers from sticking their head or arms out the windows. As signs suggest, car did serve World's Fair. Neuberger collection.

4001 (one car)

This experimental pre-PCC car built by Pullman, and its companion car 7001 built by Brill, were built to CSL specifications that were few and simple. The idea was to give the carbuilders a lot of leeway to come up with the most modern car possible. The door arrangement was fixed at three front doors for loading, and two center doors and a single rear door for unloading. Seats for 58 passengers were specified, and a length of about 50 feet was called for. But within those limitations the builders were told to come up with as fine a car as the state of the art would allow.

The Pullman car, though single-end, had nearly identical front and back ends. Another feature immediately noticeable was how the sides and ends sloped in towards the roof. The windows were permanently sealed, with blowers providing a complete change of air every three minutes.

Trucks were of special all-aluminium construction, as was the entire carbody. It was said that more aluminium was used in building this car than any other up to that time. Car weight was only 29,600 lbs, about 40 per cent lighter than standard Chicago cars. Braking was dynamic, but an auxilliary air brake held the car still when stopped, and could also be used in conjunction

Slightly awkward when viewed head on, car 4001 presented this sleek shape when seen from the side. The nearly symmetrical design of the car is also evident in this CTA photo. Color scheme was blue and silver. This door arrangement was adopted for the prewar PCC cars.

• Above. A. C. William's shot clearly shows how one of the twin center exit doors was removed on the pre-war PCCs and replaced by an extra body panel and window. • Opposite page. Construction photos show motorman's controls, top, and how steps folded into body to preserve unbroken body line. Pullman-Standard photos of car 4001. • Below. Yes, at least one PCC car — 4051 — did run on Milwaukee Avenue. It was equipped with three rear entrance doors, a single center exit, and two front exits. Successful tests determined door arrangement of postwar cars. CTA photo.

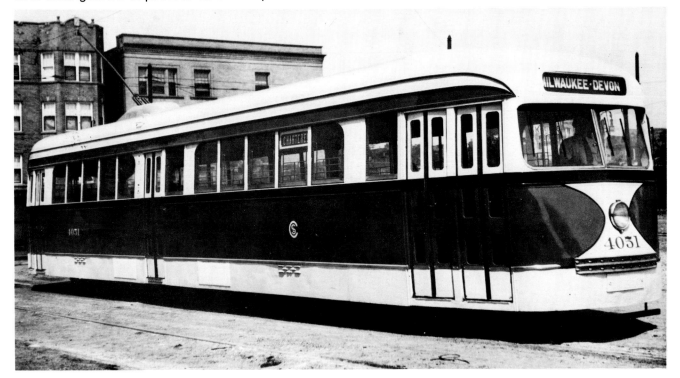

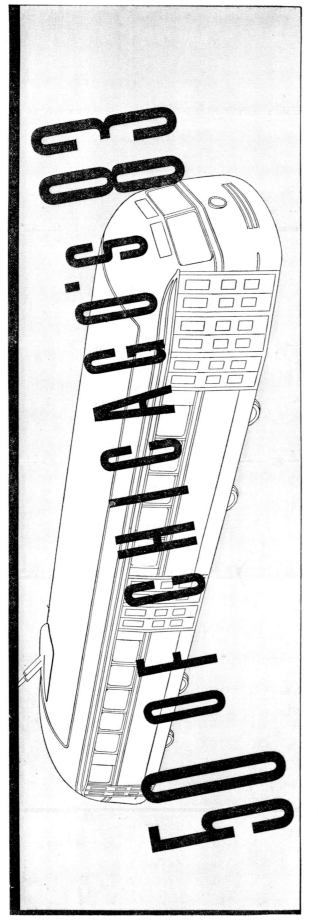

50 OF CHICAGO'S 83

Electrically Equipped by **Westinghouse**

Westinghouse Congratulates the People of Chicago on being able to enjoy the all-around advantages provided in a new fleet of 83 modern, electric street cars . . . now going into service on Chicago's Madison Street Line. Marvels of beauty, quietness and riding-comfort, these cars will establish new standards of convenience and utility in metropolitan transportation.

Westinghouse Congratulates the Officials of the Chicago Surface Lines on their foresight and enterprise in providing, on behalf of their patrons, car-riding facilities of such all-around excellence. Not only will these cars, by reason of their spacious accommodations and rideability, add fresh meaning and lustre to the phrase, "Chicago's Street-Car Service;"

but they will unquestionably usher in a new era of operating efficiency . . . by reason of their easy maneuverability in traffic, and by their capacity for *adequate speed with safety.*

The Westinghouse Electric & Manufacturing Company is proud to have played a genuine part in equipping this imposing street car fleet. 50 of these 83 new, modern, electric street cars are furnished with complete electrical equipment by Westinghouse, including both motors and control. Compact and powerful, these motors provide almost unbelievably smooth *acceleration,* at rates up to 4¾ miles per hour per second. The control apparatus is also of the very latest modern design, and provides *deceleration*

through a combination of electric dynamic braking, track brakes, and air brakes.

For 50 years Westinghouse has rendered a highly specialized service to the Transportation Industry . . . on land, on the sea and in the air . . . attested by its work in connection with the New York, New Haven and Hartford Railroad's streamlined train, "The Comet," and the Pennsylvania Railroad's main line electrification from New York to the Nation's capital. It is singularly appropriate that in its Golden Jubilee Year, the Westinghouse Electric & Manufacturing Company should be able to make this new and important contribution to Chicago's modern electric transportation.

with the dynamic brake to bring the car to an emergency stop.

The car had four 50 HP (some sources say 60 HP) Westinghouse 300 volt motors, permanently connected in series for operation on 600 volts DC. Drive was double reduction, similar to type WN. Both acceleration and braking were at 4.75 mph/sec, and top speed was 40 mph. Control was through a master controller with only three power points — switching, full field, and short field — and only two brake positions — hold and braking. The motorman could select a range of acceleration rates from 1.50 to 4.75 mph/sec. He could also select braking rates up to 4.75 mph/sec.

The motorman controlled the car's three front doors, which were not interlocked with the control circuit. For small groups of passengers he could open just a pair of doors, and for bigger crowds all three. The conductor could open or close either of the center doors. They were interlocked with the control circuit to prevent car movement while they were open. The treadle-operated rear exit was also interlocked with the control circuit. In regular service it could be opened only when the conductor had the center doors open. However, the conductor could cut in the treadle mechanism to work independently of the center doors by pushing a switch. He also had the option of opening the rear door even if a passenger were not on the treadle. The streamlined, rounded body of this car made folding steps necessary.

Car 4001 was designed for two-man operation. Passengers entered through the front doors, and paid their fare as they passed the conductor. He was stationed just ahead of the center exit doors. The car was used in revenue service on Clark-Wentworth, Through Route 22. It was also used to serve the Century of Progress.

Arriving on the Surface Lines in early July of 1934, car 4001 made its first official trip on July 9 with a party of engineers and newsmen aboard. It stood out from the other CSL cars not only because of its styling but because of its light royal blue and silver paint job, with black striping.

After a brief career this car was retired and made into a storage shed at the 77th and Vincennes yards. It is now preserved at the Illinois Railway Museum at Union.

4002-4051

With this lot of 50 cars, built for Chicago Railways, and an identical lot of 33 cars, built for the Chicago City Railway Co., the Surface Lines entered the era of the President's Conference Committee cars. Commonly known as PCCs, these cars resulted from extensive research conducted on behalf of a committee of street railway presidents. Because these cars represented a radical departure from previous designs, their mechanical and operating characteristics are given fuller treatment in the preceeding chapter. A detailed scale drawing of one of these cars is included at the back of the book.

As originally delivered, these St. Louis Car Company 1936 models had seats for 58 and were designed for two-man operation. Entrance was through the two front doors and exit was through the double center doors or single rear door. The conductor was stationed just ahead

• Opposite page. Manufacturers of components for the pre-war PCC cars were so proud of them that they ran ads like this in a special section of the *Chicago Tribune*. Nick Kalman collection. • Above. Car 4044 at the Madison-Austin terminal of the Madison Street line on January 10, 1937. A. C. Williams collection.

CSL 4006 in the original standard colors of dark blue and cream with a red belt rail. G. Krambles collection.

of the center doors, and fare collection was Pay-As-You-Pass. When converted to one-man operation in 1952, seating capacity was increased to 61. These 4002-4051 series cars were identical to the 7002-7034 series assigned to Chicago City Railway Co.

These cars might have been built by any of four car-builders. CSL sent specifications for 100 PCC cars to Pullman, Brill, St. Louis and Budd on May 27, 1935. Westinghouse and GE got requests to bid on the electrical equipment. As the prospective owners of the cars, two of the companies underlying CSL had to ask the Federal court for permission to order them, since the underlying companies were bankrupt. Specifications called for the cars to reach a speed of 20 mph within 60 feet after starting from a stop, and to reach 30 mph in 180 feet.

Passenger comfort was assured through high-intensity interior lighting, forced-air ventilation, low steps into the car, leather upholstery, smooth acceleration and braking, and a body that "floated" on rubber.

Braking was by a combination of dynamic brakes, magnetic track brakes, and air brakes. The air brakes were only an auxiliary system, to prevent heat damage to the resilient rubber wheel "sandwich" from excessive brake shoe friction. The new cars were to weigh 10,000 lbs. less than the 1929 Peter Witts, the reduction to come through the use of Cor-Ten steel.

CSL later modified the specifications to match more closely those of the Brooklyn & Queens Transit Corporation, which was ordering its first lot of PCC cars then. As finally accepted the bid was for 83 cars at a cost of $1.3 million. The City of Chicago objected, but Federal Judge Wilkerson ruled in favor of the Surface Lines on February 27, 1936. CSL promptly notified St. Louis Car to begin construction. At that time St. Louis was building all of the 200 PCC cars then on order from street railways all over the United States.

Condensed specifications for the 1936 PCC Cars		
Seating capacity	58	
Total weight	36,000	lbs.
Acceleration	4.00 to 4.75	mph/sec.
Balancing speed	42	mph
Maximum service brake rate	4.75	mph/sec.
Maximum emergency brake rate	8-9	mph/sec.

CSL's first PCCs were 4', 5" longer and 5" wider than the standard PCCs being built by St. Louis Car for Brooklyn and Baltimore. The extra length was used to add another entrance door (three rather than the standard two), and to add a single rear exit door. The extra width made it necessary to mount the car bodies 3" off center on the trucks so two cars could pass each other. This resulted in the bodies overhanging the right hand rail 3" more than the left. As Chicago's cars were to be two-man, the motorman didn't have to make change or issue transfers. So hand controls for acceleration and braking were used, rather than the pedals used in other PCC cars. With all their advantages, CSL's PCCs cost about $16,000 each, $1,000 less than the Peter Witts purchased in 1929.

The first six cars got a big greeting from Chicagoans on November 12, 1936, when CSL staged a night transit pageant along Madison Street featuring the new cars. Prior to the parade, CSL President Guy Richardson was host for lunch served to newsmen aboard the cars as they made trial runs — and not a drop of coffee was spilled. On November 13 the public had a chance to inspect the cars, which were on display at State and Madison and State and Adams in the Loop.

• Top. Wings, chevrons, and stripes of all types decorate the noses of these 4000-series cars, painted in experimental hues in 1945. See page 105 for colors used. G. Krambles collection. • Middle and bottom. Close-ups of two of the experimental paint schemes. B. Neuberger collection.

Passengers found the cars just as attractive to ride as they were to look at. The first of the 83 cars entered service November 13, 1936, and the last was placed in service in February, 1937. Between November, 1936, and January, 1937, total CSL ridership increased 3.6 per cent. But during that same period Madison Street ridership increased 25 per cent.

Both the Madison main line and the Madison-Fifth Avenue routes got the new cars. CSL chose Madison as a test route for several reasons. It was one of the busiest in the city, had much short-haul and transfer traffic, went through the most congested parts of the Loop, ran on a narrow street with many stop lights, and already had loops at both ends for turning single-end cars.

Weekday base schedules called for 52 cars, 44 on the Madison main line and 8 on the Fifth Avenue branch. CSL sent out 90 cars during the morning rush hour, 77 on Madison and 13 on Fifth. The evening rush hour was the heaviest of all with a total of 95 cars required, 82 on Madison and 13 on Madison-Fifth. CSL gave Madison PCC service at all times, although with only one spare car to cover the evening rush hour there were times when the Peter Witts filled in on Madison during the evening rush. There were enough PCCs to give base service on Madison-Fifth, but Peter Witts had to run here in both morning and evening rush hours.

PCC operation cut from 10 to 12 per cent from the running time of Madison cars, compared to the schedules maintained by the 1923 steel cars in the 1721-1785 series, which ran on Madison prior to the PCCs. It was the spectacular 25 per cent growth in traffic that forced CSL to assign 16 Peter Witts to all PM rush hour service on Madison-Fifth, and to fill in on the Madison main line for shopped PCC cars.

Comparison of Madison Street Headway in Minutes		
	1923 cars	**1936 PCC cars**
AM rush hour	1.14	0.96
Base period	1.76	1.58
PM rush hour	1.20	0.86
Evening hours	2.44	2.23

The PCC's success in Chicago, and indeed around the country, was no fluke. It was the result of a $1 million research program funded by a group of transit company presidents and suppliers who met in Atlantic City, N.J., in the grim fall of 1929. Street railways got by during the inflation of the 1920s, as rising passenger volume helped meet rising costs. Then the auto boom hit, followed by the Depression. Passenger volume dropped, and operating costs had to be cut to the bone if the companies were to survive. The bus was, of course, by that time an alternative, and by 1936 CSL had a dozen gas bus and trolley bus routes. Like CSL, though, many transit operators had a huge investment in tracks, overhead wires, electric substations and other fixed facilities that would be of little value if they converted to bus operation. Also many transit operators, including CSL, firmly believed that nothing could match the streetcar for handling the heaviest loads.

Transit companies wanted a modern streetcar which could win new passenger business away from the automobile, while cutting costs still further. Hard specifications to meet, since it seemed that any improvements in the car to attract passengers would add to the first

The door arrangements tried out on prewar PCC car 4051 (see page 99) became the standard door arrangement on the postwar cars. The three rear doors were the entrances, and the single center door and the two front doors the exits. The Surface Lines was the only traction company to use this type of door arrangement on its PCC cars. Photo of car 4359 at 81st and Halsted from the Barney Neuberger collection.

cost, the operating expenses, or both. Why didn't the streetcar builders come up with a modern car? They were geared to making the lowest bid on the specifications furnished them by transit operators for what amounted to custom-built cars. Carbuilders spent next to nothing on research and development, since its cost would have to be figured into the bids, and might make them too high to get the order.

But the prospect of building a standardized streetcar which could be sold by the thousands to a nationwide market persuaded the carbuilders and suppliers of streetcar components to join the transit companies in financing the basic research for a modern car design. Less than seven years later the first true production model PCCs were in operation.

Almost every part of the PCC car was new: blinker doors which folded out of the passengers' way; stainless steel window sashes that didn't stick; luxurious leather seats; a heating system that used waste heat from the motor control resistors as a heat source; and welded rather than riveted bodies. Even the trolley pole, trolley wheel, and trolley catcher (retriever) were of new, streamlined design.

Brooklyn & Queens Transit Corp. ordered the first production-model PCCs in July, 1935. CSL was next, with their order for 83. CSL was so pleased with its 1936 PCCs that President Guy Richardson announced plans to buy a total of 1,035 PCC cars.

CSL even had a part in testing a pre-production model PCC. PCC model "A" was really only the first pair of PCC trucks mounted under a streetcar borrowed from the Brooklyn & Queens Transit Corp. PCC Model "B" was built by Pullman to the specifications of the Transit Research Corp., developers of the design. Model "B"

ran in Chicago in 1934 on the Windsor Park line. Together with Model "A" and CSL's pre-PCC experimental cars, Model "B" went on display at a street railway convention in the fall of 1934 in Cleveland.

Painted dark blue from the belt rail down, the 1936 cars picked up their nicknames of "Blue Geese" and "Blue Devils" from their paint. The belt rail stripe was red, and the body above the belt rail, including the roof, was cream, with a stripe of blue on the lower part of the letterboard. The hourglass figure on the front dash, first used on the Peter Witt cars, was also applied to the dash of the 1936 PCCs to indicate a front-entrance car. But on the PCCs the hourglass was outlined in red.

Straphangers got a chance to choose the colors they thought would look best on the postwar PCC cars. To aid them CSL in 1945 repainted a half-dozen 1936 PCCs in various color schemes. Car 4010 was a reddish brown with an orange belt rail, 4018 was green with an orange stripe, 4020 was yellow with an orange stripe, 4022 was salmon red, 4035 was traction orange with a maroon stripe, and 4050 was yellow with an orange stripe. All cars had a cream roof. The colors chosen for use on the postwar PCCs were Mercury Green (light green) and Croydon Cream, with the belt rail painted Swamp Holly Orange.

CSL added three wide cream stripes edged with red across the dash of the 1936 cars in 1945. They curved around the dash and tapered away after running across the front doors. Known as "Tiger Stripes," they were intended to warn approaching motorists that the cars were wider than they seemed. They blended quite well into the hourglass design on the dash, and gave the cars a racy touch. The 1936 PCCs were the only CSL cars to get such striping. Before they entered service as one-

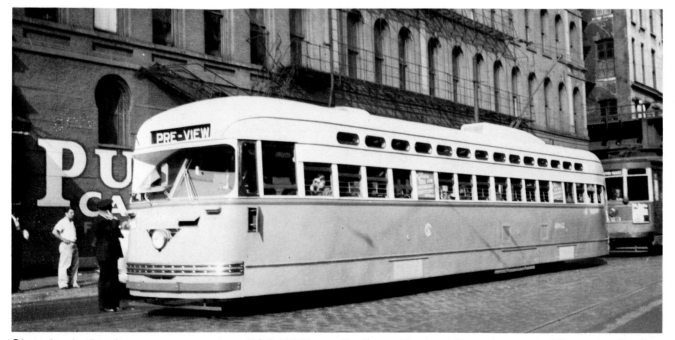

Gleaming in the afternoon sun, postwar PCC 4062 is on display on Harrison Street just east of State shortly after its arrival in Chicago. Old Pullman car behind the PCC points up how streetcar styles changed over a period of four decades. Sign in PCC car window proclaims that car 4062 is just one of 600 new streetcars Chicago received after WW II. All were out of service by 1958. Neuberger collection.

man cars on the Cottage Grove line on May 11, 1952, CTA repainted them Everglade Green and Croydon Cream.

Through the years the cars received various mechanical modifications, including truck work, ventilation alterations, and replacement of the trolley wheels with trolley shoes during their first few years of service. Cars 4032 and 7026 received roof cowling similar to that on some Boston cars in a forced-ventilation experiment: they were not air conditioned.

In 1940 triple rear doors were cut into car 4051, and the conductor's station was moved to the rear of the car from in front of the center doors. One of the two center doors and one of the three front doors was removed, with sealed windows replacing them. After conversion the car had three rear doors, a single center door, and two front doors. As built they had a single rear door, two center doors, and three front doors.

Car 4051 ran in experimental service on Milwaukee Ave. as a rear-entrance, front exit car. No other 1936 cars received this modification, but this door arrangement was used on CSL's postwar PCCs, the only cars in the country to have this arrangement. In 1941 car 4051 was rebuilt with its original door arrangement, but it was not restored to its exact original form. An extra window was added behind the rear door, moving it forward one window space from its original position.

Among other cars of interest was 4041, which had special destination signs for making trial runs on the Ashland and Indiana routes. PCC cars never ran on these routes in regular service. When the other cars were

• Above. The Pullman Company built PCC Model "B" in 1934, the same year they outshopped CSL experimental car 4001. Car "B" was run in Chicago on the Windsor Park line. In this Barney Neuberger photo it is southbound at 73rd and Stony Island, about to take the switch for a turn onto 73rd Street on a short turn run to South Chicago. • Below. Signed for operation in Chicago, car "B" demonstrates its front entrances and center exits in this photo from the collection of Stephen D. Maguire.

scrapped at 47th and Morgan in 1956, CTA held back car 4021. It is still in storage, waiting to go on display in the CTA's own transportation museum, which may some day be built.

During their two decades of service, the 1936 PCC cars were assigned to the Madison, Madison-Fifth, Madison 10¢ Shuttle, 63rd, Cottage Grove, and Western routes. They entered service on Madison November 13, 1936. As previously noted, they filled all base schedules on the Madison main line and the Fifth Avenue branch, but evening rush hour schedules required the use of Peter Witt cars. PCCs were also assigned to the Madison 10¢ Shuttle service, which began on October 15, 1949 and ended August 1, 1951.

Displaced from the Madison Street lines by the arrival of the postwar PCCs, the 1936 cars moved to the 63rd Street route on April 11, 1948. They did not completely replace the Old Pullmans on this route.

From 63rd the cars went to Cottage Grove, where they replaced the Peter Witts. Before reassignment CTA converted the PCCs to one-man operation. This involved sealing one of the two center doors and replacing it with a window. At this time they received the standard postwar PCC paint scheme. On car 4016 the rear exit door was sealed during conversion to one-man operation.

On June 19, 1955 Cottage Grove became a bus line, and the PCCs moved to Western. They displaced two-man postwar PCCs which ran weekdays, and buses on weekends, since Western had been a weekend bus line since December 7, 1952. The 1936 cars lasted less than a year on Western, which was converted to bus operation on June 17, 1956.

Although not regularly assigned to these routes, the 1936 cars did run on Milwaukee, Ashland, Indiana, Clark-Wentworth, and Stony Island. They may have run on other routes experimentally or to fill in gaps in the service, as they did when they were diverted from 63rd to Stony Island.

4052-4061

These 10 cars, built by St. Louis Car Co. in 1947, were assigned to Chicago Railways. They were identical to cars 4372-4411, built for Chicago Railways in 1948 by St. Louis, and to cars 7035-7274, built by St. Louis in 1947-1948 for Chicago City Railway Co.

As delivered, these cars were equipped for two-man operation. The conductor was stationed opposite and slightly forward of the three rear doors. The single center door and the two front doors were exits. Between May 8 and September 18, 1952, all cars were converted to one-man operation. As two-man cars they had seats for 57, and as one-man cars they had seats for 61. In October, 1954, the last three cars in this series (4059-4061) were converted back to two-man operation. In May and June of 1955, all cars in the series were converted to optional one-man/two-man operation, with seats for 57 or 58.

St. Louis Car Co. received all ten cars back in the first two months of 1957. Parts from the cars were used to build CTA's 6000-series rapid transit cars.

4062-4371

The 310 cars of this class represent all the PCC cars Pullman built for the Chicago Surface Lines. This total does not include car 4001, which was an experimental pre-PCC car built by Pullman in 1934. Two series make up this class: 4062-4171 (1945-1946), and 4172-4371 (1946).

A width of nine feet, a length of 50 feet, and six doors all contributed to the uniqueness of these cars among PCCs. With the 300 similar cars built by St. Louis, Chicago had the largest fleet of new PCC cars — 600 — in the United States. Counting the prewar cars, Chicago had a total fleet of 683 PCCs.

The postwar cars were the mainstays of two of the heaviest routes in the city, Clark-Wentworth and Broadway-State. The cars needed on just the Broadway-State route in the 1950s were more than the total PCC car fleet of San Francisco.

The crowd-swallowing capability of these cars was astonishing. Loading was through the three rear doors, with exit through the single center door or two front doors. The conductor stood just ahead of the rear doors on the opposite side of the car. In effect this gave these cars a rear platform, where passengers could stand before paying their fare.

At busy stops the cars loaded quickly and got moving as soon as the last passenger had squeezed inside. While the car ran to its next stop passengers would file by the conductor and pay their fare. The natural rear-to-front passenger flow was aided by making the center and front doors exits. The center exit was controlled by a treadle, the front doors by the motorman.

Use of a wye track at 81st and Halsted Streets led to some unusual maneuverings to turn Clark-Wentworth cars at their south terminal. After discharging passengers on 81st Street, the cars turned and ran north on Halsted for a few hundred feet, ran back south across 81st Street, then turned and ran east on 81st Street. The maneuver was aided by a small back up controller located below the rear window.

On February 17, 1953, car 4240 was sent to St. Louis Car for conversion into a PCC-type rapid transit car for Chicago's "L"-Subway system, also under CTA control. From that time until the end of 1955, all 310 cars were sent to St. Louis. The car bodies were scrapped, but the trucks, seats, controls, and other parts were incorporated in the CTA's 6201-6510 series rapid transit cars. The last 40 cars to see service were 4062-4101 on the Wentworth route in 1955.

More than two decades after conversion — and nearly three decades after they were built — these partly reincarnated cars still run on the CTA's rapid transit system.

4372-4411

These 40 cars were the St. Louis-built equivalents of cars 4052-4061 and 7035-7242. They were Chicago Railways cars.

● Above. One of the last PCC cars delivered to Chicago, CTA 4391 arrived in 1948. It is shown on the off-street loop at the south end of the Western Avenue line just north of 79th Street in this photo from the Barney Neuberger collection. On August 1, 1948 the Western line was cut back from 111th to 79th on the south end and from Western and Howard to the Schreiber loop at Clark and Devon on the north end, with PCC cars replacing conventional equipment. In December, 1948 the north terminal was changed to the Western-Berwyn off-street terminal. ● Below. Interior of car 4381, sent to St. Louis Car in October, 1952 for conversion to an experimental rapid transit unit. St. Louis Car photo.

St. Louis-built car 4400 rests in the open storage yard behind the 69th and Ashland carhouse after a run on Western Avenue. Delivered as a two-man car, it was still in two-man service when the picture was taken and, unlike some of the other postwar cars, remained two-man until it was scrapped by the CTA in 1959. Photo from the Barney Neuberger collection.

Thirteen cars in this series went to St. Louis Car Co. for conversion: 4372-4377, 4379-4380, and 4382-4386. Car 4381 went to St. Louis in October, 1952, but was scrapped without conversion in March, 1953. Car 4394 was sent to Pullman, also in October, 1952, and was scrapped without conversion in March, 1953.

Of the other cars 4378, 4399, and 4411 were scrapped by the CTA. Cars 4387-4390, 4392, 4395-4398, and 4401-4410 were scrapped by Merchants Steel and Supply Co. The Electric Railway Historical Society preserved car 4391 in 1959. The only postwar PCC to be preserved, it is now in operation at the Illinois Railway Museum at Union, Ill. Car 4406, which retained its light green color scheme to the end, was used on an enthusiast's special sponsored by the Central Electric Railfans' Association on October 21, 1956.

5001-5200

This series began a class of large, double-truck, deck-roof wooden cars that at its peak totalled 600. These cars were the Chicago City Railway Co. standard design, as the Old Pullmans of the 101-700 series were the Chicago Railways standard design. Built in 1904, they were known as the "Little Brills."

Cars 5044 and 5076, built by CCRy, went to the commercial carbuilders as samples. Car 5044 went to American; car 5076 to Brill. The earliest modification to any car in this class was 5022, converted to a cable car but re-converted to electric operation. It was scrapped in 1948. Although not built as PAYE cars, the 200 cars in this series were converted to PAYE in 1908.

A fire in the Archer barn in April, 1916, claimed cars 5169 and 5194. From 1916 to 1945 the remaining cars stayed on the roster, serving the South Side CCRy lines, until five were scrapped in 1945. One car survived the scrapping that continued through the late 1940s. Car 5031 became salt car AA-99 on August 20, 1948, and survived until 1956. By the end of 1948 all the other cars had been scrapped.

5201-5600

The first 100 cars of this series, built in 1906, continued the CCRy design established by the 5001-5200 series. They were converted to PAYE in 1908. Cars 5301-5600 were built as PAYE cars — Chicago's first — in 1907-1908.

After the San Francisco earthquake and fire of 1906, cars 5201-5250 were sent from the J. G. Brill factory to the United Railroads in San Francisco. They became Market Street Railway 1500-1549, and ran there until the late 1940s. Brill built a second lot of 50 cars for Chicago.

For such a large series of cars (400), remarkably few were written off the books during their half-century of service. Car 5239 was destroyed in 1914, car 5303 burned in the Archer barn fire of 1916, and 5358 was destroyed by fire in 1944. Aside from those three cars, the entire series was intact when scrapping began in 1945. By the end of 1951 all the cars were gone except for 5517. Made into a storage shed at South Shops, it lasted until 1957. The only unusual car in this cookie-cutter series was 5522, which had 54 rather than 40 seats.

5601-5650

Built by J. G. Brill in 1910, these 50 cars bore a strong resemblance to the Old Pullmans of the 101-700 series, although 5601-5621 were CCRy cars and 5622-5650 were Southern Street Railway Co. cars.

CCRy car 5606 was destroyed by fire on December 24, 1944. All other CCRy cars were scrapped between 1945 and 1948. All 29 Southern Street Railway Co. cars remained on the roster until scrapped in 1947-1948.

5651-5665

Built as single-end cars by Kuhlman in 1907, these cars first ran on the Chicago & Southern Traction Co. as 126-140. Acquired by CCRyCo in 1912, they were rebuilt into double-ended PAYE cars. Aside from 5664 and 5665, destroyed in the 1938 Lawndale barn fire, the series ran intact until one car was scrapped in 1941, and another in 1942. The remaining 11 were scrapped in 1946. On the C&ST these cars made the suburban runs to Crete, and on CSL they ran on Ashland Avenue.

5701-5702

These two cars represented CCRyCo's first experiment with maximum traction trucks. Built in CCRy's own shops, they had Brill 39-E maximum traction trucks with 34" and 22" wheels. Both cars were built in 1910. Car 5701 was destroyed in the Archer barn fire of 1916, and car 5702 was scrapped in 1948.

5703-5827

Known as "Nearsides," these cars also were called "Muzzleloaders" because both entrance and exit were at the front. They were two-man cars, with the conductor stationed behind the motorman.

Car 5703 was tested in Philadelphia where the builder, J. G. Brill, had its plant. Upon delivery the cars were assigned to the Cottage Grove line, which had also received the first PAYE cars in 1908. Twenty-six cars were rebuilt for optional one-man/two-man operation in 1933 and 1935. They were all low numbered cars from 5703 to 5731 (cars 5706, 5710, and 5718 were not converted).

After a collision with a railroad train at 94th Street and Cottage Grove Ave., car 5765 was retired in 1913. Car 5808 was rebuilt with a treadle door at the rear and seats for 53.

The first cars in this series were scrapped in 1946, and the last in 1949. From the first days of their service these cars were mainstays of operation on the Cottage Grove line, and later ran on other southeast side and South Chicago district routes. The first car to arrive in Chicago was 5703, which was placed in service on Cottage Grove.

The Nearside was a favorite in Philadelphia, where it carried a large front route sign box, a feature taken over by the Chicago Nearsides. (The 5900 series CSL cars, built by Brill in 1913, also later carried these large sign boxes.) This type of car was also used on the International Railways of Buffalo before its introduction in Chicago. Not a very fast car by Chicago standards, the Nearsides did not run well when placed in mixed service with other types of car on the same line. In addition to their slowness, they had a front entrance, which confused Surface Lines riders who boarded all other cars

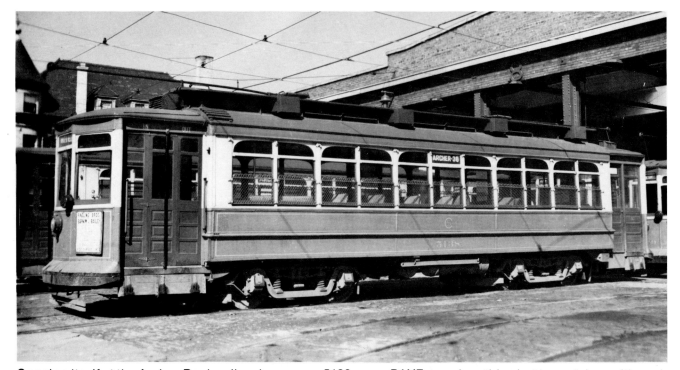

Sunning itself at the Archer-Rockwell carhouse, car 5138 was a PAYE car when this photo was taken, although it began life as a conventional car. Neuberger photo from Railway Negative Exchange.

except the Sedans and PCCs at the rear. The cars ran briefly on the interstate lines during the 1930s.

The cars got their name from their design as front entrance cars, supposedly easier to load when they stopped to pick up passengers on the near side of street intersections. The design also took some of the pressure off the conductor who, though he stood directly behind the motorman, was no longer responsible in any way for starting or stopping the car. CCRy claimed that the Nearsides reduced platform accidents 91 per cent, comparing April, 1912, with April, 1913. Accidents of all kinds reportedly fell 37 per cent. The reductions came despite a six percent increase in passengers.

Among other advantages claimed for the cars was a 25 per cent increase in seats compared to the Brill PAYE cars, achieved by eliminating one platform. Raise sash permitted a wider aisle, since the window pockets and arm rests used with drop sash were not needed. Through the use of two-motor maximum traction trucks the car steps were dropped two inches nearer the ground. There were some disadvantages, too. People wouldn't move to the rear of the car, jamming the front entrance. They couldn't use the rear exit, because this was for emergencies only.

5900-5999

These large arch-roof cars, 1913 Brill products, had a seating capacity of 55 and rode on Brill 39-E-1 maximum traction trucks with 34″ and 22″ wheels. They were CCRy cars.

As a series these 100 cars remained intact until one — 5939 — was scrapped at the end of 1945. Four were scrapped in 1946, two in 1947, and the remaining 93 in 1948.

6000-6137

Identical to Chicago Railways 3000-3091, these 138 Chicago City Railway cars were part of the first order built under CSL management for Chicago's street railways. Cars 6000-6133 had Brill 39-E-1A maximum traction trucks, while cars 6134-6137 had Baldwin maximum traction trucks. Both trucks had 34″ and 22″ wheels.

On February 22, 1933, car 6062 caught fire at 90th and State Streets. Rebuilt, it was scrapped July 20, 1951. Car 6043 was used for storage at the lower level Hamlin Ave. yards of the Lake Street "L" line. Sent to Hamlin on April 28, 1950, it was scrapped May 5, 1955. Car 6113 was taken off its trucks and used for storage at the 38th and Halsted material yard from May 11, 1950 until June, 1956, when it was scrapped.

6138-6154

The first nine cars in this series, 6138-6146, replaced cars destroyed in the Archer carbarn fire of 1916. They were built by American Car Co. in 1918. The other eight cars, 6147-6154, were built by CSL in 1919. The weight, motors, control, and trucks vary widely from car to car in this series, and they were aptly given the official designation "The Odd Seventeen." During 1951 nine cars re-

Nearing the end of its career, car 5234 waits for departure time at the 79th and Brandon lakefront terminal of the 79th Street line. Barney Neuberger photo from Railway Negative Exchange.

• Above. Car 5309 is starting to show its age as it rumbles down this beautiful, tree-shaded street on a streetcar enthusiasts outing (probably the Electric Railroaders' Association trip of 1949). Photo from the Barney Neuberger collection. • Below. In better days the Big Brills looked like this: freshly painted, neatly striped, dents ironed out, and daily grime washed off. George Krambles collection.

• Above. The crew changes ends on car 5335 at the Western Avenue terminal of the 79th Street line. The car didn't remain long on the CTA roster: it was scrapped September 25, 1950. Neuberger photo from the Railway Negative Exchange. • Below. Interior shot of car 5209 clearly shows the two doors in the bulkhead, a PAYE trademark. Note heater, also on bulkhead. George Krambles collection.

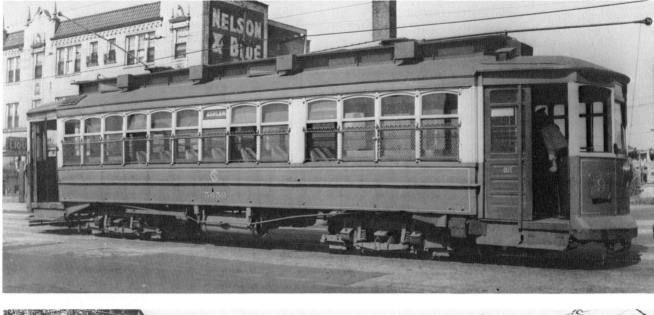

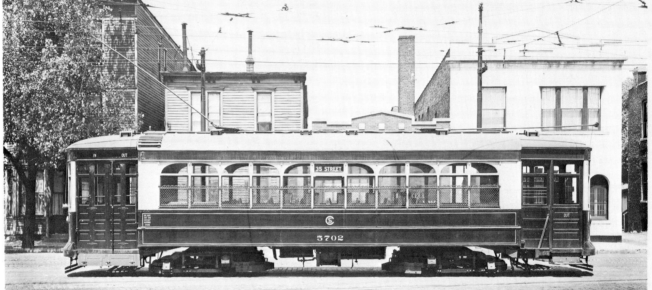

114

The Nearside cars were the mainstays of the Cottage Grove routes for many years. Here car 5736 makes an inbound run on TR 5, Cottage Grove-South Chicago. Barney Neuberger collection.

• Opposite page. Top. After the Crete suburban cars were acquired from the Chicago & Southern Traction Co. in 1912 they were rebuilt into PAYE cars from their original single-end design. In this shot from the Neuberger collection, car 5659 is at the 95th terminal of the Ashland line. • Middle. One of two cars built by the CSL in 1910, car 5702 was scrapped May 20, 1948. Its mate, car 5701, was retired after being damaged in the Archer carbarn fire of 1916. Chicago Transit Authority photo. • Bottom. Equipped for one-man operation in 1935, car 5726 was scrapped by the CTA on April 21, 1949. The "Visit Museum of Science and Industry" dash sign was typical of the dozens of such signs the CSL used to encourage off-peak riding. Allan C. Williams collection.

At the north end of Through Route 17, Kedzie and Bryn Mawr, car 6034 awaits its time to leave for a run to 67th and Kedzie. Barney Neuberger photo from the collection of A. C. Williams.

Known as part of the "Odd 17" series of cars, 6140 was one of nine cars (6138-6146) built to replace cars destroyed in the Archer carbarn fire of 1916. R. H. Kennedy photo from A. C. Williams.

• Opposite page. Top. CSL 6162 was built by J. G. Brill in 1923 as a two-man car, and is running as such in this photo from the author's collection. On October 5, 1949 the CTA converted this car to one-man operation. It was scrapped February 9, 1953. • Middle. Built as a multiple-unit car in 1924, car 6207 was permanently converted to one-man operation in 1930. CTA scrapped it on September 4, 1951. Photo shows car on Dorchester Ave. just south of 63rd Street. Neuberger collection photo. • Below. CSL 6148 on Lake Park Avenue at 56th Street, south terminal of Through Route 1, Cottage Grove-Broadway. Converted to one-man operation on July 6, 1951, the car was scrapped August 13, 1954. Note Illinois Central Railroad electric suburban train at 55th-56th-57th station. Neuberger photo from A. C. Williams.

CTA 6203 was eastbound on the 93rd-95th Streets line when this photo was taken on 95th Street near State. Car had been in one-man service since 1930. Barney Neuberger collection photo.

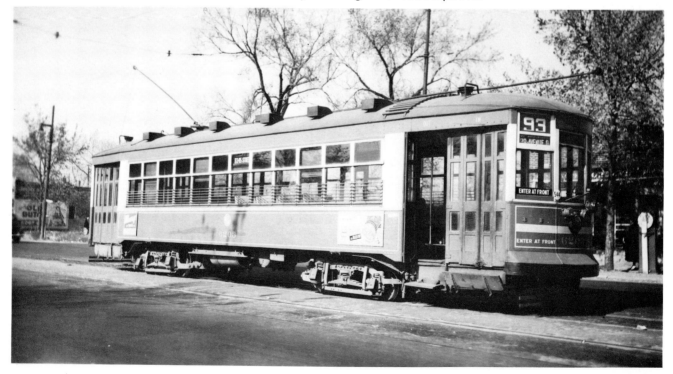

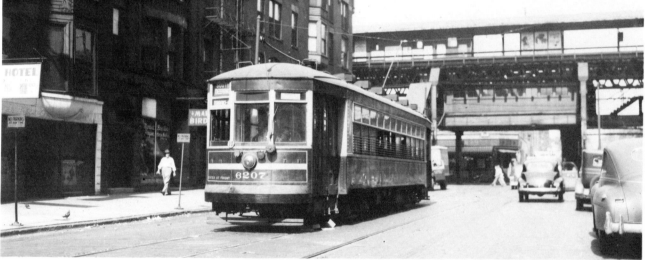

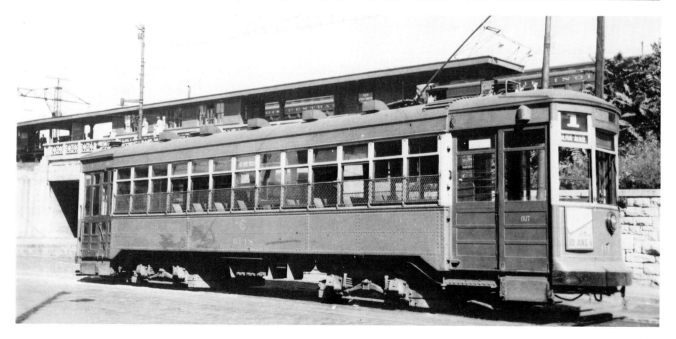

Westbound on the 93rd-95th Street line, car 6272 bounces across the NYC&StL (Nickel Plate) railroad tracks under the watchful eye of a crossing flagman. A. C. Williams photo on May 6, 1951.

Side view of CSL 6281 taken at South Shops shows triple front entrance doors and triple center exit doors. Conductor was stationed between the center exit doors. Chicago Transit Authority photo.

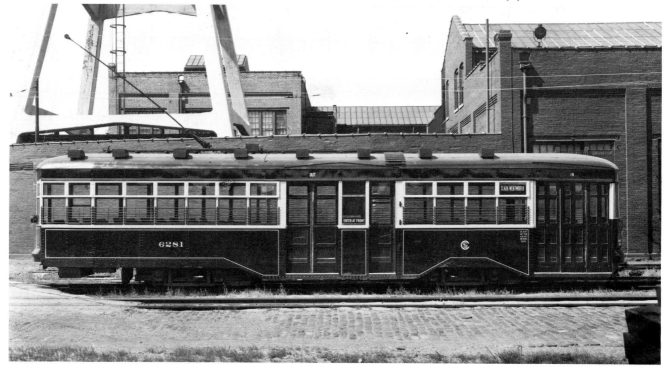

The last assignment of the Peter Witt cars was on the Cottage Grove line. After PCCs began to take over the Cottage line in 1952 the remaining Peter Witts were scrapped. Barney Neuberger collection.

A handsome car in a scenic setting, CSL 6298 is southbound on Clark St. near Lincoln Ave. making a run on the Clark-Wentworth line. Neuberger collection from A. C. Williams.

ceived Pullman 150 trucks and GE-216 motors. All cars were scrapped between 1946 and 1954.

6155-6198

In 1923 CCRy received a total of 44 cars from three builders. They were identical to Chicago Railways 1721-1785 and 3119-3178 cars. None of the cars in this series were equipped with Van Dorn couplers, to pull trailers.

During 1949-1950 they were converted from two-man to one-man operation, except for 6197, which was scrapped in 1948. All cars were scrapped by the end of 1954.

6199-6238

The first 19 cars of this series, 6199-6218, were built by Chicago Surface Lines. The Lightweight Noiseless Streetcar Co., a Minneapolis, Minn., concern, built the other 19. All cars ran on Brill 39-E-2x maximum traction trucks with 28″ and 22″ wheels. All 40 cars were outshopped in 1924.

Identical to the Chicago Railways series 3202-3261, the bodies of these cars were similar to Chicago Railways 3262-3321 and Chicago City Railway 6240-6279.

Built as multiple-unit cars, they ran in two-car trains. They could MU with cars 3202-3261, 3262-3321, and 6240-6279. When train operation ended in 1930 the Tomlinson couplers were removed and the cars used for one-man operation. As built the cars could run one-man, two-man, or three-man in a two-car train.

Like cars in their sister series, these cars were built without bulkheads. Each platform had a single folding door, treadle-operated. In the early 1930s these cars were converted to one-man only operation. Scrapping began in the late 1940s, and was complete by the end of 1953.

6239 (one car)

Built by CSL in 1924, this CCRy car replaced wooden car 2726, which was wrecked on February 18, 1924. Car 6239 had two sets of motors during its career, four GE-275-I and four GE-80-A. The replacement car was built without bulkheads. It was scrapped in 1948.

6240-6279

The product of three builders, this series of 1926 cars was assigned to the Chicago City Railway. Identical to Chicago Railways 3262-3321, the bodies of this series were the same as Chicago Railways 3202-3261 and CCRy 6199-6238. See listings for those series for details.

After train operation ended in 1930, these cars were converted to one-man operation. All were scrapped between 1948 and 1952.

6280-6319

Built in 1929 by Brill, Cummings, and the CSL, these CCRy cars were Peter Witt types, the same as Chicago Railways 3322-3381. They differed from other CSL cars because of their front entrance and center exit, with the conductor's station at the center of the car.

In a short-lived experiment, cars 6303, 6305, 6310, and

Pulling away from its connection with the Englewood "L" at 59th and Wentworth Ave., CSL Peter Witt 6288 moves south on the Clark-Wentworth Through Route. Photo from the Neuberger collection.

6319 were equipped by CTA for one-man operation. Never used as one-man cars, they were scrapped in 1953. Car 6319 got a green and cream paint job.

First to be scrapped was 6280, in 1946. Most of these cars were scrapped in 1952, when the Cottage Grove line received the pre-war PCC cars. The four experimental cars mentioned above lasted a year longer.

7001

An experimental, pre-PCC type, car 7001 was built by Brill in 1934. Brill did not later adopt the PCC design, and built its own version of a modern, lightweight streetcar.

Exhibited at the Century of Progress in Chicago in 1934, car 7001 also ran in revenue service carrying visitors to the Fair. It was taken out of service shortly after the Fair ended, and was retired. It was a CCRy car.

Car 7001 had an appearance closer to that of its successors — the 1936 St. Louis-built PCCs — than did its Chicago Railways counterpart, Pullman-built 4001. Car 7001 was the last car Brill built for the Surface Lines. Similar cars, known as Brilliners, served routes in Philadelphia, Pa., and Atlantic City, N.J. The Brilliners built for the Philadelphia Suburban Transportation Company (Red Arrow Lines, now SEPTA) still run in the western suburbs of Philadelphia.

The car came from the rather unusual specifications CSL gave to J. G. Brill and Pullman in 1933. Each was to design and build the most modern car it could, making it quieter, faster, smoother riding, lighter in weight, and more comfortable than any streetcar previously built.

Brill called on artist and designer Otto Kuhler, who came up with a streamlined design similar to that adopted for the CSL's 1936 order of PCC cars. Both the Brill and Pullman cars had 58 seats, were single-ended, two-man operated, and had three front entrances, two exit doors at the center of the car, and a single rear exit.

The Brill car arrived in Chicago in early 1934. It made a run for the press on March 20, stopped at City Hall for inspection by the mayor and city council on March 21, and later went on display for the public on Adams near State. It entered service with two-day trial runs on the Clark, Broadway, and Madison lines. Everywhere it went, riders commented favorably on its sleek shape, set off to advantage with a paint scheme of aluminium and two shades of green with orange trim.

The triple brake system was actuated from a single pedal. First the motors were turned into generators with the car's own resistances providing the load (dynamic braking). Next the magnetic track brakes took hold, and lastly the power-assisted hydraulic brakes came on. An emergency application of the brakes by pushing the brake pedal all the way to the floor brought all three brakes into use at once.

Brill used steel structural sections and steel pressings to frame the car, compared to the all-aluminium body of the Pullman experimental car. The Brill 95-E trucks were also of steel, with rubber cushions in the steel wheels. Around the bolsters, journal boxes, and springs much other rubber was used to cushion shocks and reduce the transmission of vibration to the car body.

The GE-1178 motors were originally developed for use in gas-electric railcars and trolley buses. Drive was single-reduction, through helical gears. The automatic commutator control had 127 full field steps and 20 field

The last car J. G. Brill built for the Surface Lines was experimental pre-PCC 7001, delivered in 1934. R. H. Kennedy took this photo of it at 81st and Halsted. A. C. Williams collection.

Front-to-rear view of 1936 PCC car 7002 shows longitudinal seating at front of car and conductor's station just ahead of the twin center exit doors. Car cards were evidently applied by the builder, since this is a St. Louis Car Co. photo taken at their plant.

Another photo of car 7002, taken in Chicago, demonstrates loading through the three front doors, and unloading through the twin center exits and rear exit door. This design speeded loading, since passengers didn't have to stop and pay fare immediately upon boarding. St. Louis Car Co. photo.

Cars 4032 and 7026 were equipped by the Surface Lines with roof cowling to house pressure ventilating equipment. They were not air conditioned. Car 4032 was made one-man on April 16, 1952, and was sent to a commercial scrap dealer on August 13, 1956. Car 7026 was scrapped October 26, 1956. G. Krambles collection.

This Chicago Transit Authority photo shows CSL 7002, first of the 1936 PCC cars built for the Chicago City Railway by the St. Louis Car. Co. After a career of two decades on Chicago streets, during which it was converted to one-man operation in 1952, car 7002 was sent to a scrap dealer on July 13, 1956.

● Top. Shortly after delivery from the St. Louis Car Co., car 7261 moves south on Western near the 79th Street terminal in August, 1948. R. De Groote, Jr., photo. ● Middle. Jeff Wien snapped CTA 7210 as it emerged from under the St. Charles Air Line (Illinois Central) viaduct at 16th and Clark. ● Bottom. CTA 7195 southbound on the Clark-Wentworth line on Clark Street, passing Lincoln Park. CTA photo.

shunt notches. Eddy current or dynamic brakes reduced speed to about five mph, followed by the hydraulic brake. Because brake shoe heat would damage the rubber sandwich in the composition wheels, the hydraulic brake acted on the motor shaft. Magnetic brakes were used as supplements to dynamic braking in both service and emergency applications.

7002-7034

The first true PCC cars on the Chicago City Railway roster, these 33 cars were identical to the Chicago Railways 4002-4051 series. Both series were built by St. Louis Car Co. in 1936. For technical data see cars 4002-4051.

Like the 4002-4051 series, cars 7002-7034 were converted from two-man to one-man operation in 1952. Conversion increased seating capacity from 58 to 61. A double seat was placed where one of the two center exit doors had been removed, and a single seat was squeezed in behind the rear exit door. A drawing of this series is included in this book.

All cars in this series were scrapped at 47th and Morgan Streets in 1956, except the following: car 7011 scrapped in 1955, 7019 scrapped at South Shops, 7027 retired at South Shops in 1955, 7028 burned at Western and Roscoe in 1956, and 7033 retired at South Shops in 1955.

7035-7274

This Chicago City Railway Co. series was the last group of streetcars built for the Surface Lines. Although CSL ordered the cars, CTA had taken over the Surface Lines before delivery. Identical to Chicago Railways 4052-4061 and 4372-4411.

In 1952 cars 7035-7044 were equipped for optional one-man/two-man operation. In 1955 cars 7235-7259 were equipped for optional one-man/two-man operation.

Thirty-three persons were killed and many injured when car 7078 hit a gasoline truck at 63rd and State on May 25, 1950. The car was completely destroyed in the resulting fire.

This series established a number of last runs on CTA streetcar lines. Car 7158 was the last streetcar on Clark Street on September 8, 1957, 7201 made the last Broadway run on February 16, 1957, and 7213 was the last streetcar to run in Chicago when it ended service on the Wentworth route on June 21, 1958.

All cars in this series, except for the following, were sent to St. Louis Car Co. for use in building rapid transit cars: car 7078, destroyed by fire 5-25-50; 7205, wrecked, rebuilt with parts from 7078; 7217 and 7218, scrapped by CTA in 1959.

8000-8060

The first 31 cars in this series of trailers were built by the Surface Lines in 1921, followed by 30 cars from J. G. Brill in 1922. They were assigned to Chicago Railways.

Without motors and controls these cars weighed just 13 tons, compared to the nearly 28-ton weight of the rebuilt Old Pullman motor cars which pulled them. They were one-man cars.

Cars 8007 and 8014 were destroyed in the Devon carbarn fire of 1922. Chicago City Railway trailers 9040-9046 were built from the salvage of these two cars, and from seven other trailers which were destroyed in that fire. When train service ended in 1930, the cars were used for storage at the North-Cicero and 77th-Vincennes carbarns. All have been scrapped.

9000-9046

These Chicago City Railway trailers were built in three lots. The Surface Lines built 9000-9019 in 1921, J. G. Brill built 9020-9039 in 1922, and the Surface Lines built 9040-9046 in 1923 as replacement for trailers of both the 8000 and 9000 series destroyed in the Devon carbarn fire of 1922. Mechanical specifications were identical to the Chicago Railways trailers of the 8000-8060 series.

Cars 9000, 9007, 9010, 9011, 9012, 9014, and 9015 burned in the 1922 Devon carbarn fire. CSL salvaged parts from these cars (and 8007 and 8014, also burned at Devon) to build trailers 9040-9046 in 1923.

Like their sister cars in the 8000 series, several of these cars became storage sheds at the North-Cicero or 77th and Vincennes carbarns. All are now scrapped.

CSL's trailers initially made one morning and one evening rush hour round trip on various lines, including Through Route 22. Such service put a strain on the motors and air compressors of the rebuilt Old Pullmans, but a layover of three hours or so between round trips was enough to cool them.

General specifications for both series of cars were 47', 6" long, weight of 26,000 lbs., seats for 62 passengers, and Brill 67-F trucks with 22" wheels and a 4', 4" wheelbase. The cars had cast steel underframes and steel sides up to the window rail, with the superstructure of wood above the window rail to save weight. Entrance and exit were through either of the two center doors. There was an electric door interlock control on both the motor and trailer to prevent starting the train with any door open. Both motor and trailer cars carried two Van Dorn couplers.

The Old Pullman motor cars were equipped with air-operated folding doors. The bulkheads were removed, and the conductor was stationed on the car floor, rather than on the platform. Removing the bulkheads made room for an additional cross seat on each side, as well as for two folding platform seats, increasing seating capacity from 40 to 54.

Clark-Wentworth was the first line to get motor-trailer trains, with regular service starting September 1, 1921. As more trailers became available they went into service on the Pulaski, Grand, Ogden, Madison, Cicero, and Halsted lines. The last trailers ran on Halsted September 9, 1930. (For details of trailer service on the other routes, all of which gave up trailer service before Halsted did, see the individual route histories). In service the two-car trains carried a three-man crew: a motorman and conductor in the first car and a conductor in the rear car.

This savings in crew costs, compared to the need for four men to run two conventional cars, plus the extremely light weight of the trailers, made operation economic. A further savings was made by converting some of the Old Pullmans to trailer-haulers, rather than buying new cars designed to pull trailers.

Trailer use did present some operating problems on lines without loops or wyes for turning the trains. On these stub end routes the motor car had to uncouple, run around the trailer, and recouple in order to reverse direction. The unpowered trailers were also troublesome to switch in yards and shops, although the radial tightlock couplers did connect the air and the electrical circuits automatically. Since the trailers had no air compressor, air had to be supplied from the motor car's tanks. Because the trailers had no trolley poles, their light, signal, and heating current had also to come from the motor car.

After the Devon carbarn fire of 1922 destroyed some of the rebuilt Old Pullman motor cars, CSL equipped 72 cars of the "169 Cars" of 1923 with Van Dorn couplers for trailer hauling. However, the development of two-car multiple unit trains ended interest in trailers. Although put in storage in 1930, some trailers came out on the streets again in 1933 to serve the Century of Progress. Not long after they were removed from service, CSL made plans to equip the trailers with motors, controllers, air compressors, and trolley poles, making them into regular two-man cars. Nothing came of this plan, and the trailers remained in storage. During WW II CSL also thought of putting the cars back on the street, but they remained in storage, ending life as material storerooms at North-Cicero and 77th-Vincennes.

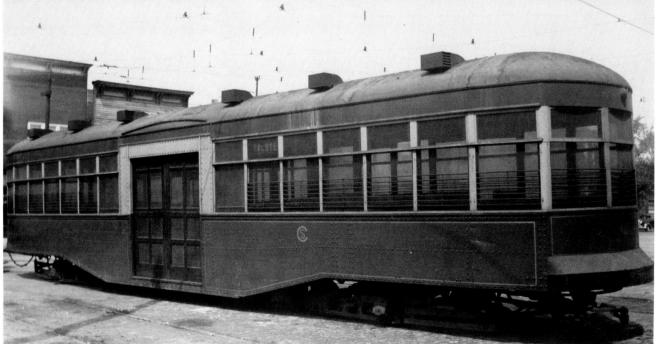

126

• Opposite page, top. Trailer 8000 was built by the Surface Lines in 1921, the first car in the 8000-8030 series. CTA photo. • Bottom. Signed for Halsted, where trailer operation ended on September 9, 1930, car 9028 was a 1922 Brill product. Neuberger collection. • Above. Old Pullman motor cars in the 501-610 series were rebuilt in 1921 to haul the trailers then under construction. This Barney Neuberger collection photograph, supplied by Jack Doyle, shows such a combination. The trailers were built to be as light as possible, but even so they put a strain on the motors of the Old Pullmans, which were not designed for trailer-hauling. • Below. After all trailer service ended in 1930, many of the trailers became storage sheds. Car 9037 wound up as a shed at South Shops. Neuberger photo from Railway Negative Exchange.

CSL Work Cars and Utility Equipment

Just as the electric streetcar met the passenger needs of the Chicago Surface Lines for many years, a variety of work equipment filled the "freight" needs of the company. In later years automotive work equipment cut into the rail work car fleet, reducing the need for wreck cars, line cars, and supply cars. Even so, the 1941 roster showed 3,659 passenger cars and more than 400 rail work cars.

CSL work cars were identified by a combination of letters and numbers. The letter indicated the type of equipment. The number indicated ownership and identified particular cars within a series.

For example, the prefix N indicated a dump car. If the number following the letter N was between 1 and 199, the car belonged to Chicago Railways. If the number following the letter N was between 200 and 299, the car belonged to the Chicago City Railway Company. Cars with numbers in the 300 series belonged to either the Calumet & South Chicago Railway Company or the Southern Street Railway Company.

Within each alphabetical series cars differed widely. Their common bond was function, not design. For example, street sprinklers of 1,400, 3,000 4,000, and 6,000 gallon capacity were all placed in the D series. Another example is the E series, which included both single and double-truck snow sweepers.

In the early years of CSL operation work cars were employed for an amazing variety of tasks. One basic job was keeping the streets open during Chicago's blizzard winters. Single and double-truck E series sweepers, their rattan brooms twirling, were a common sight on Chicago streets during snow storms. For stubborn drifts the F series plows were called out. Sprinkler cars in the D series, once used to keep dust down on the streets, later fought winter storms as snow plows.

Up to the final years of streetcar operation the AA series salt cars went out to deliver salt to terminals and passenger loading points. However, the main job was to salt the tracks with eight bags of salt per mile for each rail. Men aboard the cars dropped the salt on the rails through chutes cut in the floor. Some salt cars had wing plows, and special windows to permit crews to guide the plows around obstacles such as parked cars. Many salt cars retained their scarlet and cream passenger colors as work cars. In fact, many were not renumbered into the AA series for years after they had begun to haul salt. Other work equipment was painted dark green.

The R series sand cars saw winter service filling sidewalk sand boxes placed near hills and other slippery spots along the car lines. Compressed air forced sand out. The cars also delivered supplies of sand to carhouses for use on streetcars during slippery weather.

• Opposite page. Chicago City Railway snow sweeper E-224 clears the way for passenger cars along State Street in downtown Chicago. Plows were called out to handle the deeper drifts. CTA photo.

Many types of work car helped to build and repair track. Among them were A series concrete mixers, I series dirt or garbage cars, J series electric shovels and cranes, K series lumber cars, L series electric locomotives, N series dump cars, S series supply cars, T series rail grinders, U series cupola cars, W series construction cars, and X series derricks. Non-rail work equipment such as Q series belt loaders and Z series steam rollers also aided construction work.

In the early years of CSL operation, the P series wreck cars, converted from street railway mail cars, and the V series line car hauled away disabled passenger cars and replaced downed overhead wires. In later years automobile wreckers and tower wagons handled these chores. Obviously automotive equipment was superior to rail-bound vehicles in handling derailments and overhead wire repairs.

When the Surface Lines was formed, the streetcar companies still generated some of their own electric power, and many carhouses and shops were heated by coal-fired boilers. To serve these facilities the Surface Lines had C series coal cars, G series cinder cars, and L series electric locomotives, which pulled standard railroad coal cars. The locomotives also handled boxcars of supplies, flatcars loaded with new passenger cars, and gondola cars loaded with the remains of scrapped cars.

Miscellaneous work equipment included B series cars for delivering newspapers, H series street railway mail cars for pickup and delivery of mail to post offices, M series money cars to pick up cash receipts from carbarns, one O series meter test car to test the current consumption meters in passenger cars, and S and Y series supply cars for delivering to carbarns such items as transfers.

When they reached the end of their usefulness as passenger equipment, many cars were converted to work service. An example is the AA series salt cars. In the chapter on passenger cars, conversions to AA series cars are noted for each series of car.

Old Surface Lines buses were sometimes converted to work equipment. All received two-letter prefixes beginning with the letter B. The only exception was the medical examination unit, which received the prefix MEU. This bus was outfitted as a doctor's examining office, and was used to give periodic medical examinations to bus drivers. Other prefixes used on converted buses were: BA — salt and sand bus, BW — work bus, BR — radio-equipped work bus, BS — school instruction bus, and BT — training bus.

In the CTA era, when all local transit companies were consolidated under one management, work equipment moved between the Surface Division (former CSL and Chicago Motor Coach lines) and the Rapid Transit Division (former Chicago Rapid Transit Co. lines). For example, BW series work buses were used on Rapid Transit Division projects, and the MEU bus was also used to examine Rapid Transit motormen and conductors.

A direct exchange of work equipment between the Surface and Rapid Transit Divisions took place in 1958. CTA Surface Division locomotive L-202, formerly the same number on the Surface Lines and C-50 on the Chicago City Railway, was rebuilt to a Rapid Transit Division locomotive. It later was renumbered S-343. Shopmen at the Rapid Transit Division's Skokie Shops used only the subframe of the old car. Everything else was new on the rebuilt locomotive, including rapid transit trucks and motors and a new car body and cab. As originally built the locomotive drew its power from an overhead trolley wire. As rebuilt it could draw power from either the third rail or overhead wire. As a Surface Division locomotive its last assignment was at 77th Street, switching cars of supplies from the railroad interchange near 87th and Wentworth to the yard and shops at 77th and Vincennes. On the Rapid Transit Division it switched cars of material from the Penn-Central (New York Central) interchange to the 63rd Street yards of the Jackson Park "L".

In the pages that follow the CSL's work cars are examined in order. They are presented in alphabetical order by prefix, which does mix cars of different ownership together, but groups cars together by function.

'D' Series Sprinkler Cars

As part of the Settlement Ordinances of 1907, the street railway companies were required to sprinkle the streets to keep down the dust and flush away horse droppings. For this purpose CCRy built 12 steel sprinklers in its own shops in 1908, and numbered them starting with D-1.

The motors, brakes, and tanks themselves were built elsewhere and assembled in the shops. The motors, control equipment, brakes and sanders were the same as those used on the CCRy's Brill PAYE cars: four GE-80 motors, with K-28-E controllers at each end. However, the sprinklers were mounted on two MCB trucks with six-foot wheelbases rather than the Brill's McGuire 10-A trucks. The 4,000-gallon tanks could be filled in 16 minutes under normal city water pressure. With the discharge valves fully open, the cars could spray a strip 17 feet wide for 40 minutes.

'E' Series Snow Sweepers and 'F' Series Snow Plows

Although a few Surface Lines employees greeted winter storms with relish, anticipating long hours of extra duty with overtime pay, most employees and riders loathed winter blizzards. For CSL the storms meant badly delayed cars, derailed equipment, closed lines, intolerable traffic congestion caused by motorists driving on the freshly-cleared tracks, and extra expense. For passengers the bad weather meant long waits on cold corners, overcrowded cars, and impossibly long travel times.

Take, for example, the storm that struck December 18, 19 and 20 in 1929. Fifteen inches of snow fell, whipped into drifts by winds up to 66 mph. CSL fought the blizzard with 5,000 men assigned to snow fighting. They manned 100 snow sweepers, 176 snow plows, and 26 sprinklers equipped with wing plows. Each snow-fighting piece of work equipment carried a 12-man crew to dig out snow by hand whenever required. Some 2,000 tons of salt were spread on the streets during the storm.

Fifteen regular wreck wagons, supplemented by some borrowed from the construction and electrical departments, answered some 1,000 calls for help a day. CSL estimated the storm cost it a half-million dollars, including the cost of removing the snow, damage to equipment, and loss of revenue. Early in 1930 CSL was crippled twice by snow and ice storms, one of which required 10,000 men and 4,000 tons of salt to clear.

During the 1920s and 30s CSL equipped some of its snow plows with air-operated side wings and ice breaking shears with tool steel teeth. Unfortunately even these shears could not dent the ice formed in the March, 1930 storm, and lines were out of service for several days while they were dug out by hand. Fifty-eight snow sweepers also received steel side wing plows during this period, following the successful test installation of wing plows on sprinklers in 1924. To protect operators, wood and steel cabs were added to seven sprinklers equipped with side plows. Ten sprinklers, 58 sweepers, and three plows also got electric cab heaters in this period.

United States Railway Mail Cars

Chicago was not the first city in the United States to have trolley mail collection and delivery. That distinction belongs to St. Louis, where the first regular mail car operation on a streetcar line began in 1891. Chicago's first mail-carrying line was Madison Street, which began service with a combination mail and passenger car on May 25, 1895. Since Madison was a cable line at that time, the postal car was a trailer hauled behind a cable grip car. Painted a gleaming postal white and richly decorated in gold, the Pullman Palace mail car made its inaugural run in a special cable car train carrying the mayor, aldermen, postal officials, and Pullman Company executives.

Labor trouble was expected on the first run, so the Chicago postmaster carried a special permit from the mayor on the first trip. The streetcar men and some Chicago aldermen, including Bathhouse Coughlin, saw in cable car mail service more than a faster way to deliver mail. By an Act of Congress street railway post offices were designated as official postal routes in 1895, and union men and their political supporters remembered well how the Pullman Strike of 1893 had been broken by the Federal government under the pretext that strikers were interfering with mail carried on passenger trains. Union leaders feared that Chicago carmen would have difficulty striking if mail were carried on streetcars. However, no trouble was met on the first trip, and the carrying of mail seems to have had no effect on subsequent labor negotiations.

The first Madison street mail runs served two post offices, one at Racine and one at Western. A second car was added on November 4, 1895 and at the same time the line was extended west to serve the post office at

Pulaski. Unlike the first car, this second trolley post office was a full postal car without space for passengers. Like the first car it was pulled behind a Madison Street grip car until Madison Street was electrified in 1906.

A route change was made in 1899 to serve the post office at Jackson and Canal. Cars ran from State and Madison via State, Washington, Clinton, and Madison. When the post office at Madison and Pulaski was moved to Lake and Springfield in 1901, the Madison route cars are reported to have run on Lake Street to serve it. This would have required some switching, as the Lake Street line was electrified at that time, but the Madison line was still cable operated. Service was extended further west along Lake to the Austin post office at Lake and Waller soon after. Schedules called for the cars to make eight to 11 trips six days a week and two Sunday runs. Only four of the weekday trips ran as far as the Austin post office. Service to downtown Chicago ended in 1911, with all cars terminating at the post office at Washington and Canal. After 1911 night trips on Madison used part of the Millard Avenue line for the return run to Washington and Canal. Madison trolley post offices continued to run between the four post offices on the route described until

all service in Chicago ended November 21, 1915.

In November of 1895 the North Clark Street railway post office began to run. Its official name was "Chicago, Ill., Clark Street and Lincoln Avenue RPO." As the title indicates, the original plans called for service to operate via Clark, Armitage, and Lincoln. In March, 1896, the Lincoln routing was replaced by one up Clark as far as Diversey. The name of the route was changed at this time to "Chicago, Ill., North Clark Street RPO." The south terminal for this route was Clark and Monroe.

When the main Chicago post office was temporarily relocated at Washington and Michigan in 1901, the North Clark RPOs ran from Washington and Clark. Various routings via Sedgwick and Larrabee were used in this period. With the electrification of the Broadway route in 1901, North Clark cars began to run to north suburban Evanston via Clark, Lincoln, Halsted, and Broadway. Eight of the fourteen round trips on the Clark line were routed past the North Western railroad station at Kinzie and Wells, then via Sedgwick to Clark. Three other trips were routed via Larrabee to the post office at Belmont and Clark. Service to Evanston was discontinued in 1903, and the line's north terminal became the

Chicago Railways concrete mixer A-1, built in 1908-1909, shown at work on the Montrose Ave. track extension on October 21, 1930. Chicago Transit Authority photograph.

Chicago City Railway snow plow D-212 began life in 1908 as CCRy D-12, a sprinkler car with a 4,000 gallon steel tank. Carrying number D-212 on the Surface Lines, it was one of 11 cars in the D-201 to D-213 series converted to snow plows by the Surface Lines. This Barney Neuberger photo from Roy Benedict shows D-212 at the 69th and Ashland carhouse.

Chicago City Railway D-202 is part of the same D-201 to D-213 series as car D-212 shown above. It too was built as a 4,000 gallon sprinkler car by CCRy in 1908, and converted to a snow plow by the Surface Lines. But note that its frame was not lengthened and its cabs were not extended, as they were on D-212. This Barney Neuberger photo, taken at South Shops, was supplied by Allan C. Williams.

All four companies that formed the CSL owned their own work equipment, just as they owned their own passenger cars. Snow plow D-304, for example, was owned by the Calumet & South Chicago Railway. Built as a 4,000 gallon sprinkler car, it was converted to snow plow use. This Barney Neuberger photo from the A. C. Williams collection shows the car at the Burnside carhouse.

This photo of Chicago City Railway sprinkler car D-208, taken by R. H. Kennedy on November 2, 1941, shows how the series D-201 to D-212 looked as sprinkler cars. Car D-208 was one of the few cars in this series not converted to a snow plow, although in later years there was no need for sprinkler cars. Allan C. Williams supplied the photo from his collection.

● Above. Chicago City Railway snow sweeper E-227 needed its full complement of brooms, wing plows, and side sweepers to fight this Chicago blizzard. Note line of CSL passenger cars waiting for slow-moving sweeper to pull in. Credit this chilling winter shot to the Barney Neuberger collection, courtesy of Bill Richmond. ● Opposite page, top. Chicago Railways snow sweeper E-55 was part of the E-1 to E-56 series built by Brill, Lewis & Fowler, and McGuire-Cummings. Photo at 38th and Halsted material yard from the Neuberger collection. ● Opposite page, below. Sweeper at work on Chicago Ave. Chicago Transit Authority photo.
● This page, below. For most of the year the snow sweepers, plows, and salt cars rested inside carbarns or out in the open storage yards adjacent to the carbarns. Here CCRy E-222, a McGuire-Cummings snow sweeper, shares a carbarn stall with another sweeper and bags of salt. A. C. Williams provided this photograph, originally a part of the Neuberger collection.

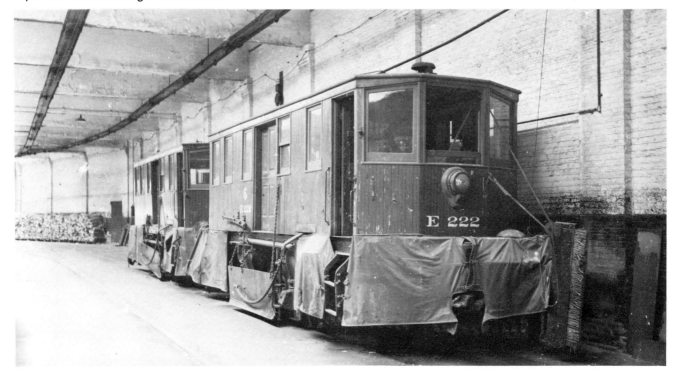

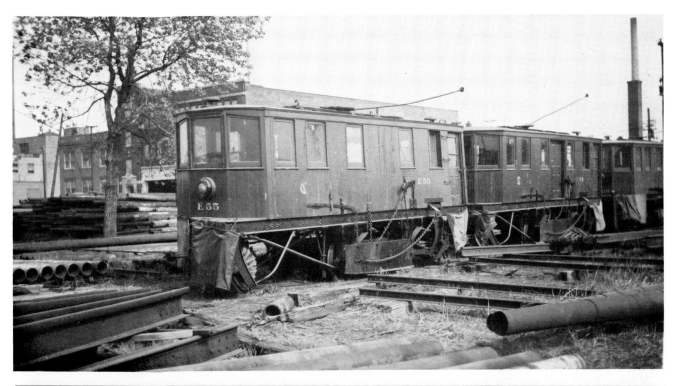

• Above. CRys small single truck snow plow F-1 was built by Taunton Locomotive Manufacturing Co. Barney Neuberger, from the Jack Doyle collection. • Opposite page, top. Surface Lines plows were more than a match for all but the biggest blizzards. CTA photo. • Opposite page, below. Chicago Railways sweeper E-18 at Division and Austin in 1943. S. D. Maguire collection. • This page, below. Plow F-303 was originally South Chicago City Railway 1, later Calumet & South Chicago Railway F-303. This Neuberger photo shows a lineup of snow fighting equipment at the Burnside barn.

Looking more like a railroad boxcar than a street railway snow plow, F-301 began life as a Calumet Electric Street Railway plow around 1898. Before receiving the number F-301 it was Calumet Electric Street Railway 81. This Neuberger collection photo, taken at Burnside carhouse yard, was supplied by the Railway Negative Exchange.

F-202 was a Chicago City Railway single truck snow plow. Part of the F-201 to F-205 series, it was built by Wason in 1908, and at first carried the number F-56. Small as it was, this car carried a full complement of front and side wing plows, and did its share to keep far South Side lines open. Photo at Burnside carhouse from the Neuberger collection/Railway Negative Exchange.

post office at Rogers Park.

With the opening of the Kinzie Tube Station in 1904, the south terminal of the Clark line became Kinzie and Orleans. All mail to and from the main post office was dispatched by pneumatic tube at this station. In 1912 the Kinzie Tube Station was abandoned, and a new tube station opened on Chicago Avenue. However the cars continued to run, without the mail, to the old Kinzie terminal before changing ends. The only exception was the night circuit trip, which ran via Clark, Belmont, Milwaukee, and Kinzie. On this trip mail was carried for North Western station. Meanwhile in 1908 the north terminal of the line was cut back from the Rogers Park post office to the re-located Edgewater post office at 5501 Broadway. All service was discontinued November 21, 1915.

The Milwaukee Avenue RPO entered service on November 11, 1895, with two cars on an hourly schedule between the main post office and outlying stations at Carpenter St. and at North Ave. The route was from La Salle and Madison via La Salle, Lake, and Milwaukee to North. Like the Madison Street RPOs, this line's cars were trailers pulled by Milwaukee Ave. grip cars. Unlike the first Madison Street RPO, these two cars were full railway post offices without a passenger compartment.

An 1898 rerouting brought Milwaukee cars past the newly-built post office at Canal and Adams. This must have required some switching, as Milwaukee Ave. cars were still cable hauled at this time, while the routes that passed the new post office were electric. The cars made eight daily round trips and two on Sunday in 1898.

A change in route brought the Milwaukee cars to a new downtown terminal at State and Randolph. The route was via State, Lake, and Milwaukee to Fullerton to serve the Logan Square post office at Fullerton. In 1902 the line was extended to Irving Park to serve that post office with six of the 14 daily round trips.

Like the North Clark cars, Milwaukee RPOs were cut back to Kinzie and Orleans when the Tube Station there opened in 1906. The new route was via Kinzie and Milwaukee to Fullerton. (In 1905 the line had been cut back from Irving Park to Fullerton when the North Western Railway began to handle mail to the Irving Park post office.) One trip a day continued via Milwaukee and North to North and California.

With the opening of the Canal post office in 1911, the south terminal of the Milwaukee RPOs was shifted from Kinzie and Orleans to Canal and Madison. Mail to and from the main post office was handled from the Canal post office by pneumatic tube. Fifteen day trips and three night trips were scheduled in 1911. The night runs were via a combination of the Milwaukee and North Clark routes. All service ended in 1915.

Cottage Grove was the first CCRy post office route, starting May 7, 1896. This was a heavy route right from the start, and the cars originally assigned were full postal types with sorting cases, tables, and pouch racks. Car 1 was named after Chicago Postmaster Washington Hesing, and car 2 after Assistant Postmaster John M. Hubbard. Both cars were painted postal white and had gold seals and trim. Like the Madison RPO, they were products of the Pullman Palace Car Co. The route was from Adams and Wabash to 55th and Cottage Grove via Wabash, Cermak, and Cottage Grove.

In 1901 the south terminal was changed to 55th and Lake Park. Clerks aboard the cars made up pouches for postal stations along the Illinois Central Railroad as far south as West Pullman on the Blue Island Branch of the IC's suburban system. The pouches were forwarded to the IC through the Hyde Park post office. Starting in 1904 mail to and from the main post office went through the 22nd Street post office, via pneumatic tube. However, Cottage Grove RPOs continued to run to downtown to exchange pouches of mail with other trolley RPOs. In 1906, the same year Cottage Grove switched from cable to electric power, the RPOs were cut back to the south fringe of the Loop at Wabash and Van Buren. In 1907 the line was extended to serve the Jackson Park post office at 528 E. 63rd Street.

From eight round trips in 1896 the service increased until by 1907 there were 15 round trips daily. Cottage Grove holds the record for both the heaviest single trip and the greatest volume handled on one day, both records set during the Christmas Season. On December 24, 1908, three cars assigned to one Cottage Grove trip received 420 pouches and sacks of mail for distribution. On December 23, 1909, Cottage Grove RPOs handled 3,260 pouches and sacks.

To spread the load of mail over a longer period, a night circuit RPO route was established in 1909. It used portions of the Cottage Grove and Wentworth lines. Starting from State and Van Buren the night cars ran via Van Buren, Clark, 22nd, Wentworth, 31st, Halsted, 63rd to Woodlawn, (change ends), Cottage Grove, Indiana, Wabash, and Van Buren. Cars ran on the night circuit at about two hour intervals from 8 p.m. to 3 a.m. The night cars permitted a cutback to nine round trips during the day. In 1913 the circuit line was discontinued and absorbed into the schedules of the Cottage Grove and Wentworth RPOs. This increased the Cottage Grove schedules to 15 trips on weekdays. However, the two Sunday and Holiday round trips continued to use the circuit route. All Cottage Grove service ended in 1915.

Although it was the fifth of six routes to be started, Wentworth Avenue became the longest in Chicago, with the most RPO cars assigned to it. Service began April 10, 1900. The route was from Clark and Washington to 63rd and Wentworth, and served post offices at 22nd, Armour (31st and Wentworth), Brighton Park (35th and Halsted), Stock Yards (42nd and Halsted), and Englewood (63rd and Wentworth). The first run left Clark and Washington at 5:31 a.m. and reached the Englewood post office at 6:17. The route was via Clark, Cermak, Wentworth, 63rd, Halsted, 31st, Wentworth, Cermak, and Clark to Washington. There were 12 daily trips, four Holiday trips, and three Sunday trips.

Three electric RPOs began the service, with a fourth held in reserve for heavy loads. Each car carried seven mail clerks. Like cars 1 and 2 running on Cottage Grove, cars 3 through 7 had names as well as numbers. Car 3 was Charles Emory Smith, car 4 was James A. Gary, car 5 was Perry S. Heath, and car 6 was William S. Shallenberger. All the cars were built by Pullman.

In 1901 the new Jackson Park post office on 63rd near

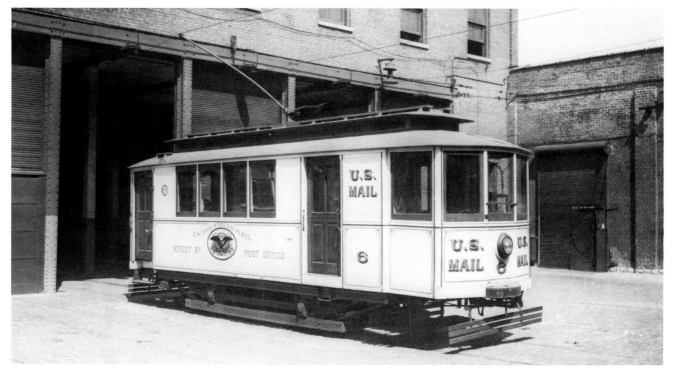

The only Chicago mail car preserved was Chicago Railways Number 6, shown here pulled out on the carbarn lead at 77th and Vincennes in 1958. Preservation is complete, and the interior of the car contains sorting cases and racks for mail sacks. On August 22, 1946, car 6 was brought out for the American Philatetic Society convention at Chicago, and mail was cancelled aboard the car. S. D. Maguire collection.

Chicago Union Traction mail car 8 was painted the traditional postal white color, the same as the steam railroad United States Railway Mail cars of the period. Note elaborate lettering, striping, and post office symbol on car. Chicago Transit Authority photo.

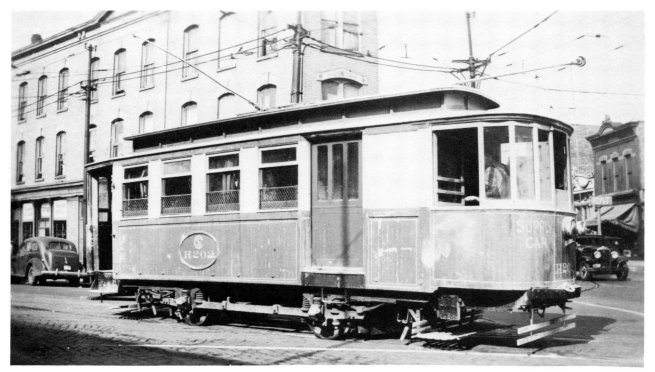

When street railway mail service in Chicago ended in 1915, many of the postal cars then on the roster were retained for conversion to work equipment. An example is Surface Lines supply car H-202, which began life as CCRy mail car A-4 in 1907. Its postal car origin is clear from its general design. Photo taken at the Lincoln-Wrightwood carhouse. From the A. C. Williams collection.

Though obviously no longer in mail service, Chicago Railways H-2 still is lettered for postal work. It was built ca. 1895 by the West Chicago Street Railway, and numbered in their 1 to 3 series. Neuberger collection photo courtesy of Roy Benedict.

Woodlawn was added to the Wentworth route, lengthening it by three miles. In 1907 the Cottage Grove RPOs took over collection and delivery to the Jackson Park post office.

The growth of the post office pneumatic tube system allowed mail to and from the main post office to be sent through the 22nd Street post office starting in 1904. The Stock Yards post office got tube service in 1907, and all mail for the Armour and Englewood post offices was sent to Stock Yards by tube thereafter. The north terminal of the Wentworth RPO became State and Van Buren in this period, and here pouched mail was exchanged with the Cottage Grove RPOs. In 1909 the night circuit RPOs entered service on a combined Cottage Grove-Wentworth route. Details of this service are given under the Cottage route above.

Millard Avenue was the last Chicago RPO route to enter service, starting February 1, 1902. It got its name from the post office at the end of its run, not because it ran on Millard Avenue (it never did run on that street). The route was from State and Randolph via Randolph, Dearborn, Lake, Clinton, Harrison, Blue Island, Racine, 18th, Ashland, 12th, and Ogden to Harding. The cars changed ends at the carbarn at Ogden and Harding, returning via the above route. The first schedule called for 15 trips a day. Pouched mail was exchanged with other cars downtown, except for the exchange with the Madison RPOs, which took place at Adams and Clinton.

Terminal points were changed several times. In 1908 the downtown terminal was moved to Clinton and Washington, and in 1910 was changed to Clinton and Adams. In 1911 the line was extended along Ogden to serve the Hawthorne post office at 3647 Ogden. All service ended November 21, 1915.

Railway post office service in Chicago had many of the advantages of such service on the steam railroads of that era. The chief advantage was that the mail could be sorted while the cars were enroute. It was sorted not only for post offices on the route of that particular car, but also for the other street railway post office routes in the city. Each line exchanged pouches of mail with other lines in or near the Loop.

Offsetting these advantages were many disadvantages. The cars were small, they were tied into the traffic pattern of the streetcar lines they ran on, and they required the services of a motorman and a trolley boy. In Chicago and other cities with trolley post offices, there were frequent disputes between the streetcar companies and the Post Office Department about the proper rates for use of railway mail cars. Trolley RPOs did have a speed advantage over the horse and wagon, but with the development of the motor truck and the better paving of streets they lost their speed edge.

Chicago's trolley RPO service was revived for one day on August 22, 1946 when Chicago Railways mail car 6 was brought out of retirement. The occasion was the annual convention of the American Philatelic Society at Chicago. A letter posted from the car appears as an illustration in this section. Car 6 is still preserved by the Chicago Transit Authority as part of its collection.

Equipped with a clamshell bucket for handling sand, gravel, and other construction material, this electric crane was well suited for its work at the 38th and Halsted material yard. Note wooden framing at end of boom to prevent short circuit should boom touch 600 volt overhead wires. Photo from the Barney Neuberger collection, courtesy of Roy Benedict.

● Above. CRys mail car 6 on its way back to storage at the Lincoln-Wrightwood carbarn after a week on display at the Ford City shopping center February 13-19, 1967. CTA photo. ● Below. CCRy steam shovel, apparently number J-204, although that number does not appear on the rail car roster, awaits its date with the torch on the scrap line. Barney Neuberger photo, courtesy of Bill Richmond.

Like the other types of CSL work equipment, the only bond most locomotives had was their function of pulling other equipment. Center cab L-203, for example, was a former passenger car: drop platforms and steps betray its origin. Barney Neuberger photo, taken at South Shops, from the Allan C. Williams collection.

Locomotive L-204 was a single truck box cab type, built by the Chicago City Railway in 1903. At first it carried the CCRy number C-35, later changed to Surface Lines L-204. Tiny body almost seems to be shorter than its trolley pole. Barney Neuberger collection, from Jack Doyle.

Locomotives L-201 and L-202 were designed to haul trains of standard steam railroad freight cars at low speeds. Built by CCRy in 1908, they were assigned to the 38th and Halsted material yard and to South Shops. This 1938 Neuberger photo shows L-202 at South Shops. Photo from Roy Benedict.

Tiny locomotive L-1 was North Chicago Street Railroad cable grip car 286, converted to a locomotive by Chicago Union Traction in 1908. This photo shows it switching an out-of-service postwar PCC car at South Shops. Barney Neuberger collection, from Roy Benedict.

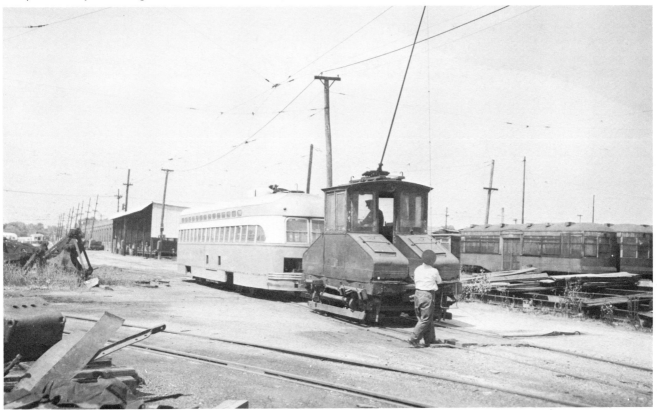

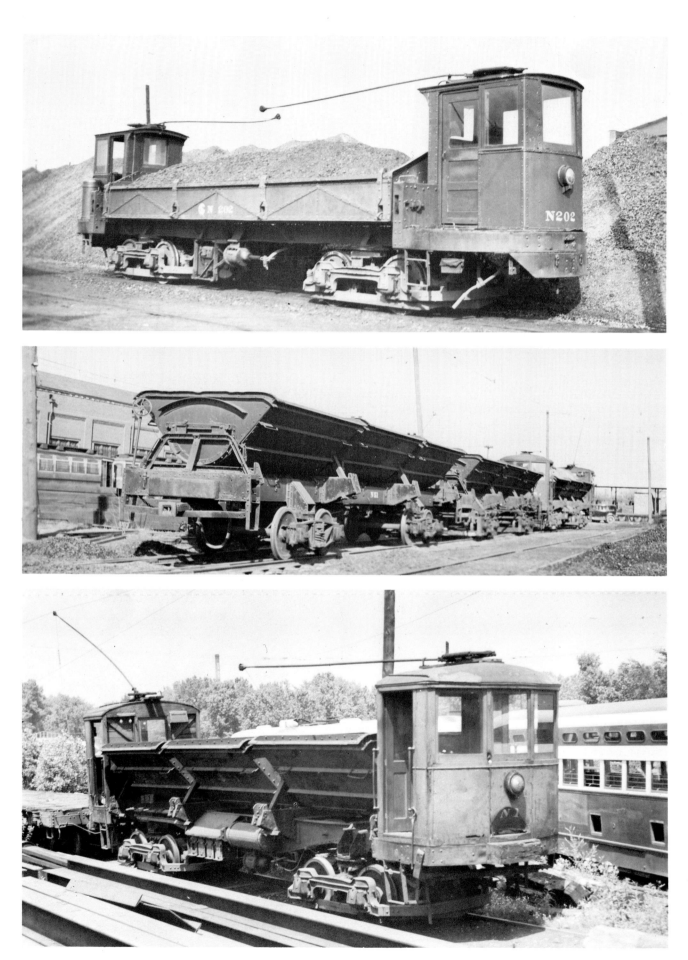

146

Electric Locomotives (L-Series)

Among the longest-lived work cars were the two electric locomotives built by CCRy in 1908. The 40-tonners saw service as switchers in the 38th Street material yard and at the South Shops at 77th and Vincennes. They were designed to haul trains of 400 to 500 tons at speeds of less than seven mph. During heavy snows they were sometimes sent out to push inprovised plows.

The locomotives had a steeple cab design, a center cab with sloping hoods on either side. The all-steel underframe and 10 tons of cast iron weights beneath the hoods gave the locomotives extra weight for better traction. One hood also carried two air tanks for the brake system, and the other contained the control rheostats.

Four GE-73 motors, wired two in series, powered the locomotives through a single K-14-E controller centrally mounted in the cab. A 72:16 gear ratio was used. For operation on streetcar girder rail, the wheel flanges were turned down to three-quarters of an inch, and the treads beveled. The locomotives carried an air whistle, bell, and MCB couplers mounted at the standard height of 34½ inches above the rail.

On the Chicago City Railway the locomotives carried the numbers C-49 and C-50. The Surface Lines numbers were L-201 and L-202. As previously described in the introduction to this chapter, L-202 was rebuilt into a rapid transit locomotive in 1958.

Money Cars (M-Series)

The Surface Lines collected the cash receipts from its carhouses with its own fleet of money cars until 1925. In that year it contracted with an armored car service to make the collections and deposit them in downtown banks. Several of the money cars remained on the roster in other service until at least 1941.

Oil Car (O-Series, became Meter Test Car)

To save money through bulk purchasing, Chicago Railways began to buy and store large quantities of oil in 1913. Oil was delivered direct from railroad tank cars, and stored in Chicago Railway's tanks with an aggregate capacity of 50,000 gallons.

For delivery to carhouses, shops, and generating stations the oil was pumped from the tanks into an oil delivery car. There were four 950-gallon tanks on the car, two for black oil, one for cylinder oil, and the fourth with a compartment for engine oil and another for compressor oil. Heated to 70 degrees by electric grids, the oil was kept under 65 lbs. to 85 lbs./sq. inch pressure by the car's air compressor. Before delivery the oil was forced through a screen by the air pressure as a final filter to remove impurities.

In 1924 the Surface Lines converted car O-1 from an oil tank car to a meter test car. Its new work was to house the equipment that tested, cleaned, calibrated, and maintained the watt-hour meters which had been installed on all passenger cars in 1923. The meters were carefully checked to see how economical each motorman was in using electric power. To equip the car for its new assignment, the tanks were removed and a motor-generator set, batteries, and testing panels installed.

Meter test car O-1 ran on a regular schedule to visit all carhouses. Watt-hour meters were removed from the cars and brought to O-1 for testing and repair. Each meter was checked approximately every nine months.

Sand Cars (R-Series)

CSL used much sand during bad weather, CCRy lines alone using 100 cubic yards a day before the unification of 1914. On the CCRy it was distributed from the 77th and Vincennes yard to the carhouses. At the carhouses it was loaded into sand boxes on the cars. The sand aided

• Opposite page, top. Chicago City Railway side dump car N-202 was built in 1915 by the Arthur Koppel Car Company. • Opposite page, center. Three section side dump car N-1 pulls a train of identical three section side dump trailer cars through the yard at South Shops. • Opposite page, below. Showing signs of wear after more than 40 years of service, CRys N-1 awaits further work in the South Shops yard. • At right. Built by Chicago Union Traction in 1911 as supply car 5, this piece of work equipment became CRys M-1. It was a money car, used to pick up receipts from the carbarns in the days before armored trucks were assigned to this work. All four of these photos are from the Barney Neuberger collection.

Meter test car 0-1 began life as CRys oil car 0-1, built in 1912 to haul nearly 4,000 gallons of oil to the various carhouses, shops, and electric generating stations. In 1923 the Surface Lines installed watt-hour meters in all its passenger cars to measure current consumption, and car 0-1 was converted into a meter test car to repair those devices. Neuberger photo from A. C. Williams.

After their service as United States Street Railway Mail Cars ended in 1915, many of the mail cars were converted to work service. Two such cars, made into supply vehicles, are shown on page 141. This Chicago Railways mail car was made into wrecker P-5. Compare this photo with that of Chicago Railways mail car 6 on page 140. This photo was taken at the North-Cicero carhouse on October 7, 1941 by R. H. Kennedy, and is reproduced here courtesy of Allan C. Williams.

Calumet & South Chicago Railway work car W-302 uses a drawbar to push a Q-series belt loader mounted on a W-series four wheel trailer flatcar. Note safety precautions: warning flag at front of train, employee riding front car to direct motorman, and work car conductor riding outside the cab to act as a second lookout. Barney Neuberger photo, courtesy of Bill Richmond.

Quite possibly the strangest looking pieces of CSL work equipment were the two R-series sand cars. Car R-201, built by CCRy in 1911, is shown here turning north on Vincennes Ave. at the entrance to the South Shops yard. It was built by CCRy as their C-46. The steel tank carried 10 cubic yards of sand from South Shops to various carhouses for use aboard streetcars during slippery weather. Barney Neuberger collection, from Allan C. Williams. R-201 and R-202 were the only two sand cars of this type ever used by CSL.

Supply car S-1 was built by Chicago Railways in 1909 as their number 1. Its half open, half closed design allowed it to deliver almost any sort of supplies from its home base at West Shops. In this photo, taken at the Lincoln-Wrightwood carhouse, a load of wheels is visible. Neuberger collection.

S-54 was a Chicago Railways supply car, built by Chicago Union Traction in 1905 as their car number 8. Here it carries its old CRys logo and "Supply Car" lettering, but has the CSL "S54" lettering also. Barney Neuberger collection, from Bill Richmond.

Chicago Railways S-51 is the twin to S-54 shown at the bottom of the preceding page. It was built as CUT number 6 in 1905. Note differences between the two cars: on S-51 trolley pole has been changed, headlight moved from roof to dash, and fenders removed. Neuberger collection, from Roy Benedict.

CCRy S-201 was a versatile supply car which could switch, haul trailers (as it is doing here with W-252), or travel by itself to deliver supplies to carhouses. Built by CCRy in 1908, it at first had the number C-45. Photo at Burnside carhouse from the Neuberger collection, supplied by Roy Benedict.

motormen in starting and stopping on slippery rail.

At first three roofed gondola cars of seven cubic yards capacity transported the sand. They were hard to unload, and the sand tended to get wet. In January, 1912, two new cars, originally assigned C-series prefixes, entered sand service. Built by CCRy, they were single-truck cars with a motorman's cab at each end and a steel tank for 10 cubic yards of sand in the middle. The cars had two GE-80 motors and two K-28-A controllers. In addition to supplying air to the brake system, an air compressor kept the sand tank under pressure of 40 lbs. sq. inch.

Sand was blown out of a three-inch discharge pipe just below the front bumper at one end of the car. A heavy-duty hose attached to the pipe permitted delivery of sand within 50 feet of the car.

CRys Utility Car/Garbage Trailer

Chicago Railways experimented with a dual-purpose utility and garbage trailer in 1910. It was of all-steel construction, 34 feet long, and divided into three sections with a capacity of 20 cubic yards each. Chicago Railways standard Baldwin-Pullman 150 trucks were installed, without motors. During the day the car hauled construction and maintenance material, such as wet concrete, to CSL construction sites. At night it collected and disposed of garbage under contract with the city of Chicago. I-series dirt cars were also used to haul city garbage.

Work Cars: What Might Have Been

Several novel uses for CSL work cars were proposed in the WW I era. The Municipal Markets Commission in a 1914 report to the City Council recommended that Chicago's street railways and interurban lines be used to bring farm products into the city. It also proposed a system of wholesale markets to replace the one central market along South Water Street in Downtown Chicago. Electric railway freight cars would serve these outlying markets, bringing in fresh food from suburban poultry,

CCRy line car V-201 was the only car of its type the Surface Lines had. It was built by CCRy in 1907 as car C-5. Allan C. Williams took its picture at South Shops on April 22, 1951.

dairy, fruit, and truck farms.

This freight could be handled, the Commission said, between 11 p.m. and 5 a.m. without interfering with passenger traffic on the streetcar lines. The Commission asserted that the farmers would benefit by getting more direct access to the market, and the consumer would benefit by having a wider choice of fresher foods to choose from.

As far as is known, nothing came of this proposal. Although truck farms did spring up around Chicago, some quite close to CSL lines, street railways never played a role in moving farm products. However the interurban lines, including the one to Kankakee that used CSL track, did transport food, particularly milk.

The Surface Lines itself tried to interest large department stores in using its cars to deliver merchandise. Under the proposal the streetcars would have taken the packages from the downtown main stores to distribution centers, and trucks would deliver the merchandise from the distribution center to the customer's home. To avoid interference with its passenger operations, CSL planned to run merchandise service only after midnight.

The department stores gave the plan a cool reception. They pointed to their own large fleets of delivery trucks, which handled all their distribution without any intermediate transfer. The trucks also had advertising value for the stores. But most important, the stores felt that they had to continue their policy of same-day delivery.

CSL replied that the public, stirred by the patriotic fervor that accompanied WW I, would permit a day's delay in package delivery. The Surface Lines had the backing of several aldermen, who objected to the noise and pavement damage done by the delivery trucks. The aldermen went so far as to request the corporation counsel to draw up an ordinance permitting both the "L" and the Surface Lines to carry freight. The stores won out, and CSL never got into the package delivery business.

Surface Lines Utility Equipment

Certainly the most exciting work on the Surface Lines and its predecessor companies was being a crew member of the wreck wagon. In the early days the wreck wagons

CSL's T-series cars were rail grinders. Their job was to smooth out rail roughened by the passage of millions of car wheels. This CTA photo was taken at the Hamlin "L" yards near CSL's West Shops on April 1, 1931.

Even cars in the same series, built at the same time, had minor differences that set them apart. Note awnings and fenders on W-1 above, missing on W-6 on opposite page. Neuberger collection photo.

Opposite page. On hand at the beginning of many a street construction project, W-6 also was there when cars had to be scrapped. A. C. Williams snapped W-6 at South Shops on just such a "last mile" assignment.

Small enough to be pushed around by hand if necessary, the single truck work cars of CRys W-61 to W-102 series could be found anywhere on the system. Neuberger collection from Roy Benedict.

were exactly that: horse drawn wagons. Later automotive trucks took over.

In the early CSL years following the unification of 1914, removing broken down wagons and trucks from the street was the biggest job the wreck wagons had. More often than not, CSL crews were called out to tow disabled vehicles out of the streetcar tracks, and not in direct aid to the cars themselves. But when streetcar service itself was in trouble, the wagons could re-rail derailed cars, lay hose bridges over fire department hoses at fires, and repair overhead wires. CSL maintenance standards were so high that the wreckers seldom had to pull away a disabled streetcar.

Before the first Chicago electrification in 1893, some 10,000 horses supplied the motive power on all but the heaviest lines, which were cable-operated. In 1906 the last horses in passenger service were retired, but that was far from the end of horse power in Chicago transit work. Horses continued to pull many of the utility wagons for nearly two decades after total electrification. The last CSL horse wasn't put out to pasture until 1925.

The following table shows the great savings in men and pieces of equipment the Surface Lines made when it switched some utility wagons from horse to automotive power.

Conversion of CSL Utility Equipment		
Type of Equipment	Horse	Truck
Tower Wagons	4	2
Reel Wagons	2	1
Horses	14	0
Drivers	6	3
Crewmen	22	9

A Day in the Life of a Work Car Motorman

In many respects the life of a work car motorman was easier than that of his brothers on the passenger cars. He did not have to wear a uniform, and did not have to punch transfers and make change as one-man car operators did. He had some time to relax while other employees loaded or unloaded his car, and he usually had no fixed running schedule. Other advantages were regular hours of work, no trips during the rush hours, and few trips to the downtown area where traffic was thickest. Many work car motormen held the same job for many years, and one set a record when he piloted locomotive L-201 for more than 30 years.

CHICAGO RAILWAYS COMPANY Roster of Work Equipment Under Surface Lines Numbers

Car numbers	Renumbered from	Rebuilt from	Builder	Date	Single or double truck	Motor or trailer	Type	Renumbered or rebuilt to see footnotes
A-1	1	—	CRys	1908-09	ST	M	Concrete mixer	
A-2 to A-9	2 to 9	—	CRys	1908-09	ST	T	Concrete mixer	
C-1 to C-3	60, 70, and 80	—	CRys	1908-09	ST	M	Coal, center dump	
C-4 and C-5	90 and 100	—	CRys	1909-10	ST	M	Coal, center dump	
C-51 to C-67	2 to 44 various	—	CUT	1901-09	ST	T	Coal	
D-1 to D-6	26 to 31	—	McG-C*	1908	DT	M	Sprinkler, steel tank, 4000 gal.* converted to snow plow	
D-7 to D-10	32 to 35	—	McG-C*	1909*	DT	M	Sprinkler, steel tank, 6000 gal.* converted to snow plow	
D-51 and D-55 to D-66	1, 2, 3, 12, and 14 to 25	—	CRys CUT	1908 1907	ST	M	Sprinkler, steel tank, 3000 gal.	
D-52 to D-54	6 to 8	—	NCStRR, WCStRR	1896-97	ST	M	Sprinkler, wood tank, 3000 gal.	
E-1 to E-56		—	Brill, Lewis & Fowler, McG-C		ST	M	Sweeper	
E-57 and E-58	—	—	Russell	1930	DT	M	Sweeper	
F-1 to F-27	2 to 51 various	—	NC St RR, WC St RR		ST	M	Plow, open body	
F-28 and F-29	—		McG-C	1922	DT	M	Plow	
F-30	—	—	CSL	1926	DT	M	Plow	
G-1 to G-10					ST	M	Cinder	
H-1 and H-2	2 and 3	—	WC St RR	c. 1895	ST	M	Mail	
H-3 and H-8	4 and 9	(a)			ST	M	Mail	(a)
H-4, H-6, H-7, H-9, and H-10		(a)			ST	M	Mail	
H-5		(a)			ST	M	Mail	(1)
J-51					DT	M	Welding	
K-1					ST	M	Lumber	
L-1	1	NC St RR grip car 286	CRys	1908	ST	M	Locomotive, steeple cab	
L-2					ST	M	Locomotive	
M-1	110	Supply car 5, ex l	CUT*, CRys	1911	ST	M	Money	
M-2	111	Supply car 9	CUT*, CRys	1905* 1911	ST	M	Money	
N-1	1	—	Arthur Koppel Car Co.	1910	DT	M	Dump, side, 3 section	
N-2	2	—	McG-C	1910* 1911	DT	M	Dump, single section	(2)
N-3 to N-5		—	Arthur Koppel Car Co.	1915	DT	M	Dump, side	
N-51 to N-55	—	—	Arthur Koppel Car Co.	1918	DT	M	Dump, side, 3 section	
O-1	—	Oil car O-1	CRys* CSL	1912*	DT	M	Converted in 1923 to meter test car	
P-1 to P-5		Some from H series mail cars			ST	M	Wreck	
P-6 to P-9					ST	M	Wreck	
R-1 to R-10					ST	M	Sand	
S-1 and S-2	1 and 2	—	CRys	1909	DT	M	Supply, half open	
S-3 and S-4	3 and second 4	—	CRys	1911	DT	M	Supply, half open	
S-51 and S-54	6 and 8	—	CUT	1905	ST	M	Supply, closed	
S-52					ST	M	Supply	
S-53	10	—	CRys		ST	M	Supply, closed	
S-55	First 4	—	CUT		ST	M	Supply, closed	
T-1					ST	M	Track grinder	
U-1							Cupola	

CHICAGO RAILWAYS Roster of Work Equipment Under Surface Lines Numbers

Car numbers	Renumbered from	Rebuilt from	Builder	Date	Single or double truck	Motor or trailer	Type	Renumbered or rebuilt to see footnotes
W-1 to W-17	2, 51 to 56, and 58 to 67	—	CRys	#2 in 1906 #51-67 in 1908-09	DT	M	Work, two cabs except W-7 and one other. (3)
W-18	—	Passenger car 1609	CRys*CSL	1912* 1946	DT	M	Work, one cab
W-31 to W-33					ST	M	Work
W-51 to W-55					DT	T	Work
W-56	—	Passenger car 1636	CRys*CSL	1912* 1946	DT	T	Work
W-61 to W-102					ST	T	Work
X-1		Work car 57	CRys*	1909*	DT	M	Derrick, two cabs rebuilt in 1910
X-2	—	Passenger car 1405 ex CUT 4934	St.L*CSL	1906*	DT	M	Derrick
X-3	—	Work car W-16	CRys*CSL	c. 1909* 1927	DT	M	Derrick (4)
X-4	—	Dump car N-2	McG-C*CSL	1910* 1946	DT	M	Derrick (5)
AA-1 to AA-25	—	(b)	CUT*CSL	1899-1900*	DT	M	Salt, converted in 1931
One car					ST	T	Sweeper
1 and 2		CUT 4419 (c)	American; CSL	1892*	ST		Whitewash
1466	—	CUT passenger car 4511	CUT* CRys	1899-1900* 1913	DT	M	Instruction
Arcturus and Sunbeam		C&P passenger cars 7 to 24 var.	Pullman*	1891*	DT		Party, later used for storage

CHICAGO CITY RAILWAY Roster of Work Equipment Under Surface Lines Numbers

Car numbers	Renumbered from	Rebuilt from	Builder	Date	Single or double truck	Motor or trailer	Type	Renumbered or rebuilt to see footnotes
A-201 to A-204	†M-1 to M-4	—	Drake	1907	DT	M	Concrete mixer
A-205		Supply car †C-56	CCRy*	1900*	DT	T	Concrete mixer (6)
B-201	†B-1	Mail car †A-2, ex 2	CCRy*	1896*	ST	M	Newspaper
B-202 and B-203		Passenger cars			ST	M	Newspaper
C-201	†C-53		CCRy	1901	DT	M	Coal, side dump
D-201 to D-212	†D-1 to D-12	—	CCRy	1908	DT	M	Sprinkler, steel tank, 4000 gal. (d)
D-213	†D-13 ex C&ST 400, purchased 1912	—	McG-C	1909	DT	M	Sprinkler, steel tank, 4000 gal. (d)
D-251 to D-259	†D-38 to D-46	—	CCRy	1895	ST	M	Sprinkler, wood tank, 1400 gal.
E-201 to E-230	†E-1 to E-30	—	McG-C	ca. 1908	ST	M	Sweeper (e)
E-231 and E-232	†E-31 and E-32	—	McG-C		ST	M	Sweeper (7)
E-233		—	McG-C		ST	M	Sweeper
E-234	†E-34 ex C&ST 503, purchased 1912	—	McG-C	1901	ST	M	Sweeper
E-235 and E-236		—	McG-C		ST	M	Sweeper
E-237	—	—	Russell	1930	DT	M	Sweeper
F-201 to F-205	†F-55 to F-59	—	Wason	1908	ST	M	Plow
F-231 to F-284	†F-1 to F-54	—	CCRy, Wells & French		ST	T	Plow, open
H-201 to H-204	†A-3 to A-6	—	CCRy	1907	ST	M	Mail
I-201 to I-217			CCRy		ST	T	Dirt
I-218	—	Concrete mixer A-205	CCRy*CSL	1900* 1941	DT	T	Dirt
J-201 and J-202					ST	M	Shovel
J-203					ST	M	Crane
K-201	†C-142	—	CCRy	1909	ST	M	Lumber

CHICAGO CITY RAILWAY Roster of Work Equipment Under Surface Lines Numbers

Car numbers	Renumbered from	Rebuilt from	Builder	Date	Single or double truck	Motor or trailer	Type	Renumbered or rebuilt to see footnotes
K-251 to K-255	†C-137 to C-141	—	CCRy	1908	ST	T	Lumber	
L-201 and L-202	†C-49 and C-50	—	CCRy	1908	DT	M	Locomotive, steeple-cab	(8)
L-203		Passenger car			DT	M	Locomotive, cab on flat	
L-204 and L-205	†C-35 and C-36	—	CCRy	1903	ST	M	Locomotive, box cab	
M-201		Mail car †A-1, ex 1	CCRy*	1896*	ST	M	Money, converted in 1897*	
M-202	†C-136	(f)	Pullman* 1910		ST	M	Money	
N-201 and N-202		—	Arthur Koppel Car Co.	1915	DT	M	Dump, side	
N-251 to N-254	—	—	Arthur Koppel Car Co.	1918	DT	M	Dump	
P-201 to P-203					ST	M	Wreck	
P-251					ST	T	Wreck	
R-201 and R-202	†C-46 and C-47	—	CCRy	1911	ST	M	Sand, steel tank	
R-203 to R-205	†C-127, C-131, and C-133		CCRy	1900-05	ST	M	Sand	
S-201	†C-45	—	CCRy	1908	DT	M	Supply, closed	
T-201 to T-203					ST	M	Track grinder	
U-201 and U-202						M	Cupola	
U-251			CCRy		ST	T	Cupola	
V-201	†C-5	—	CCRy	1907	DT	M	Line, closed	
W-201 to W-227	†C-7 to C-21 and C-23 to C-34	—	CCRy	1907-08	DT	M	Work, two cab	(9)
W-228 to W-230			CCRy		DT	M	Work	
W-251 and W-252			CCRy		DT	T	Work	
W-261 to W-299			CCRy		ST	T	Work	
X-201	†C-22		CCRy	1907	DT	M	Derrick, one cab	
2626	—	—	CCRy	1901	DT	M	Instruction	

CALUMET & SOUTH CHICAGO RAILWAY Roster of Work Equipment Under Surface Lines Numbers

Car numbers	Renumbered from	Rebuilt from	Builder	Date	Single or double truck	Motor or trailer	Type	Renumbered or rebuilt to see footnotes
D-301					DT	M	Sprinkler, steel tank, 6000 gal.	
D-302	CE 2			c. 1907	DT	M	Sprinkler, steel tank, 4000 gal.	
D-303					DT	M	Sprinkler, steel tank, 4000 gal.	(10)
D-304					DT	M	Sprinkler, steel tank, 4000 gal.	(g)
E-301 to E-309					ST	M	Sweeper	
F-301	81 ex CE 4	—		c. 1898	DT	M	Plow	
F-302	CE 6			c. 1898	ST	M	Plow	
F-303	SCC 1			c. 1899	ST	M	Plow	
F-304		—	Wason	1913	ST	M	Plow	
F-305	—	Sprinkler D-303	CSL	1930	DT	M	Plow	(11)
P-301					ST	M	Wreck	
R-301	CE			By 1905	ST	M	Sand blast	
U-301	CE 58			By 1905	DT	M	Cupola	
V-301					ST	M	Line	
W-301	41 ex CCRy purchased 1909	—	CCRy		DT	M	Work	(12)
W-302					DT	M	Work, two cabs	
W-311					ST	M	Work	

CALUMET & SOUTH CHICAGO RAILWAY Roster of Work Equipment Under Surface Lines Numbers

Car numbers	Renumbered from	Rebuilt from	Builder	Date	Single or double truck	Motor or trailer	Type	Renumbered or rebuilt to see footnotes
W-316 and W-317					ST	T	Work	
Y-301 and Y-302	1 and 2	—	Kuhlman	1910	DT	M	Funeral	(13)
Y-303					DT	M	Supply, closed	

SOUTHERN STREET RAILWAY Roster of Work Equipment Under Surface Lines Numbers

Car numbers	Renumbered from	Rebuilt from	Builder	Date	Single or double truck	Motor or trailer	Type	Renumbered or rebuilt to see footnotes
E-331 and E-332	E-231 and E-232 ex †E-31 and E-32	—	McG-C		ST	M	Sweeper	

CHICAGO TRANSIT AUTHORITY 1948 RENUMBERINGS

Car numbers	Renumbered from	Rebuilt from	Builder	Date	Single or double truck	Motor or trailer	Type	Renumbered or rebuilt to see footnotes
AA-26 to AA-56	—	(h)	St. Louis* CSL	1903-05*	DT	M	Salt	
AA-57 to AA-63	—	(i)	St. Louis* CSL	1906*	DT	M	Salt	(14)
AA-64 to AA-90	—	(j)	CUT*CSL	1899-1900*				
AA-91	—	Passenger car 1545	CRys*CSL	1911-1912* 1947	DT DT	M M	Salt Salt	(15)
AA-92	—	Passenger car 2826, ex C&SC 811, ex CE 121	Kuhlman*	1905*	DT	M	Salt	
AA-93 to AA-97	—	(k)	Jewett* CSL	1903* 1943	DT	M	Salt	(16)
AA-98 and AA-100 to AA-107	—	(l)	SCC*	1907* 1943	DT	M	Salt	(17)
First AA-99	—	Passenger car 2807, ex C&SC 707, ex †2536	St. Louis*	1901-02*	DT	M	Salt storage	
Second AA-99	—	Passenger car 5031	American* CTA	1905-06* 1948	DT	M	Salt	

NOTES

(a) Five cars in H-3 to H-10 group rebuilt from C&P passenger cars 1 to 4 and 6, American* 1891* c. 1900. Cars H-3 and H-8 rebuilt to wreck cars P-5 and one other?

(b) Cars AA-1 to AA-25 rebuilt from passenger cars 1430, 1431, 1433, 1435, 1437, 1440, 1441, 1443 to 1448, 1459, 1462, 1474, 1475, 1482, 1483, 1488, 1492, 1493, 1496, 1501, 1502 respectively, ex CUT 4475 to 4550 various.

(c) Indicates origin of one of the two whitewash cars.

(d) Eleven cars in D-201 to D-213 group converted to snow plows.

(e) Sweeper E-223 sold to Richard N. Lukin in 1958; now at Illinois Railway Museum.

(f) Rebuilt from passenger car 2273, ex 2471 to 2497 group until 1908, motorized from cable trailer in 1906.

(g) D-304 converted to snow plow.

(h) Cars AA-26 to AA-52 rebuilt from passenger cars 1107, 1142, 1145, 1166, 1183, 1198, 1205, 1213, 1215, 1219, 1220, 1224, 1231, 1235, 1239 to 1241, 1243, 1248 to 1250, 1252, 1255, 1259, 1260, 1266, 1277 respectively, ex CUT 4636, 4671, 4674, 4695, 4712, 4727, 4734, 4742, 4744, 4748, 4749, 4753, 4760, 4764, 4768 to 4770, 4772, 4777 to 4779, 4781, 4784, 4788, 4789, 4795, 4806 respectively.

(i) Cars AA-57 to AA-63 rebuilt from passenger cars 1306 to 1311 and 1374 respectively, ex CUT 4835 to 4840 and 4903 respectively.

(j) Cars AA-64 to AA-90 rebuilt from passenger cars 1451, 1453 to 1455, 1457, 1458, 1463, 1465, 1467, 1468, 1471, 1472, 1477, 1478, 1480, 1481, 1484, 1487, 1489, 1494, 1495, 1497 to 1500, 1503, 1504 respectively, ex CUT 4475 to 4552 various.

(k) Cars AA-93 to AA-97 rebuilt from passenger cars 2841 to 2845 respectively, ex C&SC 826 to 830 respectively, ex SCC 321 to 325 respectively.

(l) Cars AA-98 and AA-100 to AA-107 rebuilt from passenger cars 2846, 2848, 2849, 2851 to 2856 respectively, ex C&SC 831, 833, 834, 836 to 841 respectively, ex SCC 332, 334, 335, 337 to 342 respectively.

* Indicates origin before rebuilding.

† Indicates CCRy number.

CCRy service cars existing before 1905 carried unknown numbers in the 5000 series. Renumbering to prefixed numbers was completed in 1907 or thereafter.

Car J-1, a power shovel on caterpillar type treads, is not part of the rail equipment roster.

(1) To #6 in 1942
(2) To X-4 in 1946
(3) W-16 to X-3 in 1927
(4) To RT in 1955, scrapped
(5) To RT S-344 c. 1954, to ERHS in 1963, to IRM in 1973
(6) To I-218 in 1941
(7) To SStRy E-331 and E-332
(8) L-202 to RT L-202 c. 1957, rebuilt 1958, renumbered S-343
(9) W201 to RT S-317 in 1954. W-223 to RT S-309 in 1952.
(10) To F-305 in 1930.
(11) To ERHS, to IRM in 1973
(12) To RT S-314 in 1953
(13) To passenger cars 2857 and 2858 in 1919
(14) AA-63 to ERHS in 1958, to IRM 1374 in 1973
(15) AA-72 to ERHS, to IRM 1467 in 1973
(16) AA-95 to ERHS, to IRM 2843 in 1973
(17) AA-98 to ERHS, to IRM 2846 in 1973.

● Above. Chicago Railways derrick car X-2 was built from Chicago Union Traction passenger car 4934 (CSL 1405). This 1941 photo comes from the S. D. Maguire collection. ● Below. Lifting CSL's heavy girder rail was one of the jobs derrick car X-3 was built to handle. Built by Chicago Railways as work car W-16 ca. 1909, it was rebuilt by CSL as derrick X-3 in 1927. Sent to the Rapid Transit system in 1955, the car was later scrapped. In this photo, taken in October of 1942, X-3 is at work on a large track renewal project in downtown Chicago. Note sheet metal housing over derrick-end headlight. Photo from the S. D. Maguire collection.

• Above. Soon after the abandonment of streetcar service west of Narragansett on the 63rd/Argo routes, CTA sent former Chicago Railways derrick car X-3 out to take up the rail for scrap. Note that the rail used on this private right-of-way was railroad T-section, not the usual girder rail CSL used in city streets. Barney Neuberger photo from Roy Benedict. • Below. Derrick car X-201 was built by the Chicago City Railway in 1907 as their car C-22. It was the only derrick on the CCRy roster. This photo from the Barney Neuberger collection was taken at the 38th and Halsted material yard. Photo courtesy of Roy Benedict.

● Above. Whitewash car H-1 began life ca. 1895 as a West Chicago Street Railroad mail car. Its last assignment was to coat carbarn walls with whitewash. Neuberger collection from Bill Richmond. ● Opposite page, top. Calumet & South Chicago supply car Y-303. R. H. Kennedy photo from A. C. Williams. ● Center. Two former mail cars, converted to a supply car and a whitewash car. Neuberger collection. ● Bottom. Car 1466 was an instruction car, used for training new operating employees. It began life as CUT passenger car 4511. It was scrapped March 9, 1951. Neuberger collection from Bill Richmond. ● Below. Built in 1891 as a party car, Arcturus or Sunbeam ended its days as a storage shed. Neuberger collection.

Car 1305 was the last car in the 1101-1305 series, built by St. Louis Car in 1903. When built it was Chicago Union Traction 4834. CSL converted it to salt service, adding a wing plow and a special window for observing the plow. In 1948 the CTA gave this car the salt car number AA-56. J. Buck photo from the Allan C. Williams collection.

Salt car AA-46 began life as Chicago Union Traction 4779, became Chicago Railways 1250, and was given the salt car number AA-46 by the CTA in 1948. Although from the same series as car 1305 shown above, and although assigned to the same work as car 1305, AA-46 was scarcely modified at all for its new function. Neuberger collection from Railway Negative Exchange.

The Surface Lines converted car 1475 to salt service, and renumbered it AA-17 on October 1, 1941. It was built by the Chicago Union Traction Company ca. 1899-1900, and scrapped by the Chicago Transit Authority on October 30, 1951. Note the car's excellent condition, even though in work service. Barney Neuberger collection from the Railway Negative Exchange.

Car AA-102 began life as South Chicago City Railway 337, became Calumet & South Chicago 836, then CSL 2851, and finally AA-102. It was scrapped by the Chicago Transit Authority on August 10, 1951. Of the 11 cars in the 2846-2856 series, the nine that survived beyond 1947 became salt cars. Barney Neuberger collection from the Railway Negative Exchange.

• Above. Back in 1893 the street railways of Chicago used 10,000 horses to pull passenger and utility equipment. Horse drawn tower wagons like the one shown were in use until 1925. Neuberger collection photo. • Below. CSL utility trucks spent much of their time removing obstructions from the tracks, as this CRys combination wreck, tower, and hose bridge truck is doing on Ashland Ave. CTA photo.

In April, 1944, an Electrical Department overhead line crew was called out to work on the trolley wire over Clinton Street near Madison. They arrived in CRys tower truck 123, a White 3½ ton vehicle. Photo courtesy of the Chicago Transit Authority.

• Above. CRYs tower truck 123 provides the platform on which a line crew tightens the trolley wire at a feeder span. Trees on far side of street get attention, too: perhaps they interfered with the feeder cable. Photo courtesy of the Chicago Transit Authority. • Below. No doubt about it, the 23 CSL automobiles lined up for this 1942 photo all have radio sets: just look at the antennas sprouting from the roofs. CSL's own FM radio station, WAYH, went on the air June 1, 1942, and CSL supervisors in their scout cars could have two-way conversations with the radio dispatcher. Like other equipment, the automobiles were owned by the companies underlying the CSL. Chicago Transit Authority photograph.

CTA 7205, a postwar PCC, went through an open switch at Root and State Streets on Sunday, July 17, 1949. It derailed and smashed into a safety island, wrapping its middle around the light pole at the end of the island. Thirty-five passengers were injured, none seriously, according to a newspaper account of the accident. The St. Louis Car Company, which built the car, circulated these two photos to demonstrate the crashworthiness of their product. Car 7205 was rebuilt, using parts from car 7078, destroyed by fire after a collision with a gasoline truck at 63rd and State on May 25, 1950. As these photos show, it took several CTA wreck wagons to pull car 7205 back on the track.

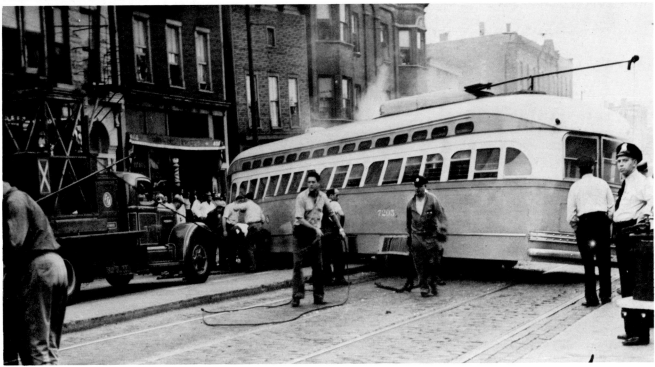

• Opposite page, top and bottom. The difference between the old and the new styles in combination wreck, tower and hose bridge trucks was mainly in the cab. Newer model 164 was built with an enclosed cab, old 150 originally had an open cab. Both photos courtesy of the CTA. • Above. Bus and streetcar hose bridges in use. Buses, of course, could always detour around a fire scene, but streetcar hose bridges were needed to keep trolley service going at major fires. CTA photo. • Below. CTA converted some CSL buses into work equipment. This one became salt spreader BA-85. Photo courtesy of the CTA.

• Above. In an attempt to keep the streets clear of snow along trolley bus lines, the CSL equipped one of its Brill trolley buses with a snow plow. The experiment wasn't successful, and automotive utility trucks with snow plows were used to keep electric bus lines open. G. Krambles collection. • Opposite page. Punctured tires caused by stray scraps of metal on the street caused both the CSL and the CTA to send out magnet-equipped buses to sweep the streets. CSL's magnet bus picked up as much as 20 lbs. of scrap per mile, although the average was some 7.5 lbs. per mile. Top photo from the Neuberger collection/Railway Negative Exchange. Bottom photo from CTA. • Below. CTA continues to convert. MEU-1 was converted from a CTA bus built by White. Chicago Transit Authority photo.

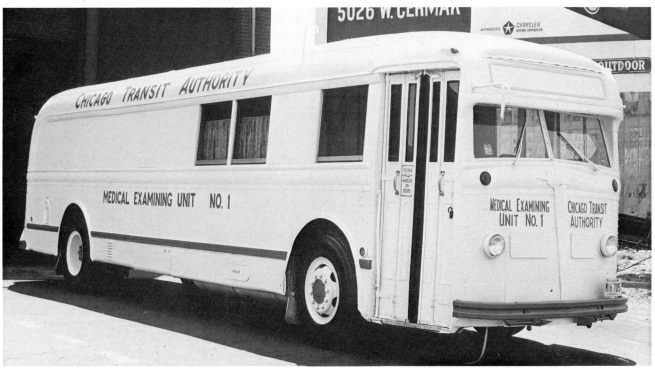

An introduction to CSL routes

Although it may seem to be going back a little bit too far, the history of the Chicago Suface Lines can be traced back some four million years, back to when Chicago lay beneath the tepid waters of a tropical sea. The shells and skeletons of trillions upon trillions of the tiny animals which swam in this sea fell to the bottom, and became the Niagara limestone bedrock upon which the city's skyscrapers rest. Stony Island on the Southeast Side of the city is an outcropping of Niagara limestone, and it gave its name to a street and to a Surface Lines streetcar route upon that street. After the glaciers of the Ice Age had come and gone, they left sheets of waterproof clay over the Niagara limestone, setting the stage for Chicago's swamps, sloughs, and marshlands.

Atop the clay the retreating and advancing glaciers formed deposits called moraines — rocky, irregular ridges. One such ridge is Blue Island, which extends along both sides of Western Ave. from 85th Street to the Sag Canal in the town of Blue Island. CSL cars climbed steep slopes between 85th and 87th Streets on the Western Ave. line, and along 111th Street on the Halsted Street line to reach the top of the Blue Island moraine. The cliffs at the 87th Street end are 35 feet high, increasing to 40 feet at the south end.

The last stage of Lake Chicago, known as the Tolleston Stage, created a cliff along Michigan Ave. between 100th and 115th Streets. CSL cars on the State line rode the top of this cliff, while cars on the 103rd, 111th, and 115th Street lines climbed the cliff to cross it. The Tolleston stage shore line is traceable as a beach ridge which runs northwest from north of 95th and Michigan to 55th Street and Kedzie. It confronted CSL with grades of varying steepness and height for the dozen crosstown lines which intersected it.

During the Glenwood, Calumet, and Tolleston stages of Lake Chicago the Wilmette, Rose Hill, and Graceland spits made their successive appearances. The Graceland spit extends 12 miles from Chicago Ave. to north Evanston, and is about a mile and a half wide. Although it intersected nearly all of the major North Side lines, its gentle slope caused no operating difficulties for the cars.

As previously noted, Chicago is poorly drained, with many square miles having no drainage at all. At the same time it is a true continental divide: the rivers and streams which flow east into Lake Michigan belong to the St. Lawrence River system; those that flow to the west join the Mississippi and drain into the Gulf of Mexico. The Illinois and Michigan Canal was built to connect these two river systems over Chicago's continental divide.

Chicago rests on the Chicago Plain, 5 to 15 miles wide and 40 miles long. Once the bed of an inland lake, the plain averages some 25 feet above the level of Lake Michigan, with a maximum height of 60 feet. This broad, flat plain helped in the rapid settlement of outlying areas. The street railways aided this dispersion of the population by making it possible for workers to live many miles away from their work, yet reach it in a reasonable time.

As noted in the Introduction, Chicago has a basic gridiron street pattern, with several important radial streets. The North Side predecessor streetcar lines were largely radial, focusing on bringing passengers to downtown Chicago. The South Side lines, on the other hand, were largely on the grid streets, and did not have quite the downtown orientation of the North Side lines. This section of the book is organized by individual line. The lines are listed in alphabetical order, followed by those lines which ran on numbered streets.

Chicago Railways and Chicago City Railway began through service over their first joint route in 1910. This was TR 2, from the Riverview amusement park to 79th and Halsted via Clybourn, Clark, Wentworth, and 79th. The route was 15 miles long, with 26 cars assigned to operate it. (Both the Chicago Railways and the Chicago City Railway ran additional local cars on their portion of the route). Through cars were furnished according to each company's share of the total mileage. Chicago Railways supplied 10 cars to TR 2, Chicago City Railway 16 cars. The fare was 5¢, with transfer privileges to the local cars of either company.

Since the Through Routes had been established by the Chicago City Council, CSL had to operate them. However, many were on long headways, such as 15 minutes, with local cars filling in the gaps in service. An example of such an arrangement was TR 22, where CSL would run three or four of its own identical Clark-Wentworth cars during rush hours between each scheduled TR 22 car. Most Through Routes started between 1910 and 1914; many ended in 1924.

On most CSL cars the front roller sign showed the destination only, with the side signs indicating the route. On a few types of car both the route name and/or route number appeared on the front destination sign, together with the destination. Through Route cars carried metal signs on the front dash with the route number only. Other cars carried metal dash signs reading "Stock Yards Direct," "Union Station," "North Western Station," or "Via 14th Street."

Short-turn cars, those that didn't go to the end of a line, had a special indication on the front roll sign. The white route number had a diagonal red line through it, followed by the short-turn terminal. There were two types of short-turn, scheduled and emergency. Many lines had regular short-turn runs. For example, CSL ran the following such lines in 1928.

• Opposite page. Small Pullman 909 eases to a stop at State and Madison, and a knot of passengers is already forming near the rear of the safety island to board the car. The crowd waiting to board is rather small on this warm day a little before noon, and the car will soon be headed south once again. David R. Phillips collection.

CSL Short-Turn Terminals: 1928

Route	Direction	Short-Turn Terminal
Ashland	Northbound	Cortland & Wood
Ashland-Downtown	Southbound	69th; 79th
Belmont	Westbound	Cicero
Chicago	Eastbound	Lake Shore Drive
	Westbound	Crawford; Cicero
Clark-Wentworth	Northbound	Devon
	Southbound	63rd; 80th
Crawford	Northbound	Elston
Fullerton	Westbound	Cicero
Grand	Westbound	Austin
Halsted-Downtown	Northbound	Chicago
	Southbound	79th
Harrison	Westbound	Cicero
Harrison-Adams	Westbound	Cicero
Milwaukee-Devon	Northbound	Central
Morgan-Racine-Sangamon	Southbound	21st & Racine
North	Westbound	Cicero
Ogden	Westbound	Crawford
Roosevelt-Downtown	Westbound	Crawford; Cicero
Roosevelt-Wabash	Westbound	Crawford; Cicero
State	Southbound	63rd; 79th
Stony Island	Southbound	64th; 80th
Western	Southbound	Archer; 63rd
	Northbound	Roscoe; Lincoln
47th Street	Eastbound	Cottage Grove
63rd Street	Westbound	Western; Central Park
67th-69th Street	Westbound	69th & Western

Twenty-three of the 97 lines running in 1928 had short turns. As the table shows, some had two or more short-turn terminals, making a total of 37 such terminals. If Chicago routes were counted as Pittsburgh counts its routes, there would be at least 134 CSL routes in operation in 1928. However, the author follows CSL practice by including these short lines within the full-length route.

In addition to the scheduled short line cars, CSL turned back cars on its lines in emergencies to avoid flooded underpasses, reroute cars, restore normal headways, avoid major fires or accidents, etc. Even though it might not have any scheduled short line cars, a route always had crossovers strategically placed to reroute or turn back cars. Cars always carried on their destination signs a number of unscheduled terminals for emergency display.

More often than is now done, cars were pulled off one route to fill in service on another whose headways had been badly interrupted. For example, a 63rd Street PCC car would sometimes be sent down Stony Island, al-

though PCC cars never were assigned to Stony Island. One disadvantage of single-end cars, the Nearsides, Sedans, and PCCs, was that they could only be run on lines that had either loops or wyes. They could not reverse ends at simple crossovers as double-end cars could.

Today, when gasoline and oil rationing is common, it is some small comfort to know that CSL faced fuel rationing back in 1918. In that year the United States Fuel Administrator decreed reductions in fuel consumption. CSL cut back its schedules every Monday, running the Holiday schedule instead of the weekday service, but had to add cars to keep up with the demand.

Through the years CSL ran many services not listed in the route guides, but which carried passengers and issued transfers just as the regular routes did. These were not routes in the normal sense, rather they were the barn movements of cars to and from their regular routes. At one point during CTA management, Western Ave. cars travelled nearly four miles to get to and from the 77th and Vincennes carhouse. Although not running on the Western line, they were still "in service" and had to stop to pick up and discharge passengers. Transfers from the route they were assigned to were issued to those who boarded these pull-in and pull-out runs, but they were punched in the "D" square to indicate a depot or carbarn trip. To motormen and bus drivers anxious to reach their route on pull-outs, and anxious to quit on the pull-ins, the rule about picking up passengers was frequently ignored.

Other unusual services included the "Fresh Air Cars" CSL ran in 1915 at the request of City Health Commissioner John D. Robertson. Five of the cars were assigned to each of 12 lines. They ran with all their doors and windows open, and carried large signs announcing their healthful breeziness. Good public response to the 12 fresh air cars already in use on the Chicago Elevated Railways was said to be the reason for the Commissioner's request. Both CER and CSL discontinued the cars during the winter of 1915-1916.

Large crowds attending religious revival services gave CSL some service headaches in the early months of 1918. Evangelist Billy Sunday drew 50,000 persons to his services on Sunday, March 10. His tabernacle near the intersection of Chicago Ave. and Lake Shore Drive was served principally by CSL's Chicago Ave. line, although some worshippers used the Grand Ave. cars which ran parallel to Chicago Ave. four blocks south. CSL eased the congestion along Chicago by building a new crossover, which created a stub track with a capacity of 25 cars.

Another track change, this time on a much larger scale, expedited crowd movement to and from Navy Pier. In 1916 CSL extended its Grand Ave. line along the upper level of the brand-new Navy (municipal) Pier. The tracks ran along either side of the pier's upper level, terminating at a loop at the far end where the recreation area began. Another loop near the land end of the pier served as a short-turn terminal during winter months. CSL had about three miles of track on the pier, most of it of open or railroad type construction.

To give the city more room to stage an exhibition, CSL removed its tracks from the upper deck and rebuilt them along the lower roadway, using mostly material salvaged

• Above. Emerging after a run of a little less than two miles under the Jackson Park "L" structure, Old Pullman 473 heads west along 63rd Street on the 63rd Street line. Surface tracks leading off to the right were the CSL's connection to the "L's" ground-level yard. The elevated structure running across the photo was an incline which connected the "L" structure and the ground-level yard. Barney Neuberger collection from the Railway Negative Exchange. • Below. After running under the Lake Street "L" for several miles, CSL's Lake Street route ran parallel to the "L" (now at ground level), then crossed it at Lake and Pine, ducked under the North Western's Galena Division tracks, and resumed running west on Lake to Austin. Old Pullman 118 waits for the gates to clear behind an eastbound Lake "L" train. Neuberger photo.

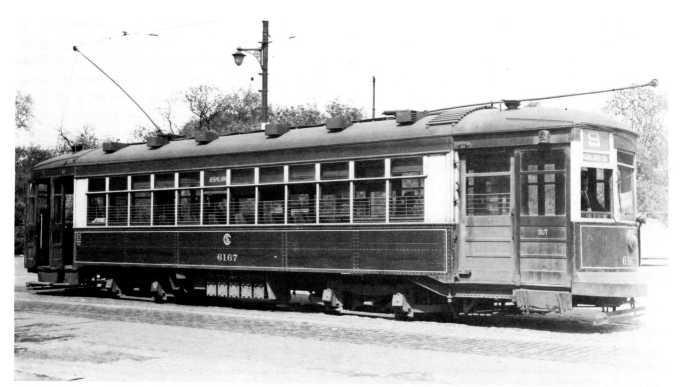

CSL 6167 running south on Ashland Ave. on Through Route 9, waiting for departure time from the north terminal at Southport and Clark. Note car in two-man operation on this heavy trunk line, with folding rear doors and sliding front door. Compare with car during one-man operation, shown below. Author's collection.

• Opposite page. Top. Car 3120 is northbound at Clark and Wells, running on the heavy Broadway-State route. Barney Neuberger collection. • Bottom. Car 3200 is in one-man service on the Cicero line at the three-way intersection of Milwaukee-Irving Park-Cicero. Alan W. Simms collection.

Compare CTA 6167 in one-man service on the 67th-69th-71st Street line with CSL 6167 above. Note folding front doors and dash stripe on CTA car, which is at the 71st and California terminal. Author's collection.

Chicago Railways 576, a 1938 ACF model H-13-S bus, poses for an official photograph at Foster and Tripp while making a run on the Foster Ave. route. CSL service along this portion of Foster Ave. began July 1, 1937 as part of the route between Milwaukee and Broadway. Photo courtesy of the CTA.

Four buses in the Chicago Railways 592-625 series pose in front of the General Motors plant in Flint, Mich., before delivery. These 1941 Yellow Coach model TG 2706 buses were assigned to North and Northwest Side lines. General Motors photo from the Jack Doyle collection.

Taken from the Rock Island Railroad viaduct at 87th and Vincennes, this photo shows passengers transferring from a 6200-series bus on the 87th Street Extension run to a waiting 87th Street one-man car. Streetcar will run east along median strip right-of-way; bus will make a U-turn and run back west. Neuberger collection.

Line extensions were often marked by civic celebrations. When the Roosevelt Road extension into Grant Park opened August 1, 1933, Chicago Mayor Edward Kelly piloted the first car across Michigan Ave., up the incline, through the Illinois Central Railroad's trainshed, and into the park. As the destination sign and the dash sign indicate, the line was built to serve the World's Fair. Author's collection.

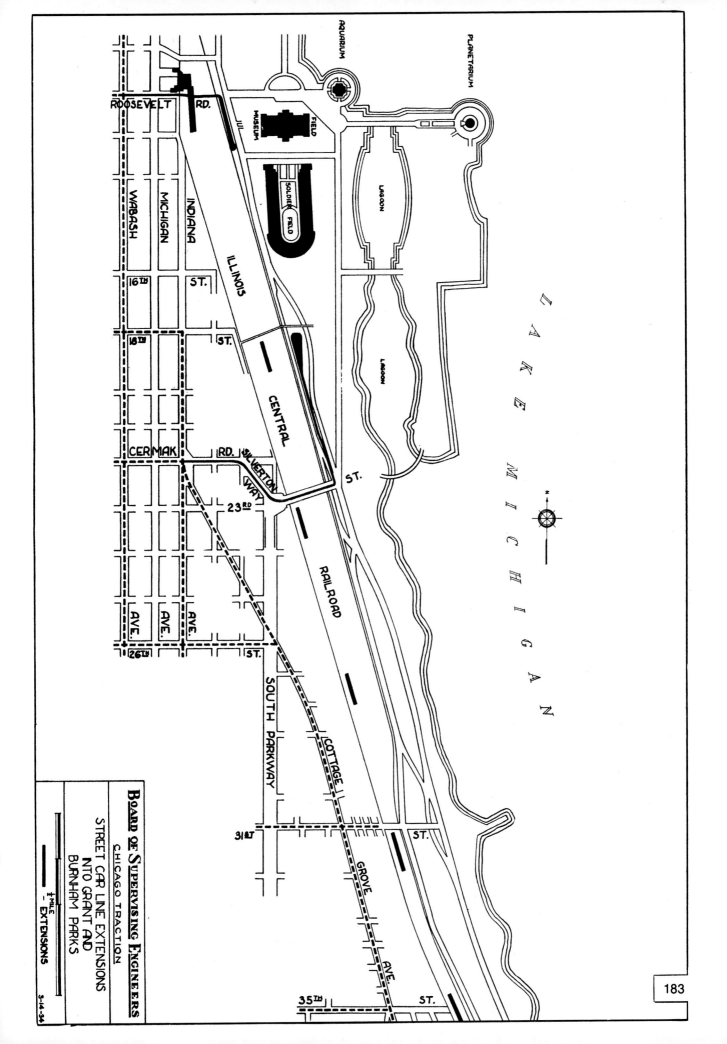

AQUARIUM

PLANETARIUM

MUSEUM

JUL

FIELD

SOLDIER FIELD

LAGOON

LAGOON

ROOSEVELT RD.

WABASH

MICHIGAN

INDIANA

ILLINOIS

16TH ST.

18TH ST.

CENTRAL

CERMAK RD.

SILVERTON WAY

23RD

AVE.

AVE.

AVE.

26TH ST.

ST.

RAILROAD

L A K E   M I C H I G A N

N

SOUTH PARKWAY

COTTAGE

31ST ST.

GROVE

AVE.

35TH ST.

183

BOARD OF SUPERVISING ENGINEERS
CHICAGO TRACTION
STREET CAR LINE EXTENSIONS
INTO GRANT AND
BURNHAM PARKS

¼ MILE

— EXTENSIONS

3-14-34

from the upper deck line. At the same time another loop, known as the Streeter Drive terminal, was built to the south of Grand Ave. on land adjacent to the pier entrance. Work to reconstruct the pier tracks and to build the new terminal took less than a month, and both were opened in June, 1921.

At the same time CSL extended the Chicago Ave. cars east across Lake Shore Drive and south along the lakefront to a terminal loop north of Ohio Street and adjacent to the pier. The CSL's only track along the lakefront, this five-block stretch was of railroad-type construction, with open ballasted track and center poles. This extension opened October 1, 1921.

CSL service to the Century of Progress expositions in 1933 and 1934 involved the building of two new terminals on the lakefront and the rerouting of several lines to serve the terminals. The first plan to extend Roosevelt Road streetcar service into Grant Park was put forward by E. J. Noonan, an engineer for the City Council's Railway Terminal Committee. To avoid crossing Michigan Ave. at grade, Noonan proposed a subway, but this idea was rejected by CSL.

The City Council passed the Roosevelt Road extension ordinance on May 24, 1933, and operation began August 1. The extension crossed Michigan Ave. at grade, climbed a short, rather steep grade on earth fill, made an "S" curve, and ran through the Illinois Central Railroad's passenger train shed. The girders which carried the cars through the train shed can still be seen today at the abandoned IC station. After emerging at the east side of the train shed, the cars continued on trestlework over the IC tracks to a loop in Grant Park. The west side of the terminal loop was built on trestlework and the east side on solid fill, since the space between Lake Shore Drive and the IC tracks was not wide enough to accommodate the entire loop. The loop had a single unloading platform, served by one track, and two loading platforms, served by two tracks.

The Cermak extension ordinance passed the City Council on May 17, the city construction permit was issued May 20, and the line began operation June 1. To meet this tight schedule required 24-hour-a-day work for most of the construction period. The target was to have the line open on the fair's opening day, June 1, 1933, and that date was met. Although the Cermak Road extension began at Cottage Grove, the extension ordinance required CSL to rebuild and relocate its tracks from just east of Wabash Ave. to Cottage Grove. The Cermak extension terminated at the 18th Street loop, which had two tracks serving two unloading platforms, and two tracks serving two loading platforms. Fare collection booths were built at 18th Street, but normal procedure was to use on-board fare collection at both the 18th and 12th terminals.

Luckily for the Surface Lines, travel to the Century of Progress came largely in non-rush hours. Most fairgoers did not arrive until after the morning rush hour, and most stayed until after 8:00 p.m., well after the evening rush hour. A small homeward surge at 4:00 p.m. and a sharp homebound peak at 10:00 p.m. were handled without much fuss by CSL.

In addition to the Cermak cars, CSL routed certain Broadway, State, Madison, and Wentworth cars to the 18th Street terminal. With platforms 300 feet long, that double-track loop could load 12 cars and unload 12 others at the same time. Roosevelt Road cars used the 12th Street terminal, together with some rerouted Clark Street cars. The Fair entrances at 31st and 35th Streets were served by CSL car lines on those streets, as well as by local and Through Route Cottage Grove cars. All cars serving any of the entrances carried a dash sign reading "World's Fair Direct."

• Above. CSL 5276 gets ready to leave the west terminal of the 74th-75th Street line at 74th and Ashland Ave. Between October, 1917 and August, 1918, 74th-75th Street cars ran beyond Ashland to a terminal at Damen Ave. to serve a war production plant. Photo from the Neuberger collection/Railway Negative Exchange. • Opposite page. Two CCRy standard Brills pass on Clark Street in this photo taken in June, 1922. These Wentworth-Clark cars had to run up a short grade to reach the level of the Roosevelt Road viaduct. Author's collection.

• Above. Shift changes at Chicago's hundreds of factories brought crowds that filled CSL cars to overflowing. Here workers fight for a foothold on the open rear platform of car 734. Location is the industrial district at 26th and Rockwell on the Blue Island Ave. line. George Krambles collection. • Opposite page. CSL 1895 turns south on Kedzie from the Arthington Street stub track which served the Sears headquarters and warehouse. Note woman seated on one of the platform seats. Alan W. Simms collection. • Below. Grand Ave. car, left, pulls out of Navy Pier, while CTA 1099 on the Stony Island line rests at the Streeter Drive loop.

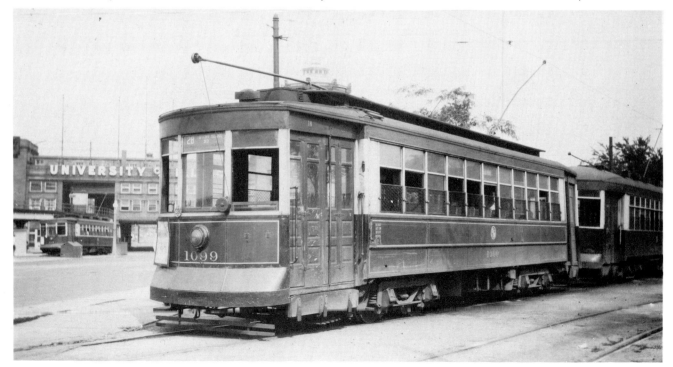

CSL credited the fair with a large part of its increased traffic during 1933 and 1934. Depression years which otherwise might have shown traffic losses. For example, in July, 1933 CSL's total traffic was up more than 6 million, a 13 per cent increase compared with July, 1932.

To handle the car riders among the 50,000 or so fans who came to a Cubs ballgame in the 1930's, CSL ran a total of 70 cars along Clark Street after the game. Regular service along Clark called for 15 cars southbound and 15 cars northbound about the time the game would end. CSL added to this 25 extra southbound cars and 15 extra northbound cars, for a total of 40 southbound and 30 northbound cars.

Quite possibly the man who enjoyed this extra service most was a man who might not have used it at all. He was the CSL employee who sat inside the park watching the game. His job was to call out the extra cars, timing his call so that they would arrive just as the fans streamed from the ball park. Men with the same job of calling out the extra cars were assigned to Comiskey Park to call out extra Clark-Wentworth and 35th Street cars after White Sox games, and to the Chicago Stadium to call out extra Madison Street cars after Black Hawk games.

Sometimes extra service was provided according to the temperature. This was true in summer, when the crosstown lines serving the lakefront beaches got extra service on days when the temperature favored swimming and picnicking. This extra service was under the jurisdiction of the station superintendent. He sent out as many cars as he thought were needed, drawing crews from men who were on the extra list. These newly-hired men usually did not qualify immediately for a regular run, so they came to the depot and waited to be called to fill an extra run, or the run of a man sick or on vacation. The 74th-75th Street line is an example of a route with fairly long headways which got much additional warm weather service by extra cars. Extra service was also given on lines like Harrison, which served the County Hospital. Extra cars ran on visiting nights at the hospital.

During the Christmas season CSL made every effort to add as many extra cars as possible. During one year every car on the CSL was in service during one day, and in many years virtually all the cars were in service. This remarkable record is covered more fully in the section on carhouses and shops. Extra late evening and early morning cars, known as Owl runs, came on the streets New Year's eve. They ran with rush-hour frequency to clear the Loop of revelers quickly.

Chartered cars were similar to extra cars, but they were rented to private groups traveling together. An itinerary was worked out in advance, with CSL charging so much an hour for the car and the crew. The largest charter movement in CSL history carried 5,000 Lane Technical High School students from the old school and its three branches to the site of the groundbreaking for the new school at Addison and Western. Fifty chartered cars, running out of the Lincoln, Limits, Division, and Noble barns, carried the students without a hitch on Tuesday June 24, 1930. With the advent of CSL bus service the use of charter streetcars declined, until in the last years they were used only by streetcar buffs making farewell journeys.

No section on CSL routes would be complete without mention of transfers. These flimsy strips of newsprint were issued by the millions each year. One reason was the sheer size of the CSL system. For many years it had over 1,000 miles of track and over 3,000 cars, plus several hundred trolley buses and motor coaches. There were no isolated routes on the system. Each line connected with at least one other CSL route, making it possible to board at any one point and ride to any other point, subject only to a few restrictions on reverse riding, circuitous routes, and stopovers. Unlike many other cities Chicago had no fare zones, and there was no extra charge for a transfer. (In the 1930s CSL began to issue and accept transfers to and from the "L", and in later years to Chicago Motor Coach, issuing them for extra fare.)

With the start of Through Routes between Chicago Railways and Chicago City Railway on March 17, 1908, a new transfer was put into use which showed the direction of travel. Two months later the Chicago City Railway adopted a similar transfer for all its local lines. The transfers were printed on paper stock of four different colors to aid conductors in identifying the initial direction of travel. Transfers issued from southbound cars were printed on manila stock, from northbound cars on salmon, from eastbound cars on pink, and from westbound cars on green.

Many of the rules governing CSL transfers continued in effect for many years. Some of these rules were: transfers were issued only at time fares were paid, they were good for an unlimited number of rides in the same general direction only, although direction could be reversed at any junction point, but only as far as the next junction, after which the transfer was invalid and the rider was supposed to leave the car.

The new transfers had a space for punching half-fares for children under 12. One child could ride for 3¢, two children for 5¢. When two children paid 5¢ it was rung up as one fare, but two transfers were issued.

These early CSL transfers were neither issued nor accepted in the downtown district, defined in an ordinance as the area bounded by Lake Michigan on the east, 12th Street on the south, and the Chicago River on the west and north. However, conductors could issue emergency transfers to passengers if their car broke down in the downtown district. These were good only on following cars of the same route.

Conductors were given leeway to honor invalid transfers if they believed the issuing conductor had made a mistake, or if they thought that the passenger had been delayed by an accident, traffic jam, or other circumstance beyond his control.

To stop transfer cheating, Chicago Railways mounted a campaign against both the vendors and the users of illegal transfers. The campaign began in 1908, and during the first six months 500 arrests were made. Some 450 miscreants were convicted, and were liable to fines ranging from $5 to $100. However, it seems that few if any were convicted for violating the transfer ordinance. Rather they were convicted under the catchall of disorderly conduct and fined $2 plus $6 court costs.

One weapon in this battle against transfer cheating

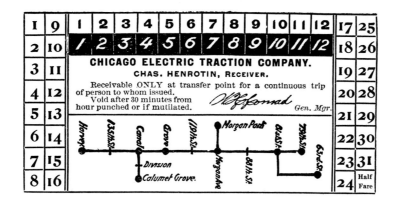

CHICAGO ELECTRIC TRACTION COMPANY.
CHAS. HENROTIN, Receiver.
Receivable ONLY at transfer point for a continuous trip of person to whom issued. Void after 30 minutes from hour punched or if mutilated. *Gen. Mgr.*

NOT A STOP-OVER CHECK.—Not Transferable. This Transfer good only for a continuous trip of person to whom issued—from point of intersection—on first connecting car—over any line of this Company receiving transfers from car indicated on the margin—limitation of direction shown by punch marks. Accepted subject to the rules of the Company.

CHICAGO CONSOLIDATED TRACTION CO.

OCT 5 — NORTH EAST — SOUTH WEST

067360 SEPT 27

668591 AUG 24

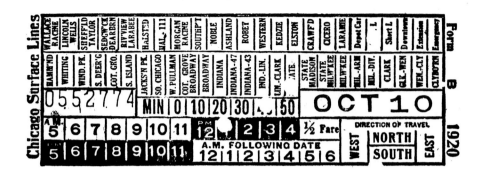

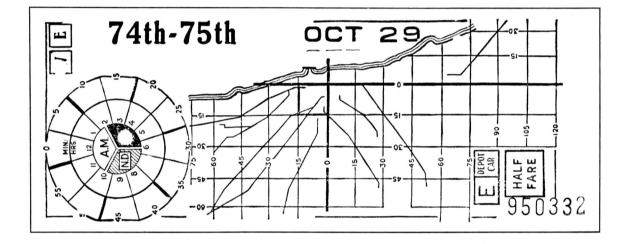

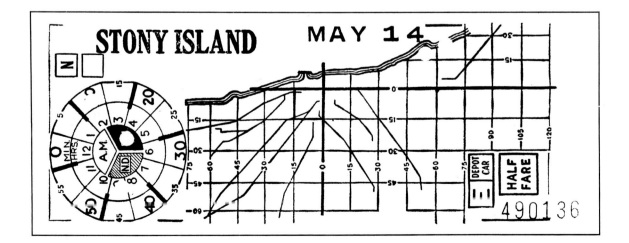

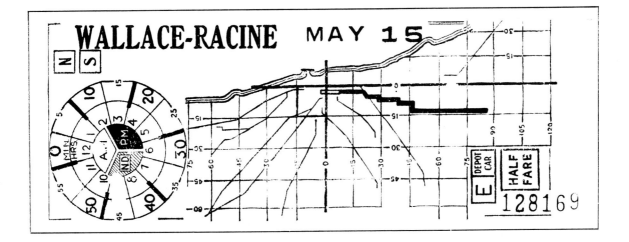

WALLACE-RACINE MAY 15

128169

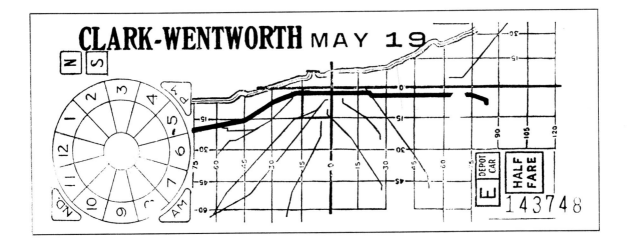

CLARK-WENTWORTH MAY 19

143748

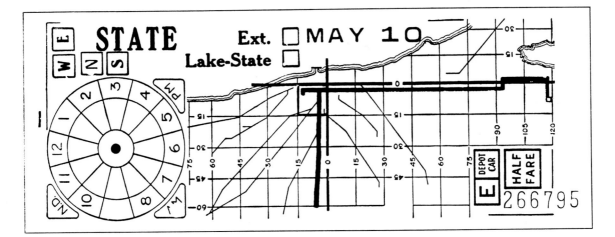

STATE Ext. ☐ MAY 10
Lake-State ☐

266795

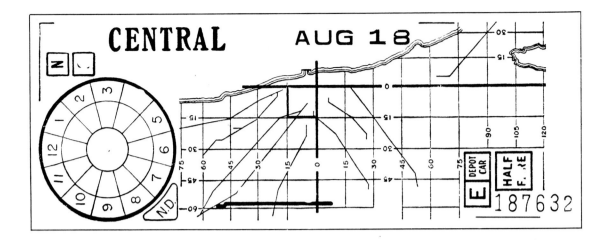

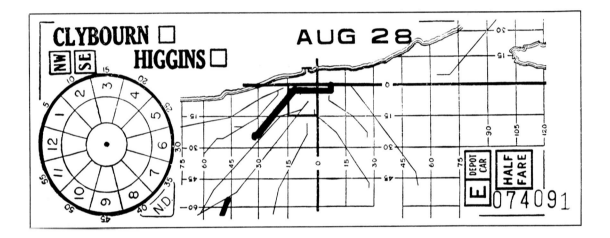

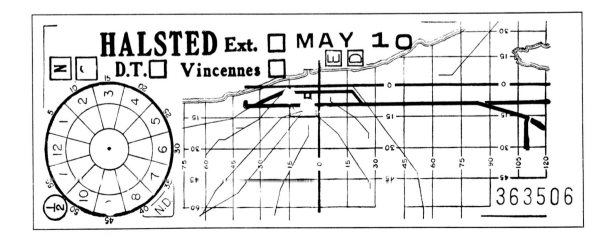

192

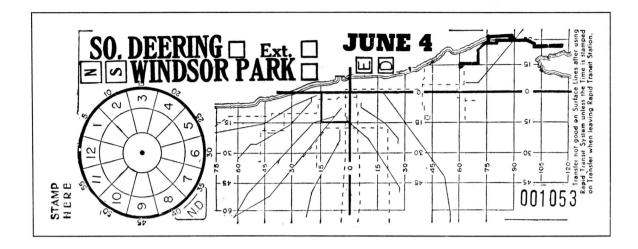

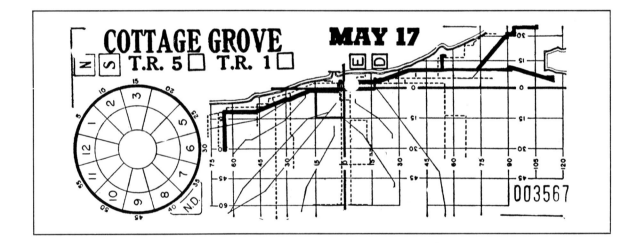

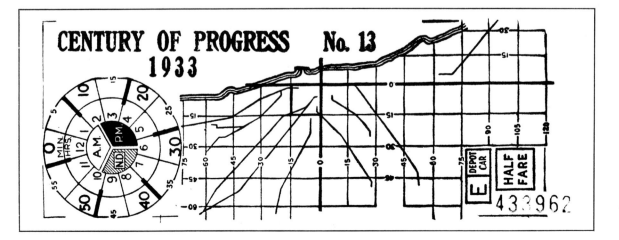

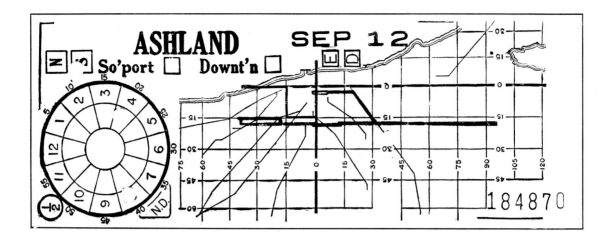

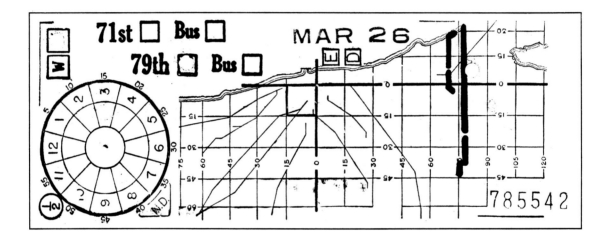

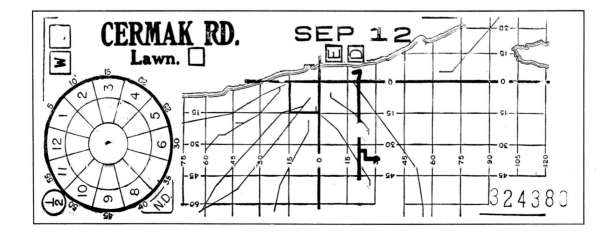

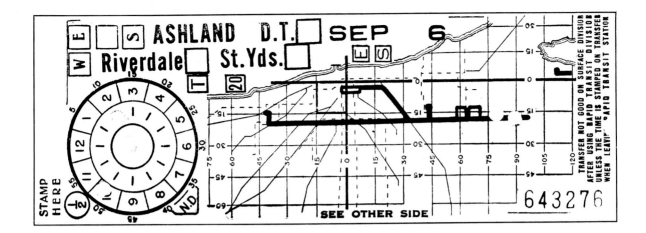

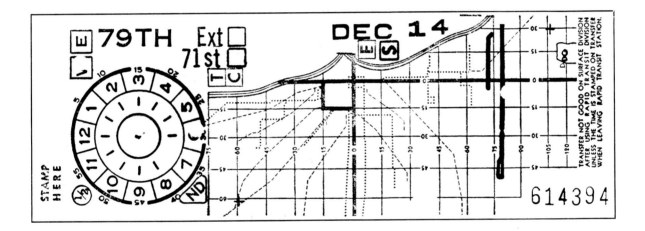

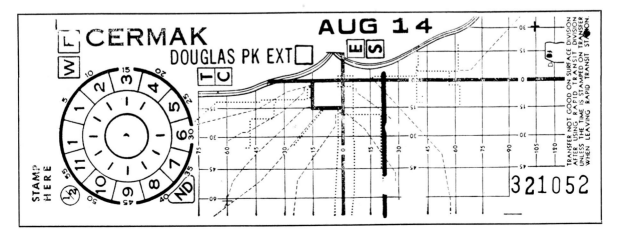

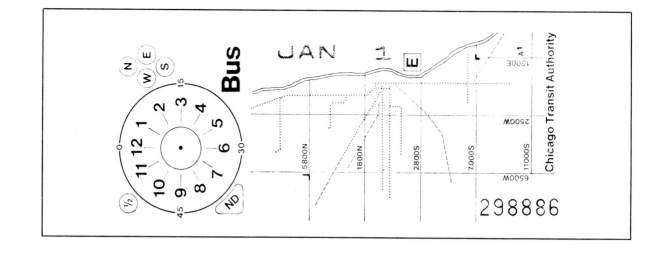

• Page 189. Top. Chicago Electric Traction Company transfer, tan in color, with map showing routes into Chicago's south suburbs. Numbers running up and down the sides of the transfer are the days of the month; numbers running across the top are the hours of the day. • Next down. Buff color Chicago Consolidated Traction Company transfer. Routes are listed across the top and bottom. Morning hours from 5 am to noon are shown along right edge, afternoon and evening hours from 1 to 12 are shown along the left edge, and Owl car hours from 1 am to 4 am were indicated by punching box at upper left. Some of the lines listed became part of Chicago Railways, others became part of County Traction. • Next below, and bottom. Type of CSL transfer issued from the Unification of 1914 until 1920. Top transfer, on orange stock, was issued for all north-south routes. Bottom transfer, on salmon stock, was issued for all east-west lines. Variations of the basic routes were indicated by punching the short line, through route, or downtown boxes.

• Page 190, top. Surface Lines transfer issued for all north-south routes between 1920 and 1932. • Middle. A sample of the first white, clock-type transfer, first issued October 1, 1932. Classified in this book as Type I. • Bottom. A Type II transfer, first issued in January, 1933. Note heavier type on clock face.

• Page 191, top. Route lines made their first appearance in May, 1933. They were printed in red. This is the Type III transfer. • Middle. A simplified clock face is the most noticeable change marking Type IV transfers, first issued in Feburary, 1934. Also note that the AM, PM, and ND pie slices were moved out of the center of the clock face and placed around the outside of the clock. • Bottom. In July, 1934 the Type V transfer appeared. A dot appeared at the center of the clock, and an outline map of the northern portion of Lake Calumet appeared on the underlying grid map of Chicago. The transfer was also shortened to the same length as Type III.

• Page 192, top. In April, 1938 the clock face was revised again, resulting in Type VI. The AM and PM triangles around the clock face were removed, and AM indicated by punching two slightly overlapping holes in the center of the clock, with PM indicated by one hole. • Middle. The addition of numbers outside the clock face distinguished Type VII transfers, introduced in January, 1939. • Bottom. Type VIII represents the last change CSL made in their standard white car-to-car transfer. In early February, 1943 the Emergency and Depot Car squares were modified and moved from the lower corner and placed below the date. The Half Fare square became a small circle containing the figure ½, placed near the top of the clock.

• Page 193, top. Starting September 22, 1935, blue transfers were issued to CSL passengers wishing to transfer to Chicago Rapid Transit lines. A 1946 South Deering and Windsor Park blue transfer is illustrated. Note space designated "Stamp Here" for use in Rapid Transit transfer validating machines. • Middle. Pink 1945 Cottage Grove transfer, issued to CSL passengers who wanted to transfer to Chicago Motor Coach lines. Note Motor Coach routes represented by dashed lines on underlying grid map. • Bottom. Special Century of Progress transfer issued in 1933. "Number 13" referred to a special event at the Fair.

• Page 194 and 195. Page 194 has CSL transfers, while page 195 has CTA transfers issued for the same lines. Note changes in clock face, in route combinations, and the appearance of a Rapid Transit bus extension on the Cermak CTA transfer.

• Page 196. Newest type of CTA bus transfer, issued starting January 6, 1974 (this transfer with January 1 date is a printer's sample). Note similarity to Chicago Surface Lines Type I transfer, illustrated on page 190.

was the following notice, printed in English, German, and Polish, and posted in large factories and stores along major lines.

> Our employees are warned that it is unlawful to misuse transfer tickets issued by the street railway companies. The city ordinance says: "It shall be unlawful to give away, or to receive for use, or to sell, barter or exchange transfer tickets. Penalty, from $5 to $100 for each offense." There must be no exchange of such transfers on or about our premises. We will assist in the enforcement of this ordinance.

Among the greatest offenders against the transfer ordinance were newsboys. As they sold their papers along heavily-travelled car lines they would offer to sell a transfer and a newspaper together. In this way they made an extra $1 to $3 a day, not a small sum in 1909. One older criminal mastermind, a veritable Fagin, was bound over to the grand jury on a conspiracy charge for recruiting newsboys to solicit and re-sell transfers.

Most of the arrests were made by Chicago Railways employees, undercover men, who were empowered to make arrests aboard the cars as special policemen. Little resistance was reported among the offenders as they were led away from the cars to the police station. After six months of crusading against transfer abuses, Chicago Railways felt they had the problem pretty well licked. The organized gangs had been broken up, and a scare had been thrown into those who stooped down to pick up a transfer discarded by someone else. According to the transfer ordinance, those who threw away a transfer without tearing it in two were also guilty of an ordinance violation.

Just as the Chicago Railways was making headway against transfer cheats, the Chicago City Railway reported a rash of counterfeit transfers. These 1909 fakes were pretty good, conductors reported, but their lack of serial numbers made them hard to pass.

Use of the familiar white clock-type transfer by the CSL began October 1, 1932. The outline map of the city was divided into zones, with zone lines fifteen standard city blocks apart. The conductor issuing the transfers punched the zone where the passenger boarded the car. He also punched the time on the transfer clock when the car would leave that zone. Ten minutes was allowed for each zone crossed. The central business district was allowed fifteen minutes, and an additional ten minutes was allowed for transferring.

The transfer issued on the first ride was good for fare for the entire trip. It was presented to the conductor on each line ridden for his check and the validating punch mark. The conductor validated the transfer for the next ride by punch-marking the zone in which a change of cars was made.

The first clock-map transfer contained the route name, but did not show the route line (Type I). In January, 1933 the clock face became more pronounced with the use of heavier lines and larger numerals within the clock face (Type II).

In May, 1933 red route lines were put on the transfer (Type III). This transfer style was used until February, 1934, when the clock face was simplified (Type IV). AM, PM, and ND (next day) were no longer punched within the center of the clock, but in separate triangles located outside the clock. The transfer length was increased by three-eighths of an inch.

In July, 1934 the transfer was again changed (Type V). The original length was restored, and a dot shown at the center of the clock. The outline of Lake Calumet was added to the underlying grid map of Chicago. This style was used until late April, 1938 when the clock face was revised (Type VI). The AM and PM triangles around the outside of the clock were removed. AM was now punched with two slightly overlapping holes in the center of the clock, and PM with one hole. During January, 1939 numbers indicating five-minute intervals were placed around the outside of the clock. (Type VII).

In August, 1942 as an economy in the printing of transfers, two or more lines were grouped on a single transfer. Where practical the lines were from the same depot. Prior to the grouping there were 72 CSL transfers in use. The number was reduced to 51.

It should be noted, however, that since the inception of the clock-map transfer, there were several lines grouped on transfers.

The last change made by the CSL on their white car-to-car transfers was in early February, 1943 (Type VIII). The Emergency and Depot Car squares were modified and moved from the lower left hand corner and placed below the date. The Half Fare square became a small circle containing 1/2, moved to the upper left hand portion of the clock area.

Blue clock-map transfers were issued to CSL passengers desiring to transfer to Chicago Rapid Transit lines effective September 22, 1935. Appearing with the grid map of Chicago was the system of rapid transit lines. Route names and lines were the same as on the white transfers.

Starting October 1, 1943 pink clock-map transfers were issued to CSL passengers transferring to the Chicago Motor Coach Co. These transfers contained the network of motor coach routes with the grid map. Route names and lines were also the same as on the white transfers.

During the Century of Progress fair in 1933-34, the CSL issued transfers at the fairgrounds to people boarding cars at the gates. These transfers were identical to regular CSL transfers used except "Century of Progress" appeared in place of a route name.

In November, 1935 the CSL started issuing a special events transfer for functions held at Soldier Field. This transfer was also like the regular transfer except that Soldier Field appeared in place of a route name. Below "Soldier Field" appeared the numbers 1 thru 9. Each event held there was assigned a number 1 thru 9 by the CSL, and this event number was punched.

When the suburban lines of Chicago Railways were taken over by County Traction in 1910, transfer privileges and through routes were ended at several points. One of these was at Clark and Howard, where the through Evanston line was cut. For details see the

Broadway route listing in the route chapter. In the Western suburbs the villages of Oak Park, Maywood, and River Forest filed separate suits against County Traction and Chicago Railways. The suits sought to force them to issue inter-company free transfers. All suits were decided in favor of the companies, and transfers were not issued.

The Illinois Public Utilities Commission, in an order issued January 3, 1921, allowed CSL to use one-man cars on light lines that didn't serve the Loop. One-man operation was allowed during the day on all lines where the headway was seven or more minutes during the morning rush hour. Night cars could be one-man on lines where the headway was 15 minutes or more. When the order was issued, CSL already had 10 single-truck safety cars (Birneys) on hand. Some of them went into service on the West Division line, joining an equal number of two-man cars. The date of one-man service on Division was February 18, 1921. The chart on page 199 shows conversions to one-man cars from 1921 through 1955, when the last one-man conversion was made by CTA.

Although the table shows that many routes were converted to one-man operation before CTA took over on October 1, 1947, as a percentage of the CSL system the number of one-man routes was small. Chicago was almost alone in ordering two-man PCC cars after WW II. At the end of the CSL era something under six per cent of the car miles were operated by one-man cars.

The table shows that one-man cars were used both to start new routes and to replace two-man cars on light lines. Of the latter 79th Street is an extreme case, with four conversions and reconversions from two-man to one-man cars. This route first got one-man cars on April 1, 1923, but at the urging of the City Council CSL restored two-man cars on August 15, 1926. Twenty-six one-man cars were replaced by two-man cars on that date. On April 6, 1936 there was a partial restoration of one-man service on 79th, with full one-man service restored October 23, 1949 by CTA. The Racine and the 35th Street routes were also converted to one-man, then re-converted to two-man operation. Some one-man cars ran on shuttles: Fifth Avenue (Sundays only), North Avenue, and Roosevelt are examples.

In the 1940s CSL operated the following cars in one-man service: 3092, 3093-3118, 3202-3261, 3262-3321, 2904-2922, 6199-6238, 6240-6279, and some cars in the 1200, 1400, and 5700 series. Other cars, normally two-man, ran in Owl service as one-man cars. Examples are some cars in the 2500-2800 series. As part of the CTA's modernization program, several hundred two-man cars were converted to one-man in 1949 and the early 1950s. Among the modifications were removal of the bulkheads and the replacement of sliding doors by pneumatic folding doors with safety edge strips. For details see the passenger equipment chapter.

To let the public know where its cars stopped, CSL hung signs from the trolley span wires reading "Cars Stop Here." In 1921 CSL discontinued the signs, which could not be seen at night and which occasionally fell to the street. Line poles painted with a white band and lettered "Cars Stop Here" in black replaced the car stop signs. One pole on either side of the street at some 8,000 stops was painted, with the band being about two-thirds of the way up the pole. In later years the black lettering

CTA 3270 in one-man service about to cross the Illinois Central Railroad's electrified South Chicago branch at 79th and Exchange Ave., just a few blocks from the east terminal of the streetcar line at 79th and Brandon. Photo taken by Richard N. Lukin in June, 1951. Photo supplied by A. C. Williams. The 79th Street line switched from two-man to one-man cars four times between 1923 and 1949. See table on next page for details.

Chronology of One-Man Car Assignments

Date	Route	Explanation
February 18, 1921	Division Extension	First use of one-man cars by CSL
March 13, 1921	Devon	
April 1, 1921	Division Extension	Full use of one-man cars on this route
April 1, 1921	Laramie	Cars 1415 and 1416 assigned
November 1, 1921	Noble	
January 1, 1923	Armitage	
January 26, 1923	Halsted Extension	New CSL route with one-man cars
April 1, 1923	71st Street	
April 1, 1923	87th Street	
April 1, 1923	North Ashland	
April 1, 1923	Milwaukee Extension	Made a two-man line 10/1/27
April 1, 1923	51st Street Extension	Made a two-man route 7/17/27
April 1, 1923	79th Street	See 1926, 1936, and 1949
July 16, 1923	Diversey	New route begun with one-man cars
November 8, 1924	S. Deering Extension	New route begun with one-man cars
August 9, 1924	Taylor-Sheffield	Made a two-man route 9/14/24
May 1, 1925	Webster	
August 9, 1925	Fulton-21st	
August 15, 1926	93rd-95th Street	
August 15, 1926	79th Street	Made a two-man route
October 1, 1926	106th Street	
December 1, 1926	103rd Street	
October 15, 1930	87th Extension	New route begun with one-man cars
April 24, 1932	Fifth Avenue	Sunday shuttle service only
August 7, 1932	Morgan-Racine	
August 7, 1932	Pershing	
August 7, 1932	South Deering	
August 7, 1932	Windsor Park	
August 7, 1932	18th Street	
August 7, 1932	43rd-Root Street	
August 14, 1932	59th-61st Street	
August 14, 1932	67th-69th-71st	
August 21, 1932	26th Street	
August 21, 1932	51st-55th Street	
September 4, 1932	Montrose	
September 4, 1932	Hammond	
September 4, 1932	Whiting-East Chicago	
November 9, 1932	Wallace-Racine	Later restored to two-man service
December 4, 1932	35th Street	Later restored to two-man service
October 7, 1934	Pershing Extension	Ran between Ashland and Western only
April 6, 1936	Riverdale	
April 6, 1936	Chicago Ave.	Partial substitution
April 6, 1936	Lawrence Ave.	Partial substitution
April 6, 1936	79th Street	Partial substitution
June 9, 1940	S. Chicago-Ewing	As replacement for interstate lines
July 3, 1949	North Ave.	East of Halsted only
August 22, 1949	North Damen	
October 23, 1949	79th Street	All service now by one-man cars
October 23, 1949	Lake St.	
December 18, 1949	Ogden	
January 29, 1950	Lawrence Ave.	All service now by one-man cars
April 9, 1950	Cermak Road	Saturdays and Sundays only
April 9, 1950	Elston Avenue	Saturdays and Sundays only
June 24, 1950	Chicago Avenue	All service now by one-man cars
September 11, 1950	Cicero Ave.	Weekdays only, buses on weekends
August 12, 1951	Roosevelt Road	East of Wabash Ave. only
September 16, 1951	Cermak Road	All service now by one-man cars
May 11, 1952	Cottage Grove	Line equipped with one-man PCC cars
June 19, 1955	Western Avenue	Line equipped with one-man PCC cars

NOTES: The North Ave. and Roosevelt Road one-man lines were short shuttles. The rest of these two routes were converted to trolley bus operation.

was dropped, and the white band alone was painted on the poles.

Although Chicago's Loop district became increasingly crowded year by year, starting at least as far back as the 1890s, the street railways began to complain vigorously about the situation only after the unification of 1914. In early 1915 CSL President Busby testified before the Illinois Public Utilities Commission that the physical capacity of the tracks through downtown Chicago had been reached. In December of 1915 CSL ran newspaper ads urging an end to parking in the Loop. "This problem," said CSL, "can best be solved by those who drive automobiles. Their slight personal convenience causes the serious inconvenience of the great majority who do not drive automobiles."

CSL's attack on Loop congestion caused by parking helped bring about Chicago's first Loop anti-parking ordinance on May 1, 1918. The law banned parking by all

types of vehicles on any downtown street used by street-cars from 7 am to 10 am and from 4 pm to 7 pm. During the first month the law was in effect, police arrested about 1,000 parking violators. The streetcar lines using State Street and Wabash Ave., including Through Routes 1 and 3, benefited most from the parking ban.

A further speed-up of streetcar schedules resulted from the CSL's own general rerouting of cars on September 14, 1924. The CSL was under an Illinois Public Utility Commission order of January 3, 1921 to prepare plans for reducing Loop congestion through rerouting of cars through the Loop and short-turning cars before they entered the downtown district. As finally approved by the Illinois PUC and the City of Chicago, the changes involved 1,600 cars running on 35 routes. CSL spent $100,000 for new curves to form new loops, made alterations to 100 mechanical switches, and removed 24 electric switches and installed 21 new ones.

The basic objectives were: to eliminate left-hand turns by streetcars and to reduce the number of right-hand turns; to carry North-South lines through the Loop before turning them back; to replace State Street with Dearborn as the north-south leg in the turning loops for West Side cars; to reroute minor lines away from the business district; and to combine lines entering the loop into through routes whenever possible. Unfortunately, the 140 men who volunteered to change carhouses (because of a change in car assignments) lost all their seniority in making the move, and had to take the worst of the runs at their new carbarns.

Three major changes made at this time involved Broadway, Halsted-Downtown, and Chicago Avenue cars. Broadway cars were rerouted to turn back at Harrison rather than at Madison in the heart of the Loop. Halsted-Downtown cars began to turn at Chicago Ave. rather than at Madison. On Chicago Avenue itself the east and west routes were consolidated and the Chicago-Downtown car eliminated. Several Through Routes were discontinued during the general rerouting: Clybourn-Wentworth, State-Milwaukee, State-Madison, Ogden-Clark, Blue Island-Wells, and 12th-Ogden-Wells. For other changes see the individual lines in this chapter.

The 1924 rerouting included designating State, Clark, and Wells for through-the-Loop traffic only, eliminating 20 places where cars made left turns and 12 places where they made right turns, and ending the use of the stub terminals on Van Buren and Adams.

An even more dramatic speed up in schedules was made possible by the installation of co-ordinated traffic lights in the Loop on February 8, 1926. CSL claimed that it could increase speed by 25 to 50 per cent after the new lights went in. From a control room in the basement of City Hall traffic lights were controlled at 49 Loop intersections. The cycles, which lasted from 60 to 80 seconds, were keyed to expedite streetcar movements. Cycles were not set up to give each direction of traffic an equal crossing period. For example, at State and Lake, 56 per cent of the cycle was used for State Street traffic and 44 per cent for Lake Street traffic. The cycle used at all other State St. intersections (except State and Jackson) gave State St. 61 per cent of the cycle. Surprisingly, pedestrians did not have to obey the traffic lights, which were for vehicles only. Policemen at each corner directed pedestrian traffic.

The co-ordinated traffic light system was designed by two CSL engineers, E. J. McIlraith and H. B. Cammack. The $230,000 system was completely automatic, once the cycles were programmed into it, and drew much attention nationwide. Engineers and traffic police from several cities came to see the Chicago system, and McIlraith developed a nationwide reputation as a traffic engineer.

While the subject of CSL schedules could fill a book, a few words about that subject are appropriate in this chapter on routes. In the CSL era the "Big Five" car lines were Halsted, Clark-Wentworth, Madison, Ashland, and Milwaukee. They had the heaviest passenger traffic, the shortest headways, they all ran two car trains when CSL used this solution to giving better service on heavy lines (Ashland never ran two-car trains), and again with the exception of Ashland and Milwaukee they all were equipped with PCC cars. All were among the last lines to be converted from streetcar to bus, and all used two-man cars until the end of service. Among other well patronized routes were Archer, Broadway-State, Cottage Grove, Indiana, Kedzie, Roosevelt, Lincoln Ave., Western, and 63rd. A glance at the table of one-man routes will show which lines were the lightest, since they were among the first to receive one-man cars.

Most Chicago streetcar lines ran 24 hours a day, seven days a week. The table on page 202, taken from a 1928 CSL route guide, shows the Owl service for all lines. When no Owl service was given, that is also indicated.

In order to accurately reflect the level of service, the term Owl car was restricted to all-night service in the table. Even under this restrictive definition, 60 of the 97 routes provided 24-hour a day service in 1928. The frequency of service is amazing. The Archer and Madison lines had cars every 10 minutes through the early morning hours, and many other lines had 15 minute service. Owl cars on Broadway and Chicago ran as often as every 8 minutes, but these headways increased to 10 and then 15 minutes as the night went on. Fullerton also had cars at 8 minute intervals, changing to 24 and 30 minute intervals in the early morning hours. Other lines with finely graduated Owl service were Halsted-26th, Harrison, Indiana-51st, Irving Park, Lawrence, Lincoln-Bowmanville, Madison-Fifth, Montrose, Van Buren, Wallace-Racine, and 14th-16th. Some lines ran short-turn Owl cars to give intensive service to the central portion of the route where traffic was heaviest. These lines were Archer, Ashland, Clark-Wentworth, Cottage-Pullman, Halsted-Downtown, Kedzie (TR 17), Milwaukee-Devon, Roosevelt-Downtown, State, and 63rd.

Some lines did not give Owl service on portions of

Opposite page. The solid line of streetcars stretching from Madison up to Washington on State Street gives this photo from the David R. Phillips collection a rush hour feeling. However, it's only 11:20 in the morning on a busy shopping day in the Loop.

Line	Hours of Owl Service	Frequency of Owl Service
Archer-South Cicero	1:12 am to 5:27 am	Six cars an hour to Cicero-Archer
Archer-38th Street	1:15 am to 4:45 am	Two cars an hour to 38th-Central Park
Argo	No Owl service	Last car ran 12:30 am from Argo
Armitage-Center	1:08 am to 5:00 am	A car every 15 minutes
Ashland (TR 9)	From 1:00 am to 4:45 am a car ran every 15 minutes from 69th-Ashland to Clybourn-Southport. Alternate cars ran over the entire line from 95th-Ashland to Southport-Clark, giving 30 minute service on the outer portions of the line.	
Ashland-Downtown	No Owl service	Last car left Loop 11:11 pm
Ashland (North)	No Owl service	Last car left Clybourn 1:03 am
Belmont	1:05 am to 4:35 am	A car every 30 minutes
Blue Island	12:51 am to 4:42 am	A car every 25 to 30 minutes
Broadway	12:32 am to 5:21 am	At 8, 10, and 15 minute intervals
Chicago	1:05 am to 5:18 am	At 8, 13, and 15 minute intervals
Cicero	12:50 am to 5:00 am	At 20 to 30 minute intervals
Clark-Wentworth	For Owl service between 1:00 am and 5:00 am this line was divided into two segments. Cars ran from 81st-Halsted to Chicago-Wells every 15 minutes. Cars ran from Clark-Howard to Clark-Madison every 30 minutes.	
Clybourn	1:10 am to 5:06 am	A car every 25 minutes
Cottage-Broadway	No Owl service was given on Through Route 1. A night car did run from 55th-Cottage to 64th-Stony Island from 1:01 am to 4:30 am. Service was at 15 minute intervals.	
Cottage-Pullman	Night service on this route was divided at the south end, with alternate cars going to 115th and Cottage and 108th and Ewing. From Randolph to 71st frequency varied from 10.5 minutes to 15 minutes, half that frequently on the two lines beyond 71st. Owl hours were from 1:07 am to 5:25 am.	
Cottage-South Chicago	Owl service provided by alternate Cottage-Pullman cars.	
Crawford	1:00 am to 4:30 am	A car every 30 minutes
Devon	No Owl service	Last car left Kedzie 1:19 am
Diversey	No Owl service	Last car left Milwaukee 12:48 am
Diversey Extension	No Owl service	Last bus left Laramie 12:03 am
Division-Downtown	1:02 am to 5:02 am	A car every 30 minutes
Division-Wells	No Owl service	Last car left Division-Wells 12:28 am
Division-Austin	No Owl service	Last car left Austin 1:10 am
Elston	1:00 am to 4:43 am	A car every 30 minutes
Ewing-Brandon	No Owl service	Last car fr. Brainard at 12:25 am
Fullerton	1:04 am to 4:43 am	At 8, 24, and 30 minute intervals.
Fulton-21st	No Owl service	Last car fr. Western 11:51 pm
Grand	1:00 am to 5:00 am	A car every 30 minutes
Halsted-Downtown	From 79th-Halsted to 111th-Sacramento service was every 30 minutes. From 79th-Halsted to Chicago-Wells service was every 15 minutes. Owl hours were 1:08 am to 5:27 am.	
Halsted	For Owl service, see Halsted-26th Street listing below.	
Halsted-26th Street	Service from 26th-Halsted to Halsted-Broadway at 11, 16 and 22 minute intervals northbound and 22 minute intervals southbound. Owl hours between 1:08 am and 4:53 am.	
Halsted Extension	No Owl service	Last car left 119th at 12:38 am
Hammond	No Owl service	Last car left 63rd at midnight
Harrison-Adams	No Owl service	Last car left Monroe at 1:37 am
Harrison	1:05 to 4:47 am	At 18, 23, and 30 minute intervals
Indiana-51st	1:03 am to 5:32 am	At 11, 15, and 18 minute intervals
Indiana-Lincoln	No Owl service	Last car left Lake Park 12:14 am
Indiana-43rd	No Owl service	Last car left Oakenwald at 8:05 pm
Irving Park	12:28 am to 5:15 am	Cars at 15 to 20 minute intervals
Kedzie-California	1:19 am to 4:20 am	30 minute intervals
Kedzie (TR 17)	Owl cars ran every 15 minutes from 47th-Kedzie to California-Milwaukee. Alternate cars went through to either Roscoe-California or Bryn Mawr-Kedzie on the north side, and to either 47th-Kedzie or 67th-Kedzie on the south side. Owl hours were from 1:00 am to 4:30 am.	
Laramie	No Owl service	Last car left Harrison 11:07 pm
Lawrence	1:00 am to 4:30 am	At 10, 20 and 30 minute intervals

Line	Hours of Owl Service	Frequency of Owl Service
Lincoln-Bowmanville	1:01 am to 5:39 am	At 12 and 20 minute intervals
Lincoln-Rosehill	Shuttle service only from Irving Park to Rosehill Cemetery. Owl hours 1:05 am to 4:50 am. A car every 30 minutes.	
Madison	1:01 am to 5:20 am	A car every 10 minutes
Madison-Fifth Avenue	Last through car left Crawford Ave. at 12:40 am. After that departure cars ran shuttle only between Fifth-Crawford and Fifth-Madison. Last car left Fifth-Madison at 2:00 am. No further service on this line after 2:00 am.	
Milwaukee-Devon	Some cars ran between Devon and Dearborn, others between Gale and Dearborn. 15 minute service between Devon and Dearborn, 30 minute service between Gale and Dearborn. Owl hours were 1:05 am to 5:35 am.	
Milwaukee-Armitage	No Owl service. Last car left Dearborn at 12:50 am. All night service provided by Armitage-Center line.	
Montrose	1:05 am to 5:00 am	At 25, 30 and 60 minute intervals
Morgan-Racine (TR 23)	On the segment between Pershing Road-Morgan and Erie-Ashland the last car left Pershing-Morgan at 9:40 pm. However, service continued between 21st-Racine and Erie-Ashland until the last car left Erie-Ashland at 1:45 am.	
Noble	No Owl service. Last car left Noble-Milwaukee at 8:40 pm.	
North	1:30 am to 4:38 am	A car every 30 minutes
Ogden	1:11 am to 5:11 am	A car every 30 minutes
Pershing Road	1:20 am to 4:50 am	A car every 30 minutes
Pershing Extension	No Owl service	Last car left Western at 7:18 pm
Riverdale	No Owl service	Last car left Leyden at 11:55 pm
Riverview-Larrabee	No Owl service	Last car left Dearborn at 2:03 am
Robey (Damen)	1:45 am to 4:40 am	A car every 35 minutes
Robey South	No Owl service	Last car left 47th at 12:18 am
Roosevelt-Downtown	Between Cicero and Canal cars ran every 15 minutes. East of Canal alternate cars ran to Adams-Dearborn or Roosevelt-Wabash, giving 30 minute service to those terminals. West of Cicero alternate cars ran to Austin, giving 30 minute service to that terminal. Owl hours were 1:14 am to 5:14 am.	
Roosevelt-Wabash	See Roosevelt-Downtown service above for Owl car schedules.	
South Deering	Owl service was operated only between 63rd-Dorchester and 112th-Torrence. Cars ran every 50 minutes between 1:34 am and 4:54 am. Between 112th-Torrence and 124th-Torrence the last car left 124th at 12:41 am.	
State	Between Division-Wells and 79th-State cars ran every 15 minutes. Alternate cars went through to 119th-Morgan, giving 30 minute service between 79th and 119th. Owl hours were from 1:11 am to 4:42 am.	
State-Lake (TR 16)	No Owl service	Last car left 63rd at 12:35 am
Stony Island	No Owl service	Last car left Randolph at 12:47 am
Taylor-Sedgwick	1:00 am to 4:45 am	A car every 30 minutes
Van Buren	1:03 am to 4:42 am	At 15, 24, and 30 minute intervals
Wallace-Racine	1:01 am to 5:25 am	At 24 to 30 minute intervals
Webster-Racine	No Owl service	Last car left Fullerton-Racine at 12:27 am
Western	1:00 am to 4:30 am	A car every 30 minutes
Whiting-E. Chicago	No Owl service	Last car left 63rd at 1:00 am
Windsor Park	1:59 to 4:35 am	A car every 50 minutes
14th-16th Streets	1:29 am to 4:50 am	At 24, 28, and 30 minute intervals
18th Street	1:25 am to 4:55 am	A car every 30 minutes
22nd Street (Cermak)	1:10 am to 5:14 am	A car every 15 minutes
22nd-Lawndale	No Owl service	Last car left Wabash 12:11 am
26th Street	No Owl service	Last car left Cottage 12:26 am
31st Street	1:00 am to 5:22 am	A car every 15 minutes
35th Street	1:23 am to 5:25 am	A car every 30 minutes
43rd-Root Streets	1:00 am to 5:18 am	A car every 20 minutes
47th Street	1:03 am to 4:53 am	A car every 15 minutes
51st Street	12:12 am to 5:16 am	A car every 20 minutes
59th-61st Streets	1:02 am to 5:17 am	A car every 15 minutes
63rd Street	Owl cars ran every 15 minutes between Stony Island and Central Park. Alternate cars went through to Melvina Ave., giving 30 minute service between Central Park and Melvina. Owl hours were from 1:01 am to 4:46 am.	

67th-69th-71st	Owl service only from 69th-Western to 71st-South Shore Drive. A car every 15 minutes. Owl hours were from 1:05 am to 4:55 am.	
71st Street	No Owl service	Last car left Cottage at 1:05 am
74th-75th Street	1:15 am to 5:15 am	A car every 30 minutes
79th Street	Owl service only between Ashland and Lake Michigan. Owl hours were from 1:50 am to 5:20 am.	
87th Street	No Owl service	Last car left Commercial at 1:10 am
93rd-95th Street	1:03 am to 5:03 am	A car every 30 minutes
103rd Street	No Owl service	Last car left Vincennes at 1:43 am
106th Street	No Owl service	Last car left State Line at 12:08 pm
111th Street	No Owl service	Last car left Vincennes at 12:48 am
115th Street	No Owl service	Last car left Halsted 11:50 pm
119th Street	No Owl service	Last car left Vincennes 11:02 pm

NOTES: Although some routes did not themselves offer Owl service, yet Owl service was provided over all or almost all of their route by Owl cars on other lines. Lines having such full-route service were: Ashland-Downtown, Cottage Grove-Broadway, Indiana-Lincoln, Indiana-43rd, State-Lake, and Lincoln-Rosehill. Lines having partial-route Owl service provided by other lines were: Hammond, Harrison-Adams, Milwaukee-Armitage, Riverview-Larrabee, Stony Island, and Whiting-East Chicago.

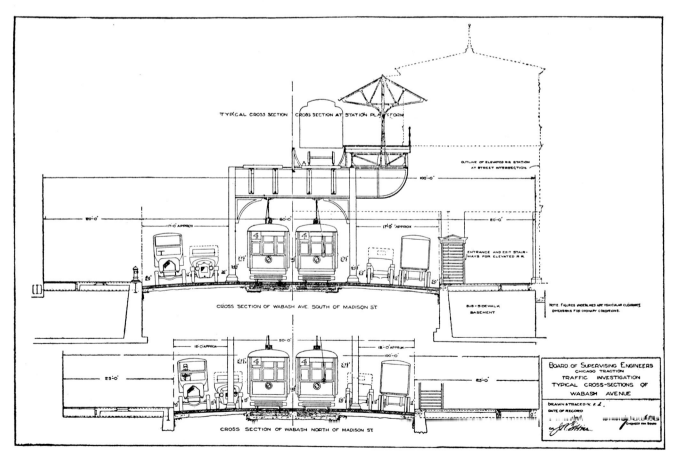

North of Madison Street along Wabash Ave. each sidewalk was five feet wider than it was south of Madison. Diagram shows how this narrowing of the street cut off two lanes of traffic. From a BOSE report.

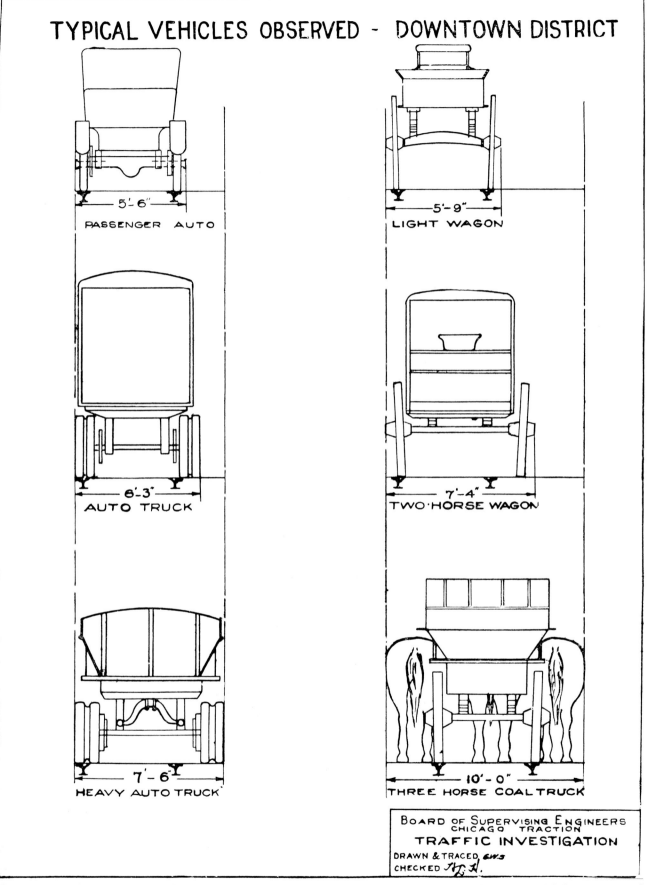

TYPICAL VEHICLES OBSERVED - DOWNTOWN DISTRICT

5'-6"
PASSENGER AUTO

5'-9"
LIGHT WAGON

8'-3"
AUTO TRUCK

7'-4"
TWO-HORSE WAGON

7'-6"
HEAVY AUTO TRUCK

10'-0"
THREE HORSE COAL TRUCK

BOARD OF SUPERVISING ENGINEERS
CHICAGO TRACTION
TRAFFIC INVESTIGATION
DRAWN & TRACED GWS
CHECKED

This drawing from a Board of Supervising Engineers report shows how the width of various vehicles compared with the width of streetcar track. Note that a three-horse coal wagon blocks two lanes of traffic.

their route. Examples are Cottage-Broadway, Halsted, Lincoln-Rosehill, Madison-Fifth, Morgan-Racine-Sangamon, South Deering, 67th-69th-71st, and 79th. It should be noted that the hours listed for Owl service are the time the first Owl car was scheduled to leave either terminal and the time the last Owl car was scheduled to leave either terminal. Obviously Owl cars and regular cars operated over the routes at the same time for short periods.

In 1924 CSL introduced the form of operating (or employees') timetable which became the standard used until the end of the CSL era. It showed in one place all the information a crew needed to know about their run. A copy of such a timetable, known as a run guide, is reproduced as a full-page illustration. It is shown in white on black because the original run guides were made on blueprint paper which gave a white on blue image. Reference to the run guide will make the following explanation easier to follow.

This Chicago Railways timecard shows rather long Owl car headways on major routes. From Jim Prokes.

The run number is in the upper left-hand corner of each rectangular box. This identified the job in that rectangle, and was the number that appeared on the metal disk or run tag which the motorman or operator fastened to the front of his vehicle just below the right-hand front window. The run tag identified the schedule the car was running on for CSL street supervisors, City inspectors, and others interested in transit schedule-keeping.

The number of hours' pay the job was worth appears in the upper right-hand corner of the rectangle. For pay purposes an hour was divided into 10 parts. A number 8^4 meant that the run paid 8 hours, 24 minutes' wages. The next line gave the time the crew was to report to the depot, usually 10 minutes before the car was scheduled to leave. The crew used this time to check out their car, sign in, get their transfers, and check the bulletin board.

The next line gave the time the crew was to leave the depot. Below that was a timetable for the run, showing arrival and departure times from the terminals. Most runs had considerable time off for the crews. These split runs allowed the CSL to meet the peak rush hour travel demands by putting as many cars as possible in service during the two rush hours, and running far fewer cars the rest of the day. In the run guide chosen as an illustration (Belmont Ave. in the Fall of 1932), many runs required a total time of more than 12 hours, but were paid for 8 hours or less. Run 415 is an example.

In that era the crewmen were paid only for their "platform time," i.e. the time they spent actually running the car. Many runs had a four or five hour mid-day gap that was not paid for because the crew was not on the car. The split runs led to many reliefs of crews in the street, and missing a relief was considered a serious offense. Some reliefs took place in front of carbarns, but they could be made at either terminal or at some intermediate point. CSL employees were not allowed to "moonlight" on second jobs, and were discouraged from visiting taverns. To give the men some place to go between trips, the Surface Lines provided elaborate club rooms, gymnasiums, and libraries in some of its carbarns. These recreational facilities are mentioned in the chapter on carhouses and shops.

A study of the Belmont run guide shows that the run numbers did not correspond with the arrival and departure times at terminals or at intermediate points. CSL supervisors carried a different sort of operating timetable which showed the times at the terminals and the time runs were due at several intermediate "time points." To illustrate how supervisors' timetables differed from employees' run guides, a supervisors' timetable for the Kedzie line in 1924 is shown on page 208.

Of particular interest in this timetable is the use of three terminals: 47th and 67th Street for regular runs, and 22nd Street for short-turn cars which went to the Kedzie carhouse on their next northbound run. Note also the extremely short headways at Van Buren Street, as little as 30 seconds between cars. CSL regularly scheduled cars at 30 second intervals. One can readily see how even minor traffic congestion could disrupt such closely-timed schedules.

Another feature of CSL scheduling practice was the use of a half-dozen or more running times for a line.

CHICAGO SURFACE LINES
RUN GUIDE

APPROVED BY

LINE **BELMONT AVE.**

Division No. **12**

Depot **LIMITS**

No. **B-5. REV.** **WEEKDAY**

DATE - Effective *Sept. 12-1932*

REVISED " *Oct. 12-1932*

REVISED "

REVISED "

Term.	Arr.	Lv.	Arr.	Lv.	Term.

400 ... 8¹

REPORT AT 4:00 A.M.
LEAVE DEPOT AT 4:10 A.M.

401 ... 8⁰

402 ... 8¹

403 ... 8¹

404 ... 7⁵

405 ... 7⁵

406 ... 8²

407 ... 8¹

408 ... 8²

409 ... 7⁵

410 ... 8³

411 ... 8¹

412 ... 7⁵

413 ... 7⁵

414 ... 8³

415 ... 7⁵

416 ... 8²

417 ... 8⁴

418 ... 7⁵

419 ... 7⁵

420 ... 8²

421 ... 7⁵

422 ... 7⁵

423 ... 8¹

424 ... 8⁴

425 ... 7⁵

426 ... 8²

427 ... 7⁵

428 ... 8²

434 ... 8⁵

435 ... 8¹

436 ... 8²

437 ... 8²

438 ... 8⁰

439 ... 8²

440 ... 8¹

441 ... 8⁰

442 ... 8⁰

Supervisors' Timetable for the Kedzie Avenue Line: 1924					
Run No.	South Terminal	Terminal	47th	Van Buren	Milwaukee
544	47th		7:28½	7:55½	8:17½
550	67th	7:18	7:30	7:57	8:19
610	22nd	7:46½		7:57½	Depot
528	22nd	7:47½		7:58½	Depot
512	67th	7:20½	7:32½	7:59½	8:21½
547	22nd	7:49		8:00	Depot

depending on street traffic. Schedule-makers also took into account union contracts of CSL crew members; starting and quitting times of schools, offices, and factories along a route; the weather; season of the year; the type of vehicle assigned to the route; capacity of terminals to handle the cars scheduled; the availability of manpower at each operating carbarn; and the financial ability of the Surface Lines to provide service. CSL had its own quota of "franchise runs" required by city ordinance (the Through Routes), and schedule-makers had to see that enough cars were assigned to the Through Routes to comply with ordinance requirements. In the case of one-man cars there were the orders of the Illinois Public Utilities Commission (later Illinois Commerce Commission), which also had jurisdiction over the general level of CSL service.

It seems a paradox, but one easily understood, that CSL could provide its fastest service in places where the fewest riders wanted service. CSL had quite a bit of private right-of-way and side-of-the-road operation, but these tracks were located at the far end of such lines as Argo, 63rd, Stony Island, Cottage Grove, Riverdale, Halsted, and Hegewisch, where traffic was comparatively light. But as the cars got closer to the city center their tracks shifted to city streets, and the cars fought a losing battle with traffic congestion.

All cars approaching the Loop from the North or West had to pass one final barrier that delayed many of them: the Chicago River. Chicago's early growth was largely the result of its port on Lake Michigan. Inbound traffic included lumber, iron, manufactured goods, and passengers. Grain was the principal outbound commodity. By 1869 as many as 300 ships arrived at Chicago within a 12 hour period. The ships passed through many swing

• Above. New Pullman 949 climbs a steep grade as it emerges from the south portal of the LaSalle Street tunnel on LaSalle near Randolph. This portal has been sealed, and the street paved over. Barney Neuberger collection. • Opposite page. Outbound Clark Street cable train, at right, takes the curve at Randolph and LaSalle while inbound two-car Clybourn Ave. train reaches the south portal of the LaSalle tunnel. Absence of Lake St. "L" structure dates this photo prior to October, 1894. David R. Phillips collection.

bridges to get to the warehouses, lumber yards, and grain elevators that lined the banks of the Chicago River. While they passed, pedestrians, wagon drivers, and horse car crews waited and fumed in lines 1,000 feet long.

The answer was to build tunnels under the river. The Washington Street Tunnel was the first, completed in 1867 after several failures. Although the approaches were single bores, the river section had three tubes, two for vehicles and one for pedestrians. It was 1,520 feet long, including approaches. On August 12, 1890 the Madison and Milwaukee lines of the West Chicago Street Railroad began to use the tunnel, to the exclusion of other traffic.

The LaSalle Street Tunnel was the next to be built, opening in 1871. Its triple tubes accommodated two streams of wagon traffic and a single pedestrian walkway. On March 23, 1888 cable cars began to run in the vehicular tubes, which were restricted against all other traffic from that date. The total length of the tunnel was 1,887 feet. Three lines of the North Chicago Street Rail-

road — Clybourn, Lincoln-Wells, and Clark — used the LaSalle Tunnel.

Built between 1890 and 1894 by the West Chicago Street Railroad, the Van Buren Tunnel was the only one of the three constructed as a cable car facility from the start. It was also the last to open, on March 4, 1894. Including approaches it was 1,517 feet long. The West Chicago's Blue Island and Halsted routes used it.

The bed of the Chicago River was some 18 feet above the top of the three tunnels when they were built. As part of a sewage disposal project, the flow of the Chicago River was reversed in 1900. Dredging the river to lower the bed enough to aid the reverse flow caused the tunnels to stick up above the river bed. In 1904 Congress declared all three to be hazards to navigation. With the end of cable car operations in 1906, the tunnels were closed: Van Buren on July 22, Washington on August 19, and LaSalle on October 21. While they stood empty the three tunnels were replaced by new tunnels which dipped further under the river. The Washington and

● Though taken near the end of the LaSalle tunnel's life, this CTA photo shows it to be in remarkably good condition. View is from the south portal. ● Opposite page. These Board of Supervising Engineers drawings show a section through the dock walls and various sections and elevations of the pump house which kept the LaSalle Street tunnel dry. These drawings are of the new 1912 tunnel. From a BOSE report.

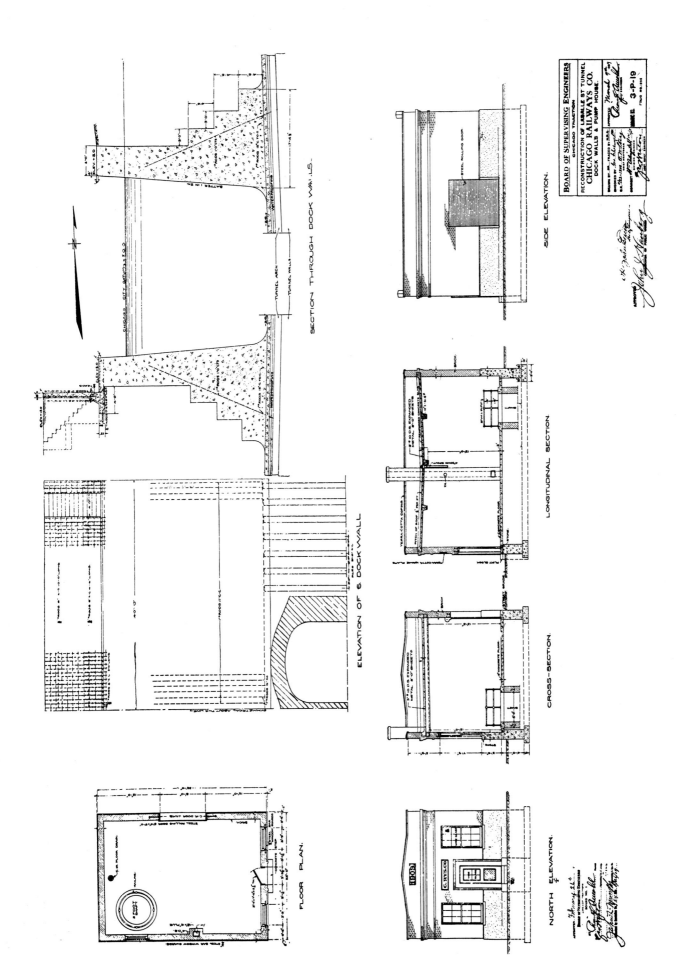

SECTION THROUGH DOCK WALLS.

ELEVATION OF S. DOCK WALL.

FLOOR PLAN.

NORTH ELEVATION.

SIDE ELEVATION.

LONGITUDINAL SECTION.

CROSS-SECTION.

BOARD OF SUPERVISING ENGINEERS
CHICAGO TRACTION
RECONSTRUCTION OF LASALLE ST TUNNEL
CHICAGO RAILWAYS CO.
DOCK WALLS & PUMP HOUSE.

3-P-19

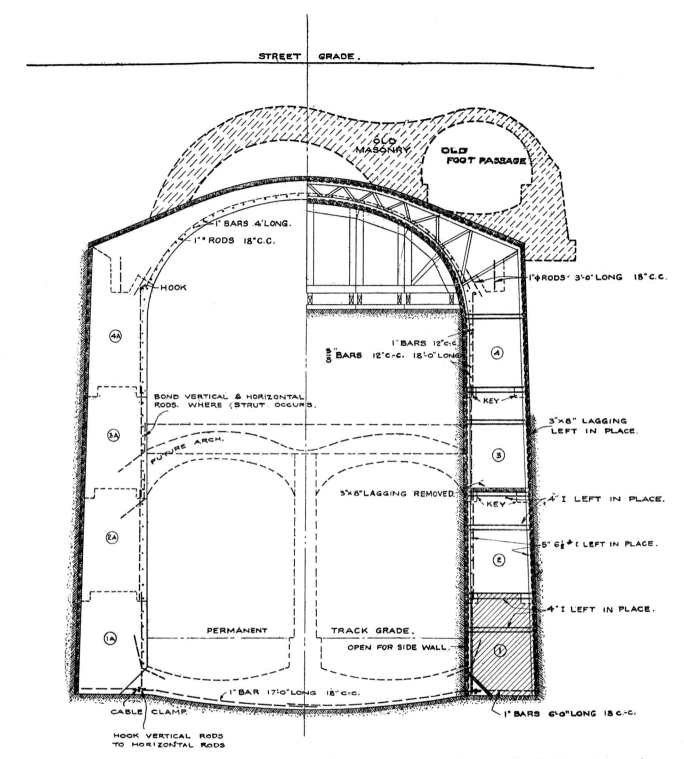

This BOSE drawing shows how the old Washington Street tunnel was underpinned while the new tunnel was built. The original Washington tunnel was built in 1867 for vehicles and pedestrians, and was later used by cable cars. The new tunnel opened on January 29, 1911.

Opposite page. Plan, profile and cross sections of the new LaSalle Street tunnel plainly show its relation to the old tunnel, built in 1871 for wagon and pedestrian traffic and used exclusively by pedestrians and cable cars starting March 23, 1888. Note that different scales are used for horizontal and vertical distances on the profile.

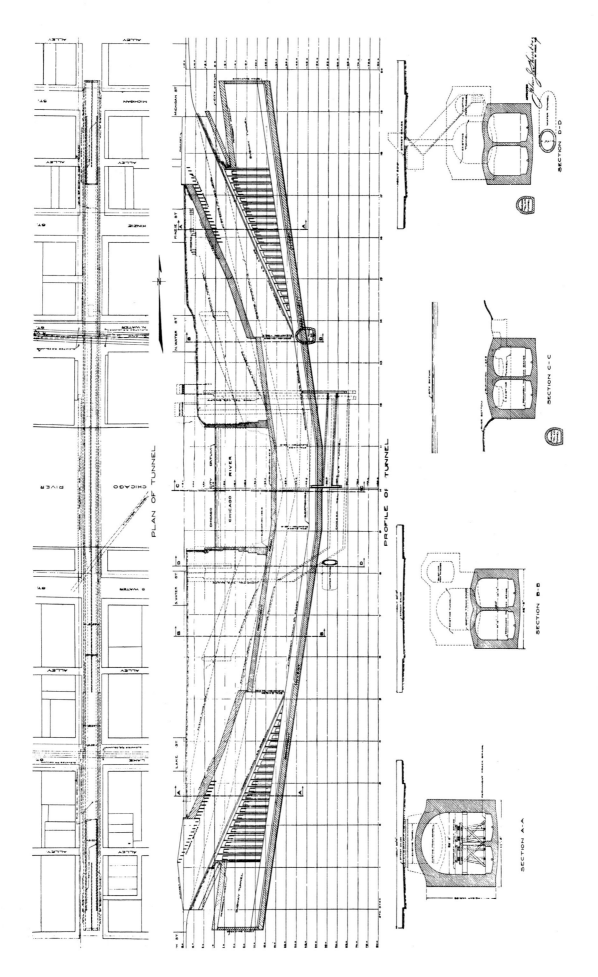

PLAN OF TUNNEL

PROFILE OF TUNNEL

SECTION A-A

SECTION B-B

SECTION C-C

SECTION D-D

213

Van Buren tunnels were built under the existing tunnels. See drawings on pages 212, 214, 215, and 217 for details.

The LaSalle Tunnel was completely new and built elsewhere, in a drydock, then floated into place on the river. On April 2, 1911 the new steel tubes were lowered into a trench at the bottom of the river. Built of steel plate, the twin 278-foot long tubes were gently guided into place, then filled with water to sink them. Cables from barges anchored to each riverbank guided the descent, which was aided by the complete absence of a current in the river. Seven hours earlier the dams at Lockport had been closed, bringing the river to a halt.

Each tube weighed about 3,000 tons, and was large enough to accommodate a Chicago "L" car. The tubes came to rest against headings on each shore. Work began at once to connect the tubes to these headings, and the tunnel opened for regular service on July 21, 1912. Among the routes using the tunnel were the Broadway local, Clark local, Clybourn, Lincoln-Bowmanville, Lincoln-Rosehill, Riverview, and Larrabee. The last lines to use the tunnel were the Lincoln Avenue routes, which were rerouted over the Wells Street Bridge on November 27, 1939. Today the tunnel still exists, although the south portal has been sealed. The north portal was used as an entrance in building the Dearborn Street rapid transit subway, and remains open today.

Provisions were made to link the LaSalle Tunnel with

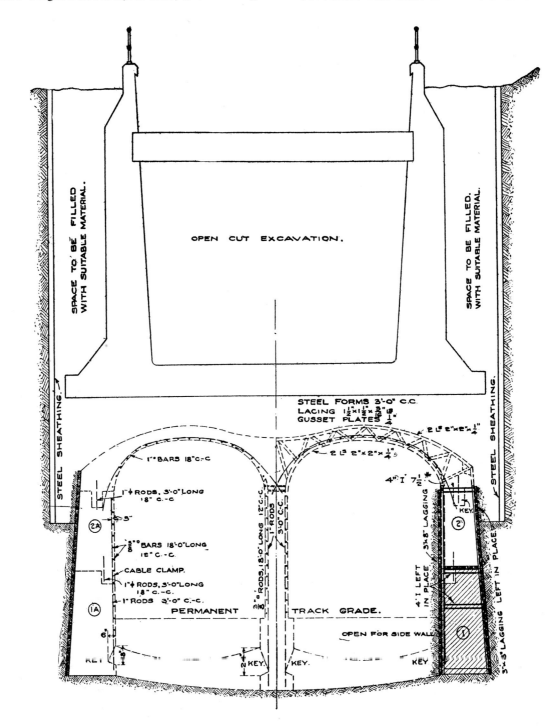

streetcar subways on both sides of the river. The permanent grade of the tunnel approaches was three per cent, but concrete struts across the walls of the subway brought the tracks up to the portals on a nine per cent grade. The streetcar subways were never built, and until the end of service in 1939 cars climbed out of the tunnel on these "temporary" ramps.

The Milwaukee and Madison routes were the primary users of the Washington tunnel, which re-opened on January 29, 1911 after rebuilding. Like the LaSalle Street Tunnel, the re-built Washington bore was designed for eventual connection with a downtown streetcar subway. Cars ran up steep nine per cent grades at either end, carried above the subway invert by falsework. Two-car trains ran through the tunnel regularly on both the Madison and Milwaukee routes, and to limit their speed timing circuits were installed. They were not block signals but simple timers. When a motorman braked his car so that he passed only green timing lights, he was holding his speed down to a safe 8 to 11 mph.

The Van Buren Tunnel opened for streetcar service in June, 1910, and was used primarily by Blue Island streetcars. On May 22, 1915 the tunnel was again closed, this time to lower its west approaches so that they would clear the baggage subways of the new Union Station to be built on the west bank of the river. The tunnel re-opened on May 14, 1916, but was closed again to regular traffic on September 14, 1924, when the Blue

Island cars were rerouted via the Monroe Street bridge. The tunnel was maintained for use in emergencies, and when bridges were open. It was also used by car 1466 in training runs for new CSL operating employees. All service through the tunnel ended March 11, 1952. The west portal of the Van Buren tunnel has been sealed, and the Sears Tower now stands where the east portal used to be.

It is also hard to find evidence of the Washington tunnel, although it, too, still exists under the river. The east portal was sealed in 1954, and the west portal, though still open, is hidden under the viaduct which carries North Western Station over Washington Street.

A 1917 study declared that the maximum safe capacity of the tunnels was 120 cars per hour in one direction. This was calculated by assuming the following conditions: a car entering one of the tunnels at 10 mph runs away on the downgrade and loses both its brakes and its electric power. (If only the brakes failed, the motorman could still stop the car by reversing the motors.) With cars entering the tunnel at a uniform rate of one every 30 seconds, a runaway car could not overtake the car ahead of it.

In theory this worked out well, because in 1917 none of the three tunnels was scheduled to take more than 108 cars an hour in the same direction. But in practice schedules were often disrupted, causing bunching of cars with as many as four at one time making the same ascent

• Opposite page. This cross section shows the open cut excavating technique and the reinforced concrete walls in the open approaches to the new Washington Street tunnel. The open approaches were only temporary, as the plan was to link the streetcar subways with new subways under Loop streets. However, these other subways were never built. • Below. Cross section under the bed of the Chicago River shows how the new Washington Street tunnel was driven below and through the existing tunnel. The pneumatic tunneling method (under air pressure) was used in building this portion of the tunnel. Both drawings from a BOSE report.

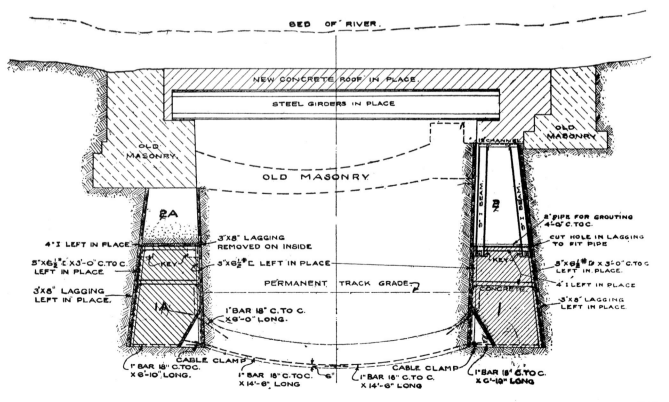

or descent. In any case, no serious accidents seem to have happened in the tunnels.

Through the years various plans were put forward to link the tunnels with streetcar subways. In its report to the City Council of October 29, 1913, the Board of Supervising Engineers recommended a U-shaped streetcar subway. Entering the Loop via the Washington Tunnel, it would have continued under Washington to Michigan, south under Michigan to Jackson, west under Jackson to Franklin, south under Franklin to the Van Buren tunnel, and then under the river. The 1913 report also recommended a north-south streetcar subway under Clark from North Avenue to 19th Street. This would have used a new Clark Tunnel under the river.

As late as 1946 a modification of the 1913 plan was proposed. Under the 1946 plan the Washington Tunnel would have been part of a Washington Street subway between Clinton Street west of the river and a terminal loop in Grant Park on the east edge of the Loop. The Van Buren river tunnel was to connect with a Jackson subway via a tunnel under Franklin Street. Like the Washington line, the Jackson subway was to run east to a loop in Grant Park.

Starting from street level at Clinton, cars using the Washington route would have dipped some 65 feet below street level under the river, then risen on a three per cent grade, barely clearing the top of the proposed low-level Wells Street rapid transit subway. Just east of Wells the line would have climbed to 25 feet below street level, and continued at this level to a loop in Grant Park north of Washington.

From street level at Clinton the cars using the Jackson subway would have also dropped some 65 feet below street level to cross under the river, then risen on a 4.1 per cent grade to clear the proposed low-level Wells Street rapid transit subway. Continuing their climb on a gentle 0.5 per cent slope, the cars would have reached 25 feet below street level at Clark, continuing at this level to a loop south of Jackson in Grant Park.

Each subway was to have two tracks, with continuous side platforms from Wells to Michigan to facilitate loading. At Clark and at State both streetcar subways were to

have passageways linking them to the mezzanine ticketing level of the Dearborn and State Street rapid transit subways. (The Dearborn, State and projected Wells subway were all lower than the streetcar subways.) The Grant Park terminal platforms would have connected with the Illinois Central Railroad's suburban stations: the Washington subway with the Randolph station and the Jackson subway with the Van Buren station.

Lines to be routed through the Washington subway were Milwaukee, Armitage-Downtown, Division-Downtown, Elston, Lake, Madison, and Madison-Fifth. The Jackson subway was to carry the Harrison-Adams, Ogden, Van Buren, Blue Island, Ashland-Downtown, and Roosevelt-Downtown routes. Both streetcar subways were designed with bulkheads placed at strategic points in anticipation of eventual conversion to bus operation. Before conversion the bulkheads would have been removed and fans and air shafts installed for ventilation. The Chicago Department of Subways and Superhighways estimated the cost of building and equipping both subways at $20 million in 1947.

Between 1913 and 1946 several transit studies had recommended building streetcar subways in one form or another. What killed the streetcar subways was their exclusion from the crucial 1938 agreement between the City and the Public Works Administration. In 1938 the PWA made an initial grant of $18 million for subway construction in Chicago. By 1948 the Federal share had been raised to $26 million (both figures represented 45 per cent of the estimated cost of the initial or first-stage subway system).

Without Federal funding the idea of the streetcar subways faded away. However, CTA did revive the idea of a Jackson subway in the mid-1950's. This time it was to be a high-level rapid transit subway, connecting with the Eisenhower Expressway median strip rapid transit line near Halsted and extending across the Loop under Jackson to a terminal loop in Grant Park. It was estimated to cost some $20 million. CTA also revived the idea of a Washington subway at this time. It would have been a high-level bus subway from Canal Street to Michigan Avenue. CTA estimated its cost at $15 million.

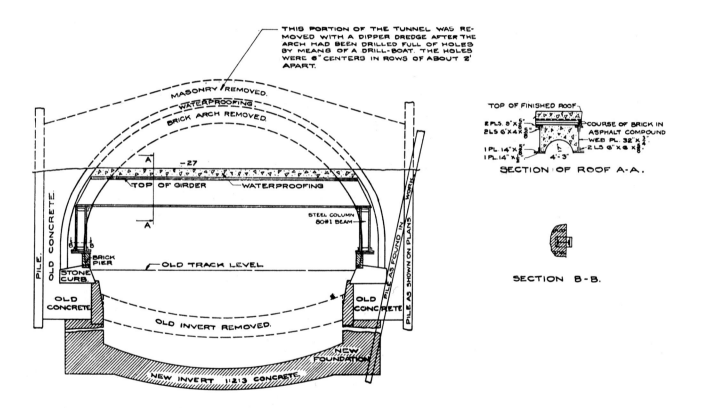

Like the new Washington Street Tunnel, the new Van Buren bore was built under and through an existing streetcar tunnel. This cross section under the bed of the Chicago River shows how the old tunnel roof was sliced off, the old invert removed, and a new concrete invert poured. The building of all three new tunnels was made necessary by a Federal ruling that held the old tunnels to be hazards to navigation. From a BOSE report.

Opposite page. Although the destination sign indicates that this postwar PCC car is westbound on the Madison Street line, it is actually rising from the east portal of the Washington Street Tunnel at Washington and Franklin Streets. As late as 1947 plans were under consideration to connect this tunnel with a subway under Washington Street that would have terminated in Grant Park. CTA photo.

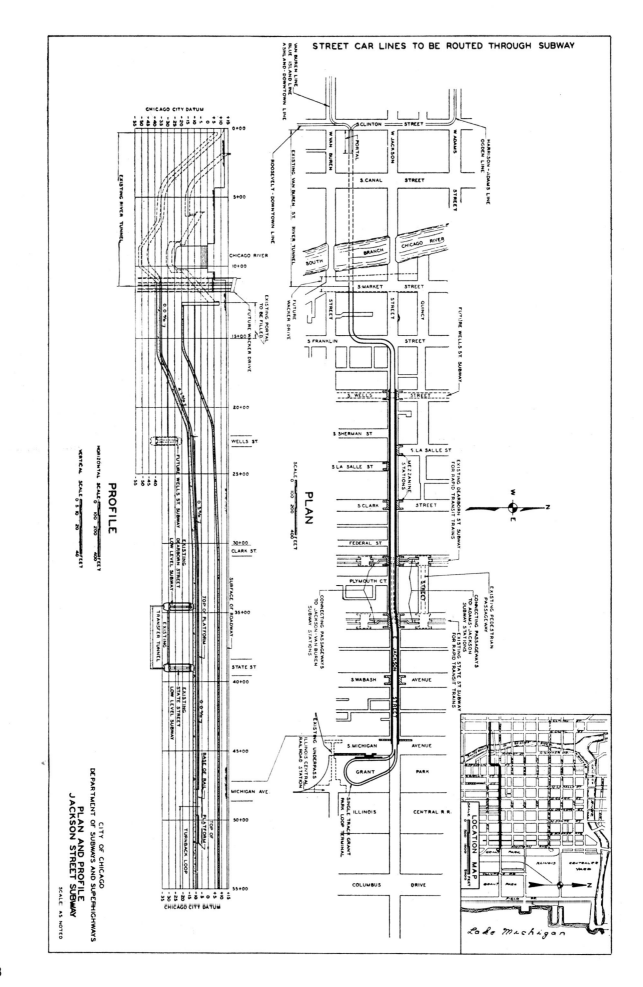

STREET CAR LINES TO BE ROUTED THROUGH SUBWAY

PLAN

PROFILE

HORIZONTAL SCALE

VERTICAL SCALE

CITY OF CHICAGO
DEPARTMENT OF SUBWAYS AND SUPERHIGHWAYS
PLAN AND PROFILE
JACKSON STREET SUBWAY
SCALE AS NOTED

LOCATION MAP

Lake Michigan

218

• Above. In 1958 the Chicago Transit Authority proposed a high level, rapid transit subway under Jackson Blvd. from a connection with the Eisenhower median strip rapid transit line near Halsted to a loop under Grant Park. The drawing shows it crossing the State Street subway. CTA drawing. • Opposite page. In 1947 the Department of Subways and Superhighways of the City of Chicago prepared this drawing of a streetcar subway under Jackson Blvd. from a connection with the Van Buren Street Tunnel to a loop in Grant Park. • Below. In 1958 the CTA proposed a bus subway under Washington St. from Canal to Michigan Ave. It was never built.

Where the cars and buses ran

Archer Avenue

We pick up the story of this major line in 1906. Back then it was an electric streetcar route from Archer and Cicero on Chicago's Southwest Side to State and Lake in the Loop. The downtown loop was a clockwise operation via Lake, Wabash, and Randolph.

In December, 1917, CSL routed the Archer cars into an off-street terminal at Archer and Cicero. For many years this was a joint terminal with the interurban cars of the Chicago & Joliet Electric Railway. To clear up downtown congestion, Archer cars were rerouted to loop via Polk, Dearborn, and Lake on August 14, 1924.

One of CSL's first extension bus routes opened June 25, 1934 along Archer from the Cicero terminal west to Neva Ave. No further changes were made in Archer service until CSL began express bus service October 21, 1946 between State and Wacker and 64th and Keating. CTA replaced the streetcars — and the extension buses — with local buses on May 30, 1948. Some track on Archer remained in service for the Ashland-Downtown and Halsted-Downtown routes.

Archer-38th Street

Transit service on this route began in 1887, when horse cars started to run from 38th and Kedzie to Wabash and Lake via 38th, Archer, State, Madison, Wabash, Lake, and State. The horse cars were hauled behind cable cars on State from Archer to downtown. Streetcars replaced the horse cars in 1894, and the line was extended from Kedzie to Central Park in 1898. In 1906 a new downtown loop was begun via Lake, Wabash, Randolph, and State.

On September 14, 1924 cars got another downtown routing via the Polk, Dearborn, Lake, and State loop. The line was cut back to a shuttle only between Archer and Central Park on December 12, 1930, although some rush hour trips to downtown were restored on September 16, 1931. All service ended February 15, 1948.

Argo

CSL began what became Argo service on July 10, 1904 between Archer and Cicero and 63rd and Central via Cicero and 63rd. On January 3, 1911 the line was extended via Central and 63rd Place to 63rd Place and Archer (Argo). Thus Archer became both the east and west terminal for this "L"-shaped line.

Opposite page. Both the United States Courthouse and the Brill streetcar are long gone, but both were important parts of life in Chicago when this photo was taken. View is northeast up La Salle from the corner of Jackson Blvd. David R. Phillips.

On October 1, 1929 Argo cars were cut back and ran only from Oak Park west to Archer. The Cicero branch became a separate route. West 63rd buses replaced all Argo service on April 11, 1948.

Armitage Avenue

This North Side crosstown line was a streetcar shuttle connecting with Milwaukee Ave. cars until 1906. The new route was from Armitage and Kostner via Armitage, Milwaukee, and Clinton to a downtown loop via Randolph, State, and Washington. In 1912 the line was extended west on Armitage to Cicero, and on March 29, 1914 the downtown loop was changed. The new route was via Milwaukee, Desplaines, Washington, Dearborn, Randolph, State, and Washington.

On June 19, 1914, a new east Armitage route was established. It connected with the other Armitage line, but instead of running down Milwaukee it ran east on Armitage from Campbell. When it came to the west side of the Chicago River it jogged over to Paulina, Cortland, and Racine before resuming its run on Armitage to Clark. The east terminal was a loop via Clark, Menominee, and Wells.

The west line (downtown) cars were extended west along Armitage to Grand on August 15, 1914. A new downtown loop for these cars via Washington, Franklin, and Randolph went into service September 1, 1920. Franklin replaced Dearborn as the west leg of the loop. In the general rerouting of 1924, the downtown loop was again changed, this time to a clockwise loop via Washington, Dearborn, Madison, and Clinton. In a cost-cutting move, Armitage-Downtown Sunday service was ended May 1, 1932.

One-man cars went into service on the east route April 1, 1923. On February 2, 1925 east route cars were extended west along Armitage to Grand, which was also the terminal for the west line (downtown) cars.

On February 26, 1951, buses took over the section east of the Chicago River from Southport and Cortland to a new loop at Ogden and Lincoln. On June 24, 1951 the remaining Armitage trolley line west of the Chicago River was converted to bus from Cortland and Southport to a new western terminal via Cicero, Cortland, and Lamon. Armitage-Downtown cars were also discontinued on this date.

Ashland Avenue (Through Route 9)

This north-south trunk route began as three separate lines, which took many years to unite. There was a North Side line originating at Irving Park and Ashland which ran downtown via Lincoln, Armitage, Clark, and Wells. A middle section ran from Cermak and Ashland north to Cortland and Ashland via Ashland, Roosevelt, Paulina, Lake, and Ashland. The south segment ran

• Above. Car 5371, westbound on the Argo line, stops before crossing the Indiana Harbor Belt tracks near the west end of the Argo line. Conductor will drop off front platform to flag the car across the railroad tracks. Neuberger collection photo. • Below. From 1895 to 1906 Archer Avenue electric streetcars were hauled behind State Street cable car trains from Archer and State to a loop via Madison, Wabash, and Lake to State. In this photo all but one two-car cable train has an Archer streetcar in tow. Photo from David R. Phillips.

• Above. Two one-man cars at the end of the Armitage Avenue line near Grand and Armitage. Armitage was one of the first CSL lines to be equipped with one-man cars on April 1, 1923. They ran at first on the east section between Campbell (Milwaukee Ave.) and Clark, which was a separate route at that time. On February 2, 1925 the east route cars were extended along Armitage to Grand Ave., which was also the terminal for the west line (Armitage-Downtown) cars. Neuberger photo. • Below. Car 5372 eastbound on the rural Argo route. Neuberger collection.

● Above. Chicago Union Traction car 5798 ran on the middle section of the Ashland line from Cortland and Ashland to Ashland and Archer via Ashland, Lake, Paulina, Roosevelt, and Ashland. Note the Ashland & Paulina route sign. Chicago Transit Authority photograph. ● Below. Two CCRy standard Brills pass on the Ashland line at 74th Street. Although the near car is almost empty, it is running all the way to the end of the line at 95th and Ashland. Western Ave. PCCs used this part of Ashland on runs from the 69th Street carbarn to 79th.

• Top. Experimental car 7001 ran in August, 1936 on Ashland to celebrate the opening of the Chicago River bridge. R. H. Kennedy photo from A. C. Williams. • Middle. The light North Ashland line was among the first to receive one-man cars on April 1, 1923. On August 21, 1936 the North Ashland line was absorbed into Ashland as the route used by alternate Ashland cars. R. H. Kennedy photo from A. C. Williams. • Below. Former Chicago & Interurban Traction Crete suburban car 5651 runs north on Ashland at 47th Street. Originally single-end cars on the C&IT, they were rebuilt into PAYE cars after the CCRy acquired them in 1912. Barney Neuberger photo.

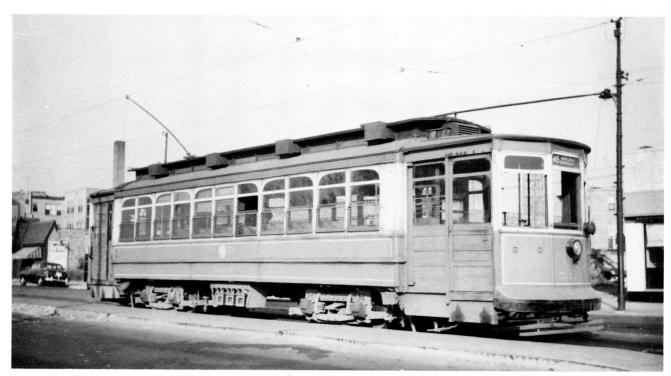

• Above. One of the first PAYE cars to run on the CCRy, car 5377 nears the end of its career running as a CTA-owned vehicle on route 45, Ashland-Downtown. This Neuberger photo from the Railway Negative Exchange shows it at the 95th Street terminal. • Opposite page, top. Former C&IT Crete suburban car 5657 signed for Ashland-Archer (Ashland-Downtown) near the 95th Street terminal. Neuberger collection. • Middle. West end of the Belmont line at Belmont and Central with New Pullman 1027 loading passengers. CTA photo. • Bottom. Pressed Steel car 714 at the west end of the Blue Island-26th Street route at 26th and Kenton Ave. Designed for operation through streetcar subways that were never built, the Pressed Steel cars in the 701-750 series ran out their days on the Blue Island-26th line. Neuberger photo. • This page, below. A bright afternoon sun throws all of car 5661's detail into strong relief as it awaits its departure time at 95th and Ashland for a run on the Ashland-Archer (Ashland-Downtown) route. None of the cars in the 5661-5665 series lasted long enough to run under CTA management. Neuberger photo from Bill Richmond.

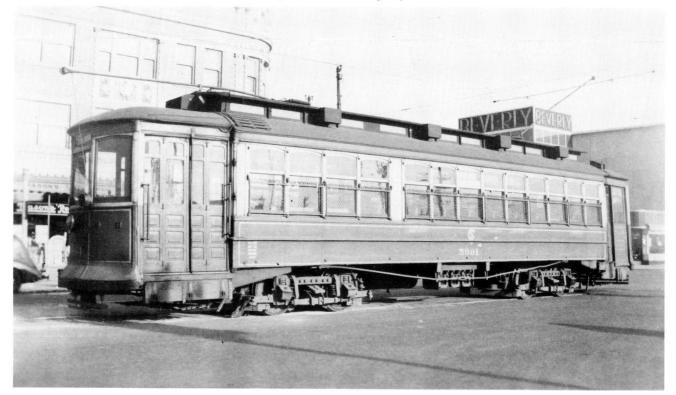

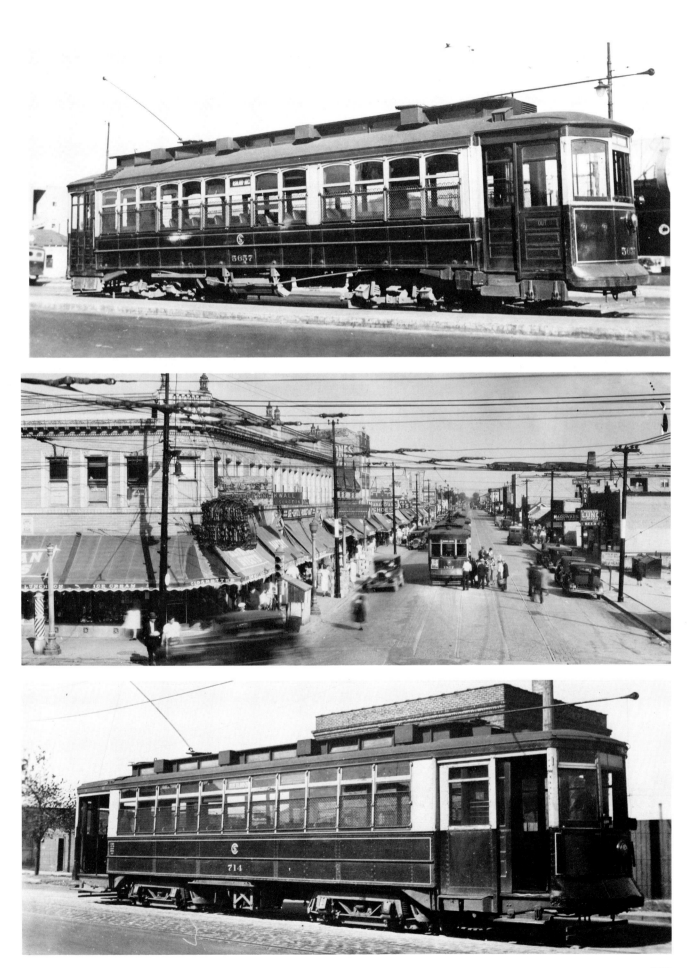

north from 70th and Ashland to State and Lake via Ashland, Archer, and State.

In 1896 the gap between Cermak and Archer was closed when the middle section was extended. But it wasn't until September 4, 1908 that cars were through routed between 70th and Ashland and Cortland and Ashland via the south and middle segments. On the same day the middle section was extended to Clybourn and Southport via Cortland and Southport, crossing the Chicago River on Cortland. On October 16, 1912 the line was extended up Southport to Clark. The 1908 changes created an Ashland-Downtown route via Archer, which was the original south segment route.

On the north segment, the cars were cut back from downtown to Lincoln and Wrightwood on February 1, 1889. By July, 1913, service was again cut back, this time to Belmont and Ashland.

Meanwhile the cars on the through-routed portion, including downtown cars, were extended south along Ashland from 70th to 71st on November 23, 1908. On October 12, 1913 service was extended south to 74th. A South Ashland shuttle line went into operation from 74th to 79th on February 18, 1915. On December 31, 1915 shuttle cars began to run to 87th. On November 1, 1916 the shuttle car route from 74th to 87th was absorbed into the through route, with service from Southport and Clark to 87th and Ashland.

On the North Side route, service was extended a mile south from Belmont to Fullerton on March 20, 1915. A further south extension, to Clybourn, opened October 1, 1917. N. Ashland became a one-man line April 1, 1923.

As part of the 1924 general rerouting, Ashland-Downtown cars began looping via State, Polk, Dearborn, and Lake on September 14. This loop replaced the loop via State, Lake, Wabash, and Randolph used since 1906. On February 1, 1926 Ashland cars were extended to 89th, and on July 6 to 95th. As a cost-cutting measure, CSL discontinued Ashland-Downtown Sunday cars on May 1, 1932.

On August 21, 1936 CSL consolidated the north and south routes. Half the cars used the old North Ashland route via Ashland, Irving Park, and Southport to Southport and Clark. The other half used Cortland and Southport to Southport and Clark. The consolidation ended nearly two decades of parallel operation by the Ashland and North Ashland cars just two blocks from each other on Southport and Ashland.

On August 31, 1947 CSL abandoned the Cortland routing, sending all cars via Ashland, Irving Park, and Southport to Southport and Clark. On May 11, 1952 CTA began weekend bus service on both the main line and the downtown branch, with some slight route changes. The weekday downtown streetcar got a longer loop when Kinzie replaced Lake as the north leg on November 16, 1953. The entire route was switched to bus on February 13, 1954.

Car 3134 got its nickname as a "Broadway-State" car because of its assignment to that route. In this photo it is running on the Broadway-State Through Route, about to change ends just south of 79th Street on State. Until the postwar PCC cars took over this line, 79th was a regular short-turn destination. Neuberger collection.

Austin Avenue

CSL began gas bus service over this North Side line from the Wabansia, Mason and North loop to Higgins via Austin on September 6, 1942. On January 9, 1944 the line was cut back from Higgins to Gunnison, and rerouted via Gunnison and Nagle to a loop at Higgins and Foster. The last change under CSL management came on August 15, 1946, when service was extended north on Nagle to a loop via Milwaukee and Haft (near Milwaukee and Devon).

Bell & Howell

The line opened December 1, 1942 as an extension of the Kedzie car line from Catalpa (near Bryn Mawr) and Kedzie to Peterson and Kedzie. Four days later the line

Pressed Steel car 718, outbound on the Blue Island-26th line, running westbound on Adams Street on the fringe of the Loop. Barney Neuberger photo from the Railway Negative Exchange.

Sun Parlor 3201, northbound on the Broadway route at State and Wacker Drive, is bound for the outer terminal at Devon and Kedzie. This car was once fitted with experimental multiple-unit equipment. Neuberger collection photo.

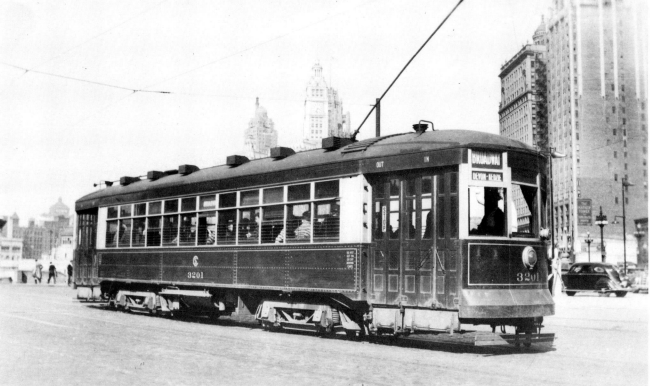

was extended to give rush hour service to the Bell & Howell plant. Routing was via Peterson, Lincoln, Kedzie, Devon, and McCormick to the Bell and Howell plant at Lunt and McCormick.

On June 30, 1943 buses were rerouted to a south terminal loop via Kedzie, Bryn Mawr, Kimball, and Peterson. CSL discontinued the circular terminal routing and sent rush hour buses to a new south loop via Peterson, Christiana, Thorndale, Kimball, and Peterson on October 1, 1945.

This was the last change made in the route under CSL management.

Belmont Avenue

This North Side crosstown route opened July 6, 1895 between Halsted and Milwaukee. During some period in their early history, Belmont cars ran via Halsted and Clark to the Limits carhouse, where they connected with Clark cable cars for downtown Chicago. On June 25, 1914 service was extended west two blocks to Pulaski, and on January 2, 1917 one mile west to Cicero. A third extension, a mile west from Cicero to Central, opened December 7, 1924. The streetcar part of the line was now at its maximum length.

On April 17, 1930 CSL inaugurated extension bus service from Central to Harlem. Trolley buses replaced the gas buses on the extension from Parkside (near Central) to Harlem on May 30, 1931, and were through-routed beyond Harlem to Pacific on a one mile extension of the line. On September 16, 1935 the trolley buses began to use a new east terminal at Parkside, on the south side of the street.

CTA substituted trolley buses for streetcars on the east part of the route from Halsted to Central on January 9, 1949. The change required a new loop terminal at Halsted. On the west end a new terminal opened at Cumberland, a half-mile west of the old terminal at Pacific. Parkside and Pacific terminals were taken out of service and a new short terminal opened at Octavia.

There was also an east Belmont route, inaugurated by CSL on February 17, 1947. It ran from a loop via Clark, School, Wilton, via Belmont to a loop via Lake Shore, Briar, and Sheridan. No change was made in this route under CSL management.

Blue Island-26th

We pick up the story of this major Southwest Side line on July 22, 1906, when streetcars took over from cable cars along the entire route. Streetcars had been running as feeders to the cable line from Cicero to Leavitt on 26th, with the cable cars running from Leavitt to Dearborn and Adams. The line also got a new route that

Opposite page. The Broadway-State Through Route wasn't established until June 29, 1923. But State Street was busy enough with its own cars and with the West Side cars. Kaufman & Fabry photo.

bypassed the Van Buren Tunnel used by the cable cars. The new route was from Cicero and 26th via 26th, Blue Island, Harrison, Clinton, Van Buren, Dearborn, Adams, Franklin, and Van Buren.

In June, 1910 the streetcars went back to the tunnel route via Clinton, Van Buren Tunnel, Franklin, Van Buren, Dearborn, Adams, and Franklin. CSL cut back the west end of the line from Cicero to Kenton on May 21, 1917.

On January 29, 1922 the downtown loop was revised again via Van Buren Tunnel, Franklin, Monroe, Dearborn, Adams, and Franklin. Blue Island-26th streetcars made their last regular runs through the Van Buren Tunnel on September 13, 1924. The next day, as part of a general rerouting, they began to run via Clinton, Monroe, Dearborn, Adams, and Clinton.

CTA discontinued weekend streetcar service on September 3, 1949, replacing the cars with buses and moving the terminal three short blocks east to Kostner. When CTA eliminated all streetcar service on the line May 11, 1952, the replacement buses ran to Kostner only.

Blue Island-Wells (Through Route 12)

This route linked the near North Side with the near Southwest side. It began at Blue Island and Western and ran to North and Clark via Blue Island, Harrison, Clinton, Adams, Wells, and North. On August 16, 1912 the line was extended west on 26th to Kenton. As part of a general rerouting the line was discontinued September 14, 1924.

Broadway

In 1906 this North Side trunk route ran from Clark and Howard at the city limits to a loop in downtown Chicago via Clark, Devon, Broadway, Clark, Randolph, LaSalle, Monroe, Dearborn, and Randolph. At this time streetcars to north suburban Evanston also ran on the Broadway route from the old Limits carbarn at Drummond and Clark to Central and Bennett in Evanston. The route was the same as the Broadway cars to Howard, then via Chicago, Dempster, Sherman, and Central to Bennett.

On July 24, 1907 the Evanston line was extended west from Bennett to Lincolnwood Dr. On the same day a single-track extension line known as the North Shore & Western Railway began service via Lincolnwood and Harrison to the Glenview Golf Club west of the Chicago River.

The local Broadway cars and the Evanston service to Lincolnwood Dr. were operated by the Chicago Union Traction Company, a Yerkes property. The track north of Irving Park was owned by the Chicago Consolidated Traction Company. (The North Shore & Western was owned by some men with a stake in the golf club) On February 25, 1908 CUT was reorganized as Chicago Railways Company. On December 27, 1910 Chicago Railways sold its suburban lines to the County Traction Company. At midnight on that date the track connection between the Broadway line, still under CRys, and the Evanston line was cut at Clark and Howard. Through passengers had to walk across a 30-foot gap in the track from the Evanston cars, now in local Evanston service only under County Traction, to the Broadway cars, still under Chicago Railways.

Because of a franchise requirement of one of the underlying companies, free transfers from Evanston to Broadway cars were issued starting December 31, 1910. County Traction was split into two companies on August 5, 1913: Evanston Traction and Chicago & West Towns

Railway Co. Evanston Traction became Evanston Bus Company.

On the Broadway local route itself, a new downtown routing via Illinois, LaSalle Street tunnel, Monroe, Dearborn, Randolph, LaSalle tunnel, Illinois and Clark went into operation on July 21, 1912. On January 2, 1918 Broadway cars began to use the terminals at Broadway and Ardmore (off-street loop) and Clark and Arthur (east of the Devon carhouse, not the Schreiber loop) for short turn cars. On January 29, 1922, Madison replaced Monroe as the south leg of the downtown loop,

---

REROUTING
of cars on
CHICAGO SURFACE LINES

Effective

Sunday, September 14, 1924

These changes in street car routes were ordered by the Illinois Commerce Commission in an order handed down June 24, 1924, "to promote the safety, convenience and general welfare of the public."

Issued by the
Chicago Surface Lines
CHICAGO

What Rerouting Does

BY the rerouting of cars in the loop district 20 left-hand turns, 12 right-hand turns and 2 stub terminals are eliminated.

State street, Clark street and Wells street are used for through routing.

Cars from the west side loop back on Dearborn street instead of State street.

Available street space is increased on State, Clark and Wells streets, expediting car movements and helping traffic conditions generally.

The new plan represents the best judgment of traffic engineers and the Illinois Commerce Commission. Although the Surface Lines have spent months getting ready for it, some confusion and inconvenience may reasonably be anticipated in inaugurating such extensive changes in routings. Passengers are urged to be patient and by familiarizing themselves with the new routes, to cooperate in maintaining orderly, efficient service.

CHICAGO SURFACE LINES,

President

A map showing the rerouting of cars in the loop district may be obtained by writing to the Chicago Surface Lines, 231 South La Salle Street

and Clark replaced Dearborn as the east leg of the loop.

Broadway-Wabash service began December 18, 1922 from the Broadway and Ardmore terminal to 18th and Wabash via Broadway, Clark, Division, State, Lake, and Wabash. The Broadway-State route replaced Broadway-Wabash on June 29, 1923. The new route was south on State from Divison to 18th. On September 14, 1924 Broadway-State was discontinued, and the Broadway cars took a new route via State, Lake, Wabash, Harrison, and State.

On the North end of the line, Broadway cars were rerouted west on Devon past Clark to Kedzie on July 10, 1932. On August 19, 1937 Broadway cars were through routed with State cars to form a new Broadway-State route. This line ran from Devon and Kedzie to 119th and Morgan via Devon, Broadway, Clark, Division, State, 95th, Michigan, 119th, Morgan, 120th, Halsted, and 119th. On May 15, 1939 cars on this route were shifted to run via State, Grand, Wabash, Lake, and State while the State Street bridge over the Chicago River was replaced. The old route over the new bridge was not resumed until May 28, 1949.

THE following are all of the street car routes changed by the order of the Illinois Commerce Commission under date of June 24, 1924. Routes not given here have not been changed and will operate as at present. All of the changes will take effect beginning with the first cars operating on the schedules of Sunday, September 14.

ARCHER AVENUE, ASHLAND AVENUE, WALLACE-RACINE

These lines will operate north on State to Polk, to Dearborn, northbound on Dearborn to Lake, to State, and southbound on State over regular route.

ARMITAGE AVENUE

See under MILWAUKEE AVENUE.

BLUE ISLAND AVENUE

Blue Island cars will operate north on Clinton to Monroe, eastbound on Monroe to Dearborn, to Adams, and westbound on Adams to Clinton, and then over regular route.

Transfer to cars operating on State street at Monroe or Adams streets.

BLUE ISLAND-WELLS—Through Route No. 12

This route will be divided, the west portion being merged with the Blue Island avenue line and the north portion with the Lincoln-Wells line.

BROADWAY

Broadway-Downtown cars will operate south over regular route to Clark and Division, turning on Division to State, to Lake, to Wabash, southbound on Wabash to Harrison, to State, northbound on State to Division, to Clark, and then over regular route.

The Broadway-State route will be merged with the Broadway-Downtown route and will operate to Harrison street.

CHICAGO AVENUE

All Chicago avenue cars will operate to and from terminals east of State street, and service from Chicago avenue to the loop will be given by Halsted and Wentworth cars on Clark street.

CLARK-WENTWORTH

The routes of cars marked "Clark-Wentworth" and "Through Route Number 22" are not changed. Certain cars from the north marked "Clark-Downtown" will turn back at Madison street during the rush hours, operating west to La Salle, north to Illinois, then to Clark. Certain cars marked "Wentworth-Downtown" will operate during the rush hours north on Clark to Illinois, to Wells, to Chicago, to Clark, then south over regular route.

COTTAGE GROVE-BROADWAY — Through Route No. 1
INDIANA-LINCOLN—Through Route No. 3

These routes will operate on Indiana avenue to 18th street, to State, northbound on State to Divi-

sion to Clark and then over regular routes. Southbound Through Route No. 1 will operate as at present. Through Route No. 3 will turn east from Clark on Division to State, south on State to Lake, east on Lake to Wabash and then over regular route.

DIVISION-DOWNTOWN

Division-Downtown cars will operate on Milwaukee to Desplaines, to Randolph, eastbound on Randolph to Dearborn, to Washington, and westbound on Washington to Desplaines, to Milwaukee, and then over regular route.

Transfer to cars operating on State street at Randolph or Washington streets.

ELSTON AVENUE

Elston cars will operate eastbound on Lake street to Dearborn, to Randolph, and westbound on Randolph to Clinton, to Milwaukee and then over regular route.

Transfer to cars operating on State street at Lake or Randolph streets.

FULTON STREET

See under 21st-CANAL.

HALSTED-DOWNTOWN

Halsted-Downtown cars northbound will continue on Clark to Illinois, to Wells, to Chicago, to Clark, and southbound on Clark to Archer.

HARRISON-ADAMS

Harrison-Adams cars will operate east on Adams to Clinton, to Monroe, eastbound on Monroe to Dearborn, to Adams, and westbound on Adams over regular route.

Transfer to cars operating on State street at Monroe or Adams streets.

HARRISON-STATE

Harrison-State cars will operate east on Harrison to Clinton, to Van Buren, eastbound on Van Buren to Dearborn, to Harrison, and westbound on Harrison over regular route.

Transfer to cars operating on State street at Van Buren or Harrison streets.

INDIANA-LINCOLN—Through Route No. 3

See under COTTAGE GROVE-BROADWAY.

LAKE STREET
STATE-LAKE—Through Route No. 16

The Lake street line becomes a part of a new through route marked "State - Lake - Through Route Number 16." Cars will operate east on Lake street to State and south on State to 63rd, returning over the same route. During the morning rush hours certain turnback cars marked "Lake-Downtown" will operate east on Lake to Dearborn, to Randolph, to Clinton, to Lake, and then west. During the evening rush hours certain turnback cars will operate south on State from Grand to Lake and west on Lake from State.

Meanwhile CTA had cut back the thru route from Devon and Kedzie to the Devon carhouse loop via Devon, Ravenswood, Schreiber, and Clark on December 15, 1947. CTA substituted buses for streetcars on weekends over the entire route from Devon to 119th on September 5, 1954. On December 5, 1955 the South Side part of the through route on State Street south of the Loop was discontinued. Weekday Broadway cars and weekend Broadway buses turned back at the south fringe of the Loop via State, Polk, Dearborn, Kinzie, and State. CTA made the final bus substitution for the week-day Broadway streetcars on February 16, 1957.

South California Avenue

This West Side bus route opened December 2, 1945 on California between Fulton and 72nd. The north terminal was a loop via Fulton, Francisco, and Walnut; the south terminal was a loop via 71st, Fairfield, and 72nd. An extension to the line under CTA management brought the line north to a terminal at Sacramento and Chicago

---

LINCOLN-CLARK
LINCOLN-WELLS
These lines will be combined from Center street south, operating south on Wells to Illinois, through the La Salle street tunnel to Madison, to Wells, and north on Wells to Center.

MADISON STREET
Madison cars will operate eastbound on Madison to Dearborn, to Monroe, and westbound on Monroe to Clinton, to Madison, then over regular route.
Transfer to cars operating on State street at Madison or Monroe streets.

MILWAUKEE AVENUE
ARMITAGE AVENUE
Milwaukee avenue and Armitage avenue cars will operate eastbound on Washington street from Desplaines street through the Washington street tunnel to Dearborn, to Madison, and westbound on Madison to Clinton, to Milwaukee, and then over regular route.
Transfer to cars operating on State street at Washington or Madison streets.

OGDEN AVENUE
Ogden avenue cars will operate eastbound on Randolph to Dearborn, to Washington, and westbound on Washington to Desplaines, to Randolph, and then over regular route.
Transfer to cars operating on State street at Randolph or Washington streets.

OGDEN-MADISON-CLARK—Through Route No. 11
This route will be divided, the west portion being merged with the Ogden avenue line and the north portion with the Clark street line.

RIVERVIEW-LARRABEE
Riverview-Larrabee cars will operate southbound as at present to Dearborn and Randolph, then to Wells, to Kinzie, and north over regular route.
Transfer to cars operating on State street at Randolph street.

ROOSEVELT-WELLS-CLARK — Through Route No. 14
This route will be divided, the west portion being merged with the Roosevelt Road line and the north portion with the Clark street line.

SEDGWICK-DEARBORN
See under TAYLOR-WELLS-SHEFFIELD.

SOUTHPORT AVENUE
ASHLAND AVENUE
Service on the north portion of the Southport route will be given by Ashland avenue cars, which will continue north on Southport to Clark street instead of turning back at Clybourn. The downtown portion of the route will be merged with the Clybourn avenue line.

STATE-MADISON—Through Route No. 7
The present service on State street afforded by Through Route No. 7 will be given by cars operating on the new State-Lake—Through Route No. 16. (See under LAKE STREET.)
On Madison street, the service will be given by the necessary cars on the Madison line.

STATE-MILWAUKEE—Through Route No. 6
The present service on State street afforded by Through Route No. 6 will be given by cars operating on the new State-Lake-Through Route No. 16. (See under LAKE STREET.) On Milwaukee avenue the service will be given by the necessary cars on the Milwaukee line.

TAYLOR-WELLS-SHEFFIELD
SEDGWICK-DEARBORN
These routes will be consolidated under the name "Taylor-Sedgwick-Sheffield," and cars will operate southbound on Lincoln to Sedgwick, to Orleans, to Austin, to Wells, and then over regular route to Taylor and Western; northbound on Wells to Kinzie, to Orleans, to Sedgwick, to Lincoln, and then over regular route.
Racine and Webster avenues will be served by cars operating around the loop formed by Webster avenue, Lincoln avenue, Fullerton avenue and Racine avenue, transferring to all connecting lines.

21ST-CANAL
FULTON STREET
These routes will be consolidated under the name "21st-Canal-Fulton," and the cars, starting at Western avenue eastbound, will operate over Fulton to Morgan, to Monroe, to Clinton, to Harrison, to Canal, to Canalport, to Halsted, to 21st, and west on 21st street to Marshall boulevard, returning over the same route.

VAN BUREN STREET
Van Buren cars will operate east on Van Buren to Clinton, to Adams, eastbound on Adams to Dearborn, to Van Buren, and westbound on Van Buren over regular route.
Transfer to cars operating on State street at Adams or Van Buren streets.

WALLACE-RACINE
See under ARCHER AVENUE.

WENTWORTH-CLYBOURN—Through Route No. 2
This route will be divided. The south portion will be merged with Through Route No. 22, providing an increase in the number of trips on that route. The north portion will be merged with the Clybourn avenue route and will operate over that route.

State Street Transfer Points
Transfers to west side lines will be accepted on Dearborn street at those streets where each line loops back.

• Above. Postwar PCC 7056 pauses at 119th and Michigan before making a right turn onto 119th for the last leg of its run to 119th and Morgan. A. C. Williams photo on November 26, 1954. • Below. Postwar PCC 7113 rests at the short-turn loop at 84th and State. Neuberger photo. Both these photos are of Broadway-State cars.

Running on the "wrong" side of Dearborn Street (which was one-way northbound), a Broadway car rolls across the Chicago River on a northbound trip. Broadway again became a separate route on December 5, 1955 when the State portion of the Through Route was discontinued. Stephen D. Maguire collection.

Chicago Surface Lines car 1735, southbound on Broadway just south of Lawrence Ave., is making a short-turn run on the Broadway line which will terminate at Wabash and Harrison. For this run the car is displaying the Broadway-Wabash sign, a line which officially lasted less than a year. Chicago Transit Authority photo.

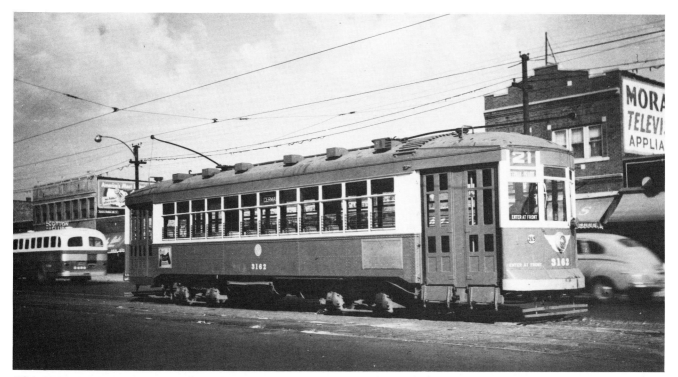

CTA 3162 at the Cermak-Kenton west terminal of the Cermak Road line. This car was one of the few conventional CSL streetcars to receive a CTA green and cream paint job. Built in 1923, the car was converted to one-man operation in 1949 and scrapped in 1954. Photo from the S. D. Maguire collection.

Three CSL streetcars, one on each of the three tracks, and two Chicago Motor Coach buses show that even during the Depression, off-peak transit service along State Street was frequent. Taken at 1:20 pm, this photo from the George Krambles collection looks north on State from Washington Street.

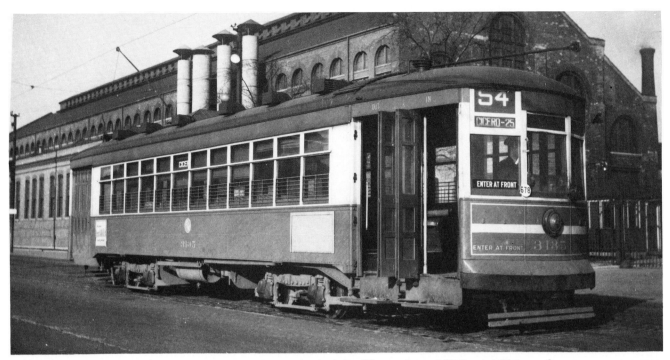

CTA 3135 in one-man service near the south terminal of the Cicero line at 25th and Cicero. One-man cars were put on this route September 11, 1950, running weekdays only (buses handled weekend runs).

via Fulton and Sacramento on October 17, 1948. At this point the buses connected with the Kedzie-California car line. CTA cut back all but weekday and Saturday rush hour and midday service to the former Fulton, Francisco, Walnut, and California loop on November 29, 1964.

Canal-Wacker

CSL began this short line from the Loop to the near South Side on May 8, 1947. The route began at a "U" turn at Wacker and Wabash and ran via Wacker, Lake, Canal, Lumber, Cermak, and Canal to a loop via 23rd Pl. and Archer. Service ran Monday through Saturday only. On September 25 the buses were rerouted via Wacker, Randolph, and Canal. This was the last change under CSL management.

Central Avenue

This north-south route on the West Side began as a Chicago Motor Coach line between Central and Lexington and Milwaukee and Lawrence on October 3, 1928. The route was via Central. Lawrence, Long, Higgins, Milwaukee, and Lawrence.

CSL substituted trolley buses for the CMC buses on June 8, 1930. The new route began at the Lexington wye used by CMC, continued north on Central to Higgins, then via Edmunds to a wye at Avondale. On August 30, 1930 CSL dropped the Edmunds-Avondale route and sent the buses to a new terminal loop via Central, Milwaukee, Foster, and Central. This was the last route change made under CSL management.

Central Avenue Extension

CSL began this gas bus extension to the Central trolley bus line October 7, 1940. Extension buses shared the Milwaukee and Foster loop with the trolley buses. From the loop they ran north on Central and Lehigh to a loop at Devon and Caldwell. On June 24, 1942 the line was extended along Lehigh to a wye at Tonty.

Cermak Road (22nd Street)

The tracks west of the Chicago River along this major South Side crosstown line were owned by the Southern Street Railway Co., one of the four companies which made up the Surface Lines. As we pick up the story on October 21, 1906, the line had just been slightly shortened on the east end from Cottage Grove to Wabash. The west terminal was Kenton.

In anticipation of handling the large crowds expected for the Century of Progress, the line was extended east via Cermak, Silverton Way, 23rd Street bridge, and private right-of-way to a terminal at 18th in Grant Park. (For full details see the previous chapter.)

On March 9, 1949 CTA discontinued streetcar service into the Grant Park Terminal and made Prairie the east terminal. One-man cars took over weekend operation April 9, 1950, and all service was given by one-man cars starting September 16, 1951. On May 30, 1954 CTA converted the line to bus operation.

Cermak-Lawndale

This line began in 1896 from a connection with the

22nd Street cars at Rockwell and 22nd to 35th and Lawndale via Rockwell, 25th, and Lawndale. In 1897 and 1898 a double-deck car provided service. On May 6, 1909 this line became a branch of the 22nd Street route, operating from 33rd and Lawndale via Lawndale, 25th, Kedzie, and 22nd. The track along Rockwell and 25th used by the former route was abandoned at this time. On June 29, 1931 non-rush hour service was reduced to a shuttle from 22nd and Kedzie to 33rd and Lawndale. Kedzie-Homan buses replaced the cars on October 1, 1945.

Chicago Avenue

This near North crosstown line had several interesting short branches, as well as a Downtown car. We pick up its story on August 7, 1915 when the line was extended east from Clark to Lake Shore Drive. The west terminal was California for cars originating at Lake Shore Drive (east route). Chicago-Downtown cars (west route) ran from Chicago and Austin via Chicago, Milwaukee, Lake, State, Randolph, Dearborn, and Lake.

On March 11, 1918 the Downtown cars were rerouted off Milwaukee and run east via Chicago to Wells. Randolph, Clark, Washington, and Wells. The Downtown route loop was changed again on August 1, 1920 with Kinzie replacing Randolph as the north leg of the loop.

A little-known extension brought the east route cars across Lake Shore Drive and south on open track along the lake to a terminal at Grand. This loop in front of Navy Pier was on the north side of the street and was used exclusively by Chicago cars. Service to Navy Pier was discontinued March 15, 1937.

In the general rerouting of September 14, 1924 the east and west lines along Chicago were consolidated and the Chicago-Downtown car discontinued.

Multiple-unit cars in two-car trains ran on Chicago between October 13, 1924 and February 1, 1925, and again between December 18, 1926 and November 1, 1929.

This one-man car, CTA 6169, is running westbound on the Cermak Road line at Cermak and Kedvale on December 30, 1953. At this point Cermak cars ran along either side of a central parkway. Allan C. Williams.

• Above. Westbound on the Chicago Avenue line, CTA Old Pullman 442 pauses at La Salle Street while an alighting passenger walks to the curb. Barney Neuberger photo, from the Railway Negative Exchange. • Opposite page. Westbound Chicago Avenue car, and its blurred eastbound counterpart, are dwarfed by the tall buildings at Chicago Ave. and Fairbanks Court, just east of Michigan Ave. This area is part of Chicago's posh lakefront Gold Coast. Hedrich-Blessing photo, courtesy of Jack Hedrich. • Below. CTA 1764 is at the west end of the Chicago Avenue line at Chicago and Austin. As early as April 6, 1936, one-man cars were used on Chicago Avenue, but all service was not given by one-man cars until June 24, 1950. Barney Neuberger.

• Above. CSL's only articulated streetcar, number 4000, was used to handle rush hour traffic on the Cicero line. Conductor sat opposite the front door of the rear car. W. R. Keevil collection. • Below. CSL 5177 pauses near Midway Airport while running on the South Cicero shuttle line. Chicago Transit Authority photograph.

Under CTA management one-man cars went into service on June 24, 1950. Trolley buses took over all service on May 11, 1952. They ran from a wye at Fairbanks to a wye at Mayfield. On July 20, 1952 the trolley buses began using the Mayfield loop, and on December 31, 1952 east end operation was extended to a loop at Fairbanks and Ontario.

Chicago-State (Through Route 19)

This number was set aside to designate a through-routing of the Chicago Avenue and State Street lines. However, the consolidation did not take place and the route was never used.

Cicero Avenue

This West Side streetcar line reached 25th, its southernmost terminal, in 1895. But it wasn't until January 1, 1913 that the Cicero line was extended north from Madison to Irving Park and through-routed to 25th. (As early as 1891 cars ran on Cicero from Lake to Madison as part of a West Side loop line via Cicero, Madison,

Harlem, and Lake. In 1895 a Cicero-Chicago car went into service from Lake and Cicero to Chicago and Austin via Cicero and Chicago.) On January 4, 1926 the north terminal was extended from Irving Park to Montrose.

Motor-trailer operation began May 7, 1923, and lasted until May 21, 1930. Multiple-unit trains went into service in 1924, and ran until November 28, 1926.

CSL's only articulated streetcar was used on Cicero, and was particularly effective during the evening rush hours at Western Electric's Hawthorne plant. In one 20 minute period between 5:00 and 6:00 p.m., Cicero cars were loaded and dispatched at 15 second intervals. Since CSL used street collectors at this point, car 4000 could be loaded through all four doors.

In normal operation the passengers entered at the front door of the rear car, opposite the conductor's station. Passengers could leave through any of the four doors, with the rear doors of each car being treadle-operated exits only.

For the mechanical specifications and paint scheme of car 4000, look in the chapter on CSL cars.

CTA replaced the streetcars with buses on weekends starting December 4, 1949. On September 11, 1950 one-man cars began to run on weekdays. Complete bus substitution came on November 25, 1951.

A Clark-Wentworth car, Old Pullman 182, is running southbound on Clark at Madison in this photo taken April 7, 1926. Note motor-trailer train turning south on Dearborn from Madison. Photo from David R. Phillips.

243

North Cicero Avenue

This Northwest Side bus line linked CSL's Montrose and Peterson routes. Buses started to run March 24, 1947 from a loop via Montrose, LaCrosse, and Sunnyside along Cicero to a loop via Caldwell and Peterson. The line also served as a feeder to the Cicero streetcars. No changes were made under CSL management.

South Cicero Avenue

This short South Side shuttle line opened on May 22, 1904 from Archer (52nd) to 63rd along Cicero. Two months later cars began to turn west on 63rd and run one mile to Central. They shared the tracks with 63rd Street extension cars, which had begun to run to Central in 1902. The service along 63rd lasted until October 1, 1929, when the line was cut back to its original length as a shuttle between Archer and 63rd along Cicero.

CSL replaced the streetcars with a bus shuttle on January 6, 1941. A south extension opened as far as 75th on October 5, 1942, and a rush-hour-only north extension to 22nd and Kenton via Cicero and 22nd opened February 8, 1943. The south extension served the Dodge-Chicago defense plant. The north extension served the Hawthorne Works of Western Electric and made connection with the CSL's Cermak Road streetcar line.

On April 14, 1943 buses began to run a block further south, to 76th, and on July 26 they started to run to a terminal at 76th and Kilpatrick, two blocks east of Ci-

cero. This was the last change made in the route under CSL management.

Clark Street (Including Clark-Wentworth, Through Route 22)

This major north-south trunk line had a long and interesting history. Begun in 1859 as a horse car line from just north of the Chicago River to Kingsbury and Division, Clark used cable cars and battery streetcars before the entire line was electrified and through-routed to downtown on October 21, 1906. The through route was from Clark and Howard via Clark, Randolph, LaSalle, Monroe, Dearborn, and Randolph.

On March 17, 1908 Clark was through-routed with the South Side Wentworth line via Clark, Archer, Wentworth, Vincennes, 79th to Emerald. In November, 1911 the Clark Street local cars began to use the newly-completed Clark-Schreiber loop at the Devon carhouse.

On July 17, 1912 through route cars stopped turning west on 79th to Emerald and continued south on Vincennes to an off-street loop at 80th. On July 21 North Side short turn cars began to use a loop via Clark, Illinois, LaSalle Street tunnel, Monroe, Dearborn, Randolph, La Salle tunnel, Illinois, and Clark.

The Clark-Howard off-street loop opened on May 19, 1915. On July 24, 1919 through route cars began using 81st and Halsted as the south terminal, but the loop at 80th and Vincennes was retained for short turns.

For a little over two years CSL operated motor-trailer

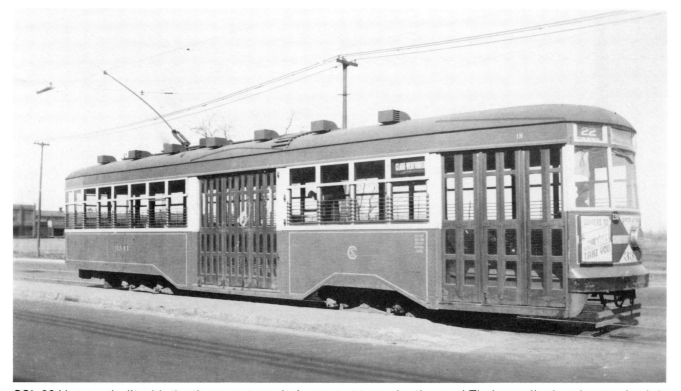

CSL 3341 was rebuilt with the three center exit doors next to each other and Timken roller bearing trucks. It is shown here running on Clark-Wentworth. Barney Neuberger collection, courtesy of Bill Richmond.

trains on Clark-Wentworth (known also as Wentworth-Clark in the early days of through operation). Service began September 21, 1921, and ended October 13, 1923.

There were no other changes in the basic route for 30 years, until CTA rerouted the northbound cars via Harrison, Dearborn, and Kinzie on November 16, 1953. The change was caused by the creation of one-way streets in the Loop. On September 5, 1954 buses replaced the streetcars on weekends over the entire route. Buses took over for streetcars on September 8, 1957 on the Clark portion of the through route north of Harrison Street. The Wentworth local cars operated as far north as Kinzie before looping back to the south.

In addition to the Century of Progress service described in brief in the previous chapter, Clark-Wentworth cars later served the Field Museum of Natural History and Soldier Field by running east on Roosevelt Road to the loop in Grant Park. For this purpose the postwar PCC cars were equipped with a front destination sign reading "Museum."

Clybourn Avenue

We pick up the story of this Near North radial line on its conversion from cable car to streetcar on October 21, 1906. The electric route ran from Clybourn and Belmont via Clybourn, Division, Wells, Randolph, Dearborn, Monroe, LaSalle, and Randolph. On July 21, 1912 cars were rerouted via Wells, Illinois, LaSalle Street Tunnel, Randolph, Dearborn, Monroe, La Salle Tunnel, Illinois, and Wells. Another rerouting on July 1, 1914

took the cars to a stub terminal at Harrison and State via Wells and Harrison. During the 1930s cars ran to the Riverview loop via Western.

CSL converted Clybourn to bus operation on May 4, 1947. The north terminal was a loop on Clybourn, Western, Melrose, and Oakley. The downtown loop was via Division, Orleans, Franklin, Monroe, State, Adams, and Franklin.

Clybourn-Wentworth (Through Route 2)

This line ran from 79th and Halsted to Clybourn and Belmont via 79th, Vincennes, Wentworth, Archer, Clark, Division, and Clybourn. Service began June 6, 1910. On July 17, 1912 the cars were rerouted along Vincennes to the off-street terminal at 80th. A new downtown routing put the cars on Clark, Illinois, Wells, and Division on February 1, 1914. All service ended September 13, 1924.

Cottage Grove-Broadway (Through Route 1)

This route entered service September 30, 1912 between a loop via Harper, 56th and Lake Park to the Arthur loop via 55th, Cottage Grove, Indiana, 18th, Wabash, Lake, State, Division, Clark, Broadway, Devon, and Clark to the Arthur terminal. It was extended up Clark to the Howard terminal on February 1, 1916. On June 29, 1923 northbound cars were rerouted via 18th, State, and Division.

The off-street loop at 80th and Vincennes was a regular short-turn terminal for Clark-Wentworth cars and later for the Wentworth route, the last streetcar line to operate in Chicago. Bill Richmond collection.

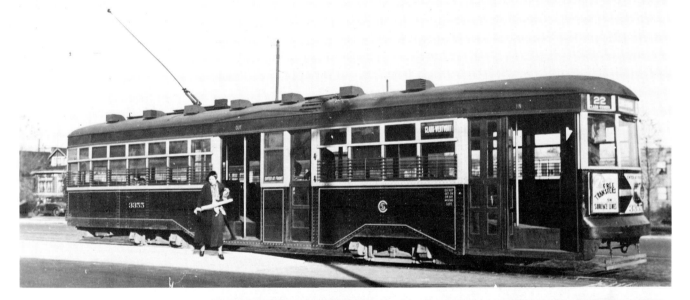

Experimental car 4001 on a regular revenue trip on Clark-Wentworth. Car is at the south terminal of the line, on Halsted Street just south of 81st. R. H. Kennedy photo taken in October, 1935, from Allan C. Williams.

• Opposite page, top. Postwar PCC 7090 in its original light Mercury Green paint scheme awaits departure time on 81st Street just east of Halsted in this Barney Neuberger photo. • Middle. R. H. Kennedy captured Sedan 3355 discharging a passenger at 80th and Vincennes on October 3, 1935. Photo from the Allan C. Williams collection. • Below. Although the wye arrangement at 81st and Halsted was not suitable as a terminal for single-end cars, CTA continued to use it until the end of service in 1958. A. C. Williams snapped this shot.

CSL 5601, outbound on the Clybourn-Wells route on October 8, 1935, at the intersection of Belmont, Clybourn, and Western. R. H. Kennedy photo from the Allan C. Williams collection.

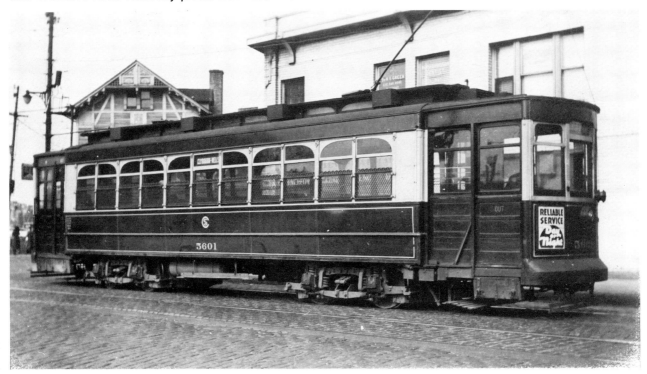

• Above. Sun Parlor 3198 was a large, modern steel car, with seats for 54 passengers. Photo was taken on September 27, 1935, when the car was running on Through Route 1, Cottage Grove-Broadway. R. H. Kennedy photo from A. C. Williams. • Opposite page. CTA 7008 at State and Van Buren, running inbound on the Cottage Grove line. A. C. Williams photo, taken on June 15, 1955. • Below. CSL 6153 running inbound on Cottage Grove-Broadway at Devon and Western during the mid-Thirties. George Krambles collection.

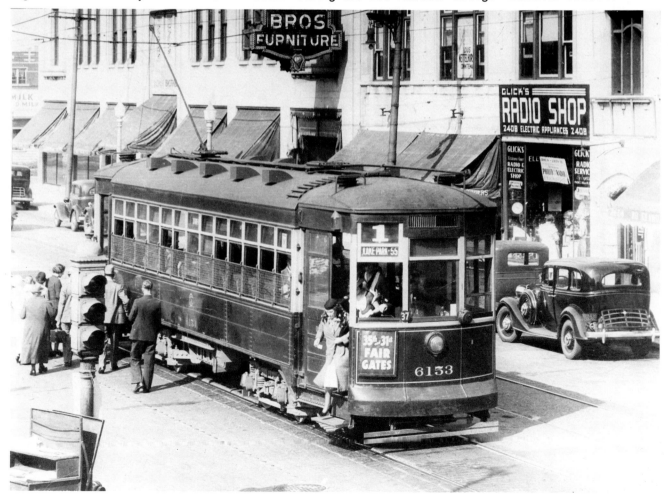

● Above. CSL Nearside car 5741 inbound on one of the Cottage Grove lines at Cottage Grove and Cermak Road. Allan C. Williams collection. ● Opposite page, top. Converted to one-man operation for use on Cottage Grove, CTA prewar PCC car 4014 pauses at the Midway Plaisance as the operator answers a prospective passenger's question. Author's collection. ● Opposite page, below. Prewar PCC 4046 at the Brookline off-street loop at 72nd Street east of Cottage Grove Ave. Note operators' toilet building and sand storage boxes at left. For an earlier view of this loop with a Nearside car, see page 9. This photo was taken on December 30, 1953 by Allan C. Williams. ● Below. The Cottage Grove routes were noted for their use of many different types of streetcar. Standard Brill PAYE cars, the first to run in Chicago, ran on Cottage Grove. The lines on this street also used the Nearsides, the Peter Witts, the Sun Parlors, and PCCs, filling in with Old Pullmans and Odd 17 cars. Here a one-man Nearside runs outbound on Cottage Grove-South Chicago (TR 5), followed by a TR 1 car on Cottage Grove-Broadway. Neuberger photo taken at 35th and Cottage Grove.

Service was cut back from the Howard terminal and cars routed west on Devon to Kedzie on July 11, 1932. On November 4, 1934 northbound cars were routed via 18th, Wabash, Harrison, and State. On May 15, 1939 southbound cars began to run via State, Grand, Wabash, and 18th, and northbound via State, Lake, Wabash, Grand, and State. Service ended October 7, 1946.

Cottage Grove-Pullman (Through Route 4)

It wasn't until August 12, 1918 that portions of the Cottage Grove, West Pullman, and 93rd-Pullman lines were put together to form a continuous route from the Garland Court loop to the 115th loop. The route was from Garland Court and Randolph via Randolph, Wabash, 18th, Indiana, Cottage Grove, 95th, Cottage Grove, 115th, St. Lawrence, 111th, and Cottage Grove.

CSL rerouted the cars via Wabash, Harrison, State, Lake, and Wabash on March 28, 1947. The Garland Court loop was retained for Owl runs only. On May 11, 1952 one-man PCC cars entered service, replacing two-man Peter Witt cars. On June 29 the CTA gave the cars a new downtown terminal via Wabash, Grand, State, Lake, and Wabash. The cars returned to their loop via Wabash, Harrison, State, Lake, and Wabash on March 16, 1953.

The entire line was discontinued on June 19, 1955, with the bus replacement line rerouted off Cottage Grove north of 35th because of construction work.

Cottage Grove-South Chicago (Through Route 5)

This route branched off the Cottage Grove line to serve the industrial community of South Chicago on Chicago's Southeast Side. It began on February 23, 1913 from a loop via South Chicago, 93rd, Baltimore, and 91st via South Chicago, Cottage Grove, Indiana, 18th, Wabash to a loop via Washington, Garland Court, and Randolph. On April 10, 1927 the cars were extended via South Chicago, 95th, and Ewing to a wye at 108th. Loops or wyes were necessary at both ends of this line, since it used single-end Nearside cars. On October 1, 1930 the line was rerouted via South Chicago, 91st, Commercial, and 95th.

Although the inauguration and termination dates are not known, route guide information indicates that during 1933 TR 5 cars ran from 18th and Wabash to the wye at 108th and Ewing, and that in 1934 they ran from 38th and Cottage to the wye. These cutbacks applied only to evening and Sunday service.

CSL rerouted all but the Owl runs to a new loop via Harrison, State, Lake, and Wabash on March 28, 1947. On July 14 the cars were cut back from 108th to a loop via 91st, Baltimore, 93rd, Commercial, and 91st. CTA ended streetcar service without direct replacement on December 4, 1949.

• Above. Car 3312, southbound on the South Damen line at 63rd Street, was a former multiple-unit car fitted with new trucks and motors as part of an experiment that also involved four of its series mates. Neuberger photo from Bill Richmond. • Opposite page, top. One of the Matchbox cars in two-man service on the North Damen line. Neuberger photo from Bill Richmond. • Below. Chicago Railways bus 6805, running on the South Damen bus extension, met Chicago Railways one-man ex-MU car 3226 at the end of the South Damen streetcar line at 74th and Damen. Barney Neuberger photo.

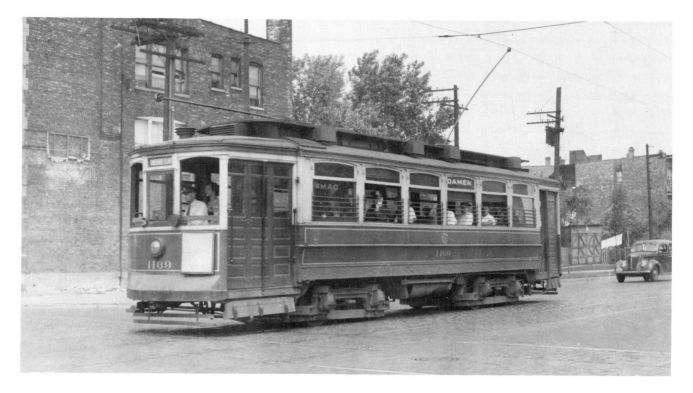

North Damen Avenue

We pick up the story of this line in 1910, when cars on the south section between Blue Island and 18th were linked to cars on the north section from 14th to Fullerton and through-routed. The south terminal of the new line was Blue Island, the north terminal was Fullerton.

On June 16, 1947 CSL opened a bus extension from Elston and Fullerton to a loop via Byron, Seeley, and Irving Park. As a substitute for Lincoln-Rosehill street-car service, the Damen bus was extended north again via Damen, Balmoral, Ravenswood, Bryn Mawr, Ashland, Olive, Clark, and Bryn Mawr on August 1, 1948.

On December 12, 1948 buses took over from street-cars between Blue Island and Fullerton. However, the substitute buses were not through-routed with the extension buses, as the replacement buses ran on Saturday and Sunday only. One-man streetcars went in service all week in 1949, replacing both the two-man weekday cars and the weekend buses.

Buses took over all service May 13, 1951. The streetcar route and the bus extension were through-routed, and a new south terminal loop established via Coulter, Hoyne, Blue Island, and Damen.

South Damen Avenue

One of the last streetcar routes built, this light line was one of the first to be replaced by buses under CTA management. The first two-mile segment between 47th and 63rd opened in 1917. On December 28, 1930 the line was extended to 69th, and on February 15, 1931 to 74th.

On August 12, 1946 a shuttle bus extension went into operation between 74th and 87th. CTA replaced the streetcars with buses on January 26, 1948. The main line and the extension were through-routed, and the buses ran to a new north terminal via 48th, Seeley, and 47th on January 26, 1948.

Devon Avenue Shuttle

This short North Side shuttle started operation May 20, 1917 from Clark to Western. One-man cars took over the service March 13, 1921. A west extension opened December 14, 1925 from Western to Kedzie, and an east extension opened from Clark to Magnolia January 30, 1928. When Broadway cars began to run to Devon and Kedzie on July 10, 1932, the Devon shuttle car service was discontinued.

Diversey Avenue

This North Side crosstown line began as a one-man shuttle between Kimball and Pulaski on July 16, 1923.

CSL started an extension bus from a wye at Harding just east of Pulaski, to a wye at Laramie on August 11, 1927.

On April 17, 1930 Diversey became CSL's first trolley bus route. The electric buses replaced the streetcar line, the bus extension, and a Chicago Motor Coach bus line. (For details of the CMC bus operation, see the chapter on Competition and Co-operation.) The new route started at a loop via Diversey, Kimball, Parker, and St. Louis via Diversey to a wye at Narragansett.

Two westward extensions of the trolley bus line were quickly made. The first, on November 22, 1931, was to a wye at Nagle. On June 19, 1932 a further extension brought the buses to a wye at Neva. On October 4, 1938 an off-street terminal loop replaced the wye at Neva.

Diversey trolley buses began to run to a new east terminal at Western on September 12, 1935. The former east terminal loop via Kimball, Parker, and St. Louis was used for short turn buses until it closed May 29, 1940.

CTA discontinued trolley bus service June 19, 1955. The former trolley bus route and a former Chicago Motor Coach line to downtown Chicago were through-routed from Downtown to Neva and Diversey.

Division Street

By 1896 this North Side crosstown line had local electric cars running between Mozart and Wells, and a Downtown car from Mozart via Milwaukee. During the cable car era the east line was cut back from Wells to Clybourn for a while. A separate extension car route opened December 16, 1914 from Grand to Cicero.

No change was made in local car service until August 19, 1937, when the route was extended via Division and State to 21st and State. A rerouting on August 24 sent the local cars west on Van Buren to Clinton, then west

on Harrison to a wye at Jefferson. On October 11, local Division cars were through-routed with local Van Buren cars to form a U-shaped continuous local route from Division and Mozart to Van Buren and Kedzie.

On May 15, 1939 Division-Van Buren cars were rerouted via State, Kinzie, Dearborn, Lake, and State because of the closing of the State Street bridge. Service was restored via the new State Street bridge on May 28, 1949. CTA discontinued the through route and substituted buses from Division and Austin to a downtown loop via Randolph, Dearborn, Wacker, and State on February 4, 1951.

From the beginning of Downtown service on June 27, 1890 until 1896, Downtown horse cars were hauled behind the Milwaukee Ave. cable cars. In 1896 the Downtown route was electrified and the cars began to run via Milwaukee and Lake to a new loop via State, Randolph, and Dearborn. By 1902 the direction around the loop was reversed, to Dearborn, Randolph, State, and Lake.

The loop was changed to Clinton, Randolph, State, Washington, and Clinton by July, 1913. On March 29, 1914 the loop was changed to Desplaines, Washington, Dearborn, Randolph, State, and Washington. On August 1, 1920 the Downtown cars began to loop via Lake, State, Randolph, Dearborn, and Lake. In the general rerouting of September 14, 1924 the Downtown car got a new route via Desplaines, Randolph, Dearborn, Washington, and Desplaines. To cut costs the Downtown cars ended Sunday service March 6, 1932.

On August 23, 1940 cars were rerouted via Division, Elston, and Milwaukee, returning to the Division-Milwaukee route October 30, 1941. Downtown cars were routed off Milwaukee and onto State January 13, 1950. The new route was via Division, State, Lake, Dearborn, Kinzie, and State. The entire Division-Downtown route was abandoned February 4, 1951.

The separate west Division line between Grand and Cicero was extended west to Austin November 25, 1915. On February 18, 1921 three one-man cars were added to three two-man cars on this segment.

A shuttle bus to link the Division and West Division streetcar lines began operation October 1, 1941. The east terminal was a loop via California, Thomas, and Mozart, and the west terminal was a loop via Grand and Central Park. The shuttle bus and the West Division car line were combined into one through-routed bus line on July 9, 1946.

Elston Avenue

This Northwest Side line ran on Elston from Milwaukee to Montrose from 1894 to 1897, when it was extended west on Montrose to Knox. At the same time it was extended south on Milwaukee to Downtown. The route was via Montrose, Elston, Milwaukee, Lake, Dearborn, Randolph, State, and Lake.

On November 28, 1914 the line was extended northwest along Elston to Lawrence, and the line on Montrose was abandoned. (Montrose cars continued to use the tracks.) On September 14, 1924 the cars were rerouted via Lake, Dearborn, Randolph, Clinton, and Milwaukee.

Multiple-unit train service ran briefly on Elston. Service started April 1, 1926, and stopped September 3 that year. On July 1, 1930 Elston Extension trolley bus service began from a wye at Gunnison and Elston to a wye at Holbrook and Elston.

CTA cut back Elston cars to a shuttle between Milwaukee and Lawrence on October 7, 1949. However, rush hour cars did continue to run downtown. Weekday service to downtown was resumed on January 30, 1950

• Above. Cook County Hospital Car 1, on its way from Cook County Psychopathic Hospital at Harrison and Wood to the Dunning Asylum, turns west on Irving Park from Elston Avenue. Note trolley bus overhead for movement of Elston Extension buses to and from Elston carbarn. For more details on Cook County Car 1, see pages 15 and 16. Neuberger photo, courtesy of Bill Richmond. • Opposite page. CSL Sewing Machine 2909 at Division and Grand Ave., east terminal of the West Division extension line. Barney Neuberger from the Roy Benedict collection. Note outbound Grand Avenue car at right.

via a new route over Elston, Division, Crosby, Larrabee, Chicago, Wells, Kinzie, Dearborn, Randolph, and Wells. On April 9, 1950 one-man cars took over weekend shuttle duties between Milwaukee and Lawrence.

CTA converted both the Elston car line and the Elston Extension trolley bus route to bus operation on January 21, 1951. The new weekday route was from a loop via Miami, Milwaukee, and Holbrook along Elston, Division, Crosby, Larrabee, Chicago, Wells, Kinzie, Dearborn, Randolph, and Wells. Weekend and evening buses ran from Holbrook via Elston and Ashland to a loop via Haddon, Milwaukee, Division, and Ashland.

Ewing-Brandon (Hegewisch)

This line served the far Southeast corner of Chicago. It began as the Hegewisch streetcar service from 108th and Ewing to 118th and Avenue M via Ewing and 118th, inaugurated January 22, 1918. On May 11 the line was extended via 118th and Burley to 122nd and Burley. Extensions were made to both ends of the line on February 1, 1919. On the north end cars began to run on Ewing, 95th, and South Chicago to a loop via Commercial, 92nd, and Baltimore. On the south end the cars started to run past 122nd and Burley via Brandon to Brainard (Hegewisch).

On April 10, 1927 the Hegewisch cars were cut back, running only from 108th and Ewing to Hegewisch. Another cutback, on April 8, 1945, restricted Hegewisch cars to 118th and Burley on the north end. CSL

replaced the streetcars with buses on October 21, 1946. The bus route was from a loop via Commercial, 91st, South Chicago, and 92nd then 92nd, Ewing, 109th (or 113th), Avenue O, 134th, and Brandon to Brainard. On October 23, 1946 the Hegewisch bus got a loop on the south end via 134th, Brandon, 132nd, Baltimore, Brainard, and Brandon to 134th.

Even when it was a shuttle between 118th and Brainard, Hegewisch was always a two-man streetcar route, because the CSL required two cremen on cars which crossed heavily-used steam railroad tracks. The Argo and 111th Street routes used two-man cars for the same reason. One-man cars could be used on 93rd-95th because a watchman was stationed at the crossing.

The line between 118th and Ewing and Hegewisch was on dedicated streets. However, it was open track on a high fill through a swamp, paved only at the passing sidings.

Foster Avenue

CSL began Foster bus service between a loop at Milwaukee and the Berwyn loop on July 1, 1937. This far North Side crosstown line looped via Lovejoy, Gettysburg, and Milwaukee on the west end, and via Broadway, Berwyn, Winthrop, and Foster on the east end.

On January 27, 1943 CSL through-routed the Foster and Northwest Highway buses. See the Northwest Highway route for details.

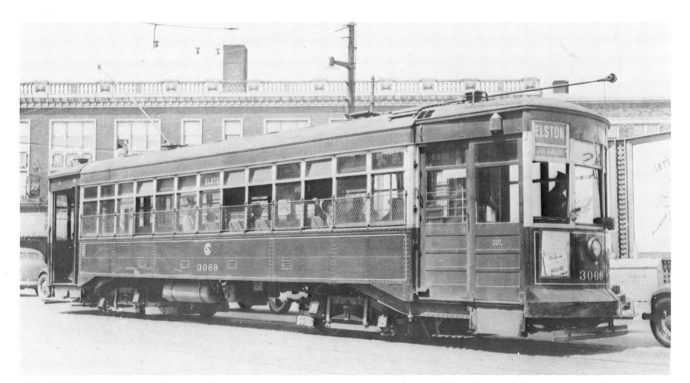

CSL 3069 loads passengers at Elston and Lawrence, outer terminal of the Elston streetcar line. Passengers wishing to go further northwest on Elston changed here to the isolated Elston Extension trolley bus line. Begun on July 1, 1930 as one of the pioneer trolley bus lines in Chicago, the trolley bus line and the Elston streetcar route were combined and converted to motor bus operation on January 21, 1951. Photo taken May 25, 1942. S. D. Maguire collection.

• Above. A Hegewisch (Ewing-Brandon) car, two-man 2518, connects with a one-man South Chicago-Ewing car at the 118th and Burley terminal. This terminal point was established April 8, 1945, when Hegewisch cars were cut back from 108th and Ewing and South Chicago-Ewing cars were extended to 118th and Burley from 108th and Ewing. Barney Neuberger photo. • Below. Two-man cars had to be used on the Hegewisch line, lightly patronized though it was, because CSL would not permit one-man cars on lines that had unattended railroad grade crossings. Here the conductor of 2518 prepares to flag his car across the Pennsylvania Railroad.

Fullerton Avenue

This near North Side crosstown line ran along Fullerton from Halsted to Milwaukee from 1895 to 1909, when it was extended west to Pulaski. On September 9, 1914 the line was extended further west from Pulaski to Cicero.

An extension car line opened from Cicero to Long on March 16, 1918. On October 21 the extension was absorbed into the basic route, with cars through-routed from Halsted to Lotus. A final west extension, from Lotus to Central, opened on October 10, 1928.

CTA converted the entire line to trolley bus on December 4, 1949. The route was from Parkside terminal, just west of Central, to an east loop via Lincoln, Orchard, and Fullerton.

West Fullerton Avenue

CSL opened this feeder to the Fullerton car line on June 24, 1942. The route was from a U-turn at Parkside to a loop via Mulligan, Grand, Narragansett, and Fullerton. On March 30, 1946 the west loop was changed to Fullerton, Grand, Narragansett, and Fullerton.

The feeder bus began to use the just-completed Parkside terminal on December 4, 1949, sharing it with the Fullerton trolley buses.

Fulton-21st Street

CSL consolidated the Fulton-Downtown and 21st-Downtown routes on September 14, 1924. The new routing took the cars out of the congested Loop area. The line began at 21st and Marshall Blvd. and ran to Fulton and Western via 21st, Halsted, Canalport, Canal, Harrison, Clinton, Monroe, Morgan, and Fulton. An oddity on this line was the one car an hour that ran southbound via Harrison, Jefferson, 14th, and Canal, and northbound via 14th, Jefferson, Roosevelt, Clinton, and Harrison. One-man cars entered service August 9, 1925. Sunday service was discontinued on January 19, 1947, while all service ended without replacement on May 7, 1947.

Grand Avenue

This major Near North crosstown line had two services running on it in 1912. The Grand-Downtown car, discontinued June 14, 1916, ran from Grand and Harlem via Grand, Halsted, Lake, Dearborn, Randolph, State, and Lake. By July, 1913 the downtown loop was reversed, via Lake, State, Randolph, and Dearborn. The local cars ran from Halsted to Peshtigo Court. Local service was extended west to Western in 1914, and east to Lake Shore Drive in 1916.

In anticipation of the end of the Grand-Downtown service, half of the local cars were extended west from Western to Harlem on June 8, 1916. At the same time the local cars began to operate to a loop at the east end of Navy Pier via tracks on the upper level. In June of 1921 the tracks were re-laid on the lower level of the Pier, and a new terminal in front of the Pier on Streeter Drive was placed in service. Service on the Pier itself was suspended September 28, 1941, and the tracks were removed August 14, 1943.

Now Pullman 944 waits for passengers to board at the west terminal of the Fullerton line at Fullerton and Central. This North Side crosstown line connected with CSL's heavy Lincoln and Halsted lines at its east terminal, served the busy Fullerton station of the North Side "L" near its east terminal, and was within walking distance of the Sacramento and Logan Square stations of the Logan Square "L" at mid-route.

Both motor-trailer trains and multiple-unit trains operated on Grand. The former ran from July 13, 1922 until May 4, 1923. The latter ran from November 18, 1926 until January 3, 1928.

CTA began a supplemental bus service along Grand from Navy Pier to a loop via Franklin, Illinois, Orleans, and Grand. This short shuttle served the Grand Ave. stations of the Ravenswood "L" and the North-South subway, relieving congestion on the Grand streetcars. Weekend bus service over the entire line began December 4, 1949 from Navy Pier to a loop via Nordica, Altgeld, and Neva.

On April 1, 1951 CTA substituted buses for weekday streetcars along the entire route. The supplemental buses were discontinued at this time.

Halsted Street

Many routes used this major north-south trunk line. (Some are listed here, others under their Through Route number.) In 1912, for example, there was the Halsted-Downtown car. It ran from 111th and Sacramento via 111th, Monterey, Vincennes, Summit, Halsted, Archer, and Clark to a terminal at Clark and Washington. There was also a local streetcar between Root and Milwaukee along Halsted, as well as a local car between 23rd and Broadway.

On February 1, 1914 the Halsted-Downtown cars began to loop via Monroe, Dearborn, Washington, LaSalle, Randolph, and Clark. Eighteen days later the cars began to turn via a new loop on Clark, Monroe, LaSalle, Washington, and Clark. On January 29, 1922 they began to run via Madison, Dearborn, and Monroe

to Clark. In the general rerouting of September 14, 1924, Halsted-Downtown cars were sent north of the Loop, and reversed direction via Clark, Illinois, Wells, Chicago, and Clark.

On June 3, 1925 certain Downtown cars began to run through the Loop via Clark and Halsted to the Waveland loop used by the local Halsted cars. They later ran northbound on Clark and Halsted to the terminal, and southbound on Broadway to Clark after leaving the terminal.

The Downtown cars and the local cars began to exchange south terminals May 24, 1931. Prior to this, local Halsted cars had run from Broadway to 79th; Downtown cars had run from Downtown or Waveland to 111th and Sacramento. On May 24 local cars began to run to 111th and Sacramento, while some Downtown cars were cut back to 79th.

CTA ended the practice of running some Downtown cars to the Waveland terminal on November 20, 1947. All Downtown cars looped via Clark, Illinois, Wells, Chicago, and Clark. On December 4, 1949 all service south of 79th was replaced by the Vincennes-111th bus.

Buses took over weekend runs on the Downtown route from 79th on November 25, 1951. CTA rerouted the weekday Downtown streetcars and the weekend Downtown buses to a new loop via Clark, Harrison, Dearborn, Kinzie, and Clark on May 11, 1953. The final bus substitution for weekday Downtown streetcar service came on May 29, 1954.

Several short terminals were placed in operation in 1912 to serve both Halsted and Through Route cars that used Halsted. They were the loop via 63rd, Union, and 63rd Place, and the loop via 79th, Emerald, and private right-of-way. On April 28, 1915 Halsted local cars began

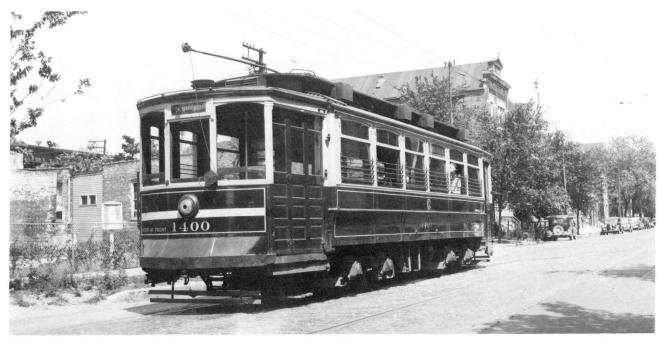

Fulton-21st Street was a light line serving the near West Side of the city. It was born through the consolidation of the Fulton-Downtown and 21st-Downtown lines on September 14, 1924, but the new line skirted the edge of the downtown district on a twisting route that used nine streets. One-man cars such as 1400, shown here at the 21st and Marshall Blvd. terminal, serviced the line from 1925 to 1947. Neuberger collection, from Allan C. Williams.

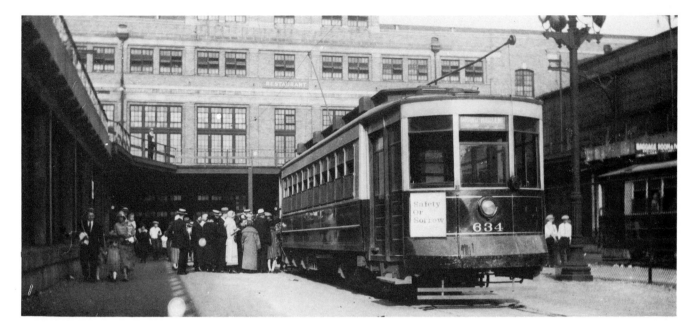

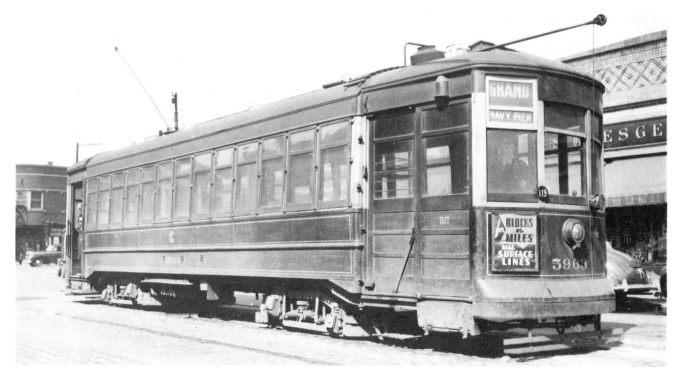

• Above. Postwar PCC 7057 leaves the Waveland terminal for a run to 79th Street on the Halsted line. Neuberger photo. • Opposite page, top. Old Pullman 634 takes on a load of homebound merrymakers at the east end of the Grand Ave. line on Navy Pier. This 1924 photo is from the B. A. Rossbach collection. • Middle. Two-car multiple-unit trains were assigned to Grand Ave. from 1926 until 1928. G. Krambles collection. • Below. CSL 5963 loads at the west terminal of the Grand Ave. line at Grand and Harlem. Neuberger photo from Allan C. Williams. • This page, below. The 79th Street terminal of the Halsted line was used by both Halsted and Halsted-Downtown cars. George Krambles collection.

Old Pullman 201 ready for a run to 111th and Sacramento on the Halsted line. Neuberger photo.

Opposite page. Three CCRy standard Brills wait to pull ahead and change ends while a fourth car is about to join the line-up at the 111th and Sacramento terminal of the Halsted line. Car 5219 will soon pull through the spring switch at the crossover and pass the other cars as it starts its northbound run. Though this photo was taken in the CTA era on September 10, 1949, it gives an indication of how busy and important the Halsted line was during the years it was a Surface Lines route. The cemeteries along both sides of the street at this point added much traffic to the Halsted line in its early days. Credit this outstanding photo to Alan W. Simms.

After flagging his car across the Rock Island Railroad's suburban line, the conductor of CTA 5475 hops back on the front platform of the car as it bumps across the tracks. This shot of winter operations along the Halsted route was taken on 111th Street east of Longwood Drive. Theodore P. Taetsch collection.

to use the Halsted-Waveland loop at the north end of the line.

From February 5, 1925 until September 9, 1930 motor-trailer trains ran on Halsted. They ran on the local route from Waveland to 79th.

On May 24, 1931 the local cars were through-routed from Broadway to 111th and Sacramento. On December 4, 1949 all service south of 79th was replaced by Vincennes-111th buses. CTA put weekend buses in service on the remaining route from 79th to Waveland on November 25, 1951. Buses took over all service on May 29, 1954.

Halsted Extension — Vincennes

Although also known as the South Halsted route, this line ran on Vincennes from 111th to 119th. It is called Halsted Extension here to avoid confusion with the bus route, started in 1938, which *did* run on South Halsted. The Halsted Extension — Vincennes cars were one-man shuttles that began to run on January 26, 1923. They connected the Halsted car line with the West 119th Street cars. CSL converted the line to bus on July 22, 1946, through-routing it with the West 119th route.

South Halsted Street

CSL began this feeder service on October 17, 1938. Buses ran from a connection with the Halsted car at 87th and Summit to a loop via 122nd, Emerald, and 123rd. On November 2, 1945 the line was extended south to a loop via 126th, Emerald, and 127th.

All Halsted streetcar service south of 79th ended December 4, 1949, and South Halsted buses were extended to the 79th terminal on that day.

Halsted-Archer (Through Route 13)

Begun on January 13, 1911, this line linked the North and Southwest Sides. It ran from Halsted and Grace to Archer and Cicero via Halsted and Archer. On July 16, 1912 it became a short-turn Halsted route, running from Halsted and Grace to a loop via 63rd, Union, 63rd Place, and Halsted. By July, 1913 the north terminal had been cut back from Grace (Broadway) to Clark, but on April 28, 1915 the north terminal was moved up to the Halsted-Waveland terminal. Service was discontinued in 1924.

Halsted-Madison (Through Route 18)

On January 3, 1910 service linking the North and West sides began on this route. The line ran from Grace and Halsted to Madison and Austin via Halsted and Madison. The route became a Halsted short line operation on August 16, 1912, running from Grace to 26th. On April 28, 1915 cars began to use the Waveland terminal. Official records indicate that the route was discontinued on July 3, 1933. However, it is still listed in the 1938 route guide. It may have been dropped as an official Through Route in 1933, but continued by CSL as an unofficial short-turn of the Halsted route.

• Above. CTA Old Pullman 192 crosses the North Branch of the Chicago River while running north on the Halsted line. Neuberger photo from the Railway Negative Exchange. • Opposite page. Old Pullman 324 turns west on Kinzie from Dearborn for a one-block run to Clark, where it will turn south and begin its run back to 79th and Halsted on the Halsted-Downtown line. From 1925 to 1947 some of the Halsted-Downtown cars ran through the Loop and up to the Halsted-Waveland terminal. After 1947 they turned back just north of the Loop, on Chicago Ave. at first, then via Kinzie Street. All Downtown service ended May 29, 1954. Neuberger photo.

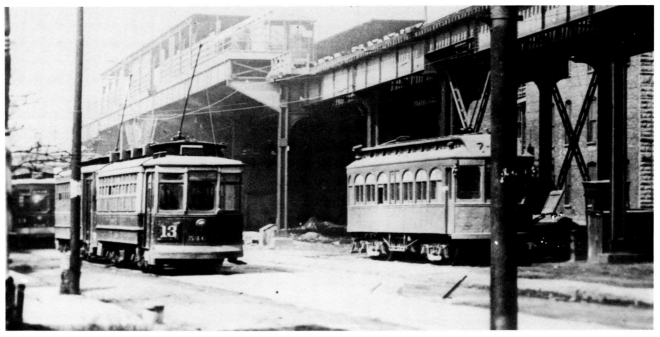

For most of its life, Through Route 13 was a short-turn run on the Halsted line. The north terminal was Halsted-Waveland and the south terminal, shown here, was the loop via 63rd, Union, and 63rd Place. The CCRy standard Brills share 63rd Place with a Chicago and Interurban Traction car. Note two-car wooden "L" train at the Halsted station of the Englewood "L" line. Photo from the Barney Neuberger collection.

Halsted-63rd (Through Route 8)

This was not the familiar Halsted route of recent years, but a short-lived Through Route begun December 13, 1911 and discontinued July 16, 1912. It ran from 63rd and Stony Island to Halsted and Grace via 63rd and Halsted.

Hammond

Hammond and Whiting-East Chicago were the two interstate lines operated jointly by the Surface Lines and the Hammond, Whiting & East Chicago Railway. Through service from Hammond, Ind., to 63rd and Stony Island began May 15, 1896 via 106th, Ewing, 92nd, Commercial, Baker, Exchange, 79th, and Stony Island to 63rd. It is possible that the through cars ran to 63rd and Dorchester from the start of through service, although the terminal at this point wasn't opened until 1906. In 1908 the cars were probably rerouted, running via 106th, Ewing, 92nd, Commercial, 91st, South Chicago, and Stony Island.

On June 10, 1914 the cars were rerouted via Ewing, 92nd, Commercial, 91st, South Chicago, and South Park to the 63rd and Vernon terminal. By 1915 the south end routing was changed from Ewing, 106th to Ewing, Indianapolis. One-man cars went into service on September 4, 1932. CSL ended all service to Hammond on June 9, 1940. For details of the replacement service see the South Chicago-Ewing route.

On the Indiana side of the state line, cars ran via Indianapolis, Calumet, and Sheffield to a loop in downtown Hammond. For car assignments, fares, corporate history, and other details of Indiana operations, see the Whiting-East Chicago route listing.

Harlem Avenue

This north-south line, serving the far North Side, opened on October 2, 1945. The bus ran from Touhy and Overhill via Touhy and Harlem to a loop via Farragut, Montclare, and Berwyn (near Foster). On May 23, 1946 the line was extended west on Foster to a loop at Ozanam, Farragut, and Canfield. This routing was changed on October 28, 1946, when the buses were extended south on Harlem to a loop via Altgeld, Neva, and Grand (near Fullerton).

Harrison

By 1912 this near South Side line extended from Cicero and Harrison to State and Adams. The route was via Harrison, Clinton, and Adams. There was a connecting car operated by the Suburban Railroad that ran from Cicero to Austin, but it was discontinued during 1912.

On November 13, 1914 CSL extended the Harrison cars to Central. The cars got a new downtown loop via Harrison, Clinton, VanBuren, Dearborn, and Harrison in the general rerouting of September 14, 1924. On February 29, 1948 CTA replaced the Harrison cars with buses from Dearborn and Harrison to a west loop via Lotus, Flournoy, and Central.

Harrison-Adams

When we pick up the story of this West Side line on July 1, 1906, streetcars had just replaced horsecars. The electric cars ran from Harrison and Western to Adams and State via Harrison, Racine, and Adams. By 1913 the cars extended west on Harrison from Western to Cicero. In 1914 they reached Central, although short line cars stopped at Cicero. The general rerouting of September 14, 1924 put the cars on a loop via Adams, Clinton, Monroe, Dearborn, and Adams.

Franklin replaced Clinton as the west leg of the loop on September 13, 1927. As a Depression-era economy measure, Sunday cars were restricted to that part of the route north and east of Racine and Harrison on March 20, 1932. CTA replaced the streetcars with buses on February 29, 1948.

Higgins Avenue

Branching off from a loop via Long, Lawrence and Linder, this line ran on Higgins to a "U" turn at Canfield. It served the far Northwest Side, beginning on April 21, 1935. On September 29, 1944 buses were rerouted on Higgins to a new loop via Milwaukee, Lawrence, and Long. This was the last change in the route under CSL management.

Homan Avenue

CSL began this West Side bus line on October 7, 1941 from a loop via Altgeld, Spaulding, and Wrightwood to a loop via 26th, Millard, and 25th. The route was via Kimball, Homan, Grenshaw, and Central Park. The line was suspended as a wartime economy measure December 1, 1942. It was reinstated October 1, 1945 via Kimball, Homan, Roosevelt, Central Park, 25th, and Lawndale to a loop via 30th, Millard, and 31st, replacing the Lawndale-Cermak streetcar line. On November 12, 1945 rush hour buses began to run south on Lawndale to a wye at 34th. This was the last change in the route under CSL management.

Indiana Avenue

This relatively short north-south trunk line served the densely-populated near South Side. When we pick up its story in 1906, the cars ran from 51st and South Park to downtown via 51st, Indiana, 18th, Wabash, Washington, Garland Court, Randolph, and Wabash. By 1906 there was also an Indiana Avenue-43rd Street route that branched off from Indiana at 43rd and ran east to the Illinois Central Railroad tracks (1200 E.). It was discontinued by 1933. There was also a 47th St. branch.

One might say that Indiana service had been rush hour only since at least 1933. By that time Through Route 3 Indiana-Lincoln cars took care of virtually all local passengers at all times other than rush hours. This was a

Along Vincennes Ave. south of 90th Street, Halsted streetcars paralleled the Rock Island Railroad on their own side-of-the-road tracks. A standard Brill car of the CCRy stops to discharge a passenger at one of the safety islands spaced a block apart on this portion of the line. George Krambles collection.

From 1896 until 1940 the Chicago Surface Lines and the Hammond, Whiting & East Chicago provided joint through service from Chicago to Hammond, Ind. On September 4, 1932 one-man car service began, and was continued until the end. This photo shows CSL one-man car 6207 sharing the HW&EC's Gostlin and Sheffield yard with HW&EC car 70. Author's collection.

• Above. Pausing on the Illinois side of the Illinois-Indiana state line while the operator collects interstate fares, CSL one-man car 6202 is on Indianapolis Blvd. at 106th Street. In the later years of Hammond service the fare for a through ride was 15¢, 7¢ on the CSL and 8¢ on the HW&EC. Photo by Ed Frank from the Allan C. Williams collection. • Opposite page. Inbound Harrison-Adams car clanks over the Chicago River on the Harrison Street Bridge. This photo was taken on August 9, 1947, just a few months before CTA took over the Surface Lines. Harrison was a heavy route which required the addition of tripper cars during visiting nights at Cook County Hospital. Many of the westbound rush hour cars on this line terminated at Harrison and Cicero, a mile short of the west terminal at Central. Credit this fine action shot to the collection of Alan W. Simms.

● Above. A car westbound on Harrison stops at Laramie Ave., a half-mile from the end of the line at Central Ave., to let an automobile cross. Ground-level Chicago, Aurora & Elgin interurban yards are to the right. Barney Neuberger photo from the Bill Richmond collection. ● Opposite page, top. New Pullman 1031, running west on the Irving Park line, discharges a passenger at the Irving Park station of the Ravenswood "L". Neuberger photo. ● Bottom. Flexible Flyer 1817 running eastbound on the Harrison line on the fringes of the Loop. Neuberger collection. ● Below. An Indiana Avenue-43rd Street car at its south terminal, 43rd and Oakenwald. Author's collection. There was also an Indiana-47th Street branch in operation by 1906. It was out of service by 1928, back in service by 1933, and out of service again by 1951.

very heavy Through Route which duplicated the Indiana-51st line except for about a mile at the south end.

On November 2, 1930 the cars were cut back to 51st and Indiana. On the north end the cars were extended up Wabash and over Grand to the Streeter Drive terminal on January 11, 1931. Just over a year later, on February 23, 1932, the cars returned to the Garland Court loop. On December 17, 1933 southbound Indiana cars began to use Cermak rather than 18th. Northbound cars got the same routing on November 4, 1934.

CTA put weekday rush hour and midday Indiana cars back on their 1931 route to the Streeter Drive terminal via Wabash and Grand on July 1, 1951. Evening, Owl, and weekend cars continued to use the Garland Court loop. On September 16, 1951 one-man cars went into service.

Indiana became a weekday, rush-hours-only streetcar line on June 29, 1952. Buses ran at all other times from a Lake, State, Wacker loop via Wabash, 22nd, Indiana, 61st, South Park, and 63rd, to Vernon. All streetcar service ended May 24, 1953.

Irving Park

This major North Side crosstown line began in 1896 from Halsted and Grace to Irving Park and Neenah via Halsted, Broadway and Irving Park. Some route information indicates that the line ran down Broadway to the Limits carhouse, where connections were made with the Clark cable cars. On June 15, 1924 CSL cut back service to Irving Park and Broadway. CTA substituted trolley buses for the streetcars on November 7, 1948. The west terminal remained at Neenah, but the east terminal was changed to a loop via Fremont, Dakin, and Broadway.

Jeffery-100th

One of the shorter CSL routes, this bus line was also short-lived. CSL started service on April 12, 1945, and CTA discontinued it on December 4, 1949. The route was from 93rd and Stony Island via 93rd, Jeffery, Van Vlissingen, 100th, and Torrence to a loop via 103rd, Hoxie, 104th and Torrence.

Kedzie-California (Including Kedzie Through Route 17)

This north-south trunk line was not through-routed until February 1, 1911, when T.R. 17 cars began to run from 63rd and Kedzie to California and Elston via Kedzie, Chicago, and California. In that same year local cars began to run through from 22nd and Kedzie to Elston and California.

On February 7, 1913 T.R. 17 cars began to run up Elston to Kedzie, and up Kedzie to Lawrence. On November 3, 1915 T.R. 17 cars began to run to 67th, and

on December 31 began to run via Milwaukee rather than Elston between California and Kedzie. T.R. 17 cars were extended to Foster November 1, 1915, and to Bryn Mawr on October 5, 1924. They were replaced December 4, 1949 by the Kedzie-Homan bus.

Local cars were extended up California to Roscoe on July 12, 1915. They began to use 47th Pl. as a south terminal on March 6, 1916. From 1928 to 1938 local cars ran from Roscoe to 67th. The single-track Sears stub off Kedzie at Arthington opened in 1919. It extended a block west of Kedzie to Spaulding. On Sundays and during non rush hours, local cars were cut back from 47th Pl. to Armitage, giving shuttle service on California between Roscoe and Armitage. This service began January 20, 1943. CTA began to run Kedzie-California cars between Roscoe and 67th all day, seven days a week starting December 4, 1949.

On May 11, 1952 buses replaced the streetcars on weekends. On May 29, 1954 buses replaced all streetcar service from Roscoe to a terminal at 63rd Pl.

South Kedzie Avenue

CSL inaugurated feeder bus service to the Kedzie car line on August 19, 1946. The buses ran from a loop via 66th Pl., Spaulding, and 66th Street via Kedzie to a wye at 114th Pl. On March 11, 1947 buses began to use a loop on 113th, Troy, and 114th. This was the last route change under CSL management.

Kimball Avenue

On June 21, 1931 CSL began trolley bus service along Kimball from Peterson to Leland. Buses replaced the trolley buses on July 1, 1937, and the route was extended south to a loop via Kimball, Wrightwood, Logan, Milwaukee and Kimball.

CSL routed the buses north of Peterson to a loop via Glenlake, Christiana, and Peterson on February 29, 1940. As a wartime economy move, CSL suspended service on December 1, 1942. Service was restored over the same route on October 1, 1945. No further changes were made in the route until CTA had taken over from the Surface Lines.

Lake Street (Through Route 16)

It wasn't until 1912 that Lake Street cars were through-routed from State to Austin. At that time the downtown loop was via Lake, Dearborn, Randolph, and State. While the Lake Street bridge over the Chicago River was out of service, CSL rerouted Lake cars via Lake, Clinton, Randolph, Franklin, and Lake. The bridge was out of service from March 29, 1914 until August 22, 1916.

In 1924 Lake cars were extended down State to 63rd. During rush hours they were extended to 119th and Morgan via State, 95th, Michigan, and 119th. The change in route was made September 14, 1924. This was

Running north through a manufacturing and warehouse district, CTA Old Pullman 372 approaches the Kedzie Ave. bridge over the Sanitary and Ship Canal near 33rd Street. This photo was taken on December 30, 1953 during the last winter of Kedzie streetcar operation. Allan C. Williams photo.

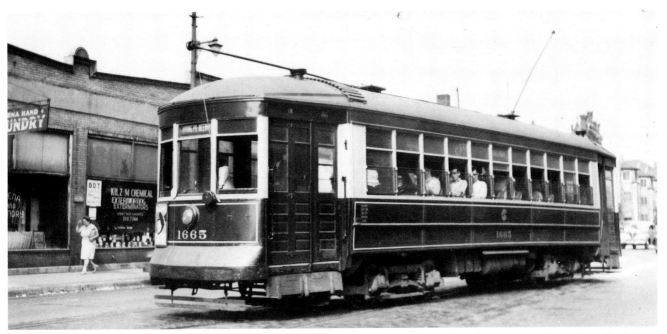

Chicago Railways car 1665 leaves the east terminal at Irving Park and Broadway for a run on the Irving Park line. Before June 16, 1924, Irving Park cars ran south on Broadway to Halsted and Grace. Even earlier, it's thought, Irving Park cars originated at the Limits carhouse. Neuberger collection.

Chicago City Railway cars in the 6000-6137 series, such as 6078, and the identical cars in Chicago Railways 3000-3091 series were often assigned to runs on the Kedzie lines. R. H. Kennedy photo, taken October 3, 1935.

• Opposite page, top. The Kimball Avenue route began as a trolley bus line between Peterson and Leland on June 21, 1931. Gas buses replaced the trolley buses on July 1, 1937, and the route was extended south. At the end of the CSL era this ACF-Brill model C-36 bus made runs on the Kimball route. On this northbound run it's picking up enough passengers to fill its 36 seats. Chicago Transit Authority photograph. • Below. Westbound Lake Street car waits a safe distance from the crossing while a three-car train of Lake Street wooden "L" cars passes over the Pine Street crossing. Neuberger photo from the Jack Doyle collection.

The nattily dressed motorman, in white shirt and dark bow tie, has CSL 6084 all to himself and his conductor as he makes a run on Through Route 17, Kedzie-California. Neuberger photo, from Allan C. Williams.

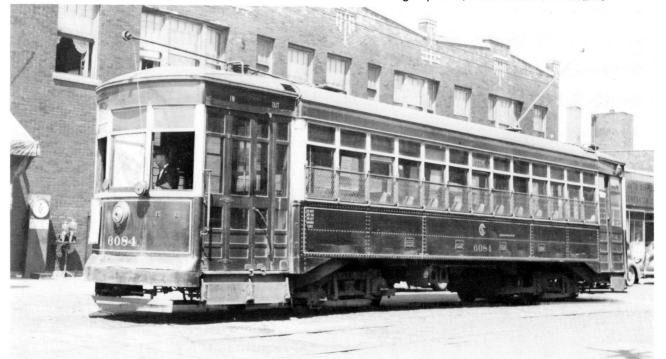

the consolidation designated as Through Route 16. Sunday and evening service was cut back to State and Van Buren on March 15, 1931, but midday cars were extended from 63rd to 79th on December 16, 1931.

All but the rush hour cars were cut back to State and Van Buren on October 7, 1946 (rush hour cars ran to 18th). On April 7, 1947 the cars were rerouted via State, Harrison, Dearborn, and Lake. CTA inaugurated a new loop via Lake, Dearborn, Randolph, Franklin, and Lake on October 23, 1949. On the same day one-man cars took over all service.

On November 15, 1953 CTA cut back Lake service to a crossover at Clinton and Lake, and from that time on no Lake cars ran into the Loop. Buses took over the entire route, including a loop via Lake, State, Randolph, and Franklin, on May 30, 1954.

Laramie Avenue

This far West Side line was one of the lightest on the CSL system. It began life as a Suburban Railroad Company streetcar line between Lake and 22nd Street on September 19, 1897. On December 21, 1912 Chicago Railways took over ownership of the line within the city limits of Chicago, between 12th and Lake. However, Laramie cars only ran between Harrison and Lake after December 21, 1912. Bus substitution came in 1937.

Lawrence Avenue

This far North Side crosstown line was opened to streetcar service between Broadway and Milwaukee in 1896. On May 5, 1917 an extension streetcar began service between Milwaukee and Austin. The two routes were consolidated on June 16, 1917. One-man cars took over all service on January 29, 1950, and trolley buses took over April 1, 1951.

Lincoln Avenue

This important radial line served the area between Lake Michigan and the North Branch of the Chicago River. The basic route was converted from cable car to streetcar on October 21, 1906. Lincoln-Bowmanville cars ran from Lincoln and Foster to downtown via Lincoln, Armitage, Clark, Randolph, LaSalle, Monroe, Dearborn, and Randolph.

The Lincoln-Rosehill cars, begun in 1897, took a different route. They ran from Ravenswood and Rosehill Drive via Ravenswood, Balmoral, Damen, Lincoln, Armitage, Clark, Wells, Randolph, LaSalle, Monroe, Dearborn, and Randolph. On July 21, 1912 both the Lincoln-Bowmanville and Lincoln-Rosehill cars were rerouted via Illinois, LaSalle Street Tunnel, Randolph, Dearborn, Monroe, and LaSalle. From this time on both routes shared common trackage from La Salle and Illinois to the Loop.

On the Lincoln-Bowmanville line cars were extended from Foster to Berwyn on April 16, 1914. The downtown routing was changed to a loop via Randolph, Clark, Monroe, and LaSalle on January 29, 1922. In the general rerouting of September 14, 1924, both routes ran from Lincoln and Damen via Lincoln, Wells, Illinois, LaSalle, Madison, and Wells. On July 26, 1931 Lincoln-Bowmanville cars were extended to Peterson.

On November 27, 1939 the downtown loop was changed to Wells, Randolph, LaSalle, Madison, and Wells. The cars got a completely new routing to a stub terminal south of the Loop on November 27, 1944. The route was via Wells, Harrison, and Dearborn to a crossover at Polk Street.

Lincoln cars began to run via Lincoln, Larrabee, Chicago and Wells, replacing the Riverview-Larrabee cars, on September 1, 1947. The outer part of the Riverview-Larrabee line on Belmont, Damen, and Roscoe to Western was left without service. However, on September 29 certain Lincoln cars began to run over the outer portion of Riverview-Larrabee, restoring service to Roscoe and Western.

CTA discontinued the Rosehill branch on August 1, 1948. All Roscoe trips over the former Riverview-Larrabee line ceased January 10, 1949. Buses replaced Lincoln-Bowmanville cars on February 18, 1951.

Lincoln-Indiana (Through Route 3)

This busy line linking the Northwest and near South Sides opened October 5, 1912 between Lincoln and Foster and 51st and South Park. The route was via Lincoln, Armitage, Clark, Kinzie, State, Lake, Wabash, 22nd, Indiana, and 51st. This route used both 18th and 22nd. At the start of service cars ran via 22nd, but by 1913 were on 18th. In the general rerouting of September 14, 1924, southbound cars were put back on 22nd, while northbound cars remained on 18th. By 1933 both northbound and southbound cars used 18th, but on November 4, 1934 northbound cars were put on 22nd. By 1936 southbound cars had joined them via 22nd. CSL rerouted the south end of the line via 47th to Oakenwald on March 11, 1917.

In the general rerouting of September 14, 1924, southbound cars were put on State from Division to Lake, and northbound cars on State from 18th to Division. Extensions at the north end of the line brought the cars from Foster to Mozart on January 11, 1931, and from Mozart to Peterson on July 26, 1931. On the south end cars were taken off 47th and rerouted along Indiana to 51st on February 23, 1932.

Northbound cars got a new route via Harrison instead of Lake on November 4, 1934. On January 25, 1938 all cars began to run via Clark, Wells, Division, and State. Southbound cars began to run on Wells, Division, State, Grand, and Wabash on May 15, 1939. On that same day northbound cars began to run via State, Lake, Wabash, Grand, State, Division, and Wells. Both reroutings were to avoid the State Street bridge, which was out of service for replacement.

A final northbound rerouting put the cars on Wabash between Grand and 22nd on March 28, 1947. All cars were now off State and on Wabash through the downtown area. CTA ended all streetcar service on the route

CTA New Pullman 1007 has changed ends and waits for departure time from the Lincoln-Peterson terminal for a run to Dearborn and Polk in Downtown Chicago. It will make its run on the Lincoln-Bowmanville route, last of the Lincoln Avenue lines to be converted to bus operation. Credit this photo to Raymond De Groote, Jr.

Lincoln-Rosehill cars began their southbound runs from this terminal on Ravenswood Avenue at Rosehill Drive, at the south end of the North Western's Rose Hill commuter station. Dash sign on New Pullman 904 indicates photo was taken after September 1, 1947. Photo from the Stephen D. Maguire collection.

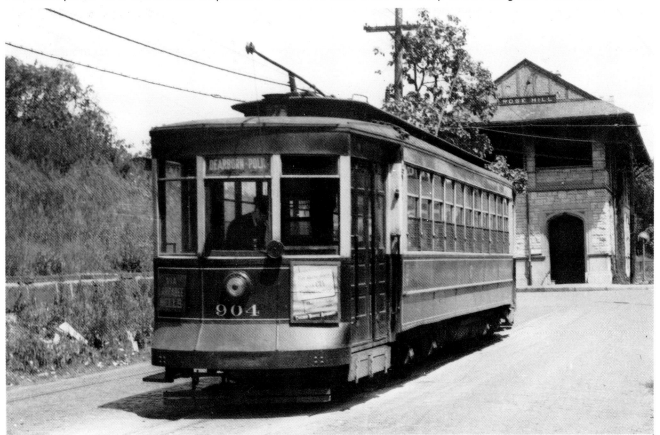

While the State Street bridge across the Chicago River was closed for replacement, for nearly eight years Lincoln-Indiana cars used the Wabash Ave. bridge, as southbound New Pullman 775 is doing in this Barney Neuberger photo. Note dash sign indicating car is on Through Route 3. From the Railway Negative Exchange.

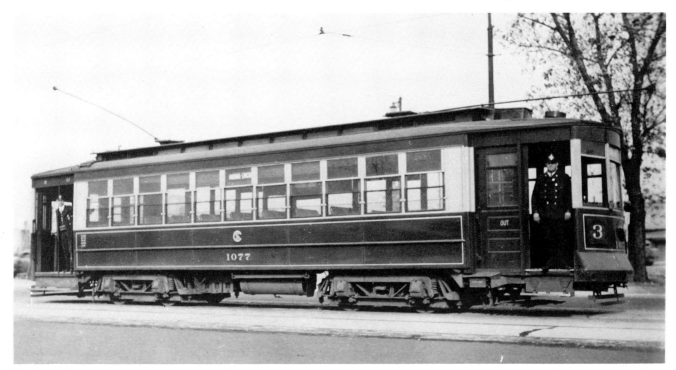

Back in October, 1935 when R. H. Kennedy took this photo, New Pullman cars such as 1077 were running on Belmont, Lincoln-Wells, Clybourn, and Division as well as the Lincoln Indiana route. Note that sign identifies the line as Indiana-Lincoln. Other Through Routes, such as Clark-Wentworth, also had reversible names. Photo from the Allan C. Williams collection.

Above. Outbound on the Lincoln-Bowmanville line, New Pullman 812 waits for a break in streetcar traffic on Clark Street at the intersection of Clark and Wells. Barney Neuberger collection.

Chicago City Railway cars saw service on Lincoln-Indiana. Here CCRy standard Brill 5082 turns east on 47th Street from Indiana Avenue, bound for 47th and Lake Park Avenue. George Krambles collection.

March 11, 1951. Through-routing to 51st was discontinued, with replacement buses running only from Peterson to Adams.

Madison Street (Through Route 20)

This major crosstown street is the dividing line between the North and South Sides of Chicago. It is also one of the oldest transit streets in the city, going back to the start of horse car service in 1859. Madison was also one of the heaviest streetcar lines in the city, using both motor-trailer and multiple-unit trains. It was the first line to get PCC cars, the entire prewar lot of 83 cars being used on this line.

We pick up the story on August 19, 1906, when streetcars took over from cable cars from Madison and Springfield via Madison to a loop via Franklin, Washington, State, and Madison. At the same time the Fifth Avenue shuttle from Pulaski to Madison was extended along Madison to the Loop. Main line Madison cars were extended to Austin on December 27, 1910, and began to use the off-street loop there in July, 1921. This was Through Route 20.

On February 29, 1914 Madison cars got a new loop via Dearborn, Washington, State, and Madison. Franklin

replaced Dearborn as the west leg of the loop on August 1, 1920.

Motor-trailer trains began to run on Madison October 14, 1923. They were discontinued July 19, 1930. Experimental multiple-unit trains went into service on July 13, 1924.

On September 14, 1924 cars got a new downtown loop via Madison, Dearborn, Monroe, Clinton, and Madison.

As a Depression-era economy measure, Madison-Fifth cars began to run only between Pulaski and Madison on Sundays, starting April 24, 1932. On October 9, 1936 Fifth Avenue cars began to loop via Fifth, Pulaski, and Harrison. The loop was used in anticipation of PCC cars running on this line.

CTA began a new streetcar service, designated as the Madison-10¢ Shuttles, on October 15, 1949. Their work was to carry passengers between North Western Station on the west edge of the Loop to the heart of the business district. During the morning rush hour, cars ran on Madison, Dearborn, Monroe, Clinton, and Madison. In the evening rush, cars ran via Washington, Dearborn, Madison, Desplaines, and Washington. The fare was 10¢, and PCC cars were used. CTA ended the service on August 1, 1951.

Service cutbacks on the main line began December 5, 1950, when the short turn loop at Springfield closed. On

On a clear January day in 1929 an outbound Lincoln Avenue car has just passed the Lincoln Square (Paulina) station on the Ravenswood "L" route. The Lincoln Ave. line also crossed the Ravenswood "L" near the Wrightwood, Addison, Irving Park, and Western stations. Note the Surface Lines tower wagon at left. It made repairs to the overhead wires. Photo from the Barney Neuberger collection.

• Opposite page, top. The Madison-Fifth Avenue line held great interest for the student of urban transportation. Starting life as a horse car shuttle in 1893, it outlasted the Madison Street main line, whose tracks it shared off and on until 1953. Madison-Fifth ended life as a shuttle service, too, with one-man cars such as 78. Renumbered because of a conflict with the 1700 series of CTA buses, car 78 was formerly car 1780. This Barney Neuberger photo shows car 78 on Fifth Avenue, fulfilling schedules on the shuttle line which lasted only from December 13, 1953 until February 22, 1954. • Below. CSL 6157 appears to be on some sort of test run as it halts on Madison at Kedzie. Note coupler for hauling trailers on this heavy line. Note also sign at right, promoting CSL World's Fair service. CTA photograph.

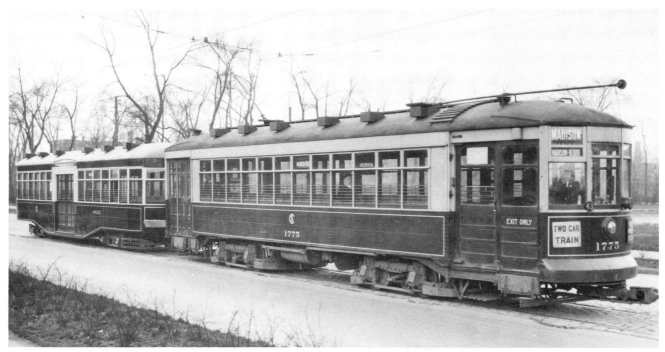

• Above. Two-car Madison Street train, motor car 1775 and trailer 8023, appear to be headed for the carbarn at Kedzie and Van Buren in this Chicago Transit Authority photograph. • Below. Because of a shortage of 1936 PCC cars, Peter Witt cars were regularly assigned to runs on both Madison and Madison-Fifth. The PCC shortage was caused by the unanticipated growth in traffic those cars brought to the Madison Street routes.

• Above. The prewar PCC cars spent so much time on Madison Street that they picked up the nickname "Madison Street cars." Car 4049 is eastbound at Franklin. Neuberger collection. • Below. Prewar PCC 4044 on Madison-10¢ Shuttle and postwar PCC on Madison-Fifth line (or on a pull-in run to the Kedzie-Van Buren barn) were snapped on Madison at Clark by Allan C. Williams on July 26, 1951.

November 10, 1951 the cars got a new downtown loop via Madison, Desplaines, Washington, Dearborn, and Madison. CTA substituted buses for the Madison main line cars on weekends only starting May 11, 1952. Franklin replaced Desplaines as the west leg of the downtown loop on January 25, 1953. On November 16, 1953 Clark replaced Dearborn as the east leg of the downtown loop.

CTA ended all Madison streetcar service on December 13, 1953, replacing it with buses. The Madison-Fifth downtown car was discontinued at the same time.

The following explanation may clarify the complex history of the Madison-Fifth Avenue line. From May 22, 1893 until August 19, 1906 Fifth Avenue was shuttle only. From 1906 until 1932 it ran downtown along Madison as a two-man route. On April 24, 1932 it continued to run downtown on weekdays and Saturdays two-man, but became a one-man shuttle route on Sundays. On May 11, 1952 it remained a two-man car route on weekdays to downtown, but became a bus route to downtown on Saturdays only, and a one-man shuttle car route on Sundays only. Fifth Avenue became a shuttle car route seven days a week on December 13, 1953 when the Madison line was converted to bus and the Madison-Fifth line discontinued. One of the cars used on this one-man shuttle was 78, a green and cream painted car formerly numbered 1781. Shuttle service ended February 22, 1954.

Milwaukee Avenue

This major radial street begins just outside the Loop at Lake and Canal and runs to the city limits on the Northwest Side. We pick up its story on August 19, 1906, when streetcars replaced cable cars between Lawrence and Milwaukee and a downtown loop. The route was via Milwaukee, Desplaines, Randolph, Wells, Washington, State, Madison, and Wells.

In 1910 the cars were extended up Milwaukee to Edmunds. On January 29, 1911 a new loop opened via Clinton, Washington, State, Madison, LaSalle, and Washington. On December 11, 1914 a separate Milwaukee extension line opened from Edmunds to Imlay. However the Imlay off-street terminal, also known as the Forest Preserve Loop, did not open until September, 1927. One-man cars were assigned to the extension on April 1, 1923. They were discontinued and the line was through-routed from downtown to Imlay on October 1, 1927.

On September 1, 1920 Milwaukee cars got a new downtown route via Washington, Franklin, Randolph, State, Washington, and Clinton. In the general rerouting of September 14, 1924, the cars got a new loop via Washington, Dearborn, Madison, and Clinton.

Milwaukee received its first two-car multiple-unit trains on March 2, 1925. They ran until May 5, 1929.

The 1936 PCC cars, and their postwar brethren, were too wide for the CSL's clearances. Both series of cars were built so that they rode off-center on their trucks, overhanging the right hand rail more than the left hand rail. As a warning to motorists that the cars were wider than they seemed, the Surface Lines added so-called Tiger Stripes to the front of the 1936 cars. Car 4009 sports the stripes at the Austin terminal of the Madison line.

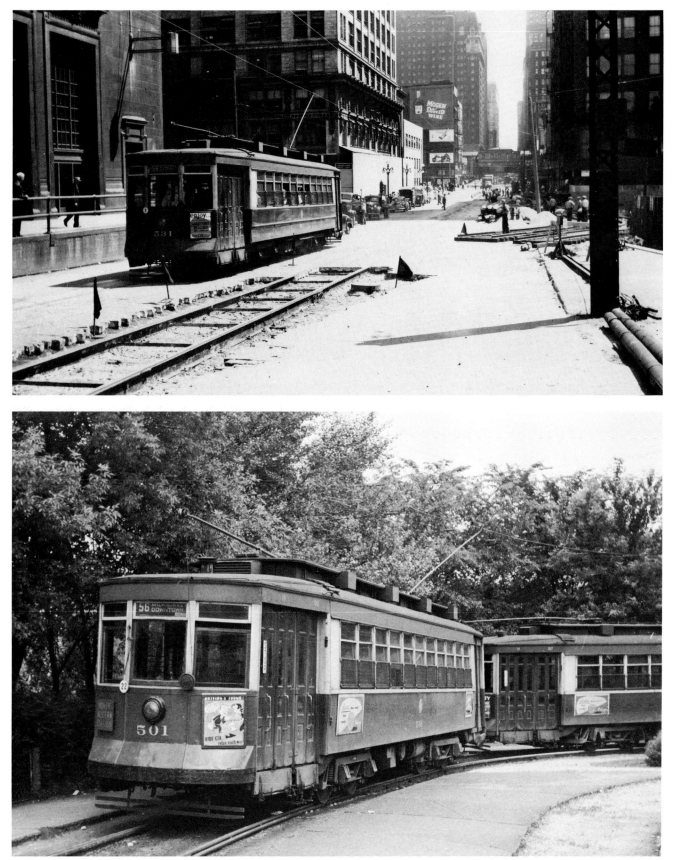

• Above. Westbound on Madison Street west of Wacker Drive, CTA Old Pullman 531 eases past the site of temporary trackwork designed to divert streetcars around the intersection. Neuberger photo, from the Railway Negative Exchange. • Below. The lowest numbered Old Pullman converted for trailer-hauling service in the 1920s, CTA 501 rests between runs at the Forest Preserve (Imlay) loop at the outer end of Milwaukee Avenue.

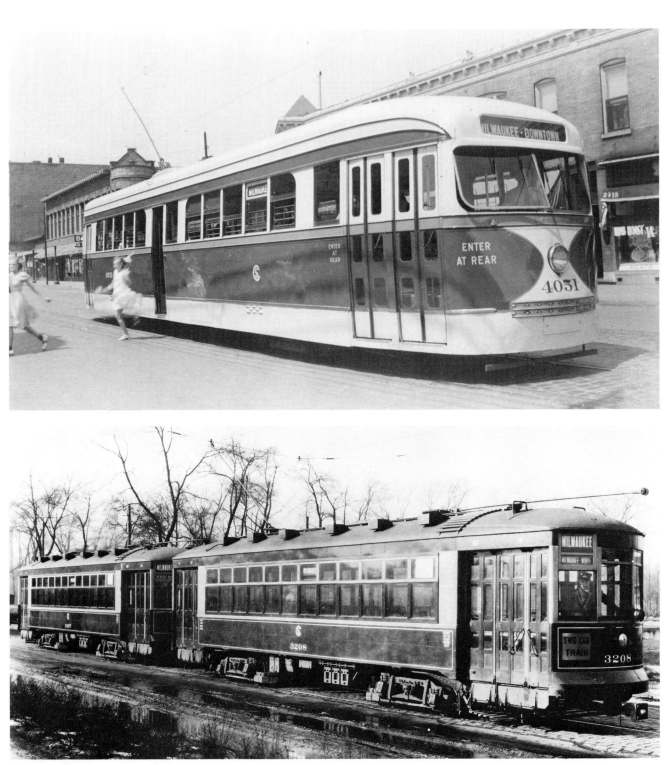

• Above, top. Prewar PCC car 4051 made runs on Milwaukee Avenue with a modified door arrangement. Although this car was later restored to conventional configuration, its experimental door arrangement was the one used on all 600 of the postwar PCC cars. Barney Neuberger collection, from Bill Richmond. • Below. Two-car multiple-unit trains, such as 3208 and 3207, ran on Milwaukee Avenue from 1925 until 1929. Chicago Transit Authority photo. • Opposite page, top. The three-way intersection of Milwaukee, Irving Park, and Cicero was the hub of a major shopping district. During the streetcar era some property at outlying carline intersections sold for more than prime property in the Loop. This photo looks west along Milwaukee, and shows two Old Pullmans, both equipped with couplers for trailer-hauling, on the far side of the intersection. To the extreme right is a 2700 series 1903 St. Louis deck-roof car, running south on the Cicero line. CTA photo. • Bottom. Old Pullman 546 turns west on Adams from Dearborn in downtown Chicago while making an outbound run on the Milwaukee Avenue line. Though their trailer-hauling days ended in 1930, these air door cars continued to run on Milwaukee Ave. until the end of service. A. C. Wiliams photo on April 17, 1952.

CSL began to supplement regular service with rush hour cars via a new downtown loop on Milwaukee, Desplaines, Harrison, Clinton, and Milwaukee on December 14, 1934.

No route changes were made until October 28, 1951, when CTA substituted buses on weekends only. On November 7 weekday streetcars got a new loop via Clinton, Washington, LaSalle, Madison, and Clinton. A rerouting put the cars on a new loop via Clinton, Monroe, Dearborn, and Adams on November 22. Complete bus substitution came on May 11, 1952.

Although it is listed as Armitage-Downtown and is shown as part of the Armitage route, the Armitage-Downtown cars were actually part of the Milwaukee line. They ran with Milwaukee Ave. cars (the air-door Pullmans), used Milwaukee Ave. crews, ran from the same barn as Milwaukee cars, and even used the same transfer.

Montrose Avenue

Streetcars began to run between Broadway and Knox on this North Side crosstown line in 1897. However, it wasn't until the 1930s that the line grew beyond its original length. It was on November 16, 1930 that Montrose cars began to run west of Knox to Milwaukee.

On January 25, 1931 CSL began an extension trolley bus line from Milwaukee to Narragansett. The streetcar line received one-man equipment on September 4, 1932. Buses replaced the one-man cars July 29, 1946, and trolley buses replaced the gas buses from Broadway to Narragansett on April 19, 1948.

Morgan-Racine-Sangamon (Through Route 23)

This near West Side line was originally two routes, Erie and Racine, each of which served downtown Chicago via Adams Street. We pick up the story on December 1, 1912, when the Erie and Racine lines were through-routed. The line ran from 39th and Morgan to Erie and Ashland via Morgan, private right-of-way, Throop, 21st, Racine, Adams, Sangamon, Hubbard, Racine, and Erie. CSL began to use one-man cars on the route on August 7, 1932. CTA substituted buses for the cars on July 25, 1948.

Narragansett Avenue

This pioneer North Side trolley bus line was begun June 29, 1930. It ran from a wye at Irving Park to an elongated loop via Wabansia, Austin, North, and Narragansett. On March 5, 1932 a new loop went into service via Wabansia, Mobile, and North. The line got a new north terminal on November 25, 1933, when it was extended beyond Irving Park to a wye at Cuyler. On December 4, 1949 CTA rerouted the Narragansett bus into a new North and Narragansett terminal. CTA substituted buses for trolley buses on February 1, 1953, through-routing the gas buses with the North Ave. gas buses.

Noble Street

One of the shortest of all CSL routes, the line began on June 11, 1885 as a horse car route from Milwaukee and Noble to Cortland and Wood via Noble, Blackhawk, Greenview, North, Ashland, and Cortland to Wood. When streetcars replaced horse cars in 1896, the line was cut to about half its former length, running only from Milwaukee and Noble to North and Ashland. One-man cars began to run November 1, 1921. Service was limited to rush hours only on July 25, 1931. All regular service ended March 5, 1932, but Elston cars on barn trips used Noble Street until February 8, 1944.

North Avenue (Including North-Downtown, Through Route 21)

This major North Side crosstown line had a local car and a downtown car. We pick up its story on June 26, 1911. On that day the local cars were extended to Lamon from Kenton. The east terminal for the local cars remained at Clark. Downtown car service began the same day via North, Milwaukee, and Lake to a downtown loop via State, Randolph, and Dearborn. The Downtown service was short-lived, ending August 14, 1912.

On October 10, 1915 CSL started a shuttle car route between Lamon and Austin. This was through-routed on November 24, 1917. The last streetcar extension, to Rossell (Narragansett), was made on November 29, 1931.

CTA replaced streetcars with trolley buses on July 3, 1949 from Clybourn loop to the Narragansett, Wabansia, Mobile, North loop. A shuttle streetcar ran from Clybourn to Clark until a trolley bus loop could be built in Lincoln Park. On December 4, 1949 CTA replaced the shuttle cars with trolley buses.

CSL also ran bus service on North from Nagle to Harlem, starting on September 1, 1942. On February 29, 1944 the buses began to run to Narragansett. CTA rerouted the buses into the new North-Narragansett terminal on December 4, 1949, and through-routed them with the Narragansett line when that was converted from trolley bus to bus on February 1, 1953.

Northwest Highway

An early Northwest Side feeder bus line, Northwest Highway service started April 21, 1935. From a loop via Ozark, Olmstead, and Overhill near the city limits it ran

Opposite page. Track reconstruction was done under traffic, and was always difficult on lines with frequent service, such as Milwaukee Avenue. Top photo from CTA. Bottom photo shows temporary track at Chicago and Milwaukee during construction of Milwaukee subway line. Neuberger photo.

One-man car 3298 has its rear pole up, and is ready to start its eastbound run on the Montrose Avenue line from the west terminal at Montrose and Milwaukee. Barney Neuberger collection.

One-man Montrose Avenue car crosses the North Branch of the Chicago River on Montrose near Rockwell St. Judging from all the open windows on the car, passengers would enjoy a cooling dip in the river.

Although officially designated as a Through Route (23), the Morgan-Racine-Sangamon line didn't have the heavy traffic characteristic of most such lines. Car 3096 is outbound on private right-of-way between Morgan and Throop. Neuberger photo.

From its start as a Through Route in 1912 until 1932, Morgan-Racine-Sangamon used two-man cars. From 1932 until the end of service in 1948, one-man cars such as 2921 handled all runs. Barney Neuberger collection.

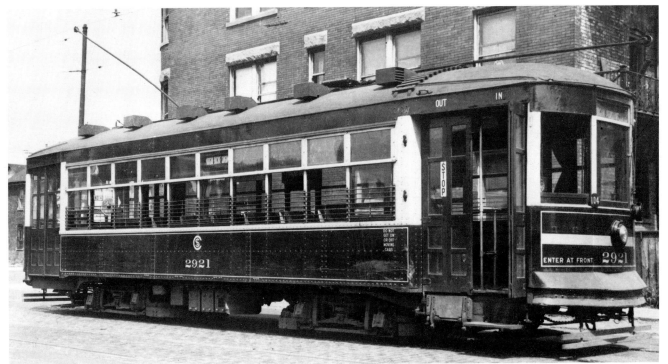

• Above. Until North Avenue trolley bus service could be extended from Clybourn to Clark, CTA ran a streetcar shuttle line between those two points. This temporary service began on July 3, 1949, and ended on December 4. In this photo a passenger is transferring from a shuttle car to a trolley bus at North and Clybourn. Neuberger photo. • Below. Westbound on the North Avenue line, CTA Old Pullman approaches the bridge over the Chicago River. Less than a mile from its east terminal the car began to pass through an industrial area, and it is now passing the north tip of highly industrialized Goose Island. Quite a contrast between Lincoln Park, at the east terminal, and this factory district so close to it. Neuberger collection from the Railway Negative Exchange.

via Northwest Highway to a loop via Milwaukee, Higgins, Gale, and Milwaukee. On January 27, 1943 Northwest Highway buses were through-routed with Foster buses from the Ozark loop to the Berwyn loop via Northwest Highway and Foster.

Ogden Avenue

This radial line connected the Southwest Side with downtown Chicago. By 1896 it extended from downtown via Randolph and Ogden to 40th Avenue. Though there was track beyond Ogden and 40th, it was a separate Berwyn-Lyons route operated by the West Chicago Street Railway. In 1911 Ogden cars were extended via Cicero and 25th to Laramie (52nd Avenue) over the existing tracks. The downtown loop was changed several times until 1914, when it became Randolph, Franklin, Lake, State, Randolph, Dearborn, and Lake.

For less than a year motor-trailer two car trains ran on Ogden. They entered service November 22, 1922, and were withdrawn October 13, 1923.

In the general rerouting of September 14, 1924, Ogden cars got a new loop via Randolph, Dearborn, Washington, Desplaines, and Randolph.

CTA put one-man cars on this line December 18, 1949. Two reroutings came in 1950. The first, on April 2, put the cars on Randolph, Clinton, Lake, Dearborn, and Randolph. The second, on September 11, 1950, set up a new loop via Lake, Dearborn, Washington, Desplaines, and Randolph. CTA put buses on the line September 16, 1951.

An Ogden bus extension ran from a loop via Clark and Wisconsin to a loop via Arcade, Paulina, and Monroe. It started to run January 17, 1938, but was suspended on December 1, 1942 as a World War II economy move. CSL reinstated service on October 1, 1945. The last change under CSL management came on October 21, 1946, when the line was extended a short distance down Ogden to a new loop via Wood, Polk, Wolcott, Harrison, and Wood.

Ogden-Clark (Through Route 11)

This line linked the near Southwest Side with the near North Side. Begun on October 26, 1911, it ran from Ogden and Pulaski to Clark and North via Ogden, Madison, and Clark. On August 16, 1912 the line was extended west to Kenton and north to the Drummond terminal (Limits carhouse loop). The line was discontinued in the general rerouting of September 14, 1924.

Pershing Road (39th Street)

Two routes provided service on this South Side crosstown street. The first to open was the east line between Cottage Grove and State in 1875. By September 27, 1896 the line had been extended to Root and Halsted via Pershing and Halsted. On March 2, 1924 CSL rerouted the cars via Wallace from Pershing to Root. One-man cars went on the line August 7, 1932. CTA replaced the cars with buses on February 15, 1948, through-routing

Another surprise along North Avenue was the use of central line poles between the tracks with bracket arms to support the trolley wires. This Neuberger photo looks east along North Avenue from California Avenue.

Chicago Railways bus 572, a 1937 Ford model 70, poses with Chicago City Railway standard wood semiconvertible 5271, an American Car Company product of 1906. The bus is signed for route 58-A, begun on January 17, 1938 between Ogden and Clark and Ogden and Arcade Place. Suspended on December 1, 1942 as a WW II economy move, the line was reinstated by the Surface Lines on October 1, 1945. On October 21, 1946, CSL extended the line down Ogden from Arcade Place to Wood Street. Photo from the George Krambles collection.

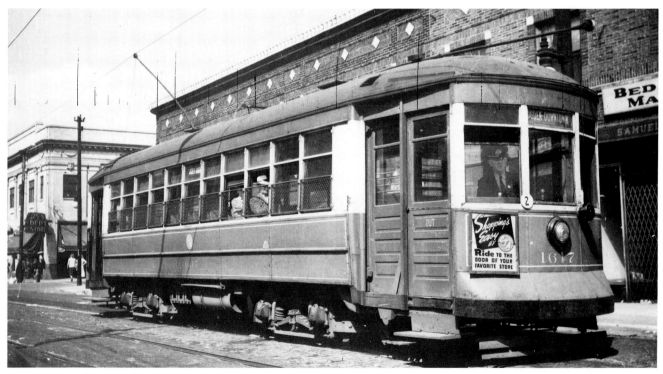

Car 1617 is at the west end of the Ogden Avenue line at 25th and Laramie in the suburban town of Cicero, Ill. The line from Cicero to Laramie along 25th was in the town of Cicero, and was used by CSL under a trackage rights agreement. Other such track in Cicero was found along Cermak (for 383 feet west of Kenton Ave.), along Cicero Ave. from Roosevelt Road to Ogden Ave., along Ogden from Kenton to Cicero, and along Roosevelt Road from Kenton to Austin Blvd. (the south track only). Barney Neuberger collection.

Near the end of streetcar service the CTA put one-man cars on the Ogden line. Here car 1733, converted for one-man service on November 18, 1949, takes the curve under the Loop "L" as it turns south on Dearborn from Lake. Ogden Avenue became a one-man line on December 18, 1949, and was converted to bus operation on September 16, 1951. During the period of one-man operation the cars were rerouted twice. See page 293 for details. In addition to one-man and two-man cars, Ogden Avenue also had motor-trailer train operation for less than a year. Neuberger photo from Bill Richmond.

The east Pershing line began here, at Pershing and Cottage Grove. Car 3245 in one-man service takes the crossover to the westbound track for its run to the Root-Halsted (Stock Yards) terminal via Pershing, Wallace, and Root. Pershing cars on the east route shared the Stock Yards terminal with cars of the 43rd-Root Street line. East and west line Pershing cars never met, and the west line was operated as almost a branch of the 35th Street line from 1919 until 1934. Gordon Lloyd took the photo September 29, 1946. Print courtesy of Jack Doyle.

• This page, top. Car 2589 is southbound on the Riverdale (Michigan-Indiana) route, and has just entered the private right-of-way south of 130th Street and Indiana Ave. Neuberger photo from the Allan C. Williams collection. • Opposite page. Car 2575 swings out from under the Illinois Central Railroad trestle at 134th and private right-of-way as it makes a northbound trip to 119th and Michigan. Alan W. Simms collection. • This page, below. This Pershing car, eastbound on the east route, takes the turn from Root into Wallace.

them with the west Pershing line.

The west line went into service on January 13, 1919 between Ashland and Western. Two weeks later it began to run to 35th and Cottage Grove via Ashland and 35th. On October 7, 1934 CSL began one-man service on this line, which was cut back to 39th and Ashland. CSL substituted buses for the streetcars on August 28, 1945.

Peterson Avenue

This far North Side bus line originally ran from Central to Broadway. Service began June 19, 1939 via Caldwell, Peterson, and Ridge to a loop via Bryn Mawr, Winthrop, Hollywood, Broadway, and Ridge. No further changes were made in this route by CSL.

Pulaski Road (Crawford Avenue)

We pick up the story of this north-south trunk line in 1911, when cars were through-routed from Cemetery Drive (5400 north) to 31st and Kostner. On September 5, 1915 the line was opened as far north as Bryn Mawr.

Motor-trailer service lasted 15 months on this line. It began July 13, 1922, and ended October 13, 1923.

On October 28, 1946 a bus extension began to run from Bryn Mawr to a wye at Glenlake. CTA cut back streetcar service to 31st and Karlov on December 4, 1949. Buses took over for the cars on weekends February 25, 1951, and CTA substituted trolley buses for all service

on September 16, 1951. The trolley buses were through-routed from a wye at 31st and Komensky to Pulaski and Peterson.

South Pulaski Road

CSL began service on this line January 25, 1937 between 47th and a wye at 63rd Pl. On August 9, buses were extended up Pulaski to a loop via 32nd, Harding, 31st, and Pulaski. CSL routed the buses into a new south terminal via 64th, Keating, 63rd, and Pulaski on June 22, 1938.

To serve the Dodge-Chicago defense plant, CSL sent the buses south during rush hours to a new terminal at 75th on July 2, 1942. To give better service to the plant, all buses were extended via 76th to Keeler, with the rush hour buses going on to Kilpatrick on July 26, 1943. This was the last change made under Surface Lines management.

Riverdale (Michigan-Indiana)

This far South Side line reached the farthest point south of any CSL route. Cars began to run in 1896 from 119th and Michigan to 124th and Michigan via Michigan. There was apparently a gap in this service, for at least the records for 1908 show no service on the line. On January 14, 1914 the line was extended south to 138th and

Leyden via 127th, Indiana, private right-of-way, 134th, Indiana, and Leyden.

CSL put one-man cars in service April 6, 1936, and substituted buses for the cars on September 9, 1946.

Riverview-Larrabee

We pick up the story of this North Side line in 1906, when the Riverview line was extended from Lincoln and Wrightwood to downtown via Lincoln, Halsted, North, Sedgwick, Chicago, Orleans, Kinzie, and Clark to Washington. Northbound cars used Kinzie, Orleans, Division, and Sedgwick. This was a restoration of downtown service on the line, which began when the line started on July 19, 1887, and stopped February 1, 1889, when the line was cut back to Lincoln and Wrightwood. The original downtown line was via Lincoln, Armitage, and Clark. The cutback of February 1, 1889 was made because on that date the North Chicago Street Railroad extended cable car service from Clark and Armitage to Lincoln and Wrightwood. The line was restored to operation downtown after the Lincoln-Clark cable car service ended on October 21, 1906.

On January 17, 1911 Riverview cars began to use the Riverview terminal west of Western and just north of Roscoe. They were later cut back to the Roscoe and Western crossover. Cars got a new downtown loop via Kinzie, Dearborn, Monroe, LaSalle, Washington, Wells, and Kinzie on July 21, 1912. On July 20, 1914 the Larrabee route was incorporated into a new Riverview-Larrabee line, and cars began to take a new route via Lincoln, Larrabee, Chicago, Kingsbury, Erie, Franklin, Kinzie, and Dearborn to Polk. A new loop via Dearborn, Randolph, Wells, and Kinzie went into service September 14, 1924.

On May 4, 1947 another rerouting put the southbound cars on Franklin, Hubbard, Wells, Harrison, and Dearborn to Polk. Northbound cars used Dearborn, Harrison, Wells, Kinzie, and Franklin. Riverview-Larrabee became a branch of the Lincoln-Larrabee route on September 1, 1947. See the Lincoln Avenue route description for further changes.

Roosevelt Road (12th Street)

This major near South Side crosstown line took the shape it was to have for many years in 1896. In that year streetcars replaced horse cars from Wabash to Pulaski, streetcar service was extended from Pulaski to Austin, and a Roosevelt-Downtown car began to run via Roosevelt, Wells, and Van Buren to State.

The Downtown cars had several route changes through the years. In 1906 they began to run via Wells, Van Buren, Dearborn, Adams, and Wells. On January 29, 1922 Downtown cars were rerouted via Wells, Adams, Dearborn, Van Buren, and Wells. Cars began to run on Canal, Harrison, and Wells to the downtown loop on December 24, 1934.

CTA discontinued the Downtown cars on weekends on July 1, 1950. On September 6 all Downtown service ended.

On the main line, Roosevelt cars were extended to Michigan on June 25, 1933. To speed the movement of visitors to the Century of Progress Exposition, Roosevelt cars were extended via a trestle to a terminal in Grant Park on August 1, 1933.

CTA substituted buses for streetcars from Austin to Michigan on August 12, 1951. The line into Grant Park was made a one-man shuttle from Wabash. The shuttle was discontinued without substitution on April 12, 1953.

12th-Ogden-Wells
(Through Route 14)

Running from Roosevelt and Kenton to Clark and Drummond, this line provided through service between the West and near North Sides. The route was via Roosevelt (12th), Ogden, Randolph, Wells, and Clark. Service began June 26, 1911. By 1913 the cars were rerouted via Roosevelt, Wells, and Clark. The west terminal was moved from Kenton and Roosevelt to Cicero and Roosevelt on July 1, 1916. All service was discontinued in the general rerouting of September 14, 1924.

• Opposite page. Inbound Riverview-Larrabee car 2733 turns east on Erie from Kingsbury on its serpentine route through the Near North Side of Chicago. Photo from the Neuberger collection. • This page, top. On August 12, 1951 CTA created the Grant Park shuttle line, which used the east end of the former Roosevelt Road line between Wabash Ave. and the Grant Park terminal. Converted for one-man service on January 5, 1950, 1923 steel car 6185 lays over at the Grant Park terminal loop. Neuberger collection, from Allan C. Williams • This page, below. Bus substitution was imminent when Ed Frank, Jr., took this photo of CTA Old Pullman 678 westbound on Roosevelt.

300

• Above. Whenever special events drew thousands to Soldiers Field, CSL was there before and after the event to handle the crowds. In this photo from the S. D. Maguire collection, Turtlebacks and Pullmans load at both the inbound and outbound platforms on April 6, 1946. Cars loading at the inbound (right) platform left the terminal on the center track, so they wouldn't be delayed by cars loading at the outbound platform. • Opposite page, top. The Roosevelt Road streetcar line had been a shuttle operation for a little more than a month when one-man shuttle car 3200 was snapped as it waited for passengers at the Roosevelt and Wabash terminal on September 23, 1951. S.D. Maguire collection. • Opposite page, below. In this photo, taken June 24, 1933, CSL air compressors AX-507 and AX-508, power shovel J-1, and two utility trucks are at work on the Roosevelt Road line extension into Grant Park. Author's collection. • This page, below. The off-street terminal near 63rd and South Park (now M.L. King, Jr., Drive) served several CSL routes. When this picture was taken, South-Chicago-Ewing and South Deering cars looped there. It was also the terminal for the Hammond and Whiting-East Chicago cars before they were replaced by the South Chicago-Ewing line. Note Chicago & Calumet District Transit bus.

South Chicago-Ewing

To give service within Chicago on the just-abandoned Hammond and Whiting-East Chicago interstate lines, CSL inaugurated this line on June 9, 1940. The line ran from the 63rd, Vernon, and South Park terminal via South Park, South Chicago, 92nd, Ewing, and 108th to Avenue F. Alternate cars ran via Ewing and Indianapolis to 106th (state line). On October 7, 1941 the runs via Indianapolis were discontinued.

On April 8, 1945 South Chicago-Ewing cars were extended to 118th and Burley via Ewing and 118th. At this new south terminal they connected with the Hegewisch cars, which had been cut back to 118th and Burley as their north terminal. The South Chicago-Ewing cars, always one-man, could not run south to the end of the Hegewisch line because of the railroad crossings south of 118th. CSL cars had to be flagged across grade-level crossings with railroads, and this required a two-man crew with the conductor doing the flagging. So the short Hegewisch shuttle was operated with two-man cars, while the much longer and busier South Chicago-Ewing line used one-man cars.

At the same time the South Chicago-Ewing cars were extended, the Indianapolis shuttle was begun from Ewing to 106th. It was discontinued on May 1, 1947.

On June 30, 1947 CSL replaced the streetcars with buses. The route was from the 63rd and Vernon terminal via South Park, South Chicago, 92nd, Ewing, 109th (or 113th), Avenue O, 134th, Brandon, 132nd, Baltimore, Brainard, and Brandon to 134th. A short-turn loop was established west on 116th to Republic Steel.

South Deering

One of the CSL routes which served the area east of Lake Calumet on the far Southeast Side of Chicago, this line ran from 63rd and Stony Island to 112th and Torrence after the changes made on December 30, 1909. These included an extension on Torrence from 106th to 112th, and the separation of service on 106th between Torrence and Ewing. Formerly a part of the South Deering route, the 106th Street segment became a shuttle line. The new South Deering route was from 63rd and Dorchester via 64th, Stony Island, 75th, Coles, 79th, Brandon, 83rd, Burley, 87th, Buffalo, 92nd, Commercial, 104th, and Torrence to 112th. By July, 1913 the cars were running from 63rd and Stony Island.

On June 3, 1914 cars began to run via Stony Island, 73rd, Exchange, and 75th. On June 22 the cars got a new north terminal via a loop on 63rd, Dorchester, and 64th.

A new loop terminal at 112th went into service in March, 1917. On November 8, 1924 a one-man shuttle car began to run on Torrence from 112th to 124th. The extension tracks ended at the foot of the incline up to the Calumet River Bridge. Although the bridge had tracks, they were never connected to the rails on Torrence. One-man cars went into service on the entire line on August 7, 1932. The extension cars stopped running on Sunday on January 1, 1939.

CSL substituted buses for the extension cars between 112th and 124th on October 21, 1946. The buses ran beyond the old streetcar terminal at 124th to a new terminal at the Ford plant at 128th. The main line between 63rd and 112th got bus service on April 25, 1948, and the buses were through-routed to 128th.

• Above. One-man car 6205 on Ewing at 108th Street enroute to the south terminal of the South Chicago-Ewing line at 118th and Burley. Neuberger photo. • Opposite page. Car 1934 southbound on State just south of Jackson Blvd. Although no route sign is visible, the car is probably a short-turn run on the State Lake line. Delays were common on this route, and a story is told of a conductor who went for a week on this line without ever reaching his far terminal. His car lost so much time that it was always turned back short of its terminal. Photo from Alan W. Simms.

• Above. CSL 3159 is at the Lake-Austin terminal of Through Route 16, State-Lake, ready to leave on a run that will take it to 119th and Morgan on the far South Side. Picture taken February 28, 1946. Neuberger collection, from Jack Doyle. • Opposite page, top. CSL 6017 heads south on State just north of Van Buren in this 1931 photo from Kaufmann & Fabry. The car is on Through Route 16 bound for 63rd and State, which was the terminal of this line in all but rush hours, when cars ran to 119th and Morgan. • Opposite page, bottom. On December 16, 1931 State-Lake cars were extended from 63rd to 79th during non-rush hours. However, Sunday and evening service on Through Route 16 had been cut back to State and Van Buren on March 15, 1931. The fact that the cars were able to change ends on a major Loop street shows how deeply the Depression had affected streetcar headways. This Barney Neuberger shot from the Bill Richmond collection shows car 3089 on State just north of 18th, bound for 79th and State. • This page, below. It's clear sailing for CSL 1636 as it runs south on TR 16 along State south of 13th during street reconstruction. Neuberger collection.

305

Southport

This North Side line began as a streetcar route from Lincoln to Clark on October 6, 1894. The line was extended south to Cortland on December 7, 1894. In 1896 Southport cars began to run downtown via Clybourn, Halsted, Division, Crosby, Larrabee, Chicago, Kingsbury, Erie, Franklin, Hubbard, Wells, Harrison, and Dearborn to Polk. Northbound cars used Wells, Kinzie, and Franklin. Some cars used an alternate route via Crosby, Elm, Franklin, and Hubbard. This alternate route ended September 2, 1912. All Southport service ended on September 14, 1924, though Ashland cars continued to use Southport from Cortland to Clark.

State Street (South)

This prime north-south street is the base line dividing Chicago streets east and west. Transit service began April 25, 1859 with a horse car route between Lake and 12th. From that time on, all extensions to the route were to the south, except for the incorporation of the North State route in 1913. This brought State cars up to Division and Wells via State and Division. The longest of the South Side extensions, and the one which gave the line its final form, came on August 12, 1918. At that time the route was extended from 79th and State to 119th and Morgan via State, 95th, Michigan, 119th, and the Morgan, 120th and Halsted loop.

On August 19, 1937 the Broadway and State lines were through-routed, and State cars began to run to Devon and Kedzie via State, Division, Clark, Broadway, and Devon. While a new State Street bridge across the Chicago River was under construction, Broadway-State cars ran via Grand, Wabash, and Lake from May 15, 1939 to May 28, 1949.

CTA put a short-turn loop in service at 84th on June 28, 1947. The 63rd terminal, in use for short turns since January, 1911, remained open and was made a loop for PCC car operation in the 1940s. On December 15, 1947, cars got a new north terminal via Devon, Ravenswood, Schreiber, and Clark.

On September 5, 1954 CTA substituted buses for streetcars on weekends. The through route was discontinued, and buses replaced State cars from 120th to downtown on December 5, 1955.

State Street (North)

Transit service on North State Street goes back to 1880 and the start of a horse car line from Clark and Division to State and Lake via Division and State. On July 14, 1895, streetcars replaced the horse cars over the same route. For a period beginning ca. 1902, cars looped via State, Kinzie, Dearborn, Lake, State, Randolph, Dearborn, Kinzie, and State. By 1905 the cars had returned to their stub terminal at State and Lake. In 1906 the line was extended from Clark and Division to the crossover at Wells and Division, and routed via Division, State, Washington, and Dearborn to a crossover at Polk. Northbound cars ran via Dearborn, Randolph,

and State. In July, 1913 Lake became the link between Dearborn and State for northbound cars. Later that year North State was consolidated with South State to form one route.

State-Madison (Through Route 7)

One of a number of Through Routes inaugurated in 1911, State-Madison began to run October 9 from 39th and State to Madison and Austin via State and Madison. On September 16, 1912 the cars were extended south on State to 63rd. Service was discontinued in the general rerouting of September 13, 1924.

State-Milwaukee (Through Route 6)

Begun on January 18, 1912, this line linking the Northwest and South Sides was discontinued in the general rerouting of September 13, 1924. The original route was from 39th and State to Milwaukee and Edmunds via State, Lake, and Milwaukee. On September 16, 1912 the cars were extended south on State from 39th to 63rd Street. Because of the closing of the Lake Street bridge from March 29, 1914 to August 22, 1916, State-Milwaukee cars were detoured off Lake.

Stony Island Avenue

This South Side trunk line operated as far south as 115th and Cottage Grove in 1893, but on January 14, 1910 service was cut back to 93rd and Stony Island. At that time the north terminal was located 150 feet south of 63rd and Stony Island.

Stony Island-Downtown service (Cottage Grove-Jackson Park line) began on July 23, 1911 as a completely separate route. It started at a loop via 63rd, Harper, and 62nd and ran via Stony Island, 56th, Lake Park, 55th, Cottage Grove, Indiana, 18th, and Wabash to a loop via Washington, Garland, Randolph, and Wabash. On June 22, 1914 the Downtown cars got a new south loop via 64th, Harper, and 63rd. Downtown cars and local Stony Island cars were through-routed on September 21, 1914.

CSL rerouted Stony Island cars via 56th, Lake Park, 47th, and Cottage Grove on October 15, 1916. On February 23, 1932 all Stony Island cars except Sunday runs were extended via Wabash and Grand to Navy Pier (Streeter Drive). Sunday cars began to use the same route five years later on July 25, 1937.

CTA began weekend bus service on December 4, 1949. The buses ran only from 93rd and Stony Island to 47th and Cottage Grove. On June 29, 1951 CTA substituted buses for cars seven days a week. All operation north of 47th was discontinued at this time.

• Opposite page, top. CTA 3197 at the Streeter Drive (Navy Pier) terminal of the Stony Island route. Neuberger collection. • Below. 3191 on Stony Island Ave. at 93rd St. A. C. Williams.

Typical of the cars assigned to the Wallace-Racine route was CSL 5040, a standard CCRy PAYE semiconvertible built by American Car Company in 1905. Gordon Lloyd photo from the collection of Jack Doyle.

Southbound on run 1186, CTA 5186 bounces across the tracks of the 51st Street line at 51st and Racine on April 3, 1948. This photo of action on the Wallace-Racine line came from the Alan W. Simms collection.

Taylor-Sedgwick-Sheffield

This line, put together in 1924, was one of the last routes started by CSL and one of the first to be converted to bus operation by CSL. It was made from parts of the Sedgwick and Taylor-Wells-Sheffield routes. The route began at Taylor and Western and ran to Sheffield and Clark via Taylor, Wells, Kinzie, Orleans, Division, Sedgwick, Lincoln, and Sheffield. Southbound cars ran via Sedgwick, Chicago, Orleans, Hubbard, and Wells. At the time of consolidation the one-man cars used on Taylor-Wells-Sheffield since August 9, 1924 were replaced by two-man cars. CSL rerouted the line via Taylor, Canal, Polk, and Wells in 1926.

CSL split the route on June 30, 1947. Service was discontinued between Taylor and Halsted and Harrison and Wells. However, streetcars continued to run on each of the two sections. Buses replaced the cars on both segments, and were through-routed to cover the entire line, on September 1, 1947.

Van Buren Street

After streetcars replaced horse cars in 1896, the new route was from State to Kedzie along Van Buren. On September 14, 1924 cars began to run via a loop on Van Buren, Clinton, Adams, and Dearborn. On October 11, 1937 Division and Van Buren were through-routed via Van Buren, State, and Division. See the Division Street listing for further details of the joint operation.

Because traffic was unevenly divided between the Division and Van Buren branches of the through route, Van Buren got extra rush hour cars over the 1924 route until after 1937. On February 4, 1951 Van Buren was separated from Division when the Division portion of the through route begun in 1937 was converted to bus. At that time Van Buren continued to run as a streetcar line, and got a downtown loop via State, Harrison, Dearborn. This period of separate streetcar operation ended when buses took over on August 12, 1951.

Wallace-Racine

Wallace and Racine cars were through-routed on September 27, 1896, three months after streetcar service began on Racine from 47th to 63rd. The route was from 63rd and Racine via Racine, 47th, Halsted, Root, Wallace, 29th, Canal, Archer, and State to a loop via Madison, Wabash, and Lake. By 1902 Wallace-Racine cars had separated from the cable line loop, and ran to their own stub terminal at Clark and Washington. On August 11, 1902 cars began to run to 75th and Racine. The downtown loop was changed to Lake, Wabash, and Randolph to State on December 17, 1906.

A half-mile extension brought the cars to 79th on April 1, 1914. CSL extended the line another mile to its ultimate terminal at 87th on April 25, 1918.

On March 2, 1924 the route was changed by using Pershing instead of Root to get between Halsted and Wallace. In the general rerouting of September 14, the downtown loop was changed to State, Polk, Dearborn, Lake, and State. One-man cars took over on November 9, 1932, but the line later became a two-man route again. On August 1, 1947 the cars returned to their old route via Halsted, Root, and Wallace.

CTA substituted buses for weekend cars on December 4, 1949. The buses ran to 47th and Wentworth only. On December 10 they were extended to a loop via 23rd Pl., Archer, and Canal. Final bus replacement for all service came on July 27, 1951.

Webster-Racine

Begun in 1878 as a horse car route from Lincoln to Racine, this very short near North Side line became a loop operation via Webster, Halsted, Fullerton, and Racine in 1884. In the 1890s the line became a testing ground for all sorts of street railway motive power. Compressed air cars replaced horse cars in 1890, electric cars that got their power from a charged rail in an underground conduit replaced the air cars in 1892, and horse cars replaced the conduit cars in 1894. Conventional electric cars, drawing their power from an overhead trolley wire, replaced the horse cars on April 1, 1895. This route was chosen for the experiments with exotic means of propulsion because it passed the North Side Company's shops at Fullerton and Sheffield.

On May 25, 1895 Webster ceased operations as a separate route, and became the north terminal of the Larrabee line via Larrabee, Lincoln, Fullerton, Racine, Webster, and Larrabee. On September 10, 1914 Webster was made part of the terminal loop of the Sedgwick line via Sedgwick, Lincoln, Fullerton, Racine, Webster, Lincoln, and Sedgwick. Webster again became a separate route on September 14, 1924. The new route was a loop via Webster, Lincoln, Fullerton, Racine, and Webster.

One-man cars entered service on the line May 1, 1925. On March 13, 1927 the line was cut back, and all service ended on Lincoln and Fullerton. The "L"-shaped line that remained ran from Racine and Fullerton to Webster and Lincoln via Racine and Webster. To allow for two-car operation, a passing siding was built on Webster near Sheffield in 1927. The siding was under the Webster station of the "L" line. CSL replaced the Webster-Racine cars with Taylor-Sedgwick-Sheffield buses on September 1, 1947.

Wentworth Avenue

We pick up the story of this major South Side trunk route on March 17, 1908, when it was through-routed with the Clark line. The route was from 79th and Emerald to Clark and Howard via 79th, Vincennes, Wentworth, Archer, and Clark to Howard.

In November, 1908 short turn cars began to use the 63rd terminal, and on September 1, 1911 certain cars began to use the 80th and Vincennes terminal. On July 17, 1912 all cars began to use the 80th terminal.

On February 1, 1914 short turn cars (which actually

formed a Wentworth-Downtown route) began to loop via Monroe, LaSalle, and Washington. On July 1, 1914 half of the cars were again sent along 79th, this time as far as Halsted. The off-street Howard terminal at the north end of the line opened May 19, 1915.

All through cars were rerouted to the 80th and Vincennes terminal on January 6, 1918. The Wentworth-Downtown cars began to run to 79th and Peoria, just west of Halsted, on the same day. On July 24, 1919 all cars began to use a new terminal at 81st and Halsted, reached via Vincennes and 81st.

Motor-trailer operation lasted a little over two years, starting on September 1, 1921 and ending on October 13, 1923.

Short-turn cars began to use a new downtown loop via Madison, Dearborn, and Monroe to Clark on January 27, 1922. In the general rerouting of September 14, 1924 the short turn cars got a new loop via Clark, Illinois, Wells, Chicago, and Clark. On June 3, 1925 Wentworth-Downtown cars began to use the Halsted, Waveland, Broadway loop. By 1928 the Wentworth local cars had been cut back to Chicago and Wells.

CTA rerouted the cars, northbound only, via Harrison, Dearborn, Kinzie, and Clark on November 16, 1953. Buses replaced weekend streetcars over the entire route on September 5, 1954. The through route was discontinued on September 8, 1957, with buses taking over the north end of the line (see Clark Street). The remaining Wentworth streetcars began to loop via Harrison, Dearborn, Kinzie, and Clark.

Final bus substitution came on June 21, 1958, ending service on Wentworth, the last streetcar route in the city. Two-man cars were used until the end, car 7213 making the last run.

New Pullman 995, southbound on Western Avenue, takes on passengers at a safety island just north of Lawrence Avenue. At right is New Pullman 982, making an outbound run on Through Route 3, Lincoln-Indiana. Note "3" dash sign on the Lincoln-Indiana car and the "Riverview Park" sign on the dash of the Western Avenue car. On July 17, 1911 Western cars began to use a new off-street loop at Western and Roscoe adjacent to the Riverview amusement park. The Roscoe terminal was discontinued on January 24, 1951. Photo from the collection of Tom Mangan.

• Above. Southbound postwar PCC uses a portable crossover to return to the southbound track after detouring around a track reconstruction project by using the northbound track. Photo taken on Western near 72nd Street on June 17, 1955 by A. C. Williams. • Below. After regular service ended, track along 69th St. was kept open so that Western Avenue cars could go to and from the 77th Street carhouse. PCC 7234 is westbound on 69th at Princeton. A. C. Williams photo on June 15, 1955.

Western Avenue (Through Route 10)

This trunk line was through-routed on September 5, 1911 between Roscoe (Riverview terminal) and 71st. On October 28, 1912 cars were extended north to Lawrence, and on May 1, 1923 Western was consolidated with the North Western route and the cars began to run through to Howard. On the south end cars reached 75th on December 1, 1924, 79th on January 11, 1931, 95th on July 26, 1931, and 111th on November 8, 1931.

CTA divided Western into three routes on August 1, 1948. PCC streetcars ran on the central portion from a loop at 79th and Western to a loop via Ravenswood, Schreiber, Clark, and Devon via Western and Devon. The north terminal was changed to an off-street loop at Western and Berwyn on December 12, 1948. However, depot cars to and from the Devon carhouse continued to use Western, north of Berwyn, and Devon. Buses operated the north and south extension routes.

On November 14, 1949 Western cars began to use the Leland terminal for short turns, and the Roscoe (Riverview) loop was discontinued on January 24, 1951.

CTA substituted buses for two-man streetcars on weekends on December 7, 1952. However, one-man PCC cars took over all service on the central portion between 79th and Berwyn on June 19, 1955. On June 17, 1956 CTA substituted buses for streetcars on the central portion, but the buses were not through-routed with the extension buses.

North Western Avenue

This extension of the regular Western route began October 18, 1915 between Lawrence and Bryn Mawr. Extensions brought the line to Devon on December 31, 1915, and to Howard on December 16, 1916. The line was through-routed with Western on May 1, 1923.

Whiting-East Chicago

Service from Whiting, Indiana, to the Illinois state line began March 12, 1894. Service into Chicago over CSL tracks began May 15, 1896. The route was on 106th, Ewing, 92nd, Commercial, Baker, Exchange, 79th, Stony Island, 64th, and Dorchester. A 1913 rerouting put the cars on Ewing, 92nd, South Chicago, South Park, and 63rd to Vernon. By 1913 the cars were running via Indianapolis rather than 106th and Ewing.

On June 6, 1914 cars were rerouted from the state line via Indianapolis, Ewing, 95th, and South Chicago to a loop via Commercial, 92nd and Baltimore. On July 18, 1916 the line was extended up 91st, South Chicago, South Park, and 63rd, to the Vernon terminal. By 1928 the 106th, Ewing route had been restored, and by 1933 the cars were running via Commercial, 95th. One-man cars went into service September 4, 1932. Service ended June 9, 1940.

Service beyond the state line was by the Hammond, Whiting & East Chicago Electric Railway Company, which later became Calumet Railways, and still later the Chicago and Calumet District Transit Company. This company also ran the through Hammond cars. Fairly frequent through service was given: every 20 minutes in 1906; and 20 minute base headways and 15 minute rush hour service in the 1930s. Of the 24 cars used in the 1930s on both the Hammond and Whiting-East Chicago routes, 16 were supplied by the Surface Lines.

In later years the C&CD charged an 8¢ fare on its lines, while CSL charged 7¢, making a total of 15¢ for an interstate ride. The extra fare was collected at the state line each way. The CSL and the HW&EC each issued

Old Pullman 113 clatters across Milwaukee Road freight tracks on Clark just north of Addison, making a southbound run on the Clark-Wentworth Through Route. Freight tracks connected with the North Side "L" at Buena Yard, where electric freight locomotives switched cars to customers along the "L".

transfers for the line, and cars in through service carried a fare register for each company. All operation within Chicago was as a regular CSL route, with CSL crews manning the cars. Among the Chicago cars used in through service were the CCRyCo's 2501-2625 St. Louis cars, C&SC's 2800 cars, the Nearsides, and the CSL's 6199-6238 multiple-unit cars in one-man service.

The route on the Indiana side of the state line (which was also the Chicago city limits), was known as Route 12 of the Chicago and Calumet District Transit Company. It ran from a wye on Forsyth, just north of Chicago Ave., via Forsyth, Schrage, 119th, and Indianapolis Blvd. to the state line.

Windsor Park

We pick up the story of this Southeast Side line in 1908, when a rerouting put the cars on 75th, Exchange, and 73rd to Stony Island, replacing the route via Coles, 75th, and Stony Island. The new route began at the 63rd and Dorchester terminal and ran via Dorchester, 64th, Stony Island, 73rd, Exchange, 75th, Coles, Cheltenham, 79th, Exchange, Baker, Commercial, 92nd, Ewing, and Indianapolis to 106th. On March 19, 1909 Windsor Park cars were rerouted to run via Commercial, 95th, Ewing, and 108th to a crossover at Avenue F.

On June 22, 1914 cars were rerouted via a loop on Stony Island, 63rd, Dorchester, and 64th. The basic route itself was changed to run via Stony Island, 73rd, Exchange, 75th, Coles, 79th, Exchange, Commercial, 92nd, Ewing, and 108th to Avenue F. Cars were cut back from 108th and Avenue F to a loop via 92nd, Baltimore, 93rd, and Commercial on April 10, 1927. By 1933 cars were looping via Commercial, 93rd, Baltimore, and 91st. One-man cars went into service August 7, 1932. CTA substituted buses for streetcars on April 25, 1948, cutting

back service from 63rd to 79th. The bus route ran from a loop via Cheltenham, Coles, and 79th to a loop via 91st, Baltimore, and 92nd.

14th-16th Street

This line was one of the last to go into service before the creation of CSL. It began January 27, 1913 from 16th and Kenton to Roosevelt and Wabash via 16th, Kedzie, Roosevelt, Damen, 14th, Canal, and Roosevelt. On May 9, 1915 Jefferson replaced Canal as the link between 14th and Roosevelt, but the old route was restored by 1928. Cars were extended one block east from Wabash to Michigan on August 1, 1933. CTA discontinued the 14th-16th route July 25, 1948, combining all of the 16th section with part of the former 18th Street route.

18th Street

We pick up the story of this near South Side crosstown line on July 22, 1906, when it was cut back to Blue Island and Leavitt. Starting in October, 1896, 18th cars had run beyond Blue Island to 26th and Pulaski via Blue Island and 26th. After the cutback they ran from Blue Island and Leavitt to 18th and State via Leavitt and 18th. One-man cars went into service on August 7, 1932. CTA used part of the 18th route to form the 16th-18th bus route on July 25, 1948. At that time 18th cars were discontinued.

21st-Wells (Through Route 15)

This short-lived through route linked the near West and near North sides. Inaugurated on December 27,

In the dawn's early light on the morning of June 21, 1958, Jeff Wien snapped CTA postwar PCC 7213 as it paused on Halsted south of 81st before pulling into the 77th and Vincennes carhouse for the last time. This 1946 St. Louis Car Company product had the honor to be the last streetcar to operate on the last Chicago streetcar line.

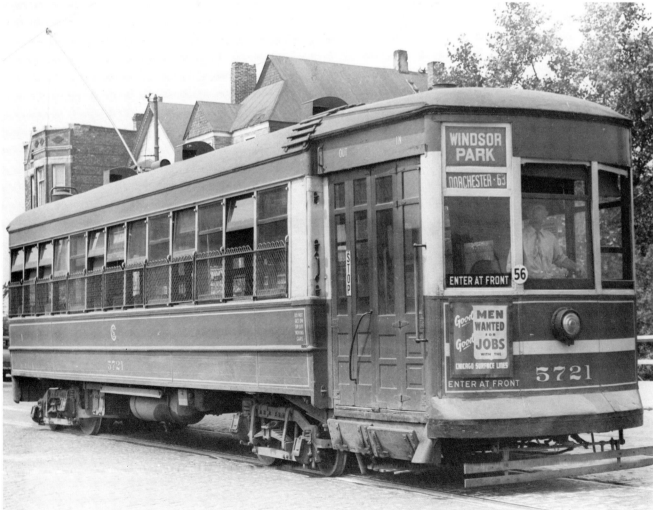

1909, it was discontinued on August 15, 1912. The line ran from 21st and Marshall to the Clark and Drummond terminal (Limits carhouse loop) via 21st, Halsted, Canalport, Canal, Polk, Wells, and Clark.

26th Street

No change was made in this route from 1888, when it began as a horse car line, to 1956, when CTA through-routed it with the 31st Street line. The horse car route ran from Halsted to Cottage Grove, and so did the streetcars which replaced the horse cars on January 4, 1895. One-man cars entered service August 21, 1932. CTA replaced the cars with buses on February 29, 1948.

31st Street

Like the 26th Street line, this route remained almost unchanged from the horse car era until it was through-routed with 26th Street on February 5, 1956. Horse car service began in 1884 from 31st and Lake Park to Pitney Court and Archer via 31st and Pitney Ct. At one point the horse cars went via Archer to Kedzie. Streetcars took over on January 13, 1895. When CTA put buses on the route on February 29, 1948, the west end was extended on Archer to a loop via Archer, Robinson, and Ashland.

35th Street

We pick up the story of this line on October 30, 1911, when the route was extended from 35th and California to 36th and Kedzie via California and 36th. The east terminal remained at 35th and Cottage Grove. On December 4, 1932 one-man cars entered service. Two-man cars later returned to service on 35th prior to 1941. CTA substituted buses for cars on April 15, 1951.

43rd-Root Street

Transit service along Root goes back to 1866, when a Root-Downtown car line via Root and State began to run. Downtown service ended in 1881, but a local Root horse car continued to run between Halsted and State. Service along 43rd from Oakenwald to State began in 1887. The 43rd and Root lines were through-routed via State by 1888, possibly when 43rd opened in 1887. On January 1, 1895, streetcars replaced the horse cars. At that time the west end of the line was extended from Halsted to a terminal in the Union Stock Yards, just west of Halsted. One-man cars began to run August 7, 1932. CTA substituted buses and discontinued the Stock Yards terminal on August 9, 1953.

47th Street

By 1896 there was streetcar service from 47th and Lake Park to 47th and Kedzie via 47th. Service west of Western was a separate route for a while after 1896. The only extension made after 1896 was on December 3, 1937, when CSL laid tracks under the Illinois Central Railroad viaduct and into Burnham Park. CTA substituted buses on April 15, 1951.

• Opposite page, top. Car 6210, in one-man service on an outbound Windsor Park run, turns west on 79th Street from Coles Avenue. Note wide spacing of tracks on this sharp curve. • Opposite page, below. Since Windsor Park was a lightly used line, it received one-man cars on August 7, 1932. Author's collection. • This page, below. Outbound on the 14th-16th Street line, Matchbox 1333 crosses the railroad yard complex just south of the Loop on the Roosevelt Road viaduct. Barney Neuberger photo from the Bill Richmond collection.

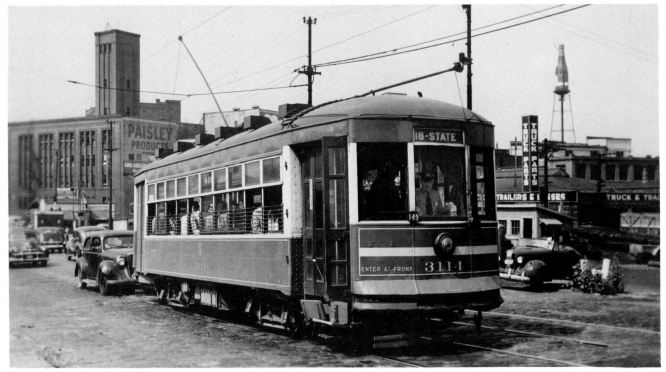

Chicago Railways safety car 3114 is running eastbound on 18th Street near Canal Street, heading for its east terminal at 18th and State. CTA used part of the 18th Street line this car is running on to form the 16th-18th Street bus line on July 25, 1948. At that time the 18th Street cars were discontinued. Less than a month later, on August 20, 1948, car 3114 was scrapped. Barney Neuberger photo from the Jack Doyle collection. • Below. Chicago City Railway Big Brill 5366 awaits passengers at the west end of the 35th Street line at 36th and Kedzie. The line jogged from 35th to 36th Street along California Ave. The car will soon depart for its east terminal at 35th and Cottage Grove. Photograph from the collection of Barney Neuberger.

• Above. Three cars wait at the west terminal of the 35th Street line on 36th Street at California Ave. Car 3206 was built by CSL in 1924 as a multiple-unit car and was used in two-car trains. The 35th Street line was one of those routes converted from two-man cars to one-man cars and back to two-man cars. Photo from the Neuberger collection. • Below. Bernard Rossbach took this photo of CTA 6184 at the Stock Yards (west) terminal of the 43rd-Root Street line during the winter of 1951-52. The terminal was just west of the intersection of Root and Halsted. From 1896 to 1948 east route Pershing cars also used this west terminal.

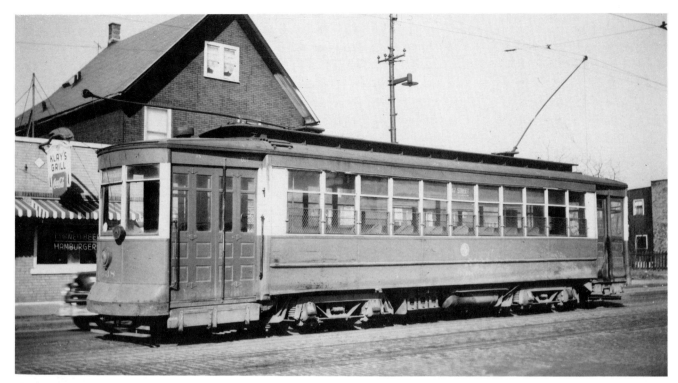

• Top. New Pullman 938 rests on 47th near Kedzie at the west end of the 47th Street line. The line reached Kedzie on October 4, 1896, and Kedzie remained the west terminal until streetcar service ended April 15, 1951. Neuberger collection from Jack Doyle. • Bottom. On December 3, 1937 CSL extended the 47th line east into Burnham Park. Richard N. Lukin took this photo of New Pullman 764 on April 8, 1951, a week before streetcar service ended. Photo from the Allan C. Williams collection.

• Opposite page, top. CTA bus 3564, ordered by the Surface Lines, was a 1947 White model 798. It is running east on 55th Street east of Cottage Grove during the period when 51st-55th Street was split into two lines, one streetcar, the other bus. Chicago Transit Authority photo. • Bottom. Car 3253 loads at 51st and Cottage Grove, the east terminal of the 51st Street streetcar line. This route ran from September 9, 1946 to May 30, 1948 from Cottage Grove to St. Louis on 51st Street. Neuberger photo.

West 47th Street

CSL began bus service that connected with the 47th Street cars on May 26, 1935. The route was on 47th from a loop via Christiana, 47th Place, and Kedzie to a wye at Kostner. No changes were made in the route under CSL management.

51st-55th Street

CSL combined the 51st Street line with track along 55th used by Cottage Grove (TR-5) cars to make the 51st-55th route on November 2, 1930. Begun in 1887 as a horse car route from King Drive to State, the 51st Street line ran from King Drive to St. Louis at the time of the through-routing. The new route began at a loop via Harper, 56th, and Lake Park and ran via 55th, Cottage Grove, and 51st. One-man cars took over service on August 21, 1932.

CSL discontinued the 51st-55th through-route cars on September 9, 1946. Buses took over the 55th Street segment, running from the Lake Park loop to 50th and Wentworth via 55th, Cottage Grove, 51st, Wells, and 50th. However, track along 55th remained in use for TR-5 cars until August 1, 1947.

Streetcars continued to run on 51st from St. Louis to Cottage Grove from September 9, 1946 until May 30, 1948. At that time the 51st cars were discontinued and buses put on a through-routed 51st-55th line.

59th-61st Street

Just before the turn of the century, on May 14, 1899, the 59th and the 61st cars were through-routed to form this line. The east terminal was at 60th and Blackstone, the west at 59th and Leavitt. Cars ran via Blackstone, 61st, State, and 59th. At the time of consolidation the 61st-63rd line via 61st, Cottage Grove, and 63rd to Stony Island was discontinued.

Extensions brought the cars to Western on July 5, 1914, to Kedzie on November 1, 1914, and to Central Park on October 1, 1924. One-man cars went into service on August 14, 1932.

An extension bus along 59th went into service March 24, 1947. It ran from a wye at Central Park to a wye at Keating. Buses replaced the streetcars on February 16, 1948, although the extension bus route was not through-routed until June 1, 1948.

63rd Street

One of the heaviest CSL lines, 63rd Street was the only South Side crosstown line to get PCC cars under CTA management. We pick up the story on September 3, 1899 when streetcars replaced horse cars on the portion between Ashland and Central Park. The line split at Ashland, and the east part between Ashland and Stony Island was another route. There was also a branch on Wentworth and 61st to State, discontinued by 1913.

CTA cut back the 63rd Street line to a west terminal at the new Narragansett loop in 1948, and placed the Madison Street prewar PCCs on the line. Still carrying its original colors of blue, red, and cream, two-man prewar PCC 4028 enters the Narragansett loop in March, 1952. Photo by B. A. Rossbach. • Opposite page. CTA 172 westbound at 63rd and Harvard. Neuberger collection.

On January 20, 1902 the west line was extended from Central Park to Central. Also by 1902, on the east segment, cars began to loop via 63rd, Stony Island, 64th, and Harper. The west line extension to Central was cut back to La Crosse during July, 1904. On August 13, 1915, 63rd cars were through-routed from Stony Island to La Crosse. On December 4, 1916 the 63rd through route was extended to Central. During the period between July, 1904 and December 4, 1916, when 63rd cars were cut back to La Crosse, South Cicero cars ran between La Crosse and Central as part of their route.

A series of extensions via Central and 63rd Pl. brought the cars to Meade on May 23, 1918, to Melvina on July 12, 1926, and to Oak Park on October 1, 1929. Also on October 1 the South Cicero cars were cut back to a shuttle between Archer and 63rd on Cicero, and the Argo cars began to run only from Oak Park west to Archer as a separate route.

CTA cut back the line to 63rd and Narragansett on April 11, 1948. A new loop terminal had been built here for PCC cars. On the same date West 63rd buses replaced the 63rd cars from Narragansett to Oak Park, and completely replaced the Argo cars. Buses took over weekend service on the remaining streetcar route between Stony Island and Narragansett via 63rd and Narragansett on December 7, 1952. Complete bus substitution took place on May 24, 1953.

67th-69th-71st Street

This South Side crosstown line was put together from the 67th Street and 69th Street lines, plus a later extension on 71st. We pick up the story on September 26,

1910, when the 67th and 69th lines were through-routed from 67th and Stony Island to 69th and Western via 67th, Rhodes, Keefe, and 69th.

On February 1, 1915 cars began to run to a new east terminal at 67th and Oglesby. The final extension was made from 69th and Western to 71st and California via Western and 71st on November 23, 1924.

One-man cars went into service on August 14, 1932. CTA substituted buses for the cars on May 24, 1953, although the track along 69th from Western to Vincennes remained open for barn movements from the Western line to 77th and Vincennes carhouse.

71st Street

This short South Side shuttle was originally a part of the Englewood & Chicago Electric Street Railway's route (by 1912 this was the Chicago & Southern Traction Company). When that route was discontinued on March 1, 1912, 71st became a shuttle car line between Cottage Grove and State. On January 5, 1916 the line was extended to 73rd and Vincennes via 71st and Vincennes. The line was an early user of one-man cars, beginning on April 1, 1923.

CSL began an extension bus along 71st, connecting with the east end of the car line, on May 10, 1935. It ran from a loop via Drexel and South Chicago via 71st, Exchange, and 72nd to a wye at the lakefront. Because of an unusual street pattern in the area near the Lake, the wye was at the corner of E. 71st and E. 72nd Streets. On September 4, 1943 a new routing took the buses to 73rd and Exchange.

The west terminal was moved west along 71st from

Drexel to a wye at Langley on December 18, 1943. On July 1, 1945 CSL moved the terminal a block west to a loop via Champlain, 72nd, Langley, and 71st.

CSL substituted buses for the 71st cars on May 22, 1947. The east extension buses were absorbed into the regular route on this date.

74th-75th Street

The 75th Street segment of this line was through-routed from the lakefront to Eggleston in 1908, and up Eggleston to 74th on August 11, 1913. Extensions brought the line to 74th and Parnell on September 14, 1913, and to Ashland on May 6, 1914. A new lakefront loop went into service in May, 1915.

To handle defense plant workers, the line was extended from Ashland to Damen in October, 1917. It was cut back to Ashland in August, 1918. CSL replaced the cars with buses on October 28, 1946, extending them to a wye at Damen.

79th Street

It wasn't until December 27, 1914 that this line was through-routed from Lake Michigan (nominally Brandon) to Ashland. On November 22, 1926 it reached its peak length, when a one-mile extension opened from Ashland to Western.

One-man cars took over service April 1, 1923, but two-man cars were restored August 15, 1926. One-man cars began to give all service on October 23, 1949, and they lasted until the end of service.

CTA substituted buses for the cars weekends only on February 11, 1951. Complete bus operation began September 16, 1951.

West 79th Street

To serve defense plants, CSL began West 79th extension bus service on November 2, 1942. Buses ran from 79th and Western to 75th and Pulaski via 79th and Pulaski. Rush hour buses began to run via 79th and Cicero to 75th and Cicero on January 21, 1943. They were cut back to 76th and Cicero on April 14, 1943. The last change CSL made was on July 26, 1943, when all-day service began from Western to a terminal at 76th and Kilpatrick via 79th, Cicero, and 76th.

83rd Street

CSL inaugurated bus service on this short Southeast Side line on September 18, 1939. The route was from a loop via Clyde, South Chicago, and 83rd to 83rd and Mackinaw. On May 13, 1940 buses were extended east to a terminal at Green Bay. During rush hours only, buses made a loop via 83rd, Green Bay, 85th, and Mackinaw starting December 26, 1944. This was the last change made under CSL management.

87th Street

CSL put together the east and west 87th Street lines in the late 1930s to form a through route. The east route was the first to open, on October 3, 1915. It was a short shuttle between Commercial and Stony Island. One-man cars entered service on April 1, 1923.

The west line opened as a shuttle route using one-man cars between State and Vincennes on October 15, 1930. On November 25, 1930 it was extended east from State to Ingleside. The gap between Ingleside and Stony Island was closed May 2, 1937, and the east and west lines were through-routed from Commercial to Vincennes.

CSL began extension bus service from Vincennes to Damen on May 5, 1935. Buses began to run to Western on July 31, 1935, but were cut back to Damen on September 30.

CSL made Western the west terminal again on May 22, 1947. A further extension brought midday and rush hour service west to a wye at Hamlin Monday through Saturday starting September 6, 1949. CTA substituted buses for 87th streetcars, and extended the bus line east to 87th and Mackinaw, on May 27, 1951.

93rd-95th Street

CSL didn't put this line together until August 12, 1918, when parts of the discontinued West Pullman and 93rd-Pullman routes were consolidated. The line ran from 89th and Avenue O to 95th and Lafayette via 89th, Buffalo, 92nd, Exchange, 93rd, Stony Island, private right-of-way, 93rd, Cottage Grove, and 95th. One-man cars went into service August 15, 1926. CSL began a bus extension to the west on May 19, 1935 from Lafayette to Claremont. The extension was through-routed with the main line when buses replaced streetcars on May 27, 1951.

103rd Street

Service on this far South Side crosstown line began in 1896 between Michigan and Racine. On April 18, 1910 cars began to run east from Michigan to the west side of the Illinois Central at Dauphin Ave. Sometime around 1924 the line was extended east under the IC tracks from Dauphin to Cottage Grove on a single stub track.

A shuttle bus went into service on May 4, 1930 from a wye at Malta to a wye at Claremont. CSL substituted buses for streetcars on October 13, 1941, through-routing them with the extension bus and with the 106th Street route (see 103rd-106th for details).

103rd-106th Street

CSL consolidated its 103rd-106th routes into this line on October 13, 1941 (see separate listings for each of these routes). The route was in two sections, split at 106th and the Calumet River by work on the bridge. A city-owned motor boat shuttled passengers across.

• Above. CSL 1416 approaches the west terminal of the 71st Street line at 73rd and Vincennes. This car began life as Chicago Union Traction 4945 in 1906, was rebuilt by Chicago Railways in 1909-10, and converted to a one-man car by CSL in 1924. Neuberger photo from the Allan C. Williams collection. • Below. CSL's 71st Street extension bus line ran from 71st and South Chicago to a wye at 71st and the lakefront when it opened May 10, 1935. CCRy 1934 White model 684 is eastbound on 71st Street at Exchange Ave. Author's collection.

• Above. CCRy 2169 is eastbound on the 75th Street line, about to cross South Chicago Ave. A northbound CCRy standard 5000 series semiconvertible can be seen inbound on South Chicago at center left. Author's collection. • Opposite page. Eastbound on the 79th Street line, car 2746 has just crested the grade leading up from under the Chicago & Western Indiana and the Rock Island Railroad viaduct at 79th and Fielding. This point was an interchange between the two commuter railroads and the Surface Lines. The few C&WI commuter trains stopped at a small station at 79th Street just out of view to the left. The Rock Island trains, on much more frequent schedules, stopped at the Normal Park station one block north at 78th and Fielding. Behind the commercial buildings on the right lay the quite lagoon along scenic Winneconna Parkway. The photo was taken in December, 1946. Alan W. Simms collection. • This page, below. For many years the west terminal of the 79th Street line was at 79th and Western, where CSL Old Pullman 123 is waiting to leave on an eastbound trip. Barney Neuberger photo from the Jack Doyle collection.

The 87th Street line was one of the last "new" streetcar routes the CSL put together. The last gap between the east and west segments of this line wasn't closed until May 2, 1937, when the gap between Ingleside and Stony Island was closed. Just two weeks before the line went from rail to rubber transit, Allan C. Williams shot one-man car 6275 eastbound on the 87th Street median strip at Normal Ave.

The west line began at 103rd and Claremont and ran via 103rd, Torrence, and 106th to the Calumet River. Beginning at the east bank buses ran along 106th to Avenue B, then south to 107th. A short-turn loop for the buses was established at this time via Corliss, 103rd Place, and Cottage Grove.

CSL was able to through-route the buses across the bridge from Claremont to a loop via Avenue B, 107th, and State Line on November 7, 1941. The last change under CSL management came on June 15, 1942, when a west extension brought the buses to a wye at Springfield.

106th Street

Although horse car service on 106th between Indianapolis and Torrence goes back to 1892, this segment was operated as part of the South Deering line from 1894 to December 30, 1909. At that time 106th became a shuttle between Torrence and Ewing. CSL didn't resume operation to Indianapolis, discontinued in 1895, until August 23, 1925. Of course, routes other than 106th ran on 106th from Ewing all the way to Indianapolis in the meantime. One-man cars went into service on October 1, 1926.

CSL substituted buses for the cars on August 13, 1941. The route was from a wye at Hoxie to a loop via Avenue B, 107th, and State Line. When the 106th Street bridge over the Calumet River closed for repairs, the portion of the line west of the bridge was suspended. Buses ran only between State Line and Mackinaw. All-bus through service on 103rd-106th began November 7, 1941. For details of the interim motorboat shuttle service, see the 103rd-106th route listing.

111th Street

It wasn't until January 5, 1911 that streetcars began to run on 111th from Cottage Grove to Michigan. On September 18 the line was opened west of Michigan to Stewart. The west terminal became 111th and Sacramento on May 9, 1917, the cars running via 111th, Vincennes, Monterey, and 111th.

CSL cut back weekday service to Cottage Grove-Vincennes only on April 4, 1918. Weekend cars continued to run to Sacramento to handle heavy visitor traffic to the cemeteries at this end of the line. Service was restored to Sacramento seven days a week on March 3, 1919. At the same time cars began to run east of Cottage to St. Lawrence. CSL cut back service to Vincennes-St. Lawrence only on July 1, 1921.

Always a schedule-maker's headache because of its single track with passing sidings, 111th Street was one of the first car lines to go bus after WW II. Another problem was its two crossings of mainline railroads. CSL required a two-man streetcar crew so the conductor could flag these crossings. However, it permitted one-man buses to run across the tracks without flagging.

CSL put on buses September 23, 1945 from a loop via Ashland, Chelsea, and Vincennes via 111th to a loop via Champlain, 112th, and St. Lawrence. A shorter east terminal loop was also opened, via 111th, Forrestville, and Cottage Grove.

111th Street Extension

CSL began bus service on this short shuttle on September 11, 1939. The bus was an extension of the

Car 2909, a 1922 CCRy safety car, heads west along 87th Street at Exchange Ave. while Matchbox 1419 in one-man service pulls into the east terminal of the 87th Street line at 87th and Commercial, one block east. This page and the page opposite illustrate three types of one-man car in service on 87th Street. Neuberger photo.

The history of the 93rd-95th Street line goes back to October 2, 1890, when streetcar service began between South Chicago and Stony Island via Exchange Ave. and 93rd Street. At one time the line on 95th Street west of Cottage Grove was part of the West Pullman route. The east part of the line was once a part of the 93rd-Pullman route, which linked Pullman and South Chicago. It wasn't until August 12, 1918 that 93rd-95th became a separate crosstown line between 89th and Ave. O on the east and a west terminal at 95th and Lafayette. The terminals remained at these locations until buses replaced the streetcars on May 27, 1951. The line was a favorite for photographers because of the private right-of-way along the Belt Railway of Chicago tracks between Kenwood and Harper. Richard J. Cook took this shot of CSL 6208 on that right-of-way crossing the Nickel Plate tracks on August 13, 1947.

Halsted-Downtown line from its terminal at 111th and Sacramento to a wye at 111th and Harding. It became part of the Vincennes-111th line on December 4, 1949, when buses replaced Halsted cars south of 79th.

115th Street

This very short line was single-track with one passing siding. Streetcar service began in 1893 from King Drive to Michigan. Extensions brought the cars west from Michigan to Wallace on October 24, 1909, and from Wallace to Halsted on May 12, 1910. CSL substituted buses for streetcars on September 23, 1945. The route was from a loop via Union, 116th, and Halsted to Champlain and Kensington via 115th and Champlain.

West 119th Street

On February 23, 1913 streetcar service began on 119th from Peoria to Vincennes. CSL replaced the cars with buses on February 3, 1946. The route was from a loop via Peoria, 120th, and Halsted along 119th to Vincennes. On July 22, 1946 the 119th bus was through-routed with the Vincennes line via Vincennes to a loop on 111th and Chelsea. Throughout its life as a streetcar route, this line ran two-man cars.

Although it doesn't have a cream horizontal dash stripe, CTA 6209 is in one-man service (note dash sign "Enter At Front"). The car is entering the private right-of-way west of Stony Island Ave. (near Blackstone Ave.) on the 93rd-95th Street line, heading west to 95th and State, the west terminal. Note wide spacing of tracks to provide clearance on this "S" curve. Barney Neuberger photo from the Allan C. Williams collection.

The conductor of car 2606, which is eastbound on the single-track 111th Street line, waits to flip aboard the back platform of his car after flagging the Chicago & Western Indiana Railroad crossing. Because this line required two-man cars to flag railroad crossings, it was one of the first converted to bus after WW II. Buses replaced the cars on September 23, 1945. Photo was taken April 4, 1942. Neuberger collection, from Jack Doyle.

Car 2571 is eastbound on the 119th Street line at 119th and Vincennes. This light line was replaced with buses on February 3, 1946. This is the West 119th Street line, not to be confused with the trackage on 119th from Michigan to Morgan used by Broadway-State cars. Ed Frank, Jr., photo from the Allan C. Williams collection.

Taken on May 11, 1931, this photo shows a 115th Street car at the east end of the line at 115th and Cottage Grove under the Illinois Central Railroad viaduct. Track curving in from the right is part of the loop track used by Cottage Grove cars to reverse direction. Photo from the author's collection.

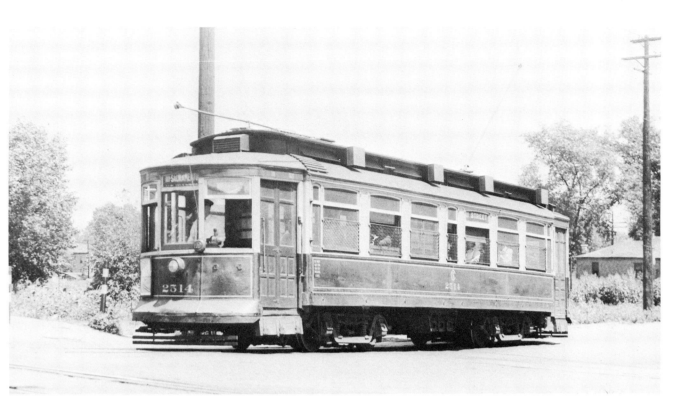

On Sundays certain 111th Street cars ran through from Vincennes to Sacramento on a part of the line normally used only by Halsted cars. This photo was taken of such a car, westbound to 111th and Sacramento, at the Rock Island Railroad crossing just east of 111th and Vincennes. Photo taken on August 13, 1944. Alan W. Simms.

The east terminal for the 111th Street line was at 111th and St. Lawrence. The 111th cars pulled into a short stub-ended siding at this point to get out of the way of the Cottage Grove cars, which used 111th Street as part of their loop. In this photo a Cottage Grove Nearside passes 111th Street car 2571. Alan W. Simms.

Because the Chicago Surface Lines was so large and so complex, this special section has been set aside for detailed route and track maps of the system. Together with the map on the inside of the dust jacket and the maps on the end papers, those presented here show the CSL system and its predecessor lines at various stages of their development.

For example, the map on this page and the one on the opposite page fill out the map on the front end paper, which does not show lines south of 79th Street.

A series of maps running from pages 334 to 343 gives much information on the CSL system shortly after the takeover by the Chicago Transit Authority. They come from a CTA official map of December, 1949. On these maps carhouses and garages are indicated by squares or rectangles, street phone locations by triangles, and phones in buildings by triangles with the letter "B". Special features include enlarged insets showing carhouse trackage and complicated intersections. Streetcar lines are indicated by solid lines, gas bus routes by dashed lines (short dashes), and trolley bus lines by lines with longer dashes.

The location of all CSL gas bus and trolley bus routes as of January 31, 1934 is found on page 344. At the time there were seven trolley coach lines and only two gas bus lines.

The map on page 345, dated January 31, 1945 shows the great changes that took place between January 31, 1934 and January 31, 1945. In 1945 gas buses ran throughout the city as replacements for some streetcar lines, and as feeders to others, while the trolley bus system shrank to six lines.

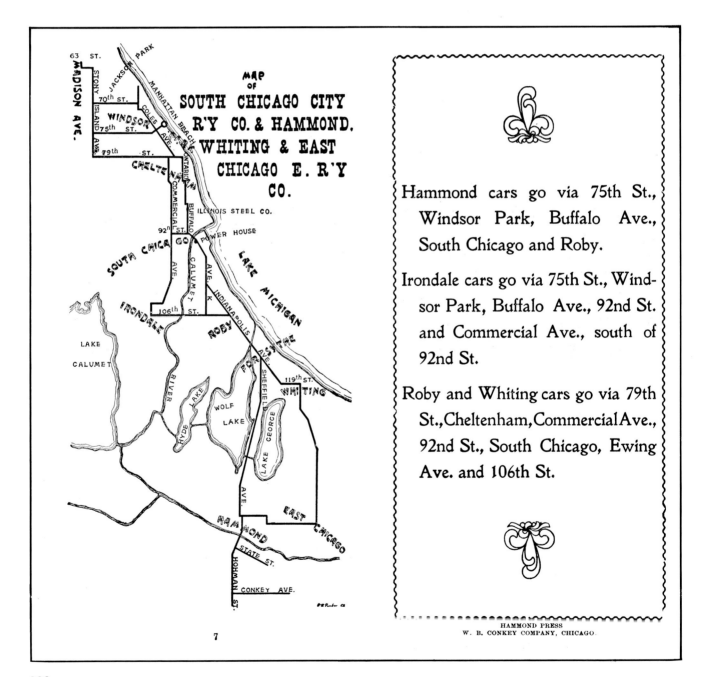

MAP of SOUTH CHICAGO CITY R'Y CO. & HAMMOND, WHITING & EAST CHICAGO E. R'Y CO.

Hammond cars go via 75th St., Windsor Park, Buffalo Ave., South Chicago and Roby.

Irondale cars go via 75th St., Windsor Park, Buffalo Ave., 92nd St. and Commercial Ave., south of 92nd St.

Roby and Whiting cars go via 79th St., Cheltenham, Commercial Ave., 92nd St., South Chicago, Ewing Ave. and 106th St.

HAMMOND PRESS
W. B. CONKEY COMPANY, CHICAGO.

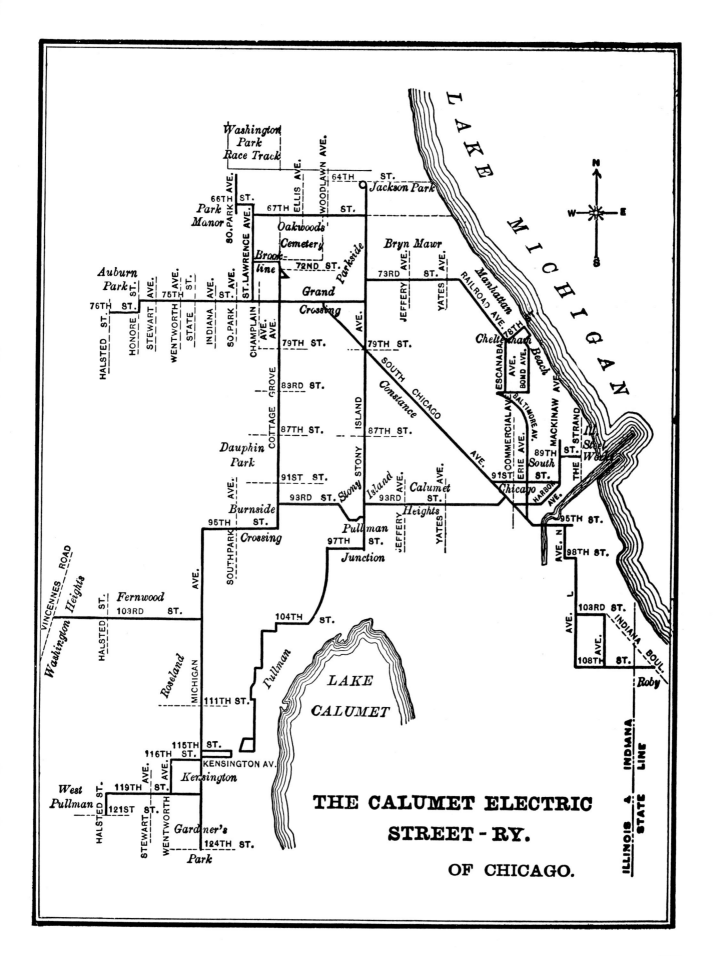

THE CALUMET ELECTRIC STREET - RY.

OF CHICAGO.

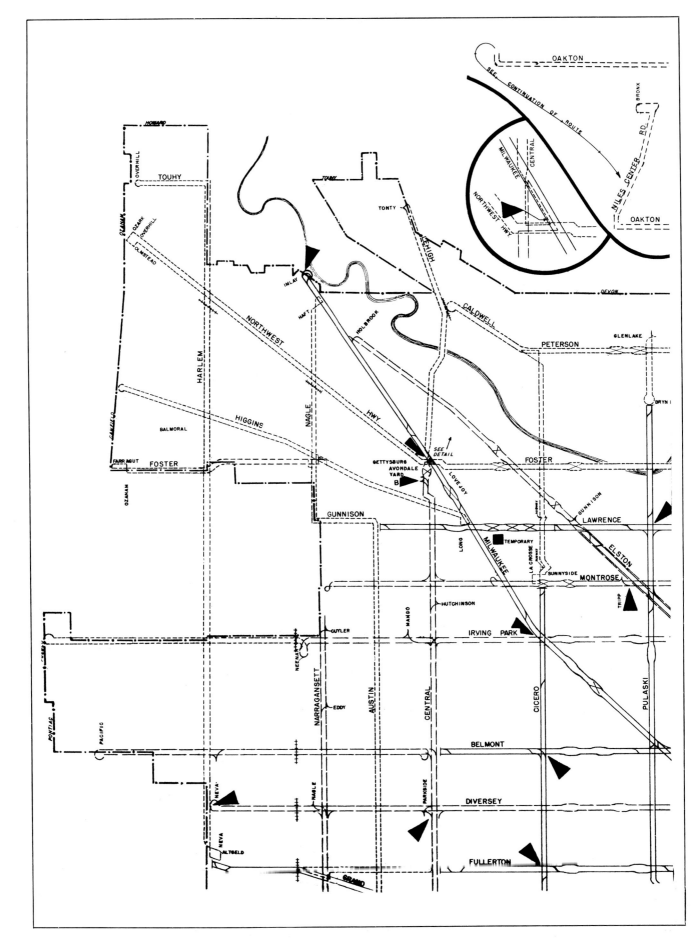

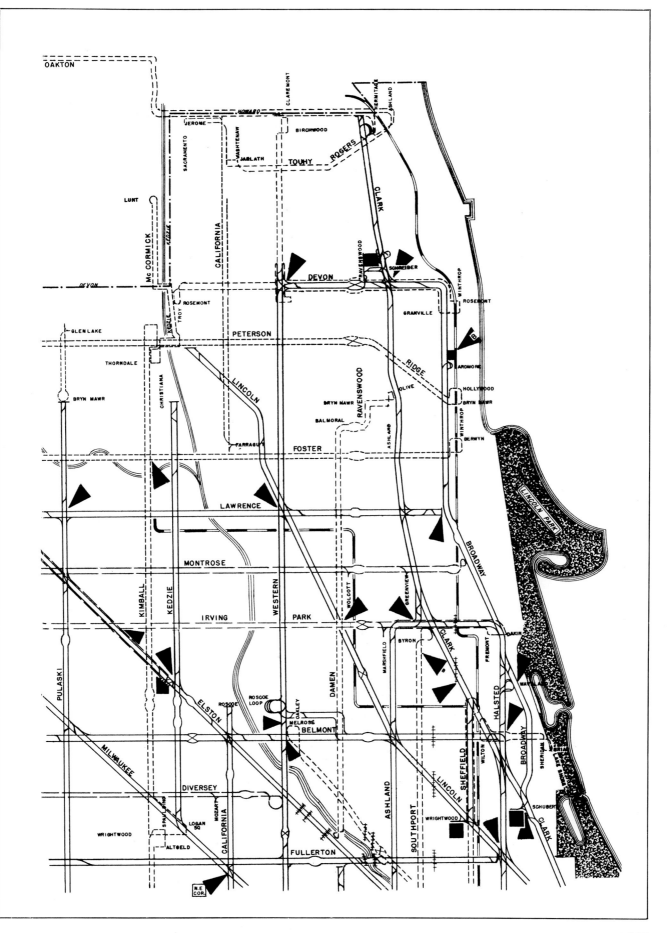

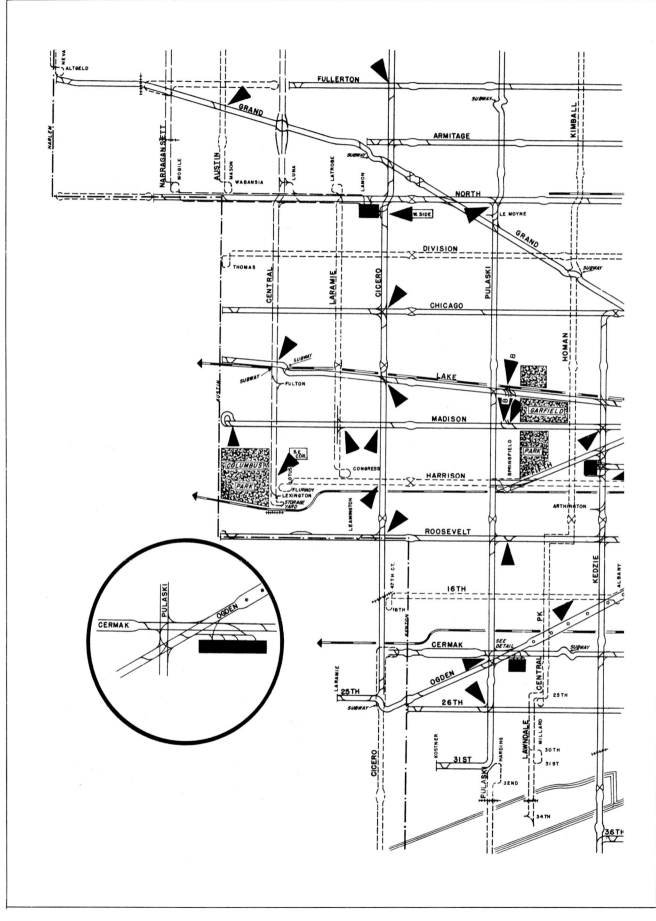

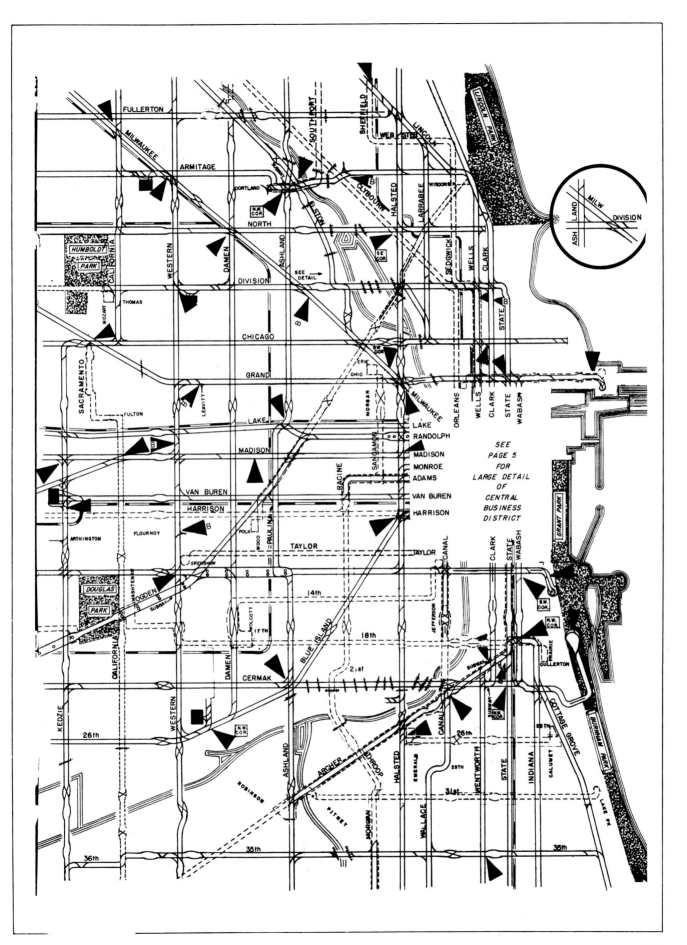

SEE
PAGE 5
FOR
LARGE DETAIL
OF
CENTRAL
BUSINESS
DISTRICT

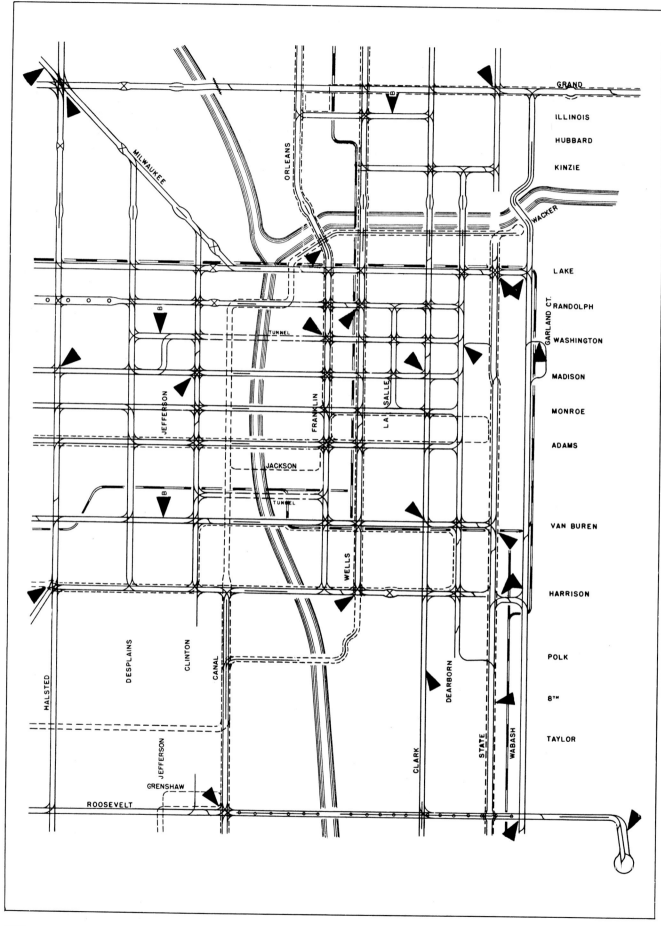

GRAND

ILLINOIS

HUBBARD

KINZIE

WACKER

LAKE

RANDOLPH

WASHINGTON

MADISON

MONROE

ADAMS

VAN BUREN

HARRISON

POLK

8TH

TAYLOR

GARLAND CT.

ORLEANS

MILWAUKEE

TUNNEL

JEFFERSON

FRANKLIN

LA SALLE

JACKSON

TUNNEL

WELLS

HALSTED

DESPLAINS

CLINTON

CANAL

CLARK

DEARBORN

STATE

WABASH

JEFFERSON

GRENSHAW

ROOSEVELT

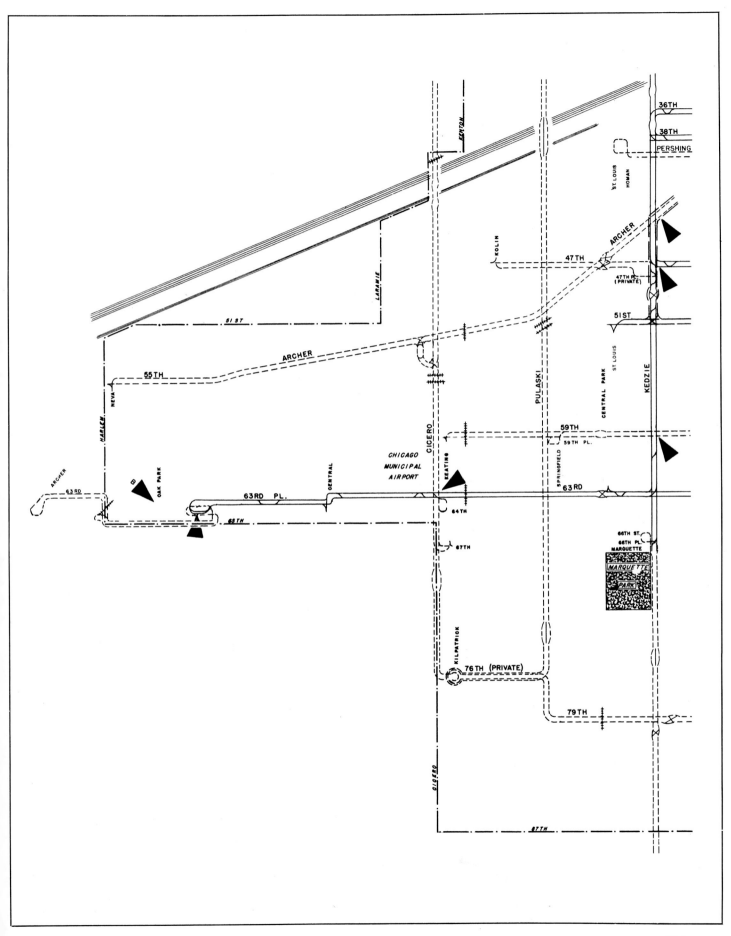

339

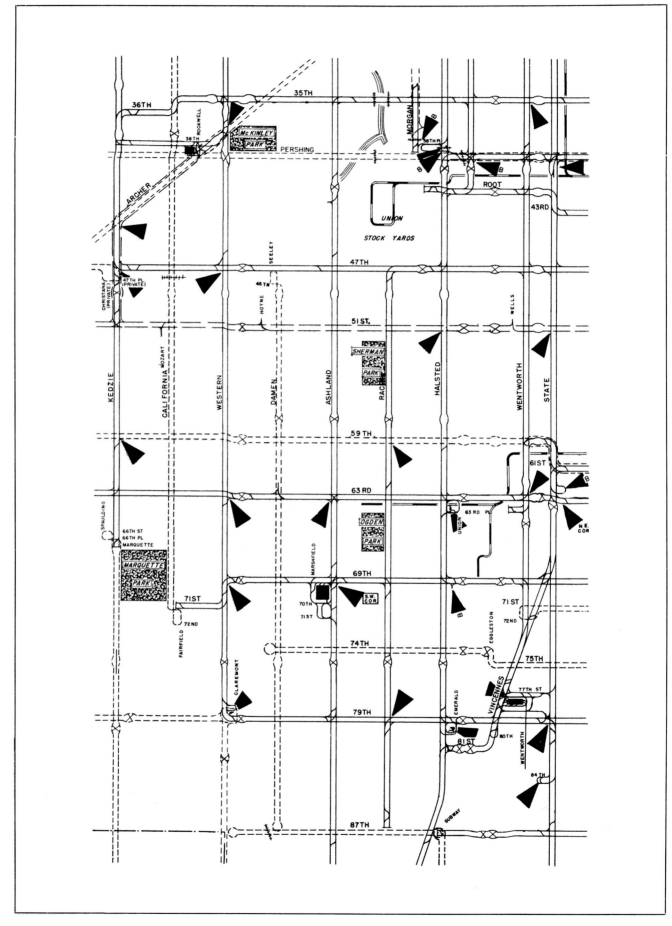

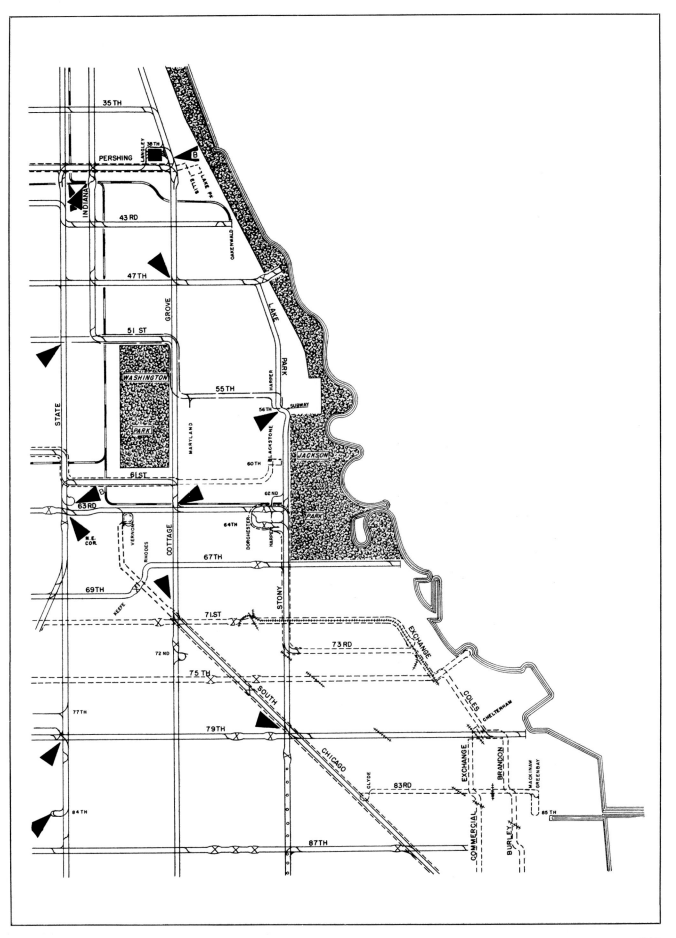

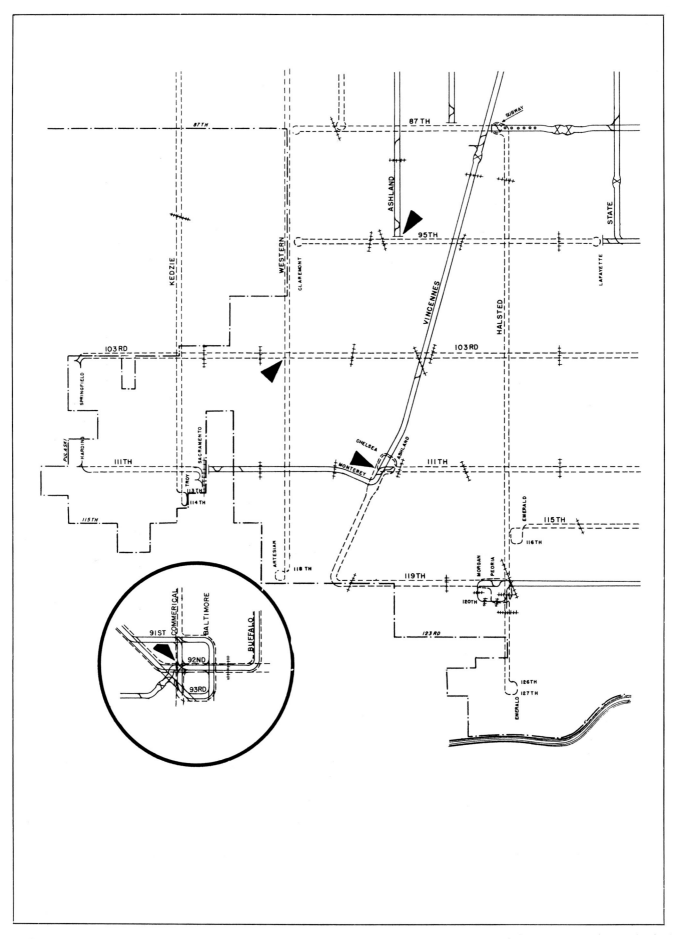

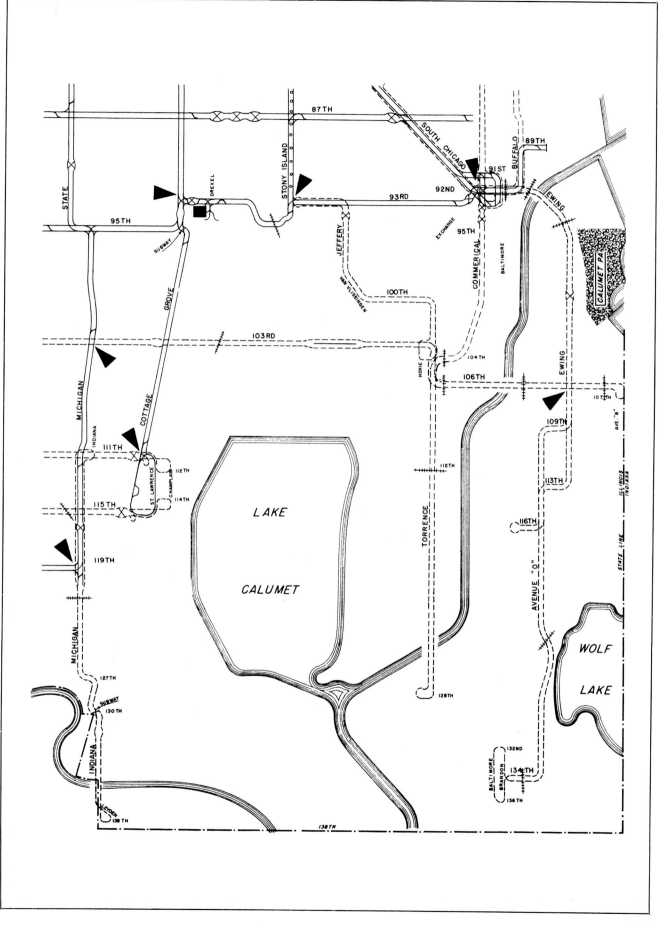

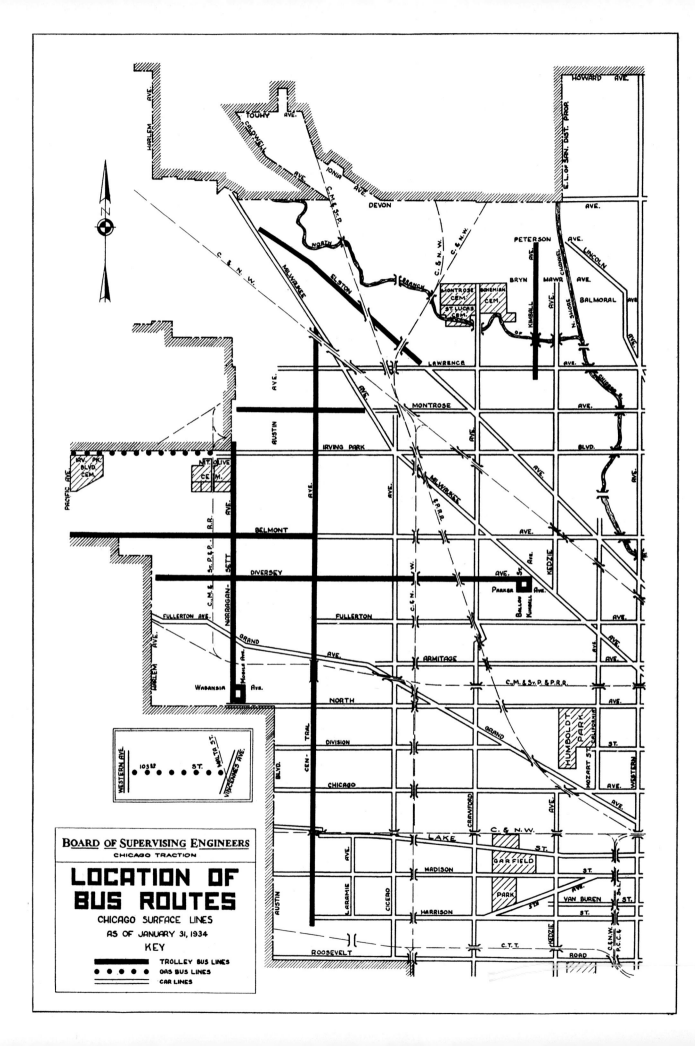

BOARD OF SUPERVISING ENGINEERS
CHICAGO TRACTION

LOCATION OF BUS ROUTES

CHICAGO SURFACE LINES

AS OF JANUARY 31, 1934

KEY

	TROLLEY BUS LINES
• • • • •	GAS BUS LINES
	CAR LINES

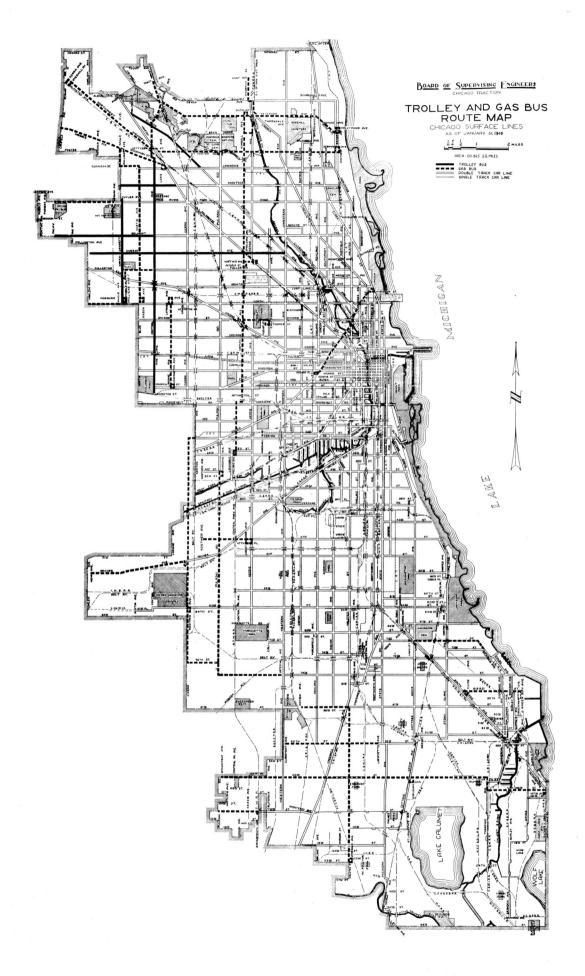

BOARD OF SUPERVISING ENGINEERS
CHICAGO TRACTION

TROLLEY AND GAS BUS
ROUTE MAP
CHICAGO SURFACE LINES
AS OF JANUARY 31, 1945

AREA - 212.863 SQ. MILES

TROLLEY BUS
GAS BUS
DOUBLE TRACK CAR LINE
SINGLE TRACK CAR LINE

Distinctive street lights, exclusive shops, the Chicago Water Tower, and at night the Lindbergh Beacon atop the Palmolive (now Playboy) Building gave an aura of elegance to North Michigan Avenue. Completing this typical scene are the swarm of cabs and the two buses of the Chicago Motor Coach Company, arch rival of the Surface Lines. The Motor Coach buses had Michigan Ave. to themselves. No streetcar dared to run here, and no subway rumbled beneath the street. The view looks north from the southwest corner of Michigan and Huron. From Hedrich-Blessing, courtesy of Jack Hedrich.

Competition and Cooperation

To give a balanced picture of public transportation during the CSL era, it's necessary to consider the other means of public and private transportation available to Chicagoans. In the CSL's early days, and to some extent even now, walking is a practical substitute for mass transit. Walking was a much more practical substitute 60 years ago, when people lived closer to their work than they do today. One of the benefits public transit brought to Chicago was the chance for workers to live in a better neighborhood, distant from the one they worked in.

Strange as it seems, the bicycle proved a strong competitor to mass transit in the 1890s. Today it is the automobile that competes with public transit for both riders and street space. CSL recognized the danger of automobile competition in the early 1920s, and fought the flivers in a number of ways.

CSL urged a ban on parking in the Loop, and better traffic control measures there. The City responded by shortening the time allowed for parking in any one spot — resulting in even bigger traffic jams as motorists jockeyed for a new spot. Early in 1926 the city put in traffic lights at 49 Loop intersections, replacing policemens' whistles. The lights were synchronized to provide a smooth traffic flow. (For details on this system, which was designed by the Surface Lines, see the introduction to the chapter on routes.)

All automobile parking was banned in the Loop effective January 10, 1928. This resulted in a speed-up of both automobile and streetcar traffic. CSL's own general re routing of 1924 also expedited traffic flow through the Loop. In 1932 Loop merchants rebelled against the parking ban, and got central ward aldermen to back a bill allowing one-hour parking for a five month trial period. The bill lost 26 to 19.

CSL also met the automotive menace with a series of ads carried as car cards in the streetcars. The ads pointed out that travel via CSL was cheaper, safer, and more dependable than by automobile, but the ads did little to deter drivers. In the end the automobile won its battle against mass transit in Chicago, as it did elsewhere. But CSL put up a good fight against it.

Steam railroad suburban service vied with CSL for customers throughout the streetcar era. When CSL was formed in 1914, nearly all the trunk line railroads entering Chicago offered suburban service of one kind or another. Even some local terminal and switching lines offered limited commuter service.

"Suburban service" is perhaps a bit misleading when applied to Chicago, since it suggests trains chugging into rural depots dozens of miles from the city. Chicago suburban service wasn't like that at all. In fact one railroad, the Illinois Central, had more "suburban" stations within the Chicago city limits than it had in the suburbs. The Rock Island, North Western, Milwaukee Road, Chicago & Western Indiana, and Wabash also had many in-city commuter stations.

Granted, even the busiest suburban line could not match the close headways of the CSL. But reduced rate commutation fares from close-in suburban stations compared favorably with CSL's flat 7¢ fare. In terms of speed and adherence to schedules, the suburban lines won hands down. Their schedule speeds were three to four times that of the streetcars (15 to 20 mph vs. 5 to 7 mph). When bad weather came and the streetcars inched their way through the storm, suburban trains sped along, scarcely affected by all but the most severe storms.

Elevated service was much like suburban service. It had higher fares and less frequent service than the CSL, but its trains were relatively fast and almost unaffected by the weather. The "L" lines did share a drawback with the railroads: they didn't service the entire city. While CSL boasted that 99 per cent of Chicago's population lived within three blocks of its lines, the "L" didn't reach the Northwest, Southwest, Southeast, or far South Sides of Chicago during the CSL era. It did reach the far North and West Sides, even reaching beyond the city limits to the suburbs.

The Chicago Motor Coach Company, known as the Boulevard Route, was another major CSL competitor. Starting life under a legal loophole which allowed it to run on boulevards under Park Board jurisdiction, the Motor Coach in the 1930s expanded its bus lines over Northwest Side streets in Chicago Railways territory. After protracted litigation, CMC was ordered to curtail its runs on the Northwest Side. Chicago Railways then took over with Chicago's first trolley bus lines.

For many years CMC charged a 10¢ fare, three cents more than CSL's 7¢ fare. This was a decided competi-

When they ran on the Chicago & Southern Traction Company as the Crete suburban cars, CCRy's 5651-5665 series cars looked like this: single-end cars with a smoking compartment. B. Neuberger.

347

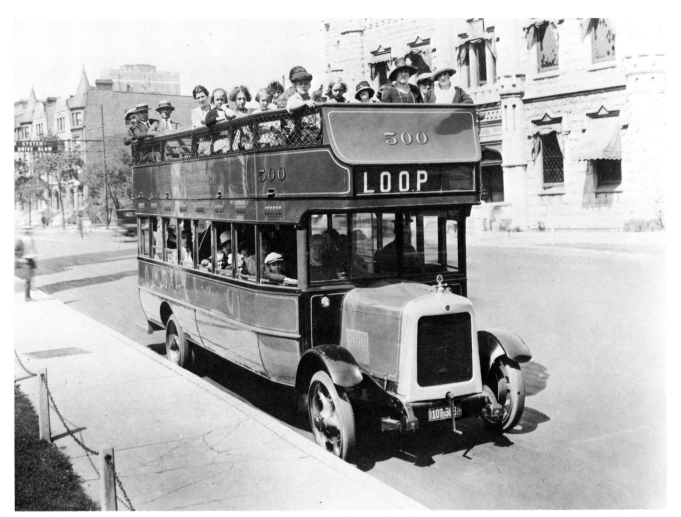

● Above, Chicago Motor Coach bus 500, Loop bound on Michigan at Chicago. Kaufmann & Fabry photo. The first open top double deck buses were put in service in 1917 by CMC, and the last double deck buses, which had closed tops, were run by CMC in 1950. Plans are afoot to run such buses in Chicago again. ● Below. Evanston Railway car 9, westbound on Central Street, at the Evanston Rapid Transit line. Barney Neuberger.

tive disadvantage to the Motor Coach. On the other hand, CMC routes tapped territory, such as North Michigan Avenue, which was poorly served by streetcars and the "L." Although CMC was best known for its North and West Side lines, it did serve the far Southeast Side with lines running to 112th and Green Bay and 92nd and Exchange. Other routes penetrated the Southwest Side as far as 61st and Cicero and Marquette Road and St. Louis. What kept CMC from being a truly citywide system was the lack of trunk lines running the length of the city to connect with their crosstown lines.

For example, suppose a Motor Coach rider wanted to get from 55th and Trumbull to 31st and Hamlin, a distance of a little over three miles. By Motor Coach the trip would have taken far more than an hour over two routes via downtown Chicago. This is a rather extreme example, but many other roundabout routings would have been necessary to reach Motor Coach points fairly close to one another. For example: Addison and Western to Logan Blvd. and Western; Logan Blvd. and Oakley to Oakley Blvd. and Hirsch Blvd.; and 26th and California to Marquette and California. One can sum up the CMC's routes by saying that most of them were radial, feeding the Loop, and that they had all the advantages and disadvantages of such a system.

Under no obligation to serve the entire city, Motor Coach made no attempt to tap thinly-settled parts of Chicago. While the Surface Lines had a number of lightly travelled, costly streetcar routes, the Motor Coach ran mostly heavy trunk lines. Even the Motor Coach shuttle services were heavily used, since they linked the near West Side railroad depots with the Loop and North Michigan Ave.; served Soldier Field and

• Above. Built by the South Chicago City Railway Company in 1907, car 336 became Calumet & South Chicago Railway Company 835 in 1908. In 1913 it became C&SC 2850. It burned at 120th and Indianapolis on the Whiting line on January 20, 1924. Photo from the Neuberger collection. • Below. At the west end of the Cermak Road line, Chicago & West Towns Rys. La Grange line cars like 138 met CSL Cermak cars.

other lakefront attractions; and carried crowds of bathers to beaches on both the North and South Sides.

There was an aura of elegance about the CMC buses which made CSL streetcars seem drab if not proletarian by comparison. Many of them were double deckers, the earliest with an open top deck, the later models with the upper deck enclosed. At one point CMC painted its fleet in three bright colors: green for the North Side lines, yellow for the West Side lines, and red for the South Side lines. Motor coach drivers, and in the days of two-man buses the conductors, wore snappy semi-military uniforms, leather Sam Browne belts, and high leather boots. By contrast the CSL motormen and conductors looked like imitation railroad conductors at best. CSL recognized that its own blue uniforms were rather dowdy when it dressed its own early bus operators in tan.

Though it lost its Northwest Side lines to Chicago Railways in 1930, CMC continued to expand its system. As late as 1949 it opened some new South Side routes. Three years later, on October 1, 1952, Motor Coach was taken over by CTA. For $16,431,000 CTA received a fleet of 595 buses and a system of 24 routes. Unfortunately, Motor Coach riders got an immediate fare increase from 15¢ to 20¢.

Both the CSL and the CMC, and to a lesser extent the South Side "L" lines, lost passengers to the jitney cabs that ran on South Park Ave. The jitneys cruised this major South Side street, picking up as many passengers as the cab could hold and delivering them anywhere along South Park (now King Drive) for a flat fare. Of course it was all illegal, but police looked the other way. CMC lost riders to the jitneys from its South Park bus lines, and CSL from its Cottage Grove and Indiana car lines.

By 1922 the Motor Coach was the second largest urban bus company in the United States. It grew because it gave one-seat service to North Side lakefront areas which had no direct streetcar service to downtown Chicago. Its double-deck buses attracted many holiday and pleasure riders, who didn't mind paying 10¢ to ride along the beautiful lakefront boulevards. Motor Coach service also appealed to women workers and shoppers: an early survey revealed seven out of ten passengers were women.

The Surface Lines also faced early bus competition on its interstate routes to Indiana, run jointly with the Hammond, Whiting & East Chicago Railway. By 1922 some two dozen buses linked Chicago with Indiana Harbor, Whiting, Hammond, East Chicago, and Gary. The bus routes ran on the same streets as the CSL-HW&EC streetcars, and used the same Chicago terminal point at 63rd and King Drive. The Hammond bus lines had 13 vehicles running every 15 minutes at a 25¢ fare for the 40 minute trip. Joint CSL-HW&EC service ran every 10

• Opposite page, above. Back when the "L" lines were really elevated railroads with steam locomotives, Lake Street engine 10, the Clarence A., posed with coach 7 at Lake and Oakley. Built in July, 1893 as a two cylinder compound type, engine 10 is now preserved at the National Museum of Transport in St. Louis, Mo. Coach 7, built by Gilbert in 1893, later became an "L" motor car. CTA photo. • Opposite page, below. Built by Barney & Smith in 1894 as motor car 711, Chicago Rapid Transit 2711 was rebuilt by ACF in 1904. It was not scrapped until February, 1957. Such long-lived equipment was common on the "L", since the Rapid Transit bought no new cars between 1924 and 1947. CTA photo. • Below. Built in March, 1892, South Side Rapid Transit locomotive 1 was a Vauclain compound type with an 0-4-4T wheel arrangement. It hauled trains of wooden coaches on the South Side Alley "L", Chicago's first elevated railway. Chicago Transit Authority photo.

WE ARE READY TO GIVE THIS SERVICE—NOW!

The Chicago Rapid Transit Company has volunteered to extend its service *immediately* upon securing authority from the Illinois Commerce Commission. The plan we propose does not in any way conflict with transfers between street cars and the Elevated Lines, or with any other traction plan now under consideration or in prospect. In fact it will be *helpful* to other traction plans if and when they are adopted.

The cost of providing buses for these extensions of "L" Service will be considerable and we want to know how much the public values their importance. FILL IN AND SEND US THE ENCLOSED CARD. It will show that you want these new "L" extensions which are designed to make Elevated transportation of far greater value to every rider and to all Chicago.

Our proposal does not preclude improvement of any other existing transportation system . . . It does not depend upon what some other company may or may not do . . . On the contrary, it is a definite, clean-cut plan from which the city will benefit *at once* and which may readily be co-ordinated into any present or future plan for transportation betterment.

For this extension of Rapid Transit Service it is proposed to purchase the very latest type of motor buses similar to the bus illustrated on the front of this folder—new, comfortable, easy-running, quiet—the finest that can be bought. Service will be operated 24 hours a day over routes shown on the map. Schedules will be co-ordinated with those of Elevated trains.

Every transportation expert who has studied Chicago's problem has agreed that the Elevated Railroads are and *always will be the* "backbone" of the city's transportation service.

Mayor Edward J. Kelly has sponsored the slogan, "KEEP CHICAGO AHEAD." If Chicago is to be kept ahead, adequate rapid transportation is absolutely imperative. The Chicago Rapid Transit Lines are ready to do their part. Do you want us to extend Rapid Transit Service? If you do, fill in the enclosed card, and mail it today (no postage required), or leave it with any "L" agent.

A. A. Sprague—Britton I. Budd, *Receivers,*

CHICAGO RAPID TRANSIT COMPANY
(The Elevated Lines)

See Back Page for Details of Proposed "L" Motor Bus Routes.

D ID you know that the Chicago Elevated Lines operate express trains that are even faster than the fastest runs in the New York subway? Did you know that "L" trains travel as much as eight miles without a single stop? There is only one form of rapid transportation in Chicago, and that is the "L". By means of the plan we propose, Rapid Transit Service will be immediately extended and made vastly more beneficial to the people of Chicago and suburbs.

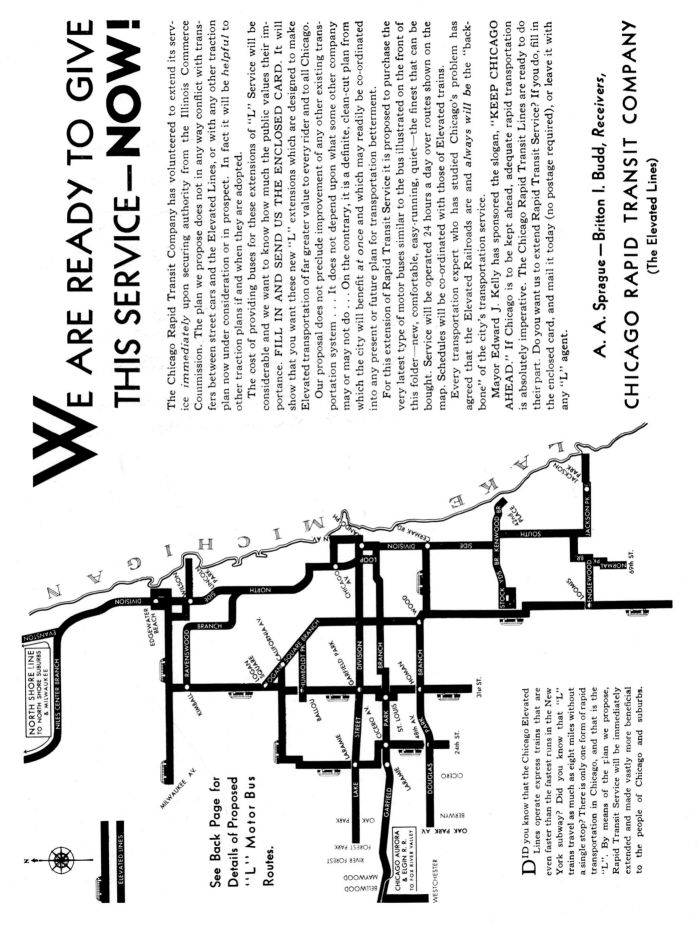

minutes at a 15¢ fare, and the cars took an hour to make the trip.

During the August, 1922 streetcar strike, a five cent bus line began service from the Loop to 53rd Street via Wabash Ave. It continued to run after the strike, using five buses on a ten minute headway.

Even counting all those in sightseeing and private service, there were only 278 buses licensed by the City of Chicago in 1922. Despite their small numbers, they were a threat to the Surface Lines. They skimmed off the cream of CSL's business, offering faster, more comfortable service at a premium fare.

The Motor Coach soon expanded its system, which in 1922 consisted of lines on only 11 miles of North Side streets, to include routes on 42 miles of South Side streets. John Hertz, president of Yellow Cab, pushed the line extensions. It will not surprise you to learn that all the buses needed for this expansion of service were built by the Yellow Coach Manufacturing Company, a subsidiary of the Yellow Cab Company, also under Hertz control. Hertz was also a part owner of Chicago Motor Coach.

Like the North Side lines, the South Side routes were over Park District boulevards. This arrangement permitted CMC to operate without a franchise from the City of Chicago. CMC did pay the city a vehicle tax of $10 a year and a passenger tax of $30 a year per vehicle. CMC also held a certificate from the Illinois Commerce Commission. The Park Board received five per cent of the Motor Coach's gross revenue for permitting buses to run on the boulevards.

On April 15, 1923 CMC began service on its first South Side route, one of 12 authorized for that part of the city. That same year CMC received permission from the Illinois Commerce Commission to begin serving the West Side. This was the start of a co-ordinated, city-wide bus service, though transfers were not issued between all lines until 1928. Late in 1923 CMC applied for permission to extend its lines. Most of the extensions were west legs branching off its main North Side lakefront routes along Devon, Peterson, Foster, Wilson, and Addison.

On March 16, 1924 CMC inaugurated its West Side service with 40 buses on three routes on Washington and Jackson Blvds. One week later three other West Side lines opened. In 1924 CMC merged with Fifth Avenue Bus Company and the New York Transportation Company to form the Omnibus Corporation of America. John Hertz was chairman of the Omnibus board. CMC had previously purchased the Peoples Motor Bus Company of St. Louis.

In addition to the two bus operation plans mentioned on page 355, the Chicago Rapid Transit Company proposed a third, much more ambitious plan which is illustrated on the opposite page. Had it been approved, this plan would have pushed Chicago Rapid Transit feeder bus lines deep into both Chicago Surface Lines and Chicago Motor Coach territory.
• At right. Near the east end of the line, CSL cars running on 63rd Street ran under the Jackson Park "L" and crossed under the Illinois Central's line.

In 1925 the City of Chicago filed for an injunction to prevent CMC from operating on city streets without a franchise, even though the bus firm had Illinois Commerce Commission approval. That same year CSL filed a complaint with the Commission claiming unfair competition by CMC in their application for route extensions into CSL territory on the Northwest Side.

Cook County Circuit Court Judge Hugo Friend upheld the city's right to require CMC to get a franchise before it could operate on city streets. Judge Friend's decision was reversed in June, 1927 by the Illinois Supreme Court. The Supreme Court held that the Illinois Commerce Commission had sufficient authority to authorize bus lines to run within a city without that city's consent. The City petitioned the Supreme Court for a rehearing, which was granted October 5, 1928. During the hearing CSL kept its Diversey bus extension running in competition with a Motor Coach route along Diversey. The Motor Coach line ran between Pulaski and Narragansett, covering the territory covered by CSL's Diversey bus extension and beyond. However, Motor

Coach buses did not pick up passengers between Pulaski and Laramie in CSL territory. The buses made local stops from Narragansett to Laramie, then ran express to Pulaski, then local to downtown.

On February 18, 1939 the Supreme Court reversed itself and found that the City of Chicago did have the right to require a franchise of bus companies running over its streets. The court made a nice distinction between regulation of a utility and requiring a franchise. A state commission could regulate the bus industry, but could not issue certificates for operation over city streets. The city could grant use of its streets to a bus company, but this did not constitute regulation of a bus company.

This legal fiction didn't last long, as cities throughout Illinois took advantage of the decision to tax local bus companies which happened to pass through their town. Supported by these smaller bus firms, CMC petitioned the Supreme Court for a second rehearing of the case, and got one.

On June 29, 1929 the Supreme Court handed down its third decision in the case — and again reversed itself. This time the Court held that the Illinois Commission did have complete authority to grant certificates of convenience and necessity for bus operation over both public highways and city streets.

It seemed that nothing could stop the Motor Coach from expanding into Surface Lines territory. It had Illinois Commerce Commission approval dating from October 2, 1928 to operate seven routes with a total of 17 miles of line in Chicago Railways (CSL) territory.

But there had been a change in state government, with a new governor sworn in during January, 1929. The new governor made some changes in the makeup of the Commission, and it re-opened the CSL-CMC case. On March 6, 1930 the Commission issued a new order in the case which reversed the order of the previous Commission and gave CSL authority to operate trolley bus feeder service on all the Northwest routes except Belmont, which was to have a gas feeder bus. The chapter on trolley buses has more details on these first CSL trolley bus routes.

Chicago Motor Coach might have gotten the right to take away all of CSL's territory, had the city gone along with its bold proposal made in 1927. At that time the 20-year franchise granted by the city to the companies

The heavy clothes worn by pedestrians and the lack of passengers on the open upper deck of the Chicago Motor Bus double decker suggest that this 1918 photo, taken at Michigan and Adams, was shot in the winter. From Kaufmann & Fabry.

354

underlying CSL expired. As an interim measure the city council on December 8, 1926 proposed a temporary six-month extension of the franchise until July 1, 1927.

On that same day Motor Coach President J. A. Ritchie offered to replace CSL's streetcars with more than 4,000 double-deck buses. His system would have served the entire city, and taken away CSL's franchise completely, reducing the Surface Lines to a company worth only what its equipment, real estate, and rail could bring at a forced sale. The man behind CMC's audacious bid for the CSL franchise was Chairman John Hertz.

Already troubled by CMC competition, the Surface Lines was threatened with additional bus competition from the Chicago Elevated Railways. In 1922 CER President Britton I. Budd proposed three CER bus routes to feed the "L". One was to serve the Logan Square station, running along Wrightwood Ave. for a mile to the west of the station. Another line was to follow a twisting route from the Fullerton station to North and Sedgwick, serving the area east of the "L". To tap an area already served by the Illinois Central and the Surface Lines, CER proposed a third route running east from the 51st station along 51st St. and Hyde Park Blvd. to a terminal at 56th and Everett.

CER announced plans to run 10 minute service on each of the three lines. The initial equipment was to be fourteen 22 or 27-passenger buses. More frequent service was promised if traffic rose enough to justify it. Free transfers were to be issued to and from the "L".

In the aftermath of the huge Stockyards fire of May, 1934, the "L" lines, now under Chicago Rapid Transit management, wanted to replace the Stockyards "L" with a bus line. The line would have run over private streets in the Stockyards with 10 buses. Should traffic rise to the pre-fire level, CRT was willing to add as many as 15 buses to the route. However, nothing came of the bus substitution plan, and the Stockyards line was eventually rebuilt.

If there was a spirit of rivalry between CSL and the Motor Coach and Rapid Transit companies, there was a spirit of co-operation between CSL and the street railways that connected with it. CSL enjoyed friendly relations with the Chicago & West Towns Railways, which served such pleasant residential communities as Oak Park, Maywood, Melrose Park, Forest Park, Riverside, and Brookfield, as well as industrial towns like Cicero.

The West Towns had always had strong links with Chicago's street railways. One of the C&WT's predecessor lines, the Cicero & Proviso Street Railway, became part of Yerkes' West Chicago Street Railroad. C&P became part of Chicago Consolidated Traction in 1899. CCT worked hand in glove with its sister Chicago properties, then under Chicago Union Traction ownership. In 1902 the Illinois Supreme Court ruled that the CCT and the CUT were the same company, and ordered the exchange of transfers between them.

CUT became Chicago Railways in 1908, and in 1910 Chicago Railways acquired all CCT property within the City of Chicago. The CCT lines outside Chicago, including the Evanston and west suburban lines, were sold to County Traction. County Traction operated its west suburban lines with cars rented from Chicago Railways. In 1912 Chicago Railways took over parts of County Traction's Harrison and Laramie lines. County Traction west suburban lines and the Suburban Railroad were taken over by new owners in 1913, becoming Chicago & West Towns Railways.

Even as an independent company, C&WT had strong ties with CSL. C&WT's five streetcar trunk lines were virtually extensions of CSL lines on those same streets.

CSL loaned C&WT 10 of its 1300-series cars in 1936 and 1937 to replace cars lost in the C&WT's Lake Street barn fire of December 2, 1936. For details, see that car series in the passenger car chapter. CSL's 3200 and 6200 multiple-unit cars, built in 1925, were similar in appearance to C&WT's 138-141 series MU cars built in 1924. On their way to the C&WT's suburban barn for scrapping, 12 C&WT cars traveled over CSL lines from the C&WT's Lake Street barn.

The Chicago & Interurban Traction Company, known as the Kankakee Line, also had a close relationship with the Surface Lines. The C&IT ran from a terminal it shared with the CSL at 63rd and Halsted to Blue Island, Harvey, and Kankakee, Ill. Of its 45 miles of main line, seven were over the Chicago City Railway between 63rd and 119th Streets.

Fourteen C&IT trains a day ran as far as Kankakee, but between 63rd and suburban Crete, Ill, there were 32 trains a day in 1912. There was a local car every 20 minutes between 63rd and Halsted and Blue Island.

On March 1, 1912 all C&IT property within Chicago was sold to the Chicago City Railway. In addition to the track, 33 C&IT cars became CCRy property. They were city motor cars 2, 4, 6, and 8, and the even-numbered city trailer cars from 10 through 32; Crete suburban cars 126 to 140; sprinkler car 400; and snow sweeper 503. All 16 city cars were scrapped in 1912. The Crete suburban cars became CSL 5651-5665, and ran on Ashland Ave. For further details on these cars, see the passenger car chapter. C&IT's double-truck sprinkler became CCRy D-13, then CSL D-213. Sweeper 503 became CCRy E-34, and later CSL E-234. As part of the deal CCRy also acquired the C&IT's carbarn at 88th and Vincennes, used for storage by CSL.

At 11:59 p.m. April 23, 1927 the C&IT abandoned its lines. Receiver W. W. Crawford cited loss of passengers to the newly-electrified Illinois Central suburban service and the loss of freight to trucks in his plea for abandonment. Another factor was the high wages paid to C&IT's 130 employees, who were paid CSL scale wages.

Schappi Bus Company of Calumet City, Ill., took over some of the C&IT routes. Today these lines are operated by South Suburban Safeway Lines buses.

The joint operation of the Indiana lines by CSL and the Hammond, Whiting & East Chicago Railway is covered in the chapter on CSL routes. In that chapter you'll also find details on CSL predecessors who operated the Evanston route. Mention should also be made of the Chicago & Joliet Electric Railway, an interurban line between those cities which connected with the CSL at the Archer and Cicero terminal, CSL cars looping on one side of the terminal building, C&J cars on the other side.

Carhouses and Shops of the Surface Lines

● Above. Two prewar PCCs and a 1914 Brill car get attention in Bay 9 of the Kedzie-Van Buren carhouse. Photo from the CTA ● Opposite page, above. Old Pullman 527 from the Ashland route and two postwar PCCs from the Western Avenue line rest at the rear of the 69th and Ashland carhouse. Barney Neuberger collection, from the Railway Negative Exchange. ● Opposite page, below. Equipped with couplers for hauling the trailers which flank it, car 1744 is between runs at the Kedzie-Van Buren carhouse. Photo from George Krambles.

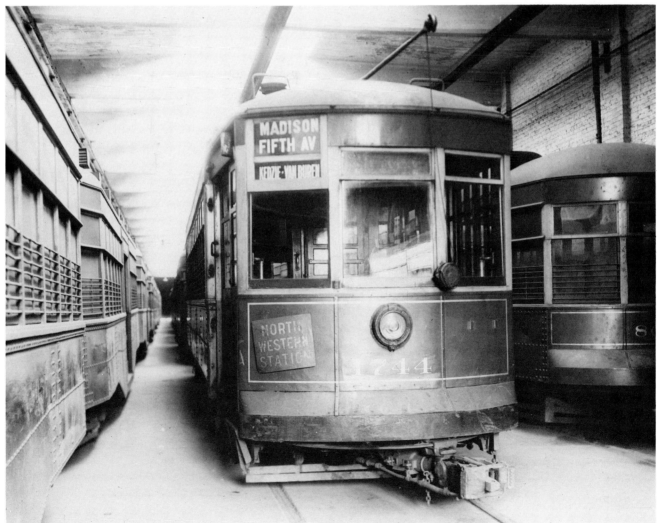

• Above. Taken from the northeast corner of North and Cicero Aves., this CTA photo shows how the North Avenue carhouse looked on April 9, 1923. Note open storage area next to barn, with the bays divided by firewalls. Note also the jog in Cicero Ave. as it crosses North Ave. This carhouse was built in 1910, and is still in use.
• Below. The Noble carbarn at Cortland and Hermitage was CSL's smallest operating carhouse. This view looks north along Paulina toward Armitage. CTA photo.

• Above. Seventeen Twin Coach buses in CRys 526-563 series, built in 1937, pose for the photographer on the lead tracks of the 77th and Vincennes carhouse. The largest of CSL's storage and repair facilities, the carhouse and South Shops complex was bounded by Vincennes on the west, Perry Ave. on the east, 77th St. on the north, and 79th St. on the south. CTA photo. • Below. After the North Clark Street portion of the Clark-Wentworth line was converted to bus on September 7, 1957, the Devon depot closed. It opened in 1901. CTA photo.

● Above. This view looks west along Wrightwood from the corner of Lincoln and Wrightwood and shows the single track carbarn lead of the Lincoln-Wrightwood carbarn, built in 1908-1910. CTA photo. ● Opposite page, top. Supposedly once the home of General Ambrose Burnside of sideburn fame, the wooden structure at the upper right was later a railroad hotel, then became the transportation building at Burnside carhouse. When Burnside closed in 1949, its 215 trainmen and 30 shopmen transferred to 77th-Vincennes. CTA photo. ● Opposite page, below. Not much to look at, the Armitage carhouse nonetheless provided shelter for the many air door Old Pullman cars, such as 507, which were assigned to the busy Milwaukee Avenue line. CTA photo.● Below. Built as a cable car barn in 1894, Elston was remodeled for electric cars in 1904. When this barn closed in 1951, only the Lawrence and Elston streetcar lines and the Elston Extension trolley bus ran from it. All 163 trainmen at Elston transferred to the North Park and Devon depots. CTA photo.

The Cottage Grove carhouse, illustrated above, and the 77th-Vincennes barn, shown on page 359, were both completed in 1908 by the Chicago City Railway Company. Both were designed as double-ended depots, with cars entering the rear of the barn after their runs, and moving through for inspection, cleaning, washing and disinfecting. By the time the cars reached the front of the carhouse they were ready to go on the street again. This view shows the Langley Ave., or rear end, of the Cottage Grove carhouse. With an inside storage capacity of 222 cars, Cottage Grove was a large barn, but it was small compared to the total of 472 cars that could fit into the old (1902) and new (1908) 77th-Vincennes carhouses. Chicago Transit Authority photo.

Opened in January, 1943 as a WW II temporary garage (to save gasoline and tire wear), the Lawrence Ave. garage closed permanently on May 30, 1954. CTA transferred its motor bus runs to North Park depot. Trolley bus runs were also assigned to Lawrence garage; however, they operated from the Central-Avondale trolley bus storage yard. In the photo above Chicago Railways 1945 Ford model 29B bus 4316 pokes its nose out of the Lawrence garage. Chicago Transit Authority photo. In the photo below a variety of Chicago Railways buses undergo repairs or await their runs in this Chicago Transit Authority photo of the interior of the garage.

A brief tour of the West Shops

Passage of the Settlement Ordinances of 1907 created a need for greatly expanded shop facilities to renovate and upgrade cars to the standards spelled out in the Ordinances. Chicago Railways met this need by just about doubling the size of its West Shops in 1910. The new shops and an adjacent carbarn occupied a tract of land 350 feet wide and 1,600 feet long between Madison and Lake east of Harding Ave. The site was a block west of Garfield Park and about five miles directly west of downtown Chicago. The design of the new shop was a joint Chicago Railways-Board of Supervising Engineers project.

In 1910 Chicago Railways had 2,160 passenger cars and 200 work cars in its fleet. Three hundred twenty-eight of the older cars were being rebuilt into PAYE cars at a rate of 25 cars a month. At this time Chicago Railways planned to build 215 Turtleback cars. All the heavy maintenance and repair work on the existing fleet, the reconstruction of the older cars, and the construction of the Turtleback cars was done at West Shops.

Three streets running through the shop property divided it into four sections of approximately equal size. A service track running along the east side of the property connected all four sections.

Seven tracks entered the property from the Madison St. (carbarn) end, and four from the Lake St. end. There was a connection at the Lake St. end with the ground-level Hamlin Ave. yard and shop of the Lake St. "L."

The section between Madison St. and Washington Blvd. was the carbarn. The next section, between Washington Blvd. and West End Ave., was the original West Shops, remodeled in 1910. This section contained the truck and wheel shop, machine shop, electrical and armature shops, blacksmith shop, brass foundry, storehouse, and offices.

In 1909 Chicago Railways completed the buildings between West End Ave. and Park Ave. These included large carpenter and paint shops, and smaller facilities for glass storage, stock rooms, and curtain and sign rooms.

Furthest north, between Park Ave. and Lake St., were the buildings completed in 1910. They housed an erecting shop with a capacity of 72 cars, a woodmill, and fender, cabinet, pattern, and tin shops. The dry kiln and boiler house were also located in this section.

Four transfer tables facilitated the movement of cars from track to track without the use of switches. They were located south of Lake St., south of Park Ave., north of West End Ave., and in the carbarn section. All except the one in the carbarn were new.

The wheel and truck shop produced three rebuilt trucks a day for converting older cars to PAYE, and repaired eight CRys standard Baldwin-Pullman 150 trucks each week. The rebuilt motors for the rebuilt

• Opposite page, above. Car 1379 gets some finishing touches of paint at CSL's West Shops. CTA photo. • Below. West Shops built hundreds of streetcars, and rebuilt or converted hundreds of other streetcars and trolley buses. This 1923 photo from the CTA shows car 1721 under construction.

trucks were run for five minutes on a test stand before reassembly into completed trucks.

The 33 men in the armature shop did all the electric repair work for the 2,360 CRys passenger and work cars. They also tested and repaired the armatures and field coils of the GE-70 and GE-80 motors for the PAYE rebuilds.

In the wheel shop, a machinist and his helper could turn 100 pairs of wheels a day (nine working hours). They used a 35 HP wheel lathe.

Almost the entire CRys passenger car fleet — 2,000 cars — went through the paint shop in 1910. The 650 cars with steel panels were sandblasted before painting to stop rusting. All car exteriors were finished in olive green with gold decorations and gold striping. Interiors were cherry wood stained to resemble mahogany. Decals were used for all lettering and for the company monogram. Two coats of body varnish, applied 24 hours apart, completed the paint job.

West Shops was also completely equipped to make repairs to air brakes, trolley poles, fenders, and other car components.

CTA consolidated West Shops with the Hamlin Ave. shops of the Lake Street "L" in 1949. Prior to the physical hookup of the two shops, all Hamlin Ave. compressor, armature, and air brake work had already been transferred to West Shops. With the consolidation, West Shops began to handle all the motor and truck repairs to Lake "L" cars.

To reach West Shops the Rapid Transit cars were sent down the incline from the Lake Street "L" into the ground-level Hamlin yard. They changed direction on a loop track at the north end of the yard and moved south across Lake Street using their trolley poles to draw current from the streetcar overhead wire. One of the transfer tables was extended six feet at either end to accommodate the "L" cars.

In 1949 West Shops also extensively rebuilt some 150 of the oldest trolley buses, all of which had been purchased by the CSL. The work included replacement of worn, broken, or rusted body panels, removal and rehabilitation of heaters, seats, flooring, and stanchions, and repairs to the motors, controls, and wiring. The buses also received complete exterior and interior paint in CTA colors. During the CSL era West Shops had done all major repair work on the trolley bus fleet. Inspection and minor repairs were made at the two carbarns which were assigned electric buses, North-Cicero and Elston Ave.

Shops got all the cars on the street at Christmas

CSL's heaviest traffic surge came in the pre-Christmas shopping period. To get the maximum number of cars on the street during the 1925 shopping period, both the West and South Shops did not accept any cars for overhauling after November 1. On that day the two shops had a combined total of 90 cars on hand for overhaul and 78 cars on hand for damage repairs. By December 4 there was just one car in West Shops and three in South Shops awaiting repairs. Despite the fact that no cars were accepted for overhaul after November 1, 40 per cent more cars got overhauled in 1925 than in 1924.

Some shopmen were sent to the 16 active carhouses to help make repairs there. Thus augmented, carbarn repair forces were able to fix cars with badly damaged platforms in just one day, often the same day they were damaged. On December 18, 1925 there were no cars held for repairs at any of the 16 carhouses.

CSL did even better during the 1926 Christmas shopping season. Normally the 16 operating carbarns held an average of 25 cars each day for minor repairs, while the West and South Shops held an average of 117 cars a day for overhaul and major repairs. On December 20, 1926 all of CSL's 3,639 passenger cars were out on the street. For the next three days all but one were on the street.

During 1927 CSL continued its good record. On December 21, 22, and 23, all 3,639 passenger cars were in service. Cars that were damaged received quick repairs. For example, car 3095 suffered a crushed platform in a collision with a cement truck on December 17. On December 21 it was back in service. An axle on car 5779 broke in an accident. The car was lifted off the track, hauled to the curb, repaired there, and set back on the track to re-enter service in just one hour and 25 minutes.

In 1927 the Surface Lines had a total shop force of 98 supervisors and 2,339 men. Thirty-four supervisors and 978 men were assigned to the West and South Shops. The remaining 64 supervisors and 1,361 men were assigned to the carbarns for light repairs and cleaning.

CSL's maintenance goal in the 1920s was to thoroughly overhaul each car every two years, or in other words to shop half the fleet each year. The actual time available to work on the cars was less than 50 weeks, since no cars were supposed to be in the Shops during the pre-Christmas shopping period. CSL approached that goal in 1927, when 45 per cent of the fleet went through the shops for overhaul.

CSL carbarns: home of the great red and cream fleet

In 1912 Chicago Railways operated out of 11 carbarns. Six were new, built to Board of Supervising Engineers standards. The six were Blue Island, Lincoln, Lawndale, Kedzie, Limits, and North Ave. The five older barns in service in 1912 were Armitage, Noble, Division and Western, Elston, and Devon. All 11 barns lasted through the CSL era (see page 367 for subsequent history).

Kedzie Ave. was the newest CRys barn in 1912. Ten local routes and four Through Routes ran from Kedzie, requiring 281 double truck cars and three single truckers. To cover extra runs and bad order cars, a total of 307 cars were assigned to Kedzie depot. After completing their westbound trips, Van Buren Street cars ran into Bay 2 of the barn, turned around, and went back to Van Buren Street for their eastbound run. All lines served by Kedzie carhouse were assigned to specific bays in the barn.

More than 1,000 trainmen worked out of Kedzie station in 1912: 510 conductors and 515 motormen. About one out of six were extra men, assigned to fill in for missing regular men.

In addition to repairing an average of eight cars a day, the shop forces at Kedzie made scheduled inspections and repairs on a time and mileage basis. Brake shoes were adjusted nightly, and controllers and trolley wheels inspected and adjusted every ten days. A general inspection was made every 1,000 miles, and the cars were lubricated every 3,000 miles.

All cars were swept and dusted every day. Every three days they got a general cleaning, including window washing, floor scrubbing, and disinfecting. Every three months each car got a more thorough scrubbing inside and out.

The Chicago City Railway, the Calumet & South Chicago, and the Southern Street Railway operated out of seven barns. Four were built after 1907 to Board of Supervising Engineers standards: Archer, Cottage Grove, 69th Street, and 77th Street. Two of the other South Side Barns, 69th and Emerald and 88th and Vincennes, were used for storage of equipment only during the CSL era. The third old barn was Burnside, which survived until the end of streetcar service on its routes in 1949.

One of the largest carhouses was opened by CCRy in late 1907 at 38th and Cottage Grove. Four hundred feet wide and 600 feet long, it had six four-track storage bays, one four-track repair bay, and one double-track utility bay. Next to the utility bay were an office, stock room, blacksmith shop, locker and lunch room, toilets, oil room, pump room, and a boiler room for heating the barn with steam.

At the opposite side of the barn were storage bins for sand, salt, track department material, and advertising car cards. This side also had six stalls for the horses used to pull emergency vehicles. Three types of emergency equipment were kept here: an overhead line wagon to fix breaks in the trolley wire; a breakdown wagon to repair disabled streetcars; and a hose bridge wagon whose bridges allowed streetcars to run across fire department hoses. (Much later all three functions were combined into a single utility truck.) One wagon driver was always on duty here, and he could call out as many barnmen as he needed to answer a call.

The Cottage Grove side of the barn was two stories high over four bays. A trainmens' room, toilets, employees' club room, and offices for the dispatcher and division superintendent were located on the second floor. At one end of the large toilet room was a barber shop. The barber paid nothing for his shop, but was limited by the CCRy to charging a maximum of 10¢ for a shave. The bootblack cleaned the toilets, and could keep all he received for shining shoes.

A club room 81 feet long by 46 feet wide occupied the rest of the second floor. It had a stage and dressing rooms for amateur theatricals. A pool table, a billiard table, two chess tables, five card tables, and a variety of gym apparatus filled the room. The reading room and the club room were open to all employees from 5:00 am to 1:00 am seven days a week. The club room furnishings belonged to a carmen's social club. More than 500 of the 750 men who worked out of the Cottage Grove barn belonged to the club. The dues of 25¢ a month paid for dances, plays, and other entertainment as well as for the furnishings.

Lines Assigned to Various Carbarns: 1947-48

Archer Avenue
Streetcars: Archer, Western, 31st.
Buses: Archer, Archer Express, Canal-Wacker, S. California, S. Pulaski, S. Cicero, 26th, 31st, Pershing, 47th, 59th-61st, 63rd-65th.

Ardmore and Lawrence Garages
Buses: Higgins, Taylor-Sedgwick-Sheffield, Southport, N. California, Kimball, N. Pulaski, Cicero, Central, North-Harlem, Touhy, Devon-Broadway, Peterson, W. Foster, Foster-Northwest Highway, Irving Park (80A).

Armitage
Streetcars: Milwaukee, Armitage-Milwaukee.

Blue Island
Streetcars: Morgan-Racine-Sangamon, 16th-18th.

Burnside
Streetcars: Stony Island-Wabash, Cottage Grove, Cottage Grove - South Chicago.

Cottage Grove
Streetcars: Stony Island-Wabash, Cottage Grove-55th, Cottage Grove-South Chicago, Cottage Grove, Lincoln-Indiana, Indiana, 35th, 43rd-Root, 47th.

Devon
Streetcars: Broadway-State, Clark-Wentworth, Western

Elston
Streetcars: Elston, Lawrence, Irving Park.
Trolley Bus: Elston Extension.

Kedzie
Streetcars: Madison, Madison-Fifth, Kedzie, Kedzie-California, Division-State-Van Buren, Van Buren, Division-Milwaukee.

Lawndale
Streetcars: Ogden-Randolph, Blue Island-26th, Roosevelt, Roosevelt-Wells (Downtown car), Cermak.
Buses: Taylor-Sedgwick, Sheffield, Kimball-Homan, S. Pulaski, S. Cicero.

Limits
Streetcars: Halsted, Halsted-Archer-Clark (Downtown car).
Buses: Clybourn, Ogden, Damen, Belmont (East), Grand (shuttle).

Lincoln
Streetcars: Lincoln-Indiana, Lincoln-Wells, Ashland, Damen, Fullerton.

North Avenue
Streetcars: Pulaski, Cicero, Belmont, North, Chicago, Grand, Lake, Armitage.
Trolley Buses: Central, Narragansett, Montrose, Belmont, Diversey.
Buses: Laramie, Austin, Fullerton, North, Division, Harrison, Harrison-Adams.

69th Street
Streetcars: Ashland, Ashland-Archer (Downtown car), Western, 63rd, 67th-69th-71st.

77th Street
Streetcars: Broadway-State, Clark-Wentworth, Halsted, Halsted-Archer-Clark (Downtown car), Wallace-Racine, 79th, 87th.
Buses: South Chicago-Ewing, South Torrence, South Deering, Windsor Park, Jeffery-100th, Michigan-Indiana, South Halsted, South Damen, South Kedzie, 71st, 74th-75th, West 79th, 83rd, 87th (87A), 95th, 103rd-106th, East 111th, West 111th, 115th, Vincennes-119th.

Name	Location	Closed
Archer	Archer & Rockwell	In use
Armitage	Armitage & Campbell	5/11/52
Blue Island	Blue Island & Leavitt	1/16/55
Burnside	93rd & Drexel	9/12/49
Cottage Grove	38th & Cottage Grove	6/19/55
Devon	Clark & Schreiber	9/7/57
Division	Western & Division	5/4/47
Elston	Elston & Addison	1/21/51
Kedzie	Kedzie & Van Buren	In use
Lawndale	22nd & Ogden	12/16/73
Limits	Clark & Dewey	In use
Lincoln	Lincoln & Wrightwood	3/7/51
Noble	Cortland & Hermitage	8/31/47
North Avenue	North & Cicero	In use
69th Street	69th & Ashland	In use
77th Street	77th & Vincennes	In use

Notes: CSL organized these 16 operating carbarns into 12 divisions for administrative purposes. CSL also had two barns used for storage of cars not needed for daily operations. They were at 69th and Emerald and 88th and Vincennes. Among other CSL facilities were the West and South Shops, material yards, the frog shop for trackwork fabrication and repair, several bus garages, and many line crew and wreck wagon locations.

Wooden cars and iron men

Nothing could better set the stage for a chapter on the men and women who made CSL go than this statement from William D. Mahon, long-time president of the Amalgamated Association of Street & Electric Railway Employees of America (now known as the Amalgamated Transit Union). The statement was made in 1952 on the 50th anniversary of Chicago Division 241.

"The history of the street railway employees prior to organization and for years thereafter is one of wrongs and mistreatment, long hours and small pay. It is a fact that in the early days the horse received much better treatment than the man who drove him. Men could easily be replaced, even at the miserable wages paid, but a horse cost money. The driver was on duty from the time he took out his run early in the morning until he pulled in late at night — sometimes as long as eighteen hours. No horse worked longer than four."

Wages and working conditions in Chicago just before the turn of the century (1898) seem to bear out many of Mahon's contentions. In that era the best paid and best treated employees were the gripmen and conductors on the Chicago City Railway Company. Their pay was from 25¢ to 30¢ an hour, and most worked an average of 10 hours a day. Their working hours included a 20 to 25 minute mealtime at the end of one run. However, if the cars were delayed, as frequently happened, the meal period could be partially or wholly lost. The cable car men were the elite employees on the CCRy, as trolley motormen and conductors received only 21¢ an hour at this time.

Gripmen had to deposit $50 as a guarantee against damage to their car, while conductors deposited $80 to pay for their uniforms, to cover the $10 in change they received each day from the company, and the remainder as security against accidents. The gripmen received six per cent interest on their $50 deposit, but the conductors got no interest on their $80 deposit.

The City Railway also provided clubrooms for employees at its carbarns. The men, organized into literary and athletic clubs, paid dues of 25¢ a month to furnish the clubrooms, and to finance social and athletic events.

West Chicago Street Railroad cable car gripmen and conductors on regular runs received 23¢ an hour, and worked an average of 11 hours a day. Meal time was not paid for. On the electric lines both conductors and motormen received 21¢ an hour.

Without a doubt the North Chicago Street Railroad was the worst company to work for. For 11 hours of continuous work gripmen got $2.25 a day to start and $2.50 a day after three months' service. Regular conductors and motormen started at $1.50 a day, got $1.75 a day after three months, $2.00 a day after six months, and $2.25 a day after two years. Extra conductors making tripper rush hour runs with extra trailers got $1.50 a day for six hours work, and $1.75 a day for eight hours work.

Discipline was harsh. For example, if a man failed to report on time for his run, he lost all seniority. If he wanted to continue in the service, he had to begin at the bottom of the extra list. Bad labor-management relations persisted on the North Chicago property (which became part of Chicago Union Traction in 1899 and part of Chicago Railways in 1908) right up to unification in 1914.

On all three properties most men worked a six day week, with Sunday off. Those who had to work on Sunday had different and usually much shorter hours. Some men were able to take two days a week off. There seemed to be no limit, though, on the hours a man could work or the number of consecutive days he could work without rest. One North Chicago employee reportedly labored on the cars for 384 days in a row.

Despite the hardships of streetcar work in those days, there were said to be long waiting lists of applicants on file at the offices of all three companies. City investigators determined that job seekers who wished to work for the North Chicago line had to sign a pre-employment agreement that they would not join a labor union. The Chicago City Railway also required a pre-employment contract, but investigators could not determine exactly what the employees had to agree to. Neither company gave copies of the contract to the employees who had signed them. Whether or not the contracts contained an anti-union clause, it was commonly understood that all three street railway companies actively prevented the formation of unions.

When the Amalgamated's first convention was held in Indianapolis in September, 1892, three Knights of Labor delegates representing the Chicago Carmen's union attended. The Knights of Labor had successfully organized streetcar men to protest against the 16-hour day, but once the 12-hour day became the standard many carmen lost interest in the union. The Knights were also felt to be inept in handling carmens' grievances. Seeing this situation as an opportunity to bring the carmen into his organization, AFL President Samuel Gompers told his organizers to begin recruiting carmen.

By 1892 Gompers thought he could move to form a street railway union, and the Amalgamated meeting in Indianapolis was held under AFL auspices. But at the convention the Knights of Labor, who claimed to represent some 3,000 Chicago carmen, were able to convince the other delegates that the new union should be independent of both the AFL and the K of L.

The first convention fixed monthly union dues at 5¢ per member per month, plus a special monthly assessment for use in supporting members of local unions who were on strike.

In 1893 the Amalgamated did affiliate with the AFL, and William Mahon became president at a salary of $800 a year. He was still president when the Amalgamated celebrated its 50th anniversary. On that occasion Carl Sandburg wrote: "So the Amalgamated now comes 50 years old. 'Well and good,' say those familiar with its record, with the main trend of its policies and programs. It is an occasion to give salutations to Bill Mahon, his able leadership, his scrupulous accounting, his sagacity and plain way of living that might to advantage have more and better imitators here and there in the American labor movement.''

Mahon contributed to the union movement in all trades through his long-time membership on the executive council of the AFL. He was also a member of the government's Federal Electric Railway Commission, and in 1933 went to Washington as a consultant in the drafting of the NRA Transit Code.

The first Chicago local to affiliate with the Amalgamated was Division 241, chartered April 1, 1902. It took in men who worked on the North and West Sides for Chicago Consolidated Traction or Chicago Union Traction. Later a charter was issued to Division 260, representing South Side employees who worked for the City Railway. Division 260 was merged into 241 with the unification of streetcar operation under the CSL. Division 241 eventually represented virtually all CSL employees, as well as those on the Chicago & West Towns and the Evanston Railways. In addition to the CSL motormen and conductors, 241 included bus drivers, shopworkers such as streetcar and bus repairmen, car cleaners, typists, clerks, schedule makers, station receivers, and even first-level supervisors. Indeed, Division 241 grew to be the largest local in the Amalgamated.

Car Men's Hall, also known as the Ashland Boulevard Auditorium, was physical evidence of the early strength of Division 241. Built at the corner of Ashland and Van Buren in 1918, it cost $400,000. In addition to its use as union offices and a meeting hall, the Auditorium was at various times a boxing arena, opera house, circus am-phitheater, ballroom, wedding reception hall, wrestling arena, and even a funeral parlor for the wakes of long-time local President William Quinn and other union stalwarts. Anna Fitzu sang arias there, and some of light-heavyweight Bob Satterfield's first bouts were fought there under arc lights.

Naturally suspicious after years of battling the companies, Division 241 kept its guard up even after it was firmly established. For example, the local frowned on some of the competition CSL tried to foster between various carhouses and shops through clubs and bands. Division 241 thought encouraging rivalry smacked of earlier efforts to divide and conquer the men. As late as the 1930s, when bus operation was just getting started, the company and the union met headlong over the issue of who would man the buses.

CSL wanted the bus drivers to be drawn from a separate roster, and to wear tan uniforms rather than the blue railroad-style uniforms the trainmen wore. Division 241 viewed these plans as a move by the company to diminish and eventually eliminate the union by changing CSL operations to an all-bus system. The union also felt the CSL was trying to create an elite corps of bus drivers who would look down their noses at mere carmen, and thus damage carmen's morale. The union insisted that motormen and conductors be given a chance to become bus drivers, and that all bus drivers be Division 241 members. CSL agreed, but retained the right to dress the bus drivers in a snappy tan uniform. Most of the tan uniforms gave way to the traditional blue uniforms be-

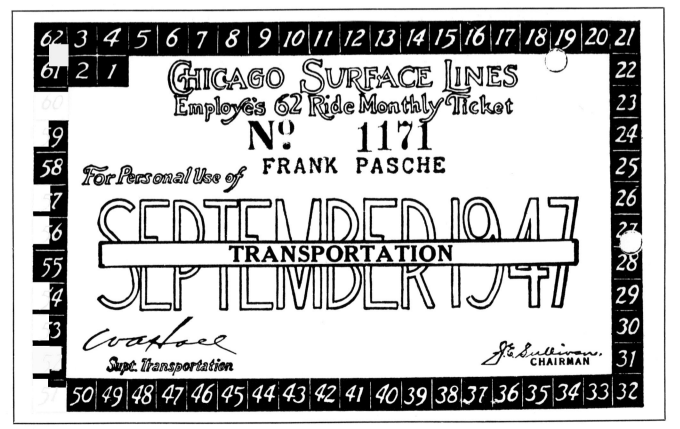

One of the fringe benefits CSL employees enjoyed was the 62-ride monthly pass. This pass, enlarged slightly, was issued for the last month CSL existed. The CTA took over the CSL in October, 1947. Pass from Walter Blix.

fore WW II.

As Division 241 grew, local politicians recognized its voting power and courted its members. Many frankly acknowledged their political debt to the members of 241. Among these office-holders were U.S. District Court Judge Michael Igoe, Illinois Secretary of State Edward J. Barrett, U.S. Representative Thomas J. O'Brien, and Circuit Court Judge Cornelius J. Harrington. By the way, Judge Harrington's uncle, Cornelius Buttimer, was one of the founders of old Division 260 at the Cottage Grove barn, and a leader in the 1903 City Railway strike.

Among the founders of Division 241, the original North and West Side Chicago union local, was William Taber. He served as the local's secretary-treasurer for many years. Other old-time union leaders whose names are still remembered are Joe Colgan, Dave Reid, Maurice Lynch, Robert Lockwood, Michael Murphy, Daniel Joyce, Fred Bisbee, Ralph Hahn, John Bradley, James Kennedy, William Sturtz, John Thorpe, Paddy McGrath, Fred Fay, Ben Lawson, Ed McMorrow, and Dick Bland. They were a redoubtable bunch, combining a flair for organization, fiery oratory, and a good punch. The latter came in handy when they tangled with company spies, spotters, strikebreakers, and hired thugs.

Other obstacles overcome by the early union organizers were the labor injunction and the rapid turnover of employees, which made organizing difficult. Long before the end of the CSL era the latter situation had turned around 180 degrees, and many CSL employees had 25 or more years of service.

While Division 241 concerned itself with local matters, the Amalgamated fought on a broader front. It was behind the eight hour day bill, which President Theodore Roosevelt urged Congress to pass in 1906. It supported the heated vestibule bill of 1907, which passed the House but was defeated by the Senate. The heated vestibule bill was an outgrowth of the enclosed vestibule program, pushed by the Amalgamated since 1894. In 1908 the big issue was to hold wages at previous levels, as companies sought to reduce wages during an economic downturn.

In the recession of 1923 the Amalgamated again fought wage cuts, regardless of the financial health of the companies. In Detroit, for example, President Mahon retained the 60¢ an hour rate and got an eight-hour day. The Amalgamated took a hard line in the Chicago negotiations of this period, but got a less satisfactory settlement.

The Amalgamated had little sympathy for the financial

In 1899 motormen on the West Chicago Street Railroad had to buy $500 surety bonds. B. Rossbach.

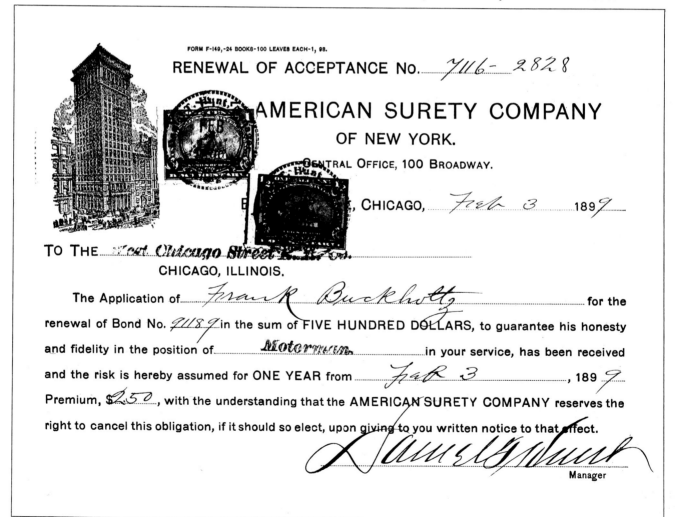

FORM F-149,-24 BOOKS-100 LEAVES EACH-1, 98.

RENEWAL OF ACCEPTANCE No. 7116- 2828

AMERICAN SURETY COMPANY
OF NEW YORK.
CENTRAL OFFICE, 100 BROADWAY.

CHICAGO, Feb 3 1899

TO THE West Chicago Street R.R. Co.
CHICAGO, ILLINOIS.

The Application of Frank Buckholtz for the renewal of Bond No. 7118.9 in the sum of FIVE HUNDRED DOLLARS, to guarantee his honesty and fidelity in the position of Motorman in your service, has been received and the risk is hereby assumed for ONE YEAR from Feb 3 , 189 9

Premium, $2.50 , with the understanding that the AMERICAN SURETY COMPANY reserves the right to cancel this obligation, if it should so elect, upon giving to you written notice to that effect.

Samuel G. Hunt

Manager

plight of the traction companies because the union felt the companies had brought their woes on themselves through over-capitalization (watered stock) and general mismanagement. In fact the union felt it was helping management become more efficient by adopting a hard line in negotiations with financially hard pressed companies. The Amalgamated argued that as wages and working conditions improved, the companies benefited through a drop in employee turnover and the creation of a loyal, stable, dependable work force.

Even during the depths of the Depression of the 1930s, the Amalgamated continued to press for the restoration of wage cuts and the shortening of the work day to spread the work. The CSL did its part by agreeing to spread the work so that no employee was discharged during the whole Depression for lack of work. Nevertheless, the shortened hours brought hardship to many of Division 241's members. As national unemployment reached the 7 million mark in 1931, Division 241 organized a relief fund. Contributions from workers in all departments went toward relief. As the Depression deepened, ultimately throwing one out of every three men out of work (national figures), Division 241's relief fund worked so well that the Union claimed not one of its members had to ask for other help.

As the nation entered the era of the New Deal, the Amalgamated supported progressive legislation: the NRA, Wagner Act, Social Security, Unemployment Compensation, and the Wage & Hour Law. Internally the Amalgamated won its men fringe benefits such as annual paid vacations, group insurance, and pensions. During the years of WW II, the Amalgamated convinced the War Labor Board to grant its members substantial pay increases, 18¢ to 20¢ an hour in Chicago and Cleveland, for example. Throughout the CSL era Chicago carmen were among the highest paid of any in the country, reaching a top wage of $1.42 an hour at the time of the CTA takeover in October, 1947. (Chicago bus drivers continue to receive top wages for their craft. Including cost of living allowances, CTA's 7,836 bus drivers were making $6.00 an hour as of December, 1973.)

Throughout the years one of the strengths of the carmen's union on both the national and local levels was the policy of offering to submit all unresolved matters to binding arbitration before calling a strike. This policy originated with President Mahon. He was canny enough to realize that his union would turn public opinion against it if it struck without making every effort to settle without a strike.

The Amalgamated also pioneered in the use of professionally prepared statistics and economic analyses to support its position. This was to counter the traction companies use of such data, prepared by an organization known as the Industrial Conference Board. The Amalgamated used the services of O. David Zimring and his firm, the Labor Bureau of the Middle West. Again it was Division 241 which led the way by first employing Zimring for local arbitration work with the CSL.

The union could also take some degree of credit for the introduction of equipment which gave some consideration to the comfort of the operator and the ease of operation. The PCC streetcar, introduced in Chicago in 1936, was an outstanding example of such equipment.

Though they worked superbly well to gain their members the economic victories they needed, the Amalgamated and Division 241 were far from perfect organizations. Right up to the end of the CSL era, Division 241 considered the Surface Lines as an enemy to be fought and beaten. To a large degree this attitude was the legacy of the early days, when the battles between labor and management were more than metaphorical. And to a degree such a tough stance was the only one possible for a union leader. After all, he represented his men and fought for their welfare. The CSL had its own selfish interests to protect and would do him few favors. Why should he do any favors for the Surface Lines?

There was also the internal need to take a hard line against management to mollify the union firebrands who thought the Division wasn't doing enough for the members. Indeed the Amalgamated itself was criticized by the leadership of other trade unions as an old mens' home and practically a company union. Perhaps the union would have been more successful in the long run had it modified its tough stance in the light of the fact that the companies underlying CSL had been bankrupt for many years, that equipment was getting older without any hope of replacement, and that all plans to reorganize the companies and grant them new franchises had failed.

Aside from trying to improve wages and working conditions, the most important function of the union was to protect its members by challenging disciplinary action taken against them by Surface Lines management. Some of the members' claims of unfair punishment were transparently baseless, but were pressed anyway to show that the union was doing its job. On the other hand a testy or vindictive operating official could always find an employee in violation of one or another of CSL's 121 operating rules, and the union grievance committee was the only place to go for redress.

The Surface Lines was a semi-military organization which placed many restrictions on its employees: they could not moonlight on second jobs without the company's consent, they had to undergo company physical exams, they were forbidden to frequent taverns even in their off hours, they had to wear the proper uniform at all times, and were discharged if their wages were garnisheed.

Many minor infractions of the rules were handled at the carbarn level. More serious problems were handled by a union grievance committee, which met with the CSL's superintendent of transportation or one of his assistant superintendents. In the early years of the union, before the formation of the Surface Lines, all discipline was meted out by the superintendent of transportation on the Chicago Union Traction Company. A strike threat by Division 241 caused CUT management to give the station superintendent authority to handle dismissals. However, in later years, under CSL management, major infractions of the operating rules went to the superintendent of transportation or one of his assistant superintendents for handling with the union grievance committee.

In most cases first offenders were reinstated if they had an otherwise good record. But even union officers admitted they couldn't do much to help men who repeatedly failed to collect and register all fares, falsified register statements, drank before or during duty hours, were discourteous to passengers, had collisions with other vehicles on straight track, or filed erroneous trip sheets.

If the grievance committee thought it wasn't getting a fair decision from the superintendent of transportation, the case would be sent to arbitration. On the whole the grievance system worked well. The use of arbitration in settling the grievances which couldn't otherwise be settled was an outgrowth of the Amalgamated's use of arbitration to settle wage and working condition disputes.

The strikes of 1913, 1915, 1919, 1920, & 1922

Though technically not a strike of CSL employees, the walkout of July 3, 1913 by County Traction and Suburban Railroad employees was closely connected with Chicago traction. Timed to hit just before the Fourth of July travel peak, the strike was successful and the two lines shut down. Employees of both these west suburban lines were members of the Chicago union. They demanded pay equal to the Chicago scale of 32¢ an hour maximum instead of their own 30¢ an hour maximum.

To avoid involvement in the dispute, Chicago Railways took the 20 cars it had leased to County Traction from County's Oak Park, Ill. carbarn just before the

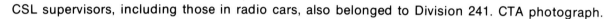
CSL supervisors, including those in radio cars, also belonged to Division 241. CTA photograph.

372

strike began.

The 1915 strike was two days long, and involved both Surface Lines and Chicago Elevated Railways employees. For a time observers thought that a walkout could be averted, since labor and management had agreed on changes in working conditions. The union wanted minimum pay of 33¢ an hour and maximum pay of 36¢ an hour. The company countered with an offer to raise the minimum wage above the current 23¢ an hour, but refused to increase the maximum wage.

CSL then proposed arbitration on the wage issue: the union declined. Amalgamated President W. D. Mahon came from Detroit to Chicago to mediate the dispute, but failed to bring the parties together. Chicago Mayor Thompson also stepped in at this point, but he too failed.

The strike came at midnight, June 13, and was completely effective in shutting down the CSL. The Chicago Elevated Railways, struck at the same time by sister Division 308, was able to provide service at 15 minute intervals between 61st Street and Wilson Avenue with older employees who refused to strike.

Suburban railroads were unable to cope with the crush of commuters on Monday, June 14, and the railroad conductors gave up trying to collect fares. On the Illinois Central's main line south, which paralleled the Surface Lines heavy Cottage Grove and Indiana car lines, commuters clung to the open platforms of the wooden cars. They hung from the outside of the cars, risking their lives to get to work.

Loop traffic choked and died as hundreds of makeshift buses poured in. Some of these buses were no more than open trucks with planks for seats.

At a regular City Council meeting on Monday, June 14, the Council passed an ordinance which made it difficult for the CSL to use strikebreakers to operate the cars. The ordinance required two to three weeks training for every new "L" or surface motorman or conductor.

Mayor Harrison met all day Tuesday, and far into the night, with representatives of the Amalgamated and the CSL and CER. The companies insisted on arbitration: the union leaders balked. They were dissatisfied with previous arbitration awards. But at 5:00 a.m. Wednesday, June 16, the unions agreed to arbitrate all remaining questions. Three men would make up the arbitration panel — a union representative, a management man, and the mayor himself. Obviously the mayor held the pivotal vote.

With the remaining issues going to arbitration, the two Amalgamated divisions called off the strike at 5:30 a.m. Wednesday June 16. It took just a bit longer than 90 minutes to get the "L" trains rolling after the settlement was announced, and service was restored to normal by 9:30 that morning. On the Surface Lines full service was not restored until noon that day. Contemporary reports say that Loop crowds cheered the first cars to arrive.

The award raised both the minimum and maximum wage, but kept a differential between them. The minimum wage went from 23¢ to 25¢ the first year, and to 26¢ the second year. The maximum went from 32¢ to 35¢ the first year, and to 36¢ the second year. Also, the maximum wage was payable after the fourth year of service rather than after the sixth year.

At 4:00 a.m. July 29, 1919, both the Surface Lines and "L" trainmen struck. The strike came as a surprise, since CSL management thought they had made a good offer. Management proposed to raise the maximum wage from 48¢ to 65¢ an hour. All wage rates below the maximum were to be raised by 17¢ an hour, and the standard day was to be eight hours with time and a half for overtime. Sixty per cent of all runs were to be completed in eight hours or less, with no runs to take more than 14 hours. The "L" employees, as was traditional, received a slightly better offer from their management. While this offer of a more than one-third increase in wages may seem very high, the offer was made during the inflationary period that followed WW I.

The Surface Lines employees agreed to time and one half for overtime, but asked for a maximum wage of 85¢ an hour. They also wanted 80 per cent of all runs to be completed in eight hours or less, no run to take more than 10 hours, and a minimum of eight hours' pay for any run, regular or extra, regardless of the actual hours worked. The CSL trainmen also wanted a maximum of six hours of work on Sundays and Holidays, to be paid at time and one half; a six day week for all employees; and fallbacks for dinner reliefs of at least 30 minutes.

Race riots had broken out in Chicago on July 27, 1919, and continued during the streetcar strike. All traffic police had been pulled from the Loop for riot service, compounding an already chaotic traffic pattern caused by the strike. Fortunately the steam suburban railroads were able to call on their entire system for passenger cars for use on their Chicago lines. They did so as soon as they heard the strike call, and the North Western, for one, was able to substantially increase its Chicago commuter service during the streetcar and "L" strike period.

To the north of Chicago, Evanston Railway employees struck July 30, after management refused to offer them whatever CSL employees might get under arbitration. To the west, Chicago & West Towns Railways averted a strike by promising its trainmen the eventual Chicago settlement.

However, AE&C (later known as the CA&E) employees struck at 3:00 a.m. July 31 after they were refused a 41¢ an hour wage increase. The strike shut down this interurban line from Chicago to Aurora and Elgin, as well as local city lines in several Fox River valley communities. Electric power service was also disrupted in several towns, including Elgin.

The Chicago Surface Lines strike ended August 1 at midnight. Full service was restored for the morning rush hour. A referendum among Surface Lines and "L" employees approved the settlement. Actually the CSL trainmen rejected the settlement by a majority of 665 votes, but they were outvoted by the 1,051 majority of "L" men who favored the settlement. With some 15,000 union members eligible to vote, 12,334 did vote, and the strike was settled by a narrow margin of only 386 votes.

Some union members fought the settlement because they were opposed to an eight hour day: it reduced their earning capacity. Working long hours for high pay was an old Chicago practice. Well before the turn of the century one employee of the North Chicago Street Railroad worked for 384 consecutive days.

A total of 300 South Shops repairmen joined electrical linemen and substation operators to strike CSL early on July 15, 1920, halting all operations. When power from the 32 CSL substations was cut off at 4:00 a.m., night cars were stranded. Supervisors did manage to get enough of the substations back on line to bring in the night cars.

By noon that day about 300 of the 1,400 scheduled cars were back in service. Some trainmen remained on the job, and the shopmen at West Shops did not join the strike right away. Later the West Shops shopmen, and trackmen, joined in the walkout.

The eventual settlement involved unionizing South Shops, but on an open shop basis, and the elimination of piecework in favor of an eight hour day with time and a half for overtime.

Hourly Rates of Pay After 1920 Strike

Blacksmiths and metal worker helpers	80¢
Metal workers night shift differential	5¢
Pavers	68¢ to 70¢
Trackmen	54¢
Line foremen	$10/day
Linemen	$9/day
Linemen helpers	$7/day
Substation operators	$200 to $210 month
Substation helpers	
First year	$120/month
Second year	$125/month
Third year	$130/month
Fourth year	$145/month

During a strike of switchmen on Chicago's steam railroads, CSL men struck on the morning of August 1, 1922. "L" employees joined the strike in sympathy. Two major issues were the hourly wage and the length of the work day. CSL offered a wage cut of 20¢ an hour — from 80¢ to 60¢ — and a standard day of nine hours with time and one half thereafter. The union wanted a cut of 8¢ an hour — from 80¢ to 72¢ — and retention of the eight hour day.

As in previous strikes, the steam suburban railroads, the Chicago Motor Bus Co., and private cars tried to take up the increased business. Some new bus lines were begun using trucks, and charging fares from 25¢ to 50¢. For the duration the Illinois Central threw out its rush hour schedules and operated trains 90 seconds apart. The IC handled 150,000 passengers each of the five weekdays during the strike, more than double its normal passenger load of 73,500. On the last day of the strike, Sunday August 6, the Illinois Central carried 63,000 passengers. It normally handled 25,725 on Sundays. The North Western saw its commuter business more than double during the strike, from 60,000 a day to 135,000. C&NW added 77 trains to its normal schedule of 166 runs. Chicago Motor Bus kept its 75 buses in service all day long, handling 40 per cent more passengers to and from the North Side lakefront area.

Never a man to miss a chance to advance his plan for municipal ownership of transportation facilities, Chicago Mayor Thompson borrowed a fleet of buses and began a 5¢ fare line from City Hall west to Kedzie Ave.

The strike ended Sunday night August 6, when the union accepted a 10¢ reduction in pay from 80¢ to 70¢ an hour. The standard workday remained at eight hours. (The wage reductions were 10¢ for all classes of trainmen: from 75¢ to 65¢ for those with six months or less of service; from 78¢ to 68¢ for those with six to 12 months' service; from 80¢ to 70¢ for those with a year or more of service; and from 82¢ to 72¢ for those on night runs.)

As part of the 1922 strike settlement, CSL relieved its conductors and operators of ticket selling duties. The Surface Lines made arrangements for some 340 stores and banks to sell the tickets, much as many years later the CTA made the same arrangements to sell its tokens.

The making of a Surface Lines man

Young, steady, sober, married, healthy, reliable, intelligent, cheerful, well-coordinated, neat appearing, well spoken: these were some of the qualities the CSL sought in its trainmen. If you were a young man applying for work on the cars, you could be sure the Surface Lines would check all of your personal references with care. Unexplained gaps in employment or other irregularities in your record would cause CSL to make further checks, perhaps writing to the bank president or postmaster in your home town. CSL wanted nothing to do with the drifters who moved from town to town and job to job. A tough, face-to-face interview with a top operating officer also helped weed out the unfit.

If you passed this preliminary screening — which eight out of ten applicants did not — you took a physical exam. If you passed your physical you had to pay the CSL a deposit on your badge and uniform.

The first day on the job was spent at a training school, the next 14 days out on the street as a student under the eyes of experienced motormen and conductors. If you passed a rules and operating exam at the end of this period, you were assigned to a carhouse and placed on the extra list. Only when you began to make irregular runs as an extra man would your pay begin: the entire training period was without pay.

As an extra man you filled in for regular men who were sick or otherwise absent. From time to time you might also be assigned to an extra car that was added to the regular schedule to meet some unexpectedly large demand, such as a run to the beach in the summer or a car to accommodate extra large pre-Christmas shopping crowds. Depending on the barn you worked from and general economic conditions — which naturally had a large effect on traffic levels — you might spend months or even a year on the extra list before you were assigned a regular run.

The regular runs were chosen in "picks." There were depot picks in which you could choose among runs out of your own depot. They were held several times a year, whenever schedules changed, routes were added or taken away from a depot, or new equipment (such as one-man cars) began to run from the depot for the first time. Less often there were system picks in which men could change their depots. In the 1920s a general pick was made every three months.

Making a pick was one of the most important decisions you had as a CSL operating employee. Your choice determined which line you ran on, what type of car you ran, what your hours would be, who you would work with on two-man cars, and how much, if any, overtime pay you'd get. Fortunately, if the run you picked didn't suit you, you could probably find a better one the next time around.

Back in 1908 streetcar men got the bulk of their formal training in two weeks of on the job instruction in actual service on the cars. They worked under the supervision of experienced motormen and conductors, known as line instructors. After their work was good enough to meet the line instructor's standards, the men were given oral and practical exams.

The motorman's examination, about five hours long, included troubleshooting artificially induced problems on an exhibit car. The trainee had to demonstrate how to cut out motors, how to make an emergency stop, and how to notch up the controller.

The conductor's examination ran about two and one half hours. While it had little to do with the physical components of the car, since that was the motorman's province, conductors did have to know the heating and lighting circuits, how to work the trolley retriever, and how to operate the bell and fare register.

An operating rule quiz was an important part of the examination. There were three sorts of question: those for motormen only, those for conductors only, and those for both.

To supplement the on the job training, CCRy opened a classroom at one of its barns in January, 1908. The exhibits included complete wiring diagrams of the 1907 Brill PAYE cars, forms commonly used by operating employees, tickets and transfers, a large-scale CCRy route map, and timetables and run guides.

Other exhibits included a wiring diagram for the older two-motor cars, a sample extra list, accident report blanks, trip sheets, lost article tags, special switchback reports, and a book with copies of all orders and operating bulletins.

Skeleton cars on display included a single truck two-motor car and a 1907 Brill. Both cars were stripped to the frame to show the motors and brake equipment. Students could operate the cars, which were suspended above the rails. The brakes applied slightly at all times to give student operators the feeling that they were accelerating a car with a load of passengers.

Formal training in the classroom was limited to two hours at the start of a student's training period. However, trainees were encouraged to return to the classroom during their two weeks of on the job training to study the exhibits and ask questions. Older motormen and conductors were also invited to drop in whenever they wished.

When the 1936 PCCs began to arrive, CSL carefully picked the motormen and conductors who would run them. After a training period at the Kedzie depot, the men took the cars out for trial runs on a loop about three miles long on streets near the depot. When six cars arrived, regular service began along Madison Street. Shopmen and engineers went along with the trainmen on the first runs to assure successful operation.

Rigid as the employment and training standards seemed, they could bend under the pressure of a changing labor market. When the Depression hit, it was obviously an employer's market for CSL. On the other hand, during WW II the labor shortage was so severe that the Surface Lines got permission to hire off-duty policemen and firemen to moonlight as trainmen. Even some men in the armed forces stationed around Chicago made runs when they were able to get into Chicago. CSL also recruited its shopmen to work overtime as trainmen, and quite a few did.

During the Depression CSL hired large numbers of men just once. Because of increased business during the World's Fair, 1,000 trainmen were hired between the fall of 1933 and the spring of 1934. In the years just prior to the Crash, labor turnover on the CSL was about 10 per cent a year, but in 1934 turnover dropped to just 3.4 per cent a year. No trainmen were fired during the Depression because of slack business. Instead CSL shortened the work week and placed a moratorium on hiring to spread the work.

During the winter of 1944-1945 the Surface Lines faced a quite different problem: it could not run all its scheduled cars because it lacked enough trainmen. Bad weather, sick men, and the callup of some 2,000 employees forced the CSL to take emergency measures to keep the system going. First the Surface Lines asked its remaining trainmen to work longer hours on their regular work days, and to volunteer for work on their days off. Six out of ten men did. Next other employees — clerks, receivers, mechanics — were asked to become part-time trainmen. Some 200 responded. Finally CSL asked policemen, firemen, and other city employees to work on the cars on their days off.

Despite these measures CSL entered 1945 short the equivalent of about 1,000 full-time trainmen. Schedules could not be filled, and rush hour cars were badly overcrowded. Worst of all, passenger traffic had doubled from pre-war levels of about 2 million riders a day to four million in 1944.

The Surface Lines force of 41 instructors was busy in 1944: it trained 1,400 new men and retrained many other employees. Trainees earned full pay while they learned, something the older heads wished they could have done.

A long look back from the end of the line

At the end of streetcar service in 1957, 120 old-time trolley men were left. Nearly all of them told the CTA and the Amalgamated they would not become bus drivers. Twenty retired with their cars. Many of the other 100 were too old for the physical strain of bus driving, or just plain refused to drive a bus even if they were able. Said one crusty veteran: "If I wanted to drive a bus, I would have gotten a job with the Chicago Motor Coach back in 1923 instead of 'going on the cars.' " So CTA gave the men who were too weak or refused bus assignments other jobs until they were old enough to retire.

What thoughts went through the minds of these veterans during their last days on the cars? Some thought of the big storms they had worked through, especially the big snows of 1917-1918 and 1939. Others recalled the kids who hitched rides on the rear of the cars, or pulled the trolley pole off the wire, or greased the rail on grades.

Other men recalled the Bank Holiday of 1933, when passengers tried to pay their fares with checks, money orders, and big bills. One passenger gave a $1 bill to Conductor J. W. Haug of 69th Street station and refused the change, saying: "All the money we have now will be soon worthless." Other passengers dug into their dresser drawers and came up with old coins to pay their fare. Conductor J. Dilworth of Devon depot got a 50¢ coin minted in 1825, and Conductor Joe Trysko of Armitage station accepted a 5¢ dividend check and 2¢ cash for a 7¢ fare.

Butchers, grocers, and other shopkeepers boarded cars to plead for change to run their business. Conductors obliged them if they had change to spare. Some merchants tendered large bills in payment of fare, pocketed the change, and got off the car at the next stop with enough change to keep their store open a while longer.

For Surface Lines management the bank closings brought some problems, too. Riding immediately dropped some seven or eight per cent. Further the banks could not legally accept the hundreds of thousands of dollars CSL collected in fares during the moratorium. The cash began to pile up in the carhouses, presenting a tempting target for thieves and robbers. CSL found a way around the problem by persuading the banks to accept the cash for safekeeping in their vaults, rather than as a regular bank deposit.

The banks closed March 4, 1933, and CSL had a payroll to meet March 10. How could the trainmen cash their paychecks? CSL solved this problem by issuing its checks as usual, but sent paymasters to all 16 barns to immediately cash the checks out of company funds.

Other old-timers remembered the crush crowds of WW II, and the fact that the Surface Lines gave free rides to men and women in military uniform during this period. The free rides were offered all day on Sundays and Holidays, and on weekdays and Saturdays during non-rush hours. The policy was begun in February, 1942, and within three years 50 million free rides had been given.

Just to keep their jobs on the cars took a lot of carbarn hopping as one station after another lost its cars as conversion to bus progressed. So the men who wanted to stay with the trolleys had to move— some as many as five times — to a barn that still ran streetcars. Many of the men had bought homes or rented apartments near their original station, and had to travel many miles to reach their new depot. One carman drove from his home in north suburban Park Ridge to the 77th and Vincennes barn on the South Side just to keep his trolley job as long as he could.

Memories sometimes wandered back to their first days with the Surface Lines, when they worked two weeks without pay while learning their craft and had to buy their own uniforms. There were good memories of the fringe benefits of the job, such as the monthly 60-ride pass and the adulation of neighborhood children who thought carmen belonged in the same Pantheon as their other heroes: the railway engineer, the fireman, the cop, and the baseball player.

Once a carman had a regular run, he had a good, steady job. During the Thirties, when schoolteachers, firemen, and police got their pay in script, trainmen got their wages in real money.

Tough men ran the cars, motormen who could tell teamsters to get out of their way and make it stick, conductors who could handle drunks and muggers. Conductors who weren't all that tough followed the maxim of elfin Herbie Kennedy, conductor out of the 69th and Ashland barn: "Always team up with the biggest motorman you can find."

Winter was the worst time of year for both motormen and conductors. Motormen carried matches, which they lit to melt holes through the thick frost which coated the front windows. Over the big black cast iron handle which opened the front door, motormen slipped tobacco sacks so their hands wouldn't freeze to the cold metal. Platform heaters and windshield wipers and defrosters later took a lot of the sting out of winter.

Conductors' winter problems began with their location — usually out on an open back platform exposed to the weather. Company rules said they couldn't wear gloves while punching transfers or making change. Some men got around the rule by wearing gloves cut off at the fingers. Others left their post on the rear platform and huddled inside the car between stops. Even with an open rear platform, winter loading was slow. These delays caused some flareups between the motormen, who wanted to get going to make the schedule, and the conductors, who didn't want to risk a passenger injury.

Summer or winter, a conductor had to beware of counterfeit money and invalid transfers. Conductors had to make good any counterfeit bills they took in.

Operating organization of the CSL

To complement the section on employees, this section briefly describes some of the management structures used by the Surface Lines and its predecessor companies.

Chicago Railways adopted a geographical division of authority on its lines in 1910. Three divisions were established: North, including all lines north and east of the Chicago River; West, all lines south of Lake Street and west of the Chicago River; and Northwest, including the lines north of Madison Street and west of the Chicago River.

Superintendents were put in charge of each division. They had responsibility for all operations in their area, as well as for the carbarns and equipment maintenance. All three superintendents reported to the general superintendent.

On the Chicago City Railway in the 1912 era, the break between the ranks of labor and management came at the position of starter. Starters ranked above motormen and conductors, but below supervisors and superintendents. Starters were stationed at major terminals and at important relief points. They made sure that cars left on schedule, and that relief crews were on hand to make reliefs promptly. In cases of extreme misconduct, starters could remove motormen and conductors from service.

Supervisors occupied the next management level. Each was assigned a district, which he patrolled by walking or by riding the cars (much later supervisors were given radio-equipped automobiles.) During rush hours all supervisors were assigned to the most congested points in their district, and at other times covered the rest of their territory. Supervisors had the authority to turn cars back short of their destination, to reroute cars when necessary, and in extreme cases to suspend trainmen.

Supervisors reported to the district superintendent, who had his headquarters in one of the carbarns in his district. In practice the supervisors had more contact with the assistant superintendent, who had the primary responsibility for maintaining schedules on his division. The assistant assumed the superintendent's full authority while that officer was absent.

Much of the division superintendent's time was spent in administrative work. He was responsible for the work of the depot clerks and receivers, including preparation of trip sheets, register statements, lost and found records, receivers' reports, and accident records. Although he did not hire or fire trainmen, he was responsible for their training and discipline. He could suspend trainmen, and in serious cases recommend that they be discharged.

A superintendent of transportation headed up the entire transportation department. He reported directly to the president, and the four division superintendents reported directly to him. All men were hired and fired through the superintendent of transportation's office.

Although the motormen and conductors would most likely deny it, it seems that CSL's supervisory force was spread rather thin. Take 1924, for example. In that year there were more than 12,000 trainmen in service, and only 96 supervisors. Of the 96, 72 were street supervisors directly concerned with streetcar service. Half of the remaining 24 were traveling motormen, the other half traveling conductors. Each of the CSL's 12 operating divisions had one traveling motorman and one traveling conductor. Their primary function was to ride with employees and help them learn the fine points of their work.

In the 1940s CSL had 15 operating districts, varying in size according to the density of streetcar operation, under patrol 24 hours a day by supervisors in scout cars. Some of these territories were quite large, particularly Districts 1 and 2 on the far South Side. To get supervisors to trouble spots quickly, CSL went on the air with FM station WAYH on June 1, 1942.

The system used was one similar to the CSL's phone dispatching operation. Crews notified the radio dispatcher by telephone of any disruptions to service. Using a city map and his intimate knowledge of transit service, the radio dispatcher sent one or more scout cars to the trouble spot. It was a two-way radio system: supervisors could report back to the dispatcher from their 50 watt sending/receiving sets.

At the time WAYH went on the air, CSL had many routes from seven to ten miles long, and one was 25 miles long. A minor delay at one point on a long route could quickly escalate into a major delay which affected the entire line for several hours. Getting the street supervisors to the scene quickly was essential.

The original installation included sending/receiving sets for all 18 scout cars assigned to the 15 districts, as well as sets in 10 tower trucks and five utility vehicles. An additional 16 service vehicles were equipped with radio sets shortly after the station went on the air. The unattended transmitter and its 250-foot antenna stood in the center of the streetcar loop at Madison and Austin, the west end of the Madison Street line. The dispatcher sat in CSL's Loop headquarters, some eight miles from the antenna and transmitter.

Near the end of the CSL era, in April, 1945, the Surface Lines reorganized its Transportation Department. Four new districts were created, each with two superintendents, to supervise all traffic within the district. Under the superintendents were 190 supervisors assigned to provide 24-hour supervisory service. Round the clock supervision was needed because of the heavy traffic to and from defense plants at all hours of the day and night.

District A covered the area between the south city limits and 59th Street, District B was between 59th and 18th Streets, District C between 18th Street and Armitage Avenue, and District D between Armitage and the north city limits.

Under the new plan the station superintendents were relieved of responsibility for the operation of the cars on the street. They retained control of station operations, including finding enough men to fill the schedules.

With few exceptions — mostly college-trained engineers — CSL management drew from the ranks of trainmen to fill its executive posts. An example of such a man was Robert J. McKinney, who entered service as a conductor on the Indiana Street (now the Grand Avenue line) in 1908. In 1917 he was made a supervisor at the North Avenue Depot, and was usually assigned to North and Crawford. Four years later he was promoted to assistant division superintendent of the 9th Division, serving at Devon-Limits and Elston-Noble, as well as at the Kedzie carhouse.

As division superintendent at North Avenue in 1932, McKinney supervised the handling of crowds to the Republican and Democratic National Conventions, both of which were held in Chicago at the Stadium that year. In 1933 and 1934 he was in charge of service to the World's Fair, and in 1935 was made assistant superintendent transportation.

Another old-timer, with a service record remarkable for its length, was John P. Burke. He joined the Chicago City Railway in the mid-1870s as an assistant to C. B. Holmes in the Transportation Department. He was promoted to paymaster in 1882, and made assistant treasurer in 1907. With the unification in 1914 he became cashier of the Surface Lines, but retained his post with the CCRy. He died March 20, 1936 with more than 60 years' service.

The buses with the sticks on top

Although the Surface Lines was the world's largest streetcar system, it also began a trolley bus system which grew to be the largest of its kind in the United States. While the electric bus network did not reach its peak, either in miles of route or in vehicles, until after the CSL was absorbed by the Chicago Transit Authority, nevertheless CSL's own trolley bus system was quite large. Until the CTA took over in October of 1947, the electric bus lines were confined to the Northwest Side of Chicago. All the buses were owned by Chicago Railways, which was the operating company for that part of the city.

Under CTA management the trolley bus lines were extended throughout the city, with the South Side 12th, 47th, and 51st-55th lines receiving the vehicles. Under the joint CSL-CTA planning program that preceeded the actual takeover, the 67th-69th-71st route and the 79th Street line, both then operated by streetcars, were to be converted to trolley bus, but nothing came of this after the CTA takeover. However the 210 trolley buses CSL planned to buy in 1945, to convert six streetcar lines, did arrive in 1948. The first to arrive were put on Montrose Ave. to replace gas buses.

Trolley bus service in Chicago came about as a result of an Illinois Commerce Commission order issued in March, 1930. Since 1928 the Chicago Motor Coach Company had run on the Northwest Side streets the Commission in 1930 gave to the Chicago Surface Lines. The Commission's reversal of its earlier decision was the result of a long court battle by the city and CSL, as well as a change in the state administration which led to a change in the makeup of the Commission. Some 30 civic groups led the fight for CSL buses against the Motor Coach service. They favored the Surface Lines because of the lower fare (7¢ vs. 10¢) and the transfers the CSL would issue good for a ride anywhere in the city. For a more detailed explanation of the litigation that led the Commission to reverse itself and award the routes to the CSL, see the chapter on Competition and Cooperation.

The Commission order covered trolley bus routes on Diversey, Elston, Central, and Narragansett. The CSL's first equipment order was for 41 electric buses to serve 17 miles of route. When delivered the fleet was the largest of its kind in the United States. The first trolley bus route was Diversey Avenue, where these buses with the sticks on top replaced two year old Twin Coach gas buses between Milwaukee and Narragansett, a distance of 3.75 miles. Thirteen buses were assigned to Diversey, giving three minute rush hour service and seven minute service during the off-peak hours.

The 41 buses came from three manufacturers, Twin Coach, Brill, and St. Louis. Both the Brill and the St.

Louis buses had General Electric equipment, while the Twin Coaches had Westinghouse motors, controllers, air brakes, and air compressors. All the buses had two 50 HP motors and four-wheel air brakes. They all had twin pedals, one pedal for the controller the other for the brakes.

Power was drawn from a positive and a negative overhead wire, spaced 24 inches apart. CSL's existing streetcar substations fed the overhead wires. This ability to use existing street railway power facilities was a strong advantage of the trolley bus. Twin trolley poles mounted well forward on the roof fed electricity to the buses. Swivel harps atop the poles allowed the wheels to remain on the wire when the bus swung in and out of traffic or pulled to the curb for passenger loading.

Some 1,835 steel line poles were used along the original four routes. A special pole-setting machine put in an average of 40 poles a day during the initial construction push by the Surface Lines, which was facing the Commission's deadline of July, 1930, to begin service on all four lines.

To get the trolley bus wires under the Chicago & North Western viaduct at Central and South Boulevard, both the subway under the North Western and the Lake Street "L" tracks (on the ground at this point) had to be lowered. Cause of the trouble was the abrupt change in wire height. The trolley bus overhead had to cross the Lake Street L's overhead wire, then dip abruptly to duck through the subway under the North Western. Lowering both the "L" tracks and the subway made the transition in height more gradual. During the 13 days the rebuilding took, Central Ave. buses were "single tracked" under alternate sides of the viaduct.

The Diversey line opened first, on April 17, 1930, followed by Central Ave. on June 8, Narragansett Ave. on June 29, and Elston Ave. on July 1. They were an immediate success. CSL met the increasing demand for service by purchasing seven more Twin Coaches and seven more Brills. Traffic continued to grow, so the Surface Lines ordered seven more Twin Coaches and eight more Brills. By the fall of 1930, when the last 15 buses were delivered, Chicago's electric bus fleet had grown from 41 to 70.

Diversey was 3.8 miles long, replacing the CSL's one-man streetcar line between Kimball and Pulaski and absorbing the CSL's gas bus line between Harding and Laramie. The line went beyond the old gas bus wye at Laramie to a new terminal at Narragansett. The east terminal was a loop via Kimball, Parker, and St. Louis. Thirteen buses were assigned to Diversey. Some 19,400 riders used the line each weekday.

Central Ave. was a major north-south line, nearly 7 miles long. It had the largest number of buses assigned to it — 25 — and its rush hour headway of a little more than three minutes between vehicles was second only to Diversey. Weekday base headways were a little under seven minutes and required 13 buses. Central was by far

Chicago

…we salute you

for keeping your transportation facilities in step with your inspiring advancement.

The development of improved transit equipment has been accomplished through the co-operation of the transit industry and the equipment builders.

Pullman with its background of over 40 years in building street cars, elevated cars, subway cars and other transit equipment, has appreciated the opportunity of contributing to these new developments.

Trolley coaches recently Built by Pullman for the Chicago Surface Lines. Now in operation on Diversey Avenue.

Built by Pullman … an assurance of advanced design and sound construction.

PULLMAN-STANDARD CAR MANUFACTURING COMPANY

Pullman Building, Chicago, Illinois

Unexcelled facilities for building traction equipment are available at

Pullman Car Works, Chicago; Hammond, Ind. and Worcester, Mass.

the heaviest trolley bus route, with 29,500 weekday riders.

Narragansett, another north-south line, was about half the length of the Central line. During rush hours the six buses assigned to this line provided service at intervals of a bit less than every seven minutes, while off-peak headways of eight minutes required five vehicles.

Shortest and lightest of the lines was the Elston Ave. Extension, a little less than three miles long. Evening rush hour service with five buses gave headways of six minutes, while midday service with three buses was at nine minute intervals.

Before the last order for 15 additional buses arrived in the fall of 1930, peak loads on each line were 40 passengers seated and 20 others standing in each bus. At the heaviest loading points street collectors were used to load the buses through the rear doors.

On the economics of trolley bus vs. gas bus operation, a CSL official claimed that if the average headway on a route was 15 minutes or less, the trolley bus was cheaper. CSL also found its first electric buses to be quieter, easier to heat, and faster in acceleration than its gas buses. Trolley buses were also longer lived, simpler to maintain, less likely to catch fire, and less in need of indoor storage than the gas bus.

Because the State of Illinois classified Chicago's pioneer trolley buses as streetcars, rather than buses, the electric buses did not need license plates and their drivers apparently did not have to have an operator's license. The trolley buses were also apparently exempt from the width and length limitations imposed by the state on gas buses.

CSL did concede some disadvantages in trolley bus operation, but they were few and minor. As pointed out above, CSL did not consider them economic when the average headway on a line was 15 minutes or more. They were also more prone to accidents than streetcars, and they did wear out the overhead wire at an alarming rate.

The public showed their liking for the buses through a steady increase in riding. For example, on the Central Ave. line riding grew so quickly that rush hour schedules were increased from a bus every three minutes in 1930 to a bus every minute by 1932. One reason for public acceptance was the modern appearance of the electric buses. Streetcar development had been at a standstill for a decade when the first trolley buses arrived with their

Two 1930 Twin Coach trolley buses undergo inspection and light repair at the North Ave. facility. Heavy repairs to the trolley buses were made at the Surface Lines West Shops. George Krambles photograph.

• Above. St. Louis Car Co. built six trolley buses, numbers 86-91, for the start of electric bus service in Chicago in 1930. St. Louis Car Co. photo. • Below. American Car & Foundry (ACF) built two trolley buses for CSL, numbers 106 and 107, in 1930. This photo shows 106 at the west end of the Diversey line at the Neva loop. Photo from the Railway Negative Exchange.

up-to-date appearance.

Winter proved difficult for trolley buses. Like CSL's streetcars they were dependent on overhead wires which could ice over or snap during a storm. But they were so much lighter than the streetcars that they couldn't buck the deep drifts even when they had the overhead wires intact. CSL kept the trolley coaches running by equipping its utility dump trucks with scraper blades 10 feet long and 20 inches wide. They were adjustable for right or left hand plowing or straight ahead bulldozing. These plow-equipped trucks were expected to run as fast as they could, consistent with traffic, or from 15 to 18 mph. CSL also equipped at least one Brill trolley bus with a snowplow. See page 173 for a picture of this unique piece of snow fighting equipment.

CSL also sent out trucks to sand bus routes during slippery weather. The sand was actually clean cinders. Usually about a ton of cinders was spread for every mile of street, but particularly bad spots needed up to two tons. Cinders were spread only at bus stops, hills, curves, and intersections.

The Surface Lines attacked the problem of excessive overhead wire wear in several ways. The trolley wheels supplied as original equipment were soon replaced by trolley shoes. The shoes stayed on the wire better, lowered maintenance costs, and reduced radio interference. But extraordinary wear of the overhead wire and fittings was still a problem. CSL solved it by equipping a tower truck with lubricating trolley poles. Various lubricants were applied to the wires, including plain light oil and several graphite mixtures.

A 1932 experimental installation of grooved overhead trolley wire cut down wear, and in 1934 CSL used such grooved wire to replace all the wire on the busy Central Ave. route. But on other lines the ordinary round trolley wire remained in service for many years.

In 1935 CSL extended the original Diversey line about 2.5 miles east from the old terminal at Milwaukee Ave. to Elston and Western. The extension connected with streetcar lines on Kedzie, California, Western, and Elston. To equip this extension CSL ordered six 40-passenger trolley coaches from Pullman. Their auto parallel rheostat control had no series-parallel transition point, and thus gave fast, smooth acceleration. The Surface Lines had previously ordered 15 electric buses from St. Louis to supplement service on existing lines. They were delivered in March, 1936.

North Avenue carhouse was the CSL's principal trolley bus barn and light maintenance facility. By early 1931 CSL had most of its electric buses based there to serve five North Side routes. Eighty-three buses were needed for rush hour schedules, leaving six spares. CSL built an open trolley bus storage area and an enclosed inspection and repair building west of the North-Cicero streetcar barn. In 1936 CSL had 125 of its 135 trolley buses based at North-Cicero, with the others at the Elston barn to supply the Elston Extension route. In strong contrast to this centralization of trolley bus facilities, CSL's 3.304 streetcars were based at 16 carhouses that same year. For heavy repairs and rebuildings, the electric buses were sent to the West Shops.

At the North-Cicero facility (actually closer to Lamon Ave.) an inspector checked each buses' controller, brakes, headlights, trolley poles, and tires at the end of each day. Light repairs and a comprehensive 5,000 mile inspection were made inside the shop building, which could accommodate 12 buses at a time.

Since the trolley buses were little more than streetcars on rubber tires, shopmen skilled in streetcar repair work had little difficulty in adapting their skills to trolley coach repair. CSL did, however, employ some automotive mechanics to work on the steering mechanism, tires, and axles.

An open storage lot for 41 trolley buses opened February 17, 1943 at Central and Lexington at the far south end of the Central Avenue line. It was the fifth lot to open in Chicago under Office of Defense Transporation orders designed to conserve fuel and tires. The other lots opened under wartime orders were at Diversey and Kedzie (12/9/42), Diversey and Neva (1/8/43), Central and Avondale (1/14/43), and at 5537 W. Lawrence (Lawrence Avenue bus garage). All except the Lawrence Garage held trolley buses.

After ten years of operation CSL was quite happy with the performance of their trolley coaches. The six routes in operation in 1940 had all begun between April 17, 1930 and July 1, 1930, except for Montrose, which began January 26, 1931, and Belmont, which began May 30, 1931. A seventh line, Kimball Avenue, ran between June 22, 1931 and June 30, 1937.

Although CSL never equalled its first total of 74 buses in 1930, it did receive 78 more in the next ten years: 40 in 1931, 6 in 1935, 15 in 1936, and 17 in 1937. Brill (56) and Twin Coach (58) built the largest number of buses. Other builders were Cincinnati Car Company (6), Pullman (6), and St. Louis (26). All 152 buses were running in 1940, and all were still in good condition.

Trolley bus service had grown to such an extent that by 1940 the Central Avenue line, longest of the routes, carried more than 50,000 passengers a day. In the morning rush hour, schedules called for a bus every 45 seconds.

Though important to the areas they served, the electric buses were not that large a factor in the overall CSL system. In 1940, for example, the 152 trolley buses made up just 3.8 per cent of the vehicle fleet (total of 3,971 streetcars, buses, and trolley buses), and they carried only 2.6 per cent of the revenue passengers.

CSL thought of running trolley buses in the State and Dearborn subways under construction in the late 1930s and early 1940s. Such operation would have been only a stopgap measure until the federal Public Works Administration could supply the $18 million needed to put rails in the tubes for rapid transit use.

In the meantime CSL went ahead with plans to convert more crosstown routes to trolley bus operation after WW II. As announced in 1945, CSL planned to purchase 210 electric buses to convert six streetcar lines. The lines were Montrose and Belmont (to complete bus operation), Fullerton, 51st-55th, 67-69th-71st, and 79th. Of these lines all were eventually converted to trolley bus under CTA except 67th-69th-71st and 79th. The first of the new buses went into service on Montrose in 1948. CTA ran trolley buses until 1973.

• This page. CSL's large trolley bus fleet was made up of many small series of buses from seven builders. A flat front end characterizes bus 167, a 1935 Pullman-Standard product. Bus 164, built by Cincinnati in 1931, has a tapered front end and a roof that dips down on either side of the destination sign. J. G. Brill built bus 155 in 1931. Note sides tapering toward the front, and the short sunscreen over the windshield. Bus 192 was also a J. G. Brill product. Built in 1937 it was part of the last order of trolley buses delivered to the Surface Lines. Note rounded front, and headlights flush with the dash. All photos on this page courtesy of the CTA.

• Opposite page, top. Pullman built bus 165 in 1935. Tom Mangan collection. • Opposite page, bottom. In order to reach West Shops, where all heavy repairs were made, CSL trolley buses used the single overhead streetcar wire: dual trolley bus overhead wire did not reach the shop. The buses made the trip with their positive pole on the streetcar wire and the negative pole hooked down. A pair of metal wheels towed behind the bus rode on the streetcar track, making the negative contact to complete the electric circuit. Note Tiger Stripes on bus 190, and compare it with plain bus 192 in the same series on this page. Photo from the George Krambles collection.

• This page, top. Diversey was CSL's first trolley bus route, opening April 17, 1930. Bus 177, a 1936 St. Louis coach, is eastbound on Diversey heading for the loop at Western. George Krambles collection. • This page, at left. Bus 86, St. Louis built, helped open the trolley coach era in Chicago as one of the first 41 buses ordered for the opening of service in 1930. Note divided destination sign and the dash illuminator headlights. St. Louis Car Co. photo. • Opposite page, top. The Central-Lexington storage yard was leased by the CSL from the Chicago, Aurora & Elgin electric interurban, whose tracks are at the left. It was opened as a WW II tire-saving measure. Before this storage yard opened, Central Ave. trolley buses had to pull in and out of North Ave., where they were stored between rush hour runs. George Krambles collection. • Opposite page, bottom. On the site of a Standard Oil station at Diversey and Kedzie, CSL stored 14 Diversey trolley buses as a WW II economy move. Other open trolley bus storage yards were at Central and Avondale (44 bus capacity) and at Diversey and Neva (24 bus capacity). George Krambles photo.

Passenger equipment appendix

Most of this Appendix deals with CSL buses, although there is a short section on streetcars beginning on page 398. Counting those buses ordered by CSL but delivered to CTA, CSL had a fleet of 960 motor buses. A total of 229 buses of 14 model designations were delivered between 1927 and 1942. A total of 731 buses of 13 model designations were delivered between 1944 and 1948. The table below gives the basic information on each bus. A complete history of CSL bus routes is given in the chapter on car and bus routes (pages 221-346).

CSL's first bus route opened August 11, 1927 along Diversey between Harding and Laramie as an extension of the Diversey streetcar line. The buses were garaged at the old Grand and Leavitt carbarn, remodeled for bus maintenance. As the bus fleet grew, other carbarns were remodeled to accommodate them. In addition CSL also operated two all-bus garages, Ardmore and Lawrence. However, they were makeshift facilities. The first new all-bus station was Beverly, which opened in 1949 after the close of the CTA era.

As WW II ended CSL began its program of converting 22 streetcar lines to bus operation: 16 were to be converted to gas bus and six to trolley bus. Many new buses were needed for the conversion program. Others were used to re-open the Kimball-Homan and Ogden lines. Still others were needed to establish new bus routes, such as Jeffrey-100th. By the time CTA took over in 1947, CSL was well on the way to becoming all bus.

Original Number	1947 Number	Owner	Year Built	Seats	Builder	Model
1 - 5	1101-1105	CRys	1927	40	Twin Coach	40
6 - 7	1106-1107	CRys	1930	40	Twin Coach	40
301-303	1108-1110	CCRy	1928	40	Twin Coach	40
401-402	2109-2110	CCRy	1934	30	ACF	H13S
403-414	3109-3120	CCRy	1934-35	32	White	684
415	2111	CCRy	1935	30	ACF	H13S
416	4104	CCRy	1936	21	Superior/Ford	51
417	5104	CCRy	1936	21	Superior/Reo	2LM
418-420	3204-3206	CCRy	1936-37	23	White	706M
421-428	3210-3217	CCRy	1937	25	White	805
429-432	2207-2210	CCRy	1938	30	ACF	H13S
433-434	3311-3312	CCRy	1939	26	White	805
435-436	1307-1308	CCRy	1942	31	Twin Coach	30G
437-440	6216-6219	CCRy	1942	32	Yellow	TG3205
446-451	6301-6306	CCRy	1942	36	Yellow	TDH3605
501-508	2101-2108	CRys	1935	30	ACF	H13S
509-516	3101-3108	CRys	1935	32	White	684
517-519	4101-4103	CRys	1936	21	Superior/Ford	51
520-522	5101-5103	CRys	1936	21	Superior/Reo	2LM
523-525	3201-3203	CRys	1936	23	White	706M
526-563	1201-1238	CRys	1937	31	Twin Coach	30R
564-575	4201-4212	CRys	1937	25	Ford	70
576-581	2201-2206	CRys	1938	30	ACF	H13S
582-591	3301-3310	CRys	1939	26	White	805
592-625	6101-6134	CRys	1941	27	Yellow	TG2706
626-631	1301-1306	CRys	1942	31	Twin Coach	30G
632-646	6201-6215	CRys	1942	32	Yellow	TG3205
801-809	2112-2120	C&SC	1935	30	ACF	H13S
810-812	3207-3209	C&SC	1937	23	White	706M
813-822	3221-3230	C&SC	1938	25	White	805
823-825	3313-3315	C&SC	1939	26	White	805
826	1309	C&SC	1942	31	Twin Coach	30G
827	6220	C&SC	1942	32	Yellow	TG3205
1400	1620	CRys	1946	34	Twin Coach	34S
1401-1404	1621-1624	C&SC	1946	34	Twin Coach	34S
1600-1606	1600-1606	CCRy	1946	37	Twin Coach	38S
1607-1608	1607-1608	SSRy	1946	37	Twin Coach	38S
1609-1614	1609-1614	CCRy	1946	37	Twin Coach	38S

Without the headlights and the "Enter At Front" lettering, it might be difficult to tell the front from the rear of Chicago Railways bus 1, a 1927 Twin Coach. Photo from Zenon Hansen.

Original Number	1947 Number	Owner	Year Built	Seats	Builder	Model
1615-1619	1615-1619	CCRy	1947	37	Twin Coach	38S
1800-1817	1800-1817	CCRy	1947	44	Twin Coach	44D
2301-2350	2301-2350	CRys	1946	36	ACF-Brill	C36
2351-2358	2351-2358	C&SC	1946	36	ACF-Brill	C36
2359-2433	2359-2433	(a)	1947	36	ACF-Bill	C36
2500-2545	2500-2545	(a)	1948	44	ACF-Brill	C44
2546-2606	2546-2606	(a)	1947	44	ACF-Brill	C44
3401-3402	3401-3402	CRys	1944	44	White	798
3403-3416	3403-3416	CCRy	1944	44	White	798
3417-3420	3417-3420	C&SC	1944	44	White	798
3421-3440	3421-3440	CRys	1945	44	White	798
3441-3485	3441-3485	CRys	1946	44	White	798
3486-3495	3486-3495	C&SC	1946	44	White	798
3496-3572	3496-3572	(a)	1947	44	White	798
3573-3697	3573-3697	(a)	1948	44	White	798
4301-4309	4301-4309	C&SC	1945	27	Ford	29B
4310-4327	4310-4327	CRys	1945	27	Ford	29B
4328-4335	4328-4335	CCRy	1945	27	Ford	29B
4336-4355	4336-4355	(a)	1947	27	Ford	69B
6401-6410	6401-6410	CCRy	1944	40	GMC	TG4006
6501-6512	6501-6512	CRys	1946	45	GMC	TD4506
6513-6520	6513-6520	C&SC	1946	45	GMC	TD4506
6521-6530	6521-6530	CRys	1947	45	GMC	TDH4507
6800-6823	6800-6823	CRys	1946	36	GMC	TGH3609
6824	6824	C&SC	1946	36	GMC	TGH3609
6825-6833	6825-6833	SSRy	1946	36	GMC	TGH3609
6834-6838	6834-6838	CCRy	1946	36	GMC	TGH3609
7100-7116	7100-7116	CRys	1947	41	Mack	C41GT

Notes: Twin Coach buses 1101-1110 were retired in late 1947. All other CSL buses were used for varying periods by the CTA. All CSL buses were owned by one of the four underlying streetcar companies, and until September 12, 1944 were numbered in a separate series for each company. Buses purchased after that received numbers in a new, unified series. This is indicated by the column headed "1947 number," the number the buses carried at the time of the CTA takeover. The note (a) indicates that the underlying ownership of the buses is unknown. Some buses were originally owned by one underlying company, then sold to another. This roster shows the 1947 ownership. Regardless of ownership, CSL used the buses everywhere in the city.

• Above. Signed for a run on the 103rd Street extension, bus 402 was a 1934 CCRy ACF model H13S. Photo from Zenon Hansen. • Below. Bus 530 was a 1937 Twin Coach model 30R. It was owned by Chicago Railways. The 38 buses in the series 526-563 were later renumbered into the 1201-1238 series. All lasted into the CTA era. Photo from the Chicago Transit Authority.

• Above. The CSL's first motor bus, Chicago Railways 1, running west on CSL's first motor bus line, Diversey Ave. Bus 1 was a 1927 Twin Coach model 40. It was out of service by the end of 1947. Photo from Jim Prokes. • Below. This is the interior of CTA bus 1305, formerly Chicago Railways 630. This was a 1942 Twin Coach model 30 G. Chicago Transit Authority photograph.

• Above. Like the streetcars, CSL's motor buses were owned by the four underlying companies. Bus 821, for example, was a 1938 White model 805 owned by the Calumet & South Chicago Railway. CTA photo. • Opposite page. Bus 623 was a Chicago Railways 1941 Yellow model TG2706. G. Krambles collection. • Below. Interior of CTA 3221, originally C&SC 813, a 1938 White model 805. CTA photo.

• Above. CRys 519 was a 1936 Superior/Ford model 51. Looking somewhat like an overgrown delivery truck, it had seats for only 21 passengers. CTA photo. • Below. Bus 601 was a Chicago Railways 1941 Yellow model TG2706, one of 34 such buses on the CSL roster. Buses in this series were renumbered into the 6101-6134 series. Photo from Zenon Hansen.

• Above. Builders of CSL's first five buses in 1927, Twin Coach supplied some of the last Surface Lines buses in 1947. Bus 1814 was a Chicago City Railway 1947 Twin Coach model 44D. CTA photo. • Below. Bus 1402 was a 1946 Twin Coach model 34S. It was owned by the Calumet & South Chicago Railway. Photo from the Chicago Transit Authority.

• Above. CSL's largest postwar order was for a total of nearly 300 White model 798 buses, delivered between 1944 and 1948. Bus 3444 was delivered to Chicago Railways in 1946. George Krambles collection. • Below. Bus 6515 was a Calumet & South Chicago 1946 GMC model TD4506. An identical series of buses, 6501-6512, was built for Chicago Railways. Barney Neuberger photo from the collection of Jack Doyle.

● Above. Bus 3405 was a Chicago City Railway 1944 White model 798. Compare its paint scheme with bus 3444, also a model 798, on page 396. George Krambles collection. ● Below. The only buses Mack built for the Surface Lines were 17 model C41GT buses built for Chicago Railways in 1947. Credit the Chicago Transit Authority for this shot of 7107.

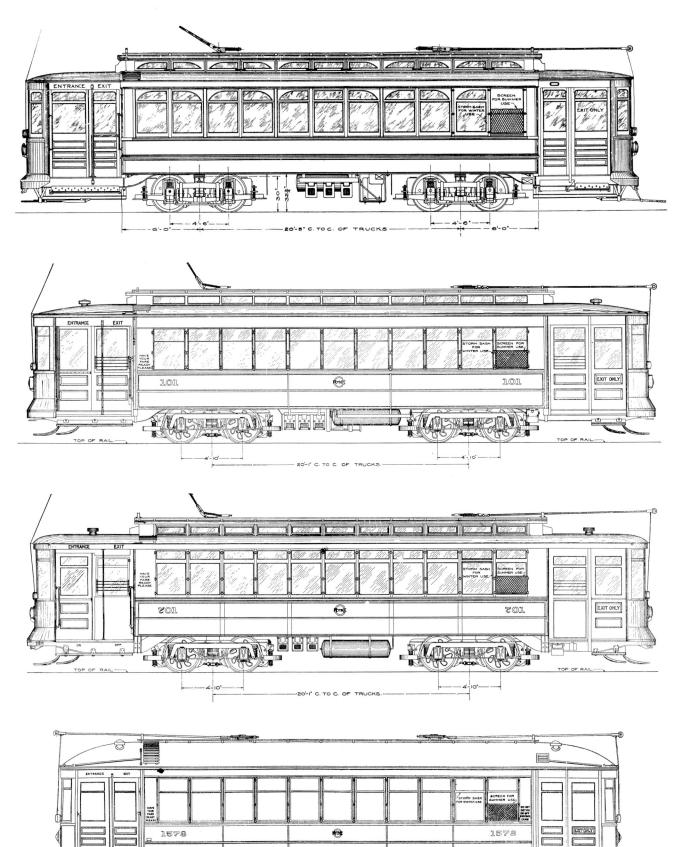

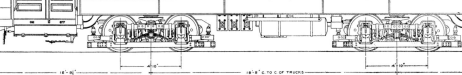

398

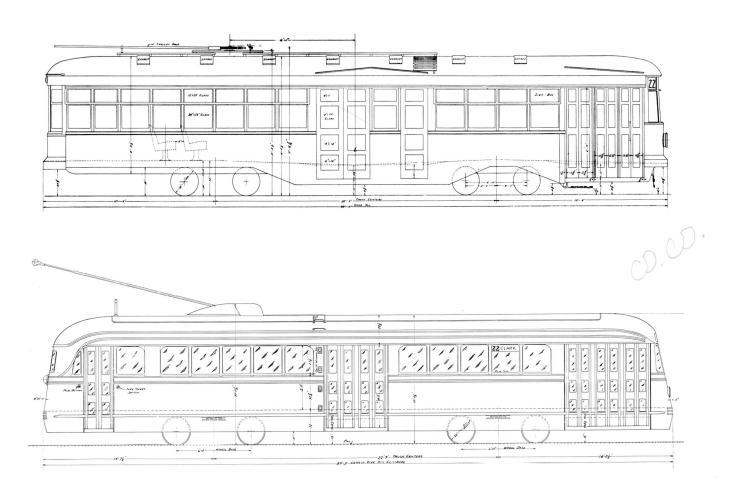

Specifications of Cars Shown on Pages 398-399

Series	5201-5600	101-700	701-750	1506-1720	3322-3381 6280-6319	4002-4051 7002-7034
Name	Big Brills	Old Pullman	Pressed Steel	Turtleback	Peter Witt	Prewar PCC
Builder	Brill American Kuhlman	Pullman	Pressed Steel	Surface Lines	Surface Lines Brill Cummings	St. Louis
Owner	CCRy	CRys	CRys	CRys	CRys-CCRy	CRys-CCRy
Built	1906-1908	1908-1909	1909	1911	1929	1936-1937
Seats	40	40	40	40	60	58
Length	48' 3"	49' 2"	49' 2"	44' - 45'	49' 0"	50' 5"
Width	9'	8' 9"	8' 9"	8' 6"	8' 6"	8' 9"
Height	11'10"	11' 8"	11' 8"	11' 9"	11' 6"	11' 2"
Weight	54,100	53,400	52,350	45,500	44,600	35,640
Motors	GE-80-A	GE-216-A	GE-216-A	GE-226-A	WH-516-D	WH-1432 GE-1198
HP	40	50	50	35	50	55
Control	K-28-E	K-35-C	K-35-C	K-35-G	GE PCM	WH Cam
Trucks	27-FE-1	BP-150	BP-150	27-GE-1	76-E-2	Clark B-2
Wheels	34"	34"	34"	34"	26"	25"

NOTES: This data applies to all cars in a series, though there were variations from car to car within a series because of rebuilding, truck changes, etc. All cars had four motors of the type and horsepower shown above. All cars shown above were built for two-man operation. This table follows the series in their order of appearance, starting at the top of the preceding page and continuing through this page. All car drawings are in HO scale (3.5 mm to the foot). All drawings came from BOSE reports, except for the 1936 PCC, which came from the St. Louis Car Co.

Chicago Surface Lines Streetcar Roster

Chicago Railways

Series	Builder	Built
101-700	Pullman	1908-1909
701-750	Pressed Steel	1909
751-1100	Pullman	1910-1911
1101-1423	St. Louis	1903-1906
1424-1428	Brill	1903
1429-1505	CUT	1899-1900
1506-1720	CRYs	1911
1721-1785	CSL	1923
1800-1999	CRys	1913-1914
2000-2005	Brill	1921
2006	CRys	1921
3000-3089	Brill	1914-1915
3090	American	1918
3091	CSL	1919
3092	CSL	1921
3093-3118	CSL	1922
3119-3160	Brill	1923
3161-3178	Cummings	1923
3179-3201	CSL	1923
3202-3231	CSL	1924
3232-3261	Lt. Wt. Noiseless	1925
3262-3281	Brill	1926
3282-3301	St. Louis	1926
3302-3321	Cummings	1926
3322-3341	CSL	1929
3342-3361	Brill	1929
3362-3381	Cummings	1929
4000	CSL	1925
4001	Pullman	1934
4002-4051	St. Louis	1936-1937
4052-4061	St. Louis	1947
4062-4171	Pullman	1946-1947
4172-4371	Pullman	1947-1948
4372-4411	St. Louis	1948
8000-8030	CSL	1921
8031-8060	Brill	1921-1922

Chicago City Railway

Series	Builder	Built
2501-2625	St. Louis	1901-1902
2701-2780	St. Louis	1903
2900-2903	Brill	1921
2904-2922	CSL	1922-1923
5001-5200	Brill	1905-1906
5201-5300	Brill	1906
5301-5600	Brill	1907-1908
5601-5621	Brill	1910
5651-5665	Kuhlman	1907
5701-5702	CCRy	1910
5703-5827	Brill	1912
5900-5999	Brill	1913-1914
6000-6137	Brill	1914-1915
6138-6146	American	1918
6147-6154	CSL	1919
6155-6158	CSL	1923
6159-6186	Brill	1923
6187-6198	Cummings	1923
6199-6218	CSL	1924
6219-6238	Lt. Wt. Noiseless	1924
6239	CSL	1924
6240-6252	Brill	1926
6253-6265	St. Louis	1926
6266-6279	Cummings	1926
6280-6293	CSL	1929
6294-6306	Brill	1929
6307-6319	Cummings	1929
7001	Brill	1934
7002-7034	St. Louis	1936-1937
7035-7114	St. Louis	1947
7115-7274	St. Louis	1947-1948
9000-9019	CSL	1921
9020-9039	Brill	1922
9040-9046	CSL	1923

Calumet & South Chicago Railway

Series	Builder	Built
2801-2815	St. Louis	1902
2816-2823	Brill	1903
2824-2840	Kuhlman	1904-1908
2841-2845	Jewett	1903
2846-2856	SCCRy	1907
2857-2858	Kuhlman	1910
2859	CSL	1924

Southern Street Railway

Series	Builder	Built
5622-5650	Brill	1910

Chicago Surface Lines Trolley Bus Roster

Series	Builder	Built
51-79	Twin Coach	1930
80-85	Brill	1930
86-91	St. Louis	1930
92-98	Twin Coach	1930
99-105	Brill	1930
106-107	ACF	1930
108-114	Twin Coach	1930
115-122	Brill	1930
123-124	Cincinnati	1930
125-129	Twin Coach	1931
130-134	Brill	1931
135-139	St. Louis	1931
140-149	Twin Coach	1931
150-160	Brill	1931
161-164	Cincinnati	1931
165-170	Pullman	1935
171-185	St. Louis	1936
186-202	Brill	1937

NOTES: The date built is the date the cars and trolley buses were constructed by the builder. Many of the cars and trolley buses were later extensively rebuilt or remodeled. In the early days much streetcar reconstruction involved converting cars to Pay-As-You-Enter types. In later years reconstruction usually involved converting two-man cars to one-man or one-man/two-man operation. Many of the early trolley buses were extensively rebuilt by the CTA in the late 1940s. See the individual series histories for details of the rebuilding of particular cars. All Surface Lines trolley buses were owned by Chicago Railways.

Supplement to the first edition

One of the pleasures of writing a book is getting reader response to it. The first edition of this work brought letters to the author from scores of readers. Many letters were complimentary, which is all well and good. Others, while flattering enough, also had the sort of questions and comments which deserve mention in this second, revised edition.

Once again Roy Benedict contributed substantially to the advancement of knowledge about the Surface Lines through his many comments on the text, rosters, and photo captions. Robert Heinlein spent six weeks digging through CSL records preserved by the Chicago Transit Authority to come up with revised dates for many route changes. He also supplied much new data on obscure operations, which is used here to expand upon matters touched only lightly in the body of the book.

Nick Kalman's sharp eye caught several errors in photo captions. Walter Keevil also noted several discrepancies in the captions, and in the text as well. John J. Kelly, Jr., pointed out several errors, also.

The problem of properly crediting photos was eased with the help of Gordon E. Lloyd. Mr. Lloyd pointed out that a dozen photos credited to the Barney Neuberger collection were his, and were sold by him to the late Mr. Neuberger in the 1940s.

Felix Reifschneider, long an electric railway enthusiast, had quite a bit to say concerning the history, policy, and practices of Division 241. His comments appear under the heading of pages 368 to 377.

Allan C. Williams, who contributed many photos to the book, sent a letter concerning several caption errors. His questions concerning certain portions of the text led to several of the clarifications and amplifications that follow.

While acknowledging the help of those mentioned above, the author takes full responsibility for the facts and conclusions presented in this supplement. Should others have further questions or comments, they are invited to write to the author through Transport History Press, P. O. Box 201, Park Forest, IL 60466.

First car in the only series of PCC cars built by Pullman for CSL, car 4062 rests at South Shops shortly after delivery from the builder. Three hundred and nine identical cars followed 4062 into service on such major routes as Clark-Wentworth and Broadway-State. Photo from Tom Mangan collection.

Page 12. In discussing the merger of the South Chicago City Railway with the Calumet Electric Street Railway, it is stated, incorrectly, that the SCCRy owned the South Chicago Avenue line. The maps on pages 332 and 333 show that the South Chicago Avenue line was owned by the Calumet company.

Page 23. The caption for the bottom photo says that Cottage Grove cable cars dropped the Indiana Avenue horse cars at 22nd and Wabash for pickup by a team of horses. The Indiana Avenue cars were actually dropped at 18th and Wabash.

Page 31. Photo caption. The Birney car is at the east terminal of the Division line, and is ready to make a westbound run to Division and Austin.

Page 34. Type 'M' multiple unit control did not have a pilot motor.

Page 51. The Old Pullmans were said here to be the last two-man conventional streetcars to run in Chicago. One who was present reports that on the last day of service on the Halsted line, at least five Odd 17 cars (6138-6154) were running on that route along with the Old Pullmans.

Page 59. Top photo caption. Rather than being northbound destined for Clark and Dewey, car 165 is quite possibly a southbound car about to leave Devon and Kedzie.

Page 59. There is a discrepancy of one car in accounting for the Old Pullmans after the Devon carbarn fire of January 26, 1922. A record of the cars destroyed, preserved by CTA, shows the same car numbers destroyed as the list on this page. Yet when added up, the number of cars surviving the fire and those destroyed in the fire comes to 601, which is not possible since there were only 600 cars built in this series. A 1934 car inventory shows 456 Old Pullmans and 98 rebuilt Old Pullmans on the roster. Evidently another unrebuilt car, number unknown, was destroyed in the 1922 fire.

Page 61. Further research gives new dates for the construction of the 1101-1423 series cars: two hundred cars ca. 1903-1904; 5 cars ca. 1905; 108 cars on the 1906 car trust; and 10 cars on the 1907 car trust. New data also shows that the rebuilding of these cars into PAYE types was spread over the years 1908 to 1913. Renumbering took place as the cars were rebuilt during these years, not all at once in 1909.

Page 65. The photos of car 804 are by Gordon E. Lloyd.

Page 68. The photo caption reference back to page 23 should refer to car 4499, not car 4399.

Page 89. Top photo. Field research indicates that this shot of car 3154 was taken at the Clark and Arthur terminal.

Page 94. Car series 3362-3321, continued from page 87. A total of 22 cars (3282-3303) are shown modified with foot operated brakes. Additional cars were so modified, but their numbers are not known. One group of cars so equipped was assigned to Montrose as one man cars.

Page 95. The two cars joined to form experimental articulated car 4000 were originally cars 4630 and 4633. Car 4630 became car 1101, then part of car 4000. Car 4633 became car 1104, then part of car 4000. (Car 4634 became car 1105, retired in 1936.) The PAYE conversion and renumbering date for car 1101 was March 22, 1911. No records were found for cars 1102, 1104, or 1105. The rebuilt "Matchboxes" that formed car 4000 retained their rebuilt St. Louis 47 trucks at one end only.

Page 120. Roster information indicated that none of the cars in the 6155-6198 series were equipped with Van Dorn couplers to pull trailers. However, car 6157 shown on page 281 appears to have such a coupler.

Page 137. Photo of Calumet & South Chicago snow plow F-303 taken by Gordon E. Lloyd.

Page 138. Plow F-301 probably built in 1896 or 1897.

Page 142. The text refers to an illustration of a letter posted from Chicago Railways mail car 6 on August 22, 1946. That letter appears on page 406.

Page 148. Photo of meter test car 0-1 by Gordon E. Lloyd.

Page 151. Photo of supply car S-201 by Gordon E. Lloyd.

Page 154. The 'W' series work cars that were motorized with cabs at both ends were chartered for State Street Christmas parades, motion picture publicity, etc.

Pages 157 and 163. Party cars Arcturus and Sunbeam were originally Cicero & Proviso passenger cars with various numbers between 7 and 24. Rebuilt into deluxe cars with observation platforms, they were used under charter for trolley excursions and parties. The car shown on page 163 is Sunbeam, identified by its McGuire-Cummings trucks. Arcturus had maximum traction trucks.

Page 162. Center photo of car H-202 by Gordon E. Lloyd.

Page 171. Top photo. The man dressed in a business suit is Joseph Mulree, a veteran transit employee. He entered service on the horse-drawn wreck wagons in 1914, and was superintendent of Utility & Emergency Service from 1949 until he retired in 1963.

Page 196. The newest type of CTA bus transfer was first used on January 7, 1974.

A new bus on a new route, CSL 3469 turns from Wacker Drive into State Street at the start of its Archer Express run to 63rd and Cicero. White built the bus in 1946 as one of their 798 models. See page 221 and supplemental route information in this section. Photo from the Tom Mangan collection.

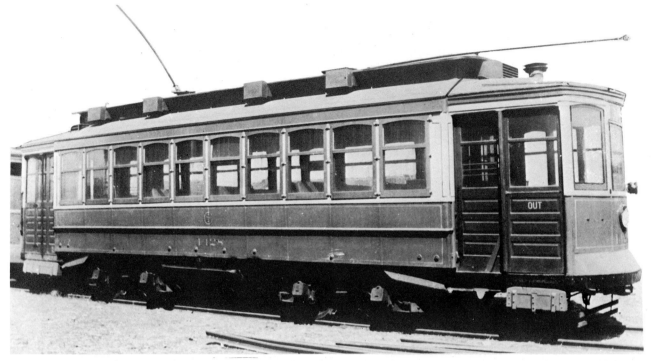

No illustration of a car in the CSL's 1424-1428 series was available at the time the first edition of this book was published. Bob Heinlein supplied this CTA photo for this second, revised edition. Car 1428, like all others in the series, was scrapped in 1937. See page 68.

Car 3322, built by the Surface Lines in 1929, was modified in 1932 with a rear exit door, treadle-operated. Evidently the change did not improve passenger flow through the car, as 3322 was the only Peter Witt so changed. See page 94. Photo from the Robert Heinlein collection.

Page 204. The 67th-69th-71st line had owl service between 69th and Western and 67th and South Shore Drive.

Page 214. The north portal of the La Salle tunnel, at La Salle and Hubbard, has been sealed.

Page 215. The east portal of the Van Buren tunnel was on the east side of Franklin Street just north of Van Buren, not on the site of the Sears Tower.

Page 220. View is northeast up Clark Street from Jackson Blvd.

Page 221. Archer cars were re-routed to a new downtown loop on September 14, 1924. The route of the Archer Express bus, inaugurated October 21, 1946, was as follows: from a loop on Wacker, Wabash and Lake via State, Archer, and Cicero to a loop via 63rd, Keating, and 64th.

Page 221. The Armitage Avenue through route was resumed with the bus substitution of June 24, 1951.

Page 221. The middle section of the Ashland line ran from Cermak and Ashland to Cortland and Wood via Ashland, Roosevelt, Paulina, Lake, Ashland, and Cortland. (This also modifies photo caption on page 224.)

Page 224. Bottom photo. The official pull-out route for Western cars leaving the 69th Street barn was via 69th to Western. However, some cars did use Ashland to 79th and 79th to Western.

Page 225. Photo caption for photo at the bottom of the page. Car 5651 is southbound on Ashland at 47th Street.

Page 231. The new route for Blue Island — 26th cars, effective July 22, 1906, was via 26th, Blue Island, Harrison, Dearborn, Adams, Franklin, and Harrison.

Page 231. The loop in use starting June 30, 1943 for Bell & Howell rush hour buses was also the mid-day circular route, replacing the route of December 1, 1942. This line became rush hour only on October 1, 1945, using the new south terminal loop described on page 231.

Peter Witt car 3368, another to have a green and cream paint job, was converted to one man service in the 1952 rebuilding program, but never ran as a one man car. See page 94 for details and identities of the other cars converted and painted. Photo from the Robert Heinlein collection.

Page 232. Although the rails connecting Chicago and Evanston lines on Clark across Howard might have been severed in 1910, they were evidently later restored. The Evanston street railway system rented CSL cars into the 1920s, and the Clark line across Howard was the only track connection between the companies.

Page 237. The photo on the bottom of the page could not have been taken during the Depression. Chicago Motor Coach bus 831, at right, was not delivered until February 21, 1939.

Page 239. Chicago Avenue east route cars were extended to Pulaski in 1914. The line along Lake Shore Drive from Chicago to Grand (Navy Pier) opened on October 1, 1921.

Page 243. The Chicago Avenue trolley bus route changes have the dates transposed. On July 20, 1952 the line was extended to a terminal at Fairbanks and Ontario, and on December 31, 1952 the trolley buses began to use the Mayfield loop terminal.

Page 243. Cicero line. The 1895 Cicero-Chicago car ran from Lake and Cicero to Chicago and Harlem.

Page 245. Trailer service on the Clark Street line began September 1, 1921. The service to the Grant Park loop via Roosevelt Road (12th Street) was by southbound cars. The route can be traced on the CTA 1949 track map on page 338. Note that southbound Clark cars could turn east on Roosevelt, and that Clark cars returning from the Grant Park loop could turn north from Roosevelt to Clark.

Page 246. The photo at the bottom of this page was taken October 29, 1955.

Page 258. The Fullerton Avenue line was extended to Cicero on September 19, 1914. On September 21, 1918 the line was through-routed.

Page 258. On the Fulton-21st Street line the one car an hour that ran over the roundabout route was run in order to hold the franchise on these tracks so that they could be used for emergency diversions from other lines. These "franchise cars" began to run on May 31, 1925.

Page 258. Photo caption. At mid-route the Fullerton line came within walking distance of the California and Logan Square stations of the Logan Square 'L' route.

Page 262. The photo of car 201 at the top of the page was taken by Gordon E. Lloyd.

Page 264. The Halsted Extension-Vincennes route was converted to bus operation on July 29, 1946.

Page 264. Halsted-Archer (Through Route 13) began December 13, 1911.

The section on Chicago Street Railway Post Office history (page 142) refers to this letter. It was mailed August 22, 1946 from Chicago Railways mail car 6, put back in service that day for an American Philatelic Society convention. From the author's collection.

Page 270. Caption for the photo at top of page. The Chicago, Aurora & Elgin interurban yards are to the right, but out of the picture. What is seen at the right across Laramie is the Chicago Rapid Transit Metropolitan Division Laramie shop and yard.

Page 272. The CTA's own published account of the Kedzie-California route states that through operation began February 1, 1911. A check of CTA files shows no evidence of an agreement prior to 1911 between the three companies whose track would be used to operate the through route. However, a record has been found of a Kedzie car involved in an accident on Chicago Avenue on January 27, 1902. This would seem to indicate through operation via Kedzie, Chicago, and California at that early date. It is certain that Through Route 17 began

in 1911, and this would mark the first time Chicago Railways cars used Chicago City Railway tracks on Kedzie. Chicago Railways owned the tracks on Kedzie between Chicago and Cermak, the Southern Street Railway owned the tracks between Cermak and 31st Street, and the Chicago City Railway owned the tracks between 31st and Marquette Road.

Page 275. Photo at top of page. Bus 2390 is eastbound on Wrightwood at Spaulding on its large, triangular terminal loop which brought it near the Logan Square 'L' station. At this point the Kimball buses shared Wrightwood with Homan Avenue buses making their terminal loop. Hence the crowd of passengers shown boarding the Kimball bus may well be transfering from the Homan bus.

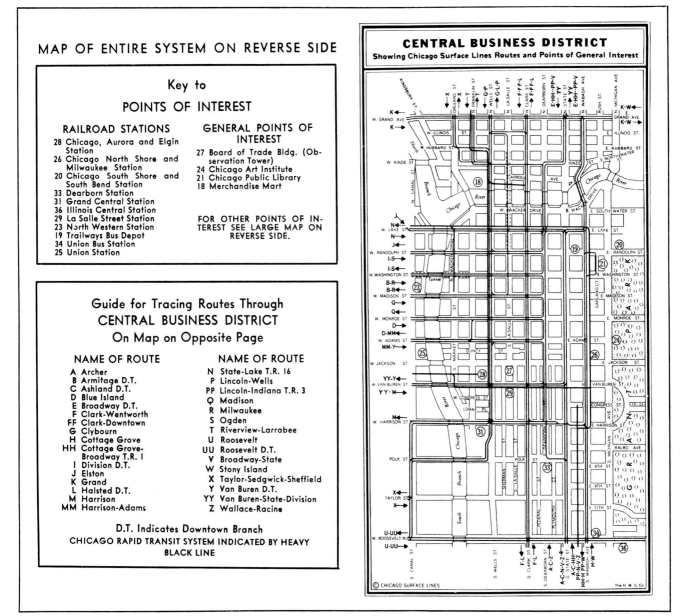

To aid the reader in tracing CSL routes through the maze of tracks in downtown Chicago, this map has been reproduced from an official Surface Lines publication. Note that 31 CSL streetcar routes served the Loop, running on every major street except Jackson Boulevard.

Page 280. The photo looks north along Lincoln at Eastwood, not at the Paulina 'L' station.

Page 280. According to Surface Lines records preserved by the CTA, Madison-Fifth Avenue remained a shuttle line until 1909. Same change on page 284, where the shuttle is once again mentioned.

Page 281. Car 78 was formerly car 1781, not car 1780. See also correction for page 284, below.

Page 284. Car 78, used on the Madison-Fifth Avenue shuttle, was one of the last two cars to run on this line. However, it was painted in the conventional red and cream color scheme (see photo on page 281.) The other shuttle car was painted green and cream.

Page 284. The Milwaukee Avenue cable cars ran from Armitage to downtown Chicago. An electric streetcar shuttle ran from Armitage to Lawrence. On August 19, 1906 streetcars replaced cable cars between Armitage and downtown, and were through-routed with the electric shuttle cars, forming an electric streetcar line from Lawrence to downtown.

Page 284. Until the Milwaukee Avenue extension from Edmunds to Imlay was double-tracked in 1927, a single track with passing sidings was used. Because of heavy Sunday and Holiday traffic to St. Adalbert's Cemetery at the end of the line, two and three-car multiple unit trains were used on the extension. This is thought to be the only use of three-car multiple unit trains on the CSL.

Page 289. On April 24, 1947 the Montrose motor bus route was extended to Narragansett, and the trolley bus extension from Milwaukee to Narragansett stopped running. Trolley bus service over the entire Montrose route from Broadway to Narragansett began April 19, 1948.

W-series work cars were sometimes chartered as rolling billboards. This car is eastbound on Madison at Canal, probably on its way from the Kedzie carbarn to the Loop. Standing next to the motorman's cab dressed in full CSL supervisor's uniform — note the leather puttees — is David M. Flynn. Entering service as a student engineer on October 29, 1935, Flynn became District D superintendent in 1945, and superintendent of transportation in 1961. He retired September 1, 1974 with 39 years' transit service. Chicago Transit Authority photo supplied by Robert Heinlein.

Page 289. The North-Narragansett terminal of the Narragansett line opened in June, 1949.

Page 289. The North Avenue extension bus began to use the North-Narragansett terminal in June, 1949 (see correction above).

Page 290. Both photos taken by Gordon E. Lloyd.

Page 291. The photo at the top of the page was taken by Gordon E. Lloyd.

Page 297. The South Pulaski Road extension of June 22, 1938 was to a wye at 64th Street, not to the loop mentioned here.

Page 298. The 1906 Roosevelt Road Downtown car route was via Wells, Harrison, Dearborn, etc.

Page 301. South Deering cars did not use the South Park loop. Car 6209 is a South Chicago-Ewing car en route to 108th and Avenue F. At the time the photo was taken, no other routes used this terminal, although it had previously been used by the Hammond and Whiting lines.

Page 304. The location of the photo at the bottom of the page is just north of Archer along State.

Page 309. The Taylor-Sedgwick-Sheffield route was split into two segments on June 30, 1947, when Taylor Street was closed for street repaving.

Page 309. Wallace-Racine was not the only line to use the crossover at Clark and Washington. This was the only downtown terminal for South Side electric cars which reached downtown under their own power. Hal-

Decked out in wartime public service advertising, car 1731 poses on the Roosevelt Road Grant Park loop for patriotic photo snapping. The car was one of ten in this series which carried messages supporting the war effort. Photo taken July 17, 1942. Print from the Tom Mangan collection.

sted and Wentworth cars, for example, also used the Clark and Washington crossover.

Page 309. In the last years of streetcar operation, northbound Wentworth cars used Cermak Road between Wentworth and Clark, while the southbound cars used Archer.

Page 312. Photo by Gordon E. Lloyd.

Page 322. The loop at the east end of the 83rd Street line, which was first used December 26, 1944, was via 83rd, Mackinaw, 85th, and Green Bay.

Page 322. The final change in West 79th Street service under CSL management came in 1943, when service was extended to 76th and Kilpatrick via 79th, Pulaski, and 76th.

Page 323. Car 1416 was made a PAYE car on September 22, 1910.

Page 325. The photo caption on page 324 refers to the Rock Island railroad's Normal Park station at 78th and Fielding. This was the Rock Island's Auburn Park station.

Page 327. The 111th Street short loop, in service September 23, 1945, was via Cottage Grove, Forrestville, and 111th.

Page 328. The West 119th Street line was through-routed with Vincennes on July 29, 1946.

Page 332. The date of this map is 1899.

Page 333. The date of this map is 1897.

Page 354. The date of the Illinois Supreme Court's first reversal of its previous decision in the Chicago Motor Coach-Chicago Surface Lines case was February 18, 1929.

Page 358. The bottom photo looks south along Paulina to Cortland.

Page 360. The Elston barn, shown in the lower photo, was never a cable car barn. It was built new for electric streetcars in 1894. The 1904 remodeling was most likely made to accommodate double-truck streetcars.

Page 363. The lower photo is of the interior of the Ardmore garage, not the Lawrence garage.

Page 365. The parcel of land north of Lake Street was also a part of the West Shops complex. Until 1917 coal was unloaded there from railroad hopper cars and transferred to street railway work cars for movement to the Washington Street powerhouse. In 1893 part of this property was leased to the Lake Street 'L' for a shop.

Page 365. Trolley bus repairs were also made at Kimball-Peterson between 1931 and 1937.

Page 366. All 11 carbarns lasted until 1947, the last year of the CSL era.

Page 367. The 51st-55th Street trolley buses were assigned to the Archer Avenue carbarn. A more complete list of barn assignments for an earlier era is included in this section on page 415.

Pages 368 to 377. Felix Reifschneider comments upon this chapter on union affairs as follows: "I can't claim to be an expert on horse car operation, although I saw

A lineup of CSL buses from the various routes which served the Dodge-Chicago defense plant, now the Ford City Shopping Center. From left are: 417, a 1936 Superior/Reo, running on the South Cicero line; 407, a 1934 White, running on the West 79th Street line; 575 and 572, 1937 Fords running on South Cicero; and 511, a 1935 White running on West 79th Street. Chicago Transit Authority photo.

•Above. CTA 2118, formerly Calumet & South Chicago 807, was still in service in 1951. Built by ACF in 1935, it was their model H13S. •Below. In mint condition, Chicago Railways 3426 was a 1945 White model 798. Both photos from the Chicago Transit Authority.

Buses of stranger shape never roamed Chicago's streets. Bus 530, above, and 1209, below, were Twin Coach mode! 30R buses built in 1937. Top photo shows the slope-back vehicle in CSL colors and with its original number. Bottom photo shows same type bus in CTA colors and number series. Both photos from CTA.

horse cars in operation in New York City as late as 1917. It is true, however, that 16 hour days were not unusual, and 18 hour days not unknown. However, many horse cars did not start operation until as late as 8:00 a.m., as few workmen rode to work on horse cars. Factory hands usually lived within walking distance of the factory. The car service was usually just a convenience. Of course, it was somewhat different in the largest cities.

"In spite of these long hours, it wasn't quite as bad as it seems. Once the car got out of the congested downtown area, the driver would frequently sit down inside the car and let the horse do the work. Horse cars as a rule would not stop for men or active boys, they would just slow down so the men or boys could hop on. Stops were made only for ladies or elderly people.

"Also, at the end of the line the men would let the horse stand outside and go in a tavern for a glass of beer or in a restaurant for a cup of coffee. [Editor's note: Many "greasy spoon" restaurants sprang up near carbarns or important terminals, and drew most of their patrons from the ranks of the Chicago carmen.] Supervision was at a minimum and lax. While drinking beer on duty would mean discharge for a trolley employee, on the horse cars it was winked at.

"There is no doubt that being a horse car driver was not an easy job, but it wasn't as bad as it might seem. Also, you must consider the times. Everyone worked long hours at low pay in those days.

"My experience has been that how union and management got along depended largely on the local union president. If he was a reasonable man, it was rare that International officers visited the property. On the other hand, if the local president was belligerent, there was always trouble, strikes, etc.

"While platform wages seemed low on an hourly basis, on an annual basis the wages of carmen compared very favorably with workers in other industries where hourly wages were considerably higher. Reason: once a man had a regular run, he had steady work. There were no layoffs for model changes, rebuilding furnaces, or anything else.

"Most carmen were recruited from the farms. While hours seem long by today's standards, they were much less than the farm boys had been accustomed to on the farm, and the work was much easier and the pay higher. Also, working on the cars in winter was much less arduous than farm work in winter (tending to the farm animals, gathering fuel in the woods, etc.).

"One thing that Mahon lost sight of was Sam Gompers' dictum that 'the worst crime against organized labor is a company that is losing money.' Gompers' counsel was wise, but Mahon didn't realize it."

Page 383. Further research indicates that a total of 11 trolley buses were housed at facilities other than the North-Cicero barn. Six trolley buses, series 86-91, were assigned to the Elston barn for use on the Elston Extension line. Five Brill buses, numbers 100-104, were stored at Kimball-Peterson for use on the Kimball Avenue line.

Page 388. Beverly bus garage opened in 1949, two years after the close of the CSL era.

Chicago Surface Lines bus 1602 was owned by the Chicago City Railway, one of the four companies which made up the CSL. It was a Twin Coach model 38S, built in 1946. Chicago Transit Authority photo.

Calumet & South Chicago bus 6518 was a 1946 GMC TD4506 vehicle. These exterior and interior photos were taken shortly after delivery, before the destination signs were installed. Note mounting bracket for fare register above and to the left of the driver's seat. CTA photos.

Lines Assigned to Various Carbarns: 1931-32

Archer Depot
Archer
Kedzie
Western
26th
31st
So. Cicero
35th-Pershing
47th
51st-55th

Armitage Avenue
Milwaukee
Armitage-Downtown

Blue Island:
Blue Island
Damen
14th-16th
18th
21st-Fulton

Burnside:
Cottage Grove
Stony Island
Windsor Park
South Deering
Hammond
Whiting
93rd-95th
Riverdale
87th-East
103rd St.
106th St.
111th St.
115th St.
119th St.
Ewing-Brandon.

Cottage Grove:
Cottage Grove
Stony Island
Through Route 1
Lincoln-Indiana
Pershing Road.
43rd-Root.

Devon Depot:
Clark-Wentworth
Broadway & Through Route 1
Lawrence

Division Street
Division
Western
Clybourn

Elston:
Elston
Irving Park
Montrose
Elston Bus
Kimball Bus

Kedzie Depot:
Madison
VanBuren
Harrison
Kedzie
Taylor-Sedgwick-Sheffield
21st-Fulton

Lawndale Depot
Crawford
Ogden
Roosevelt Road
22nd Street

Limits Depot:
Broadway &Through Route
Halsted
Belmont

Lincoln Avenue:
Lincoln-Indiana
Riverview-Larrabee
Taylor-Sedgwick-Sheffield
Fullerton
North Ashland
Webster-Racine

Noble Street:
Elston
Armitage-Center
Ashland
Morgan-Racine

North Avenue:
North Avenue
Grand
Chicago
Crawford

Cicero
Division Extension
Laramie
Through Route 16
Diversey Bus
Belmont Bus
Central Bus
Narragansett Bus
Irving Pk. Bus
Montrose Bus

69th Street
59th-61st
63rd
67th-69th
Wallace-Racine
Ashland
Damen

77th Street:
State
Through Route 16
Clark-Wentworth
Halsted
74th-75th
79th
71st
87th-West
103rd Bus

Notes: This list, compiled from CSL records, supplements the list on page 367, which was compiled from CTA records. Each barn was its own CSL operating division for administrative purposes, with the following exceptions: Lawndale and Blue Island were one division, as were Armitage and Division, Elston and Noble, and Limits and Devon.

Transit Revenue Passengers, Population, Transit Rides Per Capita, and Auto Registration Data: 1900 to 1947

Year	Originating Revenue Passengers				Population of Chicago (1)	Annual Rides Per Capita	Pass. Autos Registered in Chicago	Autos Registered per 1,000 Residents
	Surface Lines	Rapid Transit	Chicago Motor Coach	Combined				
1900(4)	282,999,580	75,849,681		358,849,261	1,698,575	211		
1901	298,008,572	95,605,693		393,614,265	1,747,236	225		
1902	322,004,332	106,538,176		428,542,508	1,795,897	239		
1903	333,008,968	114,882,261		447,891,229	1,834,558	244	Not	Not
1904	347,008,111	113,882,771		460,890,882	1,893,219	243	Recorded	Recorded
1905	376,006,224	123,664,292		499,670,516	1,941,880	257		
1906	373,900,000	131,958,605		505,858,605	1,990,600	254		
1907	372,123,199	147,263,985		519,387,184	2,039,271	255		
1908	396,073,965	150,371,374		546,445,339	2,087,942	262	5,475(2)	2.6
1909	442,511,273	152,423,961		594,935,234	2,136,613	278	7,110(2)	3.3
1910	481,822,110	164,875,974		646,698,084	2,185,283	296	9,963	4.6
1911	561,517,222	162,866,136		724,383,358	2,236,926	324	11,876	5.3
1912	589,178,708	164,314,524		753,493,232	2,288,568	329	16,857	7.4
1913	634,026,040	164,164,225		798,190,265	2,340,210	341	22,136	9.4
1914	627,731,550	165,770,135		793,501,685	2,391,852	332	26,814	11.2
1915	623,030,097	164,678,900		787,708,997	2,443,494	322	34,441	14.1
1916	686,071,644	180,649,694		866,721,338	2,495,136	347	48,358	19.4
1917	692,815,889	193,119,829	3,077,558	889,013,276	2,546,778	349	59,382	23.3
1918	685,300,718	197,436,736	4,571,374	887,308,828	2,598,420	341	58,505	22.5
1919	743,746,584	184,667,604	6,060,365	934,474,553	2,650,063	353	75,241	28.3
1920	769,025,413	190,636,873	6,395,472	966,057,758	2,701,705	358	86,670(3)	32.1
1921	750,515,622	180,626,990	7,774,953	938,917,565	2,769,178	339	137,750	49.7
1922	762,629,211	181,283,785	9,619,558	953,532,554	2,836,652	336	172,655	60.9
1923	824,850,103	203,943,551	21,916,485	1,050,710,139	2,904,126	362	218,991	75.4
1924	830,151,540	213,006,798	49,268,427	1,092,426,765	2,971,599	368	260,887	87.8
1925	842,201,453	216,045,575	57,492,529	1,115,739,557	3,039,072	367	289,948	95.4
1926	876,249,663	228,812,766	55,838,927	1,160,901,356	3,106,545	374	317,433	102.2
1927	882,458,647	226,212,172	59,270,849	1,167,941,668	3,174,018	368	335,263	105.6
1928	892,814,620	207,864,238	61,836,233	1,162,515,091	3,241,490	359	360,985	111.4
1929	897,564,354	196,774,395	69,001,990	1,163,340,739	3,308,962	352	402,078	121.5
1930	812,080,701	182,954,846	58,310,208	1,053,345,755	3,376,438	312	406,916	120.5
1931	732,095,601	152,414,248	49,571,371	934,081,220	3,378,475	276	423,786	125.4
1932	633,826,944	126,989,541	40,799,663	801,616,148	3,380,512	237	396,783	117.4
1933	651,602,518	124,855,354	49,298,578	825,756,450	3,382,549	244	367,402	108.6
1934	677,532,725	127,276,803	43,698,473	848,508,001	3,384,586	251	368,585	108.9
1935	667,900,574	127,459,188	40,019,162	835,378,924	3,386,623	247	397,023	117.2
1936	706,722,032	129,578,269	47,827,417	884,127,718	3,388,660	261	461,527	136.2
1937	706,564,952	128,005,374	55,618,162	890,188,488	3,390,697	263	504,207	148.7
1938	661,341,637	121,426,629	55,386,336	837,488,648	3,392,734	247	506,071	149.2
1939	662,904,465	121,426,629	55,386,336	839,717,430	3,394,771	247	516,128	152.0
1940	672,101,225	123,704,810	57,410,265	853,216,300	3,396,808	251	549,537	161.8
1941	695,138,697	127,133,614	60,304,813	882,577,24	3,419,224	258	585,219	171.2
1942	753,786,165	133,208,577	69,189,952	956,184,694	3,441,638	278	545,777	158.6
1943	818,815,534	140,905,171	67,835,380	1,027,556,085	3,464,054	297	467,423	134.9
1944	844,873,931	151,062,563	70,986,197	1,066,922,691	3,486,468	306	433,880	124.4
1945	847,671,449	157,275,085	75,018,686	1,079,965,220	3,508,884	308	427,779	121.9
1946(4)	921,383,351	157,876,434	72,732,022	1,151,991,807	3,531,298	326	461,721	130.8
1947(5)	888,534,530	145,800,514	85,835,806	1,120,170,850	3,553,714	315	512,810	144.3

Notes: (1) Yearly population figures accepted as standard by CTA. (2) Trucks and other vehicles included through 1909. (3) Partial year, May to December — previous years, May to April — following years, January to December. (4) Chicago Surface Lines passengers 1900-1946 based on fiscal years ended January 31 (following year). All other passengers based on calendar years. (5) CTA took over operations of Chicago Surface Lines and Chicago Rapid Transit Company October 1, 1974.

Supplement to the second edition

It's now a little more than five years since the first edition of *Chicago Surface Lines* appeared in July, 1974. That edition was followed by a second, expanded from 400 to 416 pages, in December, 1974. It is now August, 1979, and this third edition is off the press with 496 pages.

The last 96 pages of the complete third edition are also being offered as a separate, softcover book to enable those who purchased either the first or second editions an opportunity to get all the supplemental material in the third edition without buying the third edition.

This supplement continues the page numbering scheme of the first two editions, starting with page 417. In the softcover supplement, this page is numbered 1/417, and the dual system of numbers continues throughout. This scheme permits use of the comprehensive six-part photo index on pages 473-493, whichever edition or supplement the reader has.

We dedicate this third edition to the memory of Allan C. Williams, who died in early 1979. The helpfulness and friendliness with which he placed his collection of CSL photos at the author's disposal is reflected in the many superb photos from that collection in the pages of this book.

Among the many others who significantly contributed to this book were William P. Barnett, Roy G. Benedict, James J. Buckley, Joe L. Diaz, Robert E. Geis, Zenon Hansen, Robert D. Heinlein, Richard N. Lukin, Kenneth Mortimer, Norman L. Thilmont, and Thomas C. Van Degrift.

Special thanks go to Mr. Benedict for his meticulous research on thorny or obscure points in Chicago traction history, to Mr. Hansen for his highly informative equipment purchase tables covering the confused transition period between the CSL and CTA, to Mr. Mortimer for his work on the index to photos, and to Mr. Thilmont for his copious notes covering CSL operations during the World War II years.

This supplement to the second edition takes a different approach than the supplement to the first edition took. In the earlier supplement the emphasis was on page-by-

Old Pullman 142 lays over on 64th Street just west of Stony Island Avenue in this photo from Allan C. Williams. Though well into its fifth decade of continuous service, the car is still dependably filling assignments on the heavy 63rd Street crosstown route. Compare with photo on page 431.

417

• One of the most unusual passenger cars to roam the tracks of the CSL system was Cook County 1, shown here leaving its private spur on the grounds of Cook County Psychopathic Hospital to join CSL's tracks on Harrison Street. • Below. Though still bearing its number 1 and perhaps still shuttling the insane along the streets of Chicago, Cook County 1 is the worse for wear in this photo supplied by the Chicago Transit Authority. Note absence of a headlight on this car. Photo of car 1 on page 15 shows it equipped with a large, portable interurban-style headlight for operation over interurban tracks.

page notes, including corrections of factual errors and amplifications of obscure points. While there is some of this sort of material in this second supplement, there is also a new emphasis on placing the CSL in its legal and political context through an exhaustive chronology covering the years 1837-1947.

The first edition and its supplement focused on the physical aspects of the Surface Lines: rolling stock, the routes, the day-to-day operations, and in general the technology of the electric railway between 1914 and 1947. The Cottage Grove line was chosen as an example of street railway development in Chicago both before and after the CSL era in lieu of covering all 100 or so CSL lines through the same period, a project which would have required a volume twice as large as the first edition.

As a means of balancing the technical coverage of the first edition, the chronology focuses largely on political, legal, and economic aspects of local transportation in Chicago, bringing in the elevated-subway lines and the largest independently owned bus system whenever necessary. It covers the years 1837, when Chicago was incorporated, to 1947, when the Chicago Transit Authority took over the operations of both the Chicago Surface Lines and the Chicago Rapid Transit Company.

The source of the data for the years 1837 to 1926 was the chronology printed in the *20th Annual Report of the Board of Supervising Engineers, Chicago Traction*, for the fiscal year 1926. The chronology for the years 1927 to 1936 was compiled by the author from BOSE reports for those years. The data for the years 1937 to 1947 came from the *Ninth Annual Report of the Department of Subways and Superhighways* of the City of Chicago.

From 1837 to 1859, when the first horse car line opened on State Street, the chronology concerns itself with the physical growth of Chicago and the legal changes which accompanied this development. Around the turn of the century the focus shifts to the political arena and the developments preceding the Settlement Ordinances of 1907 and the Unification Ordinance of 1913.

Throughout the 1920s the emphasis is on the progress made by the Surface Lines in purchasing modern equipment, extending service to new parts of the city, and on the growth in ridership and in gross revenues. In the 1930s the picture changed radically, and the reports deal with the bankruptcies of the companies underlying the CSL, the drastic drop in ridership and gross revenues, and the failure of the City and the companies to agree on new franchises to replace those that expired in 1927.

From the 1930s on, legal and political entries dominate, as plan after plan to put Chicago's transportation system on a firm legal and financial footing failed. In this period the legal and financial maneuvers became so complex that virtually all other matters, such as new equipment for the Surface Lines, drop out of the chronology. To remedy this situation, a series of tables covering CSL equipment purchases from 1927 to 1947 has been prepared as a supplement to the chronology for those crucial years. See pages 463-466.

The complexity of these tables is an indication of the near-chaos that the war years brought to the carefully-laid plans of the CSL receivers for new equipment. To the supervision of a Federal bankruptcy judge was added the changes ordered by the Office of Defense Transportation in Washington, which cancelled some CSL equipment orders during WW II. Unfortunately the war years were also the years of transition between the privately-owned CSL and the publicly-owned Chicago Transit Authority, which added further confusion.

Because the BOSE ran on a February to January fiscal year rather than a calendar year, all financial and operating statistics in the chronology taken from the BOSE reports refer to the fiscal year. All dates connected with equipment acquisitions or physical improvements have been corrected to reflect the calendar year.

Except for correcting gross errors of fact and smoothing the style, the author has reproduced the chronology exactly as it appeared in the official records cited. Readers who go through the entire chronology will detect subtle shifts in tone and emphasis, as local transit moves from virtually unregulated status to an industry tied in legal and political knots.

In the five years since the second edition of this book came out, interest in the Chicago Surface Lines has markedly increased. The author is indebted to Roy Benedict, Zenon Hansen, and Norman Thilmont for their patient work in helping to uncover new data that has been incorporated in the page notes for this third edition. These notes are on pages 425-444.

In some cases their research has brought to light errors of fact or interpretation, or simply typographical errors. Frequently their efforts have yielded explanations and amplifications on well-established points. When their efforts have merely served to confirm a fact in previous editions, that is usually not cited in these notes.

These notes are arranged in numerical order by page number. These notes supplement the notes on pages 402-413 of the second edition; they in no way replace them.

Many of the photos in the book are credited to the Barney Neuberger collection. Recent research has revealed that his last name has also been spelled Neuburger. His death certificate was not available to the author at press time, but the preponderance of the evidence points to the spelling of Neuburger as correct.

With the assistance of Mr. Kenneth Mortimer, the author has compiled an index to photos in all three editions. The index is divided into six parts. The first part lists all CSL cars in numerical order. The second lists CSL work equipment. It is arranged by alphabetical prefix, then numerically within each prefix. Although a hyphen was not used between the prefix and the number on the work equipment, it is used in the index to make the list more readable.

The third index lists vehicles of all types that are identified as belonging to owners other than the Chicago Surface Lines. These include cars of the underlying companies as well as those owned by competing transit operators.

The fourth index lists all buses in numerical order. The number used is the number painted on the bus when the picture was taken. In some cases, the underlying ownership of the buses is shown. Trolley, gas, and diesel buses are listed in numerical order without regard to type of motive power. CSL and CTA motorized work equipment are listed at the end of this index.

• Opposite page, top. Although owned by Chicago City Railway, cars in the 2701-2780 series served on lines of the other underlying companies after the CSL Unification of 1914. Car 2757, for example, is shown here at the outer end of the Riverview-Larrabee line at Roscoe and Western. This was a Chicago Railways route. For a photo of another car in the 2701-2780 series on this line, see page 298. • Opposite page, bottom, and this page, bottom. What fire could do to a wooden streetcar is evident in this photo, believed to be of car 2713 or 2719. Both photos from James Prokes collection. • Above. Car 2760 as built for CCRY Co. in 1903 by St. Louis Car Co.

• Above. During the period 1907-1914 and again during the years 1940-1947 there was considerable shifting of rolling stock among the underlying companies that formed the CSL. The shifts in ownership during the first period grew out of the Settlement Ordinance of 1907 and the Unification Ordinance of 1913. The shifts during the later period grew out of the disruptions of WW II, formation of the Chicago Transit Authority in 1945, and the CTA's takeover of the CSL and CRT in 1947. The cars in series 2801-2815, such as 2808 shown above, were originally Chicago City Railway cars in the 2501-2625 series. They were sold to the Calumet & South Chicago Railway in 1908, where they were renumbered in 1908 into the 701-715 series, and in 1913 into the 2801-2815 series. See page 79 for details of the renumberings. Car 2808 is on the 119th Street line. • Below. Car 2808 is ready to make an eastbound trip on the 119th Street line from what appears to be the 119th & Vincennes terminal. Note drawbar carried on hooks under car body just behind front truck, used to couple cars together.

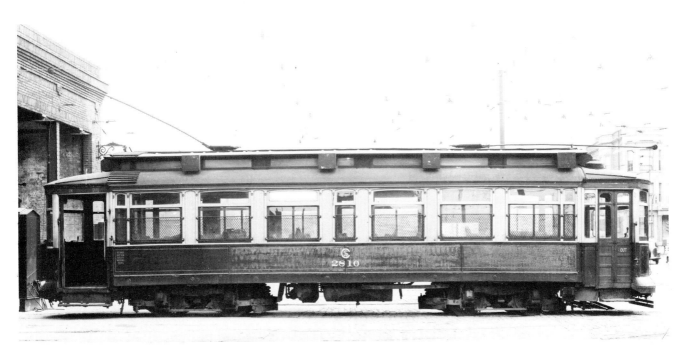

• Top. Official CTA photograph of car 2810 clearly shows the ten side windows characteristic of this series, including the odd narrow window on the right hand side of the front platform. Narrow window in the center of the car side required an offset destination sign; as shown in this view the sign is blank. Cars in the 2801-2815 series were seen on many far South Side lines over the years: this book shows them running on Ewing-Brandon (below), Riverdale (29), 106th (opposite page), and 119th (opposite page). • Bottom. In this photo of car 2814 running on the Ewing-Brandon (Hegewisch) line, the car's heavy wire window guards have been replaced by wooden sash storm windows. For many years CSL carbarns had the Fall chore of removing the window guards and installing the storm sash; in the Spring the process was reversed. The storm windows held in the car's electric heat, which though simple to produce by means of resistance coils mounted in protective metal boxes under the car seats, was also expensive to produce and put a heavy drain on CSL's substations.

• Opposite page. Throughout the period covered by this book, roughly the years 1890 to 1960, many types of cars operated on a typical CSL route. On these two facing pages, three car types operating on Ashland Avenue are shown. Car 3181, shown here at the Southport & Clark north terminal, was part of the 3179-3201 series built by CSL at West Shops in 1923. Known as "Sun Parlors," these cars had a lifespan of less than 25 years, rather short by CSL standards. Barney Neuburger photo from A. C. Williams collection. • Above. Car 5328 was part of the 5201-5600 series of Chicago City Railway cars built by Brill between 1907-1908. It was part of the sub-series 5301-5600 built as Chicago's first PAYE cars. Most of these cars ran for nearly 40-45 years; nearly all were scrapped between 1945 and 1951. Car 5328 is shown near the south terminal at 95th Street. • Below. Old Pullmans in series 101-700 were also frequently seen on Ashland Ave. Car 531 was snapped near 95th St.

The fifth index should prove of value to those interested in both the CSL's passenger vehicles and the routes they ran on. This index lists all vehicles by route. The sixth index complements the fifth by listing all vehicles shown at a carbarn or other location not on a regular route.

In all six indexes a vehicle is listed even if in the photo the entire vehicle does not appear.

Among the photos not indexed are those on the dust jacket, and the three photos on the contents page. Drawings, diagrams, tables, maps, transfers, rosters, and non-photographic illustrations are also not indexed. Some of these are listed on the contents page.

We are deeply grateful to Mr. Mortimer for allowing us to use his index; it will be, we think, a valuable addition to the book for many readers. See pages 473-493.

Page by Page Notes to First and Second Editions

Page 10. The battery cars on the connecting line that ran between 63rd and Vernon and 87th and Summit were under different corporate ownership than the Cottage Grove cable cars. The line is mentioned as a feeder route to the important Chicago City Railway cable on Cottage Grove.

The distance from the Downtown loop of the Cottage Grove cable line to the Calumet Co.'s outer terminal at 119th and Michigan was 15.6 miles.

Page 11. Car 5787 is southbound on Cottage Grove Ave. at 47th Street. It is an example of an unconverted car.

The 5703-5827 series of Nearside cars contained 125 cars, not 124.

Page 16. The single-truck passenger cars still on the property after February 1, 1914 were never used under CSL management but were held for emergency use. For photos of two types that were offered for sale, see *Electric Traction* for November 1915, page 736.

Page 28. This photo was probably taken on March 6, 1933, the same date, and at the same location, as the photo on page 200.

Page 29. The photo at the top of this page was taken by Joe Diaz.

Close comparison of PCC car 7004, operating on the 63rd Street line (bottom photo on this page) with PCC cars 7008 (page 249) and 4014 and 4046 (page 250) indicate a minor variation in the paint scheme on car 7004. On that car the green roof color appears to run along the car side from top to bottom and back to front; on the other three similar PCC cars the window area is white.

Page 31. There is no question that, when new, the 5900 series were intended to operate with closed vestibules. The rear doors and steps were operated from the conductor's position, but by mechanical linkage, not by air as with the cars built a decade later. Possibly in routine service in later years the doors were not always kept closed while the cars were running.

● Above. Nearside 5747 was part of the 5703-5827 series built for the Chicago City Railway by Brill in 1912. The cars first ran on Cottage Grove lines, such as Through Route 5, Cottage Grove-South Chicago, the line on which 5747 is running in the photo. The Nearside type of car, with its single front entrance and single front and rear exits, was never really suited to the heavy traffic conditions encountered in Chicago. The conductor's station, located behind the motorman just inside the body of the car, was a point of congestion as boarding passengers jostled with exiting riders; tne single rear exit door seems to have been unpopular with riders. ● Below. Rebuilt 1936 PCC car 4033, snapped at 115th & Cottage Grove, was typical of the cars which replaced the Peter Witts and ran until the end of service in 1955. This car was one of the 83 that inaugurated PCC operation in Chicago along Madison Street in 1936. For a list of some car types that ran on Cottage Grove, see the note to page 251.

Page 32. The photo at the top of the page was taken on 38th Street west of Rockwell Ave.

Page 58. Since the photo of car 199 was taken during the CTA era, this car could have been filling in between Nearside or Peter Witt cars on Through Route 5, Cottage Grove-South Chicago. Old Pullmans also supplemented the single-end cars of both types on Through Route 4, Cottage Grove-Pullman.

Page 59. Here, as on page 33, 12 rebuilt Old Pullmans were destroyed in the Devon carbarn fire of 1922.

Page 61. Further research on the construction of the "Matchboxes" reveals that this series (1101-1423) came from the St. Louis Car Company in six batches. Cars 1101-1200 were built in 1903, except for 1117, 1131, and 1198, which were built in 1905 as replacements for destroyed cars. Cars 1201-1240 were built in 1904. Cars 1241-1300 were also built at that time, but not purchased from the carbuilder until the following year. Five cars, 1301-1305, were built later in 1905, and cars 1306-1423 followed in 1906.

The Chicago Union Traction (CUT) numbers carried by the 1101-1423 series were 4625-4952 until renumbered in 1909.

Page 66. The Chicago cars used by C&WT were two-man cars operated by one man. CSL itself needed the 25 cars which were converted to one-man operation. There is a photo of car 1381 in Madison Street C&WT service in Gibson, *Chicago & West Towns Railways* (ERHS, 1952), page 19.

Page 68. In the 1429-1505 series, only 77 of the original 80 cars were renumbered to this series. Cars 4476, 4498, and 4526 had been retired before the renumbering. Of the 77 renumbered cars, 53 were rebuilt as shown in the table. The 24 cars not rebuilt are listed in the text on page 69.

Page 69. Continuing the clarification of the rebuilding of the 4475-4554/1429-1505 series: As built, the 80 CUT "Bowling Alleys" all had extremely short platforms (see car 4499 on page 23). Twenty-four of the cars kept the original short platforms; they are listed on page 69. The others were rebuilt with larger platforms. Cars 1429, 1456, and 1479 were sold to the Gary & Interurban Railroad, Gary, Ind., rather than to Gary Railways. Twenty, rather than 18, other cars were sold in 1917. The two cars not listed were 1486 and 1505.

Page 70. CSL's nominal voltage at substation output was 600 volts, but experienced some loss between there and the cars. Therefore car equipment was frequently rated at a lower voltage, often 10% less. Motors were tested and rated at 500 VDC.

On this page reference is made to the routes Lake, Ogden, and Division-Van Buren. It has been suggested in a letter to the author that the route designations be changed to Lake-State, Division-State-Van Buren, and Ogden-Randolph. The difference between the names used and the names suggested arises from a difference in sources for the names. This book gives preference to route names as given in official CSL and CTA documents such as route guides and internal memoranda; these "official" names were also used on most transfers. The letter to the author suggested that names displayed on the side signs on the cars be used as route designations.

The author believes that use of the printed sources is preferable to use of the car side sign readings. For example, consider the two side signs "Stony Island-Commercial" and "S. Chicago-Sheffield." They were used on the routes this book identifies as "Windsor Park" and "Hammond," respectively. The front signs of cars operating on these two routes agree with this description.

Almost all Through Routes also had different signs on their front and side sign boxes, which would make identification of a Through Route by its side sign confusing. Side signs on many lines were just a catalog of streets over which the line ran, rather than an "official" route description.

Page 73. The "Flexible Flyers" — series 1800 to 1899 — did have bulkheads, but they contained a pair of sliding doors which met in the middle, rather than the two separate doors which characterized the PAYE arrangement, which had been used on previous orders of new cars for several years. It was car 1874, rather than 1814, which had a run-in with a freight train and was rebuilt with different roof vents.

Page 75. The photo at the top of this page was taken by Edward Frank, Jr.

Page 78. The bottom photo is of a short-turn car on the Stony Island-Wabash route preparing to leave on a southbound trip from State and Wacker Drive.

Page 79. The single car in series 2824-2840 was like cars 2824-2838 because it had medium-size platforms.

Page 81. It is likely that car 2829, rather than car 2838, was selected as a test car for the PAYE design.

Page 83. The photo at the top of page 83 was taken on 38th Street west of Rockwell Ave.

Pages 83 & 165. A photo of car 2854 in service is in Buckley, *The Hammond Whiting & East Chicago Ry.* (ERHS, 1953), page 16.

Page 85. The 16th-18th line was a bus route. Cars in the 3093-3118 series ran on 18th Street, which was a car route. Only car 3110 had the rear door, which was added some years after the cars were built. CSL originally considered a rear exit unnecessary because of the cars' short length and wide aisles.

Page 88. The photo at the bottom of the page was taken at the Erie and Ashland terminal.

Page 101. Car 4001 ran on the Madison line as well as on the other routes indicated on this page. It was retired from passenger service by the CTA on April 15, 1948 and stored at South Shops. About 1955 it was removed from its trucks, painted dark green, and converted to a yard office at South Shops yard.

Page 102. The photo of car 4006 is probably a publicity photo. It is probably not on Madison Street, as there are vacant lots visible.

Page 106. Pullman-built PCC model ''B'' tested in Chicago by CSL was equipped with four GE 1178 B-1 motors of 50 hp, and had 17-1-KM-D-1 series-parallel (multipoint) type control. The car weighed 31,400 lbs. It was delivered to the CSL August 1, 1934. From then until August 20, adjustments were made to the motors, controls, and door equipment. It ran in Chicago in revenue service only from August 20 to September 5, 1934, when it was returned to Pullman with a total accumulated mileage of 1,300 miles.
Bottom photo. CSL did not use Route 2 for Windsor Park. The photos of this car in service on Windsor Park show the route number sign blank.

Page 109. Cars 4372-4411. Further research has determined that car 4400 was also scrapped by the CTA. Also, car 4393 was scrapped by Merchants Steel and Supply Co.
Cars 5201-5600. Good coverage of the San Francisco cars was published in Smallwood, *The White Front Cars of San Francisco,* Interurbans Publications.

Page 114. The photo in the middle of the page was taken on 38th Street west of Rockwell Ave. Car 5702 (middle photo) was built in Chicago by a street railway company in their own shops, but since it was built prior to the 1914 Unification, it is incorrect to say that it was built by CSL. The actual builder was the Chicago City Railway Co.

Page 115. The photo at the top of the page was taken on South Chicago Ave. at the Illinois Central Railroad (now ICGRR) underpass near 75th Street.

Page 120. There were 40 cars in the 6199-6238 series, half built by the CSL (lower numbers) and half built by the Lightweight Noiseless Streetcar Co. of Minneapolis, Minn.

Page 121. Car 7001 later ran on the Clark-Wentworth and Madison lines, and by 1945 was in storage at the Kedzie carhouse. It was officially retired from passenger service on April 15, 1948 and stored at South Shops. It subsequently became a storage shed, but unlike car 4001 it retained its trucks and faded CSL color scheme. It was scrapped on December 22, 1959.

Page 122. The posed photograph at the bottom of this page was taken at Fifth Ave. and Independence Blvd. with car 7002 eastbound along Fifth Ave.

Page 123. The photo of car 7002 at the bottom of this page was taken on Kedzie Ave. in front of the Kedzie & Van Buren carhouse.

• Opposite page. CSL 5610 stops at 81st and Stony Island Avenue to discharge a passenger while making a southbound run on the Stony Island-Wabash line. Side sign reads "Cottage Grove-Stony Island," one of several side signs in use on this line. Car 5610 was part of the 5601-5621 series built for the Chicago City Railway by Brill in 1910. Car is running on the wide, grassy median used by the line between 69th Pl. and 93rd Street. • Above. Although car 5929 was built just three years after car 5610, its arch roof and uncluttered lines give it a far more modern appearance than car 5610. This view, taken at the 93rd Street terminal, clearly shows the Brill 39-E-1 maximum traction trucks with their 34" and 22" wheels. Note "Stony Island-Wabash" sign at side and end of car.
• Below. Car 6224 was built as a multiple-unit car in 1924 for use in two-car trains. It is shown here at the Navy Pier terminal of the Stony Island line.

Page 125. Cars 7035-7274. Car 7205 was wrecked, rebuilt with parts from car 7078, and was sent to the St. Louis Car Co. for use in building rapid transit cars in series 6511-6720. Good coverage of the rebuilding is in Central Electric Railfans' Association, *Chicago's Rapid Transit Volume II,* which is currently available.

Page 136. The photo at the top of the page was taken at Pitney Ct. and Archer Ave., looking north.

Page 174. Based on evidence about the film playing at the Roosevelt Theatre, this photo was probably taken on Saturday, September 11, 1948.

Page 175. Chicago Railways and Chicago City Railway operated some through routes. One joint route, begun in 1910, was TR 2, Clybourn-Wentworth (or Wentworth-Clybourn), which ran from the Riverview amusement park to 79th and Halsted.

Page 181. Top photo. This photo was taken at Pontiac, Mich., at what was then the plant of the Yellow Truck & Coach Manufacturing Company. Today it is the location of General Motors' GMC Truck & Coach Division.

Page 189. The transfer at the top of the page is dated about 1905, as W. H. Conrad became general manager and superintendent sometime between February 1904 and April 1905. In July 1907 the road was taken over by the Chicago & Southern Traction Company. However, a transfer with the same map and differing only in other respects is illustrated in the *Street Railway Review* for September 15, 1899.

The two transfers nearest the bottom of the page were the type of CSL transfer issued from May 18, 1930 through September 30, 1932, rather than from 1914 to 1920. The top transfer, on salmon (northbound) or manila (southbound) stock was issued for all north-south routes. The bottom transfer, on pink (eastbound) or green (westbound) stock, was issued for all east-west lines.

Page 190, top. Surface Lines transfer issued for all north-south routes between 1914 and 1930, with changes made in the copy to reflect route name changes over the years.

Page 193. Chicago Motor Coach operators used punch marks in the shape of an equilateral triangle.

Chicago Rapid Transit used paper transfers between the Evanston and Niles Center (later Skokie) branches as Howard station, the transfer point, did not have prepaid station access.

The white, the blue, and the pink transfers were printed from different base plates so the shape of Lake Calumet is significant only of the date the plate was designed—not of the particular transfer specimen. Only the white transfers were frequently updated.

Page 199. Chronology of One-Man Car Assignments. April 6, 1936. The 79th Street partial one-man service was the night cars starting about 11 pm. Lawrence Av-

enue was the night cars using cars 3200-3201, whereas the two-man daytime service used small Pullmans. Chicago Avenue used cars 1994-1999 in night service.

The June 9, 1940 South Chicago-Ewing conversion was as a replacement for the Hammond line, not for the Interstate lines. On the same day, the South Chicago-Indianapolis route was converted to one-man operation as a replacement for Whiting-East Chicago (Interstate) cars.

On September 16, 1951, the Indiana line was converted to one-man operation.

On December 13, 1953, all service on the Fifth Ave. line was by one-man cars exclusively.

Page 200. The photo was taken in early March, 1933; the precise date may be March 6. This date was established through research on the movie "Grand Slam," then playing at the Roosevelt Theatre.

Page 214. The LaSalle Tunnel opened for regular service on July 21, 1912. Two routes began to use it immediately, Clybourn and Clybourn-Wentworth (TR 2). Among the routes using the tunnel a year later were the Broadway local (then known as the Evanston car), Clark local, Lincoln-Bowmanville, and Lincoln-Rosehill. The last lines to use the tunnel were the Lincoln Ave. routes, as described in the text.

Page 216. Photo. While destination signs are often incorrect, in this particular case the sign is all right. The *Transfer Reference Manual* provides that passengers may make reverse rides on routes that have downtown loops. Anyone boarding at or after Franklin Street (Monroe for north-south loops) thus needs to know the destination after the car turns around—especially on a branching line like Madison.

Page 221. On December 12, 1930, the Archer-38th Street cars were cut back to a shuttle only between Western, where the cars reversed on a crossover just north of Archer, and Central Park.

For nearly two years, between June 24, 1951 and February 1, 1953, the Armitage Ave. line was operated by motor buses, which replaced the streetcars. Trolley bus service was inaugurated on February 1, 1953.

Page 226. Caption for photo at bottom of page. The correct car series is 5651-5665.

Page 231. Broadway route. On January 25, 1908 the CUT property was purchased at foreclosure by Chicago Railways Company, which had been incorporated October 30, 1903.

Through Route numbers (1 through 24) were assigned by ordinance specifying the routes and minimum service. They were usually interline between different companies since, in most cases, the obvious routes within each company's territory were already being operated and did not need to be prescribed by the City. In some cases, the companies (especially the closely related ones) were already voluntarily operating over the tracks of one another; no Through Route numbers were used. On 22nd

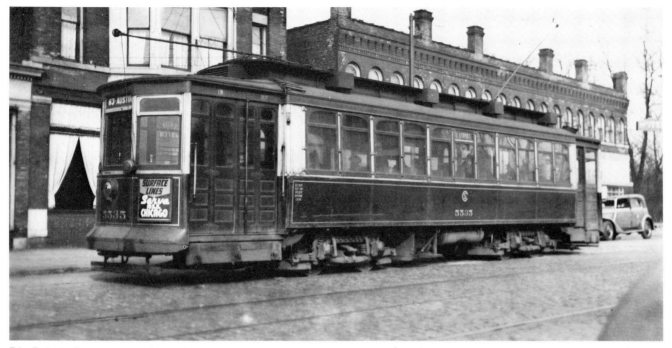

Big Brill 5535, built in 1907-1908, rests between runs on the busy 63rd Street crosstown line at its east terminal at 64th Street west of Stony Island. Compare with photo of car 142, page 417.

Street, as an early example, cars of the Chicago General Railway began using Chicago City Railway tracks in 1897, long before through routing was regulated by government.

Of the 21 Through Routes originally prescribed (not all of which were placed in operation), 14 were interline between CRys and CCRy while the others (Through Route 11, 12, 14, 15, 18, 20, 21) were on CRys tracks but over route combinations not previously operated. Through Routes 22, 23 and 24 were regarded as temporary pending establishment of other routes which were then prevented by physical conditions. Of course, Through Route 22 proved very successful and its successors operated until 1957. Many of the improbable combinations were eliminated in the route rationalization of 1924.

Page 236. The side signs on the postwar PCC cars included "Broadway Wabash." When the Broadway-State through service was discontinued in 1955, a new sign "Broadway" was spliced into the roll, and used until the line was entirely motorized. As of 1954, the only turnback route for North Side cars was via State, Lake, Wabash, Harrison, and State. This was also used for southbound diversions when there were parades on State Street, while northbound diversions operated via Polk, Dearborn, and Kinzie.

Page 237. Lower photo. Indirect evidence from the picture itself indicates that this photo was probably taken on Saturday, September 7, 1940.

The third track on State Street was eliminated when the street was rehabilitated after construction of the subway. While most of the subway was built by tunnel-ing, there was enough subsidence that the surface was done over. A track map revised October 29, 1946 shows the two tracks, while one of 1941 has three tracks.

The outside track of the three was available to loop cars from any combination of Lake, Randolph, Washington and Madison Streets, and was not connected to permit operation via State Street north of Lake or south of Madison. However, the normal routing of all West Side cars was via Dearborn after 1924, when downtown routes were extensively altered to increase capacity by eliminating many conflicting car movements.

There were shorter stretches of three parallel in-street tracks at Indiana & Cermak, State & Pershing, Cottage Grove & Pershing, 64th Street between Stony Island and Harper, and on 12th at Laramie and Austin.

Page 239. Cermak-Lawndale line. Kimball-Homan buses replaced the streetcars on October 1, 1945.

Page 242. South Cicero line. South Cicero was a lightly patronized, single-track shuttle line. It was one of the first CSL streetcar lines converted to bus operation, and thus does not appear on the 1945 track map on page 345 as a streetcar line. However, a written record of CSL track as of June 1, 1941 says that the line was single track except for a double-track portion extending 302 feet north of the north line of 63rd Street. The switch shown in the photo of car 5177 is at the end of this double-track segment, just north of 63rd Street near the original Midway Airport terminal building.

Page 243. Trolley buses replaced streetcars completely on the Cicero Ave. route on November 25, 1951. From December 4, 1949, motor buses served the line on weekends until they were replaced by the trolley buses.

Aerial view shows one of the four transfer tables at CSL's West Shops. During its long life the Shops built and rebuilt streetcars as well as repairing and rebuilding trolley buses and repairing Lake Street "L" cars.

Page 245. Clark-Wentworth route. The official date of conversion for the Clark Street portion of the route north of Harrison Street was September 8, 1957. However, because of weekend bus operation on this line, the last streetcars had operated on the north portion of the through route early the preceding day.

Page 251. Caption for bottom photo. Standard Brill cars, the first PAYE cars to run in Chicago, once ran on Cottage Grove. They were replaced successively by the Nearsides, Peter Witts, and PCC cars. Old Pullmans, Odd 17 cars and cars from other series filled in the gaps left as the Nearsides deteriorated. Sun Parlors and Odd 17 cars were common in Cottage Grove-Broadway (TR 1) service. Still other car types, from the Stony Island line, shared the tracks on Cottage Grove.

Page 254. In 1979 there is still a rush-hour service (signed "76 Diversey via Wrightwood/Logan Sq. station") via Pulaski and Wrightwood. Diversey service to downtown Chicago was discontinued February 1, 1970.

Page 255. The Division-State-Van Buren route operated from the Kedzie and Division carhouses. Some Kedzie runs pulled out via Kedzie, Chicago, and California to start their trips from the Division Street end of the line.

Page 258. Grand Ave. On April 1, 1951, CTA substituted motor buses for all streetcar operation on Grand Ave. However, as on several other lines, the motor bus substitution was temporary. On December 16, 1951, trolley buses replaced motor buses on Grand Ave.

Fulton-21st Street line. The one car an hour route was via Harrison, Jefferson, 14th, and Canal southbound, and via 14th, Jefferson, Roosevelt, and Clinton northbound.

Page 259. Halsted-Downtown route. Subsequent to the November 20, 1947 routing of all Halsted-Downtown cars to a downtown loop via Clark, Illinois, Wells, Chicago, and Clark, the loop was shortened to operate via Clark, Illinois, Wells, Kinzie, and Clark.

Page 262. The photo at the top of the page was taken on Waveland Ave. east of Halsted St.

Page 264. Division, Crosby, Larrabee, Chicago is the correct diversion for Halsted cars. It was again in use at the end of service in 1954.

Page 266. Harrison Street, although located south of Madison Street, is really a West Side rather than a South Side line. After World War II, Harrison and Harrison-Adams almost always used the Flexible Flyers, some of which (the 1800s) were based at Kedzie. During the last few months there appeared higher-numbered cars of the same type which had been at North Avenue carhouse. The 1506 series were only occasionally operated on the Harrison lines, 6000s even less often. Available information suggests that there was indeed no service on Harrison west of Cicero from December 21, 1912 until November 13, 1914. Of course, the Metropolitan "L" served the area.

Homan Avenue. The correct name of this line is Kimball-Homan.

Page 269. Car 6053, inbound on the Harrison-Adams route, is shown crossing the Adams Street bridge into downtown Chicago. Wednesday evening was the major visiting night at Cook County Hospital, and certain runs were required to make additional trips on this evening. Tripper cars were not added for this purpose.

Page 272. Indiana Avenue line. Subsequent to the 1932 downtown re-routing, which brought the cars once more to the Garland Court loop, a new terminal loop was made via Harrison, State, Lake, and Wabash, eliminating Garland Court. After the weekday rush hour and midday cars were sent up to the Streeter Drive terminal in 1951, evening, Owl, and weekend cars continued to use the State-Lake loop.

Kedzie-California line. In the late 1940s, Kedzie and Kedzie-California used 3000 and 6000-series cars primar-

Northbound Western Avenue car stops at Western and Division, site of the old Chicago Railways carbarn. Though not of the most modern design, this barn could take 125 cars in closed storage, 37 cars in open.

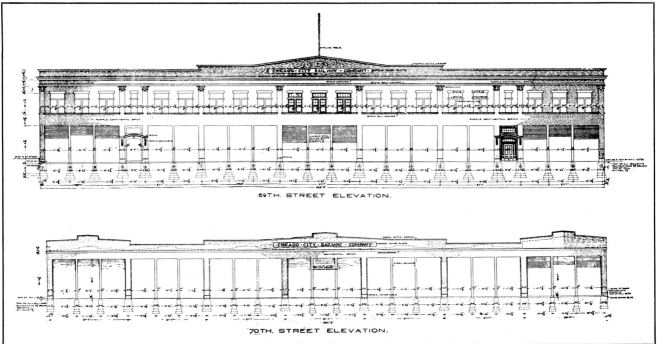

69TH. STREET ELEVATION.

70TH. STREET ELEVATION.

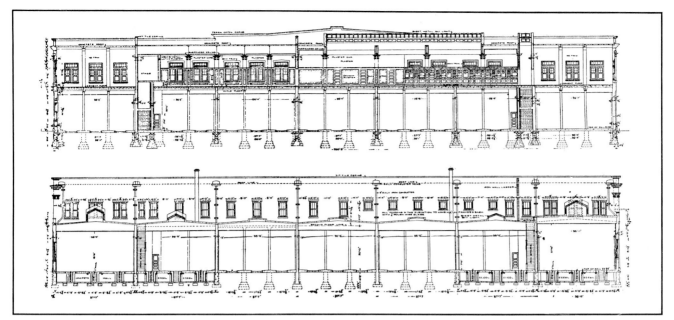

• Opposite page, top. Old Pullman 483 at the 69th Street end of the 69th & Ashland carhouse. • Opposite page, bottom. Plan shows 69th and 70th Street elevations of carhouse. • Above. Ashland carhouse had a club room for off-duty trainmen to relax in between runs. • Below. New Pullman and PCCs at 70th Street end.

• Opposite page, top. When the first trolley buses arrived in Chicago in 1930, the CSL carbarn at North and Cicero was selected as their home base. There was room to the west of the barn for an open storage area and an enclosed inspection and light repair facility (see pages 378 and 381). Here Turtleback 1633 shares the North and Lamon yard with some of the early trolley buses. George Krambles collection. • Opposite page, bottom. Air door Old Pullman 510 overhangs a transfer table pit at West Shops during the CTA era. Car 510 was rebuilt in 1921 for hauling trailers. • Above. To keep out bad weather, carhouses and shops were equipped with rolling steel doors, which can be seen behind car 5179 in this view. • Below. Although some cars were sold to scrap dealers and cut apart in their yards, many CSL cars were scrapped on the property. It looks as if car 2832 and its mate were carefully stripped of parts before burning.

438

• Opposite page, top. Three-section side dump car N-1 appears to be working as a locomotive in this photo, taken at South Shops yard. Coupled to a standard railroad flat car which is carrying one of the preserved Old Pullman cars, N-1 will perhaps haul the flatcar to the railroad interchange at 84th and Wentworth. • Opposite page, bottom. Car 1494 poses on the lead track in front of the Lawndale carbarn at 22nd and Ogden. Though closed by the CTA as an operating station in 1973, Lawndale is still in use as a training facility for shopmen, who have CTA's historic vehicle collection to work on as well as some modern buses. • Above. Elston shopmen spruce up their barn with flower boxes. • Below. Parade of four different vehicle types at South Shops.

• Above. For streetcar buffs, CSL's carhouses, shops, and yards were the place to find unusual vehicles. For example, the Archer-Rockwell carhouse was home to experimental car 5702. With its mate car 5701, this car was the Chicago City Railway's first trial of maximum traction trucks. They were Brill's 39-E model, with 34" and 22" wheels. Both cars were built in 1910 in CCRy's own shop, but 5701 was destroyed in the Archer barn fire of 1916. Car 5702 lasted until the early CTA era; it was scrapped in 1948. • Below. First of the Old Pullmans, car 101 rests at the North and Cicero barn yard. Because there were 600 cars in this series, and because they ran all over Chicago for nearly 50 years, the Old Pullmans became the symbol of the Surface Lines for many passengers. They were large, powerful, dependable cars which could buck drifts of snow that would keep more modern cars in the carhouse during winter storms.

ily, with the 1506 type occasionally and some 1800s at the end of the decade. The air-door 3091 ran here although trainmen avoided it when possible, as a commonly held myth claimed that continual use of the doors would deplete brake pressure. In 1954, service on Kedzie-California ended with Big Pullmans. Motor buses replaced all streetcar operation on May 29, 1954. However, Kedzie-California was converted to trolley bus operation on December 4, 1955, and was the last trolley bus line inaugurated in Chicago.

Page 274. Bottom photo. CSL 6084 is operating on Through Route 17, Kedzie, not Kedzie-California.

Pages 275 & 319. Buses 2390 (p. 275) and 3564 (p. 319) were both delivered to the CTA after October 1, 1947, although both were ordered by the CSL and were to be owned by the CCRy. Thus both photos date from the early CTA years rather than from the CSL era.

Page 276. Lincoln Avenue. It was the remaining North Side local service on Lincoln Ave. that was replaced on February 18, 1951. Lincoln-Indiana through cars continued to run for three more weeks. (See Lincoln-Indiana route description.)

Page 278. Caption for top photo. Lincoln-Indiana cars used the Wabash Ave. bridge across the Chicago River after the State Street bridge across the Chicago River was closed for replacement for nearly 12 years.

Pages 280 & 306. Fifth Avenue never had cable cars. See Hilton, *The Cable Car in America,* for the Chicago cable routes. Fifth Ave. began with horse cars May 22, 1893, and was electrified in May, 1896. There was no through service to downtown until August 19, 1906.

The loop line of the Cicero & Proviso Street Railway originated at Madison & Springfield, terminal of the Madison cable, and operated via Madison to Cicero, then both ways around the Cicero, Lake, Pine, Lake, Harlem, and Madison loop.

On the major streets (or those the City Council considered major), many Through Routes overlapped the same portion of the street. The idea of the Through Routes was to provide a one-fare, one-car ride between various portions of the city. Thus for a while in 1911 and 1912, cars on Madison Street went downtown (T.R. 20), downtown and then south on State Street (T.R. 7), and north on Halsted (T.R. 18).

At Madison & Desplaines the specialwork arrangement was changed sometime in 1951 so that a curve was available for the eastbound cars to turn from Desplaines to Washington. These cars were the last to operate regularly through the Washington Street Tunnel. The service was rerouted effective January 24, 1953 because Desplaines Street was made one-way southbound. As the 24th was a Saturday, the first streetcars to use the new route via Franklin operated January 26.

Page 282. Bottom photo. The last of the 83 PCCs became available for Madison service in February, 1937. In the mid-1940s, they were supplemented with 24 Peter Witts (scattered numbers in the 3322-3381 group) which were also assigned to Kedzie carhouse. They operated both to Madison-Austin and to Fifth-Pulaski as many runs made consecutive trips on both branches. However, they were all in the barn by about 8 pm each day, leaving the street to the PCCs.

On Madison Street the folding seat was usually in place across the single center door, unlike the practice on Clark-Wentworth where all doors were used.

Experimental cars 4001 and 7001 were also at Kedzie but in storage, seldom used by this time.

Page 283. Caption for bottom photo. Further research has determined that the postwar PCC car was on a pull-in run to the Kedzie-Van Buren barn. Madison Street cars which pulled in on westbound trips regularly operated via Fifth Avenue to Kedzie rather than turning left at Madison & Kedzie.

Page 284. Fifth Avenue Sunday service was a shuttle as indicated in the text, but in the 1940s was operated two-man using 1800-series cars, or occasionally a 6000. Three cars were required.

Page 286. The photo at the top of the page was taken at Milwaukee and Armitage, with car 4051 inbound.

Page 289. The service information on Noble is from the 1966 CTA publication *Historical Information.* The transfer illustrated in Johnson, *A Century of Chicago Streetcars,* page 20 is years newer although it was not issued from the Noble line. The only consistent explanation would be if the Noble service was suspended during the Depression with the expectation that it would be resumed when times were better, hence transfers were provided for it. Laramie, Noble, So. Cicero were minor lines which were grouped on trip-type transfers from their inception on October 1, 1932.

Page 298. Roosevelt Road was another major streetcar route which was converted to motor bus operation and later re-converted to trolley bus operation. On the main route between Austin and Wabash, motor buses took over on August 12, 1951. On May 24, 1953, this portion of the line was converted to trolley bus.

Page 302. South Chicago-Ewing. On October 7, 1941, runs via Indianapolis were discontinued, but some evidence indicates that they were soon reinstated with cars in the 6199-6220 series going straight through from the State Line (106th and Indianapolis) to 63rd and South Park. A rider on the cars has confirmed the restoration of through service for the years 1943 and 1944. According to Joe L. Diaz, who was a trainman at Kedzie, in April, 1945 cars 6000-6015 were sent to Burnside to be used as one-man cars on the South Chicago-Ewing line, and were replaced at Kedzie by 16 of the 5001-5200 series from some other barn. Those 5000s were then used on Kedzie and Kedzie-California.

Pages 302 & 313. S. Chicago-Ewing and Windsor Park lines. The 108th Street track seems to have had service

441

only when it suited operating convenience. The Roby line of the Calumet Electric Street Railway was extended over 108th Street on May 20, 1896. It was cut off by closure of the 95th Street bridge over the Calumet River on October 14, 1898 and/or collapse of the bridge on August 17, 1899. The line was discontinued on March 30, 1908 because of the merger with the South Chicago City Railway. Windsor Park service started here about a year later, on March 19, 1909, but only to Avenue F, not across the railroad tracks and onward to Roby. However, the July 1913 routings indicate the terminal to be Ewing & 108th, not 108th & F. A 1915 routing again shows service to 108th & F. Service was eliminated effective April 10, 1927. South Chicago-Ewing cars (successor to the Whiting-East Chicago route) began operating via 108th instead of 106th on June 9, 1940 (or in 1941?). Service finally ceased effective April 8, 1945 with the reroute to 118th & Burley.

There was little residential development in this area, especially so at a distance from Ewing, and what traffic there was could perhaps be as well served by the lines on 106th and on Ewing. Along 108th neither the tracks nor the pavement were constructed to the usual standard, with the tracks being largely along the north edge of the roadway.

Until the 1945 change, Ewing & 108th was a necessary transfer point for many riders although a natural location of traffic for only a few. A "Transfer Corner Tap," or bar of some similar name, catered to passengers and car crews who found themselves at this improbable point.

Page 306. State Street as far as 63rd was a cable line as early as May 1887, and was electrified July 22, 1906.

From 64th to Vincennes (at 68th) it was used by 69th Street horse cars and electrified January 14, 1895. On August 9, 1902 at least some cars of this line were removed from State Street and run to 68th & Cottage Grove instead, although a 1906 source indicates some cars still operating up State Street.

Between 71st and 81st, State Street was part of the route of the Englewood & Chicago Electric Street Railway (a Chicago & Interurban Traction predecessor). Battery cars were operated effective June 20, 1896 from Vernon & 63rd terminal via Vernon, 67th, Vincennes (now Eberhart), South Chicago, 71st, State, 79th, Vincennes, 81st, Halsted, Summit, Vincennes to 88th and subsequently beyond. By May 1899 the route was via 81st instead of 79th west of State. The line was subsequently worked by trolley cars and was discontinued March 1, 1912, but the tracks on certain portions including State Street were retained. The best published coverage of this line is in Buckley, *Chicago & Interurban Traction Company* (CERA Bulletin 93).

On Michigan south of 95th, streetcar service began May 30, 1892. These cars operated from Cottage Grove & 72nd to Michigan & 109th, and were subsequently extended.

The gap between 63rd and 64th Streets resulted from the level crossing with the Pittsburg Ft. Wayne & Chicago and Lake Shore & Michigan Southern (now Conrail). Cars from the south were extended to 63rd after the railroads were elevated. The gap between

Vincennes and 71st was closed September 6, 1912 when the State Street cars (operating from Lake Street) were extended to State & 79th although some of the cars by July 1913 were operating to Vincennes & Wentworth instead. The gap between 81st and 95th was filled with new track in 1918; on August 12 the State Street cars (now operating from Division & Wells) were extended all the way to the West Pullman loop via State, 95th, Michigan, 119th, replacing the Cottage Grove cars in West Pullman service. Along part of the section new in 1918, Bates expanded steel line poles were used, one of their few applications in Chicago.

Page 309. The early Sedgwick, Sheffield and Larrabee lines all served what is now the Near North Side, and were involved in routes over some of the same streets at different times.

The Sedgwick route was inaugurated in 1861 with horse cars between Sedgwick & North and Clark & Carroll via Sedgwick, Division and Clark. In 1863 it was extended to Sedgwick & Center (now Armitage). In 1882 the route was extensively changed, operating from a downtown terminal via Wells, Chicago, Orleans, Division, Sedgwick, Lincoln, Garfield (now Dickens), Racine, Center (now Armitage), Sedgwick, Chicago, and Wells back downtown. In 1887 the downtown terminal became Dearborn & Polk and was reached via Orleans, Kinzie, and Dearborn, with the route north of Chicago Avenue unchanged.

The service was electrified June 6, 1895, and operated only between Sedgwick & Center (now Armitage) and Dearborn & Washington. In 1896 it was again extended to Racine using the same loop as in 1882. By 1902 it was routed off Dearborn onto Clark, terminating at Clark & Washington. By 1905 it was back on Dearborn, terminating at Dearborn & Polk, and hauled by horses south of Dearborn & Lake. The Dearborn portion was electrified in July, 1906. The north loop was changed September 10, 1914 to Sedgwick, Lincoln, Fullerton, Racine, Webster, Lincoln, and Sedgwick.

Effective September 14, 1924, the Sedgwick portion of the route was combined into the Taylor-Sedgwick-Sheffield line, while the north loop was operated via Racine, Webster, Lincoln, Fullerton, Racine (one way) as the Webster-Racine line. On March 13, 1927 this service ceased to be a loop and cars operated both ways via Racine and Webster.

The Sheffield route was inaugurated in March, 1889 with horse cars between Sheffield & Clark and Sheffield & Lincoln. Gas cars were substituted by April, 1893, and electric cars effective October 8, 1894. In 1906 the route was extended via Lincoln, Center (now Armitage), Clark, Wells, and Harrison to the State Street crossover.

Effective July 20, 1914, the route was combined into the Taylor-Wells-Sheffield line, operating via Wells, Polk, Canal, and Taylor to the Western crossover. It was rerouted June 7, 1919 via Taylor instead of Polk. One-man operation began August 9, 1924, the closest approach of one-man cars to the city center at that early date, and ceased the following month when the line was rerouted to include the Sedgwick service area.

The Larrabee route was inaugurated in 1864 with horse cars between Larrabee & Center (now Armitage) and Larrabee & Chicago. In 1872 it was extended to Larrabee & Lincoln. It was electrified as "Larrabee-Market St." effective May 25, 1895 and extended to operate from Clark & Lake via Clark, Kinzie, Market (now Orleans), Chicago, Larrabee, Lincoln, Fullerton, Racine, Webster, Larrabee and back to Clark & Lake over the reverse route. The downtown terminus was later Clark & Washington. In 1906 the middle part of the route was rerouted via Kinzie, Franklin, Erie, Kingsbury, and Chicago. Effective July 13, 1906 a downtown loop was made via Kinzie, Dearborn, Washington, and Clark. This route was combined into the Riverview-Larrabee line effective July 20, 1914.

Van Buren St. While through cars ran to Division Street, local Van Buren Street cars normally looped via Clinton, Adams, Dearborn, and Van Buren as indicated in the text. However, some trips were signed "Washington-State" and looped via Dearborn, Washington, State, and Van Buren. Also, several cars in the rush hours were kept busy on a Union Station shuttle loop between Dearborn and Clinton or Desplaines Streets.

Page 312. Whiting-East Chicago line. Service into Chicago over the tracks of the South Chicago City Railway Company, a CSL predecessor, began on May 15, 1896.

Page 312. Abandonment of streetcar service on the Indiana side was precipitated by a sewer project in the Robertsdale area of Hammond (around Indianapolis & Calumet).

Page 315. The 47th Street line was operated by trolley bus effective March 12, 1952.

Page 317. Caption for top photo. The photo was taken at 36th Street and Kedzie Ave., not 36th and California.

Page 320. 51st-55th Street line. The track along 55th Street remained in use for Cottage Grove-55th cars, the South Side successor to TR 1, until August 1, 1947. 51st-55th Street was operated by trolley bus effective June 20, 1948. By this time the streetcar tracks had been removed along 55th Street while motor buses were detouring on 56th (one of the last cases in Chicago where the tracks were bodily removed rather than just covered over). The 51st Street portion was later resurfaced, half of its width at a time, with some shifting of the wire positions so that the trolley buses could operate during the course of the work.

Page 327. 111th St. line. As of June 1, 1941, all of 111th Street east of Vincennes, as well as all of the Hegewisch line and all of the Riverdale line were C&SC track.

Page 328. 115th Street line. King Drive is the current name for South Park Ave.

Page 332. Map. The track map reproduced on pages 334 to 343 was issued by the CTA in November, 1948, rather than in December, 1949.

70th Street never operated as it was still incomplete, although begun in 1895, when the C&SC merger took place in 1908. The 73rd Street line was an adequate alternative.

The line between 68th & Yates and Coles & 75th opened in late 1892 with two routes: via Cheltenham, Commercial to 93rd (later extended via 92nd, Ewing to 106th), and via 79th, Ontario (now Brandon), 83rd, Superior (now Burley), 87th, Buffalo, 92nd, Commercial, Notre Dame (now Commercial), 104th, and Torrence to 106th (later extended via 106th to Indianapolis). However, about 1894 or 1895 these lines were both rerouted via Stony Island, 75th and replaced with a shuttle car to 68th & Yates. It apparently operated sporadically. The track was retired on the books April 22, 1908.

Page 333. Map. On July 10, 1892 the Cottage Grove line of the Calumet Electric Street Railway was extended to the Kensington loop. By 1895 the loop was operated as a separate line on 115th, Howard (now Prairie), Kensington, Michigan (direction not known). Later it was a shuttle on 115th between Michigan and Front, still later between Michigan and South Park (now King). All of 115th was C&SC track as of June 1, 1941.

In 1892 or 1893 some cars of the Cottage Grove line were extended to loop via 116th, Wentworth, 119th, and Michigan. On April 4, 1896 the route was extended to 119th & Halsted. The southbound cars were rerouted via Michigan and 119th following the northbound route, probably in 1902.

The 93rd Street line operated to 89th & The Strand (now O) beginning in 1891, initially via 93rd, Harbor, and Mackinaw, later via 93rd, Erie, 91st, and Mackinaw, finally on March 24, 1910 via 92nd and Buffalo.

Page 355. The 111th Street line west of Vincennes was CCRy track purchased by them from the Chicago & Southern Traction Company (predecessor of C&IT).

Page 367. Lines Assigned to Various Carbarns: 1947-1948. Under Burnside add 93rd-95th. Under Lawndale change to Taylor-Sedgwick-Sheffield.

Page 367. Foster Extension bus service began October 28, 1946, although the street had service as part of the Harlem line beginning October 2, 1945.

North Park garage opened May 28, 1950 and initially issued the Skokie, Touhy, North California, Kedzie-Homan, North Western, Devon, North Damen, Kimball, Clybourn and North Pulaski lines.

Pages 379 & 383. The 210 trolley buses announced in 1945 were ordered prior to the CTA takeover on October 1, 1947, but there was no authorization for expenditure (AFE) prior to the takeover date. For a reason now unknown, these trolley buses were ordered in reverse numerical order. The first to be ordered were 369-412 from St. Louis Car Co. on July 18, 1946. The contract approval for buses 323-367 from Pullman came

November 15, 1946. The last ordered were 203-322 from ACF-Brill on June 13, 1947.

It is thought that the lowest 100 numbers (203-302) were allocated to the Chicago Railways, and the remaining 110 numbers (303-412) were assigned to the Chicago City Railway. All 210 were delivered in 1948. The 45 St. Louis buses appeared in March and April, the 120 ACF-Brills in the middle of the year, and the 45 Pullman buses arrived in November and December. All 210 coaches had 44 seats. The 45 Pullmans and the 45 St. Louis-built coaches had GE electrical equipment; the 120 ACF-Brills had Westinghouse electrical equipment.

Page 379. The postwar trolley buses under their CTA numbers were:

9203-9322	ACF-Brill, 1948	44 seats
9323-9367	Pullman-Standard, 1948	44 seats
9368-9412	St. Louis, 1948	44 seats
9413-9761	Marmon-Herrington, 1951-52	49 seats
9762	ACF-Brill, 1950	48 seats
9763 (Articulated)	Twin Coach, 1948	58 seats

Page 382. Bottom photo. This photo was not taken in Chicago. It is an ACF builder's photo taken on the Detroit Street Railway's Plymouth Road trolley coach line in Detroit. The date is November 14, 1930. ACF's bus building facilities were located in Detroit at this time. ACF reportedly built only three Model E-1 coaches like this, two for CSL and one for Brooklyn & Queens Transit. Both ACF and Yellow Coach occasionally tested new trolley coaches on the Plymouth Road line.

Page 383. Diversey line. The 1935 extension was for a distance of 1.25 miles (2.5 miles round trip).

Kimball Avenue line. The line operated as a trolley bus route between June 21, 1931 through the close of schedules on June 30, 1937.

Page 386. In the photo at the top of the page, trolley bus 177 is eastbound at Diversey and Parkside.

Page 389. There was no such bus as 2606; the last bus was 2605 in this series.

Buses 6401-6410 were GM TG-4007 models, not GM TG-4006 as shown in the table.

Page 402. See correction to page 61 in this new series of page corrections for new data on the construction dates of the Matchbox cars (1101-1423).

Correction to page 94. The car series was 3262-3321.

Page 406. Correction to page 232. Buckley, *The Evanston Railway Co.* (ERHS Bulletin 28) covers the Evanston service. He says that in the 1920s, the rental of several CSL cars was on the day of the big picnic each year.

Page 407. Kedzie-California route, page 272. Further evidence of through operation via Kedzie, Chicago, and California at an early date is a Chicago Union Traction (CUT) transfer form placed in use February 1, 1900, which lists a route named "Kedzie & California."

Kedzie-California was a CUT route, although it used some CCT tracks which are not on the front endsheet map.

The W. Chicago Avenue line of CCT operated from Harlem & Lake to 48th Avenue & Lake via Chicago. It did not connect with the other Chicago Avenue services, which operated only as far west as 40th Avenue.

Page 415. Lines Assigned to Various Carbarns: 1931-1932. Under Limits Depot add Through Route 1 (Cottage Grove-Broadway), to clarify entry reading "Broadway & Through Route." Kimball trolley buses were housed on-line, but the administrative functions were handled at Elston depot. The buses could be towed or run on the streetcar tracks and wire (see page 384) when it was necessary to transfer them.

Page 416. Note 5 to table. The Chicago Transit Authority took over the operations of the Chicago Surface Lines and the Chicago Rapid Transit Company on October 1, 1947.

Chicago Local Transportation: 1837-1947

To aid in understanding the tangled legal and political background of public transit in Chicago, the following chronology has been prepared covering the years 1837-1947. In 1837 Chicago was incorporated; in 1947 the Chicago Transit Authority took over the property and operations of the Chicago Surface Lines. Starting in the mid-1920s the history of the Surface Lines becomes so complex that as a further aid to understanding the equipment orders in this period, they have been explained in detail in the chronology itself. In addition, a series of tables prepared by Zenon Hansen is presented on pages 463-466. The tables explain the bus and PCC car orders by series, date ordered, builder, model number, underlying owner, and year delivered, from 1927 to 1947.

March 4, 1837. Chicago incorporated. On March 4, 1837, the City of Chicago, with a population of about 4,200 was incorporated by a special Act of Legislature.

March, 1856. First street railway ordinance passed. First ordinance for street railroad, passed by the City Council; granted to Roswell B. Mason, Charles B. Phillips, and others. The rates of fare were not to exceed five cents for any distance less than one mile, and not to exceed ten cents for any distance more than one mile within the city limits. Nothing was ever done under this ordinance.

July 19, 1858. Second street railway ordinance passed. Second ordinance passed; granted to Henry Fuller, Franklin Parmelee, and Liberty Bigelow. This measure was vetoed by Mayor John C. Haynes because it virtually granted a perpetual franchise to the grantees in case the city did not purchase the lines at the end of twenty-five years.

August 16, 1858. Third street railway ordinance passed. Third ordinance passed, and the first under which by aid of the legislature operation was begun; granted to Henry Fuller, Franklin Parmelee and Liberty Bigelow. The rights under this measure were subsequently affirmed to them by the legislature under the name of Chicago City Railway Company. Under this ordinance, since enlarged and modified, were constructed the principal street-railway systems of the south and west sides. Rights on the streets in the west division of the city were later deeded to the Chicago West Division Railway Company. The life of the grant was for twenty-five years and contained a "purchase by the city" clause.

Laying of tracks under the terms of this measure, however, was held up by an injunction secured in the Circuit Court on a plea that the City Council had no right to grant the use of the city's streets for railway purposes. It was contended that right rested in the legislature. This brought the question squarely before the law-making body of the state and the following year brought the solution.

February 14, 1859. Chicago City Railway Co. and North Chicago City Railway Co. incorporated. Incorporation of the Chicago City Railway Company and the North Chicago City Railway Company for a period of twenty-five years; the Chicago City Railway Company in this Act of incorporation secured all those rights and privileges contained in the ordinance passed by the council August 16, 1858. The rights of the company to the use of the streets named in the grant were affirmed, subject however to all the terms and conditions of the ordinance. The Act further gave the right to the company, under the law of Eminent Domain to extend its railway to any point or points in Cook County. The incorporation of the North Chicago Street Railway Company was provided for in Section 10 of the same Act, the same details and obligations being imposed upon this company as upon the Chicago City Railway Company. No streets were named in this Act. The designation of such thoroughfares was left to the City Council; the rights granted covering the City of Chicago and County of Cook for a period of twenty-five years. Incorporators: William B. Ogden, John B. Turner, Charles V. Dyer, James H. Rees, Valentine C. Tyrney.

May 23, 1859. Ordinance passed giving to the Chicago City Railway Company the right to occupy for street-railway purposes certain streets named in the ordinance "during all the term in the Act of February 14, 1859, specified and prescribed."

February 21, 1861. Chicago West Division Railway Co. incorporated. Incorporation of the Chicago West Division Railway Company for the term of twenty-five years; the incorporators being Edward B. Ward, William K. McAllister, Samuel B. Walker, James L. Wilson, Charles V. Brown, Nathaniel P. Wilder. This company's charter expressly prohibited it from constructing or using any tracks in the north division of the city without first getting the written consent of the North Chicago

City Railway Company. This charter expressly licensed it to acquire or enjoy any rights or privileges granted to the Chicago City Railway Company on the south and west sides.

July 30, 1863. Chicago West Division Railway Co. acquires rights on west side. All rights of the Chicago City Railway Company in and to the streets of the west division of the city acquired from it by the Chicago West Division Railway Company for the sum of $300,000; construction of certain operating equipment and rights to construct and operate railways in certain designated streets in the business district of the south side were included in the sale. The three corporations mentioned, shortly after this date, mutually pledged themselves to protect each other. They became entrenched in their respective territories each charging a rate of fare of five cents for a single ride on any of its lines. The original ordinance of August 16, 1858, and the Act of February 15, 1859, which later passed to the Chicago City Railway Company for rights on the south and west sides, provided for the fare of five cents for any distance within the city limits. When the division of the territory was made, however, through the $300,000 purchases, already mentioned, this provision was disregarded. A similar condition later arose between the north and west sides. This problem later was taken into the courts with the result that the company was obliged to issue and accept transfers between lines operating on the north and west sides of the city.

In some of the articles passed prior to February 6, 1865, there was no expressed provision and no reference as to time limit of previous ordinances—for instance the ordinances of February 18, 1861, and August 22, 1864. There was no expressed provision of time limit in the ordinances of August 22, 1864, and July 11, 1864, to the Chicago West Division Railway Company, but the grant was made subject to the conditions and regulations concerning other railway tracks in the City of Chicago. The ordinance of August 17, 1864, to the same company made a grant subject to the ordinance then in force respecting the railways in the south and west divisions. In the ordinance passed May 23, 1859, by which the North Chicago City Railway Company first acquired the right to occupy certain streets, it was provided that those rights and privileges were "to continue and be in force for the benefit of said company for the full term of twenty-five years and no longer." A supplemental ordinance was passed December 17, 1860, which presumably was intended to carry with it the time limitation. Subsequent ordinances to the same company passed January 18 and August 11, 1864, contained provisions making the grants therein named subject to the rules, limitations, restrictions, conditions, rights and privileges mentioned in the ordinance of May 23, 1859.

January 4, 1865. 99-year Act introduced. First appearance in the legislature of the so-called 99-year Act. It came up in the form of House Bill No. 66—"an Act concerning the horse railways in Chicago." The bill was referred to the committee on banks and corporations. This Act amended the corporation Acts of companies, extending their duration to ninety-nine years. The bill was passed January 20, 1865.

February 4, 1865. Veto of 99-year Act. Veto by Governor Richard J. Oglesby of the 99-year-Act.

February 6, 1865. Passage of 99-year Act. Passage of the 99-year Act over the governor's veto by a vote of 55 to 22 in the House and 18 to 5 in the Senate.

August 8, 1870. New constitution in effect. New constitution went into effect which provided that "no law shall be passed by the General Assembly granting the right to construct and operate street railroads within any city, town, or incorporated village without acquiring the consent of the local authorities having control of the road or highway proposed to be occupied by said railroad."

July 1, 1874. "The Horse and Dummy Act". "The Horse and Dummy Act" passed; required the consent of the local authorities for the location or construction of any street railroad and provided that such consent should not thereafter be granted for a longer period than twenty years. This Act was later amended by a bill hereinafter referred to and known as the "Allen bill," which was later repealed.

April 23, 1875. Adoption of the new charter for the City of Chicago; authorized the city to permit, regulate, and prohibit the locating, constructing, and laying of a track of any horse railroad in any street, alley, or public place; but such permission not to be for longer than twenty years.

March 18, 1878. $50 car license fee. Annual license fee of $50 a car established by ordinance.

1882. First appearance of cable on South Side. Up to this year only animal power was used for the propulsion of street cars, but during this year the cable system of mechanical operation of cars was put in service by the Chicago City Railway Company upon its State Street and Cottage Grove Avenue lines.

February 12, 1883. Incorporation of Chicago Passenger Railway Company.

1883. Ordinances begin to expire. During this year a large number of ordinances granted for twenty-five years expired. The Act of July 1, 1874, and the new city charter of 1875 governed subsequent ordinances, but there remained the question of the legal effect of the 99-year-Act upon the original grants, and the question came before the City Council in this year for a decision.

July 30th of this year a compromise ordinance was passed granting the three companies an extension of time upon all of their then existing lines in the city until July 30, 1903. This ordinance carried with it an annual car-license fee of $50.00 to be paid to the city for each car operated 365 days.

March, 1886. Charles T. Yerkes and his associates obtained control of the North Chicago City Railway Company by purchasing a majority of the stock of that company.

March 18, 1886. North Chicago Street Railroad Co. incorporated. The North Chicago Street Railroad Company was incorporated and a lease of all of the property of the North Chicago City Railway Company was made to the new company for a period of 999 years.

June, 1886. North Side Cable. The North Chicago City Railway Company, which had used only animal motive power up to this time, was authorized to equip all of its lines with cable power, and under this grant North Clark Street, Wells Street, Lincoln and Clybourn Avenues were successively equipped with cable power between the years 1886 and 1889.

June 18, 1887. Charles T. Yerkes and his associates secured control of the Chicago West Division Railway Company by purchasing a majority of the stock of that company.

July 19, 1887. West Chicago Street Railroad Co. incorporated. Incorporation of the West Chicago Street Railroad Company, which took a lease of the property of the Chicago West Division Railway Company for 999 years, and also took a lease on the Chicago Passenger Railway Company in May, 1888, for a period of 99 years.

February 12, 1888. West Side cable. The Chicago West Division Railway Company and the Chicago Passenger Railway Company, authorized by ordinance to install cable power; under this ordinance there were constructed the Milwaukee Avenue, Madison Street, Blue Island Avenue and Halsted Street cable lines in the five years following.

1893. First overhead trolley. The Chicago City Railway Company installed the first overhead trolley system in the city. This was followed by those installed by the West Chicago Street Railway Company and North Chicago City Railway Company. (Editor's note: In 1890 the Calumet Electric Street Railway became the first Chicago-area line to electrify with overhead wires.)

February 17, 1897. Humphrey bills introduced. Introduction of the Humphrey bills in the state legislature.

No. 148 provided for the establishment of a state commission, appointed by the governor, which should have practically exclusive control of all street and elevated railways in the state.

No. 149 provided that ordinances of all street railways in actual operation on the first Tuesday in September, 1897, should be extended forty years upon payment by the companies of $2,000 per mile in counties whose population exceeded 100,000 inhabitants and $500 per mile in counties whose population was less than 100,000 inhabitants.

This payment not to be annually, but once made was to cover the entire period.

No. 150 provided for the annual payment by the companies to the state treasurer of two percent of the gross earnings of the road for the year last preceding, two-thirds of which might, under certain conditions, be paid by the state treasurer to the city, town or village in which the lines of the corporation were located.

No. 148 was passed.

Nos. 149 and 150 were amended and combined in a new bill known as No. 258.

No. 258. Section 6 extended the power to grant franchises from twenty to fifty years.

Section 7 provided that every street-railway ordinance

then in force should be extended for a period of fifty years from and after the first Tuesday in September, 1907. It provided, further, that the street-railway corporations, in whose favor such ordinances had been passed, should have the right to charge during the life of the extended ordinance five cents for each passenger for a continuous ride for the distance or distances specified in the ordinance so extended.

The only condition imposed was that each corporation should make the following payments:

In counties not exceeding 100,000 population, 1% of gross receipts.

In counties exceeding 100,000 but not exceeding 200,000 population, 2% of gross receipts.

In counties exceeding 200,000 population, 3% of gross receipts for the first fifteen years; 5% for the next twenty years, and 7% for the next fifteen years.

May 12, 1897. Defeat of the Humphrey bills in the House.

June 4, 1897. Allen Law passed. Allen Law passed by the Senate and the House.

June 9, 1897. Governor Tanner signed Allen Law. Allen Law approved by Governor John R. Tanner. The Allen Bill was an Act to amend the title and sections 1 and 3 of the Act known as the "Horse and Dummy Railroad Act," approved July 1, 1874.

The Allen Law was drafted with a view to giving the companies distinct advantages which they did not before possess. It amended the old law, which fixed the period of the life of franchises at twenty (20) years, by permitting the city authorities to grant franchises for the period of (50) years and fixed the rate of fare for the first twenty (20) years thereof at five cents. It permitted non-competing companies to consolidate. It sought to bring about a condition which amounted to the exclusion of all competition by prohibiting "the use of the tracks of any company by any other company without the former's consent in so far as it is impracticable to construct new lines in the business district." The bill contained no provision for a state commission and did not seek to extend the ordinances then in force.

October 13, 1897. "Harlan" committee appointed. Appointment of a special Committee of the City Council of Chicago to report upon street-railway franchises and operation; this Committee was composed of Mayor Carter H. Harrison, ex-officio chairman, John M. Harlan, William Jackson, Adolphus T. Maltby, William T. Maypole, and George E. Hooker, secretary.

March 28, 1898. "Harlan" report. The "Harlan" report submitted containing a comprehensive résumé of the financial conditions of the various street-railroad companies, the ordinances under which they were operated, and general information of the conditions of transportation throughout the city.

December 5, 1898. "Lyman 50-year" franchise ordinance introduced. Introduction in the City Council by William H. Lyman of an ordinance extending for a period of fifty years the rights under all ordinances granted prior to July 1, 1897, to all street-railway com-

panies; no provisions for improved service, through routes, unified service, etc. Simultaneously with this measure were proposed the Kimbell ordinance extending the same grants to December 31, 1946, and the Hermann ordinance extending the same rights twenty years. All were placed on file six days after the Allen Law was repealed.

January 23, 1899. City Council declaration against Allen Law. The City Council passed a resolution, January 23, 1899, declaring that the Allen Law should be repealed.

January 28, 1899. Incorporation of the Chicago Consolidated Traction Company.

March 7, 1899. Allen Law repealed. The legislature, on March 7, 1899, passed an act repealing the Allen law and leaving cities with power to make street railway grants not to exceed 20 years.

May 24, 1899. C. U. T. Co. incorporated. Incorporation of the Chicago Union Traction Company.

June 1, 1899. Union Traction leases. Consolidation of the lines of the North Chicago Street Railroad and West Chicago Street Railroad companies and their operation by the Chicago Union Traction Company under leases.

December 1, 1899. Consolidated Traction Co. The Chicago Consolidated Traction Company, incorporated January 28, 1899, to take over the outlying North and West side companies, entered into a so-called operating agreement for fifty years with the Union Traction Company, this agreement bearing date December 1, 1899. The effect of this operating agreement, which dealt with both operating and financial relations between the two companies, was to give the Union Traction Company control of the Consolidated Traction Company. Instead of extending the lines of the existing North and West side systems, the Yerkes management had organized independent companies to develop feed lines, some of which extended beyond the city limits, and a certain degree of community of financial interest existed between these companies and the existing North and West side systems. The following were the seven companies thus combined into the Chicago Consolidated Traction Company: Chicago Electric Transit, Chicago & Jefferson Urban, Cicero & Proviso (consolidated), Evanston Electric, North Chicago Electric, North Side Electric and Ogden Street Railway Company.

December 18, 1899. Street Railway Commission created. Resolution passed by the City Council providing for special committee of seven, subsequently known as the Street Railway Commission, composed of Milton J. Foreman, Ernst F. Hermann, William S. Jackson, William F. Brennan, Walter J. Raymer, William Mavor, William E. Schlake, and George C. Sikes, Secretary.

December 17, 1900. Report of Street Railway Commission. The Street Railway Commission made its report to the City Council December 17, 1900, discussing questions of policy and submitting an enabling street railway bill for presentation to the legislature. This bill was later approved by the council and introduced in both houses of the General Assembly, but never was reported out of committee.

May 20, 1901. Local Transportation Committee appointed. Creation of the Local Transportation Committee by the City Council, outgrowth of the Harlan Committee and the Street Railway Commission. Nine members: Mayor ex-officio member; Frank I. Bennett, chairman; William S. Jackson, Milton J. Foreman, Ernst F. Hermann, William Mavor, William F. Brennan, Francis D. Connery, John Minwegen; membership later was increased to thirteen members. This Committee was an outgrowth of a recommendation made by the Street Railway Commission.

December 11, 1901. The new Committee on Local Transportation made its first report; outlined ordinance.

April 1, 1902. First vote on municipal ownership. First vote on municipal ownership by the City of Chicago of all street railroads within the corporate limits of said city:

For	142,826
Against	27,998
Total	170,824

May 26, 1902. Ordinance passed by the City Council authorizing the Mayor and City Comptroller to make and execute a contract with Bion J. Arnold for the rendering of services as expert engineer in furnishing information, estimates, and opinions, and in the preparation of a general report for that Committee in relation to the cost of operation and earnings of any traction company or companies.

November 19, 1902. Arnold Report. The Arnold Report submitted to the Committee on Local Transportation; in his report Mr. Arnold said that Chicago should be regarded as one city—not three—and that divisional lines should be obliterated as far as possible. He recommended the "One City, One Fare" idea, and that routes through the business district should be substituted for down-town terminals wherever possible. Two plans for a subway system were outlined in this report. Plan No. 1 provided for three north and south subways from Indiana Street on the north to 14th Street on the south, and two subways entering the business district from the west side and looping back at Clark Street. Plan No. 2, the one recommended, provided practically for the same north and south high-level subway in combination with three or more low-level subways for the west side passing under the north and south subways and reaching Michigan Avenue. He also recommended the removal of the tops of the river tunnels in the interests of navigation. A new reorganized, unified and combined subway street-railway system was also planned comprising the lines of the Chicago City Railway Company, Chicago Union Traction Company, Chicago General Railway Company, and the Chicago Consolidated Traction Company within the city limits with all the new necessary and proper connections of all parts of the proposed system. The report further stated that the operation of cars in Chicago by the electric conduit system was practicable and feasible. The report consists of 310 pages of comprehensive discussion and details, a series of fourteen maps, and a large number of charts, diagrams and tables setting forth the text.

January, 1903 and February, 1903. Negotiations opened for franchise renewal.

May 18, 1903. Mueller Law. Mueller Law passed by the legislature and signed by the governor.

It was drafted by Walter L. Fisher, assisted by George C. Sikes; introduced in Senate by Carl Mueller January 12, 1903; finally passed and approved by the governor May 18, 1903; in force July 1, 1903.

It provides that every city in the state shall have the power to own, construct, purchase, and operate street railways within its corporate limits and to lease the same, or any part thereof, to any company incorporated under the laws of the state, for the purpose of operating street cars for any period not longer than twenty years. The city is also authorized to incorporate in any grant it may make to any company to construct and operate street railways, the right subsequently to take over all or any part of said street railways or to permit a new grantee to do the same. In order to be legal in any city it must receive the majority of those voting thereon. No ordinance for a period longer than five years can go into effect until after sixty days after its passage.

For the purpose of acquiring street railways either by construction or purchase, or for the equipment of the railways, the city is authorized to issue its negotiable bonds for the cost plus ten (10) per cent, and these bonds can be issued only after they have received a two-thirds (2-3) majority of those voting. Instead of doing as above the city may issue interest-bearing certificates, to be known as "street-railway certificates," which shall be payable only out of the income of the property for which they were issued. The amount cannot exceed the cost plus ten (10) per cent. As security for payment the city may convey by trust deed or mortgage any part of the property and also the right to operate the same for twenty years after the foreclosure proceedings.

1903. Municipal ownership agitation. Municipal ownership agitation became active and municipal participation in the control of public service corporations was widely discussed. This subject, together with the problems of municipal ownership and operation, prominently marked the five-year period of negotiations between the city and the traction companies. As recorded herein in the vote on the street-railway-franchise question in 1906, the proposition of municipal ownership of the lines was indorsed by a majority of the votes cast at the election; but the question of municipal operation failed to receive the required support. Ultimate city ownership of the traction lines has figured in practically every bit of street-railway legislation since the incorporation of the municipality, but at no time was its agitation so marked as that during the preparation and passage of the Ordinances of 1907.

April 22, 1903. Receivers Appointed for C. U. T. Co. Receivers appointed in the United States Circuit Court for the Chicago Union Traction Company's properties: Rafael R. Govin, James H. Eckels, and Marshall E. Sampsell.

April 5, 1904. Vote on Mueller Law. The vote on the Mueller Law was as follows: "Shall the Act of the General Assembly of the State of Illinois entitled, 'An Act to authorize cities to acquire, construct, own, operate, and lease street railways, and to provide the means therefore approved May 18, 1903, in force July 1, 1903, commonly known as the Mueller Law, be adopted and in force in the City of Chicago?"

For	153,223
Against	30,279
Total	183,502

"Shall the City Council, upon the adoption of the Mueller Law, proceed without delay to acquire ownership of the street railways under the powers conferred by the Mueller Law?"

For	121,957
Against	50,807
Total	172,764

The result in both cases was in the affirmative.

April 5, 1904. Popular vote on licensing street railway companies under police powers. "Shall the City Council, instead of granting any franchises, proceed at once under the city's police powers and other existing laws to license the street-railway companies until municipal ownership can be secured and compel them to give satisfactory service?"

For	120,863
Against	48,200
Total	169,063

The result was in the affirmative.

May 28, 1904. 99-year Act litigation; Judge Grosscup's decision. Judge Peter S. Grosscup of the Seventh United States Circuit Court rendered an opinion on the 99-year Act. On application of the receivers the validity and effect of the 99-year Act were raised for adjudication in Judge Grosscup's court. His decision, concurred in by Judge James G. Jenkins, who had been invited to sit with him on this case, was rendered May 28, 1904. The decision sustained the validity of the 99-year Act and held that its effect was to extend to 99 years the franchise rights of the companies for the lines which had been authorized by the ordinances passed prior to the declaration on May 3, 1875, of the vote adopting the cities and villages act as the new charter of Chicago.

August 24, 1904. Tentative ordinance reported. Tentative ordinance reported for the Chicago City Railway Company by the Council Local Transportation Committee.

March 30, 1905. Employment of Bion J. Arnold by the city to prepare plans and specifications for a municipal street railway; Mr. Arnold had his specifications ready the following June.

April 4, 1905. Popular vote on tentative Ordinance. "Shall the City Council pass the ordinance reported by the Local Transportation Committee to the City Council

on the 24th day of August, 1904, granting a franchise to the Chicago City Railway Company?"

For	64,391
Against	150,785
Total	215,176

"Shall the City Council pass any ordinance granting a franchise to the Chicago City Railway Company?"

For	60,020
Against	151,974
Total	211,994

"Shall the City Council pass any ordinance granting a franchise to any Street Railway Company?"

For	59,013
Against	152,135
Total	211,148

The result was in the negative.

July 5, 1905. Mayor Dunne's "Contract" plan. Mayor Edward F. Dunne submitted to the City Council his "Contract" plan for the settlement of the street railway question, and the establishment of municipal ownership at the same time. On this date Mayor Dunne also submitted another plan which proposed an ordinance for the right to use street railway certificates and for municipal operation; both plans were referred to the Committee on Local Transportation.

The Mayor's "Contract" plan, in brief, provided for a body of trustees who should construct a municipal street railway system in behalf of the city and hold and operate it until the city had gone through the necessary procedure to acquire and operate it for itself. Later in the same year the Mayor submitted drafts of two ordinances in pursuance of his street railway certificate plan, but neither the plan nor the ordinance received favorable consideration from the Committee on Local Transportation.

December 4, 1905. "Settlement" ordinance reported. So-called "settlement" ordinance reported to the City Council by a majority of the Local Transportation Committee.

January 18, 1906. Mueller Certificate and Operation Ordinances. At the same time that a majority of the committee on local transportation submitted to the city council, Dec. 4, 1905, the third tentative ordinance, a minority of the committee submitted a report recommending the passage and submission to the people of the "city plan" ordinance transmitted to the council by Mayor Dunne on July 5, 1905. This ordinance authorized the issuance of Mueller Law certificates to an amount not exceeding $75,000,000 for the acquisition of street railways by the city. The Council on January 18, 1906, passed the ordinance recommended by the minority of the local transportation committee. The council at the same time passed an ordinance submitting to the people the question of municipal operation.

March 12, 1906. Supreme Court 99-Year Decision. The Federal Supreme Court, on March 12, 1906, reversed in respect to material points the decision of the court below on the 99-year act. The upper court held that while that act extended the corporate life of the companies to 99 years, its language was not sufficient to extend the duration of their rights in the streets of Chicago. While the legislature had the right to grant street railway franchises it gave the City Council unusual authority in regard to the control of the streets. The charter of 1851 gave the City Council exclusive control over the street. The city passed ordinances while acting under this charter, and the legislature gave the right of municipal control by confirming the terms fixed by contract in the ordinances. The effect of this decision was to give the City of Chicago practical control of the situation, March 12, 1906.

April 3, 1906. Issue of $75,000,000 in Mueller certificates authorized. Issue of not to exceed $75,000,000 in Mueller certificates authorized by popular vote; the question of municipal ownership was supported but that of municipal operation was lost.

Vote on Mueller certificate issue. "Proposed Operation of Street Railways by the City of Chicago: Shall the City of Chicago proceed to operate street railways?"

For	121,916
Against	110,323
Total	232,239

This question lost because it failed to receive three fifths (3-5) of the total vote cast as required by law.

"Proposed Approval of an Ordinance of the City Council of the City of Chicago passed January 18, 1906, making provision for the issue of 'Street Railway Certificates' not to exceed the sum of $75,000,000.00: Shall the ordinance entitled 'An ordinance authorizing the City of Chicago to construct, acquire, purchase, own and maintain street railways within its corporate limits and providing the means therefor' passed by the City Council of said city on the 18th day of January, A.D., 1906, making provision for the issue of Street Railway Certificates not to exceed in amount $75,000,000.00 be approved?"

For	110,225
Against	106,859
Total	217,084

Vote on combined municipal ownership and operation. "Proposed Question of Public Policy: Shall the City Council proceed without delay to secure Municipal Ownership and Operation of all Street Railways in Chicago under the Mueller Law, instead of passing the pending franchise ordinances or any other ordinances granting franchises to private companies?"

For	111,955
Against	108,087
Total	220,042

On the last two questions the vote was in the affirmative.

April 10, 1906. Walter L. Fisher appointed special Traction Counsel for the City by Mayor Dunne.

April 27, 1906. The "Werno" letter. So-called "Werno" letter received by Alderman Charles Werno, Chairman of Committee on Local Transportation, from Mayor Dunne. In this letter the Mayor outlined upon what basis he then favored settlement of the traction question. This letter was adopted by the council committee as embodying the general policy of the city and was accepted by the companies as the basis of negotiations for a settlement. These negotiations actively continued, and resulted in the ordinances of February 11, 1907.

June 18, 1906. Ordinance passed authorizing the temporary electrification of certain street railway lines of the Chicago City Railway Company.

July 22, 1906. First trolleyizing of cable lines. The Chicago City Railway Company changed the motive power of the State Street cable line to trolley. On the same day the Blue Island Avenue cable line of the Chicago Union Traction Company was changed to trolley.

August 19, 1906. The Madison Street and Milwaukee Avenue cable lines changed to trolley.

October 21, 1906. Cottage Grove Avenue cable changed to trolley; likewise the North Clark Street, Wells Street, Clybourn Avenue and Lincoln Avenue cable lines changed to trolley. The changes in motive power were made under temporary authority from the city.

January 15, 1907. "February 11th" ordinances reported. Traction settlement Ordinances reported to the City Council by the committee on local transportation.

February 4, 1907. Traction settlement ordinances passed by the City Council subject to the approval of the voters at the April election.

February 11, 1907. Ordinances passed over Mayor's veto. Settlement Ordinances vetoed by Mayor Dunne. Passed over Mayor's veto by a vote of 57 to 12.

April 2, 1907. Ratification by voters of settlement ordinances. The popular vote on the Traction Ordinances was as follows:

"Proposed Question of Public Policy: For the approval of ordinances substantially in the form of the pending ordinances (reported to the City Council of the City of Chicago on January 15, A.D., 1907), authorizing the Chicago City Railway Company and the Chicago Railways Company, respectively, to construct, maintain and operate street railways in said city, and providing for the purchase thereof by the said city or its licensee."

For	167,367
Against	134,281
Total	301,648

April 15, 1907. Acceptance of the "February 11th" ordinance by the Chicago City Railway Company.

April 18, 1907. $75,000,000 Mueller certificate ordinance held unconstitutional by Supreme Court of Illinois. Supreme Court of Illinois reversed the decision of Circuit Court of Cook County (Judge Windes) and held that the special street railway certificates authorized by the Mueller law would constitute a debt of the City of Chicago, notwithstanding the provisions of the statute and of the ordinance of January 18, 1906, that they should not be so considered; and held that the city could not then issue such certificates because it had then reached its constitutional limit of indebtedness.

(See Lobdell vs. City of Chicago, 227 Ill., 218.)

May 6, 1907. Charles V. Weston appointed by Mayor Busse to represent the city on the Board of Supervising Engineers.

May 7, 1907. Organization of the Board of Supervising Engineers and date of its first official meeting. The personnel of the Board then was: Bion J. Arnold, Chairman and Chief Engineer, as provided for in the Ordinances; Charles V. Weston, representing the city; and Harvey B. Fleming, representing the Chicago City Railway Company. In the month of July following John Z. Murphy joined the Board as engineer, acting for the receivers of the Chicago Union Traction Company.

1907. During the latter months of this year there was eventually determined an organization plan for the Chicago Union Traction and underlying companies. The plan submitted to the trustees and the bond holders was approved by Judge Peter S. Grosscup and John C. Gray. The following extensions of time in which to accept were granted that company by the City Council:

July 8, 1907. First extension, fifty days. This expired September 14, 1907.

September 12, 1907. Second extension, 140 days from September 14, 1907.

November 24, 1907. Pay-as-you-enter cars. First appearance in Chicago of the Pay-as-you-enter type of car, installed by the Chicago City Railway Company on its Cottage Grove Avenue line.

January 13, 1908. Resignation of Charles V. Weston from the Board of Supervising Engineers and the appointment of George Weston by Mayor Busse to succeed him as representative of the city.

January 25, 1908. Date of purchase, foreclosure sale of the Chicago Union Traction north and west side properties by the Chicago Railways Company.

January 28, 1908. Acceptance of the "February 11th" ordinance by the Chicago Railways Company.

February 15, 1908. John Z. Murphy appointed Representative of Chicago Railways Company, Board No. 1.

March 15, 1908. Report of Traction Valuation Commission composed of Bion J. Arnold and George Weston, on the values of the properties of the Calumet Electric Street Railway Company and South Chicago City Railway Company. A value of $5,000,000 was agreed upon for the tangible and intangible assets of these Companies as of February 1, 1908.

March 21, 1908. Calumet & South Chicago Railway Company incorporated. A merger of the Calumet Electric Street Railway Company and the South Chicago City Railway Company.

May 29, 1908. Calumet & South Chicago Railway Company accepts Ordinance passed by City Council March 30, 1908. This Ordinance follows the same general line laid down in the Traction Ordinances of February 11, 1907.

June 8, 1908. George Weston appointed city's representative on Board of Supervising Engineers No. 2 by Mayor Busse. A. L. Drum appointed company representative on Board No. 2.

June 17, 1908. First meeting of Board No. 2 for the Calumet & South Chicago Railway Company.

March 31, 1909. The Southern Street Railway Company accepted traction ordinance passed by City Council March 15, 1909, its operations being consolidated with those of the Chicago City Railway Company.

May 23, 1910. Chicago Railways Company in receivership.

December 10, 1910. Purchase by Chicago Railways Company of the Chicago Consolidated Traction Company. This purchase was accepted by the City in lieu of extensions required by the 1907 Ordinance for the year 1911.

December 27, 1910. Chicago Railways Company out of receivership.

January 24, 1911. Operating agreement between The Southern Street Railway Company and Chicago, Riverside & LaGrange Railroad, passed January 9, 1911.

March 1, 1912. Purchase of parts of the Chicago & Southern Traction Company by the Chicago City Railway Company. Ordinance passed January 29, 1912.

July 15, 1912. Passage of Through Route Ordinance making revisions in through routes authorized under the 1907 Ordinances.

July 15, 1912. Electrolysis Ordinance effective, passed by the City Council July 8, 1912.

December, 1912. Chicago Railways Company purchased Suburban Railroad Company. Ordinance passed Nov. 29, 1912.

February 1, 1914. Unified operation of street railways takes effect. Ordinance passed Nov. 13, 1913.

February 1, 1914. H. B. Fleming made Representative of the Calumet & South Chicago Railway Company to succeed A. L. Drum on Board No. 2.

April 28, 1914. Accounting report made by Barrow, Wade, Guthrie & Company to the City Comptroller containing adverse criticisms of the Board's interpretation of the Ordinances in respect to the accounting. The Chairman made answer to these criticisms and, after hearings conducted before the Committee on Local Transportation, the Board's decisions on accounting were upheld.

July 2, 1914. E. W. Bemis succeeds George Weston as City's Representative on Boards Nos. 1 and 2. Mr. Weston was retained as Engineer for the Board.

January 31, 1916. City Council passed Ordinance appointing Chicago Traction and Subway Commission, composed of Wm. Barklay Parsons, Chairman, Bion J. Arnold and Robert Ridgway.

May 8, 1916. F. L. R. Francisco succeeds E. W. Bemis, who was removed by the Mayor January 19, 1916, as City's Representative on Boards Nos. 1 and 2.

December 15, 1916. Report of Chicago Traction and Subway Commission on a "Unified System of Surface, Elevated and Subway Lines." The Commission recommended unified operation of all local transportation, under one management, control vested in the City Council; a nine-year construction program; a general physical plan; recapture by the City through amortization; transfers between surface and rapid transit lines, a financial plan, and enabling legislation necessary to carry out the recommendations.

November 5, 1918. Referendum on an Ordinance based largely upon the above recommendations of Chicago Traction and Subway Commission. This was defeated by a vote of 209,682 for, and 243,334 against.

November, 1918. The Surface Lines filed a petition with the Public Utilities Commission for an increase in fare. The City of Chicago, through its Legal Department, appeared before the Commission and made claim that the existing rates of fare were fixed by a contract between the City and the Companies; and asserted that the Commission had no power to change the rate. Litigation resulted in a decision by the Illinois Supreme Court holding Public Utilities Commission's Order of August 6, 1919 to be valid.

August 8, 1919. Street car fare raised from five to seven cents under Order of the Public Utilities Commission.

November, 1919. Forfeiture suits instituted by City against Companies in Cook County Circuit Court.

December 1, 1919. Cash fare seven cents, or 50 tickets for $3.00 or 10 tickets for 65¢.

December 27, 1919. Fare reduced to six cents.

June 1, 1920. Wages of trainmen increased from 65¢ to 80¢ per hour.

July 1, 1920. Order by the Public Utilities Commission fixing the rate of fare at eight cents.

July 31, 1920. Order by Public Utilities Commission of the State of Illinois, effective July 1, providing for Special Renewal and Equipment Funds and the discontinuance of payment of eight per cent of the gross receipts into the Renewal and Depreciation Funds specified in the 1907 and subsequent Ordinances. Under the final order, eight per cent of gross receipts was deposited in Special Renewal and Equipment Funds "and from such special funds each of said Companies shall pay its current renewals and shall expend the balance for the purchase of additional equipment".

November 5, 1920. Pending the entering of the final order for rate of fare, the Commission considered valuations of the street railway properties as presented by the Companies and the City; and on this date, the Commission entered its final order stating that the present value used and useful in public service, April 30, 1920, was "at least $159,113,114.56". This value was the same as the purchase price, or Capital Account, certified by the Board of Supervising Engineers. The Commission found that the Companies were entitled to earn 7½ per cent upon the present value of the properties after paying all operating expenses, taxes and setting aside a reasonable amount for depreciation. The Companies' engineers found that the cost to reproduce the property new, as of April 1, 1920, was $247,246,637.

January 2, 1921. F. L. R. Francisco resigned as City's Representative on Boards Nos. 1 and 2.

February 4, 1921. City Council passed Ordinance declaring that the surface line companies had forfeited their street railway Ordinances "because of the repudiation thereof and the refusal to keep, live up to and perform the same in essential particulars by the said Companies and each of them".

July, 1921. Two car trains (motor car and trailer) operated by Surface Lines for first time. By September 101 units were in operation.

July 1, 1921. Illinois Commerce Commission succeeds State Public Utilities Commission of Illinois.

November 23, 1921. Illinois Commerce Commission issued order establishing a 5¢ fare. The next day, Thanksgiving Day, the Companies secured restraining order.

January 9, 1922. United States District Court decided 5¢ fare was confiscatory and issued temporary injunction against 5¢ fare order.

February, 1922. Re-opening of fare case on motion of the City for further hearing on the 5¢ fare order by the Illinois Commerce Commission which had been enjoined by the Federal Court.

April 8, 1922. The commission issued an order for a 6¢ fare, effective May 1st, but the Companies secured a restraining order from the Federal Court preventing a reduction from the 8¢ rate.

June 15, 1922. Following a hearing before three Federal Judges, a temporary injunction was issued June 9th on condition that the Companies, not later than June 15th, put into effect a 7¢ fare and three tickets for 20¢.

May 22, 1923. Report to the Committee on Local Transportation by R. F. Kelker, Jr. on a Physical Plan for a Unified Transportation System.

July 2, 1923. Mayor Dever in message to City Council declared for comprehensive unified system of City owned surface, elevated and subway lines, and for purchase of traction properties at a fair price by issue of public utility certificates, principal and interest of which was to be paid out of earnings.

October 19, 1923. City Administration dismisses forfeiture suits brought against the surface lines companies by the previous Administration in November, 1919, during which four years, the City had refused to accept its 55 per cent of the divisible net receipts amounting to over $8,000,000. The day following this court action the City accepted this money.

November 28, 1923. Walter A. Shaw appointed by the Mayor as City's Representative to fill vacancy on the Board caused by resignation of Mr. Francisco in 1921.

June 24, 1924. Order of the State Public Utilities Commission of Illinois of November 5, 1920, amended so as to permit the cost of the construction of certain street railway extensions to be paid out of the Special Renewal and Equipment Funds.

September, 1924. Service with multiple unit trains of two cars inaugurated. These cars may be operated singly or in trains.

September 14, 1924. Rerouting of street cars in the downtown district which eliminated, as far as practicable, unnecessary looping of cars, left-hand and right-hand turns. This was followed by a police order prohibiting left-hand turns by other vehicles. These traffic changes removed considerable congestion in the Loop district.

February 11, 1925. Chas. V. Weston succeeds John Z. Murphy as member of the Board representing the Chicago Railways Company. Mr. Murphy passed away January 16, 1925, having represented that company on the Board since 1907.

February 27, 1925. The City Council passed an Ordinance providing for a "Comprehensive Municipal Local Transportation System" by a vote of 40 to 5.

April 7, 1925. Above Ordinance defeated in referendum by following vote:

	Ownership	Operation
For	227,554	226,681
Against	329,228	327,543
Majority opposed	101,674	100,862

This Ordinance provided for the purchase of railway properties by the City through issuance of "Municipal Railway Certificates" payable, both as to principal and interest, out of earnings, and secured by first mortgage on the property purchased. The management and operation of the system was to be in a Municipal Railway Board, composed of nine members: three to be selected by the Mayor, three by the holders of Municipal Railway Certificates and three by agreement between the first two groups. When 51 per cent of all Certificates outstanding had been redeemed by a sinking fund, this Board would consist of only seven members: four chosen by the Mayor and three by the Certificate holders. This was essentially a referendum on the policy of municipal ownership and operation.

June 10, September 23, November 5, 1925. Companies authorized under Orders of Illinois Commerce Commission to make certain extensions and reconstruct certain tracks, paying for the cost thereof from the Special Renewal and Equipment Funds. None of the cost of this work was charged to Capital Account.

February, 1926. Bond Holders Protective Committees appointed in the interest of the various bond issues of the Chicago Railways Company, Chicago City Railway Company, Calumet and South Chicago Railway Company, and Chicago City and Connecting Railways Collateral Trust.

March 18, 1926. Federal Master in Chancery Morrison approves 7¢ fare.

June 23, 1926. Additional order of the Illinois Commerce Commission to the Chicago City Railway Company, authorizing certain track reconstruction to be paid for from the Special Renewal and Equipment Fund.

November 18, 1926. Order of Illinois Commerce Commission, authorizing Chicago Railways Company to install, maintain and operate a motor bus line in Diversey Avenue from Crawford to Laramie Avenues as an extension of its street railway system, subject to the same rates of fare and with transfer privileges between bus and street railway lines. The cost of this bus line to be paid from the Company's Special Renewal and Equipment Fund. Intervening petition filed by Chicago Motor Coach Company denied.

1926. Ordinance submitted by F. J. Lisman and associates to the Committee on Local Transportation, Chicago City Council, for a twenty year franchise for the operation of a system of street railways, motor buses, subways and other rapid transit lines in the City of Chicago.

December 15, 1926. Chicago Railways Company in receivership.

January 26, 1927. Franchises, about to expire, renewed for 6 months. On January 26, 1927, five days before the expiration of the 20-year ordinances, the City Council passed an extension of the 1907 and subsequent traction ordinances for a period not to extend beyond July 31st, 1927, subject to termination at any time by the city or the companies on thirty days' notice. The companies accepted the extension on the day following its passage. The BOSE and the companies continued to function in accordance therewith.

August 11, 1927. First motor bus service on Diversey Ave. The first motor buses to go into service on the Chicago Surface Lines were put into operation on August 11, 1927, on Diversey avenue from Crawford avenue to Laramie avenue, a distance of 1½ miles, as an extension of the street car service on Diversey Avenue.

A total of five buses, Chicago Railways 1-5, were used to maintain the schedules on that extension. The fare was 7 cents, with free transfer to and from the Surface cars.

1927. Consolidation efforts continue. Attempts were made during the year to come to some understanding and agreement on the settlement of the whole traction question involving surface and elevated lines, busses and subways. Traction bills were prepared after negotiations between the Companies and the city, and efforts made to secure their enactment into laws by the state legislature. All these efforts failed, however, and the work was to be taken up anew in 1928. The Council Committee on Local Transportation is already considering a new traction program.

January 10, 1928. Complete ban on Downtown parking. A marked change in traffic regulations with immediate effect upon street railway service was instituted on January 10, 1928 when, by city ordinance, there became effective a universal and complete restriction of parking vehicles in the Central Downtown District.

1928. Operation under temporary permit continues. Since the expiration of the traction ordinances on January 31, 1927 the companies operated under permits of varying duration, in effect extending the life of those ordinances according to the time specified in the permits, which has varied from thirty to ninety days.

1928. CCRY purchases three Twin Coach motor buses with Hercules engines. Five dual motor single end operated buses placed in service on Diversey Avenue by the Chicago Railways Company in 1927 met with the approval of patrons and residents along the route. The Chicago City Railway Company purchased three similar buses, equipped with Hercules motors, in 1928 for service in outlying, heavily populated districts.

June 1, 1928. Trainmen get wage increase. On June 1 there was trainmen's wage increase of one cent an hour, and a similar increase is due to go into effect June 1, 1929. During the year there was also established group insurance for death, and sick and disability benefits.

December, 1928. Bankruptcy judge appoints Citizens Advisory Committee. In connection with the franchise question negotiations between the city and the companies were reopened during the year, with the result that in December Judge Wilkerson, in whose court receivership proceedings of the Chicago Railways Company were pending, appointed a committee for the purpose of assisting in the drafting of bills for enabling legislation to be presented to the legislature at Springfield for enactment. This committee is known as the Citizens Traction Settlement Advisory Committee. With the enactment of the necessary legislation a broader solution of Chicago's local transportation problem than has heretofore been possible with the laws as they now exist was expected.

Christmas, 1928. CSL sets new car availability record. During the week before Christmas the companies exceeded their former record by maintaining in service for five consecutive days every passenger car on the system. This was made possible by constant co-operation between all departments of the organization. The Shops and Equipment department overhauled 1,609 passenger cars during the fiscal year and these, together with the overhauled cars of 1927 and the new ones purchased in recent years placed all the passenger equipment in good condition. As a result the car mileage without failure for 1928 was 27,777, an increase of 1,893 miles over 1927.

1929. Traffic and revenues increase for 8th consecutive year. The past year was the eighth consecutive year showing a substantial gain in traffic and receipts and the Chicago street railway system retained its position as the only one showing such gains, according to reports from the principal American cities.

The gross earnings of the companies for the past year were the highest in their history, and amounted to $62,717,867.90, an increase of $321,183.66 over the year 1928.

July 1, 1929. Consolidation enabling legislation takes effect. The consolidation of the elevated, street railway and other transportation properties was made legally possible by enabling legislation enacted by the Legislature during the year and effective July 1, 1929. This legislation also authorized the city of Chicago to grant a terminable permit—the term theretofore having been limited to not longer than twenty years—and provides for subway construction by the city, the cost to be borne partly by special assessment. It also provided for a local transit commission to be appointed by the city of Chicago and having jurisdiction over the Company.

The Local Transportation Committee of the City Council, representatives of the transportation companies and counsel for the respective parties, the citizens committee and the Federal Court, began the drafting of a new ordinance following the legislative enactment. Certain financial questions and sections of the measure were referred to a bankers committee and at the close of the year substantial progress had been made.

1930. Depression breaks steady climb in traffic and revenue. The year 1930 broke the chain of eight consecutive years showing a substantial gain in traffic and receipts. The general industrial depression brought about a decrease in revenue passengers, the first decrease since the fiscal year 1921. The gross receipts for the year 1930 were $56,737,109.90; operating expenses $47,700,142.15; and net receipts $9,036,967.75; the total revenue passengers for the year was 812,080,701, a decrease of 85,483,653. The unusual heavy snow-storm in the month of March cost the companies about $1,000,000.00 in loss of revenue and added expense.

1930. Temporary permits extended until 1932. CSL operations continued under a new temporary permit, which was to expire in 1932.

April 17, 1930. First trolley buses placed in service. The Illinois Commerce Commission, on March 6th, 1930, gave authority to the Chicago Railways Company to inaugurate bus service in the Northwest section of the city. On April 17th, 1930, the first trolley buses were placed in service, and during the fiscal year five lines were put into operation. To fill the schedules on these routes, seventy-five single end, two-motor trolley buses were purchased and delivered during the year.

May 19, 1930. City Council passes new franchise ordinance. The prolonged franchise negotiations, particularly those following the enactment of enabling legislation by the state Legislature in 1929, finally ended in the passing of a franchise ordinance by the City Council on May 19, 1930, granting a terminable permit to the Chicago Local Transportation Company (later incorporated) for a comprehensive unified transportation system for the City of Chicago and its metropolitan area, which area the ordinance described as: "the territory embracing the City of Chicago and the territory within the State of Illinois lying within thirty (30) miles distant from the nearest point—marking the corporate limits of the City of Chicago." This measure obligated the new company to acquire as part of the system all of the street railway companies constituting the Chicago Surface Lines and all of the elevated companies of the Chicago Rapid Transit Company.

July 1, 1930. Citizens vote in referendum on new traction ordinance. A special election for a referendum by the citizens of Chicago on this ordinance, held on July 1, 1930, resulted in the following vote: Yes, 325,837, No, 56,690. The ordinance was approved by a vote of approximately six to one.

1931. CSL accidents lower than any year since 1919. The number of accidents reported for the year was less than any year since 1919, although the number of motor vehicles in Chicago for the year 1931 was five times that of the year 1919. The number of fatalities was the second lowest in the history of the properties. It is a matter of record that 76 per cent of the force of conductors and motormen operated through the year 1931 without a single chargeable accident. In other words, 8,984 platform men had a clean record of 100 per cent with respect to accidents.

1931. Last Western Ave. extension completed. The extension on South Western Avenue, completed during the year 1931, provides what is said to be the longest ride for one fare exclusively on one street of any street railway system. The distance between the south terminal and north terminal on Western Avenue was 22.5 miles.

March 8, 1931. Severe snow storm. The trolley bus and gas bus lines were especially hard hit during the severe snow storm of March 8, 1931.

1931. CSL adds 40 new trolley buses. An additional forty new single end, two motor trolley buses were delivered during the calendar year, making a total of one hundred and fourteen on the system. These buses were manufactured in accordance with general specifications drawn by the Chicago Surface Lines and approved by the BOSE.

All trolley buses were in operation, 53 having been overhauled, repaired, and repainted during fiscal 1931, and were utilized to fill the schedules.

The single way mileage for street routes has increased from a total of 38.86 in 1930 to 48.62 in 1931, a gain of 9.76 single way miles.

1931. Illinois Supreme Court hears traction ordinance case. Proceedings were then pending before the Illinois Supreme Court on appeal to determine the validity of the new traction ordinance approved by the voters at a special election July 1, 1930. The City Council

on December 22, 1930 extended to January 31, 1933 the time for acceptance of that measure by the new company, and at the same time passed an ordinance continuing unified operation to the same date.

1931. Operation under temporary permit continues until 1933. Operation and maintenance, construction and reconstruction of the various street railway properties continued under the provisions of the 1907 and subsequent traction ordinances, now in effect, under temporary permits of the City and approval of the Federal Court, which were to expire January 31, 1933.

1932. No employees discharged; work spread to keep all employed. A most commendable achievement of the companies during the past three years of widespread unemployment and "hard times" has been the continued pay of their 16,000 employees, made possible by the distribution of hours of work, thus avoiding the necessity of laying off any of the operating force, during a long period of constantly decreasing employment during the depression. The companies' records also show that in addition to the foregoing benefit to the community, they have maintained life, health and disability insurance for their employees without cost to them—the group life insurance alone at the close of the year totaling $16,277,000.

1932. Temporary operating permit extended until 1934.

June 1, 1933. Cermak Road Burnham Park extension opens. The most important development during the year was the construction of street railway tracks to and into Grant and Burnham Parks to provide service for A Century of Progress Exposition.

August 1, 1933. Roosevelt Road Burnham Park extension opens. The Roosevelt Road ordinance for the extension into Grant Park was passed by the City Council May 24, 1933, and operation over the extension was begun August 1.

April 3, 1934. 1930 Unified traction ordinance becomes null and void. The ordinance providing for a comprehensive unified local transportation system for the City of Chicago and Metropolitan Area passed by the City Council on May 19, 1930, and approved at a special election July 1, 1930 became null and void because of non acceptance by the new company on or before April 3, 1934, the final date set by the City Council after many extensions of time had been granted by the City.

1934. Maximum service to Exhibition; experimental cars in use. During A Century of Progress Exposition practically all passenger cars were in use, thus giving maximum service to and from the Exposition grounds as well as on all other lines in the city. This good service and courteous treatment by trainmen created a very good impression for the Chicago Surface Lines, not only in Chicago but from patrons from every section of the United States, as was evidenced by the wide favorable comment received by the companies. The two new passenger cars were in operation on short runs to and from A Century of Progress and the central business district.

Based on the experience in the operation of those two units the most desirable and practical features of each will be combined in specifications for new cars, which the companies aim to purchase. Four gasoline buses of an improved type were also purchased during the year bringing the total of gasoline and trolley buses owned to 128.

1934. Four new motor buses purchased. Four new front entrance, center exit gasoline buses, No. 401-404, were purchased during the fiscal year and placed in operation on outlying streets in the Southwest part of the city. These smaller buses were purchased to supply the needs of patrons in districts where transportation is not sufficiently heavy to demand larger buses or street cars. Whenever the rush hour traffic became too heavy for the smaller buses, one or more of the larger type were assigned to relieve the overload.

These buses were equipped with the horizontal or pancake type engines, mounted underneath the floor near the center, and were serviced from below. No gas fumes penetrated to the interior because the solid, tightly sealed floors separate it from all the operating units. The bodies, built of aluminum and steel, had no chassis, the sides being the load carrying members. The entrance doors, pneumatically operated, were placed forward of the front axle, opposite the operator and under his control. The rear doors, pneumatically treadle operated, but also under control of the operator, were placed directly forward of the rear wheels. All doors are folding and have sensitive edges.

1934. Operation continues to be by temporary permit. The Surface Lines still operated under temporary permits from the City, the last extension granted expiring June 1, 1935.

1934. CSL continues physical improvements. The street railway companies, as in previous years, maintained their properties to a high standard of physical condition, having expended during the year for maintenance and current renewals the sum of $9,653,932.30. The equivalent of more than 42 miles of single track were renewed and reconstructed. In the face of extraordinary decrease in revenue, for the years 1930, 1931 and 1932, the same high standard was followed throughout; there having been expended in the past five years for maintenance, renewals, extensions, and betterments a total of $49,560,789.23.

1934. Revenue passengers increase. The upward swing continued throughout the year 1934, which showed an increase in revenue passengers of 3.98 per cent above the year 1933. The Surface Lines, as in previous years, continued to carry 80 per cent of the total of the local transportation load. The number of revenue passengers for the year 1934 was 677,532,725, an increase of 25,930,207 revenue passengers over 1933. The second season of A Century of Progress Exposition contributed materially to the increase in car riding.

April 28, 1934. Bankruptcy judge appoints co-

receivers. All the companies continued in receiverships, and on April 28 Judge James H. Wilkerson of the U.S. District Court appointed Walter J. Cummings as co-receiver with Guy A. Richardson for the Chicago Railways Company, and Edward E. Brown co-receiver with Harvey B. Fleming for the Chicago City Railway Company, Calumet and South Chicago Railway Company, and The Southern Street Railway Company, comprising the South Side lines.

1934. CSL increases cars repaired. The number of cars overhauled, repainted, and repaired during the fiscal year of 1934 was 1,464, a gain of 128 over the fiscal year of 1933.

1934. Last single-truck passenger cars scrapped. For several years the Chicago Surface Lines held in reserve for emergency use a number of the old type single truck passenger cars that had been superseded by large modern double truck cars. These single truck cars have now been disposed of.

1935. CSL suffers decline in revenue passengers and gross revenue. The Surface Lines, as in previous years, continued to carry 80% of the total local transportation load. The number of revenue passengers for the year 1935 was 672,147,051, a decrease of 5,385,674 revenue passengers from 1934. In the years 1933 and 1934 revenue passengers reflected the additional traffic due to the Century of Progress Exposition during those years. The gross earnings for 1935 were $46,821,001.69, a decrease of $653,005.33 compared with 1934. The purchase price as of January 31, 1936 was $169,142,629.48.

September 22, 1935. CSL to exchange transfers with Chicago Rapid Transit lines. The Surface Lines and the Chicago Rapid Transit lines exchanged transfers at certain designated points, the order being effective for a one year trial period beginning with September 22, 1935.

1935. U.S. District Court appoints CSL reorganization committee. All the Companies are still in receivership, but it is expected that some definite action will be taken following the appointment by the U.S. District Court of a re-organization committee for the purpose of combining all Surface Lines properties under one financial structure through the exchange of old for new securities.

1935. Gasoline buses increase in number and route mileage. During the fiscal year 1935 there was a large increase in the number of gasoline buses and in the mileage over which they operated. The total mileage amounts to 32.88 single way miles of revenue operation on streets. This additional mileage was placed in service on new routes on 47th Street, 71st Street, 87th Street, 95th Street, Higgins Road, Northwest Highway, and a slight increase at Archer Avenue east terminal. The total revenue trolley bus mileage is 52.50, with 9.02 miles additional service mileage, and the total gasoline bus mileage is 45.35. There was also an increase of 2.75 single way miles of trolley bus operation. This additional mileage was on Diversey Avenue and Belmont Avenue. There was also an increase of 0.23 miles in the North and Lamon yard.

To provide equipment for this increased mileage there was added to the system during 1935 six trolley buses and 44 gasoline buses.

Great public interest was manifested, as usual, in these new facilities. Crowds attended the official opening of the 47th Street extension and the new line on Higgins Road. Similar enthusiasm was shown on the occasions of the opening of other lines. The Higgins Road and Northwest Highway routes are entirely new.

1935. Fatalities from CSL accidents reach all-time low. In considering the various operating statistics it is well here to point out that the number of fatalities from accidents for the year was the lowest in the history of the Surface Lines.

1936. Revenue passengers and gross income increase. The Surface Lines, as in previous years, continued to carry more than 78 per cent of the total local transportation load. The number of revenue passengers carried during the fiscal year 1936 totalled 720,301,899, an increase of 48,154,848, or 7.16 per cent over 1935. Gross earnings for 1936 were $49,777,685.51, an increase of $2,956,683.82 or 6.31 per cent over 1935.

The purchase price of the properties as of January 31, 1937, was $169,987,396.94.

February 28, 1936. First PCC cars ordered: to replace 159 or more conventional cars. Final steps were taken for securing new, most modern and up-to-date passenger cars, the development of which had been under consideration since securing the placing in operation two new type passenger cars for the purpose of experimenting with the object in view of adopting a type of equipment that would offer the most comfortable, quiet and speedy car to meet the traffic conditions in Chicago. Changes were made in the design of the experimental cars with the result that the Chicago Railways Company placed an order for fifty (50) of the new type and the Chicago City Railway Company an order for thirty-three (33), the purpose being to fully equip the heavy traffic Madison Street Line as the first step in a general plan for intensive improvement in street railway service throughout the City.

The eighty-three (83) new cars referred to will replace and cause the retirement of one-hundred and fifty-nine (159) or more of the older type cars. The cost of the new cars, approximately $1,300,000.00, will be paid out of the Renewal and Depreciation Reserve Funds of the respective companies and not charged to Capital Accounts. By that method the cash in the Renewal and Depreciation Reserve Funds will be used for the express purpose for which they were established in the ordinances of 1907.

September 22, 1936. CSL/CRT transfer exchange continued until 1937. The Surface Lines and the Chicago Rapid Transit Lines, by order of the Illinois Commerce Commission effective September 22, 1935, inaugurated a system for the interchanging and transferring of passengers for a trial period of one year. On September 22, 1936, the Illinois Commerce Commission entered orders continuing this arrangement to March 21, 1937, and subsequently to September 30, 1937. During the year three more transfer points were added by order of the Commission, making a total of 55.

1936. Twelve motor buses placed in service; 43 on order for 1937. Twelve standard-type 23 passenger gasoline buses were received and placed in service in calendar year 1936 (CCRy 416-418 and CRys 517-525), making a total of 62 gas buses of various seating capacities now in service on the system. Five additional 23 seat gas buses have been ordered for delivery and service early in 1937 (CCRy 419-420, C&SC 810-812). Thirty-three 30-32 seat capacity gas buses with engines mounted at the rear of the chassis were ordered under approved specifications, to be delivered and placed in service during the early part of 1937 (CRys 526-558). Five additional buses of the same type were ordered early in 1937. Two gasoline buses were overhauled in 1936, and seven got new steel roof panels.

1936. Fifteen trolley buses delivered; 17 on order for 1937. Fifteen new 40 passenger trolley buses were purchased and placed in service during the year in the Northwest part of the city. They were similar to those purchased in 1935, with later improvements added.

During the year 58 trolley buses were equipped with new improved type wheels, 43 with new steel roof panels and six with new steel side panels and gusset plates.

The addition of these fifteen brings the total to a fleet of 135 trolley buses.

Seventeen 40 passenger trolley buses were ordered early in 1937 under specifications approved by the Board of Supervising Engineers and will be delivered late in 1937. These buses will be equipped with one large motor instead of two of smaller size.

Fifty-five trolley buses were overhauled, repaired and repainted during fiscal year 1936.

1936. North Ashland and East 87th Street track extensions. Completion of the new track extension in North Ashland Avenue from Cortland Street to Clybourn Avenue across the new North Ashland Avenue bridge during the year provided a continuous route on Ashland Avenue from Ninety-fifth Street to Irving Park Boulevard. The distance between the South terminal and the North terminal was nearly 17 miles.

Another track connection, to be started in January 1937 on East Eighty-seventh Street between Stony Island Avenue and Ingleside Avenue, when completed will give through rail service from Commercial Avenue to Vincennes Avenue.

1936. CSL operation to continue into 1937 under temporary permit. Operation and maintenance, construction and reconstruction of the various street railway properties continued under the provisions of the 1907 and subsequent traction ordinances, then in effect, under temporary permits of the City and approval of the Federal Court, which were to expire May 31, 1937.

November 12, 1936. New PCC cars placed in service on busy Madison Street route. On the night of

457

November 12, the first six of these new cars were introduced to the public on Madison Street at a celebration in which it is estimated that 500,000 people lined both sides of Madison Street from the City Limits to the Loop.

November 21, 1936. Judge Wilkerson of Federal Court directed the proponents of the Abbott Plan, for reorganization of the Chicago Surface Lines, to make prompt application to the City for a new ordinance.

December 10, 1936. The Abbott Plan proponents requested the City to undertake negotiations for a franchise to the Chicago Surface Lines. The City took the position that the plan presented should be enlarged to include all local transportation services.

January 26, 1937. Mayor Kelly presented a Plan to the Committee on Local Transportation for a Comprehensive Transportation System for the City of Chicago and outlined the general requirements for a unified and modern transportation system.

April 28, 1937. Federal Court appointed the "Lynch Committee" to prepare the reorganization plan for Chicago Rapid Transit Company.

May 27, 1937. Abbott Plan Committee submitted outline of separate ordinance grant to Chicago Surface Lines.

June 7, 1937. The Mayor requested the Lynch and Abbott Committees to agree upon a plan for unification which the City Council might consider.

June 30, 1937. Abbott Committee again requested separate franchise for Chicago Surface Lines.

July 1, 1937. The Lynch Committee reaffirmed willingness to continue negotiations for a comprehensive and unified plan.

July 7, 1937. Mayor requested operating officials of the transportation systems to confer with the engineers of the City for the purpose of developing basis for a unified plan and a program for improvements.

October 20, 1937. Mayor presented to the Federal Court a general outline for a practicable comprehensive unification plan.

November 22, 1937. A Comprehensive Local Transportation Plan for the City of Chicago, prepared by the City's engineers, was presented to the Court. Copies were sent to each of the Companies with the suggestion that the Committee on Local Transportation be advised if the plans contained in the report can be adopted.

December 6, 1937. Abbott Plan Committee filed statement with the Court again suggesting separate reorganization of the street railway properties.

December 17, 1937. Court appointed Mr. Walter A. Shaw as Adviser to the Court, directing him to study plan presented by the City and to attempt to bring about an agreement among interested parties.

February 18, 1938. Mr. Shaw reported failure to reach agreement; recommended that report of engineers of City dated November 22, 1937, should constitute initially the basis for negotiations, and that the Companies should be directed to assign engineers and accountants to work with him in the preparation of a joint program.

February 23, 1938. Court instructed Mr. Shaw to obtain agreement or in case of disagreement to report his recommendations.

May 5, 1938. Mr. Shaw submitted to the Court an interim report on fundamental principles.

June 14, 1938. Mr. Shaw filed his second interim report, and was directed by the Court to prepare a plan for unification and present it to the Court on September 26, 1938.

July 20, 1938. City Council presented temporary ordinance authorizing receivers of street railway companies to operate property under their control. This ordinance was not accepted by the receivers.

July-September, 1938. Committee on Local Transportation met with operating officers of the transportation companies to prepare a tentative ordinance draft and many non-controversial sections were drafted.

September 26, 1938. Mr. Shaw presented his full report.

October 25, 1938. City entered into a contract with Federal Government providing for Federal aid in the construction of the Initial System of Subways.

October 31, 1938. Mr. Shaw filed suggested modifications of his report.

November 14, 1938. Mayor filed statement of City's position with reference to further procedure.

December 15, 1938. Amendments proposed to Plan of Reorganization as basis for unification and Trustee of Chicago Rapid Transit Company directed by the Court to prepare and file a plan of reorganization of rapid transit properties.

January 20, 1939. Mr. Shaw submitted modification of his report; recommended that franchise negotiations with the City be pressed to consummation as early as practicable.

February 6, 1939. Trustee of Chicago Rapid Transit Company filed a plan for reorganization providing for unification with the Chicago Surface Lines as single corporate entity.

February 23, 1939. Abbott Committee presented amendments to its reorganization plan which were later embodied in its complete plan dated March 23, 1939.

May 1, 1939. Court appointed Shaw, Richardson and Sprague as negotiators to act in behalf of Chicago Transit Company and appearance of Chicago Transit Company entered in the Chicago Surface Lines receivership case.

May 15, 1939. Order entered establishing procedure for submission of plan to security holders of the Chicago Surface Lines, and modifying plan of reorganization.

May 19, 1939. Committee on Local Transportation began meetings with Negotiators.

June 27, 1939. Negotiators submitted an ordinance draft which the City rejected.

July 14, 1939. Goldthwaite report submitted by City on findings of value of the several properties.

July 27, 1939. Negotiators and Committee jointly instructed their engineering staffs to attempt to reconcile differences as to property value, but no agreement was possible.

September 27, 1939. Negotiations resumed, leaving matter of determining capital value at any future time to the Transit Commission.

October 27, 1939. PWA representatives attended a meeting of the Committee and Negotiators, at which the status of entire traction negotiations was reviewed.

November 16, 1939. Negotiators reported to the Court that acting under their interpretation of the Court's instructions they will be unable to agree with the City's representatives as to the terms of a franchise ordinance.

November 22, 1939. Statement of Mayor Kelly as to a suggested plan for settlement of Chicago's traction problem was filed with the Federal Court.

December 18, 1939. Judge Wilkerson submitted a memorandum stating the Mayor's plan appears to offer more to the security holders than they could hope from any other course which has been suggested. The Court appointed four additional members to the Board of Negotiators: E. E. Brown, W. J. Cummings, M. H. MacLean, S. L. Castle.

January 3, 1940. The Committee on Local Transportation met with enlarged group of Negotiators and a number of meetings were held.

March 29, 1940. The Committee presented to the Negotiators its informal synopsis as to its present views with regard to all sections of the ordinance.

April 13, 1940. First discussion with Reconstruction Finance Corporation concerning loan to new company to aid in carrying out modernization program.

June 4, 1940. Revised Synopsis of ordinance prepared and discussed with Negotiators at subsequent meetings.

July 6, 1940. Draft of ordinance by the City's Staff completed with all exhibits and copies sent to Negotiators.

July 10, 1940. Public hearings on ordinance began before Committee on Local Transportation.

July 30, 1940. Meetings began at which Negotiators suggested modifications in ordinance draft.

August 1, 1940. Reconstruction Finance Corporation transmitted letter to Mayor Kelly outlining general terms upon which it would make a loan to new company for purpose of modernization.

September 20, 1940. Lawyers for the City and for the Negotiators presented a joint redraft of the ordinance.

September 26, 1940. Proposal of Motor Coach Company suggesting terms for its inclusion in unified operations submitted to the Committee on Local Transportation.

December 19, 1940. Reading of ordinance draft before full Committee on Local Transportation began.

January 8, 1941. Committee on Local Transportation gave approval to draft of the traction ordinance and recommended to the City Council that the ordinance be passed.

January 9, 1941. Draft of traction ordinance received by City Council and ordered printed in pamphlet form.

January 29, 1941. Public hearings on traction ordinance began.

January 30, 1941. Board of Negotiators reported to Federal Court that they could not recommend acceptance of the ordinance as drafted.

February 4, 1941. Committee on Local Transportation recommended to the City Council that certain amendments to the ordinance suggested by the RFC be adopted.

February 5, 1941. The Federal Court discharged the Board of Negotiators and the receivers for the surface lines companies and appointed as receivers of Chicago Railways—Walter J. Cummings and Daniel C. Green; as receivers of Chicago City Railway—Edward J. Fleming and Edward E. Brown (replaced, on resignation, by Charles H. Albers on March 28). These receivers and Mr. Walter A. Shaw, court adviser (who would act as chairman) to function as a joint Board of Management and Operation for the Chicago Surface Lines. The joint board and the Trustees of Chicago Rapid Transit Company to continue negotiations for a franchise. The order to be effective March 1, 1941.

February 5, 1941. Mayor Kelly submitted letter to Federal Court in which he stated the urgent need of transportation in a city stimulated with new industries, and recounted previous statements for settling problem. He also warned that failure to accept ordinance would leave a bankrupt elevated relegated to the scrap heap and leave Chicago without rapid transit service.

March 4, 1941. Ordinance draft with amendments submitted to new board of negotiators.

March 26, 1941. Joint board on negotiations reported to Federal Court suggesting that certain provisions in the traction ordinance draft be modified.

April 25, 1941. Mayor Kelly made statement to Federal Court showing there was substantial agreement on the terms of the traction ordinance and offered to recommend modifications to make it acceptable to the various parties at interest.

May 23, 1941. Board of Management and Operation of Chicago Surface Lines and Trustees of Chicago Rapid Transit Company, through their counsel, advised Federal Court that they had agreed on provisions which would be recommended by City officials to the Committee on Local Transportation, by way of amendment to the proposed traction ordinance.

May 27, 1941. Committee on Local Transportation approved amended draft of ordinance and authorized chairman to ask leave of City Council to substitute it for ordinance draft submitted January 9, 1941.

June 12, 1941. Jesse H. Jones, Administrator of RFC, advised Mayor Kelly that there are reasonable possibilities of a substantial loan to the transportation companies if they see fit to make application for same.

June 18, 1941. Federal Court approved wage increase to Chicago Surface Lines' employees and gave Board of Management and Operation permission to prepare a request for increased fares before the Illinois Commerce Commission.

June 19, 1941. City Council passed traction ordinance by a vote of 40 to 6. The ordinance requires unification of Chicago Surface Lines and Chicago Rapid Transit Company; and acquisition of Chicago Motor Coach Company is permissive.

July 10, 1941. Order of Federal Court approved wage increases for Chicago Rapid Transit Company employees and gave Trustees permission to begin proceedings before the Illinois Commerce Commission for increased fares.

July 11, 1941. The Federal Court (Judge Igoe) instructed representatives of the security holders to come to an agreement upon the details of a plan based upon the ordinance and to report to the Court on or before September 9, 1941, and stated that, in the event that such an agreed plan is not presented, the Court will take steps for the preparation of a plan.

August 13, 1941. Chicago Motor Coach Company ordered by Illinois Commerce Commission to show cause why there should not be a reduction in its rates of fare and hearings were started on August 19, 1941.

September 9, 1941. Attorneys for Chicago Surface Lines first mortgage bondholders and Attorneys for Trustees of Chicago Rapid Transit Company stated to Federal Court their willingness to recommend the acceptance of the unified traction ordinance of June 19, 1941, and submitted a plan of reorganization based on the ordinance.

September 11, 1941. Hearings were begun before the Illinois Commerce Commission on the petition of the Chicago Surface Lines for an increase in rates of fare.

September 11, 1941. Federal Judge Igoe stated "that the State Commission, the City and the Court, have functions of equal importance to perform in connection with the reorganization" and suggested that each select a representative to aid in coordinating and harmonizing the steps in the reorganization program.

September 22, 1941. Because of concurrent proceedings before the Federal Court and the Illinois Commerce Commission and because the submission of reorganiza-

tion matters to security holders will require more time—the City Council postponed the referendum date on the traction ordinance from November 4, 1941, to a date to be later approved.

City Council appointed Philip Harrington, Commissioner of Subways and Superhighways, to represent the City on joint City-State-Court Committee suggested by Judge Igoe on September 11th; but neither the State Commission nor the Governor ever acted upon the Court's suggestion.

October 10, 1941. The companies submitted, to the Federal Court, evidence as to reorganization values.

October 14, 1941. Hearings were begun before the Illinois Commerce Commission on the petition of the Chicago Rapid Transit Company for an increase in rates of fare.

November 7, 1941. Joint memorandum on reorganization values submitted to Federal Court by attorneys for first mortgage bondholders of Chicago Surface Lines companies and attorneys for Trustees of Chicago Rapid Transit Company.

November 27, 1941. Federal Judge Igoe gave opinion that a reorganization value of $179,348,467 for the combined surface lines and rapid transit properties was sustained by the evidence, and that the proposed division of securities of the new company between the two groups was fair and equitable.

December 12, 1941. Amendments to reorganization plan, in conformity with the Court's order of November 27, 1941, were submitted by the proponents of the Plan.

December 22, 1941. Committee on Local Transportation submitted its policy in regard to the reorganization proceedings before the Federal Court of not interfering but reserving the right to make suggestions or objections to any details which affect the interests of the public; and its policy in regard to the fare cases before the Illinois Commerce Commission that it does not approve of any increases in fare, but that if the Commission sees fit to grant such increases in fares, its order definitely should provide for and assure substantial improvements in both quantity and quality of service. This policy was approved and adopted by the City Council.

January 9 and 10, 1942. Evidence was heard in Federal Court relating to allocation of securities to the various groups of security holders under the plan of reorganization.

January 17, 1942. Final argument completed in Federal Court on reorganization plan by attorneys representing the various groups of security holders.

February 19, 1942. The Federal Court entered orders tentatively approving the plan of reorganization and ordered Trustees of Chicago Rapid Transit Company to submit the plan to the Illinois Commerce Commission in accordance with the Federal laws.

February 26, 1942. Hearings were begun before Illinois Commerce Commission for its approval of the reorganization plan as to the public interest therein and the fairness thereof; as required under the Chandler Act in the Rapid Transit Proceedings.

March 27, 1942. Illinois Commerce Commission stated that it is in favor of unification. It questioned its jurisdiction in the preliminary phase of the matter but expressed desire to return freedom of action in respect to issues relating to final details of the plan of reorganization.

April 3, 1942. M. E. Gilmore, Commissioner of Public Works, Federal Works Agency, expressed approval of reorganization plan and of the traction ordinance and asked that the ordinance be submitted to the voters at a referendum at an early date.

April 14, 1942. Federal Judge Igoe approved orders providing for submission of reorganization plan to security holders, and in an opinion stated that the reorganization plan is feasible and fair. He stated there should be no delay so that the unified company may contribute its improved transportation service to the war activities of the community.

April 15, 1942. City Council amended traction ordinance by providing for referendum on June 1, 1942.

April 20, 1942. Illinois Commerce Commission granted the Chicago Surface Lines permission for a temporary increase in fares to 8 cents.

May 25, 1942. Results of overwhelming approval of reorganization plan and the traction ordinance by security holders presented to Federal Court.

June 1, 1942. Unification ordinance approved by the electors with 238,571 voting for and 22,626 voting against the proposition.

June 22, 1942. Federal Judge Igoe appointed William P. Sidley, Francis X. Busch, Henry F. Tenny, Thomas L. Marshall and William J. Friedman as members of a committee to initiate the proceedings before the Illinois Commerce Commission to secure approval of the reorganization plan.

July 22, 1942. Committee appointed by Federal Judge Igoe filed a petition with the Illinois Commerce Commission on behalf of the new company to acquire the properties of the Chicago Surface Lines and the Chicago Rapid Transit Company and to issue the securities provided for under the reorganization plan.

July 30, 1942. Hearings were begun before the Illinois Commerce Commission on the reorganization plan.

August 5, 1942. The City Council passed an ordinance authorizing the temporary use by the Trustees of Chicago Rapid Transit Company of the Initial System of Subways for local transportation purposes, subject to approval at a referendum on November 3, 1942.

November 3, 1942. Ordinance authorizing the temporary use of the subway for local transportation purposes, by the Trustees of Chicago Rapid Transit Company, approved by the electors with 877,198 voting for and 137,311 voting against the proposition.

November 5, 1942. City Council extended date of acceptance, by the new company, of the ordinance providing for a comprehensive unified local transportation system to January 2, 1943.

December 21, 1942. City Council extended date of acceptance, by the new company, of the ordinance providing for a comprehensive unified local transportation system to February 2, 1943.

City Council extended date of acceptance, by the Trustees of Chicago Rapid Transit Company, of the ordinance authorizing temporary use of the Initial System of Subways, for local transportation purposes, to March 2, 1943.

February 1, 1943. Examiner for the Illinois Commerce Commission in a report stated that the reorganization plan of Chicago Transit Company was basically unsound and should be disapproved.

February 11, 1943. Federal Judge Igoe entered an order giving Trustees of Chicago Rapid Transit Company permission to accept ordinance authorizing temporary operation of the subway to the Trustees.

February 13, 1943. Trustees of Chicago Rapid Transit Company filed acceptance of subway ordinance with City Clerk.

March 16, 1943. Hearings concluded in traction reorganization before the Illinois Commerce Commission.

May 3, 1943. Illinois Commerce Commission approved permanent 8-cent fare for Chicago Surface Lines.

Illinois Commerce Commission in an opinion and order rejected the petition of Chicago Transit Company for approval of the reorganization plan.

May 17, 1943. Federal Judge Igoe approved petition for rehearing of traction reorganization plan to be filed with Illinois Commerce Commission by attorneys for Chicago Transit Company.

May 27, 1943. M. E. Gilmore, Commissioner of Public Works, FWA stated that he concluded that the Chicago Transit Company under the proposed plan of reorganization "will start business in an unusually strong cash position and will enjoy ample credit where, as and if needed, to carry forward the eight-year modernization program contemplated in the unification ordinance."

June 1, 1943. Honorable Jesse H. Jones in a letter to Mayor Kelly stated that to permit the City to proceed with the unification, the RFC will give consideration to a loan of $39,860,320 conditioned upon receipt of a formal application from the new transit company.

June 2, 1943. Petitions for rehearing of traction reorganization plan filed with Illinois Commerce Commission by City of Chicago and by attorneys for Chicago Transit Company.

June 11, 1943. City of Chicago submitted supplement to Application for rehearing of reorganization plan to Illinois Commerce Commission requesting that letter of June 1, 1943, from Honorable Jesse H. Jones to Mayor Kelly be given consideration.

June 22, 1943. Illinois Commerce Commission rejected petitions for rehearing of traction reorganization plan.

July 13, 1943. Judge Igoe submitted memorandum on steps to remove traction companies from receivership and asked that proposals be submitted to the Federal Court on September 20, 1943. Also ordered appeal taken from order of Illinois Commerce Commission rejecting the reorganization plan.

July 20, 1943. Appeal filed in Superior Court of Cook County by City of Chicago and by Chicago Transit Company from Illinois Commerce Commission order rejecting the reorganization plan.

July 28, 1943. City filed petition with Illinois Commerce Commission asking for entry of order providing for transfers between surface routes and subway routes.

August 21, 1943. Appeal filed in Superior Court of Cook County by City from Illinois Commerce Commission order granting Chicago Surface Lines permanent 8-cent fare.

September 8, 1943. Illinois Commerce Commission entered order for exchange of transfers between all intersecting lines of Chicago Surface Lines, Chicago Rapid Transit Company, including the subway, and Chicago Motor Coach Company to be effective by October 1, 1943.

September 20, 1943. Chicago Surface Lines first mortgage bondholders submitted plan to Federal Court for separate reorganization of Chicago Surface Lines.

September 21, 1943. Mayor Kelly issued public statement announcing that City is opposed to separate reorganization, will grant no franchise without unification, and urging that Chicago Surface Lines first mortgage bondholders make concerted effort to produce a constructive response from the Illinois Commerce Commission. Mayor hinted at revolutionary proposal that might be necessary if they fail to achieve unification immediately.

September 29, 1943. The City Council on Mayor Kelly's recommendation instructed the Corporation Counsel to advise the Federal Court that the City could not give consideration to the granting of any transit franchise that did not require unified operation and modernization of all forms of service.

October 4, 1943. The Federal Court was advised that the City could see no hope for city-wide improvement of local transportation if a separate reorganization plan for the Chicago Surface Lines were granted. The Federal Works Agency also opposed separate reorganization.

October 13, 1943. Mayor Kelly presented to the City Council a plan for acquisition and operation by the City of Chicago of all local transportation systems, together with alternative plans for solution of Chicago's traction problem. This plan summarized the advantages of Public Ownership of Local Transit with operation under an independent transit board.

October 17, 1943. Revenue operation of the new subway was inaugurated. The temporary operation by Trustees of Chicago Rapid Transit Company is under the terms of the Ordinance of August 5, 1942.

October 26, 1943. Federal Court appointed "Sidley Committee" to negotiate with City in the matter of purchase by the City of the Chicago Surface Lines and Chicago Rapid Transit Company properties.

October 26, 1943. Major General Philip B. Fleming, Administrator PWA, commended the City Administration for continuing its effort to find a solution (municipal ownership plan proposed by Mayor Kelly) to the complex local transportation problem.

November 3, 1943. Negotiators began series of conferences with the Committee appointed by the Mayor in regard to proposed purchase of local transit systems.

November 6, 1943. Chas. A. McDonald, Special Master in Chancery of the Circuit Court of Cook County, issued report on application for an injunction by the Chicago Rapid Transit Company, in which he stated a 2-cent increase in fare and a 1-cent inter-company transfer to be just and fair return on an $80,000,000 evaluation of the Chicago Rapid Transit Company properties.

November 13, 1943. The Sidley Committee appointed by the Court presented a memorandum to Judge Igoe expressing the opinion that the equity proceedings involving the Chicago Surface Lines afforded ample means for transfer of title to the properties to the City of Chicago or any other purchaser free and clear of all existing liens. The Committee further stated that the various Committees representing security holders entitled to participate in the reorganization had sufficient power to work out the program and details necessary to transfer the title.

November 16, 1943. Mayor's special committee outlined procedure for preparing draft of an ordinance for public ownership of local transit lines and for negotiating purchase price of the properties of Chicago Surface Lines, Chicago Rapid Transit Company and Chicago Motor Coach Company.

November 17, 1943. The City ownership and operation of the local transportation systems proposed by Mayor Kelly on October 13, 1943, was approved in principle by the City Council. The Council authorized the Mayor and Local Transportation Committee to begin negotiations immediately to put into effect the public ownership plan.

November 22, 1943. City of Chicago, State of Illinois and Illinois Commerce Commission filed objections to Special Master McDonald's report.

December 2, 1943. Special Master McDonald overruled all objections to his report of November 6, 1943.

December 6, 1943. The Sidley Committee reported to the Federal Court on progress of negotiations for purchase of local transit properties by the City and advised that they have asked the City to submit proposals as to purchase price. The Court approved the progress and instructed the interested parties to consider modification of the reorganization plan for operation under the 1941 ordinance in the event that plans for public ownership should fail.

TABLE 1
Sources of 1,410 Cars and Buses on Order to 10/47

```
200 PCC Planned   × 3 =  600     600 PCC
270 Bus On Order  × 3 =  810    ⎰ 600 Motor Bus
                                ⎱ 210 Trolley Bus
─────────────────
470 (10/17/44)    × 3 = 1410    1410 Ord. to 10-1-47
```

Sometime in 1945, the quantities of equipment on order 10/17/44 were tripled.

TABLE 2
CSL Bus Procurement: 1942-1947

Models	CRys	CCR	C&SC	Totals
Mack LC	14	5	1	20
Mack LD	16	4	—	20
Yellow 3606	18	2	—	20
ACF 36s	15	10	—	25
ACF 41s	4	12	9	25
White 788	12	8	—	20
Twin 41 G	13	7	—	20
X by ODT 1942	92	48	10	150
(Auth. 5/25/42)	(78)	(43)	(9)	(130)
White 798	67-2	24-14	4-4	95-20
Ford 29-B	18	8	9	35
GM 4007	—	19-10	1	20-10
Option 1943	85-2	51-24	14-4	150-30
On Order 1944	177	99	24	300
—ODT Release	-2	-24	-4	-30
On Order 10/17/44	175	75	20	270

TABLE 3
PCC Car and Bus Orders by Underlying Owner

```
CRys  ⎰ 59.3% ⎱  100%
CCR   ⎱ 40.7% ⎰
        ⎰ CCR   81.79%              ⎰ C&SC ⎱
100% ⎨                  ÷ equally ⎨ SSR   ⎬ 6.07% each
        ⎱ Rest  18.21%              ⎱ C&W  ⎰
```

	CRys	CCR	Totals
PCC Orig. (Auth. 3/16/45)	120	80	200
Add (Auth. 12/5/45)	240	160	400
Total PCC	360	240	600

	CRys	CCR	C&SC	Totals
Bus	445	345	20	810
PCC	360	240	—	600
	805	585	20	1410
		20		
		605 South Side		

TABLE 4
Changes in Original 1944 Equipment Plans

Bus Plan	CRys	CCR	C&SC	Totals
Orig. 1944	175 ⎱285	75 ⎱160	20	270 ⎱465
Add 1945	110 ⎰ ⎱210	85 ⎰ ⎱195	—	195 ⎰
Trolley 270 ⎰	100 ⎰ ⎰270	110 ⎰	—	210
Add 1947 ⎱	60 ⎰	75 ⎱	—	135
	445	345	20	810
Bus Orig.	175	75	20	270
Add	270	270	—	540
	445	345	20	810
Motor Bus	345	235	20	600
Trolley Bus	100	110	—	210
	445	345	20	810

1-23-45 Joint Board voted to purchase: 270 Motor Bus "Firm orders awaiting ODT release;" 100 Trolley Bus "Awaiting Bids;" 200 PCC "Awaiting Bids."

3-16-45 Authorized 195 Motor Bus, 200 PCC, bids still out on 100 Trolley Bus.

10-8-45 Authorized to solicit bids, 10-17-45 Authorized to order:

270 Motor Bus; 400 PCC; 210 Trolley Bus; expenditure authorized 12-5-45, except bids not received on 210 Trolley Buses.

210 Trolley Buses ordered 1946-47 as authorized 10-17-45, but no authorization for expenditure prior to 10-1-47.

TABLE 5
Old Series CSL Buses 401-837 by Owner and Model

401-440	CCR	Listed p. 388; 435-445 (36002)	—
441-445[1]	CCR	Mack LC 32 pass.	5
446-451	CCR	Yellows p. 388 (36006)	—
452-453	CCR	Yellow TG 3606 36 pass.	2
454-457	CCR	Mack LD 35 pass.	4
458-467	CCR	ACF 36s 36 pass.	10
468-479	CCR	ACF 41s 41 pass.	12
480-487	CCR	White 788 40 pass.	8
488-494	CCR	Twin 41 G 41 pass.	7
501-646	CRys	Listed p. 388; 626-660 (35007)	—
647-660[1]	CRys	Mack LC 32 pass.	14
661-676	CRys	Mack LD 35 pass.	16
677-694	CRys	Yellow TG 3606	18
695-709	CRys	ACF 36s	15
710-713	CRys	ACF 41s	4
714-725	CRys	White 788	12
726-738	CRys	Twin 41 G	13
801-827	C&SC	Listed p. 388; 826-828 (37000)	—
828[1]	C&SC	Mack LC	1
829-837	C&SC	ACF 41s	9

[1] 20 Mack LC ($10,541.89) ordered 10-15-41 along with 9 Twin 30 G's, 20 Yellow TG 3205's and 6 TDH 3605's which were delivered. 130 remaining units listed above, ordered 5-25-42, never delivered.

TABLE 6
CSL Buses by Owner and Model 1944 and 1945

On Order 10-17-44	CRys	CCR	C&SC	Totals
White 798	65	10	—	75
Ford 29-B	18	8	9	35 } 110[1]
GM 4007	—	9	1	10
Mack LC	14	5	1	20
Mack LD	16	4	—	20
Yellow 3606	18	2	—	20
ACF 36s	15	10	—	25
ACF 41s	4	12	9	25 } 160[2]
White 788	12	8	—	20
Twin 41 G	13	7	—	20
Totals	175	75	20	270

	CRys	CCR	C&SC	Totals
1943 Options	83	18	9	110 } 195
Repl. Orders	62	14	9	85
Open	30	43	2	75
	92	57	11	160
Totals	175	75	20	270

	CRys	CCR	C&SC	Totals
Open 3-45	30	43	2	75
Add 1945	110	85	—	195
Auth. 12-5-45	140	128	2	270

[1]110 Authorized 3-16-45, originally ordered 1943.
[2]160 Not built as ordered, replaced.

TABLE 7
Bus Purchases Authorized 12/5/45 and 9/16/47

Auth. 12-5-45	CRys	CCR	C&SC	Totals
1600-1619	—	20	—	20
1800-1817	—	18	—	18
3503-3572	38	32	—	70
6521-6527	7	—	—	7
6800-6838	24	15	—	39
7100-7105	6	—	—	6
	75	85	0	160
(BOSE Acct. No.)	(35123)	(36088)		
1400-1404	1	4	—	5
3800-3824	—	25	—	25
4400-4465	50	14	2	66
6528-6530	3	—	—	3
7106-7116	11	—	—	11
	65	43	2	110
(BOSE Acct. No.)	(35164)	(36120)	(37037)	
Total Auth.	140	128	2	270
Trolley Buses	100	110	—	210
Auth. 9-16-47				
2359-2433	—	75	—	75
2546-2605	60	—	—	60
Total Auth.	60	75	—	135

TABLE 8
Bus Purchases Authorized 3/16/45

Auth. 3-16-45	CRys	CCR	C&SC	Totals
3421-3495	65	10	—	75
4301-4335	18	8	9	35
1943 Options	83	18	9	110
3496-3502	—	2	5	7
2301-2358	50	6	2	58
6501-6520	12	6	2	20
Repl. Orders	62	14	9	85
Total Auth.	145	32	18	195
(BOSE Acct. No.)	(35117)	(36083)	(37022)	

TABLE 9
Chicago Surface Lines Motor Buses: 2-1-47

Auth.	3-16-45	12-5-45	Totals
CRys	145	140	285
CCR	32	128	160
C&SC	18	2	20
Total	195	270	465

TABLE 10
Chicago City Railway Co. Buses

3-45	12-45		
—	4	1401-1404 (To C&SC)	
—	7	1600-1606	
—	2	1607-1608 (To SSR)	
—	6	1609-1614	
6	—	2351-2356 (To C&SC)	
10	—	3486-3495 (To C&SC)	
8	—	4328-4335	
6	—	6513-6518 (To C&SC)	
—	1	6824 (To C&SC)	
—	9	6825-6833 (To SSR)	
—	5	6834-6838	
30	34		64 Del.
—	5	1615-1619	
—	18	1800-1817	
2	—	3496-3497	
—	32	3541-3572	
—	25	3800-3824[1]	
—	14	4450-4463[2]	
2	94		96 On Ord.
32	128		160 Auth.
-22	-16		- 38
10	112		122

[1]Cancelled, replaced — 3573-3597; 9-15-47.
[2]Cancelled, replaced — 2535-2544 (10), 4351-4354 (4); 4-15-47.
Cancelled postwar buses were of the following types: 3800-3824 White 32 pass. model 784, 4400-4465 Ford 31 pass. This model not put into production, probably due to reorganization of Transit Bus Sales/Transit Buses Inc.

TABLE 11
Chicago Railways Co. Buses

3-45	12-45		
—	1	1400	
50	—	2301-2350	
65	—	3421-3485	
18	—	4310-4327	
12	—	6501-6512	
—	24	6800-6823	
145	25		170 Del.
—	38	3503-3540	
—	50	4400-4449[1]	
—	10	6521-6530	
—	17	7100-7116	
	115		115 On Ord.
145	140		285 Auth.

[1]Cancelled, replaced — 2500-2534 (35), 4336-4350 (15); 4-15-47.

TABLE 12
Calumet & South Chicago Railway Buses

3-45	12-45		
2	—	2357-2358	
9	—	4301-4309	
2	—	6519-6520	
13	—		13 Del.
5	—	3498-3502	
—	2	4464-4465[1]	
5	2		7 On Ord.
18	2		20 Auth.

[1]Cancelled, replaced — 2545, 4355; 4-15-47.

TABLE 13
CSL Bus Deliveries: 1945-1948

	3-16-45	12-5-45	9-16-47	Totals Del.
1945	55	—	—	55
1946	133	59	—	192
1947 (To 10-1)	7	120	60	187
1947 (Post 10-1)	—	20	75	95
1948	—	71	—	71
Totals Auth.	195	270	135	600

TABLE 14
Number of Buses by Type of Transmission
10-1-47

Gas/Mechanical	600	600 Mech.
Gas/Hydraulic	57 + 166 On Order = 223 }	259 Hyd.
Diesel/Hydraulic	36 +36 }	
	693 + 166 = 859	859

TABLE 15
Chicago Surface Lines Motor Bus Deliveries

	CRys	CCR	C&SC	SSR	Totals	
1927	5	—	—	—	5	
1928	—	3	—	—	3	
1930	2	—	—	—	2	
1934	—	4	—	—	4	
1935	16	11	9	—	36	
1936	9	3	—	—	12	
1937	50	10	3	—	63	
1938	6	4	10	—	20	
1939	10	2	3	—	15	
1941	34	—	—	—	34	
1942	21	12	2	—	35	
1944	2	24	4	—	30	
1945	38	8	9	—	55	
1946	132	18	31	11	192	
1947	140	41	6	—	187	(To 10-1)
10-1-47	465	140	77	11	693	
On Order						
1947	—	95	—	—	95[1]	
1948	35	35	1	—	71[2]	
Total	35	130	1	—	166	
Totals	500	270	78	11	859	

[1]CSL order delivered to CTA after 10-1-47: 2359-2433 (75), 3553-3572 (20).
[2]CSL order delivered 1948: 2500-2545 (46), 3573-3597 (25).

Where the first CTA buses came from: Under provisions of a City Ordinance passed September 28, 1944, the Department of Subways and Superhighways placed orders for 500 buses and 65 three-section articulated rapid transit cars. The 500 buses were: 160 45-passenger GM diesels, 100 44-passenger gas Twin Coaches, 100 45-passenger gas Macks, and 20 36-passenger gas ACF-Brills, all ordered October 4. Twenty Ford Transits were ordered October 5, and 100 44-passenger gas Whites were ordered October 23. An Ordinance of May 23, 1947 conveyed rights to these options to CTA, which put 460 of the buses up for bid October 28, with the bids due December 16. The 20 ACF-Brills and the 20 Fords were not put up for bid. On December 20, the CTA ordered 100 Twin Coaches (1700-1799), its first bus purchase, and they began to arrive January 31, 1948. On January 3, 1948, CTA ordered the 100 Whites (3598-3697) and 160 GM diesels (6531-6690), but the last 60 GMs (6631-6690) were cancelled March 9, 1948 because of a fuel shortage. The Mack bid was rejected, as were the ACF-Brill bids against both Twin and Mack on the above options. The Department of Subways and Superhighways ordered 35 articulated subway cars from Pullman and 30 from St. Louis Car Co., but both orders were cancelled. CSL's underlying companies were liquidated February 15, 1950, their certificates were cremated June 22, 1960, and the legal case was closed with the sending of a BK-74 to Washington on September 30, 1969.

TABLE 16
Chicago Surface Lines Bus Account Scheme: 1945-47

```
CCR  ⎰110 Trolley              CRys ⎰100 Trolley                      = 210 Trolley Buses
195  ⎱ 85 (36088)              175  ⎱ 75 (35123)                     = 160 (Auth. 12-5-45, 1st Grp.)
            CRys ⎰145 (35117)  CCR ⎰32 (36083)  C&SC ⎰18 (37022)     = 195 (Auth. 3-16-45)
            210  ⎱ 65 (35164)  75  ⎱43 (36120)  20   ⎱ 2 (37037)     = 110 (Auth. 12-5-45, 2nd Grp.)
       75 (2359-2433)      60 (2546-2605)                            = 135 (Auth. 9-16-47)
       ─────────          ─────────            ─────────              ─────────────────
       270 CCR            270 CRys             270 CSL                810 Ordered to 10-1-47
```

	Orig. Auth.				Adjusted		1927-44		
CRys	345		—		345	+	155	=	500
CCR	235	−	38	=	197	+	73	=	270
C&SC	20	+	27	=	47	+	31	=	78
SSR	0	+	11	=	11	+	0	=	11
	600 Motor	(1945-1947)				+	259	(1927-1944)	=	859

TABLE 17

CSL Bus Order Changes by Builder: 1945-1947

	On Order 10-17-44	Totals	
Ord. 1943	White 798	75	⎱ 110 1943 Option Blt. as Ordered (Auth. 3-16-45)
	Ford 29-8	35	⎰
	GM 4007	— 10	10 GM (Repl. 6521-6530) Auth. 12-5-45
Auth. 10-15-41	Mack LC	— 20	⎱ 40 Mack-17 (7100-7116) = 23 Not Repl., 17 Auth. 12-5-45
	Mack LD	— 20	⎰
	Yellow 3606	— 20	20 Yellow (Repl. 6501-6520) Auth. 3-16-45
Auth. 5-25-42	ACF 36s	— 25	⎱ 50 ACF (Repl. 2301-2350) Auth. 3-16-45
	ACF 41s	— 25	⎰
	White 788	— 20	20 White/Gen. Am. Option 1945 (Auth. White 12-5-45; X Gen. Am. 9-16-47)
	Twin 41G	— 20	20 Twin + 23 (Repl. Mack) = 43 Twin Auth. 12-5-45
	Totals	270	160 Replacements Ord. 1945
			270 Original Orders by Builder As Replaced 1945

TABLE 18

Grand Summary of CSL Bus Order Changes by Year and Equipment Builder: 1942-1947

	1942	1943	ODT Release	10-17-44		Add 1945	2-1-47	1947	10-1-47
White	20	+ 95	=115 −20	= 20+ 75= 95+		7+75	(20)=177		177
ACF	50		50	50	50+	8	= 58	+46+135	=239
Yellow/GM	20	+ 20	= 40 −10	= 20+ 10= 30+		39	= 69		69
Ford		35	35	35	35+	66	=101	−46	= 55
Twin	20		20	20	20		+23 = 43		43
Mack	40		40	40	40		−23= 17		17
Gen. Am.							(20)[1]		
Totals	150	+ 150	= 300 − 30 = 270	150+120=270		+195	=465	+135	=600

[1]Twenty General American Aerocoach model T-361 tentatively ordered in 1945 when that company announced its projected transit bus, but due to protracted development these were never officially ordered. On September 12, 1947 authorization to purchase these along with 135 ACF-Brills was requested from the bankruptcy court, this authorization being granted September 16 for the ACF's but denied for the General Americans. This action was apparently a move to release CSL (soon to be CTA) from any possible obligation to purchase in the future rather than a serious intention to acquire the buses. Numbers were assigned in the 8100 series, 8100-8112 (13) Chicago Railways and 8113-8119 (7) Chicago City Railway.

December 7, 1943. The special committee for transit negotiations reported to Mayor Kelly on progress. It was agreed that steps be taken by the City to determine a reasonable fair commercial value of the Surface Lines and Elevated properties and that lump sum purchase prices be submitted to the Court's committee for transmittal to the Federal Court for consideration and approval.

January 7, 1944. Commissioner Harrington submitted to City's traction subcommittee his recommendations for lump sum offers to be made to owners of Chicago Surface Lines and Chicago Rapid Transit Company properties.

January 28, 1944. Mayor Kelly advised the Sidley Committee that the City's traction subcommittee authorized him to suggest that the City pay for the Surface Lines properties the lump sum cash price of $75,000,000, with the owners of Chicago Surface Lines to retain cash in excess of $27,500,000 estimated at approximately $8,000,000 or a total of $83,000,000. He suggested for Chicago Rapid Transit Company properties (except certain non-transportation property carried on the Company's books at $3,500,000) the lump sum cash price of $11,000,000.

The Sidley Committee submitted this suggestion to Judge Igoe who expressed the Court's desire that the plan for public ownership be carried out; but asked that plan for reorganization under private ownership with operation under the 1941 Traction Ordinance be revised for resubmission to Illinois Commerce Commission, to insure action on traction settlement in the event that the public ownership plan is not completed.

February 19, 1944. Commissioner Harrington in a statement to the Committee on Local Transportation recommended drafting of the major terms of an ordinance for public ownership so that the complete situation could be presented to the Federal Court. The Committee authorized drafting of the ordinance.

March 6, 1944. Sidley Committee submitted suggestion to Federal Court for amendments to 1942 reorganization plan, providing for a reduction of first mortgage bond interest to four percent on both Series A ($72,718,350) and Series B ($7,002,290), with only two percent interest on Series A being fixed; remaining interest and sinking fund being contingent on earnings. Other equities would be represented by 996,279 shares of no-par common stock.

May 5, 1944. The Court heard evidence on certain objections to the plan particularly to the effect that a 5 percent interest rate on first mortgage bonds was justified. In a statement by Mayor Kelly which was presented to the Court, it was stated that if the utilities are unable to bring forth an assured improvement program the solution must be found in requiring the owners to find a buyer who can and will finance the required improvements.

May 19, 1944. Judge Igoe in a memorandum on the proposed amendments to the reorganization plan stated "I am firmly of the opinion that if reorganization is to be accomplished in these foreclosure suits we must start the financial structure of the new company with a first mortgage bond issue limited to $45,000,000 with 4 percent interest per annum."

June 2, 1944. Surface Lines' first mortgage bondholders expressed dissatisfaction with the proposal that first mortgage bonds issued by the new company be limited to $45,000,000. They suggest that the Surface Lines be permitted to complete their own reorganization first and ask that every effort be made to determine as speedily as possible whether municipal ownership can be effected.

June 9, 1944. In response to a request for a continuance to allow time to determine whether an acceptable public ownership plan could be developed, the Court granted the continuance but stated that the corporate reorganization plan must also go forward. The Court stated that the suggestions filed in that regard were of no assistance to the Court at all and suggested that the interested parties study the petition for bankruptcy.

June 23, 1944. Plan proposed by Mayor Kelly presented to Court for City purchase of transit properties. The prices having been discussed with practically all of them, this plan apparently had the approval of the chairmen of most of the security holders' committees. Draft of Public Ownership Ordinance filed on this date. The court indicated concern over the method of transferring title to the properties to the City under the pending equity foreclosure proceedings and stated that under the existing condition, as related to the reorganization attempts, the Court was obliged to grant a hearing to the petitioners in the bankruptcy suit.

June 30, 1944. Counsel for the City expressed the opinion that the only solution left was the sale of the properties by the private owners to the City under the equity proceedings and that placing the Surface Lines in bankruptcy would delay consummation of a sale by a year or more.

August 8, 1944. In the report and recommendation for Expediting Settlement of Chicago's Traction Problem submitted to Committee on Local Transportation by Commissioner Harrington, the suggestion was made that the City offer to pay $75,000,000 for Surface Lines properties with City to receive CSL renewal funds and that the City offer to pay $9,650,000 for Rapid Transit Properties, with CRT to retain their cash and non-operating property and the City to assume CRT taxes prior to 1940.

August 15, 1944. City Council passed resolution by 41 to 0 vote, approving Commissioner Harrington's report and the formal presentation of the City's offer to the Court.

August 16, 1944. Report on Public Ownership and the City Council's formal price offers were presented to the Federal Court by counsel for City and taken under advisement by the Court. Counsel for bondholders' groups indicated that they were interested in the City's offer but suggested no procedure to expedite matters. The Court expressed the opinion, with which the City's counsel differed, that bankruptcy proceedings would expedite matters.

September 6, 1944. Commissioner Harrington submitted report to Mayor Kelly and Chairman Quinn on "Program for Immediate Post-War Improvement in Transit Service," and suggested that inasmuch as it appeared from the legal proceedings in the Federal Court that it would require one or two years before the Elevated and Surface properties could attain a status whereby they could be acquired by the City and that, since money rates and other conditions may materially change, the pending price offer of the City for these properties should be withdrawn for the present.

September 8, 1944. The City Council acting on Commissioner Harrington's report of September 6, directed the Corporation Counsel to present a copy of this suggested program for immediate improvement in service to the Federal Court and the Receivers and Trustees of Chicago Surface Lines and Chicago Rapid Transit Company.

September 18, 1944. Federal Court approved the petitions on Bankruptcy under Chapter X for the Surface Lines Companies and appointed Thomas J. Friel and Charles C. Renshaw as trustees in bankruptcy for Chicago Railways Company; and Edward J. Fleming and Charles H. Albers as trustees in bankruptcy for Chicago City Railway Company and Calumet and South Chicago Railway Company. The Court also requested representatives of the Surface Lines and the Rapid Transit Company to report their views on the recommendations of Commissioner Harrington for immediate improvement of these properties.

September 21, 1944. Committee on Local Transportation recommended passage of an ordinance authorizing Commissioner Harrington to place priority orders on behalf of the City for 500 buses and 130 subway-elevated cars; and recommended withdrawal of City's offer to purchase the local transportation properties.

September 28, 1944. City Council passed above ordinance and resolution.

October 31, 1944. Trustees of Chicago Surface Lines and of Chicago Rapid Transit companies reported concerning the status of their endeavors to obtain new equipment and their program for the acquisition of such new equipment.

November 10, 1944. City Council extended date for acceptance of 1941 traction ordinance to February 1, 1945. In granting this extension the Council cited, among other things that "In authorizing a relatively short extension of time for acceptance of said ordinance, the City of Chicago will retain the right to refuse further extensions of time and the right to permit said ordinance to lapse if, in the opinion of the City, the new corporation which would be established under any plan of reorganization will not be able financially to provide the transit improvements contemplated in said ordinance."

November 15, 1944. Judge Igoe in a memorandum offered suggestions for a new plan of reorganization under Chapter X with unification of Chicago Surface Lines and Chicago Rapid Transit Company and operation under the 1941 traction ordinance and directed the trustees to present a complete plan.

November 29, 1944. Trustees of Chicago Surface Lines companies and of Chicago Rapid Transit Company present plan for reorganization and unification with proposed capitalization of new company consisting of $45,000,000 first mortgage 4 percent Series A bonds, $40,264,310 first mortgage 4½ percent Series B, income bonds, and 996,279 shares of no-par common stock. The plan provides that holders of the $72,718,350 existing Surface Lines first mortgage bonds would receive the $45,000,000 of new Series A first mortgage bonds and $33,262,020 of the new Series B income bonds with the proviso that the latter may be reduced to $27,718,350 if the Court finds it feasible to distribute $3,635,000 in cash to these security holders.

November 29, 1944. Commissioner Harrington reported to Committee on Local Transportation that orders had been placed by him on behalf of the City with manufacturers for 500 transit-type buses and 65 three-compartment elevated-subway cars (equivalent in capacity to 130 present cars). The chairman of the committee transmitted copies of these orders to Trustees of Chicago Surface Lines and Chicago Rapid Transit Company and advised them that each of the orders contains a provision whereby the City may assign the order to any transportation public utility authorized to operate within the City of Chicago without loss to such assignee of the City's production priority position. The City's hope was expressed that the Trustees would develop programs for providing, next year, improvement in service which may include the taking over of these priority orders.

December 13, 1944. Counsel for Securities and Exchange Commission expressed desire to Federal Court that valuation of properties and allocation of securities should not be bound by previous orders in the equity cases.

December 19, 1944. In Federal Court it was determined that the Trustees should meet with the various objectors to the reorganization plan to ascertain if common agreement can be reached.

January 15, 1945. The Federal Court authorized Trustees of Chicago Rapid Transit Company to place orders with manufacturers for a train of four articulated motor cars (equivalent in capacity to eight of the present steel cars).

January 16, 1945. City Council extended time for acceptance of 1941 traction ordinance to May 1, 1945.

January 19, 1945. The Federal Court granted the City permission to file a plan for public ownership in the bankruptcy proceedings as soon as the complete plan is drafted and approved by the City Council. Hearing was held on objections to the Trustees plan of reorganization.

January 26, 1945. The Federal Court, in an order to the Joint Board of Management and Operation of Chicago Surface Lines, ordered the Board to make every effort to obtain priority for orders of 200 streetcars, 100 trolley buses and 270 gas buses.

February 9, 1945. The Federal Court entered an order for the Trustees of the transit companies to submit the reorganization plan of November 29, 1944 to the

Illinois Commerce Commission for review as to the public interest therein; and an order submitting the plan to the Securities and Exchange Commission for its advisory report.

February 17, 1945. Governor Green and Mayor Kelly agreed to propose, to the various legislative bodies, a comprehensive transit plan providing for a Metropolitan Transit Authority which may acquire and operate all local transportation (except steam and electric interurban railroads) in Metropolitan Cook County.

February 26, 1945. Committee on Local Transportation approved Proposal for acquisition of Surface Lines and Rapid Transit Lines and Plan of Distribution to security holders; also recommended to City Council the passage of a resolution approved the proposal of Governor Green and Mayor Kelly for establishment of a Metropolitan Transit Authority.

February 27, 1945. City Council adopted the Proposal and Plan for public ownership and passed resolution approving the proposal of Governor Green and Mayor Kelly.

February 28, 1945. The City's Plan and Proposal for Public ownership was filed with the Federal Court.

March 3, 1945. The Federal Court authorized the Joint Board of Management and Operation of Chicago Surface Lines to enter into contracts with specified manufacturers for 200 new streetcars and 195 new buses.

April 2, 1945. Answers to objections and suggestions to City's Plan and Proposal filed in Federal Court by City.

April 9, 1945. City presented testimony in Federal Court as to fairness of its offer for properties of Chicago Surface Lines and Chicago Rapid Transit Company.

April 12, 1945. Governor Green signed the Transit Authority Act, which was passed by the State Legislature on April 5, 1945.

April 16, 1945. Draft of Ordinance, granting to Chicago Transit Authority the right to operate a Local Transportation System within the City of Chicago, presented to City Council and ordered by it to be deferred and published. City Council extended date for acceptance of 1941 traction ordinance to June 11, 1945.

April 19, 1945. Committee on Local Transportation approved final draft of ordinance to Chicago Transit Authority.

April 23, 1945. City Council passed ordinance granting exclusive right to Chicago Transit Authority to operate a local transportation system within the City of Chicago by 44 to 0 vote.

April 23, 1945. Federal Court certified City's Proposal and Plan for public ownership as being worthy of consideration and submitted it to Illinois Commerce Commission for report as to the public interest therein; also to Security and Exchange Commission for report by them.

April 30, 1945. Mayor Kelly signed traction ordinance

granting exclusive rights to Chicago Transit Authority.

May 23, 1945. Illinois Supreme Court in an opinion approved the basis on which a 12¢ fare was sought by Chicago Rapid Transit Lines, but petitions for rehearing were filed later by City and other interested parties.

June 4, 1945. The voters at a referendum approved the Metropolitan Transit Authority Act and the City ordinance granting exclusive rights to Chicago Transit Authority, by a six to one vote.

June 6, 1945. Illinois Commerce Commission found the Trustees plan of November 29, 1944, for private ownership, as not in the public interest and approved City's Plan of February 28, 1945, for public ownership and stated it to be most likely to bring about needed improvements in transportation.

June 8, 1945. The Federal Court stated that the 1941 ordinance, so far as the bankruptcy case is concerned was at an end. At that time the Court signed an order submitted by Mr. J. F. Elward, representing $2,100,000 principal amount of Northwestern Elevated Railroad Company bonds, giving leave to adopt the City's plan on the condition that earnings after April 30, 1945 shall go to the benefit of security holders and that the elevated Trustees keep the property in a physical condition at least equal to that of April 30, 1945.

June 11, 1945. The 1941 traction ordinance expired— last date for acceptance.

June 13, 1945. City Council approved amendment to City's plan in accordance with Mr. Elward's suggestion of June 8. The amendment was subsequently filed in Federal Court on June 28th.

June 14, 1945. Deliveries of 75 new buses for Chicago Motor Coach Company started.

June 20, 1945. Governor Green's appointment of John Q. Adams, Philip W. Collins and George F. Getz, Jr., to Chicago Transit Board was confirmed by the State Senate.

June 21, 1945. Mayor Kelly's appointment of Philip Harrington, Irvin L. Porter and James R. Quinn to Chicago Transit Board was confirmed by the City Council.

June 26, 1945. Mayor Kelly's appointment of William W. McKenna to Chicago Transit Board was confirmed by the City Council.

June 28, 1945. First meeting of Chicago Transit Board, Philip Harrington selected as chairman, William W. McKenna selected as secretary and Irvin L. Porter selected as treasurer.

July 10, 1945. Chicago Transit Board accepted ordinance of the City of Chicago of April 23, 1945 granting to the Authority the exclusive right to acquire, construct, reconstruct, maintain and operate facilities for local transportation within the City of Chicago for the term of 50 years and thereafter until terminated. The Board also consented to the assignment to the Authority of the rights of the City of Chicago under the City's proposal and plan of February 28, 1945, as amended to date, to acquire the Surface Lines and Rapid Transit properties. The Board also passed an ordinance providing for the issuance of $90,000,000 revenue bonds for the acquisition of a transportation system and for the execution and delivery of a trust agreement.

July 12, 1945. The State's Attorney of Cook County, in the name of the people of the State of Illinois, instituted two causes in the Circuit Court of Cook County. One was an action at law in quo warranto questioning the franchises and powers of the Chicago Transit Authority and the right of the members of Chicago Transit Board to hold their offices. The other was an information in chancery seeking to enjoin the Chicago Transit Authority from issuing bonds and from expending certain moneys appropriated by the City Council of the City of Chicago.

July 24, 1945. Governor Green approved the "Park Acts." These were amendments to the Chicago Park District Act giving Chicago Transit Authority the right to operate buses on boulevards and driveways of the Park District subject to compensation payments agreed upon between the Authority and the Park District.

July 30, 1945. Judge Miner of the Circuit Court of Cook County in an opinion reviewed the legal points presented by the two informations filed by the people. All of the objections made by the people were overruled and a motion to strike the information in each case was sustained.

August 2, 1945. Notice of Appeal of Chicago Transit Authority cases filed by State's Attorney of Cook County in Illinois Supreme Court.

August 13, 1945. Securities and Exchange Commission submitted its advisory report to the Federal Court on the City's Plan and Proposal of February 28, 1945 as amended. It was the conclusion of the Commission that the upset price proposed for the properties of Chicago Rapid Transit Company is fair and the upset price proposed for Chicago Surface Lines would be fair if the City waives its claims to the City Compensation Fund and if the Trustees are permitted to retain net earnings up to the date of the transfer of the properties.

August 14, 1945. Chicago Transit Board adopted a statement of policy to lay plans and take steps as promptly as possible to initiate a program designed to secure adequate and modern transit facilities in Chicago and in such other municipalities in the Metropolitan Area as may so desire.

August 17, 1945. Judge Igoe entered an order that Chicago Transit Authority be substituted in the place of the City of Chicago under the Proposal and Plan of the City dated February 28, 1945.

August 27, 1945. Brief and Argument filed with Illinois State Supreme Court by States' Attorney of Cook County in Chicago Transit Authority test case.

September 8, 1945. Brief and Argument filed with Illinois State Supreme Court by Chicago Transit Authority and the City of Chicago in Transit Authority test case.

September 19, 1945. Groups of Surface Lines Security Holders met with Chicago Transit Board and agreed to draft modifications of City's Plan and Proposal of February 28, 1945, in accordance with recommendations of Securities and Exchange Commission.

September 21, 1945. Oral argument in Chicago Transit Authority test case before the Illinois Supreme Court in Springfield.

September 24, 1945. The Federal Court stated that it would consider a modified plan and proposal of Chicago Transit Authority for purchase of Surface Lines, based on recommendations of Securities and Exchange Commission.

October 8, 1945. Amended Proposal and Plan of Chicago Transit Authority for purchase of Chicago Surface Lines filed in Federal Court.

October 15, 1945. Amended Proposal and Plan of Chicago Transit Authority for purchase of Rapid Transit Lines filed in Federal Court. Hearings begun on Surface Lines and Rapid Transit Plans.

October 17, 1945. Judge Igoe of the Federal Court entered an order (which was endorsed by Chicago Transit Authority) authorizing Trustees of Surface Lines to spend up to $15,000,000 for transit equipment.

October 22, 1945. Committee on Local Transportation recommended that City Council pass ordinances waiving claims against Chicago Surface Lines and Chicago Rapid Transit Company (subject to similar waivers of Trustees or Companies for claims against the City) if Chicago Transit Authority's Proposal and Plan for purchase of properties is made effective.

October 25, 1945. Both of above ordinances passed by City Council by unanimous vote.

November 13, 1945. Representatives of western suburbs appeared before Chicago Transit Board for discussion concerning local transportation in their communities.

November 21, 1945. Illinois Supreme Court, in an opinion, upheld legality of Transit Authority Act.

November 23, 1945. Chicago Transit Board authorized the Chairman to appoint a committee to negotiate with Chicago Motor Coach Company for the purchase of that property. The Chairman of the Board appointed Mr. Collins (Chairman), Mr. Porter and Mr. Quinn as members of this committee.

November 23, 1945. Mr. John Q. Adams elected Vice-Chairman of Chicago Transit Board.

November 30, 1945. Chicago Transit Board's Committee on Acquisition of Chicago Motor Coach Company held first meeting with company representatives.

December 11, 1945. Chicago Transit Board authorized employment of W. C. Gilman & Co., by Committee on Acquisition of Chicago Motor Coach Co., to study and report on that property and to advise the Committee. Negotiations with Motor Coach Co. representatives continued through the remainder of the year.

December 13, 1945. Amendment to Chicago Transit Authority's Proposal and Plan for purchase of Chicago Surface Lines filed in Federal Court, providing for agreed settlement with holders of minority capital stock of Chicago City Railway Company.

December 28, 1945. Taking of testimony completed in Federal Court on proposal of Chicago Transit Authority to purchase Chicago Surface Lines.

January 14, 1946. Final oral arguments presented in the District Court on Chicago Transit Authority's Proposal and Plan to acquire Chicago Surface Lines. Arguments were presented by attorneys for the Authority, the security holders who joined in and adopted the plan and by attorneys for objectors. Arguments were held from January 14th to January 18th, 1946.

February 8, 1946. Securities and Exchange Commission filed in the District Court its supplementary report on Amended Plan of Chicago Transit Authority to acquire Chicago Surface Lines and stated that in its opinion the plan is fair except for the proposed allowance to holders of Chicago City Railway Company's minority stock.

February 15, 1946. Judge Igoe of the District Court filed opinions holding Chicago Transit Authority's Plan for purchase of Chicago Surface Lines (as modified in accordance with the suggestion of S. E. C.) and its Plan for purchase of Chicago Rapid Transit Lines to be fair and equitable, and feasible, and warranted their submission to the security holders.

February 19, 1946. Chicago Transit Board authorized the Chairman to appoint a committee to negotiate for acquisition of South Suburban Safeway Lines, Inc.

February 27, 1946. The District Court entered "Findings of Fact, Conclusions of Law and Orders Approving Plans" for acquisition by Chicago Transit Authority of Chicago Surface Lines and Chicago Rapid Transit Lines.

March 11, 1946. The District Court entered orders approving certain documents to be sent to the security holders providing forms to indicate their approval or disapproval of the reorganization plans of Chicago Surface Lines and Chicago Rapid Transit Lines.

March 20, 1946. Illinois State Supreme Court held the ten cent fare of Chicago Rapid Transit to be confiscatory and directed the Illinois Commerce Commission to fix a rate of fare which would provide sufficient revenue to meet operating expenses.

March 28, 1946. Notice filed in the District Court by counsel for Chicago Railways Consolidated Mortgage Series B bondholders of intention to appeal from the orders of the District Court in the Surface Lines Reorganization Plan; similar notice filed by minority stockholders of Chicago City Railway Company.

March 29, 1946. Chicago Transit Board authorized the Chairman to appoint a committee to ascertain the possibility of acquisition by it of the properties of Bluebird Coach Lines, Inc., and of Suburban Transit Company.

April 19, 1946. A Board of Arbitration granted Chicago Surface Lines operating employees a wage increase of 18 cents an hour for 2-man car operators and 20 cents an hour for 1-man car operators and bus drivers. This increase to be retroactive to March 17, 1946.

May 15, 1946. Trustees of Chicago Surface Lines and Chicago Rapid Transit Company filed reports in the District Court stating that security holders expressed their approval of the reorganization plans by assents ranging from 91 percent to 100 percent of the various classes voting.

May 20, 1946. Judge Igoe entered an order authorizing Trustees of Chicago Surface Lines to request Illinois Commerce Commission for increased fares.

May 24, 1946. Chicago Rapid Transit Company fare increased from ten cents to twelve cents in the City of Chicago after Judge Finnegan of the Circuit Court of Cook County had entered the order in People ex rel Sprague v. Biggs in compliance with the mandamus writ issued against him by the Supreme Court. Trustees of Chicago Rapid Transit Company filed schedules covering such increased rates with the Illinois Commerce Commission and the matter is pending.

Chicago Transit Board adopted a resolution requesting Illinois Commerce Commission to give prompt consideration to the necessity for current income of local transit lines requisite to successful consummation of the plans for public acquisition.

May 28, 1946. Trustees of Surface Lines petitioned Illinois Commerce Commission for a temporary increase in fare to 9 cents and a permanent 10 cent fare.

June 10, 1946. W. C. Gilman and Company began a survey of the properties of Chicago Surface Lines and Chicago Rapid Transit Lines for the purpose of advising prospective investors in the revenue bonds of the Authority.

June 17, 1946. The District Court entered an order confirming the Plans for purchase of Chicago Surface Lines by Chicago Transit Authority. (Appeals were taken from this order by Series "B" bondholders of Chicago Railways Company and minority stockholders of Chicago City Railway Company).

July 10, 1946. Transcript of the record on the appeals from the orders of the District Court on Chicago Surface Lines reorganization plan filed by appellants in the Circuit Court of Appeals.

July 16, 1946. Hearings on Chicago Surface Lines fare case began before Illinois Commerce Commission.

September 5, 1946. The Mayor of the City of Chicago appointed William W. McKenna, as a member of Chicago Transit Board to succeed himself, for the term beginning September 1, 1946.

September 16, 1946. The first of the 200 new type

streetcars for use on the Clark-Wentworth line was placed on public exhibition.

September 30, 1946. A petition of the City of Chicago for certain motor bus extensions and substitutions was heard by Illinois Commerce Commission pursuant to an agreed program between Chicago Transit Authority, Chicago Surface Lines and City of Chicago to provide definite routes for 265 buses delivered to the Trustees during the last half of 1946. (Subsequently orders were entered by the Commission approving the service which started on most of the routes).

October 3, 1946. Service suspended on Chicago Motor Coach Lines because of employees strike.

October 7, 1946. Chicago Transit Board adopted a resolution outlining its policy with respect to extension of service and new routes in municipalities within the Chicago Metropolitan Area. The resolution suggested that in order to promote and expedite negotiations looking to public acquisition of transit properties, which public operation is desired by a municipality, that all franchise ordinances granting rights to privately-owned companies be revocable by the municipality upon reasonably short notice.

October 17, 1946. The filing of briefs of appellants in the Circuit Court of Appeals in the Surface Lines Reorganization case was completed.

November 11, 1946. Briefs of the Appellees viz: Chicago Transit Authority, Bondholders Committees and Securities and Exchange Commission were filed in the Circuit Court of Appeals in Chicago Surface Lines Reorganization Plan.

November 22, 1946. Chicago Motor Coach service resumed after a fifty-day suspension.

November 25, 1946. Oral arguments were heard by the Circuit Court of Appeals on the Chicago Surface Lines Reorganization Plan and the cases were taken under advisement by the Court.

January 4, 1947. United States Circuit Court of Appeals in ruling on the Surface Lines reorganization plan stated that the order of the District Court approving the plan and the order confirming the plan must be affirmed.

February 26, 1947. United States District Court entered an order for confirmation of the Plan for purchase of Chicago Rapid Transit System by Chicago Transit Authority.

March 7, 1947. Sale of Surface Lines set by order of the United States District Court for April 22, 1947. The sale to be conducted by Walter A. Wade, who was appointed Special Master for this purpose.

March 19, 1947. Sale of Rapid Transit Lines set by order of the United States District Court for April 22, 1947.

March 31, 1947. Mr. John Q. Adams resigned as a member of the Chicago Transit Board.

April 3, 1947. Attorneys for certain Surface Lines "B" bondholders filed a petition with the Supreme Court of the United States for a writ of certiorari in the matter of the opinion of the United States Circuit Court of Appeals of January 4, 1947.

April 14, 1947. United States Supreme Court denied petition of appellants for writ of certiorari on motion of Chicago Transit Authority to dismiss.

April 21, 1947. United States Circuit Court of Appeals dismissed an appeal of certain "B" bondholders from the order of sale of Chicago Surface Lines.

April 22, 1947. Sales to the Authority (as sole bidder) of the properties of Chicago Surface Lines and Chicago Rapid Transit Company, contingent upon the sale of bonds by the Authority were held by Special Master Walter A. Wade at the Cook County Court House.

April 29, 1947. 9 cent fare became effective on Chicago Surface Lines by order of Illinois Commerce Commission.

May 2, 1947. Order entered by United States District Court confirming sale of transit properties to Chicago Transit Authority.

May 9, 1947. Appointment of Mr. Frank McNair, as a member of Chicago Transit Board for term expiring September 1, 1949, became effective.

May 23, 1947. The City Council of the City of Chicago, by ordinance, authorized the conveying to Chicago Transit Authority of rights to priority orders of 500 motor buses.

May 27, 1947. Mr. Frank McNair appointed to the position of Vice-Chairman.

May 27, 1947. Chicago Transit Board adopted a transit modernization program for the period 1947 to 1955 inclusive.

June 27, 1947. Mr. Walter J. McCarter appointed as General Manager of Chicago Transit Authority, effective as of the date when the Authority sells its initial issue of bonds.

July 10, 1947. The First National Bank of Chicago designated as the Trustee and the Chicago paying agent of the Authority's Series of 1947 bonds.

July 10, 1947. Official Statement of Chicago Transit Authority offering its Series of 1947 bonds was approved by the Board.

July 10, 1947. Harris, Hall & Company, Inc., First Boston Corporation and Blyth and Co., Inc., appointed to act as fiscal or bond agents to assist the Authority in the sale of its $105,000,000 Series of 1947 bonds.

July 21, 1947. Last day for filing petition for writ of certiorari in U.S. Supreme Court to review dismissal by the U.S. Circuit Court of Appeals of the appeal from the order of sale. No petition was filed.

July 22, 1947. George F. Getz resigned as a member of Chicago Transit Board.

July 23, 1947. First Advertisement published for sale of $105,000,000 series of 1947 bonds on which bids were to be received on August 5, 1947.

July 24, 1947. Appointment of Mr. Guy A. Richardson as a member of the Chicago Transit Board for the term expiring September 1, 1947 became effective.

August 5, 1947. This was the date for receipt of bids for the sale of $105,000,000 series of 1947 bonds. No bids were received; whereupon the Board immediately instituted proceedings for the sale of the bonds on the most advantageous terms obtainable.

August 5, 1947. Bond sale agreement entered into by the Authority with Harris. Hall & Co., First Boston Corporation and Blyth and Co., Inc., whereby this banking group agreed to buy all of the bonds on stated terms if subscriptions for 80 per cent of the bonds were received by September 12, 1947.

August 11, 1947. United States District Court set the date for the closing, preliminary to the transfer of the properties of Chicago Surface Lines and Chicago Rapid Transit Lines to the Authority, for September 30, 1947.

September 1, 1947. Appointment of Mr. Guy A. Richardson was made effective, as a member of Chicago Transit Board for the term expiring September 1, 1954.

September 2, 1947. The banking group deposited a check with the Authority in the amount of $2,100,000 as a good faith deposit, pursuant to the terms of the agreement of August 5, 1947 and stated that all series of 1947 bonds have been subscribed.

September 26, 1947. An ordinance was adopted by the Board prescribing the rates and charges for the transit system operated by Chicago Transit Authority effective as of the date when the Authority acquired the local transit properties. Under this ordinance adult fares for rides within the city of Chicago were set at 10 cents on the Surface Division and 12 cents on the Rapid Transit Division while the combination Rapid Transit/Surface ride can be made for 12 cents.

September 26, 1947. An ordinance was adopted by the Board providing for the acquisition and operation by the Authority of the transit systems and for the issuance of revenue bonds in connection therewith and for the execution and delivery of a trust agreement for the series of 1947 bonds.

September 26, 1947. An ordinance was adopted by the Board providing for the authentication and delivery of the series of 1947 revenue bonds and providing for the allocation of the proceeds therefrom.

September 26, 1947. Resolutions were adopted by Chicago Transit Board providing for the appointment of general officers and for the transfer of employees of Chicago Surface Lines and Chicago Rapid Transit Company and Board of Supervising Engineers to the service of Chicago Transit Authority.

September 30, 1947. The trust agreement between the Chicago Transit Authority and the First National Bank of Chicago, Trustee securing the Series of 1947 bonds was executed and the bonds were delivered by the Authority to the Trustee. The bonds were authenticated and delivered by the Trustee to the purchasers and the purchasers delivered payment for the bonds. Whereupon payment was made by the Authority to the Special Master for the Trustees of Chicago Surface Lines of $75,000,000 for the purchase price of those properties and payment was made to the Special Master for the Trustee of Chicago Rapid Transit Company of $12,162,500 for the purchase price of those properties. Payments were also made for various adjustments. The Special Master then delivered bills of sale and property deeds to the Authority.

October 1, 1947. Operation of the properties formerly known as Chicago Surface Lines and Chicago Rapid Transit Company was begun by Chicago Transit Authority as a unified system.

Chicago Surface Lines Passenger Car Index by Car Number

Car	Route	Location	Page
78	Fifth Avenue Shuttle	Fifth & Madison	281
101	———	North Avenue Barn	440
113	Clark-Wentworth	Addison	312
114	(Instruction Car)	(Interior)	59
118	Armitage-Downtown	Grand	51
118	Lake	Pine	177
123	79th	Western	324
134	63rd	Narragansett	52
142	63rd	64th & Stony Island	417
157	Roosevelt	Michigan (Two Photos)	182

165	Broadway	Clark & Dewey	59
172	63rd	Harvard	321
182	Clark-Wentworth	Clark & Madison	243
192	Halsted	North Branch, Chicago River	265
199	———	Cottage Grove Barn	58
201	Halsted	Waveland East of Halsted	262
204	Western	Probably Just North of 79th	52
225	———	———	48
229	Cermak	18th Loop	53
269	North	Chicago River	292
272	63rd	Narragansett	52
324	Halsted	Kinzie & Dearborn	264
367	Racine	State & Congress	57
372	Kedzie	33rd (Sanitary & Ship Canal)	273
373	Armitage-Downtown	Grand	1
391	63rd	64th & Stony Island	30
442	Chicago	La Salle	241
473	63rd	Calumet	177
483	———	69th & Ashland Carhouse	434
499	Milwaukee	Grand	288
501	Milwaukee	Devon	285
507	———	Armitage Barn	361
510	———	West Shops Transfer Table	437
522	Ashland	Roosevelt & Paulina	56
527	Ashland	Ashland Barn	357
531	Ashland	———	424
531	Milwaukee	Madison & Wacker Drive	285
537	Milwaukee	Grand	288
542	———	South Shops (Scrapping)	56
546	Milwaukee	Dearborn & Madison	287
560	———	———	54
593	Milwaukee	Grand	288
620	Western	79th	4
627	Cermak	Kenton	55
634	Grand	Navy Pier	260
640	Ashland	95th	54
644	North	Dayton	57
678	Roosevelt	Wolcott	299
700	———	At Pullman Plant	50
700	———	At Pullman Plant	51
714	Blue Island-26th	Kenton	227
718	Blue Island-26th	Van Buren & Clinton	229
730	———	Lawndale Barn	61
734	Blue Island-26th	26th & Rockwell	186
738	Blue Island-26th	26th & Kenton	60
750	———	Blue Island Barn	60
755	Indiana-Lincoln	(Experimental Uniforms)	62
764	47th	Burnham Park	318
775	Lincoln-Indiana	Wabash & River	278
804	Cottage Grove-Broadway	Limits Car Barn	65

804	South Cicero	———	65
810	Fullerton	Central	62
812	Lincoln	Clark & Wells	278
813	———	69th & Ashland Carhouse	435
904	Lincoln-Rosehill	Ravenswood & Rosehill	277
909	———	State & Madison	174
922	———	(In Old Green CSL Colors)	64
938	47th	Kedzie	318
944	Fullerton	Central	258
949	———	LaSalle & Randolph	208
952	———	(Publicity Photo)	63
982	Lincoln-Indiana	Lawrence	310
995	Western	Lawrence	310
1007	Lincoln	Peterson	277
1027	Belmont	Central	227
1031	Irving Park	Ravenswood L Station	271
1044	Western	Devon	64
1077	Indiana-Lincoln	———	278
1099	Stony Island	Navy Pier	186
1169	North Damen	———	253
1305	———	(As Salt Car)	164
1317	31st	Archer	67
1333	14th-16th	Roosevelt & Clark	315
1348	———	(Showing Curved Side)	66
1379	———	West Shops (Paint Shop)	364
1400	Fulton-21st	Marshall	259
1407	87th	Vincennes	67
1415	Webster-Racine	Racine & Belden	33
1416	71st	Vincennes	323
1419	87th	Exchange	327
1428	———	———	404
1433	———	———	68
1466	———	(Instruction Car)	162
1494	———	Lawndale Carhouse	438
1513	Taylor-Sedgwick-Sheffield	———	70
1590	———	Elston Barn	69
1617	Ogden	Laramie	294
1633	———	North Avenue Carhouse	437
1636	State-Lake	13th & State	305
1665	Irving Park	Broadway	273
1721	———	(Unusual Paint Scheme)	72
1721	(Under construction)	West Shops	364
1730	Broadway-State	119th & Sangamon	73
1731	Chartered (Victory Special)	Roosevelt & Grant Park	409
1733	Ogden	Lake & Dearborn	295
1735	Broadway-Wabash	Lawrence	236
1739	Ogden	21st & Lawndale	71
1744	Madison-Fifth	Kedzie Barn	357
1756	———	(Pulling Trailer)	35
1762	State	Washington	237

1764	Chicago	Austin	241
1775	Madison	(Motor-Trailer Operation)	282
1775	State	Adams (Recruiting Car)	34
1779	———	(Interior)	72
1781	Madison-Fifth	(Re-numbered to 78)	281
1817	Harrison	Franklin	271
1825	Grand	Harlem	74
1895	Kedzie	Sears Stub (Arthington)	187
1934	State-Lake	Jackson	303
2004	———	North Avenue Barn	32
2006	———	———	75
2514	119th	Vincennes	331
2518	Ewing-Brandon	(Passing Car 2599)	77
2518	Ewing-Brandon	118th & Burley	257
2518	Ewing-Brandon	PRR Crossing	257
2571	119th	Vincennes	330
2571	119th	St. Lawrence	331
2575	Riverdale	134th & PRW	297
2589	Riverdale	130th & Indiana	296
2599	111th	Halsted (Passing 2620)	76
2599	Hegewisch	(Passing 2518)	77
2606	111th	C&WI Crossing	329
2615	106th	Torrence	76
2619	Hegewisch	127th & Brandon	76
2620	111th	Halsted (Passing 2599)	76
2715	———	———	78
2719	———	(Fire Damage/Interior)	420
2719	———	(Fire Damage/Exterior)	421
2720	74th-75th	75th & Coles	78
2733	Riverview-Larrabee	Erie & Kingsbury	298
2746	79th	Fielding	325
2757	Riverview-Larrabee	Western & Roscoe	420
2760	———	(As Built for CCRy)	421
2776	Stony Island-Wabash	State & Wacker	78
2802	(Chartered car)	Halsted & 63rd Place	80
2808	119th	East End	422
2808	119th	(Vincennes?)	422
2810	———		423
2811	Riverdale	PRW South of 134th	29
2814	Ewing-Brandon	(C&SC Car)	423
2827	115th	Cottage Grove	330
2829	31st	Archer & Pitney Court	80
2832	———	(Being Scrapped)	436
2847	———	———	75
2851	———	———	75
2853	———	(As a Work Car)	83
2859	———	(C&SC Railway Car)	82
2902	———	(Light Color Scheme)	82
2906	———	38th West of Rockwell	83
2909	West Division	Grand	254

2909	87th	Exchange	327
2915	87th	Vincennes	181
2921	Morgan-Racine	Erie & Ashland	291
3034	————	(Interior)	86
3049	Halsted	Limits Barn	87
3069	Elston	Lawrence	256
3085	Kedzie	Bryn Mawr	86
3089	State-Lake	State & Archer	304
3091	————	(Replaced 1360)	88
3092	————	38th West of Rockwell	32
3094	Morgan-Racine	Erie & Ashland	88
3096	Morgan-Racine	Throop	291
3110	North Ashland	————	225
3114	18th	Canal	316
3120	Broadway-State	Clark & Wells	179
3134	Broadway-State	79th & State	228
3135	Cicero	25th	238
3154	Clark-Wentworth	Clark & Arthur	89
3159	State-Lake	Lake & Austin	305
3162	Cermak	Kenton	237
3172	Ashland	95th	89
3179	Stony Island	Navy Pier	84
3181	Ashland	————	425
3189	Cottage Grove	Cottage Grove Barn	89
3191	Stony Island	93rd	307
3197	Stony Island	Navy Pier	307
3198	Cottage Grove-Broadway	(Taken 9/27/35)	248
3200	Cicero	Milwaukee & Irving Park	179
3200	Roosevelt	Wabash	300
3201	Broadway-State	Wacker & State	229
3206	35th	36th & Kedzie	317
3207	Milwaukee	(Two-Car MU Train)	286
3208	Milwaukee	(Two-Car MU Train)	286
3226	South Damen	74th	253
3236	Armitage	Grand (Experimental Paint)	42
3237	North	Clybourn	292
3245	Pershing	Cottage Grove	295
3245	Pershing	Root & Wallace	296
3249	————	————	92
3253	51st	Cottage Grove	319
3266	67th-69th-71st	71st & California	90
3270	79th	Exchange	198
3287	————	(Interior)	90
3298	Montrose	Milwaukee	290
3303	Armitage	Grand	91
3311	67th-69th-71st	Ashland Barn	91
3312	South Damen	63rd	252
3314	Grand	(Two-Car MU Train)	260
3320	Grand	(Two-Car MU Train)	260
3322	————	(Rear Exit Door)	404

3341	Clark-Wentworth	79th (Three Adjacent Center Doors)	244
3355	Clark-Wentworth	80th & Wentworth	246
3358	Clark-Wentworth	———	93
3362	Madison	Clinton	282
3368	———	Kedzie Barn	93
3368	———	(One-Man, Green & Cream)	405
3376	Madison	Kedzie Barn	42
3825	———	Noble Barn	358
4000	———	———	94
4000	———	(Interior)	95
4000	Cicero	(Interior)	242
4001	———	———	36
4001	———	(Interior)	96
4001	———	(Side View)	97
4001	———	(Interior)	98
4001	Clark-Wentworth	81st Street & Halsted	247
4006	———	Kedzie Barn	93
4006	Charter Trip	———	102
4009	Madison	Austin	284
4010	———	(Experimental Colors)	103
4014	Cottage Grove	Midway Plaisance	250
4018	———	(Experimental Colors)	103
4020	Madison	Austin	103
4020	———	(Experimental Colors)	103
4020	———	Kedzie Barn	356
4021	———	Cottage Grove Barn	362
4022	Madison	Austin	103
4022	———	(Experimental Colors)	103
4028	Cottage Grove	(Center Door Change)	99
4028	63rd	Narragansett	320
4032	———	69th & Ashland Carhouse	435
4033	Cottage Grove	115th	426
4034	63rd	Ashland Barn	39
4035	———	(Experimental Colors)	103
4044	Madison	Austin	101
4044	Madison — 10¢ Shuttle	Clark & Madison	283
4046	Cottage Grove	72nd & Cottage Grove	250
4049	Madison	Hamlin Boulevard	Front End Paper
4049	Madison	Monroe & Franklin	283
4050	———	(Experimental Colors)	103
4051	Milwaukee	Car Barn	99
4051	Milwaukee	Milwaukee & Armitage	286
4062	(On Display)	Harrison & State	105
4062	———	South Shops	401
4219	(Rear View)	South Shops	144
4359	Clark-Wentworth	81st & Halsted	104
4372	Clark-Wentworth	81st & Halsted	246
4381	———	(Interior)	108
4391	(Three-Quarter View)	Illinois Railway Museum	48
4391	(Front View)	Illinois Railway Museum	49

4391	———	ERHS Carbarn	49
4391	Western	79th Loop	108
4395	Western	72nd (On Portable Crossover)	311
4400	Western	Ashland Barn	109
5023	———	Jackson & State	2
5025	Racine	Ashland Barn	27
5040	Wallace-Racine	———	308
5082	Lincoln-Indiana	47th & Indiana	279
5138	Archer-38th	Archer Barn	110
5177	South Cicero	61st Street	242
5179	———	Archer Barn	436
5186	Wallace-Racine	51st & Racine	308
5209	———	(Interior)	113
5212	Wentworth-Clark	Clark & Roosevelt	185
5219	Halsted	111th & Sacramento	263
5225	———	(As CTA Car)	26
5225	Halsted	79th Loop	261
5232	Indiana-43rd	43rd & Oakenwald	270
5234	79th	Brandon	111
5251	Halsted	South of 90th	267
5253	Halsted	79th Loop	261
5263	———	77th Car Barn	359
5271	———	At Car Barn	294
5276	74th-75th	74th & Ashland	184
5309	Charter Trip	(ERA, 1949)	112
5328	Ashland	———	424
5335	79th	Western	113
5366	35th	Kedzie	316
5371	Argo	IHB Crossing	222
5372	Argo	Probably 76th Ave.	223
5377	Ashland-Downtown	95th	226
5426	Ashland	(With Wreck Truck 129)	166
5433	———	Noble Barn	358
5465	Halsted-Downtown	Clark & Polk	26
5475	Halsted	111th & Longwood	262
5518	Ashland	74th	224
5535	63rd	Stony Island	431
5580	———	Jackson & State	2
5601	Clybourn-Wells	Belmont	247
5610	Stony Island-Wabash	81st	428
5649	———	———	112
5651	Ashland	47th	225
5657	Ashland-Downtown	95th	227
5659	Ashland	95th	114
5661	Ashland-Downtown	95th	226
5702	———	38th W. of Rockwell	114
5702	———	Archer Carhouse	440
5721	Windsor Park	93rd & Baltimore	314
5726	Cottage Grove	Cottage Grove Barn	114
5736	Cottage Grove-South Chicago	75th & South Chicago	115

5741	Cottage Grove	Cermak	251
5747	Cottage Grove-South Chicago	———	426
5779	Cottage Grove	71st (Brookline Loop)	9
5787	Cottage Grove-South Chicago	47th & Cottage	11
5798 (CUT)	Ashland	Middle Section	224
5929	Stony Island-Wabash	93rd	429
5963	Grand	Harlem	260
6017	State-Lake	State & Van Buren	304
6034	Kedzie	Bryn Mawr	115
6053	Harrison-Adams	Chicago River	269
6078	Kedzie-California	———	274
6081	———	Kedzie Barn	356
6084	Kedzie	———	274
6140	Cottage Grove-55th	———	116
6144	Cottage Grove-55th	State & Madison	200
6148	Cottage Grove-Broadway	56th & Lake Park	117
6152	Cottage Grove	111th	12
6153	Cottage Grove-Broadway	Devon & Western	248
6157	Madison	Kedzie	281
6162	Broadway-State	———	117
6167	Ashland	Southport & Clark	178
6167	67th-69th-71st	71st & California	178
6169	Cermak	Kedvale	239
6184	43rd-Root	Halsted	317
6185	Roosevelt	Grant Park Loop	299
6202	Hammond	State Line (106th & Indianapolis)	268
6203	93rd-95th	95th & State	116
6205	South Chicago-Ewing	108th & Ewing	302
6207	South Deering	63rd & Dorchester	117
6207	Hammond	Hammond Barn	268
6208	93rd-95th	NKP Crossing	328
6209	South Chicago-Ewing	63rd & South Park Terminal	301
6209	93rd-95th	PRW (Blackstone)	329
6210	Windsor Park	79th & Coles	314
6224	Stony Island	Navy Pier	429
6242	S. Chicago-Ewing	118th & Burley	257
6272	93rd-95th	NKP Crossing	118
6275	87th	Normal	326
6281	———	South Shops	118
6284	Cottage Grove	96th	10
6284	Cottage Grove	115th	119
6288	Clark-Wentworth	60th & Wentworth	120
6298	Clark-Wentworth	Clark & Lincoln	119
6518	———	(Interior)	414
7001	Broadway-State	(To World's Fair)	37
7001	Clark-Wentworth	81st & Halsted	121
7001	Ashland	(August 1936 Parade)	225
7002	———	(Interior)	122
7002	———	(Loading & Unloading)	122
7002	———	———	123

7004	63rd	PRW Near West End	29
7008	Cottage Grove	State & Van Buren	249
7020	Cottage Grove	95th	39
7022	Madison	Hamlin Boulevard	Front End Paper
7026	———	(Roof Cowling)	123
7032	Madison	Clinton	167
7033	Cottage Grove	115th	13
7053	Clark-Wentworth	80th & Vincennes Loop	245
7056	Broadway-State	119th & Michigan	235
7057	Halsted	Waveland	261
7060	Freight Interchange	84th & Wentworth	41
7090	Clark-Wentworth	81st & Halsted	246
7113	Broadway-State	84th & State Loop	235
7140	Clark-Wentworth	59th & Wentworth	38
7150	———	Ashland Barn	357
7161	Clark-Wentworth	73rd & Vincennes	6
7195	Clark-Wentworth	Clark & Wells	124
7205	Broadway-State	Root (Wreck)	169
7210	Clark-Wentworth	16th & Clark	124
7213	Wentworth	81st & Halsted (Last Run)	313
7223	Broadway	Dearborn & Chicago River	236
7234	Western	69th & Princeton	311
7259	———	69th & Ashland Carhouse	435
7261	Western	79th	124
7261	Clark-Wentworth	81st & Halsted	246
8000	———	———	126
8023	Madison	———	282
8049	———	(In Service)	35
9001	———	———	127
9028	———	———	126
9037	———	South Shops	127
Arcturus		38th & Halsted	163

Chicago Surface Lines Work Streetcar Index by Car Number

CESRY	4		(Interior)	25
CESRY	307		Pullman Plant	22
C&WT	138	(La Grange)	22nd & Kenton	349
CCRY	10		Museum of Science & Industry	45
CCRY	209		———	46
CCRY	532		Chicago Railroad Fair	46
CCRY	662	(Cottage Grove)	(Cable Car)	8
CCRY	1490		Brill Plant, Phila.	22
CCRY	2169	(75th)	South Chicago	324
CCRY	2176		Pullman	21
CCRY	2176		(Interior)	20
CCRY	2188		———	24
CCRY	———		(Cable Grip & Trailer)	21
CCRY	———		(Cable Grip & Two Trailers)	23
CGRY	54		(Interior)	18
CGRY	54		(Exterior)	19
CGRY	106		Pullman Plant	18
CRYS	6	(Mail)	South Shops	140
CRYS	6	(Mail)	Ohio & Orleans	143
CRYS	6	(Mail)	(On St. Ry. RPO Cover)	406
CRT	2711		Logan Square	350
CTA	2		(Hot Rod Paint Scheme)	41
CUT	4499	(Lake)	———	23
CUT	5798		———	224
CUT	8		(Mail Car)	140
Cook County	1		West Shops	15
Cook County	1	(Elston)	Irving Park	255
Cook County	1		On Van Buren Street	418
Cook County	1		Psychopathic Hospital	418
Evanston	9	(Central)	L Crossing	348
HW&EC	70	(Hammond)	Hammond Barn	268
LSER	7	(Lake)	Oakley (Coach)	350
LSER	10	(Lake)	Oakley (Steam Engine)	350
NCSRY	8		Chicago Railroad Fair	47
NCSRY	713	(Clark)	Randolph & La Salle	209
NCSRY	750	(Clybourn)	Randolph & La Salle	209
Pullman	B	(Windsor Park)	73rd & Stony Island	106
Pullman	B		On Display	106
SSRT	1		(Steam Engine)	351
WCSRY	4		———	47
WCSRY	4	(Ashland)	(Ashland Bridge Opening)	49

Chicago Surface Lines Gas Buses and Trolley Buses by Vehicle Number

Bus		Location	Page
1	(Diversey)	———	391
1		Side View	389
55		North Avenue Barn	381

60	Central-Lexington	387
66	North Avenue Barn	381
86	———	386
86	———	389
89	———	382
106	Plymouth Road Line, Detroit	382
109	Central-Lexington	387
128	Central-Lexington	387
135	———	378
155	———	384
164	———	384
165 (Diversey)	———	385
167	———	384
177 (Diversey)	Diversey & Parkside	386
190	(Using One Pole)	385
192	———	384
193	ERHS Carbarn	49
198 (Diversey)	Kedzie	387
303 (Irving Park)	———	7
402	———	390
407 (West 79th)	Dodge-Chicago Plant	410
417 (South Cicero)	Dodge-Chicago Plant	410
510	Midway Plaisance	5
511 (West 79th)	Dodge-Chicago Plant	410
519	———	394
530	———	390
530	South Shops	412
531	South Shops	359
541	South Shops	359
542	South Shops	359
544	South Shops	359
545	South Shops	359
547	South Shops	359
547	Lawrence Garage	363
548	South Shops	359
549	South Shops	359
560	South Shops	359
572	At Carbarn	294
572 (South Cicero)	Dodge-Chicago Plant	410
575 (South Cicero)	Dodge-Chicago Plant	410
576 (Foster)	Tripp	180
582	Lawrence Garage	363
592	———	181
593	———	181
594	———	181
597	———	181
601	77th & Vincennes	394
623	———	393
684 (71st)	Exchange	323
821	Winnecona Parkway	392
1209	Beverly Station	412
1305	———	391

All Vehicles Indexed by Route Name

Ashland	640	95th	54
Ashland	3172	95th	89
Ashland	3181	———	425
Ashland	5328	———	424
Ashland	5426	(With Wrecker Truck 129)	166
Ashland	5518	74th	224
Ashland	5651	47th	225
Ashland	5659	95th	114
Ashland	5798 (CUT)	Middle Section	224
Ashland	6167	Southport & Clark	178
Ashland	7001	(August 1936 Parade)	225
Ashland	4 (WCSRY)	(Ashland Bridge Opening)	49
Ashland	129 (Truck)	S. of Roosevelt	166
Ashland-Downtown	5377	95th	226
Ashland-Downtown	5657	95th	227
Ashland-Downtown	5661	95th	226
Belmont	1027	Central	227
Blue Island-26th	714	Kenton	227
Blue Island-26th	718	Clinton & Van Buren	229
Blue Island-26th	734	26th & Rockwell	186
Blue Island-26th	738	26th & Kenton	60
Broadway	165	———	59
Broadway	7223	Dearborn & Chicago River	236
Broadway-State	1730	119th & Sangamon	73
Broadway-State	3120	Clark & Wells	179
Broadway-State	3134	79th & State	228
Broadway-State	3201	Wacker & State	229
Broadway-State	7001	(To World's Fair)	37
Broadway-State	7056	119th & Michigan	235
Broadway-State	7113	84th & State Loop	235
Broadway-State	———	State & Randolph	43
Broadway-Wabash	1735	Lawrence	236
Central (Evanston)	9 (Evanston Ry)	Evanston L Crossing	348
Cermak	229	18th Loop	53
Cermak	627	Kenton	55
Cermak	3162	Kenton	237
Cermak	6169	Kedvale	239
Chicago	442	LaSalle	241
Chicago	1764	Austin	241
Chicago	———	Chicago & Fairbanks	240
Cicero	3135	25th	238
Cicero	3200	Milwaukee & Irving Park	179
Cicero	4000	(Interior)	242
Clark (Cable)	713 (NCSRY)	Randolph & LaSalle	209
Clark-Wentworth	113	Addison	312
Clark-Wentworth	182	Clark & Madison	243
Clark-Wentworth	3154	Clark & Arthur	89
Clark-Wentworth	3341	79th (Modified Peter Witt)	244
Clark-Wentworth	3355	80th & Vincennes	246
Clark-Wentworth	3358	———	93

Clark-Wentworth	4001	81st & Halsted	247
Clark-Wentworth	4359	81st & Halsted	104
Clark-Wentworth	4372	81st & Halsted	246
Clark-Wentworth	5212	Clark & Roosevelt	185
Clark-Wentworth	6288	60th & Wentworth	120
Clark-Wentworth	6298	Clark & Lincoln	119
Clark-Wentworth	7001	81st & Halsted	121
Clark-Wentworth	7053	80th & Vincennes Loop	245
Clark-Wentworth	7090	81st & Halsted	246
Clark-Wentworth	7140	59th & Wentworth	38
Clark-Wentworth	7161	73rd & Vincennes	6
Clark-Wentworth	7195	Clark & Wells	124
Clark-Wentworth	7210	16th & Clark	124
Clark-Wentworth	7261	81st & Halsted	246
Clybourn	750 (NCSRY)	Randolph & LaSalle	209
Clybourn-Wells	5601	Belmont & Western	247
Cottage Grove	4014	Midway Plaisance	250
Cottage Grove	4033	115th	426
Cottage Grove	4046	72nd (Brookline Loop)	250
Cottage Grove	5779	72nd (Brookline Loop)	9
Cottage Grove	6152	111th	12
Cottage Grove	6284	96th	10
Cottage Grove	6284	115th	119
Cottage Grove	7008	State & Van Buren	249
Cottage Grove	7020	95th	39
Cottage Grove	7033	115th	13
Cottage Grove	662 (CCRY)	(Cable Car)	8
Cottage Grove	5741	Cermak	251
Cottage Grove-Broadway	804	Limits Car Barn	65
Cottage Grove-Broadway	3198	Probably Devon & Kedzie	248
Cottage Grove-Broadway	————	35th & Cottage Grove	251
Cottage Grove Broadway	6148	56th & Lake Park	117
Cottage Grove-Broadway	6153	Devon & Western	248
Cottage Grove-South Chicago	5736	75th & S. Chicago	115
Cottage Grove-South Chicago	5747	————	426
Cottage Grove-South Chicago	5787	47th & Cottage Grove	11
Cottage Grove-South Chicago	————	35th & Cottage Grove	251
Diversey	1 (Bus)	————	391
Diversey	106 (Bus)	Plymouth Road Line, Detroit	382
Diversey	177 (Bus)	Diversey & Parkside	386
Division	2909	Grand	254
Division-State-Van Buren	————	State & Randolph	43
Elston	3069	Lawrence	256
Elston	1 (Cook Cnty)	Irving Park (To Dunning)	255
Fifth Ave. Shuttle	78	Fifth & Madison	281
Foster	576 (Bus)	Tripp	180
Fullerton	810	Central	62
Fullerton	944	Central	258
Fulton-21st	1400	Marshall Blvd.	259
Grand	634	Navy Pier	260

Grand	1825	Harlem	74
Grand	3314	(Two-Car MU Train)	260
Grand	3320	(Two-Car MU Train)	260
Grand	5963	Harlem	260
Halsted	192	North Branch, Chicago River	265
Halsted	201	Waveland, East of Halsted	262
Halsted	5219	111th & Sacramento	263
Halsted	5225	79th Terminal	261
Halsted	5251	South of 90th Street	267
Halsted	5253	79th Terminal	261
Halsted	5475	111th & Longwood	262
Halsted	7057	Waveland Terminal	261
Halsted-Downtown	5465	Clark & Polk	26
Halsted-Downtown	324	Kinzie & Dearborn	264
Halsted (Through Route 13)	———	63rd Place	265
Hammond	6202	State Line (106th & Indianapolis)	268
Hammond	6207	Hammond Barn	268
Hammond	70 (HW&EC)	Hammond Barn	268
Harrison	———	Harrison & Laramie	270
Harrison	1817	Franklin (?)	271
Harrison-Adams	6053	Chicago River	269
Hegewisch	2518	118th & Ewing	77
Hegewisch	2518	118th & Burley	257
Hegewisch	2518	PRR Crossing	257
Hegewisch	2619	127th & Brandon	76
Hegewisch	2599	118th & Ewing	77
Indiana-43rd	5232	43rd & Oakenwald	270
Irving Park	1031	Ravenswood L Station	271
Irving Park	1665	Broadway	273
Irving Park	303 (Bus)	———	7
Kedzie	1895	Sears Stub (Arthington)	187
Kedzie	3085	Bryn Mawr	86
Kedzie	6034	Bryn Mawr	115
Kedzie	6084	———	274
Kedzie-California	372	33rd (Sanitary & Ship Canal)	273
Kedzie-California	6078	———	274
Kimball	2390 (Bus)	Wrightwood & Spaulding	275
LaGrange	138 (C&WT)	22nd & Kenton	349
Lake	118	Pine	177
Lake	———	Lake & Pine	275
Lake	4499 (CUT)	———	23
Lake	7 (LSER)	Oakley (Coach)	350
Lake	10 (LSER)	Oakley (Steam Engine)	350
Lincoln	Lincoln & Eastwood	Lincoln Square, Ravenswood L	280
Lincoln-Bowmanville	812	Clark & Wells	279
Lincoln-Bowmanville	1007	Peterson	277
Lincoln-Indiana	755	(Experimental Uniforms)	62
Lincoln-Indiana	775	Wabash & Chicago River	278
Lincoln-Indiana	982	Lawrence	310
Lincoln-Indiana	1077	———	278

Lincoln-Indiana	5082	47th & Indiana	279
Lincoln-Rosehill	904	Ravenswood & Rosehill	277
Madison	1775	(Motor-Trailer Operation)	282
Madison	3362	Clinton	282
Madison	4009	Austin	284
Madison	4044	Austin	101
Madison	4049	Hamlin Boulevard	Front End Paper
Madison	4049	Monroe & Franklin	283
Madison	6157	Kedzie	281
Madison	7022	Hamlin Boulevard	Front End Paper
Madison	7032	Clinton	167
Madison	8023	(Motor-Trailer Operation)	282
Madison	123 (Truck)	Clinton	167
Madison-10¢ Shuttle	4044	Clark & Madison	283
Milwaukee	449	Chicago	288
Milwaukee	501	Forest Preserve Loop	285
Milwaukee	531	Madison & Wacker	285
Milwaukee	537	Milwaukee & Desplaines	288
Milwaukee	546	Dearborn & Adams	287
Milwaukee	593	Chicago	288
Milwaukee	3207	(Two-Car MU Train)	286
Milwaukee	3208	(Two-Car MU Train)	286
Milwaukee	4051	(With Modified Doors)	99
Milwaukee	4051	Milwaukee & Armitage	286
Milwaukee	———	Irving Park & Cicero	287
Montrose	3298	Milwaukee	290
Montrose	———	N. Branch Chicago River	290
Montrose	A-1	Milwaukee (Mixing Concrete)	131
Morgan-Racine	3096	Private Right-of-Way (31st & Morgan)	291
Morgan-Racine-Sangamon	2921	Erie & Ashland	291
Morgan-Racine-Sangamon	3094	Erie & Ashland	88
North	269	Chicago River	292
North	644	Dayton & Clybourn	57
North	———	California (Central Line Poles)	293
North Shuttle	3237	Clybourn	292
North Ashland	3110	———	225
North Damen	1169	———	253
Ogden	1617	25th & Laramie	294
Ogden	1733	Lake & Dearborn	295
Ogden	1739	21st & Lawndale	71
Pershing (East)	3245	Cottage Grove	295
Pershing (East)	3245	Root & Wallace	296
Riverdale	2575	134th & Private Right-of-Way	297
Riverdale	2589	130th & Indiana	296
Riverdale	2811	134th & Private Right-of-Way	29
Riverview-Larrabee	2733	Erie & Kingsbury	298
Riverview-Larrabee	2757	Roscoe & Western	420
Roosevelt	157	Michigan (Two Photos)	182
Roosevelt	678	Wolcott	299
Roosevelt Shuttle	3200	Wabash	300

Roosevelt Shuttle	6185	Grant Park Loop	299
Roosevelt	———	Grant Park Loop	301
South Chicago-Ewing	6205	108th	302
South Chicago-Ewing	6209	63rd & South Park	301
South Chicago-Ewing	6242	118th & Burley	257
South Cicero (Bus)	417	Dodge-Chicago Plant	410
South Cicero (Bus)	572	Dodge-Chicago Plant	410
South Cicero (Bus)	575	Dodge-Chicago Plant	410
South Cicero	804	———	65
South Cicero	5177	Cicero & 63rd (Midway Airport)	242
South Damen	3226	74th	253
South Damen	3312	63rd	252
South Deering	6207	63rd & Dorchester	117
State	1762	Washington	237
State	1775	Adams (Navy Recruiting Car)	34
State	7205	Root	169
State	———	State & Washington	237
State	E-224	State & Lake	128
State (Truck)	579	Root	169
State	———	State & Madison	230
State-Lake	1636	13th & State	305
State-Lake	1934	Jackson	303
State-Lake	3089	State & Archer	304
State-Lake	3159	Lake & Austin	305
State-Lake	6017	State & Van Buren	304
State-Lake	———	State & Madison	28
Stony Island	1099	Navy Pier	186
Stony Island	2776	State & Wacker	78
Stony Island	3179	Navy Pier	84
Stony Island	3191	93rd	307
Stony Island	3197	Navy Pier	307
Stony Island	5535	63rd	431
Stony Island	5610	81st	428
Stony Island	5929	93rd	429
Stony Island	6224	Navy Pier	429
Wallace-Racine	367	State & Congress	57
Wallace-Racine	5040	———	308
Wallace-Racine	5186	51st & Racine	308
Wallace-Racine	———	State & Washington	14
Webster-Racine	1415	Racine & Belden	33
Wentworth	7213	81st & Halsted (Last Run)	313
Western	620	79th	4
Western	995	Lawrence	310
Western	4391	79th Loop	108
Western	4395	72nd (On Portable Crossover)	311
Western	7234	69th & Princeton (Pullout)	311
Western	7261	79th	124
Windsor Park	5721	93rd & Baltimore	314
Windsor Park	6210	79th & Coles	314
Windsor Park	Pullman B	73rd & Stony Island	106
14th-16th	1333	Roosevelt Viaduct	315
18th	3114	Canal	316

31st	1317	Archer & Pitney Court	67
31st	2829	Archer & Pitney Court	80
35th	3206	36th & Kedzie	317
35th	5366	Kedzie	316
43rd-Root	6184	Halsted (Stock Yards)	317
47th	764	Burnham Park	318
47th	938	Kedzie	318
51st	3253	51st & Cottage Grove	319
55th (Bus)	3564	East of Cottage Grove	319
63rd	134	Narragansett	52
63rd	142	Stony Island	417
63rd	172	Harvard	321
63rd	272	Narragansett	52
63rd	391	64th & Stony Island	30
63rd	473	Calumet	177
63rd	4028	Narragansett Loop	320
63rd	5535	64th & Stony Island	431
63rd	7004	Private R-O-W	29
63rd	X - 3	West of Narragansett	161
67th-69th-71st	3266	71st & California	90
67th-69th-71st	6167	71st & California	178
71st	1416	Vincennes & Wentworth	323
71st (Bus)	409	Exchange	323
74th - 75th	2720	Coles	78
74th - 75th	5276	74th & Ashland	184
75th	2169 (CCRY)	South Chicago	324
79th	123	Western	324
79th	2746	Fielding	325
79th	3270	Exchange	198
79th	5234	Brandon	111
79th	5335	Western	113
West 79th (Bus)	407	Dodge-Chicago Plant	410
West 79th (Bus)	511	Dodge-Chicago Plant	410
87th	1407	Vincennes	67
84th	1419	Exchange	327
87th	2909	Exchange	327
87th	2915	Vincennes	181
87th	6275	Normal	326
93rd - 95th	6203	95th & State	116
93rd - 95th	6208	NKP Crossing	328
93rd - 95th	6209	PRW & Blackstone	329
93rd - 95th	6272	NKP Crossing	118
106th	2615	Torrence	76
111th	2514	Vincennes (Rock Island RR)	331
111th	2571	St. Lawrence	331
111th	2599	Halsted (Passing Car 2620)	76
111th	2606	C&WI Crossing	329
111th	2620	Halsted (Passing Car 2599)	76
115th	2827	Cottage Grove	330
119th	2571	Vincennes	330
119th	2808	(Vincennes?)	422
119th	2808	East End of Line	422

Vehicles by Carbarn of Other Location Not on a Regular Route

Location	Car		Page
Archer Barn	5138		110
Archer Barn	5179		436
Archer Barn	5702	(Compare w/page 114)	440
Armitage Barn	507		361
Ardmore Garage	547	(Bus)	363
Ardmore Garage	582	(Bus)	363
Ashland Barn	483		434
Ashland Barn	527		357
Ashland Barn	813		435
Ashland Barn	3311		91
Ashland Barn	4032	(Rear View)	435
Ashland Barn	4034		39
Ashland Barn	4400		109
Ashland Barn	5025		27
Ashland Barn	7150		357
Ashland Barn	7259	(Rear View)	435
Ashland Barn	D-212		132
Blue Island Barn	750		60
Burnside Barn	D-304		133
Burnside Barn	F-202		138
Burnside Barn	F-301		138
Burnside Barn	F-303		137
Burnside Barn	S-201		151
Burnside Barn	———		361
Central & Lexington	60	(Bus)	387
Central & Lexington	109	(Bus)	387
Central & Lexington	128	(Bus)	387
Cottage Grove Barn	199		58
Cottage Grove Barn	3189		89
Cottage Grove Barn	4021		362
Devon Depot	———		359
Diversey & Kedzie Temporary Yard	198	(Bus)	387
Division & Western	———		433
ERHS Carbarn	4391		49
ERHS Carbarn	193	(Bus)	49
ERHS Carbarn	F-305		40
Elston Barn	1590		69
Elston Barn	———		360
Elston Barn	———	(Men with flower boxes)	439
Hamlin Yard	T-1		153
Illinois Railway Museum	4391		48
Illinois Railway Museum	4391		49
Kedzie Barn	1744		357
Kedzie Barn	3368		93
Kedzie Barn	3376		42
Kedzie Barn	4006		93
Kedzie Barn	4020		356
Kedzie Barn	6081		356
Lawndale Barn	730		61
Lawndale Barn	1494		438

Lawrence Garage	4316	(Bus)	363
Limits Barn	3049		87
Lincoln & Wrightwood Barn	H-202		141
Lincoln & Wrightwood Barn	S-1		150
Lincoln & Wrightwood Barn	———		360
Midway Plaisance	510	(Bus)	5
Noble Barn	3825		358
Noble Barn	5433		358
North Avenue Barn	1633	(With Trolley Buses)	437
North Avenue Barn	101		440
North Avenue Barn	2004		32
North Avenue Barn	P-5		148
North Avenue Barn	———		358
North Avenue Barn	———		378
North Avenue Barn	55	(Bus)	381
North Avenue Barn	66	(Bus)	381
South Shops	542		56
South Shops	4062		401
South Shops	4219		144
South Shops	6281		118
South Shops	9037		127
South Shops	AA-102		165
South Shops	D-202		132
South Shops	J-204		143
South Shops	L-1		145
South Shops	L-202		145
South Shops	L-203		144
South Shops	N-1		146
South Shops	R-201		149
South Shops	V-201		152
South Shops	W-6		155
South Shops	W-201		152
South Shops	530	(Bus)	412
South Shops	209	(CCRY)	46
West Shops	Cook County 1		15
West Shops	4	(WCSRY)	47
West Shops	510	(On Transfer Table)	437
West Shops	1379		364
West Shops	1721		72
West Shops	1721		364
West Shops	8000		126
West Shops	———	(Aerial View)	432
38th & Halsted Material Yard	E-55		135
38th & Halsted Material Yard	X-201		161
77th & Vincennes Barn	5263		359
77th & Vincennes Barn	560	(Bus)	359
77th & Vincennes Barn	———	(Various Car Types)	439
77th & Vincennes Barn	6	(CRYS)	140
84th & Wentworth	7060		41
84th & Wentworth	L-202		41

Chicago Street Name Changes Connected With Street Railway History

Ann Street—see Racine Ave.

Armitage Avenue
(Between Western Ave. and Ashland Ave.)
Armitage Rd. changed to Armitage Ave.
(Between Racine Ave. and Clark St.)
Center St. changed Oct. 7, 1936 to Armitage Ave.

Armitage Road—see Armitage Ave.

Ash Street—see Neenah Ave.

Austin Avenue—see Austin Blvd. and Hubbard St.

Austin Boulevard:
Austin Ave. changed Oct. 14, 1919 and Nov. 17, 1919 to Austin Blvd.

Avenue K—see Ewing Ave.

Avenue O:
The Strand changed July 1, 1936 to Avenue O.

Baltimore Avenue:
Erie Ave. changed Apr. 14, 1913 to Baltimore Ave.

Blackstone Avenue
(Between 60th St. and 61st St.):
South Park Ct. changed Apr. 16, 1894 to Washington Ave., changed Apr. 14, 1913 to Blackstone Ave.

Bond Avenue—see South Shore Dr.

Bosworth Avenue—see Cooper St.

Brandon Avenue:
Ontario Ave. changed Apr. 14, 1913 to Brandon Ave.

Broadway:
Evanston Ave. changed July 30, 1913 to Broadway.
(Portion collinear with Halsted St.)
Halsted St. changed May 27, 1895 to Clarendon Ave., changed Nov. 1, 1915 to Broadway.

Burley Avenue:
Superior Ave. changed July 30, 1913 to Burley Ave.

Center Street—see Armitage Ave.

Centre Avenue—see Racine Ave.

Cermak Road:
22nd St. changed Mar. 15, 1933 to Cermak Rd.

Cicero Avenue:
(Between north city limits and North Ave.)
Jefferson Ave. changed Jan. 14, 1895 to 48th Ave., changed Apr. 14, 1913 to Hyman Ave., changed July 30, 1913 to Cicero Ave.
(Between North Ave. and 12th St., now Roosevelt Rd.)
48th St. changed Jan. 14, 1895 to 48th Ave., changed Apr. 14, 1913 to Hyman Ave., changed July 30, 1913 to Cicero Ave.
(Between 51st St. and 65th St.)
48th Ave. changed Nov. 1, 1895 to Cicero Ave.

Clarendon Avenue—see Broadway.

Clybourn Place—see Cortland St.

Colorado Avenue—see Fifth Ave.

Commercial Avenue—see Exchange Ave.

Cooper Street:
Cooper St. changed Mar. 19, 1917 to Bosworth Ave.

Cortland Street:
Clybourn Pl. changed Apr. 14, 1913 to Cortland St.

Crawford Avenue—see Pulaski Rd.

Damen Avenue:
Robey St. changed June 15, 1927 to Damen Ave.

Dewey Court—see Schubert Ave.

Dewey Place—see Schubert Ave.

Dickens Avenue—see Garfield Ave.

Dole Avenue—see Drummond Pl.

Dorchester Avenue:
Madison Ave. changed Apr. 14, 1913 to Dorchester Ave.

Drummond Place:
Huck Ct. changed to Sherman Pl., changed July 30, 1913 to Dole Ave., changed July 1, 1936 to Drummond Pl.

Erie Avenue—see Baltimore Ave.

Evanston Avenue—see Broadway.

Ewing Avenue
(Between 96th St. and south city limits):
Ewing Ave. changed Jan. 14, 1895 to Avenue K, changed Mar. 15, 1897 to Ewing Ave.

Exchange Avenue:
(Between 71st St. and 79th St.)
Railroad Ave. changed Oct. 23, 1911 to South Shore Ave., changed Mar. 28, 1917 to Exchange Ave.
(Between 79th St. and 83rd St.)
Commercial Ave. changed Jan. 14, 1895 to Exchange Ave.
(Between 83rd St. and 175 ft. north of 83rd Pl.)

Commercial Ave. changed Apr. 12, 1961 to Exchange Ave.

Fifth Avenue—see also Wells St.:
(Between Crawford Ave., now Pulaski Rd., and Madison St.)
Colorado Ave. changed June 7, 1920 to Fifth Ave.

Garfield Avenue:
Garfield Ave. changed Oct. 7, 1936 to Dickens Ave.

Grace Avenue—see Harper Ave.

Graceland Avenue—see Irving Park Rd.

Grand Avenue:
(Between Western Ave. and the River.)
Indiana St. changed July 23, 1914 to Grand Ave.
(Between the River and the Lakefront.)
Indiana St. changed 1913 to Grand Ave.

Grand Boulevard—see South Park Ave.

Halsted Street—see Broadway.

Harper Avenue:
(Between 50th St. and 57th St.)
Jefferson Ave. changed Apr. 14, 1913 to Rosalie Ave., changed Oct. 6, 1913 to Harper Ave.
(Between 62nd St. and Jackson Park Terr., now 65th St.)
Washington Ave. changed Feb. 11, 1895 to Jefferson Ave., changed Apr. 14, 1913 to Rosalie Ave., changed Oct. 6, 1913 to Harper Ave.
(Between 77th St. and 94th Pl.)
Washington Ave. changed Jan. 14, 1895 to Jefferson Ave., changed Apr. 14, 1913 to Rosalie Ave., changed Oct. 6, 1913 to Harper Ave.

Hubbard Street:
Michigan St. changed Apr. 14, 1913 to Austin Ave., changed Mar. 2, 1936 and Oct. 7, 1936 to Hubbard St.

Huck Court—see Drummond Pl.

Hunting Avenue—see Kostner Ave.

Hyman Avenue—see Cicero Ave.

Indiana Boulevard—see Indianapolis Ave.

Indiana Street—see Grand Ave.

Indianapolis Avenue:
Indiana Blvd. changed Jan. 14, 1895 to Indianapolis Ave.

Irving Park Avenue—see Irving Park Rd.

Irving Park Boulevard—see Irving Park Rd.

Irving Park Road:
(Between west city limits and Western Ave.)
Irving Park Blvd. changed Jan. 14, 1895 to Irving

Park Ave., changed May 27, 1895 to Irving Park Blvd., changed Mar. 3, 1937 to Irving Park Rd.
(Between Western Ave. and Clark St.)
Irving Park Ave. changed May 27, 1895 to Irving Park Blvd., changed Mar. 3, 1937 to Irving Park Rd.
(Between Clark St. and the Lakefront.)
Irving Park Ave. changed May 27, 1895 to Graceland Ave., changed Apr. 14, 1913 to Irving Park Blvd., changed Mar. 3, 1937 to Irving Park Rd.

Jackson Park Avenue—see Stony Island Ave.

Jefferson Avenue—see Cicero Ave. and Harper Ave.

Juniata Avenue—see South Shore Dr.

Karlov Avenue:
41st Ave. changed July 30, 1913 to Karlov Ave.

Kenton Avenue:
46th St. changed Jan. 14, 1895 to 46th Ave., changed July 30, 1913 to Kenton Ave.

King Drive—see South Park Ave.

Knox Avenue:
Stewart Ave. changed Jan. 14, 1895 to 46th Ct., changed July 30, 1913 to Knox Ave.

Kostner Avenue:
Hunting Ave. and 44th St. changed Jan. 14, 1895 to 44th Ave., changed Apr. 4, 1913 and July 30, 1913 to Kostner Ave.

Lake Park Avenue:
(Between 47th St. and 57th St.)
Lake Ave. changed Apr. 14, 1913 to Lake Park Ave.
(Between 71st St. and Cheltenham Pl.)
Lake Ave. changed July 30, 1913 to Lake Park Ave.

Laramie Avenue:
(Between Chicago & North Western Ry. and Madison St.)
52nd St. changed to Robinson Ave., changed to 52nd Ave., changed Apr. 14, 1913 and July 30, 1913 to Laramie Ave.
(Between Madison St. and 12th St., now Roosevelt Rd.)
52nd Ave. changed Apr. 14, 1913 and July 30, 1913 to Laramie Ave.

Madison Avenue—see Dorchester Ave.

Marianna Street—see Schubert Ave.

Michigan Street—see Hubbard St.

Nasby Avenue—see Neenah Ave.

Neenah Avenue:
Ash St. changed Apr. 14, 1913 to Nasby Ave., changed July 30, 1913 to Neenah Ave.

Normandy Avenue:
67th Ave. changed Apr. 14, 1913 to Normandy Ave.

Ontario Avenue—see Brandon Ave.

Pulaski Road:
Crawford Ave. changed Jan. 14, 1895 to 40th Ave., changed Apr. 14, 1913 to Crawford Ave., changed Dec. 12, 1933 to Pulaski Rd.

Racine Avenue
(Between Madison St. and 123rd St.):
Centre Ave. changed Apr. 14, 1913 to Racine Avenue

Railroad Avenue—see Exchange Ave.

Robey Street—see Damen Ave.

Robinson Avenue—see Laramie Ave.

Roosevelt Road:
12th St. changed May 26, 1919, June 9, 1919 and July 14, 1919 to Roosevelt Rd.

Rosalie Avenue—see Harper Ave.

Schubert Avenue:
Dewey Ct. changed Jan. 14, 1895 to Dewey Pl., changed July 1, 1936 to Marianna St., changed Oct. 7, 1936 to Schubert Ave.

Sherman Place—see Drummond Pl.

Silverton Way:
Silverton Way changed Mar. 22, 1961 to South Park Ave., changed July 31, 1968 to King Dr.

South Park Avenue:
(Diagonal portion)—see Silverton Way.
(Between 29th St. and 51st St.)
Grand Blvd. changed 1923 to South Park Ave., changed Apr. 15, 1940, Sept. 24, 1940 and Oct. 8, 1940 to South Parkway, changed July 31, 1968 to King Dr.
(Between 60th St. and south city limits.)
South Park Ave. changed July 31, 1968 to King Dr.

South Park Court—see Blackstone Ave.

South Parkway—see South Park Ave.

South Shore Avenue—see Exchange Ave.

South Shore Drive:
(Between 67th St. and 71st St.)
Juniata Ave. changed Feb. 25, 1892 to Yates Ave., changed Oct. 15, 1940 to South Shore Dr.
(Portion collinear with 71st St.)
71st St. changed Sept. 24, 1940 or Oct. 15, 1940 to South Shore Dr.
(Between 71st St. and 83rd Pl.)
Bond Ave. changed Oct. 15, 1940 to South Shore Dr.

Stewart Avenue—see Knox Ave.

Stony Island Avenue:
Stony Island Ave. changed May 20, 1901 to Jackson Park Ave., changed Nov. 4, 1907 to Stony Island Av.

The Strand—see Avenue O.

Superior Avenue—see Burley Ave.

Washington Avenue—see Blackstone Ave.

Wells Street:
(Between Chicago Av. and Kinzie St.)
Wisconsin St. changed to Wells St., changed Oct. 7, 1870 or Oct. 17, 1870 to Fifth Ave., changed Dec. 13, 1916 to Wells St.
(Between the River and 59th St.)
Fifth Ave. changed Apr. 14, 1913 to Wells St., changed July 30, 1913 to Fifth Ave., changed Dec. 13, 1916 to Wells St.

Wisconsin Street—see Wells St.

Yates Avenue—see South Shore Dr.

12th Street—see Roosevelt Rd.

22nd Street—see Cermak Rd.

40th Avenue—see Pulaski Rd.

41st Avenue—see Karlov Ave.

44th Avenue—see Kostner Ave.

44th Street—see Kostner Ave.

46th Avenue—see Kenton Ave.

46th Court—see Knox Ave.

46th Street—see Kenton Ave.

48th Avenue—see Cicero Ave.

48th Street—see Cicero Ave.

52nd Avenue—see Laramie Ave.

52nd Street—see Laramie Ave.

67th Avenue—see Normandy Ave.

71st Street—see South Shore Dr.

Note: This table was compiled by Roy G. Benedict in 1979, using the card file in the Municipal Reference Library of Chicago. The dates shown are the dates of the ordinances by authority of which the street names were changed. In some cases a name change appeared in more than one ordinance (City of Chicago or Chicago Park District or both). This data has not been verified with copies of the ordinances. Also note that on some streets the name was changed in a series of steps over several years. The list includes all streets upon which streetcars ran, as well as terminal streets for several important lines. This list covers only name changes for streets within the City of Chicago; beyond the city limits some streets retain their old names, which may or may not correspond to the name of the street within Chicago.

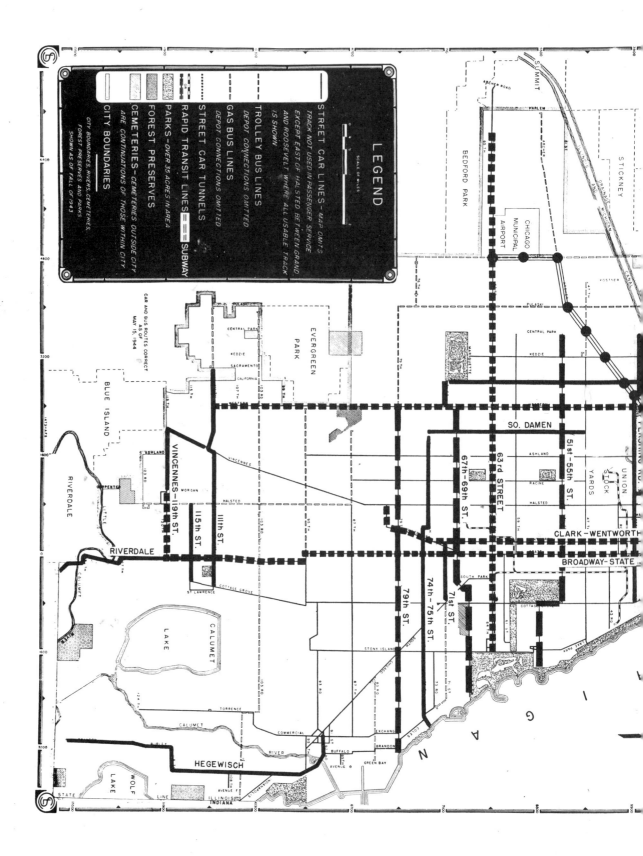

LEGEND

STREET CAR LINES – MAP OMITS
TRACK NOT USED IN PASSENGER SERVICE
EXCEPT EAST OF HALSTED BETWEEN GRAND.
AND ROOSEVELT WHERE ALL USABLE TRACK
IS SHOWN

TROLLEY BUS LINES
DEPOT CONNECTIONS OMITTED

GAS BUS LINES
DEPOT CONNECTIONS OMITTED

STREET CAR TUNNELS

RAPID TRANSIT LINES ═══ SUBWAY

PARKS – OVER 35 ACRES IN AREA

FOREST PRESERVES

CEMETERIES – CEMETERIES OUTSIDE CITY
ARE CONTINUATIONS OF THOSE WITHIN CITY

CITY BOUNDARIES

CITY BOUNDARIES, RIVERS, CEMETERIES,
FOREST PRESERVES AND PARKS
SHOWN AS OF FALL OF 1943

SCALE OF MILES

CAR AND BUS ROUTES CORRECT
AS OF
MAY 15, 1944